Wings Over the Waves

Fleet Air Arm Strike Leader
Against *Tirpitz*

The Biography of Lt Cdr Roy
Baker-Falkner DSO DSC RN

Dedication

'To the world you were but a part
To me you are all the world'

'Naomi Baker-Falkner, 1945'

Wings Over the Waves

Fleet Air Arm Strike Leader Against *Tirpitz,*

The Biography of Lt Cdr Roy
Baker-Falkner DSO DSC RN

By Graham Roy Drucker

Foreword by
Capt Eric Melrose 'Winkle' Brown
CBE DSC AFC RN

Pen & Sword
AVIATION

First published in Great Britain in 2010 by
PEN & SWORD AVIATION
An imprint of
Pen & Sword Books Ltd
47 Church Street
Barnsley
South Yorkshire
S70 2AS

Copyright © Graham Drucker 2010

ISBN 978 1 84884 305 9

A CIP catalogue record for this book is
available from the British Library

Printed and bound in England
By CPI Antony Rowe, Chippenham, Wiltshire

Pen & Sword Books Ltd incorporates the Imprints of Pen & Sword Aviation,
Pen & Sword Family History, Pen & Sword Maritime, Pen & Sword Military,
Wharncliffe Local History, Pen & Sword Select, Pen & Sword Military Classics, Leo
Cooper, Remember When, Seaforth Publishing and Frontline Publishing

For a complete list of Pen & Sword titles please contact
PEN & SWORD BOOKS LIMITED
47 Church Street, Barnsley, South Yorkshire, S70 2AS, England
E-mail: enquiries@pen-and-sword.co.uk
Website: www.pen-and-sword.co.uk

Contents

Acknowledgements

I would like to express my sincerest thanks to all those people over the past thirty years who have inspired or helped me to write this book, with especial thanks to my dear cousin Sandra 'Bunny' Coventry who gave up so much time and effort to ensure that the heroic endeavours of the father she never knew would never be forgotten. To those closest to me with especial thanks to my family and children, not least to my dear wife Ellemiek, my children Roy and Christopher, and to my father Gerald, and in particular to Roy's wife Naomi, his younger sister and my mother Leslie 'Babs' Baker-Falkner Drucker, and younger brother Capt H. de Lande 'Harry' Baker-Falkner.

A great many people have contributed their memories, letters, journals, flying log books and photographs over the years. Amongst those I would like to pay tribute are Roy's best friends and their families: Lt Cdr A.J.D. 'Titch' Harding DSC RN, Capt Edmund Squarey 'Splash' Carver DSC RN, Cdr John W. 'Ginger' Hale DSO RN, Capt Donald McEwen DSC RN, Lt Cdr Peter Pagett RN, Capt L.E.D. 'Edward' Walthall CBE DSC RN, Capt David K. Buchanan-Dunlop DSC RN, Capt F.M.A. 'Tiffy' Torrens-Spence DSO DSC AFC RN, Lt Cdr Kevin Gibney, DSC* RN, and Lt Harold Emerson Mid RNZVNR.

It is not possible to list by name all those who have assisted in some way during my many years of research. The following are amongst those who I particularly wish to thank: Lt Cdr J.W. 'Willie' Armstrong DSM; A.N.E. 'Norman' Austin; Dorothy Baden-Powell; Wing Cdr Sir D.R.S. 'Douglas' Bader CBE DSO*, DFC* MID** RAF; John 'Johnnie' Baggs; Lt Cdr John I. Baker; Capt G.C. Baldwin CBE DSC; Ray Barker; Mrs Mita Barnes; George Barnwell; Wing Cdr Roland P. 'Bee' Beamont CBE DSO* DFC* RAF; Viv Bellamy; Roy Benson; Capt W.W.R. Bentinck OBE; Lt Cdr Richard L. 'Biggy' Bigg-Wither DSC*; F. and S.G. Bingham; Lt Cdr George F. Birch; Alastair Black, Mrs Elizabeth 'Mac' S. (MacIver) Black WRNS; Air Vice Marshal D. Nigel Blair Oliphant CB OBE RAF; Mrs June 'Panda' Blakey WRNS; Phil W. Blakey; Tom Blurton; L. Boddington; Rear Admiral Alistair S. 'Beau' Bolt CB DSO DSC; Eric Bond, LS GCM*; Lt Cdr B.E. Boulding DSC; Mrs E. Boulding; Cdr N.H. Norman 'Crash' Bovey OBE DSC RNR; Lt Cdr William G. Briggs; Lt J.D. 'Jim' Britton DSC; P.J. Britton; Prof David A. Brown RNZNVR; Capt Eric M. 'Winkle' Brown CBE DSC AFC; John F. Brown; Jack Bryant; J.D. 'Buck' Buchanan; T.M. Bulloch; Don A. Bunce CGM;

Mrs Rae (Kimberley) Burge; Richard Burge; Rear Admiral D.R.F. 'Dennis' Cambell CB DSC; Lt Cdr M.J. de C. Carey; Stanley G. Carr; Lt J.A.L. 'John' Carter; Mrs Anne Carver; Capt R.H.P. Carver CBE DSC; Mark Causon, John A. Chambers; Ron Chapman; Mrs Elizabeth Cheesman; Major V.B.G. 'Cheese' Cheesman DSO MBE DSC; Grant Christie, Winston S. Churchill MP; David S. Clarabut DSC; Lt Cdr Philip N. Clark VRD RNR; E.W. 'Bill' Clayton; Lt Cdr J. Anthony Clayton; Dr Gilbert W. Clark; P. College; Stan S. Collier; Lt Cdr C.A. Conn; Eric A. Cooper; Anne (Vincent-Jones) Copeman; Cdr A. David Corkhill DSC; Cdr N. Roger Corbet-Milward; John Cortes and family; Mrs Leida Costigan; Mrs V. Crimp; B.J. 'Bing' Crosby; Peter 'Charles' Cross; Cdr R.M. 'Mike' Crosley DSC*; Air Vice Marshal Kenneth 'Bing' Cross KCB CBE, DSO, DFC RAF; Mrs Peggy Crowe; Flt Lt John A. Cruikshank VC RAF; Hugh Cundall; Lt Cdr W. 'Bill' Curtis; Lt Cdr Tom Graham Darling RCN; C.A. David; Rear Admiral Anthony Davies CB CVO; Vice Admiral Sir Peter Dawney KCVO CB DSC DL; Reginald A. DeLorey; John Dickson; Lt Cdr Harry Dixon; Air Vice Marshal Frank Dodd CBE DSO DFC DFM AFC*** RAF; Richard 'Dickie' Douglas-Boyd; Les Driver; Maurice Driver; Cdr J.A.L. 'James' Drummond; D.E. Doveston; Sir A.E. Patrick Duffy PhD MP; Cdr J.H. 'Jimmie' Dundas OBE DSC JP; Mrs GM Dunn WRNS; Admiral Sir Laurence G. 'Laurie' Durlacher KCB CB OBE DSC; 2nd Officer Catherine 'Puck' Finch-Noyes Duvall; Jack Dyson; Stuart Eadon; Lt Cdr Alastair T. Easton; Admiral Sir Ian Easton KCB DSC; Dennis W. Edwards; Lt Cdr Leslie A. 'Snowy' Edwards; D.E.F. 'Donald' Eldridge; Mr Don and Mrs Mary Ellis ATA; Larry K. Elton; R.A. Elliott; Mrs Connie Emerson WAAF, Roy Emerson; Edward C Evans-Lombe QC; Capt Roy L. Eveleigh DSC FBIM MID; Cdr Robert N. Everett OBE; B Mansell Evans; Mrs Leysa Falk; Mrs Dorothy M. Fancourt; Lt Vernon A. Fancourt; Gerald Faville; John Fay; Admiral Sir John Fieldhouse GCB GBE ADC; Sqdn Ldr Ernest E. Fitchew DFC RAF; R. 'Dick' Fitzsimmons; Tony Ford; Lt Cdr Philip S. Foulds DSC RCNVR; Air Chief Marshal Sir Christopher Foxley-Norris GCB DSO OBE RAF; Lt Charles Friend; F.W.A.G. Orkney; H.E.K. 'Windie' Gale; Peter Gaillard; Hugh Garlick; Sir William F.C. Garthwaite 2nd Bt, DSC*; Lt Bill 'Gerry' Germon; Kevin Gibney, DSC*; Mrs Winnie Gibney; Vice Admiral Sir Donald Gibson KCB DSC JP; Rear Admiral Philip 'Percy' Gick CB OBE DSC; L. Gifford; Denis Gill; Capt Jeff A. Gledhill DSC RAN; Mrs Coral Goddard; Claire Godfrey-Faussett; Cdr GRM 'Bobby' or 'Grubby' Going DSO OBE; Capt David G. Goodwin CBE DSC; Sir Charles Gordon KCB; Steve Gorrie; Capt Geoffrey Gowlland; Sir William Gladstone KG JP DL; John Grace; Mrs P.R. Leslie (Kingdon) Grace; Frank Grainger DSM; Norman B. Gray; Rear Admiral T.S. 'Gordon' Gray CB DSC; Mrs A. Green; George E. Green; Mrs Toni (Dundas) Green; Lt Cdr J.A. 'Jimpy' Greenfield DSM; Bill Grice; J. 'Honest John' Grieveson; Annelise E. Grimsey, Sussi Grimsey (née Albeck), Tim Groome; Cdr Paul R. Grotrian; Dunstan Hadley; Robert Halhead; Alan W. Hall; Capt Nigel G. 'Buster' Hallett DSC; Lt Cdr K.I. Hamilton DSC; John F. Hamlin; Frank W.

Hammett; Mrs Annette Harding; T.W.G. 'Tom' Harding; Lt Cdr Norman Harrison; W.A. 'Bill' Harrison; Tony Hart; Cdr R.C. 'Ronnie' Hay DSO DSC* RM; Sqdn Ldr Norman Hearn-Phillips AFC DFM RAF; H.J. 'Terry' Heffernan; A.P.J. Hemsley; Mrs Daphne Hemsley; Lt Cdr G.R. 'Dick' Henderson DSC; Tony Herrold; Jon Hibberd; Ron G. Hibbs; Denis Higton, Eric Hill DFC DFM RAF; Dr George S. Hislop CBE; Rear Admiral Frank D. Holford CB DSC; Norman 'Blondie' Hollis; C.J. 'Charlie' Homer DSM BEM; Joan M. Hopking; Admiral Sir Frank H.E. Hopkins KCB DSO DSC; Dr Nigel Hopkins; Lt Cdr Paul Housden RNR; David J. Howarth; H.E. Hoyte; Vice Admiral Sir Charles Hughes-Hallett KCB CBE; Michael J. Hugill; Leading Artificer Ronald F. Humphreys; O.G.W. 'Hutch' Hutchinson; Sir H.R.B. 'Dick' Janvrin KCB CB DSC; Air Vice Marshal JE 'Johnnie' Johnson CB, CBE, DSO RAF; Peter G. Jupe; Lt Richard H. 'Dick' Kendall, DSO RNVR; Lt Cdr Anthony S. 'Puppy' Kennard DSC; Mrs Laura B. Kennard; W.W. 'Bill' Kenny; Harry Kenworthy; Ernest 'Ernie' Kerridge; Lord J. Kilbracken (John R. Godley) DSC; Lt Cdr C.J.W. 'Cliff' Kindell MBE; Mrs Joy Kindell; K.R. 'Ken' King; Nigel Kinnings, Gordon Kinsey; P.L. Kirk; Lt Cdr J.H. Kneale; E.D. 'Digby' Knight; Lionel Lacey-Johnson; Lt Cdr J.B. Lamb DSC; Thelma W. Lancaster WRNS, Cdr John R. Lang; Dennis I. Leach; Admiral Sir Henry Leach GCB DL; Lt Cdr WG Leek; R. Lee-Smith, Henry Leeson; Mrs Leslie M. Leeson; Frank H. Leigh-Spencer; Mrs Betty Lethaby; George Lewis; Capt R.G. Lewis-Jones CBE; E.S. Linstead; C.A.M. Lister; Cdr J.D.C. Little; C.M. 'Clifford' Lock RNVR; Mrs Mary Lock; S.W. 'Jan' Lock DSM BEM LS GCM; Lt Cdr E.W. Lockwood; Peter Lockwood; Lt Cdr Frank K.A. Low; Mrs Eira Lord; Victoria Lord; Dr Ken R. Lown; Sue (Carver) Lyon; R.A. Lyons; Landon McAllister; Wing Cdr Prof Charles G.B. McClure, RAF; Mrs Heather McEwen; Lt Cdr Lachlan Mackintosh of Mackintosh OBE RN; J. Mahony; H. Mainwaring; Liz Mardel-Ferreira; Anthony Tony Freire Marreco; Major Alan E. Marsh RM; Mike Martyn and family of 'Moose' Martyn; Hugh Mason; Violet Matthews; Roy T. 'Nicko' Matthias; Lt Cdr Harold S. 'Matt' Mattholie, Kevin Mattholie and family; Lt Cdr J.H.D. Humphrey Maughan; Hugh R. Micklem; W. Midgley; Cdr A.D.H. 'David' Milne Home DSC; H.A.M. Mitchell; Ken J. Mitchell; Allan Monaghan; Lt Cdr Eric Monk DSM*, Derek P.R. Moore RNZNVR; Rear Admiral M.G. Morgan-Giles DSO OBE GM MP; Derek Morten DSC MID RNZNVR; Murdo Murchison, Sqdn Leader Alan D. 'Ginger' Murray DFC RAF; Mrs Edna Murray; Cdr J.B. Murray; Lt Cdr H.G.L. 'Biff' Nash; Cdr B.H.C. 'Barry' Nation; James Naylor; Mrs J. Naylor; Lt Cdr John W. 'Tweeny' Neale DSC DFC; Norman Nevard; W. and J. North; Lt Cdr Geoffrey D. Nutt DSC; Anthony M. Oakeshott; Admiral Sir William O'Brien KCB CB DSC; Cdr Stan G. Orr DSC** AFC MID; Lt Cdr C.H.C. O'Rorke; Capt Philip W.A. 'Pip' O'Rorke DSC; Mrs Joan Pankhurst; Admiral Sir Frederick R. Parham GBE KCB DSO; Mrs Joan Parham; Major R.T. 'Dick' Partridge DSO MID RM; P. Major Oliver Patch DSO DSC MID RM; Mrs June (Ruck-Keene) Payne; Nigel Perry; H.W. 'Bill' Pethick; Lt Cdr D.F.W. 'Dennis'

Phillips DSC; Lt Cdr Harry Phillips; J.J. 'John' Pinkerton; Admiral Sir C.T. 'Mark' Pize GBE KBE CB DSO; Mrs Althea Place; Rear Admiral B.C. Godfrey Place VC CB CBO DSC; Harry Plaice; Cdr J.W. 'Jeff' Powell DSC; Cdr E.O.F. Price; G.F. 'Geoff' Priestley; Cdr E. 'Ted' Pritchard; G.E. Purnell; Mrs E.V. 'Nancy' (Bartlet) Quartly; H.K. Quilter; Peter Rance; W. 'Bill' Rawstron; Rear Admiral Cedric K. Roberts CB DSO; Mrs A. (Cartmell) Robinson; Cdr Don R. Robertson AFC; Rear Admiral I.G.W. 'Ian' Robertson CB DSO DSC*; Lt Cdr W. 'Alastair' Robertson DSC*; Alfred W. Rogan; Alf 'Buck' Rogers; Charles V. Rolfe RCN; R.S. Rolph BEM; Des E. Rowe MID RNZNVR; R. Rowe; Mrs Margherita Ruck Keene; Lt Thomas Ruck Keene; Lt Cdr G. Russell-Jones DSC VRD RNR; Alan Ryman; Mrs Shirley (Hook) Salmon; Mrs Penelope (née Haworth) Salter; Peter G. Sara; R.S. 'Sandy' Saunders DSM; John S. Sawyer; Cdr J.D. Sayer OBE; L.D. Les 'Ginger' Sayer MBE DSM; Vice Admiral J.P. 'John' Scatchard CB DSC; Peter Scott; Mrs Sarah (Philip) Shaw; Cdr Donald J. Sheppard DSC RCN; E.J.W. 'Ted' Sherlock DSM MID; Mrs Marion Sherlock; Professor Graham Shipley; Derrick O. 'Shorty' Short; K.L.J. 'Ken' Sims DSM; Mrs Barbara (Walls) Sinclair WRNS; Dane 'Sinkers' Sinclair; Sam Sissman; Roger Sleigh; Mrs Hope Slessor; Ernest H. 'Prof' Sloman; Mrs Betty Smith; Wing Cdr Dick Smith OBE RAF; Sir John Smith CBE; Victor 'Vic' Smyth MID; Lt Cdr Stuart E. Soward RCN; Jan Stark; Surgeon Vice Admiral Sir Derek D. Steele-Perkins KCB KCVO; Tony Steele-Perkins; Mrs Jane (Carver) Stephens; Mrs Angela Stewart-Moore; Cdr James A. Stewart-Moore; Lt Cdr J.A. 'Jack' Stoles RCN; Capt A.W.F. 'Alfie' Sutton CBE DSC*; Fred Swain; Cdr F. Alan Swanton DSO DSC; A.E.R. 'Dickie' Sweet; P.E. Swonnell; Cdr E.W. 'Bill' Sykes DSC; Grp Capt J.B. Willie Tait DSO*** DFC; Francis Taylor; Allan H. 'Thomo' Thomson; Mrs C.F. Cathie Thomson WRNS; Lt Cdr C. 'Ginger' Topliss DSM; Mrs Anne Topliss WRNS; Rear Admiral Arthur D. Torlesse CB DSO*; L.T. Toswell RNZVR; Ron R. Tovey, Lt Commander Arthur R. Towlson DSC; Fred Townsend; Capt H.A. Traill CBE; Lt Cdr F.R.A. Dick Turnbull DSC* MID; Lt Cdr Peter Twiss OBE DSC; Peter Underhill; Capt Desmond Vincent-Jones DSC; Harry Vine; FC Walling MBE; W. Mrs D.M. Walthall; Rev Cyril Warner; Lt Cdr David W. Waters; R.H. Weir; Lt Cdr J.W.G. 'Smoothie' Wellham DSC; Arthur G. 'Willie' Wells MID; Jack Whitaker; Cdr Dennis C.B. White OBE; Gordon G.F. 'Knocker' White; E.W. Whitley, Lt Cdr W.R. 'Bill' Whitworth; Lt Cdr E.S. 'Teddy' Wicks MBE; Mrs Widecombe; C.J. 'Bungy' Williams; Dave Williams; Cliff 'Rocky' Winters; John Winton; Cdr G.A.L. 'Gerry' Woods DSO; Eric 'Zeke' Woodward; Cdr G.R. Graham Woolston; Grp Capt Sammy Wroath CBE, AFC* RAF; Capt Cecil Young, Wing Cdr J.R.C. Young AFC RAF.

I also wish to thank in Norway: Bernhard Bergersen; N. Hagen; Urban Hansson; Knut Haugland; Thor Heyerdahl; Karl Kjarsgaard; Thor-Roger Kjellbakk; Ulf Audun Larsstuvold; Reydar Martinusen; Trond-Inge Mathisen; Sigurd Myher; Harald Pedersen; Harry Pettersen; Hugo Rønring; Ole Martin

Running; Morten Sandvik; Hans Christian Søborg, Ole Sølensminde Mathias Sørensen; Monica Sørensen; Gunnar Sonsteby; Capt Knut Støre. In Germany I appreciate the assistance from: B. Gerhard Bigalke; Siegfried Breyer, T. Hoffman, Kurt Kabisch, Hans-Ulrich Lerche, Kurt Schulze, Oliver Stier and Dirk Wascher. I also wish to thank in Holland: Jan G. Boon van Ochssee MLD RNethN.

Thanks are also forthcoming to the following researchers, museum and association staff for their patience and assistance: Even Blomkvist (Alta Tirpitz museum); David Brown (Naval Historical Branch (RN); Miss D. Coffey (Air Historical branch (RAF); Mrs Moira Gittons (Fleet Air Arm Museum); Peter B. Gunn; Cdr David Hobbs (Fleet Air Arm Museum); Mrs Jan Keohane (Fleet Air Arm Museum); Cdr J.D.O. Macdonald (Fleet Air Arm Officers Association); Trond-Inge Mathisen (Hamarøy Krigsminnemuseum); Simon Moody (RAF Museum); Graham Mottram (Fleet Air Arm Museum); Mrs Brit Rasmussen (Alta Tirpitz Museum); Dave Richardson (Fleet Air Arm Museum), Dr Chris Samson; Leslie Sayer (Telegraphist Air Gunner Association); Ray Sturtivant; S.A. Thornton (Royal Aircraft Establishment Library); Mrs Allison Wareham (Royal Naval Museum); Cdr Dennis C.B. White OBE (Fleet Air Arm Museum); Mike Wood (Met Office Archives).

Finally I wish to dedicate this book to the immortal memory of Roy Baker-Falkner and his love for Naomi, and to all those brave young Fleet Air Arm airmen who failed to return, not least to those lost with him on 18 July 1944, Lt Guy Micklem DSC RN and PO Arthur Kimberley.

Foreword

by Captain Eric Melrose 'Winkle' Brown, CBE, DSC, AFC, RN –
Former Chief Naval Test Pilot

I first met Lt Cdr Roy Baker-Falkner on 1 February 1943, when he arrived as the pilot of a Barracuda II at the Royal Naval Air Station, Arbroath, where I was serving in the Service Trials Unit. He was about to undertake deck-landing trials on the aircraft carrier HMS *Illustrious* with this new type of aircraft. I knew of him by repute, for he was a distinguished Fleet Air Arm squadron commander, and a very competent pilot, who had been chosen to introduce the Barracuda II into service.

In person he was tall, handsome and personable, and after our meeting I could well envisage him as a role model for young pilots designated to be torpedo-bomber aircrew, for he had already built up a background of operational experience in Swordfish aircraft, as his award of the DSC bore witness.

After carrying out intensive flying trials with the Barracuda, not the most loved of aircraft, he became CO of the first Barracuda squadron and a wing leader in the Fleet Air Arm, and was particularly involved in attacks on the German battleship *Tirpitz* in Norway, for which he won his DSO.

With such a fine record he was earmarked to become the CO of the Naval Test Squadron at A&AEE, Boscombe Down, but sadly was lost on 18 July 1944, two weeks before he was due to take up his new posting. His final flight was on anti-submarine patrol from a carrier operating off Norway, and he failed to return in poor weather. A great loss to the Fleet Air Arm, which will not forget him.

Prologue

18 July 1944

A thick blanket of fog encompassed aircraft carrier HMS *Formidable* as she ploughed her way through the Arctic seas off the coast of Norway. On board, weary officers and men of 8 Naval Air Wing were recovering after the most recent attack on the great German battleship *Tirpitz*. Among them was Lieutenant Commander Roy Sydney Baker-Falkner DSO, DSC, RN. He was wing leader and just four months before had led Operation *Tungsten*, which had left the battleship bomb-blasted, bullet-marked and with her superstructure in shambles.

Further raids had followed with less success and another such raid had been carried out on Monday 17 July 1944. Just after midnight, Baker-Falkner had taken off from *Formidable* in his Barracuda dive-bomber to lead the strike force to Kaa Fjord where the semi-repaired *Tirpitz* was preparing to weigh anchor. This time, an effective smoke screen, aided by an almost complete lack of wind, covered the area. He later commented that if he had not been there before he might not have recognised the locality as a fjord at all. The attack was pressed home but with the majority of pilots having to drop their bombs blind in the murk, no hits were claimed although a column of smoke with a mushroom top was seen to rise above the general smoke level.

Another raid, Operation *Encore*, had been planned to take place later that day but was cancelled due to fog from seaward. Now should have been a time to relax. Baker-Falkner was on his way home to England. Having served throughout the war and seen action at Dunkirk and in the Battle of Britain, he was due to take up a non-operational appointment.

With the Fleet homeward bound, returning from the latest *Tirpitz* raid, Baker-Falkner was thinking of his wife and two small children at home in Devon. It was not to be. Intelligence was rushed to the captain reporting that there were U-boats in the area. The order went out for anti-submarine patrols to be launched. Baker-Falkner, as commanding officer of the strike force, indicated to the captain that the weather conditions were too dangerous for anyone to fly. Eventually, after characteristically biting his lower lip deep in thought, he said that if anyone had to go, it should be him.

In the early hours of 18 July, Baker-Falkner took off as part of the first anti-submarine patrol with his normal crew, Lieutenant Guy Micklem, RN, as observer and Leading Airman Arthur Kimberley as telegraphist air gunner (TAG). They were accompanied by a Corsair, piloted by Sub Lieutenant Harold 'Matt' Mattholie, RNVR. The two aircraft flew through the low cloud, fuel gauges dipping to dangerously low levels. No U-boats were encountered, and with visibility deteriorating rapidly the patrolling aircraft searched for the aircraft carrier but could not see her.

On *Formidable* Captain Ruck-Keene was getting anxious. Star shells were fired up through the clouds and search aircraft tried to relay co-ordinates to the missing pair. The only response was a fading message from Roy stating that the Barracuda was running low on fuel and he had no option except to head for enemy-occupied Norway...

CHAPTER 1

Early Days in Canada

On 3 June 1916, newspaper billboards on street corners in England and across the British Empire brought news of major disaster. On this, the 305th day of the First World War, the headlines announced more death and destruction. *The Times* of London reported 'Great Naval Battle – Heavy Losses'.

Six British cruisers had been sunk along with five destroyers and a further six were missing during a naval engagement off the coast of Jutland, it was reported.

The Battle of Jutland, fought between the British Grand Fleet and the German High Seas Fleet, was the largest naval battle of the war. It heralded the demise of the reputation of the battleship and at the same time witnessed the first use of carrier-based aircraft.

Time was to reveal that the Grand Fleet lost ships totalling 110,000 tons with over 6,000 men killed. The Germans lost ships totalling 62,000 tons with 2,500 men dead.

Meanwhile life, as encapsulated in *The Times* that day, continued: 'In the Birthday Honours it was announced the Prince of Wales had been given the Military Cross'; a certain Mr Winston Churchill had relinquished the temporary rank of lieutenant colonel on ceasing to command a battalion of the Royal Scots Fusiliers; 'Daddy Long Legs' was playing at the Duke of York's Theatre and was predicted to 'run for years and years'; Marshall and Snelgrove were advertising blouses of a particularly dainty and refined character at prices ranging from 13/9d; a substantial house in Bloomsbury, 'situated on the best side of the square', was offered for rent at £275 per annum.

In another house, in another part of England, a young couple from Canada – Sydney and Grace Falkner – were celebrating the birth of their first child, Roy.

Sydney, whose family had ties with North America stretching back over 200 years, had volunteered in November 1915, at the age of thirty-one, to join the Dominion Army of Canada. He was in England awaiting a posting to the Western Front.

The Falkners came from a family that had a long history of serving in the militia and of travelling the world. Roy's great-great-great-grandfather, Luke Falkner, had been an officer from Lincolnshire serving with the British forces during the American War of Independence, and Luke's brother was killed whilst serving in the rebellious Jersey Blues of New Jersey.

Roy's middle name was Sydney, also in honour of his grandfather, Alfred Sydney, who was driven by the family trait of adventure and travel. In the 1870s, he was one of the first farming pioneer settlers in a remote homestead at Daly in the prairies of Manitoba.

Roy's father was born there in June 1884, one of five children. Daly, a rural municipality not far from the railroad halt at Brandon, was a small grain and cattle ranching community nestling amongst rolling hills on the edge of the Little Saskatchewan Valley through which ran a tributary of the great Assiniboine River. Its appearance on maps coincided with the year of Sydney's birth.

At the time the Falkners first arrived, the explorer Captain F.W. Butler described the surrounding area in his *Narrative of Travel and Adventure in the North-West of America*: 'The region is without law, order or security for life or property; Indian massacres are unchecked even in the vicinity of the Hudson's Bay Company's post, and all civil and legal institutions are entirely unknown.'

It would be a while before Manitoba became entirely safe for the young Falkner family. The year after Sydney's birth the Battle of Batoche hit the Manitoba newspaper headlines. The battle was fought between the Métis of mostly French and Indian blood (augmented by First Nations warriors) and the North-West Mounted Police.

By then members of the Falkner family had spread far and wide from the Pacific to the Atlantic coasts of Canada, with uncles, aunts and cousins in British Columbia, Saskatchewan, and Ontario. Yet throughout the two centuries of the family's colonisation in the Americas, links were still strong with the 'Old Country', particularly in Nottinghamshire, over 5,000 miles away.

Sydney, or Sid as everyone called him, travelled to England in his youth and subsequently set up the Falkner Bros Printing Company at Houndsgate, Nottingham, with his brother in 1910. By all recollections, he was a fair-haired, blue-eyed gentle giant of a man at 6 feet 1½ inches tall. He was kind, passionate about history and loved delving into his family tree.

During this time, he assisted in church charitable work to help the poor, 'slumming' as it was called then. It was on one of the many church events in Nottingham that he met Miss Gracie Smerdon Baker. Sid and Grace were soon to marry at St Jude's Church, Mapperley, on 8 March 1913 in a double wedding with Grace's younger sister, May, and her new husband.

Grace was from a town background in the industrial English Midlands with a colourful family heritage of her own. She had developed a strong character and often got her way. She was intelligent, very involved in music and was excellent at embroidery and lacemaking.

Grace was devoted to Sydney and was a down-to-earth, no nonsense type. Some would say she was eccentric, yet she merely wanted to do what she wanted, and was ambitious for herself and Sydney. He would always give in and appreciate peace and quiet.

After the wedding both of the newly married couples returned to Sydney's birthplace in Canada for their honeymoon, and to start a new life.

Grace and Sydney settled on the farmstead Maples owned by Grace's elder sister Maud and her husband Frank Caporn, in the small farming community of Carnegie not far from where Sydney was raised.

Life was harsh for these pioneer Falkners. There was no running water, only oil lamps and few neighbours to help out in the event of emergencies. Everyone at the Maples farmstead had to join in the farm work to make it a success, Grace became adept at farming, tinkering with machinery and finding new ways of making ends meet. She was for ever setting aside things for 'a rainy day'.

In such an isolated community, whilst Sydney was working with Frank Caporn late into the night threshing the corn with their primitive horse-drawn machines, Grace would earn extra money by travelling in their horse and buggy to neighbouring homesteads to teach music. She would also play the violin for some of the dances around the farming district.

The Falkners' quiet and peaceful existence was abruptly halted on 4 August 1914, when Britain declared war on Germany. The Dominion of Canada, as a part of the British Empire, was automatically at war.

The following year, Sydney enlisted at nearby Brandon, which was the mobilisation headquarters of the 79th Overseas Infantry Battalion. Only five months later he and his battalion were at Halifax, Nova Scotia, en route to England on board the troopship RMS *Lapland*, famous for rescuing survivors from the *Titanic* disaster off the Newfoundland coast.

In May 1916, Sydney arrived in England as part of the Canadian Overseas Expeditionary Force. Grace, who was one month pregnant when Sydney enlisted, determined to return to the land of her birth and followed her husband across the Atlantic to join her family in Nottingham.

She was terrified at the thought of travelling by ship during wartime but boarded the Cunard liner SS *Orduna*. Grace's worst nightmare was that the ship would be attacked by German submarines as the SS *Lusitania* had been torpedoed and sunk only twelve months previously.

The journey across the Atlantic was rough. At one point there was an ominous thud and a jolt to the ship and Grace fell to the ground, believing that her ship had been struck by an enemy torpedo. Her fears proved groundless but she was worried that her unborn child had been hurt.

The baby, Roy, survived and was safely delivered at their temporary home, 38 Chaworth Avenue, West Bridgford, Nottingham. Just five days later – on 8 June 1916 – Sydney was ordered to report to the Canadian Army Medical Corps at the military camp at Dibgate in Kent.

He remained at Dibgate, with potential onward transfer to a field hospital on the Western Front. Grace was frantic that he would be heading off to the trenches. At Ypres earlier that year there had been more than 6,000 Canadian casualties.

On 4 October 1916, much to Grace's relief, Sydney was posted to Clivedon House, the Astor's Estate in Taplow, Buckinghamshire, where the Canadian Expeditionary Force had set up the Duchess of Connaught Canadian Red Cross Hospital for wounded troops returning from the trenches in France.

Baby Roy was rarely to see his father whilst he was with the CEF. With this early lack of a 'fatherly figure', Grace made up for this by doting on him and taking him everywhere, including her church social events and visits to his young Falkner and Baker cousins.

Soon after, Sydney was seriously injured and his lungs affected during a fire in one of the barracks. In November he was diagnosed as having pulmonary tuberculosis and hospitalised.

Sydney's health deteriorated and following the biggest disaster for the Canadian forces at Vimy Ridge, near Arras in France, in April 1917, he was transferred to No. 5 Canadian Hospital in Kirkdale, Liverpool. Sydney was invalided back to Canada on board SS *Stewart Castle* in November 1917 and was eventually discharged from the army through ill health three months later.

The first of Roy's epic travels was about to start, and he was barely a year old when Grace applied to follow her husband back to Canada. Special permission was required for the voyage as strict wartime restrictions existed at that time. Meanwhile, she personally continued to concentrate on Roy's upbringing, at a time when nannies were often the norm in middle class and well off families. After six months Grace and seventeen-month-old Roy were issued an Emergency Certificate to travel in a troopship via the United States to Canada. The young mother and her toddler travelled alone on the 2,700-mile journey by railroad for more than two days across the continent to join Sydney. By that time, he had taken up a position as Regional Secretary for the Great War Veterans' Association, in Broadview, Saskatchewan.

Soon after they arrived, peace was finally declared and the young family again settled down to life in the prairies.

Broadview at this time was a small but respectable town. According to *Wrigley's Saskatchewan Directory* of 1921, it was a community with a population of 1,000 with '6 churches, public and high school, 2 garages, hotel, bank, newspaper, 3 elevators'. The countryside was flat and grain elevators dominated the skyline, owned by the Grenfel Milling and Elevator Co.

That winter the temperature fell to 40 below Fahrenheit, and even simple tasks like chopping up meat proved difficult. The cold temperatures started to make Grace ill.

Sydney's work was to help the homecoming veterans in the Province to demobilise, processing applications for land settlement, agricultural training and loans for returned soldiers of the Canadian Overseas Expeditionary Force.

In the lead up to Christmas 1918, Sydney's thoughts returned to his career before the war, farming. As a veteran soldier he was entitled to land, and received an encouraging letter from a Great War Veterans' Association colleague at Calgary on 6 December 1918:

Dear Sid, I was very pleased to get a letter from you, and to know that you are thinking of farming. I have a half section (of property) 10 miles south east of Rural Municipality No. 10 in Happy Valley, which is partly open and partly timberland, on the west side is a big tamaracks swamp. But it is not dangerous.... Some people like the country, others prefer the prairies. I would not like to advise either way, but if you have not been out west, then come out for a vacation, and at the same time you will see what it is like. In its raw state it looks pretty rough, but give me the timber anytime in place of the prairie. I am so glad to know that you have Mrs Falkner and the baby out now, and you must not fail to give them my very kindest regards.

Happy Valley was extremely isolated – nearby Estevan had only recently been made a village. It did not appeal to the young family and they remained at least for the foreseeable future in Broadview. Roy thrived in Broadview and was fascinated by the Canadian Pacific Railway locomotives that steamed and rattled their way through the town before travelling on for thousands of miles in each direction.

At the age of five, Roy attended his first school in downtown Broadview. The school was run with a rod of iron by Mr Frost, the principal. Emily Dupont, the music school teacher, was friendly with Grace since they shared a passion for music.

Roy's brother, Harry, was born shortly after, on 3 July 1921. Up until then Roy had been receiving the attention lavished on an only child.

Leslie, Roy's younger sister, who was born years later, recalled:

With Grace being such a head-strong woman, but at the same time generous too, it helped mould Roy's character into being an independent person himself, reliable and a leader, not a follower type.

In those first few years at Broadview, the family had a horse and buggy, which Roy helped to look after and learnt to ride at an early age. He also enjoyed riding the horses on his uncle's farm whenever the family went to visit.

Later, after Harry's birth, Roy's parents bought an oasis-green Durant Star, a cheap version of a Model T Ford – or as the adverts of the day described it 'the aristocrat of low-priced cars'. Their automobile was one of the few in town which kick-started and reinforced Roy's interests in cars, locomotives and boats.

His interest in aviation also started early. Sydney and Grace entertained his old Great War veteran pals who mesmerised Roy with tales of heroic exploits on the Front. Canadians had made a major contribution to air warfare, with famous names like Billy Bishop and William Barker. The young Roy was fascinated to hear that it was a Canadian namesake, Captain Roy Brown, who had shot down the dreaded German air ace 'The Red Baron', Baron von Richthofen.

In 1923, Grace, who adored the family and would do anything for them, insisted on looking for a milder climate in which to raise the children. The family decided to move far west to the temperate coastline of British Columbia where Roy's aunt and uncle, Frank and Maud Caporn, now lived having sold their farmstead in Manitoba. They set out in their Durant Star car and drove the 1,250-mile journey across the prairies and along mountain tracks which were little more than pack trails through the breath-taking beauty of the Canadian Rockies.

For Sydney this was a major expedition and he had spent ages in advance checking and re-checking his treasured set of cloth-backed maps covered in dramatic contours. Grace came well prepared too, using her heavy beaver skin fur coat for the journey into the snowy mountains. Ahead were three mountain ranges to negotiate and deep, fast-flowing rivers to cross.

Navigating their Durant Star along the narrow, curving dirt trails, they slowly drove up to the craggy heights of the awe-inspiring mountain scenery. Harry years later recalled:

> We stayed in log cabins en route; there were howling wolves outside. In one log hut where we stayed overnight, we awoke to be asked by neighbouring settlers if we had been disturbed by the bears that frequented the building.

They finally arrived on the Pacific coast and crossed the Straits of Georgia to Vancouver Island and their new home. The sea voyage to the island fascinated Roy and kindled his love of the sea and boats.

In 1924, the family initially settled in the capital, Victoria, where Sydney took an administrative job with the Canadian Pacific Railway, and they stayed with Maud and Frank. Another newcomer to Victoria recalled that year going 'to see the Government Buildings, Governor General's House and around the city, and it impressed us as being a real nice city, so clean, wide streets and beautiful yards and boulevards, and roses and other flowers in blossom.'

Eventually, the family settled in Saanich, a small town located on a peninsula of Vancouver Island. Their first home was in Canterbury Road, a two-bedded house with a colonial-style verandah running round the building. Later, they moved only a few blocks away to 46 Sims Avenue, which was a typical cedar-shingled early twentieth century bungalow, also with a verandah where Harry recalled they had caterpillar races: 'You chose your caterpillar and gave it a prod in the back to keep it moving.'

Their homestead, which had a large cellar for the heating and for storing potatoes, was set in wooded countryside. It was quite primitive and the only water was from the well at the bottom of the drive. The boys fought over who should fetch the water and who would look after the neighbour's goat which they had to feed from time to time.

The name Saanich was derived from the native Indian word meaning 'emerging people'. The area was renowned for its cultivation of fruit and flowers. By the 1920s it was settled and prosperous, an ideal environment for the young Falkner children to grow up.

Roy was now eight years old. The boys' favourite haunt, not far away from their house, was a big wooded lake, Swan Lake, where they went swimming, boating, watching waterfowl and fishing. Years later, Roy told one of his friends, Nancy Bartlett, about his exploits of salmon fishing and catching a 40-lb fish.

Roy and Harry attended McKenzie Primary School. Their recollections were of a small building of five rooms surrounded by countryside. Roy recalled the classrooms being lit by oil lamps until Mr Routley the principal managed to organise electric lighting in 1926.

Harry remembered a child dropping a live round of ammunition which went off, hurting another child. Later Roy attended secondary school, Ctanleigh House School, and Harry went to Sims School just round the corner from their home.

Family friends included the Whites whose son played with Roy and was a boy soprano who broadcast 'O for the wings of a dove' on the wireless, to the excitement of the Falkners.

By now, Roy had become a good horse-rider despite falling off and hurting himself when out riding in the hill country on one occasion. Roy excelled in sports generally and enjoyed new sports, including water polo as Leslie recalled being told years later.

In the afternoons when back from school, at the weekend or in the school holidays, the area was a vast adventure playground for the two boys. The house was only twenty minutes' walk to the sea at Portage Inlet and about two miles away from Esquimalt Harbour and naval base where the boys used to watch the warships coming and going.

In the great forests, there were beavers that lived alongside the lumberjacks and fishermen. Roy enjoyed clambering over the logs that had been felled by lumberjacks into the river in readiness for the timber to be floated downriver to timber yards.

On 13 November 1924 there was an addition to the family when Grace gave birth to a daughter, Leslie Marjorie, at home with no female help. Roy became devoted to 'Babs' or 'Little Sis' as he called her.

As Leslie grew older, she joined the family in its musical talents. Grace and Leslie played the violin. Harry played the piano. Unlike the rest of the family, Roy was not interested in music, but played the violin – badly, according to Leslie. Before their meals, the young family would always say grace. The family frequently used to sing hymns around the pianola in their Saanich homestead, or recite in fits of laughter one of their favourite tongue-tying sayings: 'How much wood would a woodchuck chuck if a woodchuck could chuck wood?'

Come bedtime they would settle down and all kneel by their bed saying their prayers. They were a very close family, all devoted to each other. Roy and Harry rarely squabbled, the arguing was more between Harry and his mother. When she said 'white' he would automatically reply it was 'black' recalled Leslie.

Roy assumed a caring attitude towards his younger brother and sister but, even when he was ill, kept them 'under control'. Leslie remembered Roy and his school friends coming to stay and all having the mumps. Roy got Leslie doing everything in the house. 'Marj, go on do this and go and do that,' he ordered his little sister. As they all got older, Roy wrote an almost parental note about Harry and Leslie: 'I don't want either of the little devils rather blasé about money.'

At home without the outlet of school team sports, Roy and his younger brother found other distractions to keep them busy. Harry remembered one occasion when their mother was baking bread. It would not rise and was much appreciated as ammunition for Roy and Harry's catapults. On other occasions they used to go and hunt and catch harmless grass snakes. 'Harry would then terrify me by dangling them in front of my face,' recalled Leslie. Roy referred to his younger brother as a 'plucky little devil'.

Leslie would try and join in with her big brothers until one day when she was running around in the fields barefoot she was warned by a neighbour that there was a rattlesnake around.

Roy and Harry were delighted when their parents bought a new car, further strengthening their interest in cars as they helped their father look after the vehicle and explore its mechanics. Harry recollected it was 'a left-hand drive Star Six or Seven manufactured in Canada'. Victoria had only just changed from driving on the left side of the road as in England to the right side as in America.

The family used to go on car outings and for walks and camping trips to lakes as often as possible. Their favourite haunt was Lake Shawnigan, surrounded by forests of Douglas fir, where Roy and Harry were happy, messing around in boats or jumping with their little sister over the fallen logs. Leslie recalled the family visiting native Indians in a little village, and seeing rotting totem poles in the woods.

The 1920s were an exciting time in Canada and the United States for aviation. In May 1927, Charles Lindbergh made his epic flight from Long Island to Paris. This was an inspiration to Roy's parents who themselves showed an interest in aviation in the aftermath of the Great War. Money was pouring into the small aviation companies being set up by returning Royal Flying Corps veterans throughout the country.

Grace was fascinated and in 1928 intended to take flying lessons in the newly built DH.60 Moth biplanes at Victoria-Lansdowne Flying School. At that time lessons cost the princely amount of $5 an hour. When Grace planned to start flying, a pioneering passenger service had only just started up at Lansdowne airfield, and was Western Canada's first international daily air service.

However, on the day Grace was to start her course, there was a big civil aircraft accident on 25 August when a British Columbia Airways Ltd Ford Trimotor from Victoria crashed in Puget Sound, Washington, during bad weather killing all seven people.

This was Canada's first ever major air disaster and Grace cancelled her flying lessons immediately. If she had indeed learnt to fly she would have been among the first Canadian women to receive a pilot's licence, as the first in history had only just qualified five months previously. 'She would have been tickled pink to know that,' recalled Leslie who added that her mother was 'really quite adventurous and enjoyed driving cars and other mechanical things.'

Instead, as both Leslie and Harry recollected, the family consoled themselves that year with a brand-new American six-cylinder Graham-Paige automobile, with big sweeping running boards, large shiny headlamps, a rack at the back for their wickerwork picnic hamper, and plenty of room inside for a growing family. It had cost a fortune at over $1,000. They were very pleased to discover that one of their friends, Commander Percy Nelles, Royal Canadian Navy (RCN), the Senior Naval Officer at Esquimalt, or the 'Admiral' as they called him, was also one of the few other people in Victoria that owned the same type of car.

That winter season, Roy was proudly photographed in the Ctanleigh House School's winning football team for 1928–9. Although he always tried hard at team games, he never made a great effort academically in the classroom. 'He was an all rounder,' recalled Leslie.

1929 was the year of the Wall Street stock market crash and thousands of Canadian families became penniless overnight. The Depression caused much anxiety for the Falkner family and the Royal Canadian Navy seemed a good and stable job for their son. The Army was not an option after the horrors of the Great War, and the fledgling Royal Canadian Air Force at Vancouver at that time was essentially a paper civilian force with a declining number of staff. The Royal Canadian Naval Air Service (the Canadian Fleet Air Arm), which had once trained Canadian cadets in the United States and in England, had long since disbanded in 1918.

The Royal Canadian Navy, however, was at that time in expansion after Mackenzie King, the Prime Minister of Canada, realised that declining British naval strength relative to the United States was making Canada dangerously dependent upon the Americans for the security of the Pacific and Atlantic coasts.

That year, 1929, the family supported Roy's interest in the Navy, ships and boats. The Royal Canadian Navy was a much respected profession and he loved messing about in boats, and his passion was sports of all sorts. The family consulted and took the advice of Commander Nelles, their senior naval officer friend, who was about to leave for a posting at HMCS *Victory*.

The outcome was that at the age of thirteen, Roy applied to join the Navy, as an officer cadet at the Esquimalt Naval Base, inspired by knowing that Scott of the Antarctic had once served there. He sat exams and endured an interview with a table full of distinguished-looking gentlemen, characteristically biting his lower lip in deep thought, and then written examinations. Afterwards he went back to Ctanleigh House School to await the results.

Following an agonising length of time, Roy at last got news from the newly appointed Senior Naval Officer, Commander Leonard Murray, RCN, that he had been accepted. However, as training of cadets at the Royal Naval College of Canada was no longer possible, Roy was transferred to the United Kingdom on a Canadian Commonwealth Scholarship. Along with other RCN cadets, he was enrolled for officer training at the Royal Naval College at Dartmouth in Devon.

After a decade in Canada, the family was en route to England. The intention was to escort Roy to Dartmouth and then return to Canada to live once he was settled at the college.

The journey was long. They took the Canadian Pacific Railway with its 'one mile long' row of carriages out east and arrived a few days later in Montreal. The St Lawrence River was frozen so all onward voyages across to England involved a further journey to the Atlantic seaboard. That winter was particularly bitter, and Leslie recalled seeing on their visit to the Niagara Falls huge icicles and icebergs, with a vast frozen lake above the falls.

In December 1929 the family sailed on the newly completed steamship SS *Duchess of York*, Canadian Pacific Steamships Line, from St John in New Brunswick bound for Liverpool in England. This two-funnelled liner of 20,000 tons carried 990 passengers and her maiden voyage had taken place only nine months previously. The Falkners shared a lower deck cabin together, and then went up to the dining saloons for their meals. Impeccably dressed stewards served the different sittings in the main dining saloon.

The Canadian Pacific Steamships' specially printed souvenir booklets advised that: 'Meals will be served in the Dining Saloon at 8.30 Breakfast, 1.00pm Luncheon, 7.00 pm Dinner. Bugle is sounded thirty minutes before dinner. Lights extinguished in Dining

Saloon at 11 pm and in the lounge and Smoking Room at midnight.'

The children were all excited about the Atlantic voyage ahead. Roy, Harry and Leslie all remembered the all-pervading odour of castrolite diesel oil from the ship's engine room. Roy spent the voyage exploring the ship and asking the officers questions. The captain, Ronald Niel Stuart VC, fired his imagination. He was a First World War naval hero.

The ship left harbour in mid-December and was still at sea on Christmas Day. The ship was specially decorated and both the passengers and ship's crew were in a festive mood. Leslie remembered the children's Christmas party on the ship organised by the ship's crew and how each of the children received a small present.

In total the Atlantic journey took just four days. Early on Boxing Day they finally arrived at Liverpool Docks, the family travelling across the Pennines to stay with relatives in Nottingham. Their cousin, Phillip Falkner, the same age as Leslie, recalled meeting his Canadian family for the first time. For him it was an unforgettable event as the adults made him compete in a rough-and-tumble game with Leslie. She was made of sterner stuff and easily beat him. By then Grace and Sydney had instilled a hardworking and resourceful attitude into all their children.

Some of the first impressions of the differences with their home in Canada, included the hustle and bustle and as Harry recollected there were 'lots of street lights in England which were *gas* and also the house lights!'

They settled for what was intended to be just a short while in the tiny fishing village, Shaldon, on the other side of the Teign Estuary from Teignmouth in South Devon. They had picked the village due to its convenience to Roy's college and because it reminded them all of home in Saanich.

They rented a house, Penrhyn, from a retired captain. Captain Rendell was renowned as having commanded Brunel's ship the *Great Eastern*, when the first transatlantic telegraph cable was laid almost seventy years before.

Once settled in England, Grace soon realised she preferred the lifestyle there and the family soon settled down to a more permanent Devon life with the likelihood of returning to Canada getting more and more remote. Roy was ready for his college life to begin.

CHAPTER 2

Dartmouth Cadet

Roy entered the Royal Navy as a Canadian Dominion candidate and registered on 1 January 1930 at the age of thirteen. Two weeks later he started as a junior cadet at the Royal Naval College in Dartmouth on the south coast of England.

He was registered as a 'colonial' under the name 'Baker-Falkner'. The Admiralty insisted on people double-barrelling their names where there was a possibility of confusion – there was already another cadet with the surname Falkner at the college.

The college was to cost Roy's parents just under £300 a year for the next three to four years – and this was not to mention the kit and uniforms which the family had to buy. By comparison, throughout the 1930s the average salary was approximately £200 a year and a three-bedroom house cost £350. Roy and his parents had to make a special trip to London to get him fitted out at Gieves in Bond Street. His parents were stunned when they heard the high price of his uniforms but they found the money from somewhere.

Sydney and Grace, who shortly after assumed the title of Baker-Falkner which was to stay with Roy for the rest of his life, proudly arranged a portrait photograph of Roy just before the first day of term which cost the grand total of 6d.

The Royal Naval College, known officially as HMS *Britannia*, lay on the steep, wooded western flank of the ancient town of Dartmouth on the River Dart. The building was an imposing landmark, designed by George Aston Webb whose previous commissions included Admiralty Arch and the East Front of Buckingham Palace. Entering the college must have been a daunting experience for the young teenager from a small school in Canada.

The college was run by a naval captain, on a fixed three-year appointment, and the headmaster, Mr E.W.E. Kempson. They were assisted by term officers, along with masters and personal tutors of the subjects to be taught. Roy was introduced to his term officer, Lieutenant Arthur Havers, a junior naval officer who was appointed to train the cadets in naval matters. Roy's tutor was Cyril Barnes-Lawrence, or CB-L for short, the English and history master.

Each intake of cadets, or term as they were known, was named after a celebrated admiral. They kept this house title throughout their four-year period at Dartmouth – to foster a sense of belonging and team spirit. Roy entered the Greynvile XI Term, a class of about thirty-eight cadets.

Roy soon lost any shyness at college, although in the first few weeks he was bullied for his Canadian accent and even called a 'barbarian' by some of the other more snobbish cadets. But he could stand up for himself – there were no problems there!

Another young Canadian in the Royal Navy, William 'Bill' Martyn, recalled in his letters to his parents back home in Canada:

One thing that gets me down occasionally, believe it or not, is that on being introduced, it's so-and-so, 'he's a Canadian'. They look at you in an interested fashion. Makes one feel like an idiot or a tagged animal at times. Not that I'm not proud that I am a Canadian – I couldn't be prouder. But it's like an Englishman in Canada – you have to lie pretty low.

Roy was rapidly accepted as he started to pick up the naval parlance and a British accent. The cadets also recognised his strong character, spontaneous friendly nature and no-nonsense attitude to life.

Roy's closest friends were Robert Boddington, Donald McEwen and Bill Whitworth. Peter Pagett was another friend but not in the inner friendship ring. Boddington came from a well-to-do family in the Birmingham area, renowned throughout the region for their brewery. Roy's other friend McEwen was from an equally well-off family; his grandfather was one of the first ever engineers in the Navy during the time of 'Up Funnel, down Screw'. McEwen was from the Channel Islands where they owned their own aeroplane.

Another cadet in that term was Michael Cary, who later recalled:

Roy was one of the most instantly likeable people I have known. The first captain of the college, when we joined on 15 January 1930, was Captain S.J. Meyrick, later Admiral and Commander-in-Chief America and West Indies Station. I remember his wife declared herself fascinated by Roy's – at that time – soft Canadian accent.

The terms were divided into three depending on ability, with cadet captains – like prefects – assigned to each term of cadets. Bill Whitworth jokingly recalled: 'Roy was at the bottom and I was rather higher up!'

The college was run as if it was a ship at sea, officers' rooms were called cabins and they relaxed in the wardroom; divisions parade was on the quarterdeck. Roy's first day started with bugle call reveille. At dawn, an old naval pensioner was detailed to get the cadets out of bed. Roy and the other cadets then went to the wash rooms for the brine plunge – a three foot deep, wash in icy water – followed by the first lesson of the day in the 'gunroom' – the naval equivalent of a classroom.

Another bugle call and Roy and the other cadets trooped out onto the parade ground and there was half an hour of drill, followed by daily morning parade divisions on the quarterdeck – the purpose of which was to raise the white ensign to the masthead and thereby declare the day had officially begun.

Following morning classes, there was the 'stand-easy' lunch break at 1 pm, then came an afternoon of classes or sport and in the evening further classes and prep.

Roy may well have been exhausted at the hour of 'turning in' with nineteen other cadets in his dormitory, including his new-found friend Robert Boddington. He found his bed, strictly according to alphabetical order, and put his few possessions in a black, battered sea-chest carved with innumerable cadet initials.

That first night he must have felt very awed as he lay in a strange bed in a strange country surrounded by strangers.

During the week, Roy took classes in seamanship, navigation and gunnery, along with torpedo classes and signals.

One of Roy's fellow cadets at Dartmouth, John Lang, recalled:

Studies were roughly divided into vocational subjects and general education. The former comprised navigation and pilotage, seamanship including 'naval practices' and 'organisation', engineering i.e. lectures in turbines, triple expansion and diesel engines, and very elementary practical fitting, pattern-making and casting and brazing, also technical drawing.

Engineering was carried out in the workshops at Sand Quay on the edge of the Dart, reached by descending many steps. Going down was okay but returning up them in double quick time was a real sweat!

On the river, we had practical instruction in sailing all the basic naval boats of the period. We also had some experience in operating the engines of steam harbour launches and motor boats. And, of course, there was rowing, or, in naval parlance 'boat pulling'. The river had a recreational aspect too with sailing races both on the river and at sea plus boating picnics in the summer term.

As a background to the above, there were innumerable parades, rifle drills and especially in the junior years, much marching here and there! Discipline was very rigid and punishment frequent and severe for very minor infringements.

For Roy and the other new cadets, the whole atmosphere of the college was of teamwork and intense competition, upon the sports field and in the gym. Lang continued:

Games were the usual for large schools of that age – rugger in the Christmas term, hockey or soccer at Easter and cricket and/or sailing in the summer. Additional sports were tennis and squash, boxing and fencing. Rifle shooting was compulsory for all. Studies and games took place within one's own term. The exception, of course, was representative sport.

At the end of a seemingly long week, it was Friday and Roy received a whole shilling's pay for his mess bills, enough to buy two afternoon teas in the nearby village.

On Sunday Roy attended the weekend divisions' parade which featured a sixteen-piece naval band. He and the other cadets formed 'fours' then opened rank and marched. Captain Meyrick, followed by the chaplain, inspected them. All cadets were then dragooned and marched into the chapel. Sunday was the only free afternoon but everyone had to be back for the evening service.

Towards the middle of each term was the 'whole holiday' and Roy, McEwen and Boddington were introduced to the cadet tradition of rushing out for afternoon teas and walks.

Roy eagerly awaited letters from the family, collecting them in the morning from the signals office. Parents were discouraged from visiting Dartmouth. However, that first term Grace insisted on coming to check Roy was settling in.

When visiting, the main duty of parents was to order cream teas and mixed grills for their offspring but certainly not to penetrate the sacred quarterdeck without permission.

The five year-old Leslie came with her parents to visit her elder brother, and was particularly taken by the friendly hounds of the Dartmouth hunt.

After ten weeks of attending the college, at last came the end of term, which was marked by examinations and Roy's first end of term dance and his first introduction to the young ladies of the gentry in the country estates around the college.

The final morning there was the special 07.15 hours early morning train, paid for by the Admiralty. Leaving the college, dragging trunks and suitcases, the cadets would cross the river, sharing with friends to pay the taxi which brought them to the Dartmouth waterside, then to Kingswear Station. The train travelled only to Torquay where all passengers disembarked.

To get home, Roy took the London-bound train, past Newton Abbot and around the Teign estuary and into Teignmouth. Then he crossed over to Shaldon on the 1d ferry, a traditional black-and-white long narrow craft built in 1906.

Back home, he went upstairs into his top floor bedroom, built into the eaves in Penrhyn house, for four glorious weeks' leave with no uniform. Next morning, instead of the early wake up call by the Dartmouth pensioners, his father roused the family as normal with his 'Got a bone in your leg', followed by breakfast in the dining room with its inset alcoves at either end and big old iron range. Roy had to get used to the house's quirky ways, including the lighting which was powered by electricity but very old fashioned. It was possible to get electric shocks each time the big brass switches were turned on.

Now was time to explore the village. He did not have to go far from Penrhyn, which looked out over the estuary to Teignmouth. The harbour in those days was full of sailed fishing boats, steam pleasure craft, working barges filled with sand or timber, scruffy old steam tramp ships, and big many-masted sailing ships.

Shaldon was an unspoilt rural Devon village. Mr Irish owned the dairy right next to Penrhyn, where the cows were milked every evening and then walked back along the street by the herdsman, Mr Wackup.

On his return home, Roy was for ever using naval phrases, including calling toilets 'heads' to the frustration of his parents. He also used to tick off the family if they confused the term 'boat' with that of 'ship', or dared whistle on board their boat as it was bad luck in the Royal Navy. Other idiosyncratic naval traditions which Roy duly trained his brother and sister to carry out included saluting magpies 'as if they were dressed in the full ceremonial uniforms of Admirals of the Fleet,' recalled Leslie.

That first Easter, Harry also had just broken up for the end of term. His school was Lendrick School, near the front in Teignmouth. Every day he would row across the estuary to Teignmouth and school. Grace would put on the tea when she saw Harry start to row home. Leslie's school, her first, was a tiny one in Ringmore. She used to walk along the sea wall to get there, passing swans feeding in the estuary next to the school. Easter 1930 – the first English Easter for the family – included the usual Falkner tradition of searching for the Easter eggs in the house and garden.

The three children then rushed out to explore, visiting the lifeboat house on the shoreline, and asking lots of questions of the old lifeboat skipper, Alfred Stanisforth. When the lifeboat went out to sea, it had to be pushed out on wheels, and everyone in the village would rush down to watch it sail off. The fire engine used to be kept in the market place.

Roy would sit on the sea wall and chat with the old fishermen, mending their nets whilst smoking their clay pipes or making lobster pots. These characters were old world fisher folk with wind-blown leathery faces and faded 'blue' canvas smocks, or woollen jerseys, and big bushy beards. Snowy the fisherman was a particular character. Roy and the older children would help pull in the nets to the shore and in return for their help were given a small bucket of fish, especially mackerel, to take home to their mothers.

Leslie recalled: 'There would be old glass weights on the nets and old wickerwork lobster pots that the fishermen would go and place around the Ness every day.'

An inevitable favourite haunt for the children was the little sweet shop on the Strand. Close by the village green was the haunt of the old fishermen, the pub. Characters who frequented it included limping Nobby Hook, who liked to trip people up with his crutch. There were the three Sharness brothers and Giddy Thomas, the old coastguard, and others who would tell tales of fishing trips in sailing boats as far away as Newfoundland. One old chap, called Crab, used to wear a bowler hat. These old fishermen would have a field day when one of their contemporaries died and insisted on being the pallbearers.

In May 1930, Roy went back to college, perhaps a little apprehensive about his new life but now more familiar with the naval routine and what was expected of him. So he returned to the daily grind of studies and divisions. On the brighter side, Roy found that summer term also meant strawberries and Devonshire cream and lazing around swimming or rowing. He hated cricket and was no good at tennis, but enjoyed golf and horse-riding.

That second term concentrated on general studies as John Lang recalled:

> Our subjects were French, English language and literature, history – I think from Queen Elizabeth I to World War I with special emphasis on naval history, geography for the first six terms (then replaced by special trigonometry and astro navigation), mathematics, pure and applied and the sciences. Maths and science predominated in the syllabus.

The term flashed by and the summer vacation arrived, bringing with it the annual Shaldon Regatta, an ancient tradition which was first started in 1817.

Roy, Harry and young Leslie looked forward to the annual Shaldon regatta; Roy would go with his friends 'Pip' O'Rorke who was also at Dartmouth College and lived at Coombe Cellars, just outside Shaldon, and Struan Robertson, another naval cadet friend, whose family had a house at the top of the village.

One highlight was the regatta jousting in open boats. A local brunette, Naomi Lord, remembered that: 'We used to lend Daddy's boat to the old fishermen in their jousting competition.' As usual the whole village would be absolutely packed with revellers.

That summer, Roy, Harry and Leslie took utmost advantage of the fine weather. Leslie recalled:

> We used to have an old wooden boat thing, with rowlocks, oars and the works. We used to row around the Ness, past the pilots and their boats to guide ships around the dangerous sand banks and eddies, water lapping on the side of the hull.

They also used to swim a lot and Leslie was always looked after by her biggest brother, Roy. The trio would swim around the other side of the Ness, which was their favourite place. They would clamber over the rocks and go fishing for shrimps, mussels, winkles and little fish. Sometimes they saw porpoises roll over in schools on the horizon. Occasionally. they sighted big ships.

The family bought some bicycles, with the old fashioned lights, and all five of them would go on outings towards Labrador hill, three miles towards Torquay.

As the youngsters grew older, Grace and Sydney would take them on longer cycle rides for picnics all together to Dartmoor and to Fingle Bridge. They were a close-knit family and enjoyed each other's company.

One of Roy's Dartmouth instructors, Lt Cdr Vaughan Williams, the naval history tutor, would spend the summer holiday with his family at Shaldon. His children, Robin and Iona, were good friends with Roy, Harry and Leslie, playing on the beach whilst their father would spend his time making perfect replica ship models, even the detail down to a red strand of thread in the rigging which was found in full-sized naval vessels was faithfully reproduced. The Falkners were amazed by his cleverness and skill.

As the family settled down in Shaldon they got to know more about the local people and Grace became known for her 'cut and come again cake' and the whole family as the 'musical Falkners'. In one house on the hill that summer there used to be garden parties with ladies in summer frocks reminiscent of the 1920s.

For Roy's third term Lt Cdr Duncan was term officer and McEwen was term cadet captain to Roy's delight. However, by the time of the exam results Roy was only thirty-third place out of thirty-eight cadets – a non too promising position.

Even though Roy's academic skills were lacking, his sporting talents were standing him in good stead. During the winter term he was selected to play in the college's junior rugby XV. He loved the team spirit and the rough and tumble. There was the added bonus of a sausage tea after the game. The first team at that time was captained by J.P. Kirkby and included a cadet, called E.S. Carver, and it looked like Roy would remain friends with him for a long time to come.

In the middle of the winter term it was customary to hold a voluntary boxing competition; the cadets received next to no training except for the odd ten minutes in gym periods. Roy had much practice fighting with his younger brother and decided to enter. He proved a natural boxer and ended up winning in the finals and was presented with a tankard. Roy's confidence rose in leaps and bounds. He proved to be a clever boxer, who won his weight, welterweight, competitions in each of the three years at Dartmouth.

That autumn term a new cadet arriving at Dartmouth, Alexander Fraser-Harris, who had followed Roy from Canada on a Commonwealth Scholarship. His presence in the college helped Roy feel less like the only Canadian to be picked on by his fellow English cadets.

As Christmas approached there was the usual carol concert at the college. Nancy Bartlett, a close friend, recalled the event:

Roy was playing the violin – not in an orchestra – with just a few other instruments. I thought what a very special event for him and how impressed I was, the lovely voices of those young men, the choir. We sat up in the gallery as I looked down on Roy – the only violin and on the right side of the chancel. It is so clear in my memory, the wonder of the old English and European carols that Christmas and the great moment with all those voices so glorious, and Roy playing.

The college broke up for the Christmas holidays. This was the first-ever English Christmas for Roy, Harry and Leslie, and they enjoyed the traditional singing of carols on the Shaldon Green.

In the spring term, 1931, sports included association football and hockey. Roy studied navigational procedures and calculation, Morse code by key and Aldis lamp, semaphore flags and knot tying, at which cadets had to be proficient in nine different kinds.

That Easter Roy had twenty-seven days' leave at Shaldon. Easter-time included a tiny fair, even a merry-go-round with wooden horses on the green. Leslie recollected at that time small seaplanes regularly flew from the seafront at Teignmouth across the moors at Haldon. It was possible to get a flight in a biplane for 2/6d at the aerodrome.

In May, Roy and other cadets above the age of fifteen years competed for the Royal Life Saving Society medallion. They went to the college swimming baths, dived from the coconut-matted diving boards, dragged unwilling comrades half a length by the neck, and swam two further lengths in their clothes.

Roy won the Bronze Life Saving Medal, inscribed with the date – May 1931. Later he was honoured with the award of a Silver Life Saving Medal after he saw a swimmer in distress near the Ness at Shaldon. Roy organised bystanders to form a human chain extending into the water to stretch out to the person. Sadly, they could not reach the swimmer who disappeared below the waves.

Two or so weeks after the Dartmouth summer term started there was excitement as the King of Spain, Alphonso XIII, sent his nineteen-year-old son, 'Cadet His Royal Highness Prince Juan' to Dartmouth.

The Crown Prince's father and several of his daughters visited the college the following weekend. They arrived on the Saturday and listened to a special concert by a small group, which included Roy, playing the violin. After the concert Prince Juan came to Roy and said to him 'damned good, damned good show'. Roy was very proud of this and could not wait to tell his amazed family, as Leslie recollected.

That year Harry's name was in the local press:

> Master Harry Falkner, a boy of 8 years congratulated for his remarkable skill at the piano held on Thursday, 29 May 1931, at Congregational Church, Shaldon. At 6.15 pm a musical service was given by various friends, amongst those taking part were Mrs Falkner, Master Harry Falkner, Mr L. Bulley, Miss Doris Bulley, and Mr H. Rawlings (the blind preacher of Exeter).

In July it was the end of term dance. Roy fondly kept his invitation 'requesting the pleasure of the company of Cadet Baker-Falkner and party at the dance in the gymnasium at the Royal Naval College on Monday, 27th July 1931. Dancing from 8 till 10 pm.'

Roy enjoyed shooting in the winter term. He and other cadets were given service Lee Enfield rifles to practise before divisions. The college broke up for Christmas again and glorious holidays. Bill Whitworth recalled shared vacations: 'Roy spent at least three holidays with us at a farm in Sussex where we made him shoot, ride and fall twenty-three feet out of an oak tree.'

Boddington sometimes came to visit Roy. Even though Leslie was a good eight years younger she admired the good-looking Robert. The family always used to tease her and she would blush at the mere mention of his name.

It was the new term, 1932, and Roy was now in the Senior College. He came eighteenth in the order of merit – Roy was gradually catching up with his friends Boddington, McEwen and Whitworth who were all Alphas. In the end of term promotions lists, skills of leadership were starting to be recognised when he was made cadet captain for the following three terms of senior year.

These three terms were to see Roy and the other cadets going on week-long training cruises to Plymouth, Penzance, the Isles of Scilly and Wales on the college sloop, the *Fife*.

Roy now had another new term officer to teach the Greynvile Term in naval matters as Michael Cary recalled:

> Our term officer at this time was Lieutenant Douglas Holland-Martin, known to us as 'Windy'. He went on to become Second Sea Lord. Roy was a cadet captain for our tenth term and a term cadet captain for our eleventh and final term.

Roy had applied to be College Cadet Captain but he was just not quite up to scratch and was not offered the promotion. He continued to put much of his efforts into his sports. By now, he was in the first XV rugby team, played hockey and excelled in the boxing ring.

In the Senior College Boxing Championship of 1933 Roy won the Middle Weight Boxing Championship match, and was awarded the Senior College tankard.

As Nancy Bartlett recalled 'There was his boxing. He was middle weight champion and all the events he played in he won at Dartmouth.'

Roy was excelling at sport and he was also showing leadership qualities through his cadet captain role. His term officer could see that Roy was inspiring the younger cadets by his fairness and leading from example, promoting co-operation and obedience and even awe by his prowess on the track, in the boxing ring and on the rugby pitch.

Roy was maturing and soon felt that given his cadet captain position he should have his own calling cards. Leslie recalled: 'When Roy was appointed as Greynvile Cadet Captain he had printed hundreds of calling cards with "Mr R.S. Baker-Falkner" in big type.'

During that summer, there were lazy days in the sun with picnics and sailing. He and his pals visited Nancy at her home, Little Dartmouth.

Nancy, who by then had become Roy's first girlfriend, recalled:

Little Dartmouth was my home, 400 acres on the coast, with fabulous views, three miles out of Dartmouth – now a National Trust property. For years since I can remember, cadets came on Sundays for tea. They came in the early afternoon and went out on a ramble with us, the Bartletts. When we first met Roy, he came with Jim Coleridge and another cadet. Jim was the son of a girlhood friend of my mother. It hurts me to tell of his being lost in one of those big battleships when torpedoed. [He was killed in the destroyer HMS *Acheron* on 17 December 1940.] The third cadet also died during the war from illness.

They always came early afternoon and we each took a golf club 'driving' off the terrace outside the dining room – then out over the fields we set off, eight of us, along with spaniels and a Labrador, and over the two fields to cliffs and three coves, to Start Bay – and then out east or west, anywhere. We had glorious exercise each time, walking for hours and then back for tea!

Roy was always so handsome and quite outstanding, so well groomed and an air of example and leadership. Roy was so mature for his age and coming from Canada seemed more serious than most cadets – such a wonderful person to be with.

The final term 1933 saw Roy take his Passing Out examinations, and gaining a third class pass, being twentieth in a class of twenty-nine. The results of his exams were good for seamanship, navigation and gunnery with lower marks for torpedo and signals.

Roy's Passing Out Parade was a major event for the family. Sydney and Grace received a special embossed invitation card. In the evening before, Roy stood on the quarterdeck in uniform complete with white gloves, stiff shirt and sword in readiness for the end of term dance with Nancy in honour of the departing term. There was a special band and a buffet in the dining hall. As the dance came to an end, the band played the National Anthem and everyone stood rigid at attention.

Nancy recalled: 'Then of course I loved the end of term dance, always a big show. Roy was a superb dancer and host, and we waltzed around that huge quarterdeck like flying through the air. I felt so proud.'

Grace and Sydney stayed overnight in Dartmouth and the next morning they proudly watched the Passing Out Parade.

Roy was now seventeen. Within weeks of leaving Dartmouth, he was posted to his first-ever ship, HMS *Frobisher*. 'Froby' as she was known, was a Cavendish Class light cruiser of some 9,800 tons. She had been designed in the First World War for the specific purpose of hunting down and destroying enemy cruisers sent to attack British convoys. That autumn, she was used as a cadet training ship under Captain H.A. Foster. Roy and other cadets of the Greynvile Term were to spend two terms in the Mediterranean and West Indies.

Roy packed his canvas naval kit bag and met up with Boddington and McEwen before boarding the ship. In total, there were 118 cadets on board *Frobisher*. As he later noted '*Frobisher*'s cadets were piped early each morning and would be scrubbing decks by 0600.'

Donald Eldridge, 1st class stoker on *Frobisher* recollected:

The crew came from Chatham and Portsmouth. It was not a full complement of ratings because we had all the cadets on board.

When on duty in the stokehole CO_2 room or on evaporators, we had a cadet and he did all the turning on and turning off, wiping up oil or whatever. I made a bit on the side by giving extra instructions after duty. I left after a lovely trip in the West Indies.

Roy admitted to getting seasick until 'I got my sea legs' and later told Leslie 'You are bow legged once onshore again and then you roll for days in your walk once back on dry land.'

Frobisher's gunnery officer took great delight in teaching the cadets fire control, using the traditional method last used in action at Jutland. He made cadets carry out a shoot so that in future years they could boast of being some of the last of the old generation of gunners.

In November 1933, Roy won the HMS *Frobisher* welterweight cadet boxing contest and was awarded another of his growing collection of pewter mugs. Leslie recalled that Roy had a wonderful time sailing to Antigua, the West Indies headquarters of the Royal Navy since the eighteenth century, and cruising amongst the Caribbean Islands to the USA.

Roy's fellow cadet John Lang remembered: 'On leaving Dartmouth, we went for eight months in a seagoing training ship – an old cruiser – for two cruises and then went to the Fleet for two years as midshipmen.'

That winter of 1933 and into the early part of 1934, the weather was bitter. Leslie only remembers it snowing once in Shaldon, normally it was too warm. That year the sea froze at the edges.

As the Falkners settled down to life in rural Devon they decided to stay permanently. Roy was busy developing his own life and was soon to spend two years as a midshipman – to an as yet unknown destination.

Roy was about to embark upon a major adventure.

CHAPTER 3

Midshipman's Days in Hong Kong

Roy was given the rank of midshipman on 1 May 1934. Three weeks later he was posted to HMS *Kent*, the Admiral's Flagship of the Royal Navy China Fleet. The Commander-in-Chief was Admiral Sir Frederic Dreyer KCB, CBE, who had been Flag Captain of the Grand Fleet under Admiral Lord Jellicoe at the Battle of Jutland.

Kent, which was an eight-year-old battle cruiser with a displacement of 9,850 tons, was to sail to the Far East over a two-year commission and Roy was ordered to join her at Chatham Naval Docks on 24 May. His parents were delighted as it was a rare honour for any midshipmen to be posted to the Admiral's flagship.

After saying a last goodbye to his family and friends in Shaldon, Roy arrived on board *Kent* and was directed to the midshipman's mess – the gunroom – where he was allocated a 'doggie', a midshipman's assistant. With him in the gunroom were his friends McEwen and Boddington and other midshipmen, French, Whitworth, Bolton, Green and Woodward.

Roy was told to keep a 'Journal For The Use of Midshipmen', which was written in longhand with an ink pen every day over the two years. It was to reveal a way of life in the British Navy between the two World Wars at a time when Britain still had an Empire which stretched across Asia and the Far East.

Roy's very first journal entry opened with: 'HMS *Kent*: At Chatham Friday 25 May: All the midshipmen and the three paymaster cadets joined about 1900 last night. This morning Captain Tower recommissioned the ship with a complement of 728 men.'

The next day began early but not as early as his training ship, as Roy recorded: 'The midshipmen were called at 0630. How different to the "*Frobisher*" where we would have done half an hour's scrubbing decks.'

Two days later Roy recorded: '0700 all midshipmen had to run to the RNB swimming bath. Everyone enjoyed the bathing but there were very few fit legs for running.'

Sunday 3 June was King George V's birthday, which was celebrated with a parade and band. The next day *Kent* set out on her travels and Roy soon saw his first catapult trial at sea involving a two-seater Hawker Osprey seaplane: 'After a very considerable delay the plane was launched successfully. The plane was picked up and the launching was repeated till everything was satisfactory.'

Kent left Spithead on 8 June and set sail for Gibraltar. Roy commented: 'No one seemed particularly sorry to leave English soil for the last time for two years.'

His duties on board were to include gunnery practice and watch keeping. Off duty much of his time was occupied by sport and athletics as noted the following day: 'Most of the midshipmen were taking exercise in the dog watches, boxing or playing tennis with a twenty to twenty-five pound medicine ball. After this French and I boxed for a very short time.'

Two days later, Roy looked a little worse for his boxing activities: 'French and I again boxed. He caught me in the eye making me look like an Egyptian flapper.'

Almost a week later, *Kent* arrived in Gibraltar: 'We were in whites. Unfortunately not in open necked shirts and bare feet as we were last time we entered Gib.'

From Gibraltar, *Kent* sailed eastwards into the Mediterranean:

14 June. We weighed and proceeded to sea in the morning for gunnery and to Malta. Everyone felt baked but it was better when we got under way. No bathing at 4 pm unfortunately. Overend, Green, French and I played tennis with the medicine ball then boxed five minute and a half rounds and a two-minute round to end up with. It was grand, both of us are in the wars though. Then in the evening took times for star sights.

While at sea, 'All Hands to bathe' was piped in readiness for crew members to go for a swim in the sea by the ship. Roy found himself in trouble on one such occasion:

I was lowered in my whaler to attend the bathing and made a mess of the signals. First I couldn't find the boat's signal book and then thought that the first whaler's distinguishing pendant was mine, and mine was hers. Consequently the Commander required my presence on the bridge afterwards.

Four days later, *Kent* entered Malta's Grand Harbour. Roy seemed more taken with the ships in the harbour than the magnificence of the medieval fortifications.

A couple of days later *Kent* sailed for Port Said and the Suez Canal:

The usual sea routine was carried out with starboard watch cruising stations at 2030. As sunrise is about 0435 I get up at 0345 to take times for star sights. The mornings are very mild and there is a gentle breeze.

As the ship approached the Suez Canal, Roy noted:

Slipped buoy and proceeded up the canal at 5 knots. Hands bathed at 2 o'clock and again whalers were required as bathing boats. At 1230 we proceeded again and passed the War Memorial to those who gave their lives in the Great War in defence of the canal. It was a curious rectangular pile standing on a colossal stone base.

Kent took twelve hours to travel through the canal. Roy wrote: 'There is nothing to think of now but a cold bath and rest as everyone swelters. I had the forenoon watch and thought it would never end.'

As they passed through the Red Sea towards Aden temperatures rose even higher. 'Just the same terrible heat all night. Hardly any sleep at all, most people slept on deck last night. Even for relief decks the temperature was 94 degrees. In the gunroom it actually reached 104 degrees.'

Aden was reached on 29 June: 'Aden is a very rocky place of volcanic construction with the town itself nestling amongst the hills. There is not a vestige of green anywhere except the gardens. There are no proper shops, merely the usual native bazaar.'

Kent sailed for Colombo the following day; the weather became more oppressive and worsened into monsoon conditions with high seas. Two days later Roy noted:

Still the monsoon blew us on. The largest roll was about 22 degrees to port, 18 to starboard. In the evening on the quarterdeck there were silly games which everyone enjoyed, such as skinning the snake, wheelbarrow races. The gunroom raced against the wardroom.

Colombo was reached on 7 July:

Colombo is a large Indian populated but European built city. East and West vie together. Rickshaws wait alongside modern taxis. Men with hair in buns, men in turbans jostle with men with military hair cut and tailor made suits. Women in robes stand in the racecourse elbow to elbow with women in the latest Paris creations.

The next day being Sunday there were divisions and church as usual. Roy took the opportunity to play a round of golf:

The course is very expensive on balls. There are a tremendous number of lakes and ditches to play over. Then when the ball does go in, native boys fish them out with their toes and of course expect something.

That evening Roy went to the Galle Face Hotel to bathe and listen to *Kent*'s Royal Marine Band as the sun set over the sea: 'It did seem incongruous that we should be sitting in velvety darkness on the lawn listening to our own band. They were good but one hardly cares to see the same old uniforms ashore.'

The ship's unofficial diary recorded events in Ceylon:

It was a glorious tropical night and there seemed many worse things to do than to lie in a comfortable chair drinking cold beer and listen to the music. Colombo was left with a certain amount of regret on 9 July and we resumed our journey eastwards.

On 9 July, *Kent* left Colombo for Singapore. Roy wrote:

In the morning we fired three torpedoes from the fore port tubes at the first cutter. All three were quite close to her. My whaler was lowered to pick up one torpedo. We towed it astern at first but found it practically impossible, the boat kept turning to port so we had to bring it alongside.

Roy was on watch the first day *Kent* arrived at Singapore. The following day he managed some shore leave, which proved expensive: 'Everywhere in Singapore in the clubs the chit system is in force so it is very easy to spend a great deal of money without noticing it.' For all the ship's crew the memory of Singapore was of the creek where the ship lay anchored: 'a smell, that amongst all odours of the East, can hold up its head unbeaten and unbearable.'

On 17 July, *Kent* sailed for Hong Kong:

When we were leaving the land, RAF bombers exercised aerial torpedo practice. They fired six torpedoes, four from the starboard side and two from the port. There were two misses, one ahead from the port and one astern from the starboard. One got mixed up in the screw and I believe sank.

All anti-aircraft stations were exercised. Pom poms and machine guns got on – after we had been torpedoed owing to lack of information from the bridge.

On 15 July, casting off about 1315 we proceeded to sea and were 'attacked' by a RAF torpedo-bombing squadron. Six torpedoes were launched at us of which four were hits. Three other planes meanwhile sprayed us with machine guns, and we steamed steadily towards Hong Kong, where we duly entered harbour at 0600 on the morning of 22 July.

The ship entered harbour at Hong Kong for a three-day period during which time the rain never ceased. Roy noted: 'According to the news England had 0.5 inches of rain and considered it a lot. We had 4.5 inches and that was a mere average.'

The colony formed the last fortified British stronghold in the East. Roy reported:

Hong Kong itself is tucked away between mountains very much the same as Aden. It is naturally protected from attack by mountains. Long-range attack is practically impossible because of the mountains especially with naval guns, as their trajectory is low and could not drop quickly enough to land on the town.

Hong Kong is situated on an island with an area of rather less than thirty square miles, one of a group round the mouth of the Canton River. At Victoria along the waterfront for about three miles stretched warehouses, piers and office buildings. Behind them lay the city proper, the imposing Hong Kong and Shanghai Bank towering up in the midst of lofty European-style business premises.

Kent sailed onwards again via the Yangtze River towards Wei-hai-wei, arriving there on 30 July. The long journey from England had come to an end after seven and a half weeks.

Wei-hai-wei, or 'Way High' as nicknamed by the sailors, was the main anchorage and summer station for the Royal Navy China Station. Roy wrote: 'Wei-hai-wei is a small island about two and a half miles long and a mile wide in the broadest part and is about two miles from the mainland.' Wei-hai-wei was rented from the Chinese government so there were no shore facilities to speak of.

Roy may have arrived at his destination but there was work to be done: 'Aug 1: Painted ship solidly all day. Everything I touched was covered with paint consequently Sin Jelly Belly has my esteemed order for more uniforms.'

It was Roy's home for the next three months and he was excited to explore. His summer home was to be Liukungtao, a pretty and well-wooded little island about two miles in length and one in breadth. It offered facilities for all the fleet sporting events, while the canteen, Boys' Club and cinema got their full share of patronage. There were a few Chinese shops in the little village which ministered to the needs of the summer visitors and liberty men.

That first Sunday at Wei-hai-wei was marked by the ship's company landing and marching to the rifle range to attend a Drumhead Service church parade. In the afternoon Roy and others went to play golf or cricket.

The next week the gunnery programme started in earnest, including full-calibre night firing. Recreational activities centred on a sailing race which *Kent* won 'with her whaler by about eight minutes'.

Roy was becoming aware of international tensions and noted on 29 August: 'I had my first close view of the Japanese destroyers that came in yesterday. They are in war conditions practically, with no bright work of any kind.'

The next day the commander-in-chief arrived on board *Kent* and hoisted his flag. Roy recorded wryly: 'The C-in-C arrived having been pulled by his staff in the green galley from the *Suffolk*. It is very cheering to see gold braid pulling an oar occasionally.'

At the Fleet Sports on 13 September, Roy was part of *Kent*'s Obstacle Race team along with Able Seamen Cummings, Mumford and Phippen. The *Kent* team started off with a flourish, but ultimately came sixth out of the eight ships competing. Two weeks later the ship's crew faired somewhat better, as Roy wrote in his journal: 'In the communications hockey game today we beat the *Eagle* by 4–3. After a very strenuous hour and ten minutes hockey I had to go immediately to play against the boys in a gunroom football eleven.'

On 20 October, *Kent* set sail for Japan and Formosa on its Autumn Cruise in a rising wind and sea. En route with frequent rain squalls, Roy saw little of the approaching Japanese islands, the mountains and islands being generally shrouded in cloud. He therefore had plenty of time to write about current affairs in his journal and was showing increasing interest in aviation. He noted on 24 October:

> Today we heard that Scott and Black, two British airmen in the Mildenhall–Melbourne air race arrived in Melbourne. They took seventy-one hours, thus easily beating all records and also showing the world what a tremendous stride has been taken even in the last thirty years. Before that time no one could get to Australia in less than two months, now it is done in under three days.

Next day *Kent* anchored at Miyazu where the mayor and notables came on board and greeted the ship's company. Roy noted:

> During the dogwatches the ship was open to visitors and they swarmed on board like bees on a honey pot. Eight sentries were posted and the whole of the duty party was required as guides, each guide had parties of twenty-five or more.

The following day HMS *Kent* weighed and proceeded to Nagasaki where Roy went with other midshipmen into the town, led by a self-appointed guide:

> Nagasaki the town is a rambling place perched on the slopes of the hills with a two-mile harbour frontage. Piers there appear to be none, pontoons do their duty. Nowhere does there appear to be an imposing building. All life and importance is centred in the dockyard.
>
> We wandered through the streets eventually arriving at the Street of Lamps. We were jostled on every side by kimono-clad figures and rickshaw boys in their standardised costumes.
>
> The shops themselves seemed to continue the incongruity; next door to modern would-be Woolworth's were dingy little shops selling clogs or horrible-looking food. None of them were very large, however, and no building in Nagasaki exceeded two storeys in height.

As others of the ship's crew recalled: 'Nagasaki is a dirty squalid place. The shipyards were working night and day on naval and commercial work and the glare of the furnaces and welding plant lit up the night sky.'

On 31 October, *Kent* set off for Kobe, the greatest Japanese seaport, and the Inland Sea where there was a further chance to explore. McEwen later recalled:

> Roy and I did a lot together during our time in *Kent* and as subs. When *Kent* was at Kobe, in Japan, a small party of midshipmen, including B-F and myself, made a trip to Kyoto, which was then a sacred city, and saw the residence of the Emperor, all most beautiful.

Roy wrote about being invited to a gentleman's house: 'The house was twenty miles out of

Kobe, at Shoya, and it was a veritable newly built palace. Walls were all oak panelling with priceless Chinese vases and pottery arranged round all the rooms.'

McEwen continued: 'We were, as always, impecunious and all but ran out of money as we debated whether to have a final meal ashore or take a taxi back to the ship – the taxi won.'

Kobe impressed both Roy and McEwen with its large seaports and much shipping in the harbour. Roy noted that: 'The traffic is very thick and practically no rules exist. Cars pass on the wrong side of the road and cut in as they please. Tram drivers seem to take no notice of the police.'

It was the week of the Port Festival of the late Emperor Meiji and the Floral Parade of decorated cars amazed Roy:

> Ships, horses and birds were all designed in flowers. In a screened off portion of the ground were well-known scenes from Japanese history, all done in flowers, old knights on moss horses with attendants, and as a grand climax, there was a moulding of Kobe harbour with wooden models of the Japanese fleet at the Naval Review last year.

There was also a firework display which produced the effect of enormous chrysanthemums bursting into flower.

On leaving Japanese waters, Roy reflected on the country and its people:

> Before the cruise I thought that the Japanese were good looking, polite but very sly and inquisitive. Now I know them to be very charming and hospitable people with intensely patriotic minds, always ready to do anything, no matter how difficult or dangerous for their country.

In his entry for 13 November, Roy noted:

> Today according to the Press News, the naval situation at the conference is becoming very tense. The Japanese representative wants naval equality in the Pacific. The United States representative refuses to allow this as he rightly says that the United States have a very much larger area to defend than Japan. The proposal ratio is five Great Britain, five United States and three Japan. But Japan is adamant for equality, so a deadlock has ensued. The conference will probably be carried over for another year. The outcome is very uncertain with two very determined nations, resolved to have their way. Only time can tell.

By mid-November the ship was at Shanghai and secured near the Bund with its 'Million Dollar Skyline'. For many of the ship's crew Shanghai was an astonishing place, the cosmopolitan metropolis of the Far East.

At the time of *Kent*'s visit, the British had a large control in Shanghai's administration of the concessionary areas and had one battalion of troops stationed there.

General leave was given and Roy went with McEwen into town where transport was very varied – trams, buses, motor cars and rickshaws. Roy and his friends were drawn to the exotic Shanghai cabarets. Nanking Road was thronged by day with flags, hoardings and signs written in Chinese script, all a mystery to Roy and his colleagues; by night, mercury and neon signs blazed out into the sky. The night clubs were principally in the French Concession.

Roy went to a Shanghai tattooist and had a scar on his forearm covered by a tattoo of a dragon. This was much to his mother's horror when he eventually returned to England, recalled Leslie.

Kent gave an 'At Home' attended by many foreign officers. Later a dance was given for the ship's company by the British Women's Association on the Bund – rather handicapped by lack of space and 'possibly by lack of a bar' recalled Roy.

The city itself appeared very dirty after Kobe. Everywhere the untidiness of China seemed to have intruded itself into this cosmopolitan atmosphere. The same day he noted that an aeroplane had been seen flying up and down the coastline: 'The popular idea is that Japan has established an aerial base somewhere on the Finnish coast. Japan with no efforts seems to be able to terrify any of the European countries.'

Kent sailed back towards Hong Kong and en route called at Takao in Formosa. Roy wrote: 'The aboriginals still take a great delight in headhunting and think that they will not go to their Valhalla unless they have the head of a least one Chinese to their credit.'

The ship's company was given a very warm welcome by the Mayor of Takao, with presents varying from plants, to peanuts and tangerines, to coloured picture postcards all sent aboard in bulk.

By the end of the month *Kent* was back at Hong Kong when all the ships in harbour were dressed overall and illuminated in honour of the wedding of Prince George, Duke of Kent, to Princess Marina of Greece. The Commander-in-Chief gave a ball on board HMS *Kent* and HMS *Falmouth* which was attended by 400 guests. Roy reflected: 'Like all balls it was rather stately, no one dreamed of asking for a dance unless they were introduced.'

Perhaps due to disappointment and the poor sporting results of his ship, Roy failed to record in his journal that his boxing team in *Kent* was defeated in the boxing tournament with the Lincolnshire Regiment, losing nine and only winning three matches.

Christmas Day started with the usual Sunday routine of church on the quarterdeck, followed by the Commander-in-Chief and the officers making a round of the mess decks, and the messes being decorated for a dinner for all. The New Year, 1935, was welcomed by the ship's company dance at the China Fleet Club.

Roy wrote in his journal a first reference to the recently appointed Chancellor of Germany, Adolf Hitler:

> The ugly problem of the Saar plebiscite has been partially overcome by the larger nations in Europe sending military forces to act as police during the plebiscite. The Saar population consists chiefly of Germans but due to Hitler's Nazi regime the many Socialists and Communists in the Saar are bitterly opposed to being under German rule.

Following closely the news developments, he wrote two weeks later:

> The Saar plebiscite took place today. Germany was easily the most popular receiving 470,000, to status quo 46,000 and France 2,000. German occupation and rule will start as soon as possible. People who did not vote for Germany are not to be isolated or discriminated against in any way.

On 22 January, *Kent* commenced her Southern Cruise, which included visits to Manila, Bangkok, Sumatra and Japan.

Roy noted that Manila Bay was a magnificent sheet of water extending for nearly thirty miles with the fortified island of Corregidor commanding its entrance. Two years prior to *Kent*'s arrival, the United States had awarded the Filipinos independence timetabled to occur ten years later. However, the US Navy was still in force. In the harbour at Manila were a number of American vessels, including USS *Augusta* which hosted a cocktail party ashore.

Roy noted a difference between the British and American vessels ferrying people back and forth: 'They seem to be very strongly built with good engines and very ornate hulls and brass upperworks. Expense is obviously no object to the Americans.'

He revealed his own natural modesty: 'The Americans seem to have a little too much money for my taste. They do not mean to show it off but they do unconsciously in their boats, their clothes and in their very talk. Except for this, they are a very charming and friendly people.'

Roy, however, wrote: 'A great welcome has been extended the *Kent* by the Manila residents. Cocktail parties, dinner parties and dances have been arranged throughout our stay.' There was also the Santa Anna, said to be the largest cabaret in the world. This tremendous cabaret, with its magnificent Filipino band and the superb dancing of the elegant mestisas, young ladies of mixed Spanish and Filipino blood, was a venue that the Midshipmen were all looking forward to see.

Kent next sailed for Singapore, where Roy noted the creation of the Naval Base and dockyard, which was being converted from mangrove swamp:

> It is hoped to complete the dockyard by 1936, ready as a base if the Japanese take any steps at the end of the inaction period and her subsequent armament race.
>
> The Governor General of Singapore Sir Shelton Thomas in a speech ashore yesterday said that 'a large base in the East is necessary not only for the British fleet in China but for the whole of the East, including Australia'.

McEwen recollected their time in Singapore:

> I was lucky enough to do a lot of sailing as cox'n of both whalers and dinghies, and always had Roy as my crew. He was obviously very patient as I remember an occasion at Singapore when there was little wind and I required him to smoke so that I could catch any zephyr of wind which the smoke would show! We did win that race and he was a wonderful crewman on other more boisterous occasions, knowing as a seaman, what was required.

During training, HMS *Kent* was 'attacked' by RAF bombers and torpedo bombers. Following some thought, Roy wrote:

> I do not think that this attack would have been very successful as there was a clear sky and the aircraft were in sight, flying in close formation for at least ten minutes to a quarter of an hour before they actually arrived at the ship. They would have been under fire from 8 inch for 15 minutes, 4 inch for about 8 minutes and two minutes firing of the pom poms and .5 inch. The machines would also have been within range of rifles and Lewis guns when they dropped their torpedoes at about 800 yards range.

Preparations for hostilities were being built up as Roy noted when *Kent* was at Penang:

> Various members of the gunroom were invited by the Flying Club to go flying in their three Gypsy Moths. The club has only been formed about a year but already

there are a large number of pilots and members of the club. The pilots, besides civil flying, are being trained in war flying by an ex-RAF officer. Most of the men seem to be very air-minded and very keen and rather expecting the next war to arrive in a short time.

Other signs were noted by Roy:

Kent gave a cocktail party to the English residents here. Only seventy attended but that is not bad as there are only two to three hundred in the whole island. But although there are such a few, their hospitals were built for over a thousand patients. Thus they seem to think that Penang is either going to grow very rapidly or that we, the Navy, are going to require assistance in quantity.

On 1 March, Kent sailed for Sumatra. A British warship was a rarity in those parts and a large crowd arrived to greet the ship at its mooring alongside a wooden wharf. Hospitality was the order of the day. The residents took 200 of the ship's company, including Roy, into the interior of the country to Medan, dined them and gave them one of the pleasantest outings of the whole commission.

The ship's informal diary recorded: 'Britishers from remote plantations flocked into Medan until it was said, in the principal hotel, that never had so many British people been seen there before.'

Roy wrote in his journal:

We were all taken to dinner by our hosts at private houses, then went to the Hotel de Boer to attend the dance given there in our honour. The dance was a marvellous success and continued until the small hours of the following morning. I left at 0500 with my host and then was faced with a fifty-mile drive over bad roads and through jungle to his home. We covered the distance in about seventy minutes. The moonlit scenery was rather wonderful, moonbeams playing on bamboo, palms and breadfruit.

That same trip another member of the ship's company described how 'he went into the primitive jungle by night with a torch and a rifle to hunt for tigers'.

As Kent sailed for her next port of call, Bangkok, on 4 March, British Foreign Secretary Anthony Eden in the House of Commons was replying to a question of why he wanted to build up the Navy. Roy wrote:

He said that the British Navy as long ago as 1914 was 2,160,000 tons but now it had shrunk to 1,180,000 tons. The personnel had shrunk from 152,000 to 92,638. The Air Force, the greatest in the world in 1918, was now only fifth rate as regards size whereas the Army was not an army but a police force.

Eden continued that it was ridiculous to let this state of affairs continue as Germany had just been released from her inactivity and was building. Other countries were doing the same with feverish activity and Britain must increase to keep guard over her Empire.

On 9 March, Kent anchored at the mouth of the Menam River. Many of the ship's company journeyed to Bangkok to see the sights of the Siamese capital. Bangkok was regarded as a primitive place, built on a tidal marsh and intersected by tidal canals or klongs.

Roy went on the excursion and described the city: Bangkok is the capital of Siam situated on the River Menam and it contains the magnificent King's palaces and temples which are of an individual architecture.' The electric train journey to the great city saw them travelling 'between rows of native houses made of straw and built on stilts. Everything was very dirty indeed, children played in the dust with sore ridden pariahs.'

Just before *Kent*'s arrival, the Siam people had chosen a new king, a boy at school in Switzerland. These were critical days for Britain. Siam had lately been turning her attention to Japan. Roy and the other midshipmen later heard that whilst on a diplomatic mission the *Kent*'s officers dined at the Saranromya Palace, and presented to the three Regents after arriving in a procession of cars at the Royal Palace in their mess dress. The informal ship's diary elaborated:

> On reaching the Palace they drove through numerous courtyards, each guarded by armed sentries – the Minister of Defence had been wounded by an assassin only the previous week. They were ushered up a fine staircase and shown into a long room at the end of which were the three Regents, one in military uniform, the second in naval uniform, the third an elderly man with wisps of hair on his chin, baggy trousers of royal blue, a white tunic with medals, very much an Oriental statesman.

The next port of call was French-speaking Saigon where the usual hospitality was extended and various sporting competitions held, including water polo, boxing and fencing. Saigon, was an interesting town with beautiful boulevards, French-looking shops, and open-air cafes.

Roy was continuing to note international tensions:

> The question of Germany re-arming seems to be of great importance to the League in that Italy for instance has decided to partially mobilise. She has called a section of 600,000 troops together and says that she is prepared to call five more sections to arms rather than let Germany re-arm.

He added:

> Japan definitely withdraws from the League of Nations tomorrow. Naturally she is saying that her withdrawal is merely nominal and that really she is still heart and soul in the League.

Kent returned to Hong Kong, provisioned, took on ammunition and oiled. In April the ship was off on her travels again, in the Pacific Ocean along the coast of Japan. *Kent* entered Tokyo bay on Sunday 14 April. Mount Fuji was obscured by cloud. Roy was surprised to see the Canadian Pacific Line SS *Empress of Britain* already berthed alongside the custom's pier. It brought back memories of five long years earlier when he his family had sailed in one of her sister ships from Canada to England. He could not resist taking a photograph of her for his album.

Kent arrived at Yokohama on Easter Monday, 22 April, and the ship's company was invited to a cocktail party. Roy travelled with a group of officers to Tokyo by electric railway to attend the Minister of Marines' party at the Takaratzka Theatre – a very impressive affair. It was cherry blossom time and there were masses of it everywhere.

Four days later *Kent* sailed for Nagasaki. As the ship steamed down the Gulf of Tokyo, more than 100 aircraft of the Japanese Naval Air Arm flew past in formation. En route, *Kent* passed the active volcano of Iwo Jima, pouring out fumes and sulphurous gases from a recent eruption.

On 2 May – almost a year since Roy had stood on the deck of the *Kent* celebrating the birthday of King George V – the ship anchored off Shanghai, for the ship's company to take part in the Shanghai Jubilee Review for the King. The anniversary of the King's accession, 6 May, saw the *Kent* dressed overall as were all other naval ships in the harbour.

The march to the racecourse where the Jubilee Review took place proved eventful as Roy recalled:

> Thousands and thousands of Chinese followed us and pressed upon us on all sides. I was marching alongside the wheels of the rear howitzer and had continually to use my dirk scabbard to clear a way; I also had to pull people from under the wheels as they were jostled on to them.

The programme started with a roll of drums and fanfare played by massed bands, followed by a salute of twenty-one guns. It included a historical pageant, ceremonial march by 300 seamen and Royal Marines of the Royal Navy and concluded with a torchlight tattoo and the Massed Bands playing 'God Save the King'.

This was a far cry from the Falkner family back in England who wrote to Roy of their own adventures during the Silver Jubilee of 1935. Leslie recollected:

> Harry, Mother, Dad and I were invited to Hampshire to stay at the family house of one of Roy's friends, Struan Roberston, to watch the Spithead Review in honour of the Silver Jubilee of King George V. It was a hot and sunny day.

The Royal Yacht moored opposite where the Falkners were staying at Struan's family house at Seaview, near Ryde, Isle of Wight.

> As far as the eye could see there were long lines of warships off Spithead. We then watched as the Royal Yacht sailed between the ranks of anchored warships, the sailors lined up on board, and as the King went past raised their caps in unison in salute shouting 'Hip, Hip'. There was then an impressive fly-past by the aircraft of the Fleet Air Arm.

On 15 May, *Kent* joined destroyers for passage to Wei-hai-wei. Roy and other midshipmen were transferred to HMS *Diamond* as part of their midshipman training on different classes of warship.

And so ended Roy's first year as a midshipman.

CHAPTER 4

First Flight and Back to Devon

Roy's first introduction to flying was through an air course on HMS *Hermes* in May 1935, whilst the aircraft carrier was stationed with the China Fleet. *Hermes*, commissioned in 1923, was the first purpose-built carrier in the world. At the time her ship's complement included 824 Seal Squadron and 803 Osprey Squadron of the RAF.

Roy was transferred from *Kent* with Whitworth and was looking forward to flying for the first time. However, he first had introductory lectures about aviation. On 19 May, the captain inspected the midshipmen on the Short Air Course Division. Roy later recorded: 'He naturally asked us if we were going to become pilots or observers.'

Roy's instruction began at 0730 the next day with lamp and hand flag exercises, followed by a lecture on aircraft signal procedures by Lt Stratton.

Ship-to-air communication was still in the early stages of development and prone to interference, as Roy noted.

> During peacetime whilst a plane is in the air, communication has to be maintained with the ship every fifteen minutes and if W/T contact is lost the aircraft returns immediately. During war, this contact of course could not be kept for fear of giving away the ship's position. W/T silence is strictly adhered to and is only broken for enemy reports or if the interception method is used to repeat the report.

Roy was left in no doubt of the hazards of flying as his next lecture, by F/O Weir, was on salvaging an aircraft. Roy wrote:

> He described every movement in great detail and also impressed upon us the need of great care and the danger of ham-fisted seamen. He did not appear to have much faith in the powers of the Navy finding a strong enough wire to take the weight of a plane or in the skill of the seamen to put it round the boss.

The following day, Lt Cdr C.W. Byas gave a lecture on the evolution of air fighting and the advantages and disadvantages of single-seater, two-seater and three-seater aircraft. Roy's comments in his journal revealed the tactics he would later use to great effect:

> With all these planes and with any armament bombs, guns or torpedoes, the essential, of course, is surprise and a speedy get-away; and for all successful attacks, it is necessary for both pilots and observers to have plenty of practice for planes in a flight and flights to act together.

A navigation lecture followed air gunnery and Roy recorded:

Navigation alone is really a full-time job for the observer but he also has to be W/T operator and back gunner in the two-seaters and navigation and observer in the three-seaters. In peacetime, of course, navigation is really the most important.

He already showed a strong sense of duty, adding: 'In wartime, results are the most important, it would be just bad luck if he could not get back, a waste but not a terrible loss compared to the value of enemy reports.'

A lecture on the role of the Fleet Air Arm and the suitability of the various aircraft for their particular job was given by Lt Cdr J.D. Harvey.

Roy recognised the inadequacy of aircraft as he commented in his journal:

As far as I can understand the Fleet Air Arm is likely to be called upon for any job from exploring to actual dogfighting, consequently the aircraft are not properly suited to either. They have not endurance enough for long distance flying and have not speed enough for aerial fighting. Of course, they can do their most important work with fair success, spotter reconnaissance, but they were not built with two or three objectives which the plane is bound to have to do.

At last, on 23 May, Roy and Whitworth were due for their first-ever flight. They met their pilot Lt I.R. Sarel who told them to take practice air reconnaissance photographs from their aircraft.

Roy wrote:

Both Mid Whitworth and I had never been up before so naturally did not know what to expect. Whilst we were bumping along trying to take off I wondered what was going to happen next but as soon as we were in the air I felt myself to be a seasoned flyer and not in the least excited.

We took our photographs of various views round the island and then flew across the mainland. We banked rather steeply round the mast of a junk whose occupants did not appear to be too happy. We flew for about half an hour at about 1,000 feet, encountering a few bumps in the lee of Linkungtao then landed for the next lot to take over.

The next day Lt Sarel advised Roy on how he could become an aviator: 'This was particularly interesting to me as I have been considering whether to become a pilot or not.'

Further lectures continued over the next few days, including air navigation. Roy wrote: 'I think that all lecturers take a fiendish delight in proving what brains an observer must have although they say that it is very easy.'

The next day after seeing a parachute opened and being stretched and re-packed he wrote somewhat wryly:

It appears to be a very complicated job. The parachute has twenty-four strings, each tested to 75 pounds, but I don't think I should feel very safe in one. The aircraftsman doing the job said that when one of the many panels in the parachute split it went with a very hard report; this I suppose was to cheer me up and encourage me.

The next lecture involved torpedo-bombing, with a divergence of views on the hazards to be faced. Roy recorded:

Lieutenant (P) Johnstone gave us the history of torpedo-bombing and the aircraft since the war. He seemed to think that planes would be entirely unscathed by such things as pom poms and .5" guns when torpedoes were dropped.

The captain, however, who lectured on 'Future Development' immediately afterwards said exactly the opposite. The captain also said that at present there was a tremendous argument going on at home as to the relative merits of small and large aircraft carriers. He seemed to favour several of about 17,000 tons or alternatively one of about 25–30,000 with several smaller ones hold off with special planes. Thus any division of the Fleet would have its aircraft carrier.

Commander gave us his side of the carrier work and the difficulties of the RAF and RN disciplines working together and also the special duties and ratings peculiar to a carrier.

The next day Roy wrote:

Wednesday May 29th, Wing Commander gave us the connections between RAF and FAA and also the very various bases of the RAF and her developments. In India, for instance, now that the Indian Government has taken charge of the RAF there will soon be no need of the RAF as an Indian Air Force is being built up. In Iraq, for instance, the same thing is happening but we will not trust the natives enough to keep out the Russians.

On 30 May *Hermes* proceeded to sea for exercises and Roy described bombing practice:

Aircraft were ranged on deck with six Seals in front and five Ospreys behind. The Seals were loaded with eight small practice bombs and took off to bomb a target towed by *St Breock*. The Ospreys then took off for air manoeuvres. The Seals bombed from about 5,000 ft and were remarkably accurate.

Roy had the opportunity to see what could happen when matters did not go according to plan:

Another Seal was flown off by a newly joined officer and landed on. As his hook would not go down he had to land without the arrester gear and did an excellent landing stopping abreast the island. The rest of the Seals then landed with comparative ease followed by the Ospreys, one of which came in much too fast and ripped his hook off and partially smashed the tail skid. He landed successfully, however.

Roy had his second ever flight later that day:

In the afternoon the midshipmen went up in the Seals to watch the Ospreys' dive-bombing. We went two to a plane and flew off the deck and climbed to about 1,500 feet. We were then able to watch the Ospreys take off. They seemed to go very slowly and very slowly climb. They also climbed to about 2,000 feet to 3,000 feet then commenced diving straight down to about 250 feet, dropped their bombs and flattened out. From our position the practice seemed to be very accurate.

He was about to experience for himself a practice dive-bombing attack on the *Hermes*:

The Seals then flew into formation, then into line ahead for the climb up to 5,000 feet. At that height we flew over *Hermes*, did a quarter roll and dived. We reached a speed of 170 knots during the dive and flattened out at 500 feet. When we pulled out of the dive the strain must have been fairly terrific as my legs simply buckled under me.

We then circled round the ship waiting for our turn to land on. We approached from astern of the ship, floated onto the deck and were stopped by the arrester gear with scarcely a jerk.

After all the excitement of flying he was confidently looking forward to the forthcoming air course exams the following day. The next morning with only slight apprehension he sat his air course exams. He later reflected 'Everyone did fairly well I believe. The paper was much more difficult than I expected.'

As Roy and Whitworth prepared for transfer back to *Kent* the next day the commander gave them some advice: 'Pilots must join early and observers wait for a commission as subs and lieutenants.'

Two days after Roy returned to *Kent* at Wei-hai-wei, he was involved in a rescue. He wrote:

The wind was very strong and a considerable sea running so that it was practically impossible to land anyone at either pier.

During the afternoon the senior engineer's yacht went ashore but was got off by coollies and taken alongside Iron Pier. The motorboat with the Senior and Lt Campbell and duty hands went to tow her to a buoy. We took her in tow, motorboat one side and yacht the other. However, the yacht sank before she could be hauled up to it and her owners were thrown into the water. Trying to pick up the Senior and Lt Campbell, grass caught in the motorboat's screw of course jammed the engine. Eventually we cleared it but not without the boat very nearly capsizing. It was absolutely impossible to move in the boat without holding on because of her rolls.

That same day, Saturday 8 June, an Osprey got into difficulties on landing and a crew member had to be rescued. Roy wrote:

An Osprey went over the side of the *Hermes* a few days ago with the hook in the wires. The plane was held quite comfortably dangling over the side. The TAG who had cast off his anchor wire was hurled into the water and picked up by *Diamond*, the attendant destroyer.

International matters were no less dramatic, according to Roy: 'In the press news today Abyssinia and Italy are still trying to cut each other's throats over the boundary lines and also Italy's establishment of aircraft bases.'

There were other matters to be considered: 'We are all practising very hard for the regatta now. Every crew in the ship goes away at least once, usually twice a day, in all sorts of weather.

A week later he wrote: 'Two weeks exactly to the regatta and we have been given our orders re training. No drinking, no smoking, not too much food and one bath a day of three minutes duration. We also pulled as opposed to paddling a mile.'

Meanwhile, gunnery practices and exercises at sea continued as well as more humdrum chores: 'June 21: Paint ship! We painted the starboard side slowly and reverently to match the success with which the port side was painted last week.'

When the eagerly awaited regatta arrived, matters did not go according to plan and the much sought after 'Bowl' was already lost when Roy and his crew took part in the 'Allcomers' two-mile race:

> We manned our gig, were all ready to go to the starting line with loosed oars. Crash, some bright seaman had let his oar catch in the scuttle above the boat. The boom went straight through the boat. With speed, a towel was placed in the hole, the boat cleared and towed to the crane, hoisted and mended, lowered again, manned and we were off.
>
> The start was a farce, no boats obeyed orders, there was a general advance and we were off with our gig rather left at the start. The race was two miles but no one noticed the distance as we sang the whole way and cheered other boats as we passed them.

Eventually Roy's gig came in third behind *Cornwall*. Roy noted: 'Even if we can't beat *Cornwall* in ordinary races we can beat her for plain stamina and energy.'

A person Roy could admire died in early July. Roy wrote:

> Aircraftsman Shaw, Lawrence of Arabia, is dead from the result of his motor cycle crash whilst indulging in his one drug – speed. It is incredible what Lawrence did in the time he was in Arabia with a mere quarter of a million dollars and personality. He inflamed, yet kept in control, the whole of Arabia in the Arab revolt against the Turks. It is doubtful whether he was a good soldier in the best sense of the word but he certainly adapted himself to the forces he had at hand and achieved a tremendous amount of distraction work when the Turks might have been backing up the Germans in Europe.

On 16 July Roy went for his first submersion in a deep sea diving suit. He was helped into the suit and a heavy brass helmet screwed into place:

> When I got to the bottom the other diver was waiting for me. We tried to make signs to each other but I couldn't understand him. We went for a walk in the knee-deep ooze. I found it terribly difficult to begin moving but afterwards it was quite easy.
>
> We got to the end of the wandering rope and turned round to come back, at least the other diver did; my legs simply shot away from me sending me flat on my back. I managed to get to my feet again and we returned to the short rope and returned to the surface by closing the air valve and blowing myself up. It is quite easy to control the ascent by opening the valve again if you are going up too quickly. Several of the midshipmen blew themselves straight up and floated horizontally on the surface of the water quite helplessly.

On 24 July *Kent* went on her Summer Cruise, including to Tsingtao where a cocktail party was given to the local inhabitants and also to the American Navy.

On return to Wei-hai-wei in August, *Kent* had more luck in the interport sports finals when McEwen, with Roy as one of his boat crew, won the Littleton Trophy. At the Fleet Rifle Meet the ship's team virtually 'wiped the board', much to Roy's delight. The sailing regatta saw McEwen, Roy and the other midshipmen in the gunroom win the Fitzgerald cup race for whalers for the second year running.

News from Europe was becoming alarming, as Roy noted on 31 August:

> The Italy-Abyssinia question seems to be rapidly evolving into a matter of prime

importance to us. All the governments are very definitely giving the situation very careful consideration as Italy has practically openly avowed her intent to show that she is not a mediocre power that can be ignored.

This demonstration of Italy's might is of great importance to Great Britain's supremacy in the Mediterranean, as Malta is a mere step from Sicily and would be untenable in view of an Italian attack. The possession of Malta to the Italians is important because of the Narrow Gut that it commands between Italy and Africa. To England this far-off base is not of much importance except that loss would be such a colossal gain for someone else.

Britain, according to the Italians, is definitely preparing for aggressive measures in that she has brought Malta's garrison up to full-strength and has concentrated her Navy at Gibraltar, Aden and Alexandria; also they consider the presence of the Home Fleet exercising off Gibraltar instead of off Scotland as very ominous.

Two weeks later Roy wrote:

The British Government has issued a proclamation that Britons are not to fight for Italy or Abyssinia under pain of imprisonment with or without hard labour for two years and a possible fine of £500.

With Roy's recent flight in an aircraft whilst serving on *Hermes* he was increasingly thinking about joining the Fleet Air Arm. He had a heightened interest in aircraft and fast vehicles:

It is rather interesting to note that Sir Malcolm Campbell has at last broken the 300 mph mark in his giant Bluebird. He achieved 301 mph downwind with an average of 299.6 mph. Whilst slowing down a tyre burst but as he was going slowly, a mere couple of hundred miles an hour perhaps, the great weight of Bluebird was not affected by the explosion of a mere 400 pound pressure.

By October, *Kent* was about to go on her travels again and leave Wei-hai-wei:

Hostilities have opened between the Italians and the Ethiopians today as Italy's forces under General Debono invaded Ethiopia and fighting took place. War, however, has not been formally declared.

As a precaution of heightened threat of war *Kent* received a war complement of depth charges and boxes of small arms ammunition. The ship's company and officers also underwent gas mask inspection with tear gas in the sailmakers' shop.

Kent sailed for Chinwangtao on 9 October to help protect a British-Belgian-Chinese mining company from possible aggression. On arrival, Roy and McEwen walked to the Great Wall of China, a distance of twenty-five miles there and back.

Roy noted:

The wall seems to be in perfect condition, still rising sheer thirty to fifty feet on the northern side with a steep slope on the southern side with a flat top of about thirty feet wide. The wall was built a mere 2,000 years ago to protect the Chin Dynasty from the Huns. It is 1,500 miles long and every family in China is stated to have done its share of the work.

This was half the equivalent distance roughly from London to New York.

Matters between Italy and Great Britain were deteriorating. Roy wrote:

21 October: With the decision of the League of Nations to enforce sanctions as necessary, Italy has declared her intention to open hostilities against Great Britain.

With the tense European situation the captain did not permit leave to the ship's company to visit Peking, the ancient capital of China. The *Kent* returned to Wei-hai-wei the same day and back to normal routine and sports.

In December, Roy joined the destroyer HMS *Duncan* for a few weeks' training whilst sailing to Singapore and back. En route they carried out exercises in conjunction with the submarine HMS *Perseus*. After one week, Roy transferred again, this time to HMS *Daring* with midshipman McEwen.

McEwen recalled:

Roy and I did two months in *Daring*, during which we were lucky enough to make an interesting cruise from Singapore to Port Dickson and Penang, and spent some days in Port Swettenham, during which we both spent a few days and nights in Klang, inland. It was rare for us to ever get out of sight of the sea.

On the passage north to Hong Kong, *Daring* berthed alongside in Bangkok, which was most interesting; the Admiralty Pilot gave the chief import of Bangkok as 'treasure', and indeed you saw that with many gilded temple domes and rich coverings, jewels etc on the Buddhas.

Roy was very impressed:

It is hopeless to attempt to describe the beauty of the place with its dome of glazed tiles, its 160 foot spire nestling in a small hollow backed by the green of tropical trees. At one side a small enclosed pool holds several sacred fish, rather of the carp species, in green waters. These fish are extraordinarily tame, eating grass and leaves while natives splash and wash alongside them.

Inside the mosque was a central beautifully ornamented throne or rather pulpit from which the Sultan speaks every Friday.

On 12 December, Roy noted heightened conflicts in the region with the continued occupation of Japanese troops in Chinese Manchuria. 'Japanese Manchukuoan troops supported by aircraft have made a considerable advance into China without any warning.' Two weeks later Prince Teh declared the independence of Inner Mongolia.

Roy added: 'Although China is yelping for help against the Japanese encroachment and invasion, the League of Nations cannot assist.' Then on 15 January 1936, Japan withdrew from the Naval Disarmament Conference in London – the outlook was looking grim.

That same day news came through of the death of King George V. Roy recalled:

It is with greatest sorrow that we heard of the death of King George at 11.55 last night. Although we knew he was ill it doesn't seem possible that after such a troublous but happy reign he should have gone. King George will definitely go down in history as one of the greatest and most loved of our kings.

Roy wrote the following day:

A gracious message to his Navy from King Edward VIII was read on the quarterdeck and a salute of twenty-one guns was fired. At 3 pm he was proclaimed King by His Excellency the Governor of Hong Kong.

One era had ended and another began. On 1 February 1936, Roy and McEwen rejoined *Kent* for the final six months of their commission. Roy wrote: 'Thus ends a very enjoyable two months' holiday!'

By then Admiral Dreyer had recently sailed for England and Vice Admiral Sir Charles Little had assumed command of the China Station on board *Kent*.

Kent departed on 4 February for the Spring Cruise which included a visit to Manila, where horses of the US Army at Fort McKinley were loaned to *Kent*'s officers and midshipmen. Roy wrote enthusiastically: 'We were out for two hours and had splendid opportunities for gallops and jumps over sticks.'

Later that month Roy experienced a mock torpedo attack against *Kent* in the Singapore Straits, from its Ospreys flying from the RAF Station at Seletar.

> At 0630 HA parties were closed up to exercise repel aircraft. Quarter of an hour later a reconnaissance plane flew over the ship, shortly followed by six Wildebeeste torpedo bombers. Three bombers attacked the ship from each side and fired at about three hundred yards range. Five hits were secured.

Roy was beginning to assess what it would be like if he subsequently became a Fleet Air Arm pilot: 'It seems to me that as this type of aircraft are very slow and have to approach to within about five hundred yards they could easily be shot down by the close-range armament.'

Later in the day on 21 February, *Kent* secured to a battleship buoy at the Singapore Naval Base, of which 'tremendous strides' had been made in the work of completing the dockyard since *Kent*'s previous visit the year before.

Even back in England there was heightened concerns about war. Roy reported:

> In the English papers there is reported yet a fourth case of sabotage to the Fleet. This time damage was done to the destroyer *Velox*. The extent of damage was not reported. Previous ships in which sabotage has occurred are *Royal Oak*, *Oberon* and *Cumberland*.

A more cheerful event occurred a fortnight later when *Kent* sailed for Batavia and crossed the line at 1750:

> At 1930 a stentorian hail from ahead caused the ship to be stopped and a wild form came on board and was introduced as King Neptune's ambassador. Lieut. Commander Redman looked very fine in long robes and beard clasping the inevitable trident. After the usual compliments to the King and to C-in-C's flag the Ambassador left the ship after making an appointment for 0930 tomorrow.

Roy recorded the next day:

> At 0930 the ship was stopped and that royal personage King Neptune, his consort and court came on board. Neptune looked his usual well-bearded, well-rounded cheery self. His wife was looking very charming with a gown of dazzling colours hiding her excellent figure.

The light-heartened moment did not last as the international situation was worsening:

> Germany has completely thrown out the Locarno Treaty and is again arming the Rhineland. Troops, tanks, armoured cars have been thrown into the district and welcomed by Hitler.

France quite naturally is very alarmed and is trying to find some way out of her terror. She has re-armed all her frontier forts and is pressing the League of Nations to apply sanctions to Germany.

Prophetically Roy wrote: 'Great Britain as per usual will, I presume, bear the brunt of all these international difficulties.'

On 19 March as *Kent* sailed for Hong Kong, Roy was to witness his first fatal aircraft accident as 100 Squadron exercised night torpedo raids.

Three aircraft had already carried out their attacks when tragedy struck.

Roy described what happened next:

The fourth attack was carried out slightly differently as the ship was swinging. After firing his flare he circled from ahead round to starboard, found the ship swinging so turned round and dived to attack. Unfortunately, due to not knowing the height or due to some failure, he dived straight into the water. The plane went straight to the bottom leaving the body of one airman on the surface, also the remains of the plane – two wheels and the petrol tank.

Kent and the RAF tenders searched for some time with no success. The airman was brought on board *Kent* where he unfortunately died. No trace could be found of the other two occupants of the plane.

It was a salutary warning to a young man who was considering becoming a naval aviator.

The next morning *Kent* returned to the mouth of the Johor Strait and anchored, whilst a Court of Inquiry was held on board. Later, *Kent* resumed her passage to Shanghai.

On 6 May, Kent proceeded up the Yangtze with *Dorsetshire* astern. The ships anchored for the night off Chiankiang and early next morning steamed on to Nanking, the Chinese capital city, passing most of the Chinese Navy, about fifteen ships in all, lying at anchor.

Roy took the opportunity to visit the city:

We motored through Nanking city, which for the Chinese capital, is very poorly laid out with tumbledown shacks bordering pitted roads. The whole of Nanking proper is enclosed by a twenty-five mile wall which is about thirty feet high and twenty-five foot thick built of very large stone bricks. There are only two gates in the wall, both guarded by colossal iron doors about an inch thick and of course the inevitable armed sentries.

The *Kent* retraced her course down the Yangtze and steamed on to Shanghai, arriving there on 12 May. General leave was given and large numbers availed themselves of the opportunity for a spot of 'night life' before leaving for the 'rural charms' of Wei-hai-wei.

Roy's midshipman's exams were upon him and he wrote the last entry in his Midshipman's Journal on 21 May 1936: 'Semaphore reading and making, flashing, buzzing and V/S and W/T papers were our exams for today thus finishing all written work before the Great Day of the 29th when our Board sits.'

Roy took his exams and two days later the ship returned to Wei-hai-wei. *Kent*'s Summer Cruise started on 24 July, heading for Dairen, the terminus of the Trans-Siberian Railway, a well laid out town with Japanese shops.

The following week, *Kent* reached the Chinese town of Chinwangtao in the Yellow Sea. Two parties from the ship went to Peking over 200 miles away and enjoyed the visit, hot though it was. There were the usual pony races and visits to the Great Wall of China.

41

At this time Roy had a small mishap breaking his collar bone whilst riding a pony near the Great Wall. He was incapacitated for quite a while and unable to write home about his adventures or take part in his beloved sports.

On *Kent*'s return to Wei-hai-wei, there was the Fleet Sports, won for the second consecutive year by *Kent* with 120 points, the *Hermes* being second with 83 points.

Later in August, the sailing date for the return to England was announced.

Everyone began to feel and act like born-again English gents, grinning from ear to ear, checking all the purchased gifts, the kimonos from Japan, the silver-plated model rickshaw from China....and loading these goodies into canvas kit bags.

Roy's plunder for the family included a jade Buddha, intricate ivory carvings, a whale bone junk boat, a silver rickshaw cruet set, a Chinese folk tale picture set cut from traditional paper silhouettes and a green dragon jug. He had also carefully prepared three photograph albums of his adventures, one for his parents, another for Leslie and a third for himself.

En route to England their escort HMS *Capetown* was diverted to Haifa to pick up the Emperor Haile Selassie, who was fleeing for exile following the invasion of Abyssinia by the Italians.

Then at last it was back to England, entering Plymouth Sound with the paying-off pennant flying from the masthead – an inflated pig's bladder tied to the end – to keep the end of the flag out of the water.

Roy hoisted his canvas kit bag and, with the prospect of seven to eight weeks' leave, was at last on the train to Teignmouth, surrounded by the sounds of the curlews and seagulls and the smell of the Devon seaside. He was home...

CHAPTER 5

Love and RAF Ab Initio Flight

Roy was considering specialising in aviation but first romance was in the air. During the Shaldon Regatta in August 1936, Roy was sitting on the beach watching the races when his friend Struan Robertson came up to greet him. Struan was accompanied by his girlfriend, a brunette called Naomi Lord. Naomi was eighteen and had just had her fortune told by a gipsy fortune teller who spoke of her meeting a 'tall, handsome stranger'. Roy offered Naomi a cigarette and they all sat down together on the beach. Naomi later commented: 'It was a moment I would never forget.'

Naomi was a little older than Roy. She was born on 30 September 1914 at Hill, Pershore, Worcestershire, where her parents, Alice and James, had a fruit farm. Naomi's grandfather lived in Torquay, Devon, and was a Justice of the Peace. When Naomi was nine, her family moved to nearby Dawlish, and then eventually to East Cliff in Shaldon, the village in which the Falkner family were later to settle.

Naomi loved horses and became great friends with Nenee Gashin who ran a riding stable in Shaldon and whose father, Captain Bigg-Wither, was in the Army.

In 1933, Naomi's mother died of cancer and her grief-stricken father died eighteen months later. Naomi was an orphan but not penniless. Shortly after her parents' death she inherited some money from an uncle and was so able to continue living in Shaldon.

Naomi and Roy sat on the beach and talked, amongst other things about his naval training. He had decisions to make about his future – he had the choice of specialising in one of three skills, namely submarines, navigation or aviation.

Shortly after meeting Naomi, Roy received a telegram which read: 'You have been appointed Acting Sub-Lieutenant in the Royal Navy and will report to Captain H.H. Bousfield at the Royal Naval College, Greenwich on the 23rd September 1936.'

Bill Whitworth recollected: 'Sub courses were absolutely routine – we did one term at Greenwich and seven months in Portsmouth.'

Roy headed off to get kitted out by Messrs Gieves, the naval and military tailors. A new blue uniform, dress uniform, white uniform, walking stick, and a topee tropical pith helmet complete with tin hat box, together with a blue and white mess jacket, were all acquired, along with a tin trunk. There was also a sword with scabbard, neatly accompanied by the ceremonial frock coat.

He put on the dark blue, double-breasted uniform of a naval officer for the first time. Badges were sewn on his pristine uniform and he headed to a nearby photographic studio for a portrait to give his proud parents.

The course started on 24 September. Donald McEwen later reflected: 'At RN College,

Greenwich, we had our time reduced to one term of academic studies. Roy was captain of the "B" Rugby XV.'

This was one of Roy's first real tastes of leadership after being cadet captain at Dartmouth. He lived for the team and his enthusiasm both on the field and off inspired everyone else. He regarded every player as a team member to be encouraged and encouraged with enthusiasm. Being captain fostered his sense of responsibility.

Roy had a further opportunity to meet Naomi when she came with a friend to a dance at Greenwich later that year. The dance was in the Royal Naval College's Painted Gallery which was decked out with flowers and bunting in profusion. Roy looked very dashing in his new uniform. Naomi was elegant in her ball gown, dancing to the music of the service band. For the time being the couple went their separate ways – Roy remained at Greenwich and Naomi returned to Shaldon.

On 24 February 1937, Roy pursued his dream of learning to fly and submitted certificate 'CW2375/37', applying to become a naval pilot in the Fleet Air Arm of the Royal Air Force (RAF). He soon received official notice declaring that 'Sub Lt R.S. Baker-Falkner is to be attached to the RAF and to report to No. 1 Flying Training School at Leuchars, Fife not later than noon on 2 April, 1937'. At that time, aircraft and all ground crews in the services belonged to the Royal Air Force, and all naval flying personnel were obliged to have a temporary RAF commission.

Roy's imminent departure to Scotland stiffened his resolve to ask Naomi for a date. The couple first went out seriously together on Good Friday, 1937. Three days later, on Easter Monday, 1 April, Roy proposed to Naomi. Her first response was 'You're rather young aren't you?' But she didn't hold out for long and soon replied 'I think I would rather like that.'

The journey to Scotland that day was long and Roy must have had mixed feelings – leaving Naomi and at the same time preparing to fulfil his ambition to become a naval pilot.

That night, on official RAF Leuchars-headed paper, Roy wrote to Naomi: '1 April. Darling, Will you marry me? Wait for me and love me, always. All my love darling and I am so excited. DIL [Darling, I love you].'

The next day he took his entrance flying examination followed by medical tests. The chief flying instructor was Wing Commander Jackie Noakes, a Great War ace who flew combat missions with the great aviation heroes James McCudden and Albert Ball. Noakes had been an inter-war test pilot at Farnborough and performed all sorts of amazing stunts with new and untried aeroplanes.

Having completed his entrance examination, Roy returned to HMS *Excellent*, the Royal Naval Gunnery School in Portsmouth, to complete his sub-lieutenant's course. He could hardly wait to tell his two closest friends, Boddington and McEwen, about his engagement.

Roy wrote to Naomi from Portsmouth: '8 April: Mac and Boddington were absolutely incredulous when I told them about us. When they gathered that I wasn't fooling they were delighted though.'

The rest of that month was spent by Roy at HMS *Excellent*, nicknamed 'Whale Island'.

A fellow officer, Carey, remembered: 'Roy and I were together in "H" Group. We did our gunnery course late and I am afraid we were known as "f........ing 'H' Group, the worst group that's ever been on Whale Island".'

He added:

Robert Boddington wrote an extremely amusing musical play for us, 'Sub-

Lieutenant Cinders' – a spoof on Cinderella. Sub Lt Cinders herself was acted by Francis Foster. Roy and Bill Whitworth, took the parts of Pack and Drill, the field training gunner's mates. I remember the lines of their duet:

> *You dropped it on the floor.*
> *Yes, you dropped it on the floor.*
> *I might've thought*
> *You'd never done rifle drill before.*

> *And when you picked it up,*
> *All the crowd began to roar:*
> *If you drop your rifle,*
> *Leave the darned thing on the floor.*

It went down very well – except with the field training gunner, who said it was a mockery of the service.

Whilst at Portsmouth, Roy continued boxing. Leslie remembered that her father was proud when Roy won the Royal Navy Officers' Championship, and then later competed in the ring for the Inter-Services Boxing Association Championship in the welterweight division.

Among the teams was the featherweight contestant Ginger Prandy, and Charles Lamb, who was representing the RAF as a lightweight contestant. Lamb had previously competed with Roy as an RNR boxer. Roy won all his fights in the ring, and was awarded the title of the Inter-Port Boxing Champion. His trophies included a statuette of a boxing figure with 'Portsmouth Port, 1937' engraved on it. He was congratulated by the family but Grace hated him boxing and 'wasn't too pleased', recalled Leslie. When he got home to Shaldon, Leslie tried on his boxing gloves: 'I was surprised how funny they felt.'

Ginger Prandy, became the Navy's 1937 featherweight boxing champion and later went on to serve onboard HMS *Firedrake* that same year. Charles Lamb continued as an RAF officer for another year and subsequently was granted a short service commission in the Fleet Air Arm where he remained, serving with distinction.

That month Roy received his Leuchars exam results and was shocked to learn that he had failed, due to a heart flutter. He was bitterly disappointed. Leslie recalled:

Roy failed his entrance flying exams on the first try, much to his surprise and annoyance. It was at about this time that he seriously considered the future of his naval career. He had long conversations with me about what he should do. He had made up his mind that if he failed yet again in his exams he would definitely become a farm vet – he so loved animals.

Roy took the test again and passed. Naomi was in two minds about the news – she was worried at the thought of Roy learning to fly but knew it was what he really wanted to do.

On 16 May Roy received his Greenwich certificate with a good score of 3.2. and formally 'reached the seniority of Sub Lieutenant.' He celebrated with Naomi by going to the Spithead Review and Fleet Air Arm Flypast four days later, staying overnight at Yarmouth on the Isle of Wight. Naomi recalled: 'We had the day on a destroyer, HMS *Sardonyx*, with Donald McEwen and his girlfriend Heather – it was a wonderful experience.'

Donald McEwen remembered:

On completion of courses we had limited choice of where we would go. I was railroaded into being the Sub of the gunroom of *Glasgow* to my indignation. Roy went straight into flying and was soon married.

Robert Boddington fell in love with Heather Hance while *Kent* was in Hong Kong and swore to marry her. At the time there were fifteen submarines stationed in China so Robert volunteered for the S/M service and was sent to a boat in China where he married Heather.

Peter Pagett was a good rugger player so went on from Dartmouth to the Royal Naval Engineering College at Manadon where the rugger facilities were good. He later became a pilot as well and joined 820 Squadron.

The next month it was time to celebrate Roy's twenty-first birthday. It was a season of parties – he had just returned from the McEwen's Channel Islands family home in their own private aeroplane. Donald McEwen added: 'Roy came over to Jersey with Heather and me for my twenty-first birthday party.'

Around this time, Roy visited Harry at Blundell's School at Tiverton. Harry was in the Officer Cadets at school and was preparing to go to the Officer Cadet Training Unit (OCTU) and on to Aldershot at the age of seventeen. There was also a big family reunion when Sydney's brother, the Rev Phillip Falkner, Canon in Bloemfontein, came to visit from his home in South Africa.

Aviation was headline news that year. On 6 May, the Hindenburg airship, built with the financial aid of Nazi Germany, exploded and burnt whilst approaching its mooring mast at Lakehurst Naval Air Station, New Jersey. American millionaire Howard Hughes set the transcontinental speed record, flying a distance of 2,453 miles in 7 hours, 28 minutes and 25 seconds. In July, the famous woman aviator, Amelia Earhart, disappeared during a flight in the Pacific Ocean. That same month the first transatlantic commercial passenger test flights were carried out by flying boats of Pan American and Imperial Airways.

Roy prepared to start his first year at No. 1 Flying Training School, Leuchars. The Pilot (P) Training Course was run by the RAF, so Roy was given dual RAF and RN rank, flight lieutenant RAF and sub lieutenant Royal Navy. The anomaly dated back to 1 April 1918, when the Royal Navy lost its air arm – the Royal Naval Air Service and the Army's Royal Flying Corps were merged to form the Royal Air Force. As the veteran naval aviators used to recount, on that day, April Fool's Day in 1918, 55,000 officers and men transferred from dark blue uniforms to light blue, and grew moustaches! They took over nearly one hundred former RN airfields dotted around the Empire and 2,500 aircraft. The result was that naval aviation throughout the 1920s and early 1930s had been neglected, in the words of Admiral Sir Ernle Chatfield, 'to the point of insanity'. Chatfield, First Sea Lord from 1933–8, demanded the return of the naval arm to full Admiralty control as the Fleet Air Arm of the Royal Navy not the RAF.

It was against this background that Roy drove up to Scotland, looking the part of the dashing young pilot in his new MG open-topped sports car, nicknamed Molly, to join No. 39 Naval Pilots' Course on 12 September. McEwen recalled: 'At that time B-F owned an MG sports car, with just the two seats, which fitted in with the image one always had of a fighter pilot.'

On arrival, Roy learned that the RAF No. 1 FTS was the oldest military flying school in the world, being formed back in 1919 with the Avro 504K.

One young pilot on an earlier Leuchars training course, Major R.T. Partridge, remembered:

> I can well recall the officers' mess set just across the road running alongside the airfield, a collection of single-storey buildings rather suggestive of Great War army huts. But it was comfortable and adequate inside and had an atmosphere of casual informality, very different from others I had been in.

On the course was a mixed collection of Royal Navy and Royal Marines. Roy was the only one from the Dominion of Canada. They included R.E. Boulding, Rodney Carver, Frankie 'Tuck' Fryer, R.W.V 'Hammy' Hamilton, John 'Godfrey' Lincoln, Arthur Pardoe, Harry Parker, and two Royal Marines, John Snow and Eric McIver.

The welcoming talk was given by the Chief Flying Instructor, Wing Commander Down, RAF. He left Roy and his fellow pupil pilots in no doubt that they were very much on probation. If they failed to reach the required grade, they would be out.

They were told:

> Each term pupils will be divided into two sets; one will fly whilst the other does ground school and academic work. A cadet will be expected to be proficient in both academic and practical fields – exemplary progress in one only not being sufficient to succeed.
>
> You will learn how to fly and operate aircraft safely and to its limits. You will also learn how to work as a team with other students and the instructors. Bear in mind that there is a selection process, weeding with flying tests to ascertain if you reach the necessary minimum standard and what the Chief Flying Instructor says, goes.

Before being accepted for any further training, Roy and the other pupils had to pass the ab initio flying course, which would take them up to fifty hours' flying time. They were to be taught on Avro Tutor and de Havilland DH.82 Tiger Moth aircraft, before flying service naval aircraft in the second year. The course included aerobatics, cross-country navigation and fighting, augmented by end of course exams.

The course got under way and Roy was issued with flying clothing. This consisted of a flying helmet with ear-pieces and Gosport tubing for inter-cockpit communication, woolly-lined flying boots, a Sidcot suit with detachable lining; large leather gauntlets formally entitled 'RAF 1933 Pattern Flying Gauntlets' with white silk gloves to wear underneath. He was also given a parachute.

Roy was handed his first Royal Air Force Pilot's Flying Log Book, Form 414 1937 edition, in which he was told to register each and every flight detail throughout his career with the Fleet Air Arm until he retired. He was instructed to complete details of each flight by date, aircraft type, name of pilot, pupil or passenger, duty including remarks, and number of hours on single or multi-engined aircraft. Each week the Pilot's Flying Log Book would be inspected and signed by the instructors and officially stamped with approval by the Chief Flying Instructor, Wing Cdr Down.

Roy met the RAF flying instructors who at that time included Sgts Lambert and Johnstone, and Ft Lts Kidd, Southwell, Kelly and Willis.

Alastair Easton, who had been stationed at Leuchars earlier that same year, recalled:

> The instructors were all extremely proficient RAF Flight Lieutenants or Squadron

Leaders. All in all it was a Rolls Royce flying course. Of the instructors, Flt Lt Southwell, my instructor for a time on 504 Ns and Tutors in 1937, was a very nice chap and an excellent pilot.

At the end of his first day Roy wrote to Naomi: 'Monday, Well, darling, that is one day gone and we go up tomorrow. Today we did nothing except receive our flying gear and lots of books.'

Roy's first training flight took place the following morning in a Tiger Moth biplane. Sgt Lambert was the instructor pilot. Waiting for his turn to fly, Roy stood watching the proceedings, whilst biting his bottom lip, a sure sign that he was deep in thought about the upcoming experience. Once he had clambered into the back seat, the fan was turned, the instructor shouted 'contact' and then they were off. They bumped along the grass and then, according to Roy, they 'unstuck with the feeling of driving a car fast up a Devonshire hill'. Suddenly, the entire aerodrome, the coast and the river Eden and St Andrews beyond, spread out before them. The flight lasted half an hour and was intended to familiarise Roy with the local area and the general procedures adopted when flying the aircraft. This was followed later in the day with a second flight in the Tiger Moth with 'straight and level flight climbing and stalling. 45 minutes'.

Two days later, Roy was shown the Avro Tutor twin-seat biplane trainer. In the open cockpit there were only a few basic instruments, airspeed indicator, turn and bank indicator and altimeter. The aircraft had dual controls; the instructor was in front and Roy behind. The Tutor was a fairly stable aircraft with excellent handling characteristics and a top speed of 106 knots. It was responsive enough for training and fairly robust to resist heavy landings. Roy made two thirty-minute flights.

Partridge recollected: 'In my first flight it was the flimsiness of the Avro that impressed me so much, it was just fabric, wires and wood that separated me from the little square fields below. We all got rather fond of it.'

By the weekend Roy was ecstatic:

Sunday 19 September. I've got three hours in the air so far. It's wonderful and I seem to be getting into handling the machine quite well. I can't land yet but I can take off quite well and can fly her quite easily in the air turns and level flying etc. Yesterday I went for about 90 miles round the country to see what it was like.

Roy was conscious that his fiancée was worried about him and added:

I suppose you saw that we had a crash up here t'other day. Nothing serious, just cuts on the pilot's head. He's ambling around quite happily so, my darling, you see that crashing is not dangerous altho' so many people say that flying is. Darling, I have been away from you for a whole ten days now, isn't it frightful?

The beginning of the next week, the trainee pilots were again in the air, initially with spinning and then a series of take-offs, approaches and landings. Roy wrote: '21 September. Flying is going very well and at last I can land the machine quite well. Will soon be a pilot after all.'

Instruction that week included 'action in the event of fire'. By that Friday Roy had made up to eight and a half hours' flying with the instructors.

He gradually met also the other course members at Leuchars from the term above. They had started that May and included J.H. Dundas, T.W.G. French, Kenneth Gurr, D.W. Kirk,

A.J. Lydekker, B.J. Smeeton, Charles Bowman Smith, and George Villiers Tothill. He would get to know them well as time went by.

A fortnight after starting his course the instructors informed Roy that he would be flying solo later that week – this was surely to be one of the landmarks of Roy's flying career, never to be forgotten. For the next few days there were endless practice flights of thirty-minute duration and then a flight test with Ft Lt Kidd to test competence for circuits and landings.

On 30 September, Roy wrote triumphantly:

Thursday. I did my first solo test and passed today. I went up all by my little self and took her round the surface of the earth at about 1,000 feet then landed. I did a perfect landing but my left wheel jammed fast so having touched down at 60 mph I did a magnificent 360-degree skid. It was rather scaring while it lasted but anyway I eventually stopped with nothing broken on me or the plane. Pretty good I calls it.

Roy was still trying to persuade Naomi that flying was safe:

Wednesday. The flying is going quite well my darling and I seem to be getting it slowly. I did spinning today, it's great fun. You stop your engine, then go crashing towards the earth, round and round in circles. First time you spin and get a bit windy but soon it feels as if you're just diving for the earth and the earth is flying round you. There is no danger as you are about 5,000 feet up so have plenty of time to glide safely down. Another thing we did was a terrific dive in which we went over 150 mph. Quite fast?

A few days later Roy reported with relief about the results of another medical test to see if his heart was still okay after the scare of that summer: 'The flying is grand and I love it. Heart tested again yesterday. Quite definitely it is nothing and only nerves at seeing a doctor.'

Roy by now had more than twenty hours' flying experience. He wrote the following week:

13 October. This flying racket is great fun. I spun down 2,000 feet the other day and loved it. I have also got our type of aircraft speed record at 160 mph, the absolute limit at which they can go.

Yesterday was grand, although rotten weather for flying. We went up through 2,000 feet of thick cloud into brilliant sunshine with a sea of clouds below us and no land, nothing in sight. It was wonderful cruising along at 100 mph but it seemed as if we were not moving and this brilliant sunshine after the misty foggy earth.

When not flying there was an all-pervading informality about Leuchars. After the officers' mess, the most memorable place was Betty's bar, a local pub. Partridge recalled the pep talk from the Chief Flying Instructor to the newly arrived pupils: 'You won't hurt yourself flying here but for God's sake be careful driving back on a dark winter's night from Betty's bar.'

Roy may not have taken the warning too seriously as he proudly wrote to Naomi explaining about the merits of his sports car: 'Molly is marvellous, came back from Cupar in under ten minutes tonight – it's over nine miles. The wind was behind us and the speedometer was over 80 the whole way. Marvellous bus, darling.'

He was also enjoying sports, including boxing. 'I've been boxing all evening and I am taking it up seriously again. No rugger tho', got to go a bit easy doctor says cos' of my galloping pulse. It's nothing to worry about and no weakness of the heart. Just interesting he says.' However, he soon ignored the doctor and continued his passion for boxing and rugby playing for the station's rugger XV.

There was an added incentive in boxing as he wrote to Naomi:

> 28 October. I've got to box tomorrow to qualify to come down south and I am scared stiff as per usual. And of course as luck would have it, I've got a black eye from rugger today to give the other guy a very good and (painful to me) target. Isn't it just my luck?

The next day he wrote in bitter disappointment:

> I didn't lose my fight tonight. I won but unfortunately this damned competition is a team fight and Leuchars' team lost. I do feel so sick about it all, especially as I had to box pretty hard to win and only won at the cost of one quite good black eye, another teeny one and a very bloody nose. I did manage to knock my opponent down though. Anyway, our team sure managed to see theirs under the table afterwards as regards drinking.

Roy enjoyed a good social life at Leuchars with his friends including Peter, Rodney Carver and John Snow:

> Last night I went to a dance in Dundee. Had quite a good time. The best part was that the old car tootled me home fifty miles in sixty-five minutes. Pretty good going I guess, my darling. She is cold though for up here.

Roy was only twenty-one and still game for a prank or two:

> Ten males and two females (actually they are ladies) arrived in a pub in Andrews for a drink..... then we went and hunted ghosts in the local graveyard. It was great fun and we had a grand time scaring each other as the cemetery is ages old (1500 or something). We hid and played damn silly tricks on each other until the women were absolutely scared stiff. Three men were going to turn up later in sheets and scare us but they got scared themselves and didn't turn up. Incredible isn't it? My old nerves weren't even palpitating and thought it the devil of a joke. I am rather thinking that I must be an absolute fool as I never seem to get scared.

Roy played golf with his fellow pupils at St Andrews, four miles away to the south-east of Leuchars. The Royal and Ancient Golf Club extended membership privileges to RN and RAF officers. Partridge recalled, whilst training at Leuchars, playing on the Eden course at St Andrews where the green fee in his day was the princely sum of one shilling and six pence, more than twice the price of a good meal.

Through to the end of October, Roy and his colleagues practised forced landings, spins, steep turns, sideslips, gliding and instrument flying, and increasingly flying alone without their instructor.

By now, Roy tallied twenty hours' dual and thirteen hours' solo pilot in his log book. He wrote: '21 October. Flying is still going very well and I love it more and more.'

A few days later he could not resist describing his boldness in the air:

> 25 October. Just a wee bit of swank, please. Yesterday I was taught to loop the loop

and they sent me off by myself to practise. I was scared stiff the first time but ended up very confidently by doing eight loops. Not bad for the old fiancée, n'est-ce pas?'

The next day: 'Today not very much has happened as it has rained all day. I did do some blind flying, however. It was not much fun, just watching instruments and just calculating were I was going. In fact, lousy.'

On 27 October he wrote: 'Had a good day flying today, lots of loops and spins and dives etc. It was great fun. I had rather fun too diving at tiny clouds and chewing them up with my airscrew.'

Flying instruction continued for the rest of the year, weather permitting, and was as equally rigorous and detailed as the ground instruction and academic studies.

Roy and the other pilots affected a casual air towards death:

1 November. Tonight Peter and I have been celebrating the first of the month and new wine bills. Peter and I had our usual quotes 'to us and ours'. We drink to ourselves first and hope that we won't kick the bucket not for ourselves, cos' we don't care but for you darlings left rather lonesomelike. Then we drink to 'ours' – you and Elisabeth, my darling.

Roy was testing his new-found skills to the utmost:

3 November. Today I rather had a good time as the weather cleared up sufficiently for us to go flying (the first time for a week). I did my usual stuff, loops and spins and a thing called a stall where you whistle down towards the earth at about 120 mph then ease the old joystick back until you are pointing vertically at the sky then kick the rudderbar over and go sailing down in a hell-dive. It is absolutely grand and really quite spectacular. I've got some thirty-odd hours in the air now. It does seem incredible just short weeks ago I couldn't fly; now I amble round the sky quite happily by myself. It really is new wizard fun. Gosh, I do hope that it is fine tomorrow for more flying.

In his next letter he wrote:

I had great fun today as I managed to beat our course altitude record by 2,000 feet. I got up to over 10,000 feet above the earth then spun down 6,000 feet. It was great fun, although I am still slightly deaf from it, coming down too fast. I had great fun scaring myself today doing stunts which I haven't been taught such as inverted flying. Quite naturally I fell off my efforts and ended up in the most colossal dives straight for the ground at well over 160 mph. It is incredible, darling, how quickly you think when you are falling at a speed of about 200 feet per second. Everything seems to come automatically to correct yourself.

He was getting ever more adventurous. The following week he wrote:

9 November. Being more of a damn fool than the others, I managed to get up higher and spun down further than the others. There is absolutely nothing in it except that I had more patience than the others.

Today another Sub and I had great fun cos' we met quite by chance above the clouds at about 4,000 feet and started to follow each other round. Anyway, it ended up in a most grand dogfight chasing each other all over the sky and trying to get on each others tails. We did love it so especially as we didn't know who the other guy was until we landed and asked who was in plane so and so.

By now the course had developed such that for the pupils it was 'practice, practice, practice' on everything from aerobatics, spins, slow rolls, circuits, forced landings, and instrument flying.

Roy wrote: '10 November. I'm feeling really rather pleased with myself at present darling as I have managed to get slow rolls buttoned. That is turning over on your back and up again without stopping. It's great fun but rather terrifying for the first time.'

The greatest enemy to the young aspiring pilots was the weather, not only for damping their enthusiasm but also by preventing them from physically flying their flimsy biplanes. Repeatedly Roy was to write home 'No flying today, wind too high 60 mph gale or something'. As Roy later told his sister, Leslie: 'Planes did not fly in those days pre-war when it rained; we had no windscreen wipers.'

Bad weather that late autumn and early winter was to get Roy increasingly down but a bright spot on the horizon was a visit by Naomi. He wrote:

18 November: Gosh, Dearest isn't it grand to know that you are actually on your way up here. I guess that I am very extremely, terribly excited. Played rugger today in a 40 mph wind. It was damned cold but quite a good game which we managed to win. Flying this morning was a wee bit difficult in a gale (a bit bumpy) but I managed to do my usual tricks.

His next letter stated: 'We've still got this darned gale up here, so no solo flying. I went up with my instructor though and had quite good fun doing steep turns, rolls and low flying in very bumpy weather.'

He was eager to taking Naomi to the term end Christmas Dance:

I am so looking forward to you arriving in this godforsaken hole. I'm on duty tonight and have just finished work at midnight and a half. Rather late and one gets so bored by one's self....I'm beginning to think that the younger generation is showing an incredibly strong will. I'm certain that we are and that the y.g. are not as bad as they are painted by Victorian minds.

By the end of term on 3 December, 'A' Flight's course was complete and Roy had clocked up almost thirty-three hours' dual and thirty hours' solo in his Flying Log Book, including one or two cross-country flights in the final few days of term. Each pupil pilot was assessed by the Chief Flying Instructor for competence.

As Roy recalled the next month 'I seem to be pretty lucky the way I always manage to just scrape through. No fault of mine that I do pass either 'cos I am deuced lazy and no brains. No disrespect meant Billy but what intelligent children we shall have.'

At last Naomi arrived at Leuchars to Roy's delight. He had already written prior to her arrival: 'I've booked a room for you. It's rather pleasant and not a hotel.' Roy enjoyed introducing Naomi to all his new pals and they had a wonderful time at the Leuchars dance.

They then took Molly for their first ever romantic weekend alone together, in a little village called Killin in the Scottish Highlands. Killin was a pretty place set against a backdrop of the spectacular mountains of Breadalbane in the Cairngorms. They stayed at the Killin Hotel, which was surrounded by mountains, rivers, and lochs.

Both Roy and Naomi loved Killin for its quietness and peace with huge tree-less mountains coming right down to the water's edge of Loch Tay. They would have loved to explore further together but the midwinter darkness fell very early. However, there was still the rest of the month for a wonderful Christmas leave together down in Shaldon.

CHAPTER 6

From Hart to Swordfish

Roy was becoming ever more passionate about flying as the New Year, 1938, found him taking up the challenge of piloting more advanced aircraft, including the Hawker Hart and Fairey Swordfish biplanes.

On 3 January, he started the 'B' Flight four-month course under Ft Lt Kelly. He commented: 'Flew a Hart today, it's darned nearly like learning to fly again.'

The Hart, designed as a front-line bomber in the 1920s, was a strutted biplane with open cockpit and a reputation for being aerobatic. Another young trainee pilot of the time commented: 'There wasn't anything you couldn't do with a Hart except pick gooseberries!'

Two days after his first flight in a Hart, Roy wrote: 'Flew again today and I seemed to have mastered the Hart fairly safely.'

He was still trying to allay Naomi's fears about flying. He wrote to her the following day: 'Do you remember Roy Clapham, medium height, fair with moustache? He had a bit of a crash today, wrote off a machine but was entirely unhurt himself. It just shows, darling, that these flying machines aren't dangerous.'

After less than a fortnight, Roy was entirely at ease flying the Hart:

Not much news, except that I went solo for the first time in a Hart today. It was great fun. Also did night flying tonight. That also is great. All you see is a world of lights. We were flying the old machines that we had last term. I managed to go solo after the first twenty-five minutes' duo. Not bad for me *n'est-ce pas*? It was magnificent, parked up in the lonely black sky all on my lonesome except for the moving lights of two other aircraft in the distance. Night flying is surprisingly simple and you can see miles more than you would expect.

The biplane was sturdy, and Roy had great fun with loops, slow rolls, half rolls and stall turns. Roy told Leslie: 'To begin with you get vertigo and find it difficult to work out which way up you are flying, till you get used to it. You need to watch the horizon and keep your eyes on it. Later you can fly by the seat of your pants.'

That January became increasingly cold, wet and windy, hindering flight training and dampening Roy's boyish enthusiasm. He grumbled to Naomi: 'Since Tuesday I've only had twenty minutes flying and I do miss my flying so. It's been due to bad weather and my being on duty.'

Roy kept up his interest in boxing, and on 12 January was looking forward to the big fight for the World Heavyweight title in New York between the reigning champion and the British Empire Heavyweight boxer Tommy Farr. Roy wrote:

No flying today as it is too windy, practically gale force. Hope that you ring up on Sunday darling cos' I'm orderly officer and a Sunday duty is so terribly boring especially if you don't drink.

Tonight Terry and I are going to listen in to the Farr–Braddock fight if we wake up.

Roy thought it was a good fight, but the American James Braddock won after ten rounds, having come from behind to win a unanimous decision, breaking Farr's nose, cracking two of his ribs, and knocking him down three times.

During flying one evening, Roy saw the northern lights: 'It was a magnificent sight, just like search lights spread over the sky, changing colour every now and again, with lovely reds, blues and greens.'

On 18 January the weather improved: 'Had a very good dose of flying this morning. Three different machines solo and one dual period. It was magnificent and a very perfect day, lovely blue sky and could see for miles.'

The bad weather returned the next day: 'No flying today as the weather is rather foggy and misty, worst luck. It's absolutely lousy when there is no flying as there is so little to do.'

He was further experimenting in high-flying and wrote on 20 January:

Letting off a little steam after a pretty lousy game of rugger and also I may be a little light-headed from doing a spot of solo flying, only 16,000 feet up (just about three miles) cor it did look a long way to fall down again so I decided against jumping. Breathing was just noticeably different up there. The old lungs couldn't quite get enough air more or less. The view was magnificent but deuced cold, miles and miles of it. Well, my darling, I guess that's the nearest to heaven I have been in my life.

A week later he flew even higher:

Flew today and thoroughly enjoyed myself too, aerobatting. I just managed to get up just over 20,000 feet solo. The view was magnificent but breathing was definitely quite hard work and the old brain started to be slow and lazy and eyes went a bit funny so I came down again. I believe that is easily the highest anyone has been this term by about 4,000 feet. Quite a height up you know my dearest, nearly four miles. The aerodrome looked very, very tiny. Also did some low flying, whistling along about 20 feet up at 150 mph. It seemed quite fast and great fun.

On 30 January there were mid-term highjinks. Roy wrote to Naomi:

Went on a scavenger hunt tonight with a couple of other Subs you don't know. We dug a 25 ft LNER (London and North Eastern Railway) board out and deposited it in front of the R&S club golf house St Andrews and also a kipper in the 18th hole. It was great fun but how will old colonel chappies like kippers two days old with their golf?

Roy was looking forward to meeting up with his fiancée and continued: 'Billy dearest, I'll meet you in Lanark on Friday.'

But before that came tragedy as the first of the students was killed in an air crash. Roy was undoubtedly shocked but only briefly wrote about it: '1 February. Leuchars tragedy, Laybourne. No flying this morning. All this beastly wind.'

In the world news, Hitler became supreme commander of the Nazi Wehrmacht and was further testing his powers. It had long been the aim of German nationalists to incorporate all ethnic Germans within a single Greater German state. The Treaty of Versailles, made after the Great War, had left substantial numbers of German people living in countries outside the German border, most notably in Czechoslovakia. Hitler was increasingly challenging that treaty.

Roy had two weeks' precious leave with Naomi. As soon as he could leave the air station, Roy drove Molly down from Leuchars, past Edinburgh to Glasgow and then onwards to the bustling market town of Lanark in the Clyde Valley to rendezvous with Naomi – for the second of their romantic weekends together. They spent a peaceful winter's break in the hills and vales around Lanark, horse riding, walking and relaxing like any young engaged couple.

All too soon it was back to Leuchars and flying recommenced on 15 February in clear but cold skies. His service training practice was leading towards advanced naval aviation with launching from catapults at Leuchars, simulating techniques he would later have to practise from on board ship.

Roy told his family about catapult launches and Leslie recalled he considered these a highlight in his flying training:

2 March. Today has been rather fun flying as four of us were catapulted off. That is, we are given a darned great shove on a runway and get up to 50 mph in about 15 yards. It's terrifying but really great fun afterwards. We actually fly the machine off with another pupil as passenger.

This evening I was doing night flying for 1.25 hours. It was lovely up – cold but clear. The three machines up put up a bit of a record, 39 landings in 1.25 hours. That's fair whipping around. All solo too.

The most important part of Roy's short aviation career was about to take place – the dreaded exams. Wing Commander Down tested Roy on the full flying syllabus during a twenty-minute flight at the beginning of March. The final examination was then sat later in the month.

Flying now included cross-country exercises to test navigational skills in particular. Roy wrote:

3 March. Went on a cross-country today. Great fun, although the visibility was shocking and it was very bumpy. One of our blokes couldn't get through and turned back. He reckons that Lincoln and my nerves must be of iron. As a matter of fact Billy girl, I was not worried at all and it didn't make the slightest difference and I managed to finish to schedule. Chief Flying Instructor tested my flying this morning and gave me an 'OK, quite good', which is not so bad as he is rather slow with his praise. I felt quite bucked anyway.

Welcome landmarks for Roy and his fellow pilots on their cross-country flights included the distinctive pepper-pot like tower of the ancient church of St Athernase, which stood on a grassy knoll above the village, and Leuchars Castle. Further afield they could fly over Earlshall Castle on the outskirts of Leuchars. Beyond lay Tentsmuir Forest and Kinshaldy Beach with miles of sandy beaches and colonies of seals. The green expanse of Tentsmuir was bounded in the north by the vast Firth of Tay and the sprawl of Dundee. Much further west at the head of the Firth was Perth and eastwards St Andrews and the North Sea.

Two days later Roy wrote: 'Catapulted again today. Great fun and also my cross-country of 150 miles. I was exactly right in my times for the trip – 1 hour and 20 minutes. I am rather proud of that.'

He went on to add: 'Darling couldn't you find out anything for me, I want to become a member of the Haldon Aero Club. Do you think you could find the particulars for me?'

Thoughts of such peacetime activities were to be thwarted by international events. As threat of war spread right across Europe, Roy had to make a crucial decision on his future career as a naval aviator – whether to specialise as a bomber or fighter pilot. This was no simple task as it could fundamentally decide life or death – the life expectancy of the fighter pilot during wartime came to be regarded as considerably less than that of the Torpedo, Search and Reconnaissance (TSR) airman.

Roy, who was considered by his instructors to have the necessary skills and qualities to become a fighter pilot, decided to put Naomi first. He wrote to her: '10 March. Have been offered the fighter course, but chose the Gosport torpedo course for my Billy girl.'

With the preparations for a conflict in Europe, training began to be much more attuned to a war situation, rather than just flying. Flying instruction became more rigorous and Roy and his fellow pilots carried out bombing practice on the ranges at Tentsmuir Forest.

The likelihood of Roy being called on to fight for his country increased, as on 12 March German troops crossed the border to annex Austria and its large population of Germans. The Treaty of Versailles had specifically forbidden the absorption of Austria into Germany, and Britain and France might have been expected to react forcibly but in fact their response was muted.

A few days later Roy received two certificates. One, posted from London on 14 March, confirmed his rank as Flying Officer, RAF, and was signed by the new king, George VI. The second certificate, dated 1 March, confirmed his appointment in the rank of Sub Lt RN. It, again, was signed by George VI.

Shortly after, Roy wrote to Naomi that he had passed his exams and the next three weeks featured armament flying. In April, Roy's 'B' Flight course ended with a total of fifty-five hours' dual instruction, and sixty-five hours' solo as pilot, recorded in his flying log book.

Roy started to focus on the task ahead at his next posting, Gosport in Hampshire. He wrote: 'From all accounts we've heard of Gosport, it is simply wonderful and I shall be able to get a machine practically any time.'

On 24 April came the most significant moment of his flying career to date as he received his flying qualification and was authorised to wear his flying badge, his cherished wings. Ceremonially the group captain wrote into their log books 'Qualified for Flying Badge under King's Regulations with effect from 24/4/38.'

Roy went on a well-earned four weeks' leave for the Easter vacation before starting his final three months' operational training at RAF Gosport and nearby Lee-on-Solent.

He arrived at Gosport on 17 May and training began the next day with the instructors Flying Officer Jupp and Pilot Officer Hally, RAF. It was Roy's first chance to handle an operational aircraft, the famed Fairey Swordfish which had been introduced into front-line operational naval squadrons two years earlier on the fleet carrier HMS *Glorious*.

The Swordfish – affectionately known as the Stringbag – was developed in 1933. A biplane with struts and wires and fixed undercart, it looked less modern than some of the newer monoplane aircraft like the Spitfire or Fulmar but such was its handling and reliability that it remained in active service for at least the next decade.

The Swordfish was powered by a Pegasus III or 30 engine and her top speed was 135 knots, but as Roy joked 'that must have been going downhill without a load'. A more attainable speed was 136 mph or 120 knots.

It was a much loved aircraft as exemplified in a squadron song:

The Swordfish relies on her Peggy,
The modified Taurus ain't sound,
So the Swordfish flies off on her missions
And the Albacore stays on the ground.

Chorus
Bring back, oh bring back,
Oh bring back my Stringbag to me, to me,
Bring back, bring back,
Oh bring back my Stringbag to me.

Roy thoroughly enjoyed himself on his first flight in a Swordfish:

18 May. Flew today. We were just told to get into the machines and fly. They are entirely different from Tutors or Harts, are incredibly safe lumbering old things. They almost land themselves. There is no fear of my doing anything mad, my darling, 'cos you can't acrobat them as these Swordfish are much too heavy and clumsy.

Did some torpedo instruction this morning. The general atmosphere of this place [Gosport] seems to be quite gentlemanly with very little to do and all day to do it in. Not that I am complaining of course.

Roy found the Swordfish could be roughly handled. To stall one was almost impossible since it had a stalling speed of 52 knots and then would gently sink but regain flying speed immediately. The Stringbag, he jokingly later described to Leslie was 'travelling at 50 mph and slower than a walking pace when the wind was in the wrong direction'.

On 19 May, in a letter sent to his parents' house in Shaldon, Roy wrote:

No flying today, torpedo instruction instead. This evening Pardoe and I found a most magnificent little golf course in Warsash. It costs 2/6 a month and the most mammoth tea of bread, butter, honey and jam and two kinds of cake costs only a shilling. It's a magnificent find.

The month of June was spent in continuous practice and formation flying, dummy drops, night flying tests, dummy landings, tactics, and sector attacks. Tragedy occurred on 21 June when a Swordfish of TTU Gosport struck and killed Aircraftman Tew while landing.

Roy started on a Swordfish floatplane course at Lee-on-Solent with Sgt Bond as instructor. Other instructors included Ft Lt Sisson and Sgt Logan, RAF. The wheeled undercarriage of the normal Swordfish was removed and replaced with floats to transform it into a floatplane.

For the first week, Roy was reunited with his fellow Leuchars pupils who had opted for fighters. Carver, Hawks, McIver and Snow had spent the summer at No. 1 FTS, flying Ospreys, Nimrods and Harts. Now they were down for a seven-day instruction on Swordfish floatplanes.

Their route was over the busy Solent sea lanes between Southampton, Portsmouth, Calshot and the Isle of Wight. Roy wrote to Naomi: 'Thursday. Solo in floatplane. It's quite good fun but rather boring aimlessly floating round the sky.'

Once the basics of flying a floatplane had been mastered, the next stage was to learn how to drop torpedoes in a quiet patch of water often close to the Cowes coastline: 'Tuesday 6 July. Did dummy attacks on the *Dunedin* this morning. It was very good fun. I seem to have got the hang of it more or less too.'

As the course progressed, Roy was starting to become proficient at his future trade of torpedo strikes against enemy targets. He wrote: 'Dropped torpedoes today. Quite good fun altho' perfectly beastly weather.'

Roy completed the floatplane conversion course on 21 July and could now look forward to his wedding, due to take place on 22 August. However, increasing political tensions in Europe were such that it looked as if Roy may be called for action at very short notice. Preparations for his wedding were speeded up and the marriage was set for two days earlier than planned.

At 8 am on 20 August, Naomi walked down the aisle of the pretty little church of Stoke-in-Teign Head, not far from Shaldon, to join Roy at the altar. She was dressed in a navy and white suit. Roy had no best man, and no photographs were taken, such was the haste in organising the ceremony. There were just members of the family, from Roy's side – Grace and Sydney, Leslie and Harry. Naomi's family consisted of her brother, Bill.

After the wedding there was a simple wedding breakfast of eggs, bacon and tomato. Presents included a glass-bottomed tankard from Roy's Leuchars pals, incorrectly inscribed with the original date for the wedding, 22 August 1938.

There was no time for anything other than the shortest of honeymoons, at the Grosvenor House Hotel in London. Just three days after the wedding, Roy was posted to RAF Donibristle in Scotland 'for full flying duties (ffd) and deck landing training with HMS *Furious* for 811 Squadron'.

Roy and Naomi together went up to Scotland to the pretty village of Aberdour in Fife and stayed at the Old School House. They barely had time to unpack before Roy received orders to report to his Commanding Officer, Lt Cdr E.O.F. Price, RN (Sqdn Ldr RAF) who had been flight commander 403 Catapult Flight on board HMS *Kent* back in 1936 when Roy was serving onboard the ship. The instructors included W.P. Sutcliffe.

Reporting with Roy were his pilot colleagues from No. 1 FTS – Frankie Fryer and Lydekker. Also at Donibristle were Roy's other friends Rodney Carver, McIver and Snow, in 801 Squadron, and Boulding, Hamilton and Pardoe, in 822 Squadron. No's 811 and 822 Squadrons were newly equipped with Swordfish aircraft which were brand new – only two months' old. Both squadrons operated as pilot training units at Donibristle.

Immediately the dummy deck-landing training and circuits started in earnest. It was not long before there was a further accident. The squadron was operating at sea off Granton in Leith, when Frankie Fryer crashed his Swordfish coded '602' into the sea. Luckily, he escaped unhurt.

Roy's flights were less dramatic, and on 31 August, he flew Swordfish K8376 on a course steering flight with the air gunner Norman 'Blondie' Hollis in the back seat as ballast. Two days later Roy carried out wind finding with Hollis, followed over the next few days by formation flying, local flying practice, instrument flying and yet more dummy landings.

On 15 September, Prime Minister Neville Chamberlain flew to Germany to negotiate with Hitler who was demanding the secession of the Sudetenland from Czechoslovakia to Germany. A week later they met again when Hitler delivered an ultimatum requiring the annexation within five days – the Munich crisis was at its height.

During the night of 23 September, while Roy and Naomi were in their accommodation in Aberdour, there came a frantic banging at the door. It was the local policeman, and he was shouting 'You've gotta get back to camp – there's a war on.'

The next day, 811 Squadron was ordered to embark immediately on HMS *Furious* at Rosyth, as was 801 Osprey Squadron (under the command of Sqdn Ldr G.K. Fairtlough, RAF), and 822 Swordfish Squadron whose CO was Lt Cdr K. Williamson, RN. The seriousness of the situation was recognised when the crews loaded live ammunition for their guns over the next few days.

Furious was one of the veteran carriers of the Royal Navy and was known as the 'Old Lady'. Commissioned in June 1917, she had a forward flying-off deck where Sqdn Ldr Dunning made the world's first deck landing that year. She had spent her early life fighting as an aircraft carrier in the Great War. Lt C. Topliss, RN, in *Salute to the Old Lady*, wrote: 'She is the mother of all the world's aircraft carriers and was flying off aircraft for offensive operations before the Royal Air Force was born.'

Furious sailed once the squadrons had embarked, setting course for Scapa Flow in the Orkney Isles.

On 27 September, the British Fleet was mobilised and sent to War Stations. Roy wrote that day:

> HMS *Furious*: After one night of non sleep, we hung around to 3.30 when we flew out here and landed on. I fixed it all right. Then I and my Flight Commander embarked Osprey pilots and flew them back to Donib. [Donibristle] for them to bring more aircraft out. Then back to *Furious*. In all, about two and a half hours flying, bed and the morning watch. Pretty lousy, *n'est-ce pas*?
>
> As far as I can see, my darling, we shall be in *Furious* for about two weeks at least. Everyone seems to be taking a very hopeful view of the situation but we are taking no chances, hence the long time.

Chamberlain flew again to Munich for a conference on 29 September, with Hitler, Mussolini and the French Prime Minister Edouard Daladier. An agreement was reached in which Czech representatives were told they must allow German forces to occupy Sudetenland or fight Germany alone. The Czechs capitulated and Chamberlain arrived back in England waving a piece of paper bearing Hitler's signature and claiming to have secured 'peace in our time'.

The panic died down, at least for a short while. The next day was Naomi's birthday. Roy wrote: 'HMS *Furious*. Tuesday. We are going to sea for exercises tomorrow so I ain't got no idea when I shall post this (Many happy returns of the day).' The next day he wrote: 'Wednesday. At sea now darling and nothing much for me to do. This morning I played around with my engine, inspecting and tiddlying it up. Ham [Hamilton] sends his love to you.'

While at Scapa Flow, the squadrons practised their deck-landing training. Roy's first impression of locating an aircraft carrier from the air was 'like trying to find and land on a pocket handkerchief in the sea', as he later remarked to Leslie.

After several days on HMS *Furious*, with no mishaps, Roy began to feel at ease with the way the Swordfish usually 'sat down' on the deck. However, he was shaken when his friend John Snow was tragically killed whilst landing on deck.

Naomi had been nervous of Roy going off to war and was extremely relieved when two weeks later following a knock on the door at School House she was told that *Furious* with Roy on board was 'steaming up the Firth of Forth'.

The couple were happily reunited and on 10 October Roy and all the trainees completed their Deck Landing Training Course. Given the potential war setting, the instructors passed the trainee aircrew if at all reliable enough to become pilots. Then all were sent on leave to await posting as pool aircrew to be allocated to active service in operational front-line squadrons.

By now the 'class' were all going separate ways after their final training, but few were to survive the war. A.A. Pardoe went to 810 Squadron *Ark Royal* (killed on 25 April 1940), H.E.J.P. Parker went to 813 Squadron on HMS *Eagle*, T.W.G. French to 812 Squadron on *Glorious* (killed in Hal Far, 11 March 1940) W.V. Hamilton to 819 (killed on 26 November 1940) and Godfrey Lincoln to 825 (killed in January, 1939).

From now on, Roy's family rarely saw him for long. Leslie recollected:

We would get a telegram from Roy saying when he would get forty-eight hours' leave pass. He would appear with his packed canvas kit bag. All the news and stories we could only really hear in this short two-day period.

Roy received the order to report to HMS *Victory* at Portsmouth for full flying duties at RAF Gosport as a reserve pilot awaiting an operational squadron. Also posted with him were his colleagues 'Hammy' Hamilton, Pardoe and Boulding.

While Roy was in the RAF Pool, he and Naomi rented a cottage called Holmwood, in Old Street, Hillhead, in Hampshire. It would not be home for long – the next month Roy would be appointed at last to a front-line squadron on board the carrier HM *Glorious* in Malta.

CHAPTER 7

Squadron Life in Malta

Roy was posted to the crown colony of Malta in November 1938 to join the aircraft carrier HMS *Glorious* and Naomi was thrilled for him.

Malta, an island just seventeen miles by nine miles – slightly smaller than the Isle of Wight or four times larger than Manhattan – had been part of the British Empire for over a century. Its significance was its position in the Mediterranean, halfway between the British port of Gibraltar in the west and the Suez Canal in the east. To the north lay Sicily and Italy and to the south the coast of Africa.

Malta had been the headquarters and main anchorage of the Royal Navy's Mediterranean Fleet since 1814. Its capital, Valletta – among the best preserved medieval cities in the world – was surrounded by harbours on three sides. On the eastern flank lay Grand Harbour which had facilities to equip and repair any ship in the British fleet.

Roy had been to Malta before. As a midshipman on HMS *Kent*, he sailed into Grand Harbour in June 1934 and spent two days there. In his writings he had indicated he was more fascinated by the many ships around him, including HMS *Resolution* and *Royal Sovereign*, than the magnificence of the medieval city.

This time, Roy had to make his own way to Malta, travelling overland via Italy before finally boarding the steamer SS *Ionian* at Syracuse in Sicily. He journeyed with fellow Leuchars pilots Hammy Hamilton, Ken Gurr and John 'Godfrey' Lincoln.

Also travelling out to Malta at the same time was the new 812 Squadron commander, Lt Cdr J.D.C. 'Sam' Little, who was relieving Sqdn Ldr Hutchinson, the one remaining RAF squadron commander on the *Glorious*.

Once the steamer cast off, Roy settled down to write:

> 17 November. Our mad rush across Europe was most exciting except that we seemed to drink an incredible amount of wine of each country as recreation. I think that Rome will remember our passage 'cos we managed to visit an incredible number of bars in an exceedingly short time. At Syracuse, of course, Ham and I had lost our luggage, all of it. However after countless worries and problems, we have recovered them, all serene and happy, thank heavens.

Gradually the distant low-lying silhouette of the small Malta archipelago came into sight. Then after the 100-mile journey from Sicily, the steamer finally chugged its way through the narrow protected entrance to the Grand Harbour with its great pillar-like structures on either side guarding the mouth.

On one side was perched Valletta, on the top of a dramatic rocky outcrop. Its enormous fortified walls had been built by the Knights of St John in the sixteenth century. On the opposite bank lay three other fortified cities and beyond that further inland the docks and moored warships of the Mediterranean Fleet.

The steamer docked beyond the imposing Customs House below the heights at Lascaris Wharf. Roy looked out for the distinctive silhouette of his new ship, the aircraft carrier HMS *Glorious*, which lay on the opposite side of the Grand Harbour at the entrance to Frenchman's Creek.

He was not to join *Glorious* straight away. That month, the aircraft carrier's Swordfish squadron crews were disembarked at their base of RAF Hal Far air station on the south-east of the island. Roy and his travelling companions were duly met by Royal Navy transport which was to take them and their belongings across the island to their accommodation at Hal Far. The truck drove through the dockland area and then up out of the city towards Pretty Bay, past flat-roofed houses with overhanging balconies and roads bounded by rubble walls, covered with cactuses and purple bougainvillea. It was warm and dusty after Gosport.

Roy and his colleagues reported to the duty officer, and were sent to the station commander after being allocated their accommodation. Hal Far, although equipped with hangars, workshops, squadron offices and other buildings, had a grass and dirt runway. It was the only aerodrome on the island and was principally used by the Fleet Air Arm.

Roy wrote to Naomi, eager that his young bride should come and join him, though worried for her safety:

Come, darling, as soon as you can as we are here until January sometime. If P&O are booked up, try Commonwealth Line. It is small and goes at the beginning of the month, I believe, and costs about £10. If none of these are any good, overland to Syracuse might be all right, or Naples. But I shall prefer you to have a companion. Trying to find your way by train in Italy is even a little excessive. Get Bill [her brother, William Lord] to drive with you part way as company.

Once Roy had put his canvas kitbag in his cabin and further explored the camp, he wrote again to Naomi: 'Sunday: This morning Ham and I went for a walk. It was very dull, no talking and a terribly lethargic atmosphere. A hot sun and a dusty breeze.'

For his first few weeks, Roy would be a 'pool', or reserve, pilot until allocated to one of the ship's resident squadrons. Among the first people he met was one of *Glorious*'s senior pilots, Lt A.J.D. 'Titch' Harding, a short but very jovial and friendly aviator, a little older than Roy but very experienced. Lt Harding took Roy up in his 812 Squadron Swordfish for familiarisation and assessment. Harding later recorded in his flying log book Roy's twenty-five minutes as a passenger carrying out 'Air experience – navigation' in Swordfish '62' K5950.

Roy was given the green light and soon set off on his first solo in Malta, which saw him take off from the west–east runway and fly over the landscape of tiny fields surrounded by a mosaic of limestone rubble walls. The Swordfish crossed over Kalafrana Bay where the RAF had a flying boat and air-sea rescue station. Roy could see the hangars and moored flying boats below, before he flew out beyond the coast, across the ultramarine calm waters, out towards the rocky outcrop of Filfla. Flying back over the centre of Malta, he could see Rabat and the massive dome of Mosta Church and beyond that the distant hills and silhouette of Comino and Gozo islands to the west.

Even though it was mid-November, the weather was such a contrast to flying in Scotland – passing through steaming wisps of cloud being blown along above the surface of the sea up to a few hundred feet. Finally, Roy did a circuit over Hal Far before a bumpy landing, throwing up dust as he revved forwards to the hangars and the waiting ground crew.

Roy's first impressions of Hal Far were that: 'It is an aerodrome some ten miles from Valletta (the main town). It is an aerodrome or rather a damned bad landing field in a sea of rocks but still I can still land in it which is the main thing.'

He was at that time the most junior sub-lieutenant and pilot, but the seasoned officers quickly made him feel relaxed and part of the team: '19 November: Everyone is extraordinarily nice. Next week we go on board for a week's watch-keeping duties and then back to this place.'

When squadrons were disembarked to Hal Far, pilots were accommodated there – except the married ones who got permission to 'sleep ashore' when not on duty. One of Roy's first tasks was to find accommodation for his young wife who was planning to come out to Malta to live with him. Meanwhile, he stayed on the air station.

Only days after arriving, he confidently wrote back to Naomi: 'As far as I can see there are plenty of flats and houses to let in Malta. The *Malta Times* has a good list.' He added: 'It may interest you to know that Britain's sun-kissed isle (Malta) for the last couple of days has been rain ridden and lousy thunderstorms. It's raining now.'

The week went by quickly and soon he found himself travelling down to Grand Harbour and to his first duties on board *Glorious*. The aircraft carrier was berthed in her usual spot alongside Parlatorio Wharf. All around was the hustle and bustle of the naval dockyard and harbour.

Roy had his first opportunity to study HMS *Glorious* which had originally been built in 1915 by Harland and Wolff in Belfast as a battle-cruiser along with her sister ships HMS *Courageous* and HMS *Furious*. The three were known as 'the ugly sisters' due to their ungainly silhouettes. *Glorious* had been based with the Mediterranean Fleet since 1930. She was spotless, her paintwork fresh, her decks hosed down, and her brass work polished until it sparkled in the sunlight.

Roy was piped on board in brilliant sunshine, typical Mediterranean early winter weather. Commander Guy Willoughby, Commander Flying, sent for the incoming naval officers to welcome them. Willoughby was the first naval officer to take up the Commander (F) post on *Glorious* and had been a naval airman from 1925 on the 2nd Pilot's course.

Roy later met the skipper, Captain Arthur Lumley St George Lyster, a tall and imposing officer and gentleman, who had come to *Glorious* from the Admiralty the previous year. He had taken over from the much loved Bruce Fraser who had gone on to be promoted as rear admiral and C-in-C Home Fleet.

Roy learnt that during the Great War Lyste had served in the Grand Fleet, in Gallipoli, and in Italy where he had been awarded the Order of the Crown of Italy. Lyster had also been awarded the DSO when he was gunnery and executive officer of HMS *Cassandra* in the 6th Light Cruiser Squadron.

One of the next officers to meet Roy was Flt Lt Nigel Blair-Oliphant, RAF, Armaments Officer.

I recall B-F when he arrived on board ship. He was a junior officer in the Royal Navy. *Glorious* was a combined service unit. Pilots from both services flew together, respected one another professionally and were united in the job they did together. The aircraft ground and aircrew were made up of roughly two-thirds FAA to one-third RAF. All the maintenance crews were RAF, of course. Since the FAA crews had little else to do except work with their aircraft, they tended to have 12 out of 12 in working order whilst the land RAF would have 10 out of 12.

Blair-Oliphant continued:

Glorious was an extraordinarily happy ship, largely due to her skipper. The captain, affectionately known by the officers as Lumley Lyster, was an ideal choice to command our combined service unit of RAF, Royal Navy and Royal Marines' ship's company. He was very well liked by all – as was his wife, Daisy. Sadly, things were to change very much for the worse when he handed over command in mid-1939 on his promotion to rear admiral. The commander was Edward Evans-Lombe, a gunnery officer and a most able man. He later became Fraser's Chief-of-Staff in the Pacific, and a vice admiral.

Roy was given a tour of the ship and her confusing deck levels, from the bridge, to the officers' wardroom and mess, the aircrew briefing rooms, his shared cabin, and the upper and lower hangars. It was going to take a while before he would easily find his way around this massive vessel with a complement of 1,200 crew including her RAF and Fleet Air Arm personnel.

When *Glorious* was initially converted to an aircraft carrier in the latter half of the twenties, she had two flight decks: the main flight deck, and at the bow, a lower smaller 'flying off deck'. During her 1935–6 refit, this smaller forward flight deck was converted to a gun deck with anti-aircraft guns. Roy was impressed by the aircraft carrier's size, 26,518 tons, in comparison with his former ship, *Kent*, which was only 9,750 tons with 700 crew.

Another young pilot, Sub Lt William 'Bill' or 'Moose' Martyn, also from Canada, succinctly described his new ship *Glorious* in a letter to his parents:

We carry 48 aircraft and 48 officers to fly them. There are also quite a few observer officers for navigation duties in the Torpedo Spotter Reconnaissance Squadrons. I haven't learned all the seamen ranks in the Navy yet but here is a general outline: ordinary seaman, able seaman, leading corporal seaman, petty officer, chief petty officer, warrant officer, etc. up to what they call executive officers which are those officers carried for fighting duties, i.e. not doctors, accountants, etc. who have special colouring between their gold stripes in the sleeve. Doctor – red, school teacher – blue, etc.

In the ship there are three messes, i.e., Wardroom Mess for officers of rank, Sub/Lt up and Gunroom Mess for midshipmen and warrant officers and petty officers have a mess of their own. Only wardroom officers use the starboard after gangway of a ship. When a boat approaches a ship, the quarter master or a seaman shouts out 'Ahoy!' and the sailor in charge of the boat shouts back 'No! No!' or 'Aye! Aye!' meaning in first place he carries no officer or wardroom rank or in second place he does, so that officer of the watch on the quarterdeck (after section of ship) knows who is coming aboard. Officer of the watch is always dressed in frock coat and sword and has a telescope under his left armpit.

When the officer steps on the quarterdeck he salutes and the officer of the watch must always stand at the salute. Also, while officers come aboard, captains are piped off and onto a ship.

Yes, she is a very complicated life and there's a lot to learn. Smoking is prohibited in ship's boats.

In the summer we had to wear whites to breakfast and lunch. While we were flying or in the hangars we wore khaki, and in the evening for dinner of course white mess kit with stiff shirts, so we are always busy changing. Sundays all officers wear frock coats to church and till 4 pm in the afternoon.

Roy's tasks on board HMS *Glorious* included duties on the bridge under the officer of the watch, as he explained:

> November 21. We came down from Hal Far this morning for a week's ship duties watch keeping etc. On Sunday we go back for normal flying. Tomorrow we have got to get all sorts of stores out of the ship. It is going to be a thoroughly lousy job, I'll bet.

Watch keeping involved being on duty for four-hour stretches overnight on the bridge – with the daunting possibility of calling and waking up the captain in the event of an emergency. At the same time there were the soothing strains of dance music, drifting across the calm water of the harbour from a dozen waterfront bars in Valletta and from the government administration district of adjacent Floriana.

Roy found himself gazing at the bright lights of the city, most likely wishing he was drinking in a local hostelry with Hammy and Ken:

> Thursday. It is only just after midnight. In other words, yours truly has just got up and is on watch and has three and a half long hours before bed again. Ugh. We are lying so quietly in harbour too with thousands of other lights of destroyers and battleships all around. Gosh darling, I hope that my wire arrived in time for you to get your berth. It is extraordinary how little there is to say after a day's watch keeping. I didn't even get a blast to tell you about.

On the positive side, whilst aboard ship, was the opportunity to catch up with former shipmates including James Stewart-Moore who later recalled:

> On *Glorious*, I served as an observer in 823 Squadron as general watch keeper and as officer of the boy's division until the Navy took over the Fleet Air Arm from the RAF and observers became regular flying crews.
>
> I first met B-F when we both joined HMS *Kent* when she recommissioned at Chatham in May '34. I was a watch keeping lieutenant and he was a midshipman. I suppose I was about six years older than he was, and correspondingly that much more senior. The age difference was significant in those days.

The person whom Roy was most eager to see was of course Naomi. He wrote to her the next night: 'November 22. I am 24 hours nearer seeing my own beautiful wife.'

The following day Roy was given permission to go ashore and was tempted by the waterfront bars in Valletta. 'I met Beaumont and Ham (Hamilton) this evening and had not a few drinks and suffered with them. They are absolutely themselves but our "Godfrey" Lincoln is becoming terribly, terribly social, tails, dinner jackets the whole time.'

For Roy, Valletta was a city of contrast with its smart shops and restaurants in Kingsway not far from the nearby shabby tenements of St Patrick Street. The latter had washing dangling across the streets from upper floor windows. There seemed to be churches on the corners of every street, over-hanging balconies and tall, straight alleyways.

With nightfall, Roy witnessed the city come to life. The afternoon siesta was over and people flocked out into the streets of Valletta which were now ablaze with the lights of shops and restaurants. Roy, a keen horseman, would have particularly appreciated the horse-drawn 'gharries' or carriages, which with lights twinkling and bells ringing, threaded their way through the crowded streets.

In December, Roy was formally transferred to *Glorious*'s 812 Squadron, which was one of the most experienced front-line squadrons in the whole of the Fleet Air Arm. Roy felt privileged to join such a qualified aircrew.

Ken Gurr had also been appointed to the squadron and it must have been daunting for the two young pilots when they arrived at the 812 Squadron mess at Hal Far for the first time. The flying crew room resembled a cross between a cricket club changing room and a boarding school common room.

The new commanding officer, Lt Cdr Little, and the senior pilot, Titch Harding, blended their positions of authority with readiness to work and play with the rest of the crew. Yet Titch took Roy and Ken under his wing and they quickly felt at home.

Sam Little recalled:

I was CO of 812 Squadron for only about six months, if that! It was at the end of a period of major re-organisation of the FAA with RAF bods going back to the RAF and naval bods taking over – I relieved a squadron leader as CO. A few months later it was decreed that squadron COs need not be pilots. My senior observer was more senior to me in naval rank so he had to take over and – rather than step down – I left the squadron sadly for another job.

He continued:

B-F was one of the most junior pilots; considering his age and lack of experience, he was a most reliable pilot and full of good ideas for the squadron.

Titch Harding recalled:

In 1938 Roy was, of course, a young junior pilot still wet behind the ears and married! Being wet behind the ears and slightly foolish – that is youth as it should be. The drying wind of time brings experience which develops and strengthens qualities – integrity, honesty, consideration etc required not only to be a good leader but someone that can be followed with confidence – hence Roy's later name of 'Daddy'; and sometimes no doubt with others 'Mother Hen' and maybe he had Jiminy Cricket (Pinocchio's conscience) painted on his aircraft.

He had what I call likeability. He was an above average pilot, no doubt about that, and as far as I can remember never bent any aircraft with us.

Roy soon settled down and got to know three other members of the squadron very well – Lt Michael 'Tiffy' Torrens-Spence, Lt J.H. 'Jakes' Barnes, and Lt Edmund 'Cliff' Clifford – between them they had a wealth of flying experience and had all trained together at Leuchars three years previously. There was also Lt E.S. 'Splash' Carver, an observer with the squadron, who Roy recollected had been in the Rugby XV team when he joined Dartmouth, and who was destined to become a good friend. There was also a young RAF pilot, Flt Lt Alan 'Ginger' Murray.

The 812 Squadron complement also included the ground crew who were mostly RAF and naval ratings. At the head of each trade was an RAF sergeant or corporal and overall 812 Squadron NCO in charge was Flight Sergeant C. Gittens. He commanded the maintenance side with an organised ability and professionalism which inspired his ratings and led to an efficient working party for the aircraft.

At this time 812 Squadron followed the RAF tradition of dividing the squadron into two flights, 'X' and 'Y', each with six aircraft. Roy was allocated to Titch's 'X' Flight. As Flight commander Titch brought him up to date with the tricks of the trade for the squadron, Routine duties at this time involved flying the aircraft from Hal Far, mainly in the day but also with night training.

Roy's first night flight was on 26 November when the squadron lifted off from Hal Far one by one into the night sky for twenty minutes of night exercises. For Roy, the view gradually opened up and as he ascended he could even see the distant shimmering lights of Sicily to the north, before following Titch in dive and runner attacks on the Battle of Jutland veteran, the battleship HMS *Malaya*. About this time, the likelihood of war with Italy and Germany was looking increasingly probable and this led to even more day and night exercises.

Roy was flying the new Swordfish which had been operational with *Glorious* squadrons for only the previous two years. As was normal at that time, he was assigned one aircraft and crew, which also included a fitter, rigger, armourer, all caring for their charge – all intensely loyal to their own aircraft and crew. This set-up was to remain until aircraft allocation was all centralised in 1942.

He was allocated Swordfish, K8360, which was painted with a big '62' aircraft carrier identification code over a diagonal yellow band on the side of the main fuselage. This was to remain his personal aircraft for many months. In the following year and into 1940, he was still flying an individual Swordfish, K5979, and routinely flew with Leading Telegraphist Russell.

Roy alluded to the fact that he had been assigned his own aircraft in one of his letters to Naomi, ten days before her arrival in Malta: 'I haven't done much flying yet as my aircraft is doing a re-fit.'

Refits were often done at the RAF flying boat and air-sea rescue station at nearby Kalafrana rather than always at Hal Far. E.W. 'Bill' Clayton, 812 Squadron air fitter, recalled the colourful procedure involved in moving the aircraft by road:

> It fell to the rigger to wind the starter handle to get the Swordfish inertia starter whizzing round, then the fitter pulled the starter control. As soon as the engine started, a pilot came over and, with the ground crew sitting on the centre-section step planes, he taxied to the far side of the airfield and switched off.
>
> Here a handling party was waiting to fold the wings and push the aircraft through a gate onto the public road. The rigger would get in the cockpit and 'stand-by the brakes' and off they went down the hill.

Bill Clayton continued:

> The folded width of the Swordfish was just over 17 feet – about the same as the road, so any traffic we met had to pull over to let us pass. If they showed any reluctance to do this, which often was the case, it was my job to check on the brakes. The two-mile journey took about twenty minutes, by which time the pressure in the brake system had almost run out.

After the inspection, the Swordfish would be prepared for a test flight. As was the custom in those days, a rigger and a fitter were required to accompany their aircraft on test. After half an hour in the air the Swordfish returned, the pilot giving it a clean bill of health so it was returned to its normal crew.

Each day, the squadron ground crew did a daily inspection on their aircraft. Roy recognised that the fitter and rigger were as much members of the team as he was and often could be seen tinkering with the aircraft along with them. He got to know Bill Clayton and the rest of the crew well and there was mutual respect and appreciation.

For the rest of November the squadron carried out a daily routine of intensive general flying and high-level bombing at 6,000 feet onto the rocky outcrop of Filfla, just off the coast beyond Hal Far. This tiny stump of an island was regarded as ideal as it represented the approximate size of an enemy warship for the practising Fleet Air Arm aircraft.

Throughout December, Roy and the squadron continued their programme of high-level bombing exercises, interspersed by drama on 22 December when they went on a search for an aircraft reported on fire. Roy was to see nothing out of the norm.

As the days passed, Roy sometimes went on manoeuvres at sea with HMS *Glorious* under Captain Lyster. However, formally 812 Squadron and the other squadrons were stationed on land at Hal Far throughout November until 23 January the following year.

At that time, even though Hal Far and *Glorious* were increasingly replacing RAF personnel with Royal Navy crews in line with the anticipated return of the control of the Fleet Air Arm to the Navy, they still had a large contingent of RAF officers and men. For the RAF officers, there were perks of serving on board a ship and they were in no hurry to return to RAF control on land. Nigel Blair-Oliphant recollected:

> The squadrons would be detached to Hal Far and I would prefer to go to the RAF base – a seaplane port at nearby Kalafrana. Of course, I let Hal Far believe I was at Kalafrana and Kalafrana at Hal Far – I used to be a good skivver in those days.

This officer was happy to recollect his flippant youth and later went on to become air vice marshal of the RAF!

Roy would spend his leave walking, horse riding, exploring the wild and ancient ruined temples close to Hal Far or travelling in the old green buses to the surrounding coastal villages, such as Marsaxlokk – which would remind him of his youth, talking to fishermen and messing about on boats with Harry and Leslie in British Columbia and Shaldon.

That month, Naomi was making her last preparations to follow Roy to Malta, including inoculations for going overseas – although they made her feel 'really rotten'. Before leaving England, she took their new car, a blue-turquoise Riley, which they nicknamed Quis, to London's East End docks to ship it out to Malta. She ignored Roy's advice and travelled overland alone by train to Italy, getting out at Naples and spending two days there.

Writing from the Parker's Hotel in Naples she explained to Roy about her own adventures: 'I met a chap at the hotel in Naples who kindly offered to accompany me to Mount Vesuvius by cable car and also to see the Roman remains of Pompeii. They were small and not very impressive.'

Whilst Naomi was still in Naples, Roy wrote excitedly to her forwarding address: '7 December. To think that my Billy girl is actually on the way here. It's really heavenly. *Glorious* is holding a cocktail party on board tomorrow night. I expect I shall go and wish that my sweetest, most perfect wife was with me.'

The cocktail party was a grand colonial affair. The ship was decked with bunting and a canopy rigged over the flight deck. All were welcomed by Lumley Lyster and his wife, Daisy. Roy and Ken dressed in their full uniforms and all the wives and girlfriends in their finery. The Royal Marines Band played serenades which wafted across the water.

Two days later Roy wrote to Naomi: 'I received Quis yesterday in excellent condition. No extra scratches other than a broken sunblind. He started off well and is now going like a bomb.'

Roy was settling in to the Malta lifestyle, a very British affair but also with a Mediterranean flavour. Membership of the Union Club in Valletta was de rigeur for naval officers – this was for gentlemen only and past members included Sir Walter Scott and Benjamin Disraeli. There was a ladies' section known as the 'snake pit'.

Roy took advantage of the Marsa Club 'Men Only' Bathing Beach before Naomi arrived. Naomi would not miss out, as she would be able to visit the nearby Union Club's Ladies' Bathing Club Section at Qui-si-Sana. This had a quaint bye-law which 'provided that a lady might invite a gentleman to bathe there'. They would both be able to enjoy swimming together from the flat rocks into deep water at Tigne Point.

Officers also enjoyed tennis, golf, polo and attending races at the Marsa Racecourse, dining as well as dancing at the Sliema Club. The following week Roy reported to Naomi: 'Kenneth and I and Tuck (Fryer) went to the races again yesterday and had quite fun... Also naturally we got well and truly bottled before returning on board.'

There was still a boyish streak in the young pilot. He continued:

Also in the boat coming off we played a monster joke on Alan Brock. It was magnificent, darling. He was asleep on the seat and we sat down near him. The boat had to call at several other ships and Alan B. was asking if *Glorious* was next. We told him that we were alongside when actually we were at another ship. He carefully woke up and went stumbling out and onto the gangway before he realised that it was the wrong ship, fury. Then when we got to the *Glorious* he was asleep, so we quietly got out and left him. He came up about ten minutes later, absolutely purple with rage and foaming at the mouth. We laughed until we were nearly sick.

Naomi was not keen on Roy continuing his hobby of boxing. Now he wrote: 'Darling dear I've got a confession to make. I am a naughty boy again, I am afraid. I have taken up boxing again, something to pass the evenings away.'

Naomi took an Italian cargo ship from Naples to Malta, but her journey did not go too smoothly: 'I spent most of my time locked up in my cabin. Two old men kept trying to get into my cabin!'

At last Naomi arrived in Malta and it was an amazing moment for her. Apart from her recent travels, she had never been out of England before. Her experiences had been confined to the orchards of Worcestershire and the green fields of Devon, the estuary at Shaldon, and the snowy mountain lochs of Scotland. Now she was on a rocky outcrop in the middle of the Mediterranean – and an exciting new life was ahead of her. She was twenty-four years old, beautiful, healthy and deeply in love with her young and handsome husband who returned that love in equal measure.

Roy was delighted to see Naomi after so long. He was standing at the quayside waiting for her when her steamer docked at Valletta, and took her in their car, Quis, to their overnight accommodation near the island's Opera House. He had arranged for a special treat for Naomi by booking them both into a luxury hotel – 'the best on the island' according to the novelist Evelyn Waugh on his visit two years previously.

Naomi recalled: 'I was very thrilled at seeing Malta for the first time; we stayed at the Great Britain Hotel in Valletta. On waking in the morning I was enchanted at the sound of bells – it was the goats being brought in for milking. We then went house hunting.'

Their route took them along the harbour-side road past mansions with magnificent ironwork balconies, then by the stately double bell-towered Misida church, and the little creek, filled with colourful boats, and up past the police station into Rue d'Argens.

Naomi continued: 'We were lucky and discovered a very nice house called 'Roy House', which we found was a very happy place.' Roy House was in a terrace of stone, two-storey houses built in 1933, midway between Misida and Sliema. By coincidence the house had been named 'Roy', after the adopted son of a resident who originally came from Australia and later retired in the US.

Roy had rented one of two adjacent apartments, the other being rented by William 'Knobby' Clarke, another RN officer who was from Bedford. His girlfriend, Mabel, was the daughter of Lord Strickland, former prime minister of Malta.

The bow-windowed apartment had a spacious hallway with a black and white marble floor. An archway separated the front rooms, a parlour and a study with a 1930s tiled fireplace, from the kitchen galley at the back of the house. The shuttered windows opened up to overlook a patchwork of small stone-walled fields. The flat also had a little garden; a spiral stone staircase up onto the flat roof where Roy and Naomi could enjoy a drink or sunbathe.

Naomi recollected: 'We only had the ground floor – I remember the back garden, very small, but it had a small pear tree, with three pears on it. We could get up onto the roof. Roy would sunbathe there – I would not take the sun, but he could!'

For the young couple, Malta was a wonderful place with the most beautiful medieval and renaissance buildings being in Valletta. There were large Italianate palaces and churches in pale, bleached limestone. There was also a very British feel to the island with cars similar to those back home in England, English-style telephone and letter boxes with VR and GR insignia on them and English-style bobbies – yet there were also palm trees, oleander and a warm tropical atmosphere.

Pre-war Malta was a sociable place. Almost every night there were cocktail parties, receptions or dinners, either on the island or on board the Royal Navy warships lying at anchor in the harbour. Naomi's arrival was just in time for the Christmas celebrations and balls:

We went to a wonderful pre-Xmas Ball at Hal Far. I met Elizabeth Hale for the first time there, and of course all Roy's friends including Cliff Clifford, Titch Harding and Jakes Barnes and of course Splash Carver and his wife Tiny. However, I did not meet Captain Lyster till later in Alexandria. I shall never forget that evening, the most wonderful dance I have ever been to.

The Christmas period was also when Roy had a week of no flying duties. It gave Roy the opportunity also to introduce Naomi to *Glorious*'s squadron commanding officers, including Sam Little, Ginger Hale, Monkey Bryant of 802 Squadron and Robin Kilroy of 823.

Ginger Hale, a red-haired former England rugby player, recollected: 'My wife and I got to know B-F and Naomi very well. I was CO of 825 Squadron in *Glorious* from August '38 till Jan '40.'

Christmas Day was spent with their new friends Mita and Jakes Barnes at Roy House followed by dinner at a favourite haunt run by a couple called Melita and Felix. Naomi recalled that they had a wonderful evening: 'He served us chicken in wine. Jakes ate three in the one night.'

Roy was to spend a very different Christmas the next year when he reminisced wistfully about the celebrations in Malta: 'Still, my darling I've got last Christmas to make up for this one. It was grand going to Melita and Felix's with my lovely old wife.'

The squadron was working a tropical routine, which meant an early start and an equally early finish. December was still warm and balmy but with the occasional downpour. For relaxation, the aircrews frequented bars in Hal Far including Wexfords and the Gut. Beppo's bar was in a stone building on the airfield where officers could sign chits for drinks, charging them to their mess bills. Everyone who had been in a squadron at Hal Far for a year worked their names in a length of wire and hung it up on the wall. Among them was 'Tiffy' Torrens-Spence.

One of the new fighter pilots to Hal Far, Flt Lt 'Dick' Roddick Lee-Smith, recalled:

Life in Malta was ideal – up early, fly until midday, then tennis, golf, bathe, tour of the island. On one occasion, I did some authorised low-flying around Gozo island at nought feet, returning below the cliffs at Hal Far, and climbed into the circuit. I must have forgotten that I had been flying below aerodrome level, for after avoiding a Swordfish during my glide approach, I looked ahead and found the ground incredibly close.

I decided in an inspired instant, that I would start a spin – so I eased the stick back, went through two stone walls, was knocked out, and came to with petrol dripping on my face and the remains of my lovely K1581 pinning me to the ground, bent double. I felt someone touch my hand and say 'We will soon get you out, Joe'.

I remember saluting my horrified CO with a bent back, which took months to lose the pain. I was sent to the naval hospital at Imtarfa, where they stitched my head up.

Roy and Naomi settled in to married life in Rue d'Argens and became very sociable. During their time in Malta, even though Roy was the most junior of officers, forty-eight people signed their visitors' book, including Sam Little, Ginger and Mrs Hale, Lt Cdr and Mrs Brock, Captain and Mrs Lyster, Titch Harding and 'Cliff' Clifford.

Naomi thought Titch Harding was 'an absolute poppet' and regarded Cliff 'one of the loveliest people'. She recollected: 'My chief friends in Malta were Mita Barnes and I was also friendly with Lady Diana Fitzherbert-Wright, she was Ken Gurr's girlfriend but much older than him. There was also Marina Dundas and Elizabeth Hale.'

'Splash' Carver and his wife, Tiny, got on very well with Roy and Naomi and they often went out to bars, cafes and restaurants together. Naomi recalled: 'Splash looked like Roy and was often confused with him.' Splash, who later became CO of various squadrons, lived nearby with his wife at Killadinia, a flat in Creek Street, Sliema. By coincidence Splash and Roy's Leuchars' colleague Rodney Carver were third cousins.

Splash Carver remembered:

Roy joined HMS *Glorious* in the Med Fleet late in 1938 and came to 812 Squadron in which I was serving as an observer. Roy was only a Sub Lt at that time when he joined the Med Fleet and, as I had married my wife, Tiny, when I was a Sub Lt in 1936. We soon struck up a bond with them when Naomi came out to Malta shortly after Roy. Married Sub Lts were fairly rare – and not entirely approved of – I had been one myself about three years earlier. So Tiny soon went to call on Naomi at her flat in Misida and we all became good friends. We liked them both very much. They seemed to have a bit more money than most of us – and I don't think it was Roy's!

Titch Harding commented later:

However charming the young couple were, it was no married allowance until you were thirty which showed what was thought of that sort of thing in those days. It was a case of 'out of their prams' when nanny was not looking.

Other friends recalled by Naomi included Richard Dobbs, Ian Swaine and 'Puppy' Kennard. There was also Lt 'Bobby' Going who was later to lose a leg in battle, Lt Robin Grey who later died in a POW camp, and 'Feather' Godfrey-Faussett who was with Roy on a number of postings on their return from the Mediterranean.

Roy liked to keep in contact with his old Leuchars' pals including 'Frankie' Fryer or 'Friar Tuck' who by now was serving on board HMS *Ark Royal*. A pleasant surprise was when, from the HMS *Vulcan* torpedo boat depot ship, came a visit to Roy House from Lt W.B. 'Bill' Whitworth from Roy's Greynvile Term and brother-in-arms as midshipmen on the *Kent*.

A 'permanent visitor' was Mons, as Naomi recollected: 'Of course we had to rescue a dog – a huge Great Dane – who adopted us.' The couple both loved dogs and Mons was to be a favourite companion of Roy's, as seen in many photographs of the time. Mons gained some notoriety in Rue d'Argens and was remembered by a neighbour, the then fourteen year-old Joseph Mifsud. He recalled Roy and added: 'That naval officer who lived at Roy House had a very big dog. Wasn't it a St Bernard?' Seventy years later Joseph and his wife themselves were living in Roy House.

Whilst Roy was on duty, Naomi's days would be filled with tennis and swimming and meeting up with other *Glorious* wives. Naomi sometimes visited Roy on board ship whilst the aircraft carrier was in dock. She recalled: 'I had a special heavy, narrow skirt to ensure that it wasn't too light to blow over my head when going up the gangway on board ship. I used to call it my "piping on skirt".' When officers went up the gangplank, they were piped on board by the saluting 'jack-tars'.

A particularly memorable time for Naomi was an evening's entertainment on board *Glorious*:

> On one occasion Elizabeth Hale and I went for a pantomime and dance and saw Snow White and the Seven Dwarfs. Seven of the NOs [Naval Officers] dressed as the seven dwarfs and paraded round. Jakes Barnes was one of the dwarfs; Cliff was gorgeously dressed up as Snow White; Titch Harding played 'Dopey'. It was a wonderful evening.

New Year 1939 led to another round of cocktail parties and social events but it was back to business for Roy on 2 January, practising air-to-air firing and squadron formation flights the next day. This was followed by two weeks of practice attacks on the Fleet, high-level bombing, and dive-bombing trials, as well as what was known by the Fleet Air Arm aircrew as 'light torpedo attacks' on another Battle of Jutland battleship veteran, HMS *Warspite*, and on *Glorious*.

On 16 January, Roy was promoted to acting lieutenant and the same day he took part in his first massed torpedo attack of all the three Swordfish squadrons on *Glorious* off the coast of Malta. By now dummy torpedo attack practice was becoming frequent. The squadron's favourite attack method was to climb with torpedoes to about 1,000 feet above the 'enemy' or target ship, and then to dive down almost vertically, everything screaming – the Swordfish was a mass of wires – and to approach the target from all points of the compass at once, releasing the 'fish' at the last moment.

The next day, Roy and 812 Squadron were ordered to embark on *Glorious* for major manoeuvres and further massed torpedo attacks. It was to be Roy's first deck landing on this ship and he was aware that Titch and other experienced aircrew would be watching him with a critical eye to see how he faired.

In Roy's final approach in his Swordfish the ship was steaming into wind, smoke bellowing from the smokestack to show the wind movements across the deck. He lined up and came in for a textbook deck landing with no mishaps. With relief, he then went to the 'nets' to watch the other more experienced pilots land on.

The 'nets' were a viewing platform running alongside and five feet below the flight deck. Extending outboard of this was a steel wire net which was intended to catch any aircraft that went over the edge. In those days, there was no crash barrier to prevent an aircraft overshooting and plunging into the sea.

Once Roy's Swordfish was on deck, it was the job of the deck-handling party to get it to the hangar. Air Fitter Clayton recalled:

> The Swordfish were moved by manpower, with an NCO on the tail steering arm. The speed at which they had to be moved with the ship rolling about all the time, called for quick reactions, both on the part of the NCO and the man on the brakes. An aircraft had to be ready to be pushed onto the lift the instant it arrived at hangar level and, conversely, as soon as the lift brought a Swordfish down to the hangar, the handling party had to rush forward to push it to its place in the hangar.

Lee-Smith recalled the procedure for landing on *Glorious*:

> Attached to the island, and facing aft, was a huge mechanical metal cross, with variable slats whose position and colours in the form of a cross indicated to pilots the affirmative, without which they must go round again, otherwise they continued their landing.
>
> There was an elaborate system of flags, run out on horizontal masts along the sides of the ship aft, which pilots had to study, as they indicated whose turn it was to land on, and other instructions, as radio, apart from w/t to the Ospreys and the Swordfish, was not yet relied upon.
>
> In the absence of reliable radio, it follows that very careful pre-flight briefing and knowledge of flag signals was essential, and practices that involved going out of sight of the carrier necessitated that single-seat Nimrods were accompanied by two-seater Ospreys with w/t radio; otherwise they would not see their aerodrome moving in any direction at 25 knots again.

Clayton continued:

> When it came to 'striking-down' aircraft, that is, getting them back into the hangar, *Glorious*'s hydraulic lifts, manufactured by the Express Lift Company, were over ten years old and took sixty-four seconds to descend from the flight deck to the lower hangar. The more modern ships like the *Ark Royal* had electric operated lifts. With up to forty-eight aircraft to recover, landing on was a protracted business.

Getting aircraft airborne was another involved procedure as Lee-Smith recalled:

> For *Glorious*'s flying operations, orders were piped over the ship's intercom system. There were two lifts, and the flight deck officer was in charge of ranging-up aircraft in the correct order for take-off.
>
> Once on the flight deck, the aircraft were subject to the 30-knot wind speed necessary for flying. Deck handling parties had to get them to their right places and hold them down whilst the pilots ran the engines up to check full power – the

slipstream from which, of course, added to the problems of the deck-handling crew holding down the aircraft behind those being run-up against the chocks. The flight deck officer was given orders from the bridge, which on *Glorious* was a tall island to the right of the flight deck containing the main controlling authorities – the Captain, Commander Flying, signalmen etc.

For take-off, the flight deck officer would flag each aircraft off, when the pilots would open full throttle and the ground crew take away the chocks. The aircraft would do a quick circuit on becoming airborne, and join up with their leader, who took off last. Occasionally we would practise catapulted take-offs, and there were floats which were attachable to the Ospreys, used very rarely.

We did not fly in very rough seas, so did not experience the very hazardous flying conditions borne by the carrier pilots during the war.

Blair-Oliphant recalled the potential hazard of take-offs:

Total time from moving the aircraft from the hangars to starting the engines with propellers revolving was five to ten minutes. When the aircraft took off there would always be a trailing destroyer in the ship's wake to pick up any crew who had to ditch.

In an operational aircraft carrier, the captain would decide what he liked when he liked, so there was no normal leave and, as such, if the CO Flying wanted the squadron to fly at 4 am, it did do so.

Through that week, Roy and the squadrons operated off Malta with *Glorious* and then returned to Grand Harbour, allowing Roy to spend a few days at home with Naomi.

Roy was content in his work on board ship and in his home life. At sea he wrote to Naomi back in Malta:

Sometimes darling, it doesn't seem real that now that adorable and very charming prattler I used to walk with is now my own dearest beloved wife. It's a heavenly thought, Billy girl. I sure can't quite understand why you just had to marry me. An awful sucker you must be Tich.

From January onwards, the squadron flew often from *Glorious*, which went out to sea every week from Monday to Friday.

Roy found *Glorious* was a happy ship, despite some inconveniences. In the Fleet Air Arm bathroom on board, there was hot water but no cold. As there were only a dozen or so wash basins and three tin baths, long queues built up and the congestion was aggravated by the fact of having to wait for the water to cool to a bearable temperature before bathing. Quite often, the taps would deliver only steam, and this involved a further delay.

On 23 January, Roy hugged his wife goodbye and once again boarded *Glorious* at Parlatorio Wharf. Later that day the ship set course southwards for a planned month of manoeuvres off the coast of Egypt and Alexandria. Roy and Naomi would be seeing a lot more of Egypt in the coming months. The onset of war now looked as if it would be unavoidable and was predicted to be only months away.

CHAPTER 8

War Clouds in Gibraltar and Alexandria

By early 1939 war with Germany and Italy was looming. Roy and Naomi's halcyon days in Malta were drawing to a close as *Glorious* was based increasingly at Alexandria in Egypt.

For most of the time Roy was disembarked with other Fleet Air Arm personnel at the air station at Dekheila about five miles west of the city. Dekheila, later called HMS *Grebe*, had been loaned by the Royal Egyptian Air Force to the Royal Navy. Facilities were indeed very spartan.

Nigel Blair-Oliphant remembered:

> At Dekheila, I and 812 Squadron, and later the other crews too, were encamped in tents at the civil airfield with a Turkish civilian flying controller. Dekheila was a tented camp on the civil airport from which we were supposed to defend Alex.
>
> The sailors got hard time money for having to live in tents which almost caused a mutiny amongst the RAF men who begrudged the fact that they received nothing for having to use hammocks on board ship and were expected to be used to living under tent conditions without extra pay.

Like everyone else Roy was in the encamped tents, along with Titch, Splash, and the rest of the squadron. He found it much more gruelling than the luxury of his and Naomi's apartment in Malta, and missed her company, writing to her frequently.

Lee-Smith recalled:

> Our tented camp had open-air toilets – one day I entered the hessian sacking walls of the toilet to find my CO Monkey Bryant seated on his thunderbox with his naval hat on. Instinctively, recalling the naval tradition of saluting your senior officer the first time you saw him in the day, I saluted! This was the only time that I ever saw Monkey at a loss for words.

The aircrews had the occasional foray into the centre of Alexandria for a taste of the night life, being introduced to supper clubs and exclusive nightclubs. Roy, Ken Gurr and Ham, without wives or girlfriends, headed to the city bars as often as work would permit. There were many young and persistent street urchins who were keen that the airmen should visit their sisters: 'Only fifty piastres!'

Yet Roy much preferred swimming in the sea and soon found the sporting facilities to keep fit.

'Moose' Martyn, the very tall young Canadian officer also in Monkey Bryant's fighter squadron, wrote home to his parents in Calgary:

Everything out here is good and expensive. Officers always have to take the best seats in the theatres to stay clear of uniformed sailors, etc. and because the Commander etc. might see you. All the dining places in the cities etc. are set aside separately in the same way, mainly by making the shops etc. catering to officers and tourists more expensive.

The only cheap amusement is to swim or stay in camp drinking beer. If I go away for a weekend, it's hotel bills usually about $4 at least per night and meals at the same high tariff. Boy! Any place east of America certainly isn't democratic.

He went on to describe the routine at Dekheila aerodrome for the Fleet Air Arm detachment as the *Glorious*'s squadrons were known:

Troops get up at 6 and are down at 6:30 on the tarmac doing their daily inspections on aircraft. We, of course, stroll down about 7 and take an interest in what is going on and make suggested changes in the rigging, etc. We have quite a lot of able seamen who do nothing but polish so our squadron is absolutely spotless.

Breakfast at 8 to 9. At 9 we go over to the office and the CO and flight commanders work out a program (if there are no fleet requirements). Quite often the C-in-C wants the squadron to do dummy machine gun attacks on his destroyers, etc.

But on an average morning we go off by ourselves in threes doing formation flying or machine gun (camera) air fighting. Individual aerobatics or half the squadron goes off and pretends to be an invader who is attempting to bomb the aerodrome from 25,000 feet down, and we try and intercept before they arrive. The ensuing dog fight is terrific – much better fun than pounding a typewriter at a desk.

Afternoons off – lots of leisure time. There are, of course, many squadron ground duties – books, records, forms – masses of red tape – petrol, spare parts, engines, etc., and of course orderly officer duties every week – but on the whole it is very interesting.

If we want to take our aeroplanes away for a weekend it is alright – or even during the week we can visit friends at other stations providing there is not an official program to be got through on that day.

Whilst operating from Dekheila, it was routine to fly across the desert. Roy found it was like flying above any featureless sea, with the same navigation demands. He found it was best to fly to and from Dekheila in the morning, as the turbulence in the heat of the afternoon made it quite a struggle for him to hold his Swordfish on an even course.

Splash described their surroundings:

Alexandria was a good harbour though not so capacious or natural as the Grand and Sliema harbours at Malta combined. Of course, Malta was still used for the refit and docking of ships wanting maintenance and also still held the fleet's stores, ammunition, spare parts etc., requirements of these soon shipped to Alex in Royal Fleet Auxiliary ships.

There was still an attitude that war would not happen and Naomi's accountant back in England could joke about her preparations to follow Roy to Egypt. Leonard Beaumont-Smith, of Smith & Hayward Accountants, wrote to her:

20 January. I am very interested to hear that you are getting from Malta to

Alexandria for 30 shillings on a troop ship. At that rate, you'll be able to go all around the world for around £25 and incidentally, living so cheap, you will have not only capital but a lot of saved income to invest before very long.

By now, Roy and his Fleet Air Arm colleagues found their roles were changing. More emphasis was placed on night flying, night torpedo attacks and night shadowing. A search pattern was developed to include six Swordfish flying in line abreast, with a further six Swordfish dropping flares at intervals to illuminate ship silhouettes.

Moose Martyn wrote on 17 January:

On Monday 802 carried out four landings without hooks on *Glorious* for practice. I don't mind saying I had the wind up about the first but found the last three were all right.

It's really nothing but a stunt – you have to bring her in over the stern at no miles per hour over the stall or else you'll overrun the ship and if you see she is not going to stay on the deck you have to open up early or you might not have enough speed to keep from diving into the sea.

Glorious is the hardest carrier to land on in the world I believe and has funnels on the side.

American carriers are so long – it must be like landing on an aerodrome.

Blue flight, i.e. my flight, all carried out successful landings, but Lt Strange in a two-seat fighter Osprey thought he would use his brakes and promptly turned a complete somersault just below the Captain's Bridge – no one hurt but one £10,000 aeroplane written off. Only last week he was telling me, 'I have these deck landings taped now!'

To tell the truth, very few shoot a line about deck landings as one nearly always trips up at some time.

After a few weeks of living under canvas, Roy was delighted when Naomi came to Alexandria on a short visit – on an even better deal than anticipated by her accountant: 'We, the wives, managed to get on a troop ship which took us to Port Said via Haifa. I shared a cabin with Elizabeth Hale and Ann Dobbs. It took three days, cost seven shillings and six pence. I have never had such good value.'

Her pleasure was short-lived, because three days later tragedy struck. Roy and Naomi were shocked when Ann's husband, Richard, was killed, along with John Godfrey Lincoln – the second pal from Roy's Leuchars days.

Lt Alfie Sutton recalled the catastrophe:

The ship put to sea periodically and the squadron flew on board and exercised from the deck. We developed our night flying techniques – and had one big disaster when two aircraft collided at night, killing six aircrew – the two piloting the aircraft, and two passengers in each aircraft that had gone up to witness the procedure of night take-off and landing from a carrier.

Moose Martyn wrote at the time:

February 2, 1939. Four officers and two seamen were killed the other night off Alexandria. All of 825 Squadron. Two Swordfish (three-seaters) collided after doing night formation. They had just broken up preparatory to doing night deck landing when they collided. Both machines burst into flames. The two pilots were Lieutenant Newcombe R.N. and Lieutenant Dobbs R.N. Unfortunately they were giving night deck landing experience to two new pilots, Lieutenant Lincoln R.N. and Flying Officer Bridges. They were passengers in the back. So the squadron lost four experienced pilots out of twelve in one crash.

Eyewitnesses reported the aircraft hit the water with such force that they were temporarily submerged. A column of acrid black smoke rose into the air as HMS *Wishart*, the attendant destroyer to *Glorious*, rushed to the scene but was just too late to be of assistance. One crew member was recovered, dead. The other five were burnt to death, their bodies never recovered. It was the biggest Fleet Air Arm crash in history up to that time and deeply affected the morale of the aircrew.

Naomi did her best to comfort her grieving friend while at the same time becoming ever more fearful for Roy's safety. Outwardly, Roy characteristically showed no deep emotion to his fellow pilots about the loss of his friend. However, he had been severely shaken.

Changes were occurring in the fighter squadrons on board *Glorious*. Moose Martyn wrote:

February 13, 1939. My new Flight Commander Lieutenant Marmont R.N. arrived, and Campbell-Horsfall and I flew in formation with him for the first time today. He has just had two and-a-half months' foreign service leave after serving in the aircraft carrier *Eagle* in China. He must be the right type, as he said after he got down, 'I didn't think we had better do a formation loop, as I haven't flown for a couple of months.'

He went on to add:

I am night flying tonight – night formation and then individual aerobatics – rendezvous over Valletta and then a squadron quick landing.

Weather couldn't be nicer here – loads of sunshine and swimming. I think I'll turn into a beachcomber – this is luxury. I feel a terrible hog grabbing all this paradise. In fact I could die out here under a palm tree and just looking at the blue Mediterranean. Most of the time it's as flat and calm as Lake Louise (and a whole lot warmer).

We are below the north coast of Africa, i.e. on the east side of the northern tip and get wonderfully warm winds.

The Mediterranean Fleet is, of course, the cushy one. The Home Fleet is always operating in fog, cold, and rain with rough seas. I should hate to serve in her, but I probably will have to later on.

Naomi returned to Malta as Roy on board *Glorious* sailed for Gibraltar at the end of February. The carrier stayed till early March for combined exercises of the Mediterranean and Home Fleets. During that time Roy and the 812 Squadron Swordfish surprised and 'sank' *Ark Royal* with four torpedo hits in an exercise on 1 March much to the satisfaction of *Glorious*.

Lee-Smith recalled: 'Twice a year we would do combined exercises with the Home Fleet, basing ourselves at Gibraltar – at that time Home Fleet were dark grey, and the Med Fleet light grey.'

Roy wrote a deliberately light hearted letter to Naomi – war might be on the horizon but there was still an echo of his midshipman days in his off-duty activities:

The combined fleets do look impressive from the air. We had one game of hockey at Gibraltar, a rather rough and tumble sort of game altogether and have played deck hockey once at sea.

The Atlantic has been awfully kind to us and just gives us a long swell. The heat tho' is terrific until up high.

Moose Martyn wrote home to his family in Canada:

Mar. 3, 1939. Glad to receive your last letter which I received this morning when I arrived back in Gibraltar with combined Med & Home Fleets after the first part of early spring exercises. We had a mock war off the Azores with Home Fleet – flying day and night and constantly. Wonderful experience and when the Home Fleet Fighter Squadron met us in the air – Gnats, we tucked them away and put them back in their hangars!

Many the unwary Home Fleet spotter we shot down in flames on our fightah! patrols.

Have a good holiday! You couldn't spit here at Gibraltar without splashing a warship – even the Spanish across the Bay wonder where all the money comes from.

Naomi's Maltese diary was always full of entries: tennis, squash, meeting friends. A busy life helped her stop worrying about Roy.

Roy was kept busy flying but he was also meeting up with friends in Gibraltar:

4 March. Friday, I think. Last night or this evening just as you look at it, Kenneth and I got let loose slightly in the olives. We did nothing but drink, but my mouth and head feel absolutely outsized now and if there was a cat anywhere near I should throw things at it for making a noise with its feet.

Four days later Hammy Hamilton's aircraft crash-landed on its side on the lower flying off deck – fortunately he survived the accident.

A few days later Roy wrote:

Going to a party in *Ark Royal* tomorrow. It ought to be good fun. Anyway I should be with Tuck. We've done very little flying the last couple of days, you'll be pleased to hear. Today we were going up but a bad fog was reported to be near us, so we didn't. Actually where we were there was a magnificent sun and boiling hot.

I am getting so fed up with these exercises, especially when we just sit and wait. Still my darling Billy girl they are nearly over now and then back to Malta.

Moose Martyn wrote:

This is Sunday, and we are still at the 'Rock'. Beautiful morning with the Levanter blowing slightly. This is an east wind and puts a little tuft of cloud on the tip of the 'Rock'.

We have just finished 'Divisions' which is Church – a parade on flight deck in brilliant sunshine. Marine band, etc. Uniform of the day was frock coats and swords for officers. Spain is very mountainous all along this coast here. A rough map will show you the position of things. La Linea is a Spanish town slapped up against Gibraltar on the north side. Algeciras is Spanish about two miles straight west of Gibraltar – it is very picturesque with its white houses, etc. La Linea has a bull ring.

Ceuta is a rock bigger than Gibraltar armed by Franco with large 18" guns and is twenty miles south of Gib – all beautifully clear in this visibility. Of course all this part of Spain is under Franco and permission to travel in Spain is only given to officers who can get special permits, but one can only go along main roads here and then only a few miles past Algeciras along the road to Malaga. I can get permission, but don't know whether I'll bother as one has to be back in Gib before 11:20 p.m.

Moose added:

We sail tomorrow for the second part of our combined manoeuvres. We fight against Home Fleet and it is a wonderful experience for me. We will carry press reporters and cameramen this trip, so you should see pictures of us in action through Movietone, etc. Perhaps even see Willy, so keep a good eye out.

I climbed the rock again and inspected all the guns, etc. with F/O Smith yesterday afternoon. We got special permits from Captain Lyster, DSO of *Glorious*. The Mediterranean is beautiful here – as calm as a lake, and that deep blue you dream about. I bought wizard silk pyjamas in Gib for 3/6 each or about 80 cents. Duty-free port here and cheap native labour.

Also a beautifully coloured bed spread all worked in flowers and birds, etc. Gibraltar is, of course, terrifically fascinating as it still contains all the very old forts and guns by the dozen. All the coast line – i.e. along the high Moroccan Coast to the south – one can see old Moorish towers on top of every peak.

When we return in a week's time we have ten days in Gibraltar before sailing for Malta. I might visit Tangier but don't know as yet.

Roy was still missing Naomi, especially since it was difficult getting ashore as *Glorious* was anchored in Algeciras Bay due to the sheer number of warships filling up Gibraltar's harbour. But he had a chance to run ashore a few times to explore, visit the rock apes at Queen's Gate, and sample the delights of the many English-style pubs. In his next letter he wrote:

Tuck and I and Ken have been together continuously drunk, sober or with a hangover... You may be please to hear that young Leslie has won her music scolarship and they are very pleased with her at Cheltenham. Good show I think.

On 10 March, Moose wrote:

Both home and Mediterranean Fleets arrived in Gibraltar this morning at the end of spring exercises. We are to spend a week or ten days here before the Home Fleet leaves for England and the Mediterranean back to Malta (the land of the bells and smells).

We are certainly getting our share of sunshine this spring. There is a fast boat for officers at 3:45 this afternoon, so I'll go ashore for a short walk. Unfortunately we are anchored out in the Bay, so have to go ashore and return at certain times laid down in the boat routine, and not as we choose. We had our aeroplanes up on the flight deck this morning, with our mechanics and riggers cleaning them up. I love the smells associated with their petrol dope, etc.

Roy's rigger and fitter worked hard to keep his Swordfish in immaculate condition, under the beady eye of Sgt Gittens. Moose noted the same in his squadron:

I have never had such a hard-working and keen crew before. My rigger is the most senior one in the squadron and is a sergeant – very unusual to have a sergeant working on one aeroplane only – no wisecracks – I thought I heard Dad say, 'He probably needs a sergeant after Bill gives it a work out.' His name is Sergeant Duly. My fitter, or mechanic, is Leading Aircraftsman Rees. They keep my Nimrod so clean I have to wipe my feet before getting in.

In mid-March, *Glorious* headed back temporarily to Malta's Grand Harbour. En route, Italian airmen operating in Franco's Spain flew low over the ship during divisions off the Balearic Islands and gave the ship's crew 'stiff Fascist salutes – funniest thing we had ever seen' recalled a number of the ship's crew. As one pilot put it 'Too bad we couldn't thumb our noses back at them or put a six-inch shell over their bows.'

Roy wrote to Naomi at Roy House in anticipation of his return: '17 March: Do you think that when you hear aircraft scuttling over in formation you could trundle off to Hal Far to pick me up?'

International tension was increasing. Hitler had sent his army into Prague, the capital of Czechoslovakia, to establish a 'protectorate' over Bohemia and Moravia. Within days the situation with Poland had deteriorated, with the German leader threatening to invade and annex Danzig.

British Prime Minister Neville Chamberlain was still trying to avoid war but felt peace could only be preserved by a strong commitment to the use of force. On 30 March he gave Poland an unconditional guarantee Britain would come to its defence in the event of a German attack.

On Good Friday, 7 April, the Italian fascist leader Benito Mussolini significantly increased the tension throughout the Mediterranean region by annexing Albania.

Alfie Sutton recalled:

In Easter 1939 Italy invaded Albania and the Fleet was put on a war footing. I remember being the officer in charge of a working party, embarking bombs and, even now, can recall over fifty-six years later, dawn and then the rising sun as *Glorious* lay alongside Parlatorio Wharf in Malta, and I got the last few bombs on board having been working all night. That was the watershed between peace and war.

From then on it was lots of war exercises, and no more heavenly visits to places like Athens, where we swam, and sunbathed, and drank retsina and ouzo, and fed in the tavernas, and made lots of love.

Our main base became Alexandria in Egypt, which was taken over by the British from the military point of view and became a main base for war.

Nigel Blair-Oliphant recollected the changing preparations of the squadrons in his role as *Glorious*'s Armaments Officer:

Initially the cruises on *Glorious* were an interesting time preceding the outbreak of war. Based on Malta, the ship visited Gibraltar, Alexandria, the Greek Islands, Corsica and the south of France and Yugoslavia.

There was a war going on in Spain, then with the annexation of Albania it made us more warlike so that we loaded fused bombs and ammunition and carried warheads on torpedoes and often darkened ship at night.

All was not doom and gloom for the pilots as Titch Harding commented: 'The FAA was a very nice club before and during the phoney war – you name it we did it.'

By the end of the month, Moose wrote:

We (802) are disembarking this weekend to Dekheila, where we will spend some time – I hope – all I want to do is eat, fly, and lie in the sun here. Boy I could die happy. We are going back to khaki shirts and shorts as soon as we get ashore. We will live in tents as usual. I am enclosing a couple of snaps taken in Malta – one showing Barnes and self perspiring freely and another showing self about to light pipe – 'absitively' surrounded by admiring Maltese children. The 'poisonality' of the chap! The nerve!

By the beginning of the month, Roy and 812 Squadron carried out dummy torpedo attacks on *Glorious*, with protection from the ship's fighter squadrons. Moose commented:

This afternoon we were detailed to fly a fighter patrol over *Glorious* about fifty miles north of Alexandria while 825 TRS Squadron attempted to launch a torpedo attack on the ship. Luckily we sighted them early in the attack and for thirty minutes had a wizard dogfight, which worked down to about fifty feet of the Med when we called it a day.

The Captain was a bit annoyed. He couldn't use his close-range guns because of there being too many 802 keeping escort on the bombers!

However, as training intensified accidents continued to happen – including a mishap involving Roy's commanding officer. Lt Cdr Little had been night flying in his own Swordfish coded '63' with the squadron on naval exercises. As he approached *Glorious* to land, his aircraft hit the carrier's roundown and the undercarriage was torn away. Neither he, nor his passengers, Lt Norman Quill and TAG W. Nicole, were hurt, but the aircraft was a write-off.

Roy wrote about the incident:

2 May. I landed at Dekheila, Egypt, last night as the CO went splat on the deck after night-flying. I was up [in my Swordfish] for homing in the boys back to the ship and was last to land on. CO came in a bit low and hit his undercarriage and bust it, but arrived quite happily on deck. Whilst they were cleaning away his machine, the remaining aircraft had to land at Dekheila for half an hour.

Roy continued:

Then off to the ship arriving about quarter past twelve. Ugh, was I tired. Then this morning a three and a quarter hour exercise at 08.15. In consequence I went to bed at 1 o'clock and didn't wake up until 6 o'clock. Not bad eh?

I must away to bed my darling, flying again at 08.15 tomorrow.

Moose wrote about the same time:

I am attempting to write this letter in my tent under difficulties (mostly mosquitoes). The sun is really pouring down and weather here is lovely. I have been into Alexandria two or three times. The cinemas are very good and I was able to see David Niven in 'The Dawn Patrol' at the Mohammed Aly Cinema.

We are flying in the minimum clothes, mainly khaki shirt and shorts (no underwear). Even this afternoon at 15,000 feet we were very warm. We are at present forming part of a Fighter Wing here in Egypt. I am hoping that the international situation will remain fairly quiet so we can have a long stay here. The squadron landed on *Glorious* this afternoon (just so we can keep our hand in).

My co-partner in the tent is F/O Garlick, who is at present lying on his camp bed under his mosquito netting – tantalizing the mosquitoes by baring choice bits of flesh to their eyes. He has a naturally cruel streak and battalions of mosqs are infuriated.

This morning we took our fighters up for some individual flying, which consisted mainly of flying up and down Agami Beach, where wealthy Americans, etc. have their summer cottages. At no time were we higher than about 10 feet and many an admiring wave was given!' Batcher, my Marine batman, is a wizard and has constructed a wooden table in the tent. Where he pinched the wood I don't know.

Throughout that time the squadrons were working practically day and night in Egypt. The heat was terrific – over 160°F for days. It finally got to some of the airmen who suffered bad stomach problems and had to go to the Hospital Ship for up to ten days.

About the middle of the month there was yet another aircraft crash and fatalities. However, Roy failed to write about it in his daily letters to Naomi, in order to ensure she wouldn't be worried for him. Moose was more open to his family:

Sykes, one of our most experienced pilots who has just arrived out from England, crashed into the sea on Saturday and was killed.

Last week I was sent to Aboukir (RAF Depot Middle East) to superintend erection of our new fighters, which have just arrived from England. I flew mine back to Dekheila on Friday. They are the Gladiator high-performance day and night fighter specially adapted for Fleet Air Arm work. Beautifully equipped with sliding roofs and four Browning (American) machine guns firing forward. They are the fastest biplane fighter in the world, equipped with Mercury VIIIA 840 HP engines. Being a biplane, they are terrifically manoeuvrable and are rather tricky to handle. Aboukir is a very beautiful station and I enjoyed my stay immensely. Palm trees, drives and gardens all set out very tastefully. It was just off Aboukir that Napoleon's Fleet was beaten by Nelson in the Battle of Aboukir Bay.

On 24 May, the Royal Navy formally resumed control of the Fleet Air Arm. For Roy, it meant the end of his dual RN and RAF ranks as RAF commissions were cancelled.

On 1 June, Roy and 812 Squadron reported on board *Glorious* in the Grand Harbour in Malta. A few days after Roy's twenty-third birthday on 3 June, the squadron formally left Malta with the aircraft carrier and the rest of the Mediterranean Fleet for their new permanent base in Alexandria.

Naomi, who was making her own final arrangements to set up home in Alexandria, recollected waving with the crowd from the Valletta viewpoint, the Baracca, as the *Glorious* ⟩ slipped from her moorings. The aircraft carrier steamed past them – lines of sailors and officers saluting on deck – heading for Egypt. It was an emotional leave-taking for all concerned as an uncertain future lay ahead.

Moose wrote from Dekheila Aerodrome once the squadrons had disembarked:

June 10, 1939. Life is very pleasant here. We have been living in tents for some time now and I am a real camper. We are exceedingly fortunate in being situated by the sea, so we swim every afternoon. The water is unbelievably pleasant and warm, and the sand of course perfect. My sub flight has formation aerobatics really weighed up these days, and we put in many hours practising.

Once formation rolls and loops are mastered, other formation flying is comparatively easy. And one can maintain beautiful position during dives and steep turns.

We gave a party in Alexandria last night to Lt Nott, Royal Marines, who has been promoted to Captain. He is our 'A' Flight Commander and is twenty-eight. Also, a farewell to F/Os Smith, Bell and Garlick who are going home – all but Garlick, who is going to the Citadel Military Hospital in Cairo to have an appendix operation tomorrow.

Even the slightest cuts take ages to heal up out here. It think it's because of the heat and the thinning out of one's blood – I am sure it would take me a long time to acclimatise back to Canadian standards.

On 16 June, while the ship was at sea Lt Cdr Bolt, who had been an observer on *Glorious* since 1932, exercised his seniority following the lifting of the RAF ban on RN observers being able to command squadrons. He took command of 812 Squadron, replacing Sam Little who returned to the UK.

Titch Harding related: 'On the 20th, Ben Bolt took over from Little. He was the first observer squadron CO. Myself, I was first senior pilot with CO in the back seat.' Roy was delighted as he got on well with Ben Bolt, who he recognised was very experienced.

On a day to day basis, however, there was little change in the squadron and Roy had other interests to keep him going. Naomi was coming out to live with him so he busied himself arranging their accommodation. Soon after, Naomi left Malta to join Roy in Alexandria: 'I had to leave Mons the large dog behind, but my friend Diana Fitzherbert brought him over to Egypt a few weeks later.' It has now been long forgotten whether or not Naomi had to buy Mons a ticket!

Naomi and Roy's Riley car unfortunately could not be taken to Alexandria. It was stored in a garage on Malta and sold for £100 after the war. 'We were lucky to get that much,' recalled Naomi.

Nigel Blair-Oliphant, self-confessed opportunist, was more fortunate in getting his car to Egypt as he recalled:

Once finished at Malta we moved to Alex and I was detached with 812 Squadron including B-F to Dekheila, seven miles from Alex.

Luckily, I was allowed to bring my new Morris Series E – cost £127.10s – lashed to the flight deck even though such honour wasn't normally permitted except for higher ranks.

Alexandria, the pearl or mermaid of the Mediterranean, was considered the most attractive city in Egypt for its long beaches of white sand and blue water, beautiful buildings and friendly people.

Splash Carver recalled:

Naomi and Tiny both moved to Alex when it was clear that war clouds were gathering. Tiny had lived there in 1936 for two or three months, when I was in destroyers, and loved the cosmopolitan atmosphere there. Naomi booked into Le Roy Hotel in the Rue Stanboul and Tiny went back to the pension, Gordon House, she had stayed in before – eventually they shared a flat.

Both Le Roy Hotel and Gordon House lay in the hub of the city in a district called Ramleh Station, where once Cleopatra's needle stood. Le Roy Hotel was situated on the top floors of an older office building, the rickety elevator released guests into an elegant world of ballrooms and grand staircases with a dining room overlooking the city. Naomi recalled their room had a pleasant but tiny arcaded balcony overlooking the town centre. From there, Roy and Naomi could listen to the sounds of Alex, its rattling trams, the clip-clop of the horse carriages, the hustle and bustle, and distant call of the muezzin to prayers in the mosque of the old quarter of town.

Splash added:

In June 1939, Roy and I in 812 Squadron were disembarked for several weeks at Dekheila airfield – just west of the harbour. The idea behind this was that we could provide aircraft to take part in fleet, squadron, or individual ship exercises without the need for *Glorious* to go to sea every time and operate such aircraft from her deck.

Dekheila had a very relaxed flying club atmosphere. It made a welcome change from the heat and close quarters of the ship and also meant that we could live more of a married life. There were quite a number of *Glorious* wives who had moved to Alex and social life was pretty active. The threat of war was, by this time, very real and the prevailing mood was 'enjoy this time while you can'.

Splash continued:

At Dekheila we worked tropical routine, starting work at 7 am and finishing about 1 pm returning later only if there was night flying. A delightful way of life for the married men who could then take their wives swimming or golfing etc most afternoons.

Alex was more popular, from the social and entertainment aspect, with officers rather than the lower deck who missed the familiar canteen bars, dance halls etc of Malta.

Both the Alex Sporting Club and the Smouha Club had excellent sporting and leisure facilities and a glamorous collection of cosmopolitan and very decorative ladies usually present.

Lee-Smith pointed out that:

When at Alex we were feted as elsewhere abroad – all officers in *Glorious* were made members of the Alex Sporting Club for 2/6 – it cost the locals several hundreds in membership fees to enjoy the facilities of this exclusive club which included horseracing, squash, tennis, swimming, and golf, with a fabulous restaurant.

Splash felt that flying exercises also maintained the relaxed atmosphere of the time: 'In order to get in some night formation flying practice the squadron flew from Dekheila to RAF Heliopolis outside Cairo – had dinner in the RAF mess and flew back again afterwards'. Inevitably, Roy and the others flew low over the pyramids in an aerial sight-seeing excursion before it was too dark.

Roy and Naomi found Alexandria was a city of paradoxes. The young King Farouk was on the throne and the place seemed divided between its allegiance to Islam and the voluptuous lifestyle of their monarch.

From ancient times onwards the city, immortalising Alexander the Great's name, flourished as a prominent cultural, intellectual, political, and economic metropolis. It had been the royal summer capital since the days of the pharaohs. The palm tree-lined corniche ran from the magnificent palace of the Egyptian royal family, eastwards for miles past fine beaches, hotels and seaside cafes.

Naomi's first impression was that Alex was a lovely city with a lot of life to it. It was friendly, safe and fascinating, with a cosmopolitan mix of nations – Egyptian, English, French, Italian, Greek, Jewish and Armenian. Electric trams rumbled along tree-lined boulevards linking splendid mansions, hotels, arcades, coffee shops, theatres and green parks – it was easy for Roy and Naomi to forget that they were in Africa at all.

Naomi noted:

Alexandria was full of wonderful memories – life was *too* good. Husbands all came home about 3 o'clock. We all went to the sporting club – played squash, then tennis, then swimming (we also even used to go surf bathing) – then of course drinking. Then a tour of the clubs at night sometimes. It was *great*!

The Cecil Hotel in Alexandria was an important meeting point for Roy and his fellow Fleet Air Arm officers as it was where the military bus stopped to and from Dekheila and right in the heart of the bustling town centre. It was where chic French, Egyptian and English ladies sat at little round tables drinking tea and eating cream cakes. Somerset Maugham once stayed there, and the British Secret Service maintained a suite for their operations.

The Cecil Hotel was a relatively modern hotel built only eight years previously in an exotic art deco-style, with dramatic sweep of marble stairs, chandeliers and high stuccoed ceilings in the hotel lobby. It had a panoramic view of the Eastern Harbour of Alexandria.

Roy and Naomi often frequented the hotel bar with their Navy friends. This bar would later be renamed the Montgomery after Field Marshal Montgomery resided at the hotel during the North Africa Campaign. At the Cecil, Roy and Naomi found the food and drinks were reasonable. An added attraction was the old Arab man, who performed his magical tricks each evening.

Another favourite haunt was Alexandria's main beach, Sidi Bisch, where photographs capture happy images of Roy and Naomi doing handstands with their friends.

Roy and Naomi were also able to pursue their other great love, horse riding. There were two places where they rode horses, one was the city stud farm, and the other was for wonderful gallops along the sandy beach in the Corniche. Roy and Naomi would often visit the art deco-styled Pastroudis tea lounge renowned for the finest pastries in Alex. In the evenings they and their friends would go to the Smouha Club bars and restaurants, or one of the many dozen little roadside cafes. As Naomi recollected: 'Most of us kept eastern Mediterranean late hours, although some of the English still insisted on dining at seven-thirty, as if at home in Devon or the home counties.'

Soon after they arrived in Alex, the young couple went on the first of their two trips to Cairo together. The first was to celebrate Roy's recent birthday. They took the tram to Misr railway station. Roy paid for the luxury of a Pullman car, with air conditioning not found in ordinary first class – and necessary in the heat of that hot summer. They watched the desert scenery unfold as their train steamed towards Cairo. On the platform of the imposing station at Cairo waited crowds of people in a variety of costumes, with station-porters aplenty, looking for their patrons. 'Colourful people' recalled Naomi.

The fine hotels of Cairo were world famous. In the modern quarters of Cairo, the wide streets were lined on either side with trees and fine buildings – the city had the air of a great metropolis. Naomi recalled the biblical-like open markets with the hectic activity of the narrow streets, and over-laden donkeys and pack mules walking between the stalls and the crowds. There was the aroma of spices, musk, and mint tea all intermingled. As a belated birthday present for Roy, Naomi haggled for a pair of relief brass horse head murals from a shop at the Khan el-Khalili bazaar.

Both Roy and Naomi felt especially sorry for the emaciated horses in the market and heard about a new animal shelter and hospital that had been set up not long before their visit to Cairo, by the wife of a British army major general, Dorothy Brooke. Mrs Brooke had been appalled to learn that these walking skeletons were ex-cavalry horses from the Great War. In 1934 she founded the Old War Horse Memorial Hospital in Cairo. Naomi never forgot the Cairo animals, and donated to and supported the Brooke Hospital as it became known for seventy years.

The next morning they awoke to the bursts of chanting, the call of the muezzin to prayer. During their stay, they went swimming at the Gezira club, and for cocktails at Shepheard's hotel – known as the 'heart and soul of visiting English society'. Shepheard's was out of bounds to junior ranks. The bars and terraces swarmed with a lunchtime crowd of fashionably dressed Cairo ladies and officers of all nations.

Churchill is reported to have said: 'If the Germans do cross into Egypt, they will be thrown back by sheer weight of officers in Shepheard's Hotel.'

Overall, Roy and Naomi lived in Egypt for ten months while Roy was stationed near Alexandria.

Many of the other *Glorious* 's wives were constantly hampered by shortage of money. They were entertained on board ship as often as possible and practicable, and lived in the cheapest possible lodgings, such a contrast to the enormous chic of the impeccably turned out Alexandrian women. Naomi's inheritance made it much easier for her than many of her friends. Naomi recalled, Roy's pay was 4/6d a day on *Glorious*. At that time the Admiralty paid no marriage allowance to any officer under twenty-five years of age. Roy's salary was £250 a year, even with extra flying pay.

During this period Roy had the opportunity to take Naomi on board *Glorious* and introduce her to Captain Lyster for the first time. She thought Lyster was 'very nice and sweet'.

On Roy's return to Dekheila, flying exercises continued for him and the squadron. Ginger Hale recollected:

> B-F was initially a Sub Lt in 812, but used to fly with my squadron occasionally when we wanted to borrow a pilot. I remember one occasion being very anxious about him when he was overdue, but he returned later to the aerodrome with just a little petrol left.

At Alexandria there was a new influx of personnel, and Roy and his young wife were quick to make them feel at home. One of the new intake of aircrew was Alastair Easton who recalled: 'Roy was a super person and he and Naomi were a super couple.' He enjoyed their company and the visits to the Cecil Hotel bar.

The level of operational practice increased throughout this period. Roy found himself doing much night torpedo work and night formation flying. Speed during take-off and landing was of strategic importance. The time interval between aircraft landing on deck was determined by how quickly aircraft wings could be folded whilst taxiing onto the lift and taken down to the hangar; on average this could not be reduced to much less than twenty seconds.

Later, with the advent of the crash barrier, the lift could be lowered as soon as a landing aircraft had its arrester hook disengaged from a wire. The aircraft could then taxi past the barrier and be parked on the deck ahead. In this way aircraft could be brought in safely at ten-second intervals.

About this time Captain Lyster met Commander Flying Willoughby, senior observer Lt Paul Slessor, and the three squadron Swordfish COs, including Lt Cdr 'Ben' Bolt who had been made night operations co-ordinator, to develop night tactics and training. This meeting was to discuss preparations for a possible strike on the Italian Fleet at its headquarters in the port of Taranto.

As Bolt recalled:

Lyster spoke to Dudley Pound [Admiral Sir Dudley Pound] at Alexandria about the projected attack on Taranto and said that *Glorious*'s Swordfish squadrons were sufficiently trained in night torpedo work and night formation flying to carry out such an operation. Dudley Pound agreed in principle. Lyster then had a meeting in *Glorious* with the senior flying officers, and myself. We were told to maintain complete secrecy but to train the Swordfish squadrons with this end in view.

Roy and his colleagues were blissfully unaware of the preparations to attack Taranto. However, as Alfie Sutton recollected many years later:

When war finally came, we were fully war-efficient night-flying squadrons and many of the aircrew subsequently took part, from *Illustrious*, in the night attack on the Italian battle fleet at Taranto in November 1940, carrying out an attack that had initially been conceived and developed in *Glorious*.

From now on Naomi and the other wives were never told when *Glorious* would sail or to what destination, or when she would return. One morning the ship would be gone, on another she would be back. By now, it had become a guessing game by the wives whether their husbands would be in Alex or back to Malta for operational duties. Of course, Roy could say nothing.

When Roy was away at Dekheila or at sea, Naomi also had the Great Dane, Mons, for company: 'A few weeks after I arrived, the dog was brought to us and caused a great sensation. The Arabs had never seen such a big dog, and I used to get crowds looking at him wherever I left him in the parked car!'

Roy and Naomi got on well with Captain Lyster and on one social event were introduced to some of Alex's residents, including a Turkish gentleman called Ali Bey Ayeha. His title emphasised that he was of noble descent, the equivalent of 'Duke' in England.

They thought nothing more of it until a few weeks later an official 'black tie' invitation arrived. Roy and Naomi dressed for the occasion. Roy was wearing his dress uniform, cocked hat and ceremonial officer's sword, its gold bullion sword knot glittering in the light. The cummerbund was worn with the uniform. Naomi was still petite in her high heels besides her dashing 6 ft officer husband. She wore a fur-lined cape and dark silk dress.

The event was at one of the few old houses which remained of the mediaeval Alexandria near the old fort, built of ancient brick with an entrance of columns. They got the first hint that something was different when footmen opened the door – it swung open and an immense Nubian in a white galabiyeh bowed as they entered. Naomi recalled: 'It was like a film set. We were led down steps through a courtyard into a vast cellar laid out with a wonderful display of food served on golden plates.' The room was simply furnished with low carved tables and divans piled with kelims and embroidered velvet cushions.

Naomi continued:

> Everyone who was anybody was there, and everyone was at least twenty years older than us. We were the *only* ordinary people; all the rest were heads of banks or the chief of police, even the mayor. We were the only nobodies. Ali Bey was a multi-millionaire whose yacht was moored in Alexandria harbour.

There were jewels and furs, glitter of gold and diamonds, medals and moustaches mixing with the dress uniform of a dozen nations. Servants and silent house suffragi came in setting out more food on golden dishes amongst the party guests. Music started and there was a belly dancer in a diaphanous chiffon costume, the most famous dancer in the city. The servants finally brought in silver pots of mint tea and Turkish coffee, and set them out beside crystal decanters of whisky and brandy.

Naomi continued: 'I shall never forget that evening, neither of us could believe it ever happened the next day!'

Towards the end of June, the old ways began to change and not for the better. Captain Lyster had been promoted and was due to take up a desk job back in the Admiralty. In the wardroom, all the officers, including Roy, dined him out as a farewell and he was toasted by his No. 2, Cdr Evans-Lombe.

A salute and procession was arranged on Lyster's leaving the ship. Hands were mustered on the lower flying-off deck, and Roy and the other officers mustered on the quarterdeck. The ship's company led three cheers as the captain left in the first motor boat, manned by all the ship's commanders and major of marines. This was escorted by the first cutter, pulled by an officer's crew including Roy, and the second cutter with a volunteer crew from the petty officers' mess.

Captain Lyster left Alexandria and his relief and new skipper was Guy D'Oyly-Hughes, a submarine hero from the Great War. He had won the DSC in the Sea of Marmora and two DSOs, and subsequently served a year as commander and executive officer of *Courageous* in 1934. He then went to the Air Ministry on the Directorate of Air Training, before returning to the submarine service.

The ship's company on *Glorious* was looking forward to his coming. Buchanan-Dunlop, himself a submariner before joining the Fleet Air Arm, recalled:

> After two such captains as Fraser (later Admiral Sir Bruce Fraser) and Lyster, when we heard that no less a person than the old first lieutenant of Dunbar-Nasmith, VC, was to command us, hopes ran high that, if we continued to give all we had, he would prove another winner. But such was not to be.

Splash Carver recalled:

> Dear old Lumley Lyster handed over command of *Glorious* about June 1939, in Alexandria. His successor was a gallant WWI submariner named D'Oyly-Hughes. He was very charming socially and quite a good-looking man but he knew little about carriers or aviation and, what was worse, he was not prepared to take the advice of the senior air officers i.e. Commander (Air) and Lieut Cdr (Ops).

Moose wrote:

> A new captain has taken over *Glorious* – Capt. D'Oyly-Hughes DSO DSC. During the war he swam from his submarine off the Dardanelles – blew up a Turkish fortification and swam back – submerged and got away.
>
> So he is a good man. When the captains change, a flimsy is made out for the benefit of the new captain and officers personally. Mine is enclosed. Capt. Lister DSO etc.
>
> The heat here in Egypt is terrific, but I get lots of swimming in the blue Mediterranean – you should see my tan.
>
> I have been living in a tent so long now that I am beginning to feel like a desert Bedouin. Even here, though, my marine servant brings me an early morning cup of tea. I stretch out my arm through the mosquito netting and quickly recover it. An amazing thing out here is that at high altitudes it can be colder than temperatures found at that height in England, even in winter.

D'Oyly-Hughes ruffled feathers soon after taking command. After witnessing his first dummy torpedo attack on his ship, he spoke to the assembled officers, including Roy, as Ben Bolt recollected:

> The substance and manner of his talk made the most vivid impression on me and on all the other responsible officers, both ship and air, who were present.
>
> He said, in effect, that he disagreed with all the doctrine about training in the FAA, particularly on the amount of time spent in reconnaissance training and that as far as air anti-submarine operations were concerned, no aircraft had ever sunk a submarine or ever would. He showed contempt for the Fleet Air Arm and for everything that had been achieved in training for the war which we all knew was inevitable.
>
> He turned down proposals made by Willoughby and Slessor for future training programmes and would brook no discussion. In a few days, the morale of the ship was reduced to a level I had never known when serving under her three previous captains.

Immediately, flying practice in 812 Squadron changed, and that month Roy and his fellow squadron members did little more than rear gun practice in the air, pulling drogues, and carrying out searchlight patrols.

Guy Willoughby recalled:

> Whenever we went to sea for exercises, D'Oyly-Hughes used to send for me and instructed me to carry out exercises with both squadrons which he had designed with a view, as he said, to further their efficiency. These exercises were mainly rubbish, but I had the squadrons carry them out when I considered none of the aircraft taking part was endangered.

Alfie Sutton recalled:

> Daddy Lyster was a strict, efficient, pleasant man who fought hard for his ship, especially against an antagonistic C-in-C. D'Oyly-Hughes distrusted his senior officers, thought the ship inefficient, and soon had morale destroyed.

With the change of captain, even the aircrew's wives could see the morale on the ship was different. D'Oyly-Hughes was not regarded as fondly by Naomi as 'sweet Captain Lyster'.

Glorious was becoming a somewhat unhappy ship under the command of its new skipper. Titch Harding later compared Lyster's attitude with that of the new captain:

> Lyster was a very good one – right balance, right values. Lyster believed in air power but many old sea dogs did not like these things that went up in the air, as their predecessors did not like the submarine. It went underwater, was underhand and not British, sir! They wanted to fight by the rules and Hitler wanted this, while he made up and fought by his. The way of the aggressor. I can hit you but you must not hit me!

The feeling of the ship's company was that D'Oyly-Hughes would forget aircraft in the heat of battle and want *Glorious* to charge the enemy like a battleship with all guns firing. Naomi recalled Tiffy Torrens-Spence arguing: 'that the battleships' day was now finished!' Naomi could not believe it.

Naomi had her own reasons to not appreciate the new captain as Alfie recalled:

> Once whilst I was having an iced coffee after playing golf at the Smouha Club in Alexandria, Naomi came over and asked if she could sit with me. I was surprised, for I didn't know her very well, but the reason was soon evident. In those days, I was four years senior to Roy and so we didn't mix much. Roy I knew as a likable, handsome man, with a particularly pretty wife, Naomi.
>
> It became apparent that Naomi was taking refuge from the new captain of *Glorious*, D'Oyly-Hughes, who had relieved Lyster and was married. He had been pestering her all afternoon, she said. And eventually he said to her 'Well, are you coming to bed with me or not?' She was insulted but replied forcefully 'You mustn't speak to your young officers' wives like that. What would my husband say?' He replied, 'Tell your husband to go to hell. Are you coming to bed?'

Alfie continued: 'That's when she saw me and dashed over to be rescued. D'Oyly-Hughes didn't pursue her!'

In July, Commander Evans-Lombe was promoted as captain and left *Glorious*. His relief was A.E.D. Lovell, who had been D'Oyly-Hughes' submarine staff officer in Malta.

On 4 July, *Glorious* sailed on her last peacetime exercises and visits, to Phaleron and Milos in Greece, to Suda Bay in Crete and to Limassol in Cyprus, returning to Alexandria six weeks later. Roy wrote to Naomi mentioning a little about their fleet, consisting of three battleships and about two dozen destroyers.

Whilst on these visits, Moose wrote:

> August 5, 1939. We are spending next weekend in Limassol, Cyprus, and as I am officer-of-the-watch tomorrow, I shall not be on duty in Cyprus, so should be able to get ashore while there for a couple of days. As we have not been ashore for three months, it isn't bad to be able to shake the sand out of one. The only real objection

is the heat. The whole flying-off deck acts as a flat iron and absorbs all the heat, which is transmitted directly to the cabins, etc. below.

Did I hear you mention holiday in your last letter? Not a hope – until the international situation cools down, and it looks decidedly worse. Might occur any moment now. The Commander in Chief Mediterranean station has brought out a new order for tropical rig and we now wear white shorts and shirts (short sleeves and open at neck) – white stockings and shoes. The ordinary white rig – tunic and long slacks when officer of the watch etc.– I have so many naval uniforms now – the upkeep is terrific. I have had to get four sets of the new outfit. I still haven't got pukker full dress yet and am hoping to stall along by renting it from Gieves if necessary, e.g. weddings and funerals.

I must get back to Malta soon so I can get an extra set of blues in case I dump myself in the sea – as it is now I have only one set of blues. Another thing I must do is get a full insurance on the whole kit which runs to over $600 at the least. My bank balance shows £65, so I am ready for any emergency.

Naomi travelled by ferry to Cyprus from Alexandria with her friend Marina Dundas who was having problems affording the fare. Naomi recalled:

So I paid for her too. However, by then we couldn't afford first class as normal, so we had to put up with second class, which had a smell of old feet. Within 5–10 minutes, Marina had charmed the captain and we finished going first class after all.

We arrived and watched all the aircraft waggling their wings at us, and us all waving as usual trying to guess which was our own husband. Roy got special leave to meet us.

Roy took Naomi for the weekend at the Forest Inn in the cooler climate of the Troodos hill resort. They enjoyed a horse and carriage trip with Marina and other squadron members and their wives. The weather was sunny and warm.

Naomi later remembered coming down from the mountains and seeing the familiar sight of *Glorious* in port. 'We took a groundnut ship back from Cyprus to Alex. It was the *best* weekend of my life.'

Moose was also on the trip to the Troodos and wrote:

August 14, 1939. Prodromos (Cyprus), Berengaria Hotel. If you will look at your atlas of Cyprus, you will see Limassol, a port on the south-eastern tip of the island. We arrived here on Friday morning with three battleships and about twenty destroyers.

I was able to get overnight leave with a few others, so we motored up to Troodos behind Limassol. The mountain is about 6,400 feet and one climbs the whole height in thirty-two miles of switchbacks and marvellous scenery like Banff. The heat at sea level is impossible to stand. We only wear shorts and shirts, but they are soaked right through just sitting still. It has to be experienced to be believed. The whole atmosphere is wet and therefore it is impossible to get dry. Up here on the very top of the mountain it is wonderful. The island is quite a big one, 150 miles x 160 miles, and it is noted for its wines. We have done quite a lot of flying since leaving Alexandria – starting by a dawn attack on Alex from 100 miles at sea. 802 was to attempt to machine gun flying boats at anchor in harbour. We did – caught them napping just as they were trying to start engines.

Lord knows what the Alexandrians thought at 6 am while our whole squadron roared across the harbour at less than 50 feet. Anyway, it was good fun for us and a fleet exercise to the Admiralty.

We sail tonight at 9.30 pm for Alexandria or something else. Thank goodness the Cypriot drivers are good. Gippy ones would be lying by the hundred along both sides of that mountain road.

Roy and *Glorious* got back before Naomi, reaching Alexandria on 15 August.

On 25 August, Britain signed a formal alliance with Poland – war was looming ever closer. British forces in Egypt were re-enforced by the arrival of Indian troops at Suez. Flying training increased in intensity for Roy and 812 Squadron. He had to fly his aircraft by night or day as long as the weather permitted, with constant night practice to locate and attack targets.

Moose wrote:

August 30, 1939. The heat here is beginning to abate, so it is more pleasant to be alive. By the time you get this letter I suppose we will be either at war or just passing through another crisis. Boy! What we wouldn't give to get our hands on Hitler and his terrible crew of henchmen. If we don't stop him soon we will have to stop him later, if we are able to. But we might as well get it over with. Needless to say we are on the top line and ready for any eventuality.

Roy's Swordfish squadron also carried out numerous night-simulated torpedo attacks on *Glorious* and the battle fleet, using a camera system to assess the probability of a successful launch.

James Stewart-Moore reflected: 'Hitler and Mussolini kept us on the hop all through 1939 as the political crises came and went. Splash added:

In early August we re-embarked in *Glorious* and sailed with the Fleet for exercises in the eastern Med. These lasted most of that month but we were in Alex on 3 September when war on Germany was declared.

CHAPTER 9

At War in the Hunt for *Graf Spee*

The announcement that Britain was once again at war with Germany came on 3 September 1939. For most Britons scattered across the Empire, the news came on a Sunday morning on the wireless with the sombre voice of Neville Chamberlain, the Prime Minister.

'Berlin had been warned,' he said, 'that if Germany did not stop all aggressive action against Poland and begin to withdraw from Polish territory by 11 am, Britain and Germany would be at war.'

At 11.15 am Mr Chamberlain announced in his radio broadcast that: 'No such undertaking has been received and that consequently this country is at war with Germany.' Almost immediately, a siren sounded in London, its haunting monotone sending people hurrying to shelters; but it turned out to be a false alarm.

In Devon, Leslie was with her parents in their Shaldon home: 'I was in the kitchen. Mum burst into tears when she heard and that made me burst into tears too.'

Roy and Naomi were at the Cecil Hotel in Alex when news of war came through. Roy and other officers were immediately recalled to the Fleet flagship, *Warspite*, to receive orders from Admiral Pound.

James Stewart-Moore recalled:

I can remember that we were invited on board the flagship on 3 September where the Commander-in-Chief told us that war had just been declared on Germany, and gave us a brief pep talk. Then we went back to the *Glorious*, and I went ashore to play tennis at the sporting club that afternoon. The next week we were at sea for exercises, and on Sunday 10th I went ashore to play golf. I have never played either game since.

'Bobby' Going recollected:

When war was declared, D'Oyly-Hughes brought out one of those little glass-fronted boxes containing revolvers. Suddenly, one of those boxes appeared on the back end of the bridge. Guy Willoughby asked D'Oyly-Hughes what it was for. He replied it was to shoot any of his officers who failed to do his duty in action!

As Guy Willoughby was hanging out flags from the flying position, and I was running up and down the deck as flight deck officer at the time, we reckoned we would be the first two to be killed by winging shots by this gallant man! He really didn't enamour himself to anybody very much.

L/A David 'Jan' Jolliff, Leading TAG with 812 Squadron, remembered:

Glorious was in Alexandria with her squadrons on the day war was declared. The ship's programme was to sail next day for Malta to carry out self-refit. I was having a cup of tea in the mess when Captain Hughes came on the ship's broadcast system and told us that a very important broadcast was to be made from London.

Almost immediately Big Ben struck and was followed by Mr Chamberlain's broadcast telling us we were at war with Germany. Shortly after, the captain came on the system and told us that the ship was not immediately affected, the crew could go on normal shore leave and the ship would sail for Malta as per programme in the morning.

Then from the ship being almost 'still as the grave', she suddenly became full of life and conversation. The only thing to do was to go ashore and have a skinful, which most of us did, and of course the whole of Alex were informed that *Glorious* was going to Malta the next day.

Naomi said: 'All we knew at the onset of war was that the *Glorious* with Roy on board slipped out of harbour on a "hush-hush" mission somewhere in the Mediterranean.'

Splash Carver recalled:

Now that we were at war we expected the ship to be ordered to rush off somewhere – with a cruiser/destroyer escort – but nothing happened. Operations during September were mainly covering convoys heading westward through the Mediterranean.

The CO of 812 Squadron, Ben Bolt, had been ill and unfit to fly, so was invalided home. Titch Harding, as senior pilot, was temporarily in charge. Ben recollected: 'Unfortunately I was struck with acute tonsillitis and the quacks sent me home to Haslar hospital in September from where I emerged in November having then lost touch with 812 Squadron.'

His mood had not been positive when he left: 'This probably saved me from going down in *Glorious* or being sent for court martial with J.B. Heath later the next year as I could see the new captain was off his head.'

At the beginning of the war, the situation was not good as far as the Fleet Air Arm generally was concerned. The Navy had only thirteen squadrons and six old aircraft carriers, *Courageous*, *Furious*, *Glorious*, *Argus*, *Eagle* and *Hermes*. The only new carrier commissioned was the *Ark Royal*. Four others were under construction, the *Illustrious* nearing completion, and *Indomitable*, *Victorious* and *Formidable* each waiting to be launched.

In the guarded language of an official Admiralty history: 'The air equipment of the Fleet had not, by September 1939, reached anything like that stage of development which world progress in Naval aviation warranted.'

The truth was that the Fleet Air Arm was chronically short of pilots and men; aircraft were virtually obsolete and there were insufficient experienced and high-ranking officers to argue the cause for naval aviation at the top level.

With *Glorious* at sea and the buzz that she was at Malta, Naomi and Mita and other wives accepted a flight to the island in a private aeroplane owned by a rich Greek oil magnate. They were disappointed to look down and see the familiar shape of *Glorious* steaming out of the harbour just as they were circling to land.

Glorious returned to Alexandria on 16 September, and the next day came the shattering news that HMS *Courageous* had been sunk off the south-west of Ireland in the Western

Approaches. It was the Royal Navy's first serious loss of the war. *Courageous* had been leading a submarine hunt when she was torpedoed by a U-boat. The aircraft carrier went down in only twenty minutes and 518 of her 1,200 complement were lost, including her captain.

It was a bitter blow for everybody, particularly as *Courageous* was *Glorious*'s sister ship and had been her sparring partner in manoeuvres and sports for the previous ten years. Many of Roy's friends were missing. Suddenly, the impact of the war came very close indeed.

Glorious remained at Alex for the next three weeks until 9 October during which time Roy celebrated his wife's birthday with her. There were rumours that the ship was about to sail for Malta so Roy and Naomi hastily arranged the second of their two excursions to Cairo: 'We had to see the pyramids before leaving Alexandria. The pyramids are on the edge of the desert, but also near the town.'

The couple rented camels to ride right up to the pyramids under the blistering sun. The desert was like nowhere Naomi had ever been. Seen from the pyramids, Cairo seemed to be dominated by the pointed silhouette of the Citadel among a sea of roofs, domes, and minarets. The couple explored inside the pyramids. Naomi left her hat in one of the tombs and, undaunted by tales of tourists getting lost for days underground, retraced her steps to reclaim her precious possession.

Later Roy and Naomi retired to the Mena House hotel, set in gardens with the pyramids towering above. In the evening they went to Madame Badia's Cabaret, a nightclub in Giza. It was a place of intrigue as Hitler regarded Madame Badia Masabni as a dangerous spy, a secret agent and traitor.

Roy was back in the air on 7 October, flying his last ever reconnaissance flight from Dekheila with David Jolliff as his TAG. Two days later, *Glorious* steamed out of the harbour at Alexandria – the destination a secret.

Roy had left Naomi convinced that he would be only away a short while and close at hand. The captain had returned from a visit to the C-in-C on *Warspite* and announced to the assembled ship's complement in the lower deck that they were ordered to go to Malta for docking. This proved to be a distraction to prevent the true information getting into the hands of spies in Alexandria, who might pass on the details to Germany and lead to U-boats trying to sink *Glorious* just like *Courageous* three weeks previously. Once at sea, the ship altered course and steered for the Suez Canal, and passed through it that night.

Stewart-Moore recalled:

We went to sea for exercises on 9 October expecting to return to harbour that night, but instead we hurried through the Suez Canal, accompanied by the battleship *Malaya*, and set off for Aden. We spent the next few weeks patrolling from Aden around the Red Sea and off Socotra, looking for German pocket battleships without any luck.

From now on, with the extremely erratic postal system, letters from Roy arrived spasmodically. No letters were to appear from him for over three weeks. With the imposition of censorship, his letters suddenly and inevitably became vague, leaving Naomi on a continual round of guessing games as to what was meant and whether there was any hidden message.

Naomi wanted to help out the war effort so she enrolled in a Voluntary Aid Detachment

Nursing Course. The VAD course was established by the British Red Cross Society and the St John Ambulance. It led to a nursing certificate and applicants could join the front line in the Navy, RAF or Army.

Whilst Roy was at sea, Naomi's life revolved around the three Ms as Roy would call them – Mons, Marina (Marina Dundas) and Mita. Tiny, along with Mita and Marina, carried out cipher work at Naval HQ, HMS *Nile*. This was the Flag Office at Alexandria – the offices of the Admiral of the Fleet.

When it became apparent to the wives that *Glorious* was not coming back soon, Naomi agreed to share a luxury flat with Mita and Marina, nicknamed 'Rina'. They had a house servant or *suffragi*, Hassan, of whom Naomi was very fond. The flat was in a tall apartment block in Rue Salvago in a smart area of Alex, close to the Turkish Embassy. There were marble floors and heavy furniture and every room had a ceiling fan. The three were not to remain there long, as Naomi recalled. 'Mita had a monkey that bit her from time to time, Rina had two animals including a bull terrier and a puppy, and us with Mons, the giant hound of the Baskerville.' Naomi added a kitten which she had found in a gutter: 'It was covered in fleas, and rewarded me by yowling its head off. We were turned out of the flat fairly soon! So had to go back to the Le Roy Hotel.'

Naomi continued to recall her adventures back in the hotel:

Whilst we three wives were living in the Le Roy Hotel a very suspicious chap was resident there also, he always wore dark glasses, called himself Mr X – he was so suspicious that nobody took him seriously. It turned out that Mr X actually was a spy, and after being taken away by the police was as far as I recall shot for being a spy.

Perhaps luckily for Roy life was more mundane on board *Glorious*:

As you can well imagine, there is absolutely no news and even if there were, we can't put it. Anyway everything is perfectly OK and there is not the slightest reason to worry. Cliff sends his love. Well, my darling there is absolutely no news except that it is bloody hot.

The aircrews were forced to adapt to the changing climatic conditions – no mean feat given that *Glorious* had no air conditioning and below decks was like a steel oven.

Splash Carver recollected the stifling tropical heat:

It was very hot and, as you can imagine, a carrier with an acre-plus of steel flight deck, under a tropical sun is a real sweat box! In those days the only air-conditioned spaces were the sick bay and the main wireless office. I also remember that all the refrigeration efforts had to go towards keeping the magazines down to a temperature within the safe limits so we had no cold drinks and, eventually, no drinks at all as we ran out.

Glorious reached Aden on 13 October, and whilst the ship was being fuelled, some of the ship's company were given the chance for a short break ashore. Roy had a couple of hours exploring the main town before being recalled on board. The ship sailed the same day partly to avoid delays at the start of the Muslim fast of Ramadan, heading for the nearby British possession of Socotra. This was a mountainous desert island lying in the Indian Ocean at the entrance to the Gulf of Aden and close to the mainland of the potentially hostile Italian

Somaliland. *Glorious* anchored that evening on the west coast of the island, at Ghubbet Shoab bay.

Glorious, in the company of the battleship *Malaya*, and destroyer *Bulldog*, remained on station in the Socotra area for almost two months until 6 December. Their role was to form part of a global chain of Royal Navy hunting groups to cover the North and South Atlantic, and the Indian Ocean, to wait and catch the German pocket battleship *Graf Spee* and the *Deutschland*, which had both sailed from their base at Wilhelmshaven before the outbreak of war.

On 30 September, *Graf Spee* found and sank its first victim, the British freighter *Clement,* while off Pernambuco in South America, alerting all Royal Navy hunting groups around the world.

Glorious's hunting group expanded to include a *Daring* class destroyer from the China Station, and their search for the *Graf Spee* extended southwards into the Indian Ocean.

Ginger Hale recollected:

> *Glorious* went down to the Indian Ocean and was based off Aden in order to protect the approaches to the Red Sea and Suez Canal from the *Graf Spee* in case she came that way. Other focal points were protected in a similar way, *Ark Royal* off the Cape and *Hermes* off Ceylon.

Roy and the squadrons were not idle. They searched the whole time with daily three- to four-hour reconnaissance operations off Socotra investigating all passing vessels on flights at the extreme limits of the Swordfish range until 20 October. This was followed by dive-bombing practice on towed targets and ALTs until the end of the month.

Splash Carver recalled:

> This involved flying armed reconnaissance sorties throughout daylight hours searching for possible German armed merchant cruisers or even a warship if one was known to be at large e.g. *Graf Spee*. We carried 4 x 250-lb bombs for dive-bombing in case we found a Hun!
>
> We would fly sorties of about 3 hrs 45 mins which allowed reconnaissance to a depth of about 140 nautical miles from the ship. Accurate navigation was required as *Glorious* had no VHF homing beacon, like later carriers, and might not give you a bearing on request if she thought it important not to break radio silence.

When not flying, life on board was humdrum for Roy and his squadron colleagues and included visiting the cinema, listening to wireless programmes and taking part in lectures, fitness training and deck sports.

Roy wrote to Naomi:

> 6 November. As per usual I've got absolutely no news whatsoever except that we have been having PT classes on the flight deck as a means of getting some exercise. This evening I got some of the squadron onto boxing for a change. It was excellent fun but my jaw feels a wee bit tender now. Oh yes, there is a wee bit of news. I have been TT [teetotal] for nearly a week now. Marvellous isn't it. Actually, of course, we ran out of beer so it is no hardship.

In November, the position of CO of 812 Squadron was formally handed over to 812 Squadron's senior observer James Stewart-Moore as Ben Bolt was still on sick leave. He recalled:

In the pre-war days [and the beginning of the Second World War] life in the FAA was highly disturbed and confusing: the Admiralty was trying hard to expand the FAA and to form new squadrons, so we [observers] were being shifted about from ship to ship and squadron to squadron at short notice. I ended up remaining as CO of 812 Squadron for a short period while the ship was carrying out operations off Socotra.

Stewart-Moore continued:

I liked B-F very much – he was very easy to get on with, and always good company. Life was pretty humdrum, but I can remember a couple of incidents: the first was having to refuel the *Glorious* with aviation petrol for the flying machines, and the other was a run ashore on Socotra one afternoon. The refuelling was unusual because the only petrol at Aden was in forty-gallon drums: there was no bulk supply. So a couple of thousand drums had to be hoisted on board, opened, and poured carefully through a filter and a two-inch pipe. It took a long time.

Socotra was spectacularly dry sand, dull like the moon; there were no signs of habitation at all, no roads, and nothing resembling a port. We went ashore by jumping from a motor boat into four or five feet of water, and got off in the reverse sequence. Yet there were inhabitants, who appeared in their canoes and small sailing boats whenever the ships anchored, and gathered up whatever was thrown overboard. I suppose we were besieged by natives who would do anything for a box of matches, particularly.

There was no vegetation on the island, and their only fuel was probably driftwood, which would be rather difficult to kindle by friction. We flew over the island quite a lot: Italy was still neutral, and anyway there were no Italians there. There was no trace of civilisation, and we were told that the last white inhabitants of the island were two Italian lighthouse keepers, who were eaten by the locals during some hungry spell. I suppose that this was before the days of Oxfam and its associates.

With the appointment of the new CO, there was a vacancy for officer in command of 'X' Flight. Ken Gurr had learnt to fly at Leuchars one term ahead of Roy, so in order of seniority he was offered the post.

Other changes were taking place with old colleagues leaving, as Roy told Naomi in his letter of 8 November: 'Cliff and Tiffy are going. Ken is my boss now. It is lousy losing them both. We all feel hellish over it.'

Moose wrote:

November 2, 1939. This letter writing has certainly gone crazy since the beginning of the war. My last letter received from home was written on August 28. The hold-up is due to movements of the ship, or as they say, 'exigencies of the service'.

I hope to have some *Daily Herald*s to read. Hitler claimed to have sunk *Glorious* the other day, but he must have made a mistake in identification!

My promotion to Lieutenant (A) R.N. dates from 12 October, as you know and the extra £10 a month will certainly be welcome, although our income tax of 7/6 in the £ will whittle it down somewhat. What is the income tax in Canada by the way?

Roy went ashore for a visit to Socotra in mid-November, only the second time he had been ashore since leaving Naomi at the beginning of October. There was little to do and see on this desert island. The infrastructure, badly developed even in the twenty-first century, was even more basic in 1939, with only one significant town and two notable villages.

D'Oyly-Hughes often overrode his air staff and was always interfering. Roy and his colleagues were carrying out fewer and fewer sorties. Roy entered into his flying log book only three flights to the end of that month.

Splash recalled:

> To try and relieve the boredom, a beard competition was started by Lieutenant Norman 'Blood' Scarlett, one of the ship's observers. There were a lot of entries. They certainly flourished in the heat.

Roy mentioned the competition to Naomi:

> As per usual there is absolutely no news. We are doing our usual job of work and the usual exercises and nothing else except that we have started a beard-growing competition to help pass the time. The faces certainly are scruffy enough. Mine, I am afraid, is not a success and it will have to come off.

On 15 November, *Graf Spee*, which had been ordered at the beginning of that month into the Indian Ocean by Admiral Raeder, the commanding officer of the German *Kriegsmarine*, sank the British tanker MV *Africa Shell* in the Mozambique Channel. *Graf Spee* was by then only a few days, sailing south of *Glorious*.

Roy and the ship's company knew what would happen if the *Graf Spee* got within range of *Glorious*, as David Jolliff recalled:

> Captain Hughes had left us in no doubt of his war tactics. 'If we meet the whole German Navy we go straight at them with all our guns firing.'
>
> Our ship's armament consisted of 4.7″ anti-aircraft guns and some Oerlikons, little more than pop guns against an enemy battleship. You can well imagine the thoughts of 812 Squadron and its highly trained and very efficient aircrews. I dare not put them into words.

Roy remained silent in his letters to Naomi about the possibility of any impending sea battle with the *Graf Spee* so close:

> 17 November. Please excuse the writing darling but I have been boxing and exercising hard and I am all tired out…We do nothing except exercise different things on board and exercise our bodies in the evening. At least some of us do.

At last sense prevailed throughout the rest of November, when Willoughby ordered Roy's squadron to increasingly carry out torpedo and dive-bombing practice and 'strikes' on *Glorious* and on the battleship *Malaya*. Their preparations were for the increasing likelihood of an imminent attack on the *Graf Spee* if she got within range of the *Glorious*'s Swordfish. The skipper and Willoughby presumed that the *Graf Spee* was heading in their direction even though there was no fresh news of her whereabouts.

Roy's letters continued to avoid any reference to action: 'I get so miserable these days that I have to sleep on the quarterdeck in the open air.'

In mid-November, news arrived that the pocket battleship *Deutschland* was far away and no longer posed a risk to shipping in the Indian Ocean, having entered Gotenhaven

(Gdynia) on 16 November. She had been renamed *Lützow* to prevent loss of morale if the ship bearing the name 'Germany' was sunk. Now there was only the *Graf Spee*.

As the atmosphere on board ship became more strained with the likelihood of a sea battle ever more likely, Roy may have been feeling anxious and was certainly despondent:

> 23 November. Oh gosh, I don't think that I was meant to be a sailor. Quite a lot of officers (about thirty) are still very keen on their fitness campaign. In fact so much so that we were doing physical jerks in the moonlight the other day. Still no news of anything in particular. We are in a safe place, which is something to be thankful for. I ain't no hero.

On 2 December at last came fresh news of the *Graf Spee*. Having left the Indian Ocean and returned to her earlier Atlantic operational area, she had sunk the British freight steamer *Doric Star* in the middle Atlantic sea lanes. The next day she sank the British refrigerator ship *Tairoa*.

Graf Spee refuelled with the German supply ship *Altmark* and headed towards the River Plate off Uruguay to disguise her intention of actually heading back to Germany. However, on 13 December, *Graf Spee* was spotted by the British cruisers *Exeter* and *Ajax*, as well as the New Zealand cruiser *Achilles*, and a sea battle ensued and the *Graf Spee* was damaged.

The next day, *Graf Spee* arrived in Montevideo to make temporary repairs but was ordered to leave Montevideo on 17 December, as the Royal Navy was arriving in force nearby. Almost two hours later, the battleship was scuttled in the River Plate Estuary.

There was general relief all round on board *Glorious*, and Roy and his colleagues were now instructed to carry out fewer sorties, to the extent that the aircrews were not doing much flying any more.

With the definite news that the *Graf Spee* was sunk, *Glorious* received orders to weigh anchor from her Socotra anchorage and head out towards the Indian sub-continent. By now, her provisions were running low and the galley was reduced to serving dried peas and rice. Splash recalled:

> A few days before Christmas, the news came that we were to proceed to Colombo for R and R. On the way there, we continued to search the ocean but in two months we had never detected an enemy. The beard competition was wound up and my pilot, 'Shorty' Shaw, and I won the team prize for the best pair.

Colombo, the capital of Ceylon, was reached on 10 December. At long last *Glorious* dropped anchor in somewhat civilised surroundings. Roy recognised the familiar outline of HMS *Kent* in Colombo's harbour and his thoughts inevitably went back to when he was last in Colombo with his midshipmen friends. McEwen and Boddington were far away and he hadn't received any news from them for a long time.

The first thing that struck the ship's crew on reaching Colombo was the welcome sight of well-wooded countryside, a most refreshing change after days at sea and the treeless wastes of the Middle East. Suddenly, life changed dramatically for Roy. It was back to the hustle and bustle of the bewildering contrast of East and West: the rickshaws and taxis, women in robes and men in turbans, a Colombo clearly recalled by Roy from his midshipman days.

Colombo had a large naval base. There was a beach near the airfield, and a sporting club that included a rugby field to which Roy was instantly drawn. He, along with Ken and

Splash, returned to the refuge of the Galle Face Hotel which resembled an English stately home, and spent the afternoon swimming in its pool. Like the previous time he visited, that evening Roy relaxed on the lawns and in the lounge drinking Pimms.

Roy wrote to Naomi:

> 11 December. I went ashore last night for the first time in a month and only the third since leaving you. Sam and I got wonderfully happy in this port. Actually, I know it slightly so we managed to get sozzled very speedily. Was supposed to be playing rugger today but was day on. Anyway it is much too hot for anything but bathing.

Next day he wrote:

> I may be playing rugger this afternoon. I don't know yet and then I suppose a flick and supper for one. It is amazing how few people stay on board now that we are in a partially civilised place. I should think that bar receipts ashore go up about 200 per cent.

Various officers left the *Glorious* at Colombo for new postings. Alfie Sutton recalled: 'I left her at Ceylon. D'Oyly-Hughes, as captain on the outbreak of war, soon had the ship in turmoil. I travelled in an armed merchant cruiser to France and then overland by train to England.'

No. 812 Squadron also lost her CO, James Stewart-Moore, who recalled:

> I stayed with the squadron until just before Christmas, 1939. My last flight was on 8 December. From Aden we went to Colombo, where I left the ship and came home in a P & O liner requisitioned as a troopship. It was a long, slow and boring journey.
>
> We ended up at Marseilles, where we took a troop-train across France to Cherbourg. The senior officer on board was an RAF type, who arranged things so that the RAF officers got all the first-class accommodation on the train, and the naval and few army officers in the draft had to make do with the wooden-seated benches in the French third class. The train trip took 36 hrs – only the first-class had any heating, and the whole country was covered in deep snow. One of the early horrors of war.

Replacement officers also joined in Colombo, including Lt Cdr Rupert Hill, who had come out of retirement as a Ceylon tea-plantation owner. There was also an influx of 'A' Branch aircrew officers, including 812 Squadron's Sub Lt Rupert Davies, who was later to become the main BBC actor in the 'Maigret' television series. No. 812 Squadron also had a new commanding officer, Lt Cdr N.G.R. 'Cracksie' Crawford. Roy was detailed to fly CPO Pinkerton to let him supervise the arrival of new TAGs.

By now, mail was even more erratic. Roy anticipated the extreme delay in letters and sent a telegram on 17 December to Le Roy Hotel: 'Merry Christmas, all well, best love Baker-Falkner.'

Meanwhile, back in Egypt, Diana Fitzherbert-Wright asked Naomi one day to go with her by ship to India to try and catch up with the *Glorious* in the Indian Ocean, particularly as she wanted to meet her boyfriend Ken Gurr. Naomi did not think there was time so went on a tour down the Nile with four other wives.

Roy's next letter read:

> We've been about five days in port now. The other night we had a squadron party.

I picked up several of my crew and Ken and breezed off to visit the local police officers' mess. We knew perfectly well that if we didn't call on them first, we would be spending an awful lot of the taxpayers' money in them having to search for and capture us.

As it was, we breezed along at something a.m. and got back to the ship about 3 or so having fixed them completely. Drunk all their beer and beat them at darts. Needless to say, I could only just hit the wall with only the occasional miss.

On 21 December *Glorious* sailed round to Trincomalee Bay in the north of Ceylon and remained at anchorage there for a week. The Royal Naval Air Station Trincomalee at China Bay had only just been commissioned that year.

Reaching Trincomalee gave the squadrons the opportunity to re-equip with new Swordfish aircraft parts to replace the almost time-expired Pegasus engines, to the delight of Roy:

23 December. Have got a new engine now which ought to please you a bit, darling. I have supervised the fitting of it myself and screwed up the bits. Actually, Ken and I gave up a half holiday just to go and dabble in grease and things and had a cracking good time on it.

He continued:

We are nowhere again and being moderately hard worked. A good thing really as it helps one to pass the time...No news except the usual exercise in the evening and even that has almost lost all zest. Very few people do it now. I bathed once ashore and tore my body to shreds on rocks and things. So did Ken but it was rather fun tho'.

Christmas, 1939 and Roy wrote:

25 December. 10 o'clock at night and I am very fed up but still my sweet here's to a very good Christmas darling, Happy New Year and most of all to our next being together.

Roy was spending a very different Christmas from the previous year with Naomi. He reminisced wistfully: 'Still, my darling I've got last Christmas to make up for this one.'

Everyone on board had received the Royal Christmas card: 'With Our Best Wishes for Christmas, 1939. May God Bless You and Protect You. Elizabeth R. George R.' Roy wrote to Naomi: 'Elizabeth R. and George R. sent us all Xmas cards. Very nice of them but I forgot to send them one. One other item of news, my sweetest one. We are getting a marriage allowance. At least I think we are.'

Splash recalled:

Christmas was in Colombo when the ship spent one or two days there, and then went round to the naval base at Trincomalee, a beautiful natural harbour on the east coast of Ceylon where we stayed over New Year.

The *Glorious*'s Players produced an excellent music hall show and then we had orders to return to the Med.

With no flying at the latter half of December, and maybe with more time on his hands to think, the stresses of war and sea travel were beginning to tell on Roy. He wrote:

27 December. So sorry Tich that the old man is ageing so much. I've only been ashore six times since I last saw you my darling and I've had the most amazing crazes for collecting things. First one was the horses in cigarette packets and now it's watches. I suppose they may come in handy. I expect so sometime or other.

Glorious sailed from Trincomalee with *Bulldog* on 29 December, along with *Kent* and the French warship *Suffren*. On 30 December, HMAS *Hobart* briefly joined them for convoy escort duties over the next few days.

Splash recalled:

For part of the way we were to escort a French troop convoy from the Ceylon area back to Aden. Most of the troop ships were filled with Senegalese units which had been in Indo-China. We would do a reconnaissance ahead of the convoy and an anti-submarine patrol around it.

I remember that as one flew 500 ft above in our Stringbags over the Senegal-filled ships, one could literally smell them and saw the sea of upturned faces on deck.

For New Year's Day Roy's convoy was in calm seas. *Glorious* called in briefly to anchor for a while at Bombay and then set sail for Aden.

Roy wrote: 'You know that Diana arrived in Colombo the day we left Ceylon don't you? It is just Ken's luck isn't it? The poor old fool is nearly frantic.'

Naomi later found out Diana Fitzherbert-Wright's side of the story and recounted: 'She had arrived in Bombay and saw the *Glorious* finally depart for the Red Sea as her ship sailed into port. That very much "scuppered" her ideas.'

Meanwhile, Naomi and her companions had reached Luxor and also visited Aswan. Naomi commented on the tombs and the Valley of the Kings: 'I was much more impressed by these than by the pyramids at Cairo.'

Roy was now at least on his way back to join her, although *Glorious* still had a long way to go before she reached the Mediterranean. The aircraft carrier was flying its aircraft on reconnaissance flights throughout the return journey.

On 3 January, Gladiators from *Glorious* gave a fine exhibition of aerobatics just before noon and *Hobart* left them soon after. Then two days later Roy made a reconnaissance flight to the familiar land and seascape of the Socotra area.

The ship's company was getting excited at the thought of returning to Malta. Roy wrote:

Many miles are we closer, my darling, and altho' we are seventeen days off the chosen land, I'm getting so excited. I tried my new engine this evening. It went awfully well. I'm so pleased.

I've given Bobby [Dundas] a hell of a ticking off for not paying more attention to his machine. He's been terribly slack and it's only been OK because of Ken and me on several occasions.

Tich dearest, there are rumours of six weeks ashore at Hal Far with ten days' leave.

Next day he wrote:

Still no news at all darling – but we certainly are pressing ever westwards which is marvellous. Yesterday I flew ahead of the ship for some hundred-odd miles and just before turning to come back I waved to you and said that I'd be seeing you soon. It was a lovely feeling, knowing that every turn of the screw is bringing us closer and closer.

Tomorrow we reach Aden and then up the Red Sea. Last night I was DO [duty officer] and had to sleep in the hangars. As my servant had put my bed in the wrong one, I had to sleep on bare board and my cap.

Glorious reached Aden on 7 January 1940:

Aden at last and oh so pleased to get your letters altho' so old. You know, everyone says how lousy to be an NO's wife – but from all your letters I should say you have by far the best end of the stick.

You have been, as you say, very social, going to parties, dances, dinners and now at Aswan and yet husband has got his work.

Glorious's new Commander Flying, Commander J.B. Heath, joined the ship at Aden, to take over as Guy Willoughby's relief. He was one of the most experienced Fleet Air Arm officers in the Navy, having qualified in No. 1 Naval Pilots' Course as far back as 1924, and having been one of the first naval officers, as opposed to RAF, to command a flight, 447, in *Glorious*. He was a gentle, approachable and pleasant man, much liked by Roy's colleagues.

Days later *Glorious* reached Port Said, the entrance to the Suez Canal. As the ship steamed up the Suez Canal, Roy wrote:

Well we are in the Canal and cracking along. Dearest I'm absolutely living on air and I wish the ship had wings. Sorry my writing is so odd but the ship is shaking terribly as if we were going fairly fast. I hope to Malta. I'm still sleeping on the quarterdeck even tho' it's freezing just to say good-night to the stars.

Splash recalled: 'We steamed up to the Suez Canal and on to Alex. Naomi and Tiny were still there – the latter working in the cipher office at Naval HQ so she knew our movements but had to be discreet about them.'

Roy wrote to Naomi prior to arrival at Alexandria:

Billy darling, the whole ship is incredibly end of term-ish and so excited.

We passed Suez this evening and Mita and Marina came off in a speedboat to see Jakes and Bobby – but they'd already flown ashore to Ismalia so the two girls dashed back again. I'm going ashore tomorrow to see if you are at our rendez-vous.

On 17 January, *Glorious* finally reached Malta and 812 Squadron aircraft flew on to Hal Far.

Naomi had arrived back in Alexandria after her Luxor trip to find a letter from Roy saying 'Coming back from the Red Sea to Malta'. She recalled:

Us wives made a mad dash to get to Malta, sending frantic letters, packed up and headed out in a troop ship paying 15/- each.

As we got there, we earnestly watched aircraft circling over our ship as we approached, the Swordfish were dipping their wings to us wives – we knew the planes were flown by our husbands but not knowing which aircraft was your husband's, waved anyway. The ship arrived two days later. It was a dash to get our Roy House flat ready, food and drink, and in the end we only had a short time as Roy's first words were 'We are off to England in three days time'.

Diana Fitzherbert-Wright eventually returned from India and we lent her and Ken Gurr our by now well stocked up apartment. He died not much longer after that in UK. So it was nice that they had the chance to be together.

In the final months after Roy left *Glorious*, even the rank and file would be glad to get away from the aircraft carrier because she was no longer 'a happy ship'. A ditty at this time was:

> *Side! Side!* Glorious *ship's side!*
> *The Skipper looks on it with pride,*
> *He'd have a blue fit if he saw any 'git'*
> *Leave a mark on his* Glorious *ship's side!*

> *This is my story, this is my song,*
> *We've been in commission too bloody long;*
> *So roll on the* Nelson*, the Rodney, the* Hood
> *For this flat-topped bastard is no bloody good!*

When *Glorious* finally left Malta, the aircraft carrier left a small legacy which helped save the island. Left behind were four crated Sea Gladiators, in storage at Kalafrana, where they remained until pressed into service in the defence of the island when the Italians attacked six months later, on 10 June. The three surviving machines – one was shot down – became famous as *Faith*, *Hope* and *Charity*.

CHAPTER 10

Back to Wartime Sussex and Hampshire

In January, 1940, Roy ended his commission with *Glorious* and was recalled back to England for a new posting. Splash Carver was with him: 'On arrival in Malta we received appointments for about ten aircrew officers who had been in *Glorious* for some time to return to UK forthwith to join new squadrons forming up for the new carrier *Illustrious*.'

Roy and Naomi, together with Splash and Tiny, sailed from Malta to Marseille on the Egyptian liner SS *Mohamed Ali el Kebir* whilst another 300 officers and men embarked on the liner SS *Duchess of Atholl*, by coincidence the sister ship of the liner Roy was on when he returned to Britain from Canada. Naomi remembered their voyage: 'The trip started very calm with a blue sky and so we drank and relaxed in a merry way. Then a storm blew up and I felt awful. Roy said a kipper would help – it didn't.'

Splash Carver recalled:

The European winter 1939–40 was a bitter one and at Marseille there was ice around the edge of the harbour locks. Having been sweating in a carrier in the tropics only a week or two before, we all felt extra chilly.

We waited for about twenty-four hours in Marseille for a troop train. It was pretty chaotic and nobody knew what was going on or what route we were taking. We all got on a troop train bound for Paris, but once there, the onward leg to the Channel ports was delayed and overcrowded so Roy and I managed to achieve a break of twenty-four hours and the four of us put up in a hotel and had a nice evening out at a show and dance, continuing our journey next day.

This was only weeks before the fall of that city to the Germans. They stayed in a small hotel in the Concorde area and had one of their most memorable weekends together, visiting the cafes, the Tuileries Gardens and Champs-Elysées boulevard. That evening they explored the Parisian night life.

Splash Carver continued: 'Of course, Roy and I were in uniform and I can't remember what on earth happened to all our heavy baggage which must have been quite bulky as we had all been overseas for at least a year.'

They were coming home after almost one and a half years and the weather was bitterly cold. Britain, like the rest of Europe, was suffering the coldest spell since 1895. Temperatures of 20–25 degrees Fahrenheit below freezing (minus 12 degrees Celsius) were common.

Naomi recalled: 'We were able to look at war-time Britain for the first time, the atmosphere was considerably different from when we had left in 1938.' Rationing had just started in January 1940 with bacon, sugar and tea being the first items. Meat followed in March and, as one newspaper reported at the time: 'Rabbit has suddenly hopped to the top of the menu in many British households.' Leslie remembered whale meat, powdered egg, cardboard-grey bread and 'sausages like sawdust' were the everyday fare.

Trench shelters were being dug in city parks; brick and concrete shelters were in the streets. City dwellers with a patch of garden were shown how to build Anderson air raid shelters. The threat of war was so great that many children and mothers with babies had been evacuated from the cities in case there were gas attacks or air raids.

Ways were being sought to speed up the supply of women workers to the munitions' factories. That month would also see a pilot from the Women's Section of the Air Transport Auxiliary (ATA) deliver the first aeroplane from factory to depot.

People were being advised they should take cod liver oil to help them see better in the blackout. Music was changing from the earlier cocky 'We're Going to Hang Out the Washing on the Siegfried Line' to tunes such as Gracie Field's 'Wish Me Luck As You Wave Me Goodbye'.

As soon as he could, Roy contacted the Naval Assistant to 2nd Sea Lord – who was responsible for officers' appointments – to register his return, ask for some leave and find out about his next posting. Under normal circumstances he would have expected some six weeks' foreign leave. Because of the war, he was appointed for duty only two weeks after his return.

First, however, Roy had some leave in Shaldon with Naomi and the rest of the Falkner family. The fishing village had also changed due to the war. The couple's first impressions were of people carrying gas masks and boxes, of the blackout and wardens.

Teignmouth and Shaldon sea-fronts were fenced and wired off and anti-tank posts installed. An anti-submarine boom and net were placed across the entrance to the harbour, and the Shaldon-Teignmouth bridge was defended in case of invasion, with tank traps and concrete pill boxes. Even local inhabitants were prevented from going on the beach; just a small gap remained in order to file down to the ferry. Gun emplacements were on the Ness which was a tangle of wire. Their arrival coincided with air-raid warnings and eerie sirens.

Across the estuary, in Teignmouth the pier was divided to stop the enemy landing on it. The boat building firm, Morgan Giles, which had been struggling to sell and build yachts up until the war, was now receiving lucrative government orders for the construction of motor torpedo boats.

As soon as they entered Penrhyn, Roy's mother, Grace, wanted to know all about the war. Roy did not want to run any risk through 'loose talk' about *Glorious* and spoke about the good times they had in the Mediterranean, the absence of any black-out or rationing, and the fine weather. Of the whereabouts of the ship, of course, nothing could be said.

His father, Sydney, had volunteered in the Shaldon Local Defence Volunteers (LDV) – Home Guard – and been appointed a sergeant. He was called 'Grand-dad' by the other volunteers. The LDV was based in a shop in Shaldon and was under the command of Major 'Biggy' Bigg-Wither whose previous military experience included the Burma Railway Volunteer Corps.

In the early days, Sydney and the other Home Guard volunteers had no rifles and would practise drill using brooms. They would also frequently go up on the Ness and practise defensive actions. Grace thought the local Home Guard was a joke and disapproved strongly of their activities, saying: 'They are adults being no better than playing like children.'

Roy and Naomi had many a leisurely walk in the countryside and relaxed drinks huddled up in their favourite Shaldon and Stoke-in-Teign Head pubs, joking with Snowy and the other old fishermen and farmer characters. On one day, they went on an excursion to visit the fifteen-year-old Leslie at her boarding school, Cheltenham Ladies' College. Leslie recalled: 'Roy and Naomi had come back overland from Egypt – they were dreadfully tired and had just been very ill from influenza.' Leslie herself had just recovered from scarlet fever.

Naomi recalled 'Leslie had changed very little in the two years we had last seen her. We took her out to a hotel in Cheltenham for a good feed.' Leslie's house mistress thought Roy and Naomi were a lovely couple and wrote to Grace after their visit to say so.

A fortnight after arriving in the UK, Roy received his next appointment to HMS *Peregrine*, the RN Air Station at Ford near Littlehampton in Sussex. He was posted in February 1940 to 819 Squadron which had been established only the month before with Ginger Hale as CO. The squadron was destined for HMS *Illustrious*, the first of the new class of armoured aircraft carriers, which was due to replace *Glorious* in the Mediterranean Fleet in the near future. Little did the aircrew of 819 Squadron realise it at the time, but their role was to prepare for a major strike in the Mediterranean to destroy the Italian Fleet, at Taranto.

The commanding officers of the newly formed squadrons were invited to hand-pick pilots and observers who had experience for this forthcoming operation. The men of HMS *Glorious* were the first choice for Ginger Hale, as back in 1939 her then captain, Lumley Lyster, had already drawn up a draft plan to attack Taranto in the event of war. Roy was headhunted for this job as Hale had known him well when they were both serving in Swordfish squadrons with *Glorious*.

Ginger Hale recollected: 'Roy left *Glorious* at the same time as I did, and then came to my new squadron, 819, when it formed at RNAS Ford in Jan/Feb 1940.'

The first to arrive at 819 Squadron were 'Tiffy' Torrens-Spence and 'Cliff' Clifford on 14 January 1940, followed by Lt G.A. Carline a week later. James Stewart-Moore, Alfie Sutton and Bobby Going joined three weeks later.

Roy joined on 12 February along with the CO and lieutenant pilots Slater, Hamilton, Morford, Garten-Stone and Sub Lts Skelton and Lea. That same day observers were appointed, including Splash Carver, Scarlett, Haworth and Collett, and petty officer air observers Bullivant and Hyde. No. 819 Squadron was building up to form a formidable team of crack aviators.

The squadron was to be equipped with twelve Fairey Swordfish Mk I aircraft and crews drawn from not just *Glorious* but also HMS *Ark Royal*. During the first week or two, time was spent collecting aircraft.

Roy and the squadron settled down at Ford airfield, which was situated on flat land in the lee of the South Downs. The air station was well equipped with workshop and hangar facilities, together with buildings dating back to the First World War. There was also a complex of station buildings and Nissen hut accommodation. Also based there, were a number of resident squadrons which formed the Observer School with its Sharks, Osprey, Walruses and Proctors, and the Air Target Training Unit.

Not far away was the RAF Station Tangmere, with its Spitfires and Hurricanes. Naomi recalled: 'In the evenings the RAF types would often drink in the same pubs as the Fleet Air Arm chaps. The RAF types tended to have fast cars and handle-bar moustaches.'

If there was a subtle difference between the RAF officers and the Fleet Air Arm officers, there was a huge difference in their aircraft and in the lavish benefits the RAF enjoyed. Mike Crosley, a Fleet Air Arm pilot, later noted:

The RAF were complete professionals. The most impressive part of the RAF was not its flying, which was barely average by Fleet Air Arm standards, but its back-up organisation. Aircrews were briefed an hour before each flight, not a haphazard five or ten minutes.

Flying clothing was of luxurious standard. We normally flew in battledress uniform as there was nothing else. The RAF flying clothing had pockets for everything and each pilot had a magnificent pair of black leather flying boots which, if they were shot down, would readily convert into tough, unobtrusive walking shoes. The Mae West was of a more recent pattern and had a dye marker, torch and whistle, and could be automatically inflated by pulling a toggle.

Besides all this, the runways were double the width and nearly half as long again as the longest [Fleet Air Arm] runway, making formation landings and take-offs safe and easy and with no strain on the aircraft brakes. Life was very easy and relaxed compared with life aboard ship.

However, for some reason, we in the Fleet Air Arm, struggling with last year's model, were not in the least jealous of the RAF. We seemed to take it for granted that we should be the poor relation. In fact, we thought ourselves rather special being able to cope without it.

Air Gunner Harry Phillips, 819 Squadron TAG, recorded:

Once 819 was formed up, we were 'crewed up' and normally as TAGs, we flew with the same people not in the same aircraft. The observers seemed to 'float' a bit for some reason. We were kept in training in Walrus aircraft until our Stringbags arrived.

His flying log book records: '12 Feb. 1940 to 1 March 1940 – flying Walruses and Sharks on land and sea navigation, then 4 March our new Swordfish arrive, immediately night flying.'

Also among the familiar faces for Roy at Ford was Robin Kilroy who had been 823 Squadron CO on *Glorious* in 1938.

Splash Carver recalled:

After a week or two's leave in icebound England, Roy, I and the others joined 819 Squadron at RN Air Station Ford destined for *Illustrious*. Several other ex-*Glorious* aircrews were with us – John Hale as CO, 'Tiffy' Torrens-Spence and Edward Clifford my pilot in *Glorious* for nearly two years.

We shared Ford airfield with Alan Cobham's aircraft company – they were on the opposite side of the field, and I never walked as far as their outfit.

On 21 Feb. 40 was my first flight with the CO, Lt Cdr Hale, being my pilot. I was his senior observer until I left in August 1940. The programme for the squadron's formation took a couple of months. We went to an airfield at Stranraer for armament practice.

Roy was to fly with old colleagues but his air gunner was new. Air Gunner A.E. 'Dickie' Sweet recalled:

I was a 'makie-learnie' TAG with 819 Squadron when it formed at Ford. 'Sunny' Hale was our CO. The majority of us TAGs were never in the air before. We had to build up the squadron from scratch. I flew as an air gunner in 819 from Jan–May 1940 at Ford where I flew with Lt Baker-Falkner during training.

The situation was also confusing for the ground crew. E.W. Whitley, an 819 Squadron air fitter, recalled:

> The squadron was made up of twelve pilots, twelve observers, twelve TAGs , twelve AM(E), twelve AM(A), along with some electricians, armourers, store bashers and the like.
> The pilots and observers were all straight Navy, the NCOs were RAF and the mechanics mostly ex-seamen and stokers who had changed horses as we had done.
> I was a RAF apprentice at Halton. Early in 1939 I transferred to the FAA and went to the clearance camp at Puckpool on the Isle of Wight. In January 1940 I was sent to join 819 Squadron at Ford with three other young air fitters. I was most disappointed to find I was to work on Swordfish as the training had been on Spitfires and Blenheims.
> It was our job to run the petrol bowsers with their wrist-breaking Lister engines. Three years' technical training to be a garage attendant! Eventually of course we were let loose on the aircraft, painting the squadron letters on the side and applying lanolin to brace wires.

When Roy and Naomi arrived, they set up base first in a guest house near Bognor Regis, and then in Felpham at the South Downs Hotel, and later at the George Inn. Naomi recalled: 'Then we stayed at a cottage owned by Flanagan and Allen, of the Crazy Gang fame.'

Alfie Sutton added:

> Soon after we formed No. 819 Squadron we were told by Dennis Boyd, who was destined to be our CO in *Illustrious*, that our first operations would be covering the laying of the northern minefield.
> We would also be attacking the German Fleet at Kiel and Wilhelmshaven, going over in Swordfish at about 10,000–12,000 ft. This gave us a certain amount of pride, but also a very considerable shiver of apprehension, because they were notorious for having one of the most strongly defended fortresses in the world.

By 28 February, Acting Lts Hearle and Osborn, and PO Marsh had all joined the squadron bringing it to full strength. By early March, all twelve aircraft had been collected.

The situation in Europe was continuing to deteriorate. According to the 819 Squadron diary or 'line book' of 1940: 'The CO and some of the others in the squadron were called upon to leave Ford for a while to do "some work" with RAF fighters.' One of the explanations why it was called a 'line book' was because a line was written each time about some squadron misdemeanour made by aircrew members of the squadron.

On his return, Hale was ordered to instigate intensive high-level bombing practice for an impending operation against the German Fleet. So, on 9 March, Roy flew in formation with the rest of the squadron north to the icebound RAF West Freugh armament training airfield in Wigtownshire, Scotland, for an anticipated three weeks' high-level bombing practice on the RAF ranges.

Splash Carver recalled the continued familiar or relaxed atmosphere of the training:

'Most of March 1940 was spent up at RAF West Freugh near Stranraer. The wives came up and stayed at the local inn.'

Alfie Sutton added: 'I was very newly married and my wife travelled by train with Naomi. Peggy remembers Naomi telling her to take every possible opportunity to be with her husband, as these moments were golden and not to be missed.'

The wives were all pleased to meet up again after last seeing each other in Alexandria the previous year. Naomi and Roy stayed at the King's Arms in Stranraer: 'We went up to an air station on the west coast near Stranraer in the freeze up. As soon as we all arrived, us wives and our aircrew husbands celebrated a traditional but rather late Scottish New Year.'

Stranraer, the largest town in south-west Scotland, was famous as the ferry port for Larne in Northern Ireland. Stranraer and its surrounding area saw a significant amount of activity during the Second World War as it became a focus for anti U-boat work.

Alfie Sutton elaborated:

We married people all travelled daily from the King's Arms to nearby West Freugh, where we were practising bombing on the RAF Ranges.

Our job was to practise high-level bombing at 10,000 ft, the Swordfish's ceiling with a bomb load, prior to attacking the German fleet at Kiel and Wilhelmshaven.

Wilhelmshaven was a tempting target for both the Admiralty and the RAF. At its naval docks at that time there were three capital ships including *Lützow* and *Admiral Scheer*, both undergoing extensive refits. There was also the, as yet uncommissioned, battleship *Tirpitz*, launched the previous year and undergoing machinery trials in the fitting-out basin.

Ginger Hale must have given a detailed briefing to Roy and the other squadron officers about preparing for their high-level bombing of Wilhelmshaven – a briefing which was also echoed by their sister squadron, 815, which was also being ordered to prepare for the attack on the naval docks.

Charles Lamb, a young pilot in 815 Squadron who Roy had last seen pre-war in boxing competitions, recalled the briefing speech about Wilhelmshaven from his new CO, Lt Cdr Robin Kilroy who stated that there was one target which had been brought within their reach which no other aircraft other than the Swordfish could possibly attack with the same chance of success – and that was the German port of Wilhelmshaven. He elaborated that it was the enemy's main harbour, and that an attack from the sea by shipping was out of the question, and the only attack they would be anticipating from the air would be high-level bombing. He then went on to say that they were going to make an unholy mess of Germany's main maritime stronghold, and that they could do it without much difficulty and – if skillful – perhaps without loss.

The Navy School of Photography has made a scale model of Wilhelmshaven, from accurate charts and from photographs by pilots from RAF Benson. From these 812 Squadron aircrew would be able to pinpoint all the ack-ack positions, and the positions of all balloons.

The model will be kept out of sight, under lock and key, available to the squadron alone and the CO expected every officer to familiarise himself with it, until he knew each building surrounding the harbour and the position of every balloon cable.

Both 819 and 815 Squadrons began a round of intense training for the Wilhelmshaven strike. For Roy's squadron this involved endless practice at the high-level bombing ranges at West Freugh until they felt confident that the squadron could accurately bomb the enemy naval docks and its warships.

Air fitter Whitley recalled:

There was much bombing and gunnery practice. I remember the aircraft dinghies arriving and spending the Easter weekend packing twelve, one for each aircraft. The first took five hours, the last just fifty-five minutes!

The only light moment was when a CO2 bottle was inadvertently released and zoomed off round the hangar like a berserk black bee... fortunately without damaging anything.

The first of my many Swordfish flights was at West Freugh, a series of climbs up to 10,000 ft and dives on to a target in Luce bay. I tried to watch but the G-force on pull-out defeated me and I spent that part of all the subsequent dives on the cockpit floor.

Alfie Sutton continued:

That first winter of the war was extremely cold for us Mediterranean pilots. Our flying kit was all right for ordinary flying but it had not been designed for flying at a height of 10,000–12,000 feet in a hard winter. We wore woollens, balaclava helmets and anything else we could put on top of our flying kit to try to keep warm.

When we were bombing we lay on our stomachs, looking through a bombing sight, and had to work a 'Mickey Mouse' bomb-selector switch. You couldn't afford to fumble – you had to do it right, as it would be used in action – but it was very difficult when your hands were so cold.

One of the new inexperienced pilots to arrive then was Charles Friend who recalled:

I, a midshipman (A), together with H.E. Rumble, another midshipman, was in a squadron composed otherwise completely of senior lieutenants including Baker-Falkner. When he arrived to 819 at West Freugh in the throes of deep winter, I remember 'Pinky' Haworth sitting in the crew room knitting a long, long woollen scarf, he said 'for the Finns' who were at the time, fighting the Russians. What a strange and wonderful war it was!

After the heat of North Africa, Roy's health was affected almost immediately on his return. Even though he wore his 'bum freezer' flying jacket and thick sheepskin boots, the open cockpit led to ear ache – especially as Leslie later recalled: 'At that time Roy did not like wearing helmets whilst flying.'

It was only a short time before he also started to have kidney trouble and was diagnosed with haematuris. The Senior Medical Officer informed him that he had no alternative and that Roy was immediately grounded from flying. On 28 March, he was sent back down to the Royal Naval Hospital at Haslar in Gosport to recover.

Haslar was the main hospital for the sick and wounded of the Royal Navy in peace and wartime. It was old, having been built about 1745 as the first hospital for Royal Naval sailors, and with its open courtyard reminded Roy of the college at Greenwich. By the time Roy arrived, Haslar was preparing for impending British casualties and was anticipating 300 wounded a day.

The squadron and the wives had returned south to Ford two days after Roy was hospitalised. The squadron's mission to bomb the German Fleet at Wilhelmshaven was postponed pending an attack firstly by the RAF.

Group Headquarters decided to send a squadron of RAF Beauforts in the end, and 812 Squadron never discovered what happened to them because not one of them returned.

Alfie Sutton remembered:

Luckily for us, the RAF attacked first and the extremely heavy losses they sustained caused our attack to be abandoned.

We spent three weeks at West Freugh, but it turned out to be a typical example of how one can be trained for the wrong thing. We then returned to Ford.

Whilst Roy remained in hospital, world events were moving at breakneck speed. Hitler ordered the invasion of Norway and Denmark. At 8 am on 7 April, an invasion fleet was sighted by a British reconnaissance aircraft off the coast of Denmark. In the early afternoon a force of twelve Blenheim aircraft attacked the enemy warships, but failed to do any damage. With the knowledge that the German Navy was at sea in force, Admiral Forbes and the Home Fleet sailed from Scapa Flow at 20.15 that same evening towards Norway.

Shortly after mid-afternoon the next day, London warned the Norwegian government that a German attack was imminent. The next morning Admiral Forbes, leading the Home Fleet battle force, ordered some destroyers up to Narvik 'to make certain that no enemy troops land'.

On 9 April, German sea and airborne forces descended on Norway. Oslo, Bergen, Trondheim, Stavanger, and Narvik were invaded. At the same time German forces entered Denmark with little resistance. The Danish Army was not in a position to challenge German forces, and was totally unprepared for war. By the end of the day, Germany controlled the whole of Denmark but Norway was to fight on.

During the capture of Trondheim, *Admiral Hipper* and her destroyer escort attacked the destroyer HMS *Glowworm*. The severely damaged *Glowworm* rammed the *Hipper* before the destroyer blew up and sank.

While Narvik was being occupied, *Renown* and Admiral Whitworth's force of nine destroyers encountered *Gneisenau* and *Scharnhorst* en route to their patrolling position in the upper North Sea. The sighting took place at 3.30 am, and the battle that resulted, fought in heavy seas, caused the two German ships to flee northward after the *Gneisenau*'s main armament control system had been put out of action.

The first of two Battles of Narvik commenced on 10 April. In the early hours the German cruiser *Königsberg* was dive-bombed and sunk by sixteen Blackburn Skuas flying from Hatston to the Orkney Islands. It was the first time a major warship had been sunk by air attack. The second battle for Narvik took place on Saturday 13 April when the Germans lost eight destroyers and a submarine which was sunk by one of *Warspite*'s Swordfish.

The first Allied troops landed for the defence of Norway on Sunday. That same day, *Glorious*, under the command of D'Oyly-Hughes, was ordered to return from the Mediterranean. She arrived in the Clyde on the south-west coast of Scotland four days later. *Glorious* was ordered to retain one fighter squadron and one Swordfish squadron for her protection so the other squadrons, 812 and 825, were flown off. The space in *Glorious* was to be filled with RAF Hurricanes urgently needed in Norway and to keep space available to rescue Gloster Gladiators for the return voyage.

Titch Harding recollected that there was a: '...signal from the Admiralty to disembark TSR squadrons to make room for RAF Gladiators trapped in North Norway. Commander Flying Guy Willoughby flipped a coin and we in 812 Squadron flew ashore to Prestwick.'

A detachment of 819 Squadron under Ginger Hale, along with Clifford, Garton-Stone, Slater, Osborn and Hamilton, were temporarily loaned to Prestwick near Glasgow to fly these RAF fighters on to *Glorious*. As *Glorious*'s Commander Flying J.B. Heath said: 'All old hands rushed in for the job and were ferried back to shore again.'

On 23 April *Glorious* sailed from Scapa towards Norway with *Ark Royal*, and an escort of destroyers, forming the first carrier task force in the Royal Navy's history. Its sixty-nine aircraft formed the largest number of aircraft assembled in the annals of the Fleet Air Arm to date.

Experienced 819 Squadron aircrew continued to be urgently re-assigned elsewhere while Roy was still away on sick leave. Splash Carver, along with Scarlett and Howarth, was transferred to another front-line squadron.

Splash Carver recalled:

In April, the war started to hot up with the German invasion of Norway. I was appointed away to another Swordfish squadron, 815, also destined for *Illustrious*, which was working with Coastal Command from RAF Bircham Newton, Norfolk. Our main task was the carrying of magnetic mines in the Ems estuary which for various reasons we did at night.

Roy came out of hospital after four weeks. Naomi had been staying nearby, worried sick for him. She was torn between wishing Roy well and hoping he was unable to fly again. Roy made little mention to his family of his time at Haslar. However, four years later in a letter to Naomi he referred to his hospitalisation as 'enforced incarceration'.

Alfie Sutton recalled matters were difficult for Naomi and Roy after he came out of hospital and was convalescing at their flat: 'My wife remembers Naomi telling her that they had been turned out of their lodgings in Littlehampton as the landlady considered it improper to laze around spending so much time in bed!'

Roy was declared fit again for duty on 3 May, whilst 819 Squadron was on seven days' leave. The CO and his detachment returned four days later from their RAF secondment ferrying fighters to *Glorious*. At the same time the last 10,000 British and French troops were evacuated from Namsos and Andalsnes following the failure to hold central Norway.

On 10 May the war situation further deteriorated dramatically. In the early hours, ninety-two German divisions commenced their invasion of Belgium, France, Holland and Luxembourg. The Belgian defensive line, Fort Eben-Emael, had been seized by German paratroopers using gliders, allowing their forces to cross the Albert Canal. That evening Chamberlain tendered his resignation to the King George VI and formally recommended Winston Churchill as his successor. Leslie and Naomi recalled: 'The next day, we were all cheered by the appointment of Winston Churchill as the new Prime Minister.'

Churchill declared in his first speech to the House of Commons:

We are in the preliminary stage of one of the greatest battles in history, that we are in action in many points in Norway and in Holland, that we have to be prepared in the Mediterranean, that the air battle is continuous and that many preparations have to be made at home...I would say to the House, as I said to those who have joined this Government: 'I have nothing to offer but blood, toil, tears and sweat'.

The British Expeditionary Force, under General Lord Gort, had been defending the Belgium–French border since just after war was declared. The BEF managed to save the

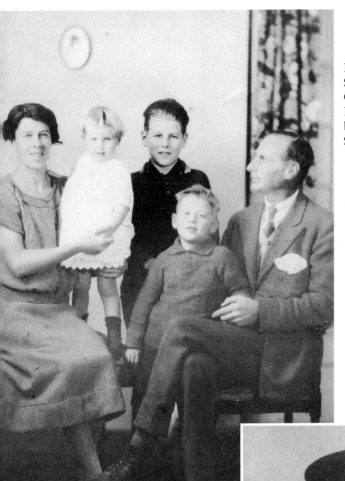

Falkner family at home in Saanich on Vancouver Island in Canada, 1926 (Grace holding Leslie, B-F standing behind his brother Harry and father, Sydney). (*Author's collection*)

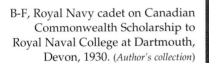

B-F, Royal Navy cadet on Canadian Commonwealth Scholarship to Royal Naval College at Dartmouth, Devon, 1930. (*Author's collection*)

B-F on parade leading the third group of cadets at Sunday Divisions, Dartmouth, 1931. (*Author's collection*)

Dartmouth sports day, 1932. B-F competing with Robert Boddington and Donald McEwen. (*Author's collection*)

HMS *Kent* in Malta while enroute to Hong Kong, summer 1934. (*Author's collection*)

HMS *Kent* gunroom midshipmen, 1934–35 (B-F top row second from the left). (*...ker-Falkner family collection*)

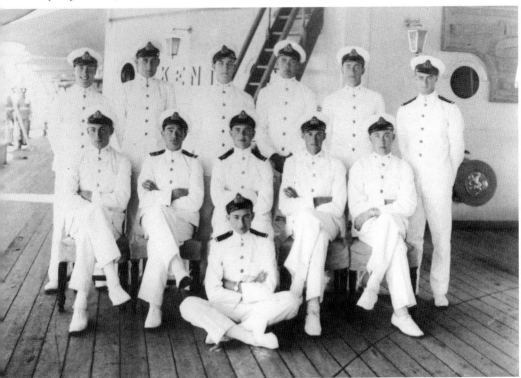

Hawker Osprey aircraft of 803 Squadron, photographed while *HMS Eagle* was on the China Station. The RE shows *HMS Eagle* herse... 1935. (R.L. Ellis, from the R. Harbord collection)

Sub Lieutenants course at Greenwich, 1937 (B-F top row, third from the right). (*Baker-Falkner family collection*)

Naomi Lord, B-F's wife.
(*Baker-Falkner family collection*)

B-F with his red MG sports car
during No 1 FTS pilot training course
1937–38. (*Baker-Falkner family collection*)

B-F in dress uniform at his
Rue d'Argens apartment
in Malta, 1938.
(*Author's collection*)

Fairey Swordfish Mk I K5933 of HMS *Glorious* in silvered prewar paint scheme flying over the Mediterranean. (*Author's collection*)

Aerial photograph by B-F of Valletta and the Grand Harbour in Malta, 1938. (*Author's collection*)

HMS *Glorious* whilst on summer exercises in Gibraltar, 1939. (*Author's collection*)

'Moose' Martyn, Ginger Murray and other FAA and RAF officers relaxing in HMS *Glorious* wardroom, 1939. (*Martyn family collection*)

F at the Rock Hotel, Gibraltar, 1939. (*Peter Pagett collection*)

Beard growing competition of HMS *Glorious* aircrews during the search for *Graf Spee* in the Indian Ocean, 1939 (B-F middle row second from right). (*Titch Harding collection*)

812 Squadron Swordfish in formation, including B-F's 'F for Freddy'. (*Titch Harding collection*)

B-F's two 812 Squadron observers, 'Pip' Philips (second from left back row) and Bruce Hawkes (fifth from left behind Titch Harding and Dick Curry) along with 'Snowball' Edwards, Puppy Kennard and other aircrew at RAF North Coates, 1940. Photograph later used by the *Daily Sketch* in its historic FAA Taranto Raid headlines. (*Titch Harding collection*)

812 Squadron senior pilot, Lieutenant 'Titch' Harding, and Swordfish pilot Lieutenant 'Shorty' Shaw. (*Cliff Kindell collection*)

Anthony Clayton with Rex, B-F's pet Alsatian and 812 Squadron mascot, at the height of the Battle of Britain, 1940. (*Cliff Kindell collection*)

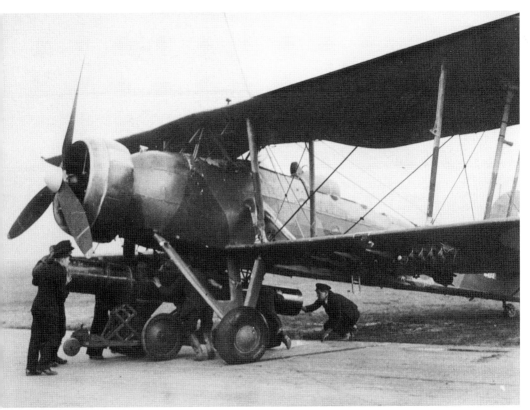

ight camouflaged 812 Squadron Swordfish with extra drum fuel tank in observer seat, preparing
r strikes off the Dutch coast, 1940. (*Cliff Kindell collection*)

F preparing to take off for an operation over the Low Countries in Swordfish 'F for Freddy', 1940.
uthor's collection)

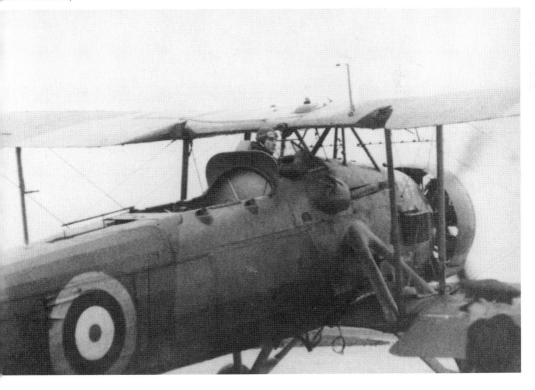

825 Squadron Swordfish 'G5P' from HMS *Glorious* captured by Germans at an airfield, 20 May 1940. (*Author's collection*)

812 crew room at RAF North Coates, 1940. (*Cliff Kindell collection*)

Lieutenant R S Baker-Falkner portrait whilst stationed at Machrihanish. (*Author's collection*)

HMS *Victorious* with *Albacore* and *Swordfish* ranged on deck, late in 1941. (*A.H. Atkins*)

Belgians for a time before being pushed back towards Calais and Dunkirk.

The German forces in the west deployed 2,700 tanks, ninety-four army divisions and 3,300 aircraft in an onslaught against the BEF and its allies. The Dutch Army capitulated on 15 May.

The next day, Churchill flew to Paris, where he found the French Government already burning its secret files and preparing for an evacuation of the capital. Churchill asked the French commanders 'Where is the strategic reserve?' The response was 'There is none'. Later, Churchill described hearing this as the single most shocking moment in his life.

With a growing sense of urgency and knowledge that life as they knew it could be disrupted for a very long time, Roy and the other 819 Squadron members made their final preparations to leave loved ones. James Stewart-Moore recalled:

> I was getting married at Clymping church near the station at Ford on 18th May 1940, a Saturday, having become engaged on the previous Wednesday to my wife, who was then in Ireland. She had to get a permit to go to Britain, and I spent all Thursday with the station padre bicycling round the See of Chichester in the mystic search for a special licence.
>
> Tiffy was the best man at my wedding. All the squadron and most of the station officers came along. The officers of the squadron kindly gave me a silver cigarette box on which their signatures were engraved. I see that B-F signed up. But the list makes sad reading: they were all very likeable chaps, and so many of them were killed soon after in the war.

Five days later, on 22 May, Roy was taken aback when ordered by Ginger to leave 819 Squadron at a time when the Low Country and Norwegian Campaigns had worsened for the Allies. As Ginger recalled: 'He was withdrawn with some other pilots and observers to replace casualties in *Ark Royal*, which had lost a number of her aircrews operating off Norway.'

The 819 Squadron diary recorded that day: 'Lieutenants Slater, Osborn, Hearle, and Baker-Falkner were transferred to Lee-on-Solent.'

After their farewells, Roy heard that six of the 819 Squadron aircraft were to fly over to Detling, a field in Kent, to operate across the southern end of the North Sea to lay mines off the Dutch and Belgium coasts before their preparations to join HMS *Illustrious*.

Roy may have been disappointed to be forced to leave his new squadron so soon but the experienced 819 Squadron aircrew from *Glorious* days were in much demand as the war situation deteriorated further. They were desperately needed elsewhere in the Fleet Air Arm, and even in the RAF.

Alfie Sutton recalled:

> I didn't stay in 819 very long but was shuffled around by telephone appointments over the next four months, including with an RAF Hampden bomber squadron in Lossiemouth Scotland where I taught them ship recognition and to fly with the leader to prevent him attacking the *Rodney* and *Nelson* instead of the *Scharnhorst* and *Gneisenau*, and a FAA Albacore (deluxe Swordfish) squadron based in Norfolk laying magnetic mines up the Ems estuary by night. All warships tended to look the same to bomber pilots.

Whilst Roy awaited his new posting and, realising that the wartime situation was getting more chaotic, he and Naomi rented rooms in the Victoria Hotel just off the seafront in Lee-on-Solent, not far from the Fleet Air Arm headquarters at HMS *Daedalus*. They urgently needed a settled base as it was clear Roy would be appointed for operational duties any day. Staying at the Victoria Hotel had one consolation if the advancing Germans started to bomb Lee-on-Solent – it was renowned at that time for storing the only fire engine in the area.

Splash Carver recalled:

I don't think Roy stayed with 819 for long as I seem to remember he joined up with 812 again at RAF North Coates. 812 Squadron were also busy minelaying by night and escorting east coast convoys. It was during this time that Roy earned his DSC.

CHAPTER 11

Into Battle from Lincolnshire to Dunkirk

In May 1940, the international situation was getting increasingly desperate. British and French troops were being beaten back towards Dunkirk and Calais by German panzer divisions.

Roy's first brush with the enemy was on the horizon. Officially, his next posting was to 763 Reserve Squadron, awaiting redeployment to an aircraft carrier. This pool squadron was based at St Peter's aerodrome at St Hellier in Jersey, and was an out station under the books of HMS *Kestrel* (RN Air Station Worthy Down, near Winchester).

Roy was formally due to commence his appointment on 27 May – on paper alone, he remained on the books of 763 Squadron until 25 June. However, events were rushing much faster than the Admiralty's army of desk generals and it would be only a matter of days before he was allocated to a front-line squadron.

L/A Kenneth King, an air gunner, recalled:

> I served in 763 Squadron and remember we started to 'form up' at RNAS Worthy Down in Hampshire on December 15, 1939. Eventually we had six Swordfish and six Albacore aircraft and I believe the commanding officer was Lt Cdr P.L. Mortimer.
>
> On March 11, 1940 the Squadron was transported to Jersey, in the Channel Islands. We were billeted in a hotel and had to be bused to the airport when we had to fly. We were a TSR training squadron, all our flying was, of course, of a training nature. We were only there for a few months, as we had to make a hasty retreat back to England on May 31, 1940.

Another of the young crew members was J.W. 'Willie' Armstrong who recalled:

> I don't think I ever flew with Lt Cdr Baker-Falkner but he was well known in the FAA. I flew to Jersey 8 May '40 with Sub Lt Sarra as pilot then daily flights with Mid Nicholson or Sub Lt Macaulay on W/T ex. My log book was signed by Lt Whitworth. I recall flying in a Swordfish on patrols between Jersey and St Malo in an attempt to deter the mighty *Luftwaffe*!
>
> As a precaution against a possible airborne invasion a motley collection of farm machinery was spread across the airport at the end of each day's flying to discourage enemy pilots from landing! Air traffic control consisted of signals from Aldis lamps or in an emergency from Verey pistols.

Whilst Roy awaited his posting, Naomi received the terrible news from her friend Marina that her husband, Bobby Dundas, had ditched and was missing. On 21 May he had been flying with 812 Squadron in one of its first operations over occupied Europe and was minelaying near Calais when his aircraft was hit and plunged into the sea 100 miles east of their base.

The squadron had lost one of its most experienced pilots and later that same day, Roy, who had been expecting to join his new aircraft carrier *Ark Royal*, received an urgent telephone call and was instead ordered to re-join 812 Squadron at its new base, RAF North Coates, to replace Dundas.

The squadron had just two weeks previously disembarked from HMS *Glorious*, which was now involved in the defence of Norway. No. 812 Squadron was temporarily loaned from the Navy to RAF Coastal Command until *Glorious* returned. Effectively, 812 Squadron was now an RAF Squadron.

Also that same day, Sub Lt Cliff Kindell, one of the new and inexperienced pilots in 812 Squadron, was appointed to cover for the loss of aircrew. He was ordered to fly to Jersey and back to East Anglia with passengers in the only aircraft that could be spared, an old Shark biplane.

Roy reported for duty at North Coates on 22 May. Lt Nathaniel 'Nat' Hearle, also joined 812 Squadron the same day and was destined to become its new 812 'X' Flight commander in the next month or so. North Coates was the one place Naomi did not want Roy to go, knowing that pilots had been killed whilst on operations from there.

North Coates, or North Cotes Fittes as it used to be called, was a remote place adjacent to the North Sea. It looked even more isolated from the air than it did from the ground; the aerodrome was a grass field separated from the foreshore by a substantial dike. Except for the nearby village of Marshchapel, there seemed to be nothing but fields and ditches for miles around. Just outside the airfield was the 'married patch' – a camouflaged row of terrace houses standing on three sides of a rectangular green. On the fourth side the mounds of two underground air raid shelters were visible.

RAF North Coates was in the area of No. 12 Fighter Command Group under Air Chief Marshal Trafford Leigh-Mallory for Eastern Counties and Midlands. The base was shared by the Beaufort IIs of 22 RAF Squadron under the command of Wing Commander F.J. St G. Braithwaite. The place was also teeming with Hawker Harts belonging to the Air Gunnery School, and these seemed to be landing and taking off every few minutes as they departed for, or returned from, the firing ranges. Flying was controlled from a weather-boarded Air Watch Office, inside which the duty pilot watched the lines of twelve old Swordfish of 812 Squadron being prepared for further operations over enemy-occupied territory.

On his return to 812 Squadron, Roy found the CO, 'Cracksie' Crawford, and senior pilot, Titch Harding, were still there. There were also several familiar faces from *Glorious* days, including Ken Gurr and his old Leuchars pal Lt George Villiers-Tothill, along with David 'Jan' Jolliff, senior TAG with the squadron. Flt Sgt Gittens, the NCO in charge of the 812 Squadron ground crews, had gone back to the RAF before the squadron arrived at North Coates. His place had been taken by Flt Sgt Robertson.

Familiar ground crew faces included Corporal 'Jock' Dyer, who was in charge of engine fitters, and Sgt Creasey (in charge of the armourers), as well as Manning, Dyer, Hazlewood, Clayton, Wilson and Hawkins.

There were also some new faces including Lt Maurice Driver:

I joined HMS *Glorious* only as she returned to UK waters in early 1940 and shortly before her departure to Norway. Shorty Shaw, Titch Harding and Dick Curry being the best remembered. They were all very senior to me and much admired by the rest of the squadron.

Shortly after her loss we were entrained to Grimsby and thence by bus to North Coates airfield, to take part in the activities of RAF Coastal Command until a new carrier should come into service.

One of Roy's TAG aircrew was also from the *Glorious*, L/A Ernest Kerridge: 'I remember him as a perfect gentleman, admired and respected by all officers and ratings. I flew often with Baker-Falkner.'

Aircraftsman Bill Clayton, air fitter in 'X' Flight, recalled that Roy arrived at North Coates just as a German invasion was thought to be imminent:

All ground crews were issued rifles and a carton of ten rounds, which we were instructed to carry with us everywhere, whether on duty or not.

We even took our meals with our rifle propped against the table! The ammunition cartons soon disintegrated, so we improvised bandoliers made out of airmen's tunic belts. Because we were working about twenty hours a day we had little time to look after ourselves. Often unshaven and with clothes the worse for wear we must have looked like a gang of desperadoes.

Titch explained to Roy that the Admiralty had started a programme where the 'dead man's shoes' would be replaced by RNVR aircrew. Cliff Kindell was the first.

Harding later added: 'These youngsters were straight from OTUs (Operational Training Units) and were to perform a magnificent job and were soon to become the backbone of the Fleet Air Arm.'

Cliff Kindell liked Roy from the start and was quick to praise him:

He was very well liked by all of us – really an outstanding personality. A tall, but well set up, man whose strong but pleasant face always reminded me of a good-looking Red Indian. I remember Roy very well with warm feelings.

Roy was allocated to 'X' Flight whose officer in charge was still Ken Gurr. He was allocated Swordfish 'F for Freddy' and Sub Lt Bruce Hawkes was appointed to be his observer. Roy was introduced to his ground crew, air fitter A.C. Wilson and rigger A.C. Hawkins, who were to support him throughout the next hectic period. He shared the armourer A.M. Eardley and electrician LAC Usher with the aircrew of Swordfish 'G for George', piloted by Lt George Villiers-Tothill, and 'H for Harry', piloted by Sub Lt R.N. David.

One major change was the appearance of the Swordfish to allow for more flying time – a huge petrol tank now protruded from the observer's seat behind the pilot. This was a potentially lethal arrangement, which would only too soon become tragically apparent.

A.C. Clayton recalled:

When the squadron had arrived at North Coates, Lt Cdr Crawford had informed the assembled ground and aircrews that the squadron had been earmarked for operations under Coastal Command. This, he told us, would involve major modifications to the aircraft and a lot of hard work for everyone. The parts had been despatched by road from the Fairey Works at Hayes, and were due to arrive that morning.

121

It began with the arrival of a number of large crates containing parts for the installation of an extra 60-gallon fuel tank. There were also modification sets for altering the rear cockpit to mount a Vickers GO (Gas-Operated) machine gun in place of the out-dated Lewis gun.

When the work of the ground crews was completed it was discovered that the extra tank, which protruded from the observer's cockpit to give the aircraft a hump-backed appearance, also prevented the electricians getting at the main electrical panel.

Clayton continued:

This meant cutting through the metal skin of the cockpit coaming and making a hinged flap to provide access to the electrics. The addition of the tank also meant that the observer would have to double up as air gunner and radio operator. When I flew on air test in 'A', I found the cockpit very cramped. How observers managed to navigate to a precise position – and minelaying had to be very precise – under such conditions was, and still is, beyond my comprehension.

Air tests revealed a tendency for fuel to surge back through the vent of the new tank during take-off, spraying the occupant of the rear cockpit with 87 octane! This was cured initially by corking the vent, but then it was discovered that the problem disappeared if the pilot took off with the fuel selector valve in the 'Main and Gravity' positions.

Roy and the rest of the squadron were informed about the nature of their work – *ad hoc* sorties under RAF Coastal Command orders on a daily basis, responding to the latest priorities as the situation in France and the Low Countries worsened. Squadron activities included anti-submarine patrols, day and night air reconnaissance and attacks against German E-boats as well as minelaying.

Clayton recalled:

We were informed of the nature of the operations to be carried out. The magnetic mine had now been perfected by Britain and was being produced in quantity. Because the RAF's new torpedo bomber, the Bristol Beaufort, had been grounded, Swordfish of the Fleet Air Arm had been assigned this task.

As well as ourselves, 815 Squadron at Bircham Newton and 825 Squadron at Detling were also involved. But, as the CO reminded us, this was only a temporary measure, as soon as *Glorious* returned from Norway we would be rejoining her to resume our part in the defence of the Mediterranean.

Roy was issued with an identification book with the latest silhouettes of potential enemy vessels – Titch Harding recalled that the observers called them 'bird books'. Roy was also brought up to date with the latest target area code names. These were sub-divided by numbers, and the names extended as time went by and more target areas were listed. The codes were named after shellfish and flowers: Oysters, Mussels, Scallops and Jellyfish, and plants such as Junipers and Zinnias. For example, Dabs and Whelks referred to the Boulogne area.

Roy was also issued with an 'Aircraft Table' which on one side stated 'for use by P/L to provide some temporary security against U-boats only' and included the codes such as 'plain van', which meant 'aircraft'. Boats or rafts were coded as 'dickey seats', Swordfish as 'tricycle' and U-boats as 'hearse'.

On the other side of the card, the main list of thirty or more coded names included such words as 'air' meaning 'I am on anti-aircraft patrol', 'Fanny' meaning 'have attacked without success', 'Popeye' meaning 'in cloud'. Some of the codes have become well known since then, such as 'bandits' which, according to the card, meant 'identified enemy aircraft'.

Roy had hardly any time to settle down before he was sent on his first operation over enemy-occupied Europe. Naomi recalled: 'Almost immediately on his return, Roy rushed off because "the Dunkirk evacuation was on", and I stayed on at the flat in Lee.'

On Thursday 23 May, half a million Allied soldiers were trapped near the French port of Dunkirk and expecting capture or death. The next day, 812 Squadron was called upon to mount a daylight bombing attack against German panzer divisions threatening the perimeter of the British Expeditionary Force's defensive positions. No sooner had the CO briefed the air and ground crews, than a signal arrived ordering the squadron to load six 250-lb bombs per aircraft and standby to attack 'land targets' near Dunkirk.

Clayton recalled:

'Bombing-up' methods were crude; it took six men – two on each end of a pole to lift, and one at each end of the bomb to steady it and hook it onto its carrier. It was a back-breaking job as it was necessary to crouch under the lower wing of the aircraft, each man lifting a load of about 65 lbs.

Five aircraft took off, led by Titch Harding in Swordfish 'A for Apples', along with Ken Gurr in Swordfish 'R for Roger', Roy in 'F for Freddy', Shorty Shaw in 'B for Beer' and George Villiers-Tothill in 'G'. They flew first to Manston in Kent, a front-line RAF Fighter Station, soon to be at the centre of the Battle of Britain.

Manston and RAF Detling were the two bases in Kent that the RAF used to refuel and re-arm during the Dunkirk evacuation. The war situation was intensifying and station defence arrangements were being tightened up; detachments of the London Irish Regiment and the Royal Artillery were arriving with anti-aircraft guns.

German forces were by this time advancing through France and were to take Marck military aerodrome on the outskirts of Calais that day. RAF Fighter Command Squadrons from Manston were now constantly patrolling over France trying to keep the *Luftwaffe* from the Dunkirk beaches.

In this chaotic situation, the aircrew of the striking force of five Swordfish learnt that a major battle was underway at the town of Gravelines, between Calais and Dunkirk. In the briefing in the Manston Ops Room, Roy and the others were informed by Titch as senior pilot that they were 'to locate and bomb enemy tanks and Wehrmacht army lorries jammed on the Gravelines road towards Calais'. Titch was very pragmatic in the briefing and recalled saying: 'Bombs and bullets they say concentrate the mind!'

He advised Roy and the others on fighter evasion tactics:

You can turn a slow aircraft in less air space than a faster one – wait until you think the fighter will open fire then turn PDQ. Charles Lamb said he put one into the sea by doing that at wave top height. The silly B..... more probably put his nose down trying to get his sights on him.

Titch ironically noted that Gravelines was where the English smashed the Spanish Armada.

The Swordfish were slower than enemy aircraft but it was hoped that the Germans would think they were actually the similar-looking Gloster Gladiator fighters and would be frightened off by them.

Roy must have been daunted with the task ahead as 'F for Freddy' and the other Stringbags took off from Manston and headed directly towards the French coast, with a fighter escort. Hawkes was Roy's observer for the operation. Flying in formation, the five Swordfish pilots took less than an hour to reach the target area, which was confirmed when they saw the smoke from the battle area, and the distinctive diamond-shaped Gravelines fortification far below them. Enemy tanks and Wehrmacht army lorries had built up on the Gravelines–Calais road. A battle was raging in Gravelines itself between the advancing Germans and the defending British Expeditionary Force and the French forces.

Titch Harding recalled: 'We found the tanks, forgotten how many but quite a few, stopped nose-to-tail on the road. They had put their flak 20-mm tracer firing guns in the fields on each side of the road to give cross-covering fire.'

Roy lined up with the other Swordfish in preparation for the attack on their primary target, the German panzer division. Titch positioned his aircraft so that the formation of Swordfish could 'lead in along the road to attack for maximum effect'. Roy was following in formation close behind.

Our bombs were set on 'Mickey Mouse' i.e. you press the button and bombs drop one after the other. So you put down a stick, five aircraft equals thirty bombs. The aircraft pulled out – explosions all around them. Five direct hits were reported on roads and three tanks were seen on fire. After the formation drop, a blue turn so that quick avoiding action away from flak and ack-ack guns meant that aircraft returned alone.

With the heavy anti-aircraft fire from enemy positions, Swordfish 'R' piloted by Ken Gurr with his observer Lt Ronald Carpmael, was hit in the fuel tank and went down in flames. Later, both men were confirmed as killed. Their bodies were retrieved and they were buried at Oye-Plage cemetery close to the site of the battle.

A retreating British Expeditionary Force eyewitness to the bombing attack by 812 Squadron at Gravelines was Jimmy Dickinson of the 6th Battalion of the Green Howard's:

On 23 May, the battle for Gravelines between Calais and Dunkirk started. The French Army was already in position and the dominant feature at our side of the canal at Gravelines was a huge stack of timber.

The bridge was on our left and we were faced all along the canal banks by thousands of refugees, who could see our every move. To confuse matters we seemed to have large numbers of the Belgian Army on both sides of the canal, all of whom seemed to be equipped with a bicycle and a series of paper parcels, paper carrier bags and very little else.

Our position was in front of a sort of warehouse-come-sawmill and there was space for lorries etc. between the canal and the buildings. A tank appeared behind us, the commander of which gave us some orders and advice that when he opened fire the blast might alarm us but not to worry. That was really our first indication that the battle for Gravelines was on.

A German tank made a short, sharp appearance to the Gravelines Bridge, and executed well-aimed shots, which must have been predetermined targets, and I was the only one who later stood up. The carnage was a sight that robbed me of sleep for years afterwards and even now in my mind's eye I can see the tank turn completely round and display for all the world to see the huge swastika flag that was draped across the rear.

The actual battle raged on all day but my part was at an end, although at HQ we got all sorts of rumours. A heartening sight was to see the French Air Force unit, who arrived to take over a section as if they had been infantry for years.

We were withdrawn at dusk and my main recollection is more marching in extended order over those flat fields, whilst aircraft, which I took to be our Fleet Air Arm, were bombing at the enemy side of Gravelines–Calais area.

After the attack, the four remaining Swordfish with Roy, Titch, George Villiers-Tothill and Shorty Shaw made their own way back. Titch's aircraft had been badly hit in the attack and he was worried he wasn't going to make it back to base:

On the way back, Shorty Shaw comes up alongside and signals 'tail feathers ruffled, put down gently like loving mother with newborn babe.' I thought this good advice, 'Will look see after landing.'

Titch had been badly shot with a 'Hole in rudder and part of the king post was shot away.'

Roy, coaxing his aircraft carefully, came over the English coastline and flew low over the South Downs escarpment towards the plateau on which RAF Detling airfield lay; the sprawl of London could be seen in the distance. The Swordfish landed, and taxied to a halt; immediately ground crew wheeled them out to dispersal pens. Relieved, Roy, Hawkes and the small band of aircrew in the Swordfish wearily clambered down from their flak-damaged aircraft. They had only been in the air one hour and thirty minutes.

Roy was shocked and shaken when he realised Ken was missing.

After debriefing, RAF Command decided it would have another go at attacking the panzer tanks the next day; 812 Squadron aircraft had taken too much damage to continue and 825 Squadron was put on the roster for the mission.

Titch recalled:

The Stringbag could take quite lot of punishment. After the Gravelines do, our tail feathers were so badly ruffled that we had to ask for a replacement aircraft. This was flown in next morning by a lovely and very, but very, young girl ferry pilot. When she took off her helmet and her hair was blown by the wind, we were dumb struck and goggle-eyed, which made her laugh as she nipped into her transport.

Roy and the other 812 Squadron aircrew were billeted overnight in a hotel in Maidstone. Roy, who was still fraught with worry by the loss of Ken whom he had known for so long, learned at this time that another friend, Lt A.S. 'Shaggers' Whitworth, now in 815 Squadron, had ditched and been rescued a few weeks previously.

The next day, Roy, Cracksie Crawford, Titch and the other surviving aircrew flew back to North Coates where they were immediately pressed into carrying out an anti-submarine search, a combined two-hour operation, before being able to land for further debriefing and then a well-earned break. Titch recollected that they were given areas to search in the Channel: 'U-boats may have been ordered in because of Dunkirk. We spaced the four aircraft out but result negative.'

The loss of such an experienced and well-trained pilot as Ken Gurr was a serious blow to 812 Squadron. Since he had been 'X' Flight commander, his position had to be urgently filled. Lt W.G. Williams, a veteran aviator from 17 Pilots' Course in 1934, was immediately called upon by Lt Cdr Crawford to take over as officer in command.

That same day, 25 May, the Dunkirk evacuation began in earnest from France, and there arrived at Detling all sorts of obsolete aircraft to help protect the retreating British forces.

Also that day, based on the debriefing of Roy and the other 812 Squadron aircrew, eleven aircraft of 825 Squadron – 812's sister squadron on *Glorious*, now under the command of Lt Cdr J.B. Buckley – took off from Detling with a fighter escort, to attack the tanks and lorries reported still jammed on the Gravelines road. On arrival over the target area, the aircraft crews found the tanks had dispersed and were by then roaring into Dunkirk. Instead, the Swordfish attacked targets of opportunity, including armoured cars, transport and AA batteries.

L/A W. Bill Curtis, 825 Squadron TAG, recalled:

> In May, there were chaotic days at Detling when we TAGs were billeted in tents, fields away from food and washing facilities and wearing a white handkerchief on our arms to show we weren't the enemy. We trudged miles to charge batteries and fill our ammunition pans, both very heavy items – no trolleys to spare!

Matters were moving at breakneck speed with the British Expeditionary Force and its allies effectively trapped in the Dunkirk pocket. A.C. Clayton recorded in his diary on 25 May: 'There was a rush to load bombs on all serviceable [812] aircraft. The squadron remained on standby until 2100 and my diary records that, for a change, I had an early night, turning in at 2230.'

The next day, Lord Gort, Commander-in-Chief of the British Expeditionary Force, received a telegram from the War Office which read: 'The only course open to you may be to fight your way back to the west where all beaches and ports east of Gravelines will be used for embarkation. The Navy will provide a fleet of ships and small boats and the Royal Air Force would give full support.'

Gort had foreseen that this action would become necessary when the counter-attack did not materialise and when withdrawal southward to the Somme became impracticable by the rapidity of the German advance. The withdrawal of the British Army began as the Dunkirk evacuation was put fully into operation.

As Hitler ordered a full-scale air and land assault on the Dunkirk area, a vast fleet of small ships, including pleasure steamers and ferries, moved across the Channel in a bid to rescue as many men as possible.

For Roy's squadron that Monday, 27 May, came a visit from King George VI.

A.C. Clayton explained that even with such esteemed presence, the squadron was preparing to defend itself against German paratroops with whatever ancient weapons were at hand:

> On Monday, we were returning from the rifle range, where an ancient gunner's mate had been brought out of retirement to instruct us in marksmanship. My rifle had seen service in the Boer War.
>
> We returned to find a procession of high-ranking officers filing through the hangars. The tall, slim figure at their head I recognised as the King. There was no ceremony; work continued and stopped only if HM paused to query what was being done. He spoke to PO Manning who was in charge of our little shooting party and seemed pleased that we were making an effort to defend ourselves.

The Detling Operations Record Book reported that day:

> At 1010 hrs, Swordfish arrived over objective to the west of Calais Citadel.

Swordfish then bombed and gunned selected targets, two enemy land batteries medium artillery. Concentration of about 500 men hit by gunfire. Enemy AA guns scattered. AA fire moderate, air activity nil. Four tanks on quay. Aircraft landed at 1046 hrs.

On 28 May, King Leopold of Belgium startled the world by surrendering to the Germans. The evacuation from Dunkirk continued in earnest. The situation in the Channel Isles looked bleak, and the likelihood of invasion inevitable within days. Jersey airport was already preparing to close down.

A.C. Clayton recollected the next 812 Squadron operation from North Coates that same day:

We were roused from our sleep at 01.25 by Flight Sergeant Robertson doing a passable impression of a town crier as he imparted the information that the squadron was moving – AND AT ONCE! 'Another Crawford's Tour!' quipped Farmer as we made our way, bleary-eyed, to the hangars.

The first priority was to get the aircraft away, all maintenance work being suspended. Both Roy and Hawkes climbed into 'F for Freddy' and took off with the other squadron aircraft. The aircraft flew the thirty-minute hop to Bircham Newton near Fakenham in Norfolk. RAF Bircham Newton was an important part of Coastal Command, the station was used for convoy protection, reconnaissance, anti-shipping and U-boat patrols and was home to 815 Squadron and the resident RAF 206 Hudson squadron. Roy and the other squadron officers were immediately ordered to report to the station armoury and be issued with firearms.

Clayton continued:

By 0825 the squadron stores and our personal kit had been loaded into two torpedo lorries, the only transport available at such short notice. We climbed on top and soon we were on our way to RAF Bircham Newton, somewhere in the wilds of Norfolk to the east of King's Lynn.

The squadron reassembled at Bircham Newton and Clayton went on:

The buzz was that we were to relieve 815 Squadron, who were leaving to join the new carrier *Illustrious*. In addition, we were told to be on the alert for parachutists, who might be in any disguise, including British uniforms. It seemed they had landed on one southern air field. The fact that this was being taken seriously was confirmed by the number of officers carrying revolvers. I came close to being arrested in the Airmen's Dining Hall because the orderly sergeant didn't recognise my uniform.

Out at dispersal we started the aircraft and they were taxied over to the tarmac where torpedoes were loaded and primed, after which we were put on standby and issued rifles and ammunition to replace those handed in before leaving North Coates. This time it was fifty rounds, in two cartons of twenty-five.

We began to wonder when we would be allocated billets, but it transpired that, until the panic was over, we would have to sleep where we could. I spent that night with a dozen others in the base of the control tower where we slept, some on camp beds, others, like me, in easy chairs, our rifles loaded and lying by our sides, but with safety catches on.

Then, on the morning of 29 May:

> At dawn we started the aircraft and once again they were taxied over to the hangars where a check was carried out on the torpedoes. After topping-up with fuel and signing for DIs we were allowed to go to breakfast. Returning afterwards we met Flight Sergeant Robertson who told us to help get the aircraft across to the tarmac, the torpedoes were to come off and we were returning to North Coates.
>
> On reflection, this must have been a situation triggered by someone in authority panicking and forming a wrong interpretation of events. Which squadron finally relieved 815 I do not know, but we were back in our old billets at North Coates by supper time.

In fact, 815 Squadron had flown down to Detling from Bircham Newton whilst the Germans were closing in on the trapped British Expeditionary Force forces at Dunkirk from all sides.

Information about enemy activities and positions at Dunkirk were pouring into the North Coates Ops Room and fed to 812 Squadron. The Detling Operations Record Book recorded that day:

> 4 Swordfish took off at 1655 and carried out 'bat' round canal and railway SW of Bergues to look for a big gun in this position. No gun was seen but AA fire met in this area from the farmhouse which was bombed result unknown. Air gunner wounded from AA fire from Dunkerque district. 15 Ju.88 bombing Dunkerque–Bergues road. 3 more Ju.88 bombing Dunkerque harbour. No damage done. Bombs dropped SW of Calais on a tank which was destroyed. Many AA guns on Sangate cliff. A/C landed between 1947 and 2030 hours.

At this time gunfire flashes in the sky over France could be seen from Jersey, a foretaste of things to come. Jersey airport was finally evacuated on 30–31 May, and 763 Squadron withdrew from its Jersey airport base to Lee-on-Solent.

Hitler was expected to follow up his rout of the French Army with an invasion of Britain within hours. As the threat of invasion grew to a critical situation, more and more of 812 crew's free time was spent digging trenches and building earthworks as defences for the hangar area. These were topped with sandbags and barbed wire.

In the event of a landing by paratroops, it was hoped ground crew might be able to hold these positions until the Army arrived. There were several false alarms when ground crew were called to stand-to, but no invaders appeared.

Meanwhile, attempts were made to further modify the Swordfish. Following the disaster of Ken Gurr's aircraft blowing up after a bullet hit his fuel tank, Lt Cdr Crawford ordered that self-sealing fuel tanks had to be fitted to all squadron Swordfish. But there was little comfort for Roy and the other aircrew as the new long-range tanks were to remain unsealed and were still potential flying bombs.

By the last day of May there were about fifty Swordfish aircraft at Detling including a detachment of 819 Squadron. The RAF Station now had at least five Fleet Air Arm squadrons, all operating under the command of RAF Coastal Command. These included two Skua squadrons, 801 and 806, as well as three Swordfish squadrons, 815 (under Robin Kilroy), 825 and 826.

On 31 May, these were due to take off on a fighter patrol across the Dunkirk beaches. The second fighter patrol of the morning was flown by Fleet Air Arm dive-bombers and two-seater fighters, comprising thirty-seven Skuas and Blackburn Rocs.

Pilot Officer Clarke, of No. 2 Anti-Aircraft Co-operation Unit, normally stationed at Gosport, recalled:

> There were not many returning – I counted six. Where were the others? One belly-flopped and I went across to see what had happened. The aircraft was a complete write-off. Bullets and cannon shells had ripped the fuselage from end to end; the after-cockpit was sprayed literally with blood. The front cockpit was worse. Two bullet holes through the back of the pilot's seat showed where he had been hit and his parachute, still in position, was saturated with blood. The instrument panel was shattered and on the floor was the remains of a foot.
>
> Of the original thirty-seven aircraft, nine came back and five were written off after inspection. The remaining four aircraft were airborne within the hour. They looked very pathetic limping back to Dunkirk all alone.

Later that afternoon, the Detling Operational Records Book recorded:

> Ten Albacores took off to carry out a raid on road junction at Westende Bain and Westende. Aircraft approached targets at 9,000 ft in sub flights in V disposed in line action. At 1607 hrs aircraft dived on targets. Hits were probably made on cars and troops near the road junction. A large open car attended by two motor cycle outriders was hit at this point. A direct hit was registered on 2 lorries. Aircraft landed at 1725.

That evening, Clarke was over Dunkirk; his orders were to patrol each night west of Gravelines-Dunkirk, dropping flares to light up any attempt by the German navy to interfere with the evacuation.

In another operation that same night, tragedy struck again for Roy's squadron. Five aircraft, again led by Titch Harding along with Roy and the other experienced pilots, went minelaying off the Dutch coast at Boomskas Deep.

Swordfish 'G for George' failed to return, having been seen going down in flames over the Rotterdam target area in a raid on Vlaardingen oil tanks. The pilot, George Villiers-Tothill, was killed. Sub Lt Shaw, the observer, managed to bail out with his parachute. He was believed to be drowned in the Nieuwe Waterweg of the River Maas. Villiers-Tothill was buried in the small village of Rozenburg, fifteen or so miles west of Rotterdam.

Charles Lamb, of 815 Squadron, had also been posted to Detling and was there during the evacuation from Dunkirk, which lasted an historic nine days and nights. His squadron, armed with bombs, ranged from the Dunkirk beaches in the smoke and flame of the battle down to Calais and up to Ostend, and then out into the North Sea, attacking E-boats wherever they could find them, and before they could close in on the floating armada for the kill.

Lamb could not but help be impressed by the spectacle of the columns of ships, ploughing endlessly between Dunkirk and Dover or Ramsgate. He described seeing, below the wings of his Stringbag, the armada of little ships of all shapes and sizes – Thames barges under full sail, paddle steamers and yachts, all of which made an incredible spectacle. Also from his Swordfish he was also able to watch the RAF save the army on the beaches, out of sight of the troops below.

Many war-weary soldiers on the beaches felt that British aircraft were conspicuous by their absence. Winston Churchill, in his speech to the House of Commons on 4 June 1940, reported what had happened:

> They (the Germans) sent repeated waves of hostile aircraft, sometimes more than a hundred strong in one formation…the Royal Air Force engaged the main strength of the German Air Force, and inflicted upon them losses of at least four to one; and the Navy, using nearly 1,000 ships of all kinds, carried over 335,000 men, French and British, out of the jaws of death and shame…
>
> We must be very careful not to assign to this deliverance the attributes of a victory. Wars are not won by evacuations. But there was a victory inside the deliverance, which should be noted. It was gained by the Air Force. Many of our soldiers coming back have not seen the Air Force at work: they saw only the bombers which escaped the protective attack. They underrate its achievements….

In all this time, Naomi, still at the lodging in Victoria Hotel in Lee-on-Solent, received little news about Roy and was frantic with worry. Her anxiety for Roy became even more extreme, as she recalled:

> Then I got a telegram from Jane Grey, wife of one of the *Glorious*' old aircrews whom I had known in Alex. The telegram said 'Robin missing can you come? Go to hotel in Maidstone.'

Naomi continued:

> I jumped on the train to Maidstone and booked into the Royal Star Hotel in the High Street. Another pilot was now also missing, and two girls with their husbands missing from a few days previously were frantically running around trying to find out any news. Someone said 'Roy is here.'

Naomi was not so sure, as he was often confused with Splash Carver. She went on: 'But amazingly it was him.'

She was delighted and so relieved that it was Roy and spent a precious couple of hours with him. She continued:

> He was exhausted having been driving [flying] up and down the English Channel during the Dunkirk evacuation. He described how he had been trying to snatch sleep whenever he could at the airfield, using his parachute as a pillow, and while his aircraft was being refuelled and rearmed. If there was time he would rest in one of Maidstone's hotels.

He subsisted on corned beef sandwiches, innumerable cups of tea and the odd gin or two.

He introduced her to his observer, Bruce Hawkes, and proceeded to tell her that they and the RAF were facing overwhelming odds, and that five aircraft from 825 Squadron had failed to return on 29 May – one of the worst wartime tragedies of the Fleet Air Arm to date – and were missing from a daylight bombing raid that day. They included that of the CO, Lt Cdr 'Jimmy' Buckley, and Robin Grey, along with Sub Lt C.S.F. Hogg and L/A L.P. Gardner. Lt Cdr Buckley's replacement was to be Lt Cdr Eugene Esmonde. Lt Alexander Desmond Neely was also lost on this raid and taken POW. He later took part in the Great Escape from Stalag Luft III, but survived the subsequent murder of fifty his fellow escapees by the *Gestapo*.

130

It subsequently transpired that the five had been bounced by the dreaded *Luftwaffe* 54 'Green Hearts Wing' fighter wing. The Messerschmitt Bf109 fighters had pounced on the Swordfish pilots in broad daylight and shot them down with ease. The air ace Adolf-Waldemar Kinzinger claimed to have shot down two Swordfish, and three other pilots in JG54 each reported shooting down one of the other torpedo-bombers.

About the same time, the renowned *Luftwaffe* air ace Helmut Wick, also in a Messerschmitt Bf109, of the *Jagdgeschwader* 3/JG2 fighter wing, reported shooting down two further Swordfish over Calais. Wick spotted the Swordfish and reportedly made a firing pass, but when the air gunner waved a white cloth he took this as a signal of surrender. As the Swordfish pilot prepared to land on French soil, Wick followed in his Bf109, but was fired on by the air gunner who thought Wick was about to attack. The Swordfish landed and overturned in a field between Calais and Gravelines. Wick then went after the other Swordfish and shot it down in flames.

Roy and 812 Squadron had been extremely fortunate in not encountering Messerschmitts in their own daylight bombing raids over Dunkirk.

As a result of the severe losses, the Fleet Air Arm ordered that Swordfish should operate over enemy territory only at night. Clayton recalled being told by his CPO that: 'The light grey under surfaces were to be painted dark earth and olive drab to render the aircraft less conspicuous at night, while IFF (Identification, Friend or Foe) transmitters were to be installed in each aircraft.'

Naomi stayed at Maidstone for a while to look after her frantic and distraught friends but eventually went back to Lee-on-Solent. Later, she and Roy were to find out that Robin Grey had survived and as a POW. Sadly, he later died in camp on 29 August 1941. Jimmy Buckley was also a POW; he met with another Fleet Air Arm pilot who had been shot down in Norway, Major Richard Partridge, and escaped in 1943.

Clayton recalled the reaction of Roy's squadron to the news of 825 Squadron's losses when it reached them at North Coates:

825, who were involved in another attack, fared even worse, losing nearly all their aircraft so that they had to be disbanded and re-formed. This was a sad day for, on top of our own losses, most of the pilots and observers in both squadrons had been flying together since first joining *Glorious* in 1937 and 1938.

The Dunkirk evacuation came to an end on 4 June. Major General Harold Alexander toured the shore line of Dunkirk in a fast motor-boat to make sure that no soldiers remained to be lifted off. Then he boarded a ship to Dover, the last Allied soldier to leave Dunkirk.

The Battle for France had been lost, now the Battle of Britain was about to begin. In an electrifying speech Winston Churchill said, 'We shall fight on the beaches, we shall fight on the landing grounds, we shall fight in the fields and in the streets, we shall fight in the hills; we shall never surrender.'

The following day, General Edmund Ironside, the new Commander in Chief Home Forces, sent a letter to Chief of Air Staff, thanking all aircrew involved in the Dunkirk evacuation. Copies of this letter were proudly distributed by Lt Cdr Crawford to Roy and his colleagues.

Letter Addressed to the Chief of the Air Staff, from the Chief of the Imperial General Staff, on 5 June 1940

> I feel I must write you a line to let you know how much we of the Army appreciate the immense efforts and the terrible sacrifices the Royal Air Force made in playing their great part in helping to save the men in the BEF. I wish I could thank all the pilots and crews personally, but as that is impossible, I can only say to you that our appreciation and thanks are very real.

Ironside himself was sent with the British Expeditionary Force to France and had a lucky escape when his Calais hotel suffered a direct hit from a German bomb.

A second letter from Vice Admiral Bertram Ramsey, Office in Charge of the Dunkirk Evacuation at the Command Centre in Dover Castle, read:

Message Addressed to Air Officer Commanding-in-Chief from Vice-Admiral, Dover

> I, and the forces under my Command who have been engaged on the evacuation of the Allied Armies, owe a deep debt of gratitude to the Royal Air Force for the support and protection which they have given us. We are fully conscious of the strain these operations have imposed on all taking part and we are filled with admiration of the courage and devotion of our comrades in the air.

Subsequently, Roy hardly mentioned his Dunkirk experience, although Naomi recalled he spoke of 'watching little boats evacuate tightly packed columns between France and Dover'.

However, he hinted at his dramatic experiences with the German panzer division encounters at Gravelines when in January 1941 he wrote to Naomi, following a discussion with his old observer Bruce Hawkes: 'People at Lee just don't believe his stories, amazing isn't it?'

Then again in 1944, the Dunkirk evacuation came to his mind during the D-Day invasion when he was on board HMS *Furious*: 'What price the news of the Second Front. Glad I'm not over Dunkirk again.'

CHAPTER 12

Gardening in the Low Countries

Throughout June 1940, Roy's squadron routinely took part in the aerial laying of mines off the Low Countries of Belgium, Holland, and parts of northern France and Germany. They were still working directly under the aegis of RAF Coastal Command as invasion by the Germans seemed inevitable.

The code name for minelaying was 'gardening' and this was to become the pattern of operations for the rest of the squadron's time at North Coates, interrupted only when there was a call for other types of operation, such as bombing or torpedo attacks.

On 1 June, Roy, with Hawkes and six other squadron aircraft, left for Operation *Cucumber* overnight. The operation was divided into two separate sub-flights in area 'Mussels' but the aircraft hit bad weather off the Dutch coast. On their return an enemy aircraft was sighted, and a replacement Swordfish 'G for George' ditched in the sea off Spurn Point. The Grimsby lifeboat and a high-speed launch were summoned to its assistance. The crew was rescued.

To the exhausted Roy's relief, no operations were held the next day. However, Aircraftsman Clayton recalled another incident that could have been fatal:

On June 4 we had loaded mines when the order came to remove them and load torpedoes. It seemed German warships had been sighted in the North Sea. When 'A' had been loaded Lt Harding came along and said he wanted to do an air test to check the trim with a torpedo on board and would I come with him in case any rigging adjustments were necessary.

As we started the take-off run, I could feel the way the machine laboured under the weight and drag of its load; suddenly there was a loud bang from the rear fuselage. At first, it seemed the self-destruct device in the IFF transmitter had been triggered (they did that sometimes), but then there was a heavy rumble from the tail before it finally lifted from the ground.

'What was that?' demanded a terse voice over the Gosport's (speaking tubes, the only form of inter-com fitted to Swordfish).

'The tail wheel tyre's burst, sir.' I wanted to ask if we were going to jettison the torpedo, for the now defunct tail wheel would take a bashing on touchdown with all that weight on board and the Swordfish might ground-loop, or end up on its nose. 'All right, we'll carry out the test and I'll do a tail-up landing,' came the matter-of-fact reply.

Twenty minutes later we landed on the two main wheels, the tail, coming into contact with the ground after flying speed had been lost, snatched this way and that, but settled down as the aircraft rolled to a stop.

On the evening of 5 June, Roy and Hawkes, in Swordfish 'F for Freddy', flew with five other aircraft on Operation *Flounders* – a 'gardening' mission of almost five hours' duration.

On their return, Titch in 'A for Apples' and 'Shorty' Shaw in 'B for Beer' encountered slight flak from Flushing and two searchlights from its aerodrome. Shorty also sighted at 21.50 hours a convoy of thirty-three enemy motor vessels with two escorts and four destroyers. Roy had a trouble-free mining operation that night.

On arrival at North Coates, they found the airfield had experienced its first air raid at midnight when two Heinkel 111s circled the area – six bombs fell about two miles east of the airfield on a dummy aerodrome at Donna Nook. Clayton recalled:

> There was some sporadic AA fire and the night was bright with searchlights which caught one of the intruders, allowing the guns to concentrate on him. I don't think he was hit, but it probably discouraged him from dropping his muck in our part of Lincolnshire.
>
> When the Swordfish returned the authorities still had the jitters and would not allow the flare path to be lit, so our pilots had to make do with their own landing lights and we guided them to dispersal with blue torches. These were useless, but the searchlight beams that were still sweeping the sky helped enormously. Even so, 'M' collided with a petrol bowser, damaging her propeller and denting her starboard wings.

In 1940 C.G. Grey, founder editor of *The Aeroplane* magazine, wrote about the part played by the Fleet Air Arm in laying mines.

> On the airfield was a squadron of Fairey Swordfish…the machine was built for Fleet reconnaissance and as a torpedo-dropper, so it is a weight-lifter, and its best cruising speed is about that of the trainers which one sees floating around the sky. These Swordfish were different. Where the navigator ought to sit was an enormous petrol tank which stuck up between the pilot and the after-cockpit. It took up all the second seat and ended in a blank wall, high above where the second seat should have been. There, beneath it in the third seat, the navigator had to sit with his legs underneath a mass of petrol, all ready to drown him in flames if an incendiary bullet caught it.
>
> At bombing-up time, just before dark, instead of the normal torpedo or bombs, huge flat-ended barrels were rolled out on trolleys and fixed between the wheels. These were our magnetic mines, far more powerful and more magnetic than the German mines of which we heard so much at the time. These barrels brought the flying speed of the Swordfish down to about 80 knots.
>
> That night, as the rest of us were going to bed, we heard the growl of the Bristols starting up, and a few minutes later the drone of the heavy stuff taking off, circling the CO's house and heading seaward. Next morning they all came back – bar one – and reported results, had their suppers at breakfast time, and went to bed, all ready to do it again the next night.
>
> Now figure to yourself that sort of courage – the 'three o'clock in the morning

courage' which Napoleon admired in our people – in the machine outrageously overloaded, carrying a mine which would leave nothing to pick up if it exploded in a crash, and carrying a truck-load of petrol to give it the thousand-mile range; its speed such that the worst anti-aircraft gunner or search-light could hardly miss it; its only protection against fighters the fact that it was too slow for them to stay with it and shoot at it; pilot and navigator without the companionship of a cabin, lonely all night on the end of a voice-pipe.

They had none of the excitement of the single-seat fighter or his interval for refreshment after a three-hour patrol, and none of the crewmanship, as it were, of the big bombers or flying-boats. If ever there was a 'solitude à deux', the minelayers in the Swordfish had it – for most of ten hours at a stretch.

They were the bravest men I have met. I have known a good many VCs and plenty of DSOs. None of these FAA lads had any decorations then. I hope they have got them since. Nobody admired our bomber crews and coastal reconnaissance people, and our fighter pilots, more than I do. But those couples in the Swordfish deserve to be recorded in history for they made so much history themselves.

Cracksie Crawford had already given the go ahead for wives to join their husbands at North Coates, as the squadron was due to embark on *Glorious* in the near future as soon as her captain, D'Oyly-Hughes, brought her back from the Norwegian campaign. As Cracksie put it to Roy and the others in the squadron: 'It will be a long while before you see them again, so make the best of it while you can.' Roy managed to get a message to Naomi to tell her the good news and she hurried to leave their lodgings in Lee-on-Solent. Other wives also coming to North Coates included her friend, Mita, and Mrs Kindell.

On 6 June, the squadron went on a torpedo mission. The North Coates Operational Records Book recorded:

Operation *Cucumber*. 6 Swordfish carried out the operation. 4 cucumbers dropped in position Xeranthemum and 2 in Zinias. 3 aircraft reported sighting 3 red stars fired from what appeared to be a ship a few miles off target. They also encountered a Hudson which flew alongside and challenged until recognised signal given.

Roy and four other pilots returned safely, but the Stringbag 'B', normally flown by Shorty Shaw, crashed on what was then a dummy aerodrome at Ouston. Fortunately, the crew were unhurt.

Clayton added:

There was another avoidable accident on the 8th when 'Jan' Creer, one of the TAGs, went to check the radio in 'Q'. On finding a cockpit cover there, he yanked it out of the way, but one of the securing cords snagged on the trigger of the Verey pistol. There was a bang, a puff of smoke and coloured balls of fire danced round the cockpit to burst through the fabric, and go bouncing along the tarmac towards a line of parked aircraft. Fortunately the fires were extinguished before any petrol or ammunition was involved.

On Sunday morning, 9 June, there was a great rush to load torpedoes on all serviceable aircraft – including 22 Squadron's Beauforts, after which they all flew to Bircham Newton.

Roy again climbed into 'F for Freddy' for the short hop to Bircham Newton, and then hung around in the ready room for the call to action. The aircrews slept fitfully that night, expecting any minute to fly, but the night passed undisturbed. Titch Harding recorded in his log book: 'Gardening, with a trip to Bircham with torpedoes on the 9 June – 30 mins and back again, next day 25 minutes.'

The aircraft returned on Monday morning with their torpedoes intact. These were promptly removed and the squadron reverted to its minelaying role.

That same day, Cracksie Crawford rushed in to the wardroom with shocking news; 812 Squadron's parent carrier, *Glorious*, had been sunk off Norway. Roy and the other veteran *Glorious* aircrew were stunned. News was sketchy at that time but it looked as if there were not many survivors.

Clayton recollected:

I was helping Beery with a thirty-hour inspection on 'B' when Lane, the CO's writer, burst into the hangar bearing the news that *Glorious* had been sunk by two enemy battleships. We stopped work in shocked disbelief, unable to believe our ears. The details were brief: *Glorious* had been intercepted by the Germans north of the Arctic Circle during the evacuation from Norway. The question on everyone's lips was, 'How could it have happened when the ship had her aircraft to give warning of the approach of the enemy?'

We all thought of our chums who had remained on board and hoped their names would be among those on the list of survivors. Someone started to say that there was little chance of anyone being picked up alive in that 'bloody ocean' but he was told to shut up.

I can only rely on memory to describe my feelings on hearing this devastating news, for there are no entries in my diary for the next three days. Shock and anger gradually gave way to relief that I had got off the ship, but this was followed immediately by a feeling of guilt that I should harbour such a thought.

Glorious had been attacked by the battlecruisers *Scharnhorst* and *Gneisenau* and sunk off Norway on 8 June 1940. The day before, *Glorious* and HMS *Ark Royal* had been operating off the Lofoten Islands, evacuating British and Allied troops and equipment from Norway. *Glorious* had taken on board twenty RAF Hurricane and Gladiator fighters which had been flown on by RAF pilots to save their valuable aircraft from the advancing German forces. On board were five Fleet Air Arm torpedo-bombers, Roy's aircraft and the squadrons normally resident on the ship were still detached to the RAF far away in the UK.

Both *Ark Royal* and *Glorious* were to have formed part of a convoy escort, but in the early hours of 8 June D'Oyly-Hughes proceeded independently to Scapa Flow along with two escorting destroyers, *Ardent* and *Acasta*. They parted company with *Ark Royal* overnight.

That afternoon, two enemy ships were sighted by *Glorious*. She increased to full speed and sounded off action stations after *Ardent*'s challenge was answered with gunfire. *Ardent* succeeded in laying a funnel smoke screen across the track of *Glorious* but the destroyer was soon hit and sunk. The German warships then both opened fire on the aircraft carrier. *Glorious* was hit by *Scharnhorst*'s third salvo. A second hit was received which killed most of the bridge crew including the captain, D'Oyly-Hughes. *Glorious* received another hit in the engine room which caused a loss of speed and a starboard list. The ship sank around 18.10 hours.

The nearest British warship, *Devonshire*, was 100 miles away. On board were the King of Norway and his ministers, and breaking radio silence would have involved serious risk in revealing her position. *Acastra* attacked with torpedoes under heavy fire, scoring a hit on *Scharnhorst*, but was herself hit and sunk. The German battlecruisers made no attempt to pick up survivors.

On 11 June, three days later, the small Norwegian vessel, *Borgund*, picked up thirty-eight men. A second vessel picked up a further four men who were landed in Norway and became prisoners of war. Ninety-four officers and 1,380 ratings from *Glorious*, *Ardent* and *Acasta* were lost, along with forty-one RAF personnel.

A Board of Inquiry was later to find that none of HMS *Glorious*'s aircraft were in the air in the twelve hours prior to or during the action. The true reasons for her loss remains secret even today and the files are not due to be opened until 100 years have passed, in 2040.

The day after the loss of *Glorious*, Norway fell to overwhelming German forces. The next day Mussolini, Italy's fascist dictator, declared war on the Allies.

The odds were stacking up against Britain's survival. Continuous operations day and night as well as the bombing raids by the *Luftwaffe*, were having an impact on exhausted aircrews. No. 812 Squadron was fighting hard while aircrew were being killed at an unsustainably high rate. Titch Harding's viewpoint, as he recollected, was 'Those that the gods love, they take early so that they will not grow old as we that are left grow old, age will not weary them or the years condemn.'

There was a brief respite while adverse weather conditions prevented any operations until 11 June, the same day *Glorious* survivors were being rescued. On that op, Roy and six other Swordfish had to return to base without dropping their payloads.

The other squadron on the air station, 22 Beaufort RAF Squadron, was at last becoming operational. On 12 June, 22 Squadron was tasked with a raid on Vaernes airfield in Norway. This was a diversionary mission to cover a raid by aircraft of the Fleet Air Arm, operating from the carrier *Ark Royal*, which were engaged in a retaliatory attack on the German capital ships *Scharnhorst*, *Gneisenau* and *Admiral Hipper*, hiding in Trondheim Fjord.

Clayton recalled:

The following Friday, June 14th, the squadron was stood off from operations so Beery and I went swimming from the beach and spent the evening in the canteen. We were about to turn in, luxuriating in the prospect of an uninterrupted night's sleep, when PO Manning came over shouting for everyone to go across to the hangars, the squadron was on the move again! We were to return to Ford!

First there were duty inspections to be done on all the aircraft and those who were going to fly with them went to draw parachutes and harnesses. Once again, Beery and I were detailed for Road Party and, five minutes later, we were back at the all too familiar task of packing up the squadron stores ready for loading onto lorries. The transport was late arriving and there were only two open lorries to convey us and our belongings, including the stores, on the 250-mile road journey.

We rolled through the gates at RNAS Ford, bleary-eyed and aching at 1035 on Sunday morning. At first we put down the solemnity of the way the Officer of the Day received us, to our unshaven appearance, but as he proceeded to outline what had been planned for us, we realised that something far more sinister was in the air: we were granted 48 hours Foreign Service leave, expiring at 0800 on Tuesday. When pressed for further details he said he knew nothing and that we had better hurry up because two and a half hours of our leave had already gone!

At last, with the squadron briefly withdrawn from front-line operations, Roy was given a well-earned leave and returned to Lee-on-Solent where Naomi was finalising the move to North Coates. She had last seen him at Maidstone during the Dunkirk evacuations: 'Three weeks or so later Roy returned to Lee. That night there was a loud air raid and bombing and he was absolutely whacked and he slept through it all.'

This was a terrible period for Roy. Not only had he only just returned to active duty after being ill and been working round the clock with the Dunkirk evacuation, but also he was devastated by news of so many of his friends killed or missing.

In haste, Roy and Naomi managed to get back to Shaldon to see the family. Trains were dashing between tunnels on the Dawlish to Teignmouth cliff section, where the tracks lay sandwiched between the beach and cliffs. They would come to a halt with a screech of brakes and hisses of steam in the shelter of the tunnels as German hit-and-run fighters chased and prowled outside.

Leslie had personal experience of the train hiding in the tunnel on one occasion:

I was in a train when the sirens were sounded in Teignmouth and the train took refuge in the tunnel until the German fighter passed.

Each of the tunnels were guarded by pill boxes at the entrances, even then the German fighters would still fire on the trains as they sped from tunnel to tunnel. These German fighters would also go into the harbour and fire on any boat. On another occasion, a German fighter flew in up the estuary and fired on a lone rower – the poor girl was so petrified that over the following weeks her hair went white.

During Roy's leave, the family was sitting and talking with him around the drawing room table, or listening to the latest BBC news bulletins on the wireless, when there was a knock at the door. Leslie recalled: 'A policeman was standing there holding a telegram, sent from the Admiralty, saying "Baker-Falkner missing at Dunkirk".' It appeared there had been a mix-up with the loss of Ken Gurr.

Soon after hearing this news, Titch tried to give an explanation for the telegram:

After enemy action in which the Swordfish dropped a bomb or mine, each aircraft returned alone to escape enemy searchlights and flak – and in bad weather or what have you, you did not always get back to North Coates. Some landed at Bircham and it was some time before they could let us know – result a bit of confusion and this leads to mistakes, including the telegram to Roy's family from Cracksie Crawford the CO at the time of Dunkirk.

At the end of leave, the squadron returned to RNAS Ford and rushed through the stores to draw tropical kit.

Clayton recalled:

After the air party had gone to man the Swordfish, we were marched to the control tower where two Bristol Bombay transports were waiting to fly us to our destination – wherever that might be! Then we were informed that we were to fly to Toulon, via Nantes and Bordeaux, where arrangements had been made for the Swordfish and the Bombays to be refuelled.

As we waited, Farmer made weak jokes about our forthcoming holiday on the Riviera then, suddenly, a staff car screeched to a halt, an officer jumped out and demanded who was in charge. He spoke briefly to the Flight Sergeant and got back in the car. It was then announced the trip was cancelled, we were to return to North Coates in the morning! It is impossible to find words to express our feelings, which were a confused mixture of relief and anti-climax.

That evening we celebrated our reprieve in Littlehampton. In the same pub were some refugees, newly arrived from France. They thought we must be crazy to have thought we could have made it, even as far as Nantes; either we would have been shot down or the *Luftwaffe* would have been waiting to take over our aircraft as they landed, and we would have remained their guests for the duration!

Titch Harding, years later, said the operation was a mystery: 'The whole squadron went to Ford on 15 June 1940 and then suddenly after a short leave the squadron was being sent back again to North Coates on 19 June.'

The squadron was pleased to be returning to North Coates and on arrival proceeded to 'beat-up' the airfield. Clayton recalled:

Sub Lt Gaillard gave a display of his own, putting Swordfish 'L' through a series of steep dives and stall turns which he rounded off with a low pass underneath the telephone wire between 'X' and 'Y' Flight hangars!

He also remembered:

On the way north someone had swiped an LNER poster and hung it in the crew room. It read: 'Nightly Service – Harwich to the Hook of Holland' but the CO ordered it to be removed because it posed a risk to security.

Sadly, our high spirits were short-lived for the next day a list of survivors from HMS *Glorious* and her two destroyers, *Acasta* and *Ardent*, was published: 38 men had been saved out of 1,519. It was hoped that some of those who were thought to have drowned might have been taken prisoner, but it turned out that the Germans rescued no one from the water; the only prisoners taken were four men picked up by a Norwegian fishing boat and landed in occupied Norway.

Shocked as they were by the loss of so many friends and colleagues, Roy and Naomi attempted to settle down to some semblance of married life. No. 812 Squadron's ground crew had been billeted in the vacant married quarters so Roy and Naomi had to find their own alternative accommodation. They first stayed at Norman's Cottage. Naomi recalled: 'The old boy who owned Norman's Cottage had evacuated his wife and family but we had to look after him.' Conditions were made a little easier for Roy at the station with the help of his steward, Sgt Hunt, who was to remain with him for the rest of the time in 812 Squadron.

Naomi continued: 'Typically, Roy would spend the day on ops laying mines and then at night he would be out on bombing raids. When Roy was on ops, I was petrified.' Throughout the day, Naomi would be a bundle of nerves. At night it was worse. Naomi would wait, listening for the roar of the Swordfish taking off; the hours would pass slowly, and eventually on the aircraft's return she would count each one of them coming back. Then the remaining minutes would seem like hours and time would appear to stop until Roy would walk in again. 'This would be repeating itself day after day, night after night,' recalled Naomi.

She had seen the stress Roy had been under since recovering from his illness. All the wives and family could see the same in their husbands. Leslie remembered: 'Roy would normally contain the pressure and just go quiet, just thinking out what to do.'

One of the few notes that Roy penned to Naomi in the hectic days of 1940 read: 'North Coates. I won't be home till about nine tomorrow morning as we are taking off in the early morning. Usual job. I've got to sleep at the camp. Just come home for clothes.'

Life fell into a certain pattern. After a night of operations, a late breakfast was followed by a walk or cycle down to where the aircraft was parked. The rigger and fitter would be working on it and after inspection of any damage, Roy would report its serviceability or otherwise to the flight office and check whether he was on the flight roster for that night.

Once she had settled down, Naomi found it such a relief to be with Roy again: 'I felt lucky to have him near me despite him being away overnight on dangerous operations.' There was also a community of wives and girlfriends at North Coates for Naomi to socialise with and share their fears. Cliff Kindell recalled: 'I remember Roy's wife, Naomi. I knew who some of the wives were because so many, including mine, accompanied their aircrew husbands. They lived in Cleethorpes and villages closer to North Cotes.'

However, because Naomi had to look after the elderly owner of Norman's Cottage, there was little time to truly relax with Roy and friends – they had their eye on moving as soon as possible but accommodation was difficult with the war on.

In many ways, the operational life at North Coates suited Roy. It had an informality not found in a warship staffed by older naval officers, and the night operations gave him the opportunity to use some ingenuity. As time went on, Roy could make his Swordfish do anything he wanted and there were times when his observer, Bruce Hawkes, subjected to some hectic manoeuvres, commented with some feeling that Roy should have been a fighter pilot.

At the end of the month, Roy and Naomi moved into Rose Cottage, a thatched cottage opposite the church in old North Coates village. Naomi recalled:

> We had been waiting to try and get it for absolutely ages. In the end, we got in there only for six to seven weeks.
>
> Bath night was quite an event. In the cottage was an antiquated bath with an old wood-fired boiler. It was a devil to light up. One had to pump the water up and it would take ages. We always had air raids whenever the bath was ready.

At last Roy and Naomi had a home where they could invite their friends. Naomi recalled:

> It was about this period after we had settled in at North Coates that we acquired an Alsatian dog called Rex. Roy bought him off an RAF type also stationed at North Coates. The dog was named in honour of the first 22 Squadron CO who had been killed in ops. Roy felt sorry for this Alsatian who had been left behind. Rex was lovely with me and Roy but aggressive with other people. Rex was especially savage with the postman. He didn't travel well. It couldn't have been at a more difficult period.
>
> Rex used to go with Roy for his daily inspection of his aircraft, and when Roy was out on ops, Roy's steward, Hunt, or the squadron would look after him. Hunt was very affectionate towards Rex; in fact the whole squadron almost adopted Rex as their squadron mascot, and many 812 Squadron members reminisced happily about Rex even fifty years later!

During her summer break Leslie came to stay and Roy told her almost nothing about his job. She recalled: 'Over that period they had long flights in open cockpits. Roy also used to complain how bitterly cold those open aircraft were.'

The ground crews were getting into the rhythm of the nightly operations. Clayton recalled:

We soon got used to the routine of seeing our aircraft off in the late evening and receiving them back in the small hours of the morning. The only difference was that air raids had become more frequent. Generally, we managed to snatch two hours' sleep after the Swordfish left before the air raid siren sounded at 2300. The alert usually lasted until daylight at 0400. No bombs were dropped near the aerodrome but the fact that bombers kept entering and leaving the area meant that we had to remain at readiness.

On 15 June, new aircrew replacements arrived including Leslie 'Snowball' Edwards:

I joined 812 Squadron at RAF North Coates near Grimsby in the rank of Midshipman (A), on completion of Observers' training at RNAS Ford. Senior pilot was Lt Harding. Sub Lt Cliff Kindell was my pilot; I was a midshipman observer navigator and wireless operator.

B-F, as Roy was affectionately known in the squadron, was a lieutenant at that time and I flew with him on engine test flights and cross-country trips. B-F was an experienced pilot, had an excellent sense of humour and was much respected by the troops.

Our operations took us as far afield as Terschelling, Texel, Ismuiden, Hook of Holland, Flushing, Rotterdam, Ostend, Boulogne and Cherbourg.

In the ops I can vouch for the extreme conditions as regards to exposure to the elements in the rear cockpit of Swordfish, particularly at night in winter time.

I remember when we were based at North Coates, another midshipman and I shared an old Austin seven (purchase price 15 pounds) which we used to get to Cleethorpes for our night off duty.

Cliff Kindell added:

Our main task now was laying mines off the coast of Europe from the borders of Germany to Le Havre. We also occasionally bombed the invasion barges waiting at Dutch ports. Additionally, we escorted east coast convoys from south of the Wash to about Scarborough. All these ops, except convoy escort, were necessarily undertaken at night in view of the Swordfish's slow speed and relative lack of firepower.

At this time the 22 Squadron RAF, equipped with Bristol Beauforts, was also staying at North Coates and were on the same task as we. However, their aircraft were powered by Bristol Taurus engines which had many failures over a period of six months, causing the Beauforts to be grounded. Our squadron and another naval air squadron based at Bircham Newton, Norfolk, were much needed.

On 17 June, Winston Churchill told the House of Commons in a speech, repeated later in a broadcast to the nation: 'Let us brace ourselves to our duty and so bear ourselves that if the British Commonwealth and Empire lasts for a thousand years men will say, "This was their finest hour".'

The next day, the second evacuation of Allied forces was completed from the French Atlantic ports. The Swordfish met little enemy opposition during this period on their nightly minelaying operations.

On Friday, 21 June, three operations were carried out that day: Operation *Convoy* with three aircraft on convoy duties over Flamborough Head; Operation *Mussels* with three aircraft flying at midnight over Dutch territory, and Operation *Oysters*, again with three aircraft on a mission, with Titch Harding in the lead. Titch and the other two aircraft sighted three powerful searchlights in the Hook of Holland area. On their return from a four-hour gardening operation, Titch Harding's Swordfish and 'B for Beer' were fired on by ground defences over the Humber estuary.

Clayton recalled:

The observers twice fired the recognition signals by Very pistol and signalled the coded letter of the day, but Titch's aircraft was hit by bullets at 1,000 ft. He managed to bring the aircraft in to North Coates with a safe landing, and with the CO fuming in the back.

What he said over the telephone to the battery commander is not recorded, but it was reported that the lines were red hot by the time he rang off!

He continued:

I was kept busy repairing the bullet-riddled flooring of 'A' – that the bullets missed both crew members and did no major structural damage was nothing short of a miracle.

Titch recalled this event: 'Cracksie lost the heal of his flying boot, shot away when I made a mistake one dark and stormy night and ended up over Grimsby. They thought that we were hostile.'

On 22 June, French armed forces surrendered to Germany. General Charles Huntziger, leader of the French delegation, signed the armistice terms, seated in the railway carriage at Compiegne where the Germans had been forced to sign the surrender at the end of the First World War. Germany gained total control of the whole of Northern France, while General Pétain was allowed to be Prime Minister of an unoccupied southern area, Vichy France. Britain was becoming increasingly isolated as Germany formally occupied all the surrounding countries in Northern Europe.

All that Roy and the rest of 812 Squadron could do was battle on – there was no option. On Tuesday, 25 June, he and six other pilots flew their aircraft to Manston before carrying out 'gardening' along the Belgian and French coasts in areas of Dabs and Clams. The operation was a success and only slight flak was encountered. They returned to North Coates where further air raids started again that night.

Two days later Roy received his official appointment to join 812 Squadron – the paperwork was beginning to catch up!

That night he flew one of six aircraft on Operation *Cucumber* in the areas of 'Mussels' and 'Limpets'. This time Bruce Hawkes, Roy's observer, flew with Titch. A three-star signal was observed over Texel and at 0240 hours a convoy of twenty to thirty ships, including a destroyer, was sighted but the Swordfish avoided their covert mining operation being discovered.

Operations were getting increasingly dangerous as German anti-aircraft resources became more organised. Overnight, on 29–30 June, Roy in 'F for Freddy', along with six aircraft, left North Coates after dark to lay mines in the areas Whelks and Dabs – the locations for invasion barges building up at Boulogne Harbour. The aircraft divided into two sub-flights of three, and first proceeded to Manston.

This was a typical mission for Roy. Following a briefing by the duty officer and the CO, Roy and Bruce Hawkes would go to the dispersal area. After checking on the serviceability of his aircraft, he would climb into his aircraft, clip on his parachute and draw the harness together.

Naomi recalled: 'He would always take with him in the Swordfish his little mascot, a model Pop-eye that I had bought for him for good luck.'

Aircraftsmen Wilson and Hawkins, his faithful fitter and rigger, would assist him. They had maintained his aircraft in adverse conditions over the past difficult operational months since Dunkirk – Wilson looking after the engine with Hawkins caring for the airframe, the pair of them always there to cosset the overworked Stringbag back to life. Wilson would wish Roy a safe journey and ask him to bring their Stringbag back undamaged. Bruce Hawkes was in the back seat. As usual on these minelaying missions, there was no room for their air gunner, Ernie Kerridge.

Swordfish 'A' took off first. Roy came next. His aircraft was heavy with the weight of the mine firmly slung under the belly of the plane. The long-range tank added to the load. Roy had to use maximum power, throttle wide open, hauling back on the stick, to enable the aircraft to lumber into the air. His rule of thumb, as Leslie recalled, was that if he had not eaten his sugared almonds by the end of the runway, he knew 'it was time to get worried as then he would never clear the ground and take off safely.' Airborne at last, all the aircraft headed to RAF Station Manston where they stayed until night.

Roy's flight took off again some time near midnight. The pilots dowsed their navigation lights almost immediately after take-off. After crossing the Kent coast, they climbed in formation at 80 knots, heading for the enemy shoreline. The Swordfish were grossly overladen, unstable and unsafe – the ASI at 60–70 knots, just above stalling speeds. The operation began with a climb to about 10,000 feet – a long and laborious task.

After one hour and fifteen minutes, Roy's main fuel tank was much lighter and the Swordfish less burdened and nearly itself again. The reserve tank was not to be used until on the way home as, when half-filled, it was particularly lethal with inflammable fumes that could easily explode if the tank was hit.

At last, they saw landfall off the French coast and the Swordfish throttled back to 65 knots. The searchlights were sweeping low over the water ahead of them. Silhouettes of the harbour installations at Boulogne became visible. The Swordfish were within range of even the lightest machine guns but had not yet been seen. There followed a long glide approach from the Swordfish's ceiling height of 10,000 ft with the engines shut off to avoid alerting the enemy. It would not do for the Germans to watch the drop, pinpoint where the mines landed and then go and retrieve them.

Hawkes and the observers in each of the other aircraft fixed their positions more accurately. Dropping towards sea level, skimming over the waves, the aircraft levelled at 50–100 feet – the dropping height. Roy and the other pilots steadied their Stringbags for the release. At a given signal, the aircraft dropped their mines one after the other. Roy activated the release button on the throttle, pressed the tit and the deadweight of nearly a ton was released from the Swordfish into the waters below. After the formation drop, Roy made a 'blue' turn, a quick avoiding action banking away from searchlights and flak. Now other Swordfish had been spotted and were coming under fire.

There was 'intense searchlight menace' as reported later, with heavy anti-aircraft fire and machine-gun bullets from both sides of the harbour – a succession of coloured 'flaming onion' tracer bullets, headed straight towards them, with the illusion of coming slowly at first towards the aircraft and then speeding as they got nearer and nearer.

Swordfish 'Q', piloted by Sub Lt C.A. Conn, was unlucky and didn't make it back to base, having believed to have plunged into the sea.

The other aircraft jinked and swerved to reach the open sea. The return journey was made with each aircraft flying alone at 5,000 ft or skimming over the waves to keep out of danger. They noted a merchant vessel of 1,000–2,000 tons partly sunk at Ijmuiden harbour and were concerned with an enemy aircraft following them for about thirty minutes – but it did not attack.

With the weight burden removed, the Swordfish went back to its normal speed of 70 knots and the controls were more responsive. The main fuel tank would be low and Roy had to switch to the extra fuel tank, remembering to order Hawkes over the Gosport voice pipe to 'out cork' – take the cork out of the air vent or no petrol would flow to the engine. Finally, the Swordfish landed at North Coates.

Clayton wrote in his diary: 'Saturday, June 29th was another tragic day for the squadron when we heard that 'Q' had been shot down over Boulogne and Sub Lt John Davies and Sub Lt C.A. Conn were posted as having been killed in action.'

As it turned out, Conn and Davies both survived and were picked up by German forces. Conn elaborated:

> I was with 812 Squadron for five weeks early in 1940, the squadron was then based at North Coates. I regret my short duration with the squadron was because I was shot down and became a POW. I am afraid I am a little hazy of the events of 1940 as, quite frankly, it has been my intention to forget this period of my life.
>
> Our mission on this particular night was to mine Boulogne harbour. One flight of three planes left North Coates during the afternoon and flew to Manston RAF Station. Thence we stayed until night and the flight took off some time near midnight. Sub Lt John Davies was with me. We arrived off Boulogne and my plane was the first to drop to sea level to drop the mine which was accomplished. Turning away I was fired on by ack-ack and was shot down into the sea about a quarter mile offshore. We swam ashore but were unfortunately picked up by a German patrol who had presumably witnessed the shooting down.
>
> John Davies and I were taken to an investigation camp, still soaking wet and worried. Davies was a little injured. From the interrogation camp, I was sent to Stalag Luft I which was an RAF POW camp on the Baltic. After a period there, obviously among RAF officers, we were after two years transferred to Sagan in Eastern Germany, Stalag Luft III was the camp.

Over the next six months, this was to be a typical nightly operation for Roy. No. 812 Squadron worked round the clock maintaining what Roy and the others now called 'Crawford's Cross-Channel Service'.

Roy later told Leslie: 'The Germans used to miss because they were so surprised that the Swordfish were so slow! But what I really hate are the search lights but for Shorty Shaw that is a different matter; he looks out for the search lights to dive on and shoot out.'

Up until then all the aircrew and their wives had done their best to live from day to day, with social events, parties and joking – they had a determination to have fun in the face of danger. The continued night-time operations, which were getting more and more hazardous, were increasing the stresses and strains.

Naomi knew Roy was not allowed to say anything; however she found it hard to accept that she should know so little. Roy was increasingly deflecting her questions about what he had been doing or how difficult and dangerous each operation had been. She presumed it was because he did not want her to be any more afraid for him than she already was.

Meanwhile, air battles were raging to the east and south of London as the *Luftwaffe* attacked the RAF airfields, trying to put them out of action before they launched an invasion. Reports were coming in of barges having been seen in large numbers in French ports, ready to carry the German army across the Channel.

Families crowded round the wireless each evening to hear the nine o'clock news and the BBC announcement of the number of German planes destroyed by the Hurricanes and Spitfires of the RAF fighter squadrons. The number of German aircraft coming over never seemed to lessen, no matter how many were shot down, and continued to pound the RAF airfields in southern England.

In July, German bombers and fighters attacked Ford, Detling and other airfields. There was to be a new series of air attacks on North Coates.

Overnight, on 1–2 July, Roy's squadron was involved in a bombing raid mounted against the oil refinery at Vlaardingen near Rotterdam. RAF Operation *34* included nine Swordfish aircraft. Titch Harding recalled:

> 812 Squadron was ordered to attack oil and petrol tanks at Rotterdam. For this we carried six 250-lb bombs and did a dive-bomb attack. Roy would have been on it.
>
> I led the squadron to the north of the town at maximum height – hoping that they might think that we were on our way to another target. Then we all turned to starboard so as to make the attack east to west so as to use extra speed in the dive for our get-away.
>
> The Germans did not want to lose their captured fuel and so had encircled the fuel tanks with searchlights and AA flak guns. On reaching the attack point – searchlights and tracer coned the target. The aircraft followed each other down to the drop-point then up again and down again and so forth.

The mission did not go well; the crews had difficulty finding the target and dropped their bombs on the searchlights and gun positions instead. 'C for Charlie' was more successful, releasing bombs at 2,000 ft, east of Rotterdam – one large blaze started and particularly intense fire was seen to the north-west of the town.

Tragically, the aircraft flown by Sub Lt John Kiddell was shot down over Amsterdam's Schiphol airport. L/A H.W.V. Harry Burt was killed and buried at Amsterdam New Eastern cemetery but Kiddell survived and was taken prisoner. He was killed later attempting to escape in July 1943 from Stalag Luft III and buried at Poznan old garrison cemetery in Poland.

The Swordfish flown by Sub Lt B.P. Grigson with observer Sub Lt Frederick Lees also failed to return – they had both been killed. Their bodies were later laid to rest in Rozenburg General Cemetery. Swordfish 'M for Mother' almost made it home but suffered engine failure and crashed while making a forced landing at Harrock Island, Orfordness. Both crew members were unhurt.

After the mission, Titch Harding wrote in his log book: 'Self, Lt Cdr Crawford bombing Rotterdam N.B.G.! trip 4.25 hrs night'.

He continued:

> At the de-briefing stayed as usual to hear reports – tail end Charlie new boy's first trip, a bit excited. 'First bombs dropped set fire to tanks so some of our aircraft were diving down into flames etc.' The de-briefing officer, who was tired like the rest of us, said: 'Oh yes, just like diving into the jaws of hell.' Our aircrew youngsters were embarrassed – had to give them a bit of a check-up to make them feel better.
>
> And so back to the mess for bacon and egg, mess staff first class – always something hot whatever the time, usually very late night and very early morning.

The remaining Swordfish that returned to North Coates found the base had been subjected to an air raid and enemy air attack by ten fighters and bombers in their absence.

The next night Roy's squadron was back on 'gardening' duties and over that month there was much to-ing and fro-ing between North Coates and Manston, often flying down one afternoon, doing an operation against a target on the Belgian coast and then returning the next day for a trip across to Kiel or the Frisian Islands.

Clayton recalled:

> As a result of this activity our aircraft were piling up the flying hours. After 180 hours a major inspection became due. Normally, this was done by the Royal Naval Aircraft Repair Yard at Fleetlands (Gosport) but, because they were inundated with work and production was being disrupted by air raids, it was decreed that such inspections should be carried out by squadron personnel.
>
> This imposed an even greater workload on the already overworked ground crews. By improvisation, compromise and goodwill on the part of all concerned, the targets were met. With so much at stake there was no question of me confining my activities to airframes for, although I had not been examined in aero-engine maintenance and operation, I had been through a longer and more thorough course of instruction than an Air Mechanic (E).

The ground crews were also ordered to distinguish for the first time Fleet Air Arm aircraft from RAF aircraft on the same air stations, so from the beginning of the month the legend 'ROYAL NAVY' had to be painted in four-inch block capitals above each machine's serial on the rear fuselage.

On Monday, 8 July, North Coates had its first daylight visit from the *Luftwaffe* when a Heinkel 111, which had dropped its bomb load somewhere inland, sighted the airfield at 1610 hours. Its aircrew decided to strafe the barracks living quarters before beating it for home.

Clayton recollected:

> It was tea time; Beery and I were walking across to the dining hall when we heard an unfamiliar engine note and, on looking up, we spotted the intruder at about 1,000 feet. We dived into a hedge bottom just as the nose and tail gunners opened fire. The pilot's fire was directed at the centre of the camp while the latter concentrated upon the area behind him, but his bullets fell to either side of us as the bomber headed out to sea.

It later transpired that the main damage was to the huts recently vacated by the Gunnery School and to one of 22 Squadron's hangars. No one had been wounded, but PO Flanagan, who was in charge of 'Y' Flight, had a bullet through his bed. He had been resting on it a few minutes before and had just gone to the Sergeants' Mess when the attack began.

For the next week, 13–20 July, 812 Squadron had a respite from exhausting and progressively more stressful night operations over enemy territory, when RAF Coastal Command ordered them to carry out local convoy duties.

By mid-July, Titch, Roy and the other old hands in the squadron had carried out up to nineteen minelaying and bombing operations with the ever increasing menace of anti-aircraft fire, more sophisticated searchlights and heavier flak as the German forces established themselves in the occupied countries. It appeared as if the number of operations would rise as the threat of invasion of Britain by the Nazis seemed inevitable.

CHAPTER 13

Battle of Britain

There was to be no let-up for Roy and 812 Squadron in the summer of 1940 as the Germans continued their push across Europe. By 25 June 1940 French resistance ended. Hitler was master of Western Europe; Britain stood alone against Germany. July was to see the beginning of what later became known as the 'Battle of Britain'. For a few weeks that hot summer the fate of the country, and of Western Europe, lay in the hands of a few hundred pilots.

The Fleet Air Arm and Roy's squadron were to play their part. Two squadrons of the Fleet Air Arm were directly under the control of RAF Fighter Command – 804 and 808 – but many naval pilots flew within RAF Fighter Command squadrons.

After Dunkirk more than thirty-eight naval pilots under training with the Fleet Air Arm were transferred temporarily to the RAF. They were sent to operational training schools in order to convert to flying Spitfires and Hurricanes. Thirty more naval pilots transferred by the end of June. At least fifty-eight naval pilots, including Roy, were formally listed as having taken part in the Battle of Britain. They wore naval uniform but for operations and discipline they were fully integrated into the RAF squadrons, and as casualties occurred, became section leaders, with RAF pilots under them.

One such naval pilot was Roy who would have been quite capable of flying Hurricanes or Spitfires, according to Flt Lt Alan 'Ginger' Murray. Ginger, who had previously flown Swordfish with Roy in 812 Squadron on board *Glorious*, himself converted to Hurricanes in June 1940 and subsequently took over command of 73 Squadron RAF in the Battle of Britain.

That summer, Roy was rumoured to have volunteered to operate briefly with 600 Squadron – a Blenheim fighter-bomber squadron based at Manston from 22 June for three months under the command of Squadron Leader David Clark. The squadron had been destroyed on 10 May when six of its aircraft had attacked Waalhaven airport near Rotterdam which had been seized by German paratroopers. Only one aircraft returned home. According to Battle of Britain RAF pilot John Young, in the urgent need to replace lost crews, Roy may have agreed to assist in one or more ops whilst he waited for his posting.

As it turned out, Roy's main role during the Battle of Britain was laying mines at the entrance to German-held harbours in order to prevent the invasion of the British Isles. Progressively, as the summer went by, Roy and 812 Squadron were also involved in the bombing of invasion barges building up in the Channel.

Lt Cdr Chapman, of 815 Squadron, emphasised the necessity of accurate minelaying: 'We're not a lot of bloody chickens, dropping our eggs indiscriminately all over the bloody shop. We've got to put them in the right place or there's no point in going.'

Meanwhile, the German offensive concentrated on pounding British airfields, particularly in mid-July. The *Luftwaffe* took advantage of cloud cover and their bombers were liable to strike at any time of the day or night.

Clayton recalled:

When we were not working on 812 aircraft, we were digging earthworks to provide defensive positions against a possible attack by paratroops. These were crude hollows in the ground by the corner of each hangar. The mounds thus produced were topped with sandbags and barbed wire and provided a parapet over which we could fire our antiquated rifles at any advancing Germans!

On 20 July, 812 Squadron carried out Operation *Cucumber* to the area code-named Xeranthemum, and included six aircraft, amongst them Roy's 'F for Freddy'. Titch Harding, with Cracksie Crawford in the back seat, recorded carrying out 'gardening' twice that day and experienced heavy flak near the Hague at 11.30 pm.

Two nights later Operation *Cucumber* missions were to the Xeranthemum and Zinnias areas over the Dutch coast and islands. Air Gunner John Pinkerton recalled:

I flew with Sub Lt Eborn to lay mines at Schiermonnikoog. We were in the air for five hours twenty minutes at night. Two days later I flew a three hour anti-submarine patrol off Flamborough during the day and that night spent four and a half hours minelaying at Texel with a different pilot.

Ralph Eborn was one of 812 Squadron's new replacement pilots, although he had already seen action against the Germans. The previous month he had participated in the evacuation of the British Expeditionary Force from Norway with 810 Squadron on board HMS *Ark Royal*. Roy and other veterans of 812 Squadron listened with dismay to his firsthand accounts of the frantic attempts by his squadron and others to search for survivors from HMS *Glorious*. During the search off Norway, Eborn's aircraft failed to return, signalling it was making a deferred forced landing at sea. Fortunately, he ditched safely and was rescued by the fishing vessel *Syrian*, which later took him and his crew to Iceland.

While Roy, Eborn, Pinkerton and the rest of the squadron were out 'gardening' over occupied Europe, a stick of bombs fell on the beach close to the airfield boundary. This was followed by a burst of machine gun fire and, last of all, the air raid siren.

Clayton recalled:

Word was passed for us to take cover in the shelters, but Beery, Meddy and I stood around at the top of the steps watching the searchlights. Suddenly, there was a strange tinkling sound; it seemed to be coming out of the darkness above our heads. Then there was a low whistle which grew in volume and we knew it was time to take cover. The trouble was we all reached the door at the same moment and fell sprawling on the ground. The sky seemed to light up then the ground beneath us heaved and shook with the concussion of several loud explosions. After that we stayed under cover until we were called out at 0320 to receive the aircraft returning from ops.

While we were refuelling and picketing them down, there was another strange rushing sound and we ran for the nearest slit trench, but before we reached it we realised it was an aircraft with its engines cut. Sparks trailed behind it and, as it passed overhead, its fuselage glowed a dull red. It was too high to land on the aerodrome but passed over the dyke to crash on the beach with an ear-splitting roar. The beach had been mined while we were at Ford; one of these must have blown up the aircraft along with any bombs still remaining on board. It was believed to have been a Do 215, hit by AA fire.

For the next two nights minelaying operations were carried out again in the areas Xeranthemum, Zinnias, Limpets, Mussels and Flounders. Flak was encountered in Holland at Borkum, and searchlights at Ijmuiden and Den Helder, as well as near Leeuwarden aerodrome.

On 25 July, Roy and the other squadron crew took turns in 'single aircraft relief' for a day-long convoy escort. Also that day, Fleet Street journalists and photographers visited 812 Squadron to interview and take photographs of them at work and rest for a later article in the newspapers. The pilots also had to carry out a squadron formation for the cameras, flying around for forty-five minutes until the perfect image was taken.

At this time, for reasons of security, all Fleet Air Arm Swordfish attacks had been ascribed to the RAF. This was designed to give the Fleet time to get away from the area before the enemy knew who had been responsible and could retaliate.

That night, three aircraft were involved in Operation *Cucumber* in the Oysters area.– Two searchlights in the vicinity of the Hook of Holland were encountered as well as extensive flak over Rotterdam. They were also challenged by an enemy flak ship with four red star bursts – but were not fired upon. The day after there was a close shave during their routine convoy single aircraft relief duties when at 1245 hours a Heinkel He111 bomber came out of the clouds at 2,000 ft but did not attack.

At the end of July there came a break in operations for Roy and the squadron, when Cracksie Crawford was asked by the local Army commander to give his men some experience of field manoeuvres whilst under air attack. Sadly, it was to end in tragedy.

Maurice Driver explained:

My saddest recollections of the North Coates days are one of an exercise we carried out when our CO, Cracksie Crawford, agreed that we should take part in a 'German Invasion Exercise'.

About six Swordfish, including mine, took off to dive-bomb supposed enemy tanks.

Clayton continued the account:

A holiday spirit prevailed as we improvised special bomb carriers to release soot-and-flour bombs on the unsuspecting infantry. The leading light in this activity was Lt Barnes, 'Y' Flight's commander, who, being of an inventive turn of mood, applied his ingenuity to the project. The flight commander spent the last afternoon of his life practising with his aircraft 'K' at a target set up on the airfield until a technique was perfected.

The squadron turned out to watch, including some of the wives, who had recently joined their husbands and rented rooms in the village.

A final touch of reality was added by the riggers, who set the streamline bracing wired at such an angle that, in a dive, they emitted the banshee wail of an attacking Stuka. I should have hated to be one of those soldiers, for a Swordfish diving straight at you at close quarters with all its wires shrieking is a terrifying experience.

The next morning, Tuesday July 30th, was dull, but the clouds were high and we all clamoured for a chance to partake in the sport, but the regular observers exercised their prerogative to fly with their aircraft; not even the TAGs got a look in!

Twelve aircraft took off at 1030 and for the next half-hour Swordfish were to be seen diving upon the fields along Sheepmarsh Lane. They kept coming in their flights and sub-flights, to peel off and swoop upon the hapless troops who could be seen running for cover in ditches and hedgerows, only to scatter when the Swordfish sought them out.

At 1100 the CO, deciding that enough was enough, fired a red Verey light – the signal to break off the exercise. One by one, the returning aircraft joined the circuit and came in to land, but two had apparently not seen the recall signal and began to dive on a fresh target. Refuelling of the aircraft had begun when, suddenly, someone shouted: 'They've collided!'

I looked up to see a wing tip spinning to the ground as a fireball rose from a field outside the boundary fence. In the same instant another Swordfish skimmed the rising ground to the south to vanish behind a clump of willows in Sheepmarsh Lane. There followed a dull thud, followed by a silence broken only by the racket of ammunition exploding in the blaze from the first crash.

That day Naomi had gone shopping, safe in the knowledge that Roy and the squadron were not out on operations. Then she heard that there had been an accident:

I could not get back fast enough to hear who was safe and what had happened. Twelve Swordfish including Roy's 'F for Freddy' had been in a mock battle practising dummy dive-bombing on 'invading troops' when two Stringbags had crashed into each other half a mile south of North Coates.

Clayton continued:

I found myself running with others, motivated by the knowledge that there might be survivors who needed help. Leaping over fences and across ditches, we passed the severed wing tip lying in a potato field. The red navigation light indicated that it had come from the port upper and the letter, L, that it was Sub Lt Gaillard and his observer, Sub Lt Andrews. They were almost certainly dead, for the heat from the blazing wreckage was so intense that we could not approach within fifty yards of it.

We skirted the field and came to the clump of willows behind which the other Swordfish had disappeared. The air was heavy with the sickly-sweet smell of high octane fuel and this led us to where the mangled wreck of 'K' lay in a ditch. At least the observer, Lieutenant Groome, was alive, for he was calling to his pilot.

A GPO van had stopped in the middle of the lane. The long tyre marks behind it told how close it had come to being hit by the aircraft while its ashen-faced driver stood helplessly by in a state of shock.

The station ambulance arrived and we helped the observer into it, disregarding his protests that there was nothing wrong with him; he only had 'a headache' and 'felt a little tired' – and no wonder for, when we returned to the wreck, we found a dent the size of a soup bowl where his head had struck the back of the overload tank.

Just then the postman produced a cigarette case and was about to light up when we yelled at him to put it away. It was then that he related how the 'bloody airyplane' suddenly burst through the hedge, upside down, and skidded across the lane in front of his van.

As he rambled on, Leading Seaman Holmes and I tore at the wreckage to get at Lieutenant Barnes, whose Irvin jacket we could just make out inside the twisted fuselage. Petrol was gushing over his legs from the ruptured main tank and we gingerly prised him free of the broken tubes and wires that entangled him. Finally we got him clear and the medical orderlies helped us carry him to the ambulance. There was no question of there being any life left in his headless corpse.

Naomi recollected:

Three crew members were killed instantly and the fourth, Jerry Groome, got out of one of the Swordfish wreckages and said he had had a good flight, not recalling the accident at all. He was rushed to the Station Sick Quarters. He was all muddled and died suddenly one hour later, with a haemorrhage.

Clayton continued:

Back at the airfield everyone was concerned for Sub Lt David and Sub Lt Cole in Swordfish 'H', which had last been seen diving on a platoon at the Marshchapel end of the lane, but soon after we arrived there was a phone message to say that they had made a forced landing in a meadow and were both uninjured.

It was a cruel twist of fate that the squadron should have come through three months of operational flying to lose two experienced crews and three aircraft in a simple non-operational exercise with the Army.

Roy and all the squadron attended the military funerals which took place on Friday afternoon at St Nicholas Church in the village of North Coates. Naomi reflected: 'Three fine young fellows were all buried in the churchyard opposite our cottage, Sub Lt Andrews, Lt Groome and Sub Lt Gaillard.' Jakes Barnes was to be buried in Chertsey. He was only twenty-six. Naomi tried her hardest to console his widow, her distraught friend Mita.

Naomi never felt the same about her cottage beside the church, looking onto the freshly dug graves upset her. For the rest of her life, she hated the sound of church bells: 'Whenever I heard the church bells ring, it always reminded me of that tragedy.'

At the end of July, Nathaniel Hearle was appointed as 'X' Flight commander, being senior to Roy, having gained his wings a year earlier. He was a good choice and was well respected by 812 Squadron ground crew. 'He was a lovely chap,' recalled Bill Grice, an 812 Squadron air mechanic who served with him after the war.

August was anticipated to see the start of the invasion of England. The month started fine and sunny and the Germans started a build-up of barges in the French and Flemish ports. In response, Roy's squadron continued to carry out attacks on barges and oil tanks being assembled at Rotterdam. No. 812 Squadron used special bombs with extended fuses to ensure they exploded above the water, in order to inflict the maximum damage on the moored vessels.

Overnight, on 4 August, an RAF operation code-named *CCOI No 50* consisting of six Swordfish, including 'F for Freddy', and four Albacores were detailed to bomb the oil tanks at Vlaardingen, near Rotterdam. They encountered very heavy defensive flak and many searchlights. Three Swordfish could not locate the target and aborted. One attacked the searchlights at Hoek van Holland and one the harbour of Dordrecht. The sixth plane, Swordfish P4007 'Q for Queenie', flown by Sub Lt Ralph Eborn and Lt Timothy Johnston, a Royal Marine, was hit and forced to ditch off the Dutch coast near Noordwijk. Both men were reported missing and later presumed killed.

The body of Sub Lt Eborn was washed ashore on Noordwijk beach on 23 August. Local policeman Ellenbaas and a few workmen collected the body by horse and cart. At the cemetery building the body was searched and a number of papers discovered. The name Ralph Churchill Eborn was found, however the rest was unreadable. Eborn was buried at Noordwjk General Cemetery, but Johnston was never found.

The Eborn family was unlucky. Molly, his sister, had a fiancé who disappeared about the same time Ralph went missing. Ralph's own Danish fiancée, Annelise Albeck, who he had met at a dance the previous year whilst on holiday in Norfolk, was never informed of his death. Even seventy years later Annelise and her daughter Sussi wondered whether there was any chance that he might have survived somewhere and not been killed in 1940.

The whole of that week in early August 1940 was taken up with convoy duties until the 9th when a new replacement observer, Sub Lt P.H. 'Pip' Phillips, arrived to join the squadron. That night six aircraft went out on Operation *Cucumber* to area Xeranthemum in poor weather conditions over Holland. The operation went without hitch.

Three nights later there were a series of deadly attacks by Stuka dive-bombers on aerodromes, including RNAS Ford and RNAS Lee-on-Solent. The next day, Detling was the target for a big *Luftwaffe* raid when eighty-six Stuka dive-bombers appeared out of the clouds. The Stukas achieved maximum surprise; each runway was riddled with bomb craters and rubble. Fires started in every hangar, destroying twenty-two aircraft. The Ops Room disappeared in one large explosion. The various taxiways and dispersal points around the perimeter of the airfield were badly bombed as well as the main runway and administration buildings. Various anti-aircraft gunnery posts were direct hits, killing all the gunners manning them. One surviving gunner is reported to have said at the time 'I preferred it at Dunkirk!' Over sixty-seven people were killed, including the station commander, Group Captain Edward Davis. A further ninety-four were injured. In retaliation, Titch, along with Roy, led a bombing attack of four hours on the German-occupied Dutch naval base at Den Helder.

The operation, code-named *CCOI No 54*, was reported in the North Coates Operational Records Book:

> Six Swordfish aircraft of 812 Squadron proceeded in company on this operation, object being to bomb the Den Helder Naval Base, situated at Willemsoord. Aircraft 'P' and 'K'/812 located target and dropped salvos of bombs. The former aircraft reported having seen bursts of bombs in the neighbourhood of the basin, and this aircraft then fired 60 rounds from its rear gun at a searchlight and light 'flak' post.
>
> Aircraft 'A', 'C' and 'H' reported releasing three salvos of bombs. Aircraft 'A' and 'H' each registered two hits on the road close to tower. The sixth aircraft failed to locate the target within the time allotted and returned without releasing bombs.
>
> All aircraft engaged on the operation reported having encountered slight searchlight opposition and inaccurate heavy and light flak in the vicinity of the target.

Roy's Stringbag and the other Swordfish returned safely to base but there was a near miss a couple of nights later. Clayton recalled:

> On the night of 14 August I was helping the crews receive their aircraft back from a bombing raid. Rotterdam again, I believe. They had brought their bombs back with them and I was directing 'G' to dispersal when 'C' overshot the flare path and ended up with a sickening thud in a drainage ditch on the eastern boundary. Luckily

for everyone, there was no fire and, although the bombs had taken the brunt of the impact which fractured their cases, none exploded. It was a near thing, and another turn on the screw as far as my nerves were concerned!

Holmes came over to us with the news that the squadron was given leave; seven days to each crew in turn. Crew 'A' first. And so started a series of leave for the ground and air crews, Roy's was scheduled for the fourth week.

National newspapers reported that air battles over Britain were continuing with unabated ferocity as the *Luftwaffe* maintained its attempt to overwhelm Fighter Command:

Goering, convinced that the RAF is at its last gasp after the hard fighting of the *Kanalkampf* (the Channel War), named last Tuesday, 13 August, as *Adlertag*, Eagle Day, when the RAF would be swept from the sky and the invasion of Britain would be made possible.

Airfields and RDF stations were hammered, but the RAF's pilots, fed frugally into the battle by Air Vice Marshal Keith Park, not only stayed in the air but had the best of the fighting, knocking down forty-six Germans for the loss of thirteen.

On 18 August, 259 Stukas and Me109s raided Thorney Island, Gosport and Ford. RNAS Ford was badly bombed by the *Luftwaffe*, putting the air station completely out of action. PO George Pett recalled being lucky to survive the attack for his clothing was torn by shrapnel. Messmates on either side of him were killed.

Titch noted:

I was gardening that day on a five hours twenty minute mission with Lt Curry, and so missed the bombers' visit to Ford. But I did lose a very nice teak carved, camphor wood-lined chest brought back from Hong Kong when serving in *Hermes* plus my first log book etc. left there for safe keeping.

The air station at Thorney Island was hit at 1400 hours. One eyewitness, Thomas Lloyd the Station Defence Officer, recalled:

What a sight met our eyes. Hangars and aircraft blazing, masses of smoke drifting westwards across the aerodrome, the sky literally thick with ack-ack bursts, vapour trails and falling aircraft, fire engines and squad tearing around and aircraft falling out of the sky, earthwards, everywhere. Every time a Hun machine hit the deck, my boys cheered. A fighter Blenheim from the station accounted for two machines. A lad from the Station Armoury accompanied by an R.E. Sapper accounted for another.

On 20 August, Winston Churchill addressed the House of Commons and praised airmen for their heroic struggle against the *Luftwaffe*:

The gratitude of every home in our Island, in our Empire, and indeed throughout the world, except in the abodes of the guilty, goes out to the British airmen who, undaunted by odds, unwearied in their constant challenge and mortal danger, are turning the tide of the World War by their prowess and by their devotion. Never in the field of human conflict was so much owed by so many to so few.

Overnight, on 21/22 August, Swordfish 'X for X-ray' was lost whilst 'gardening'. The pilot, Lt Nathaniel Hearle, and observer, Sub Lt Rupert Davies, were taken prisoner at the mouth of the River Scheldt. Nathaniel Hearle, had been acting as 'X' Flight commander for less than a month. It was a sad day for 'Cracksie' Crawford who knew, when writing to Mrs Hearle the next of kin, that Nathaniel's mother had already lost her husband two years previously.

The two airmen were taken to Stalag IXA then interrogated at Dulag Luft in Frankfurt and ultimately taken to Stalag Luft III where they were involved in escape attempts in April 1942 along with Wing Commander Douglas Bader and others. Their tunnel was discovered by the German 'goons' before completion; however, undeterred, they tried again four months later but again were caught before they could escape.

In total, Davies made three attempts to escape, although he later reported that he was involved in 'continuous escape activity'. All failed. Both airmen remained POWs until 1945. On repatriation, Hearle returned to 812 Squadron but sadly was killed in a flying accident two years later. During his captivity Davies had begun to take part in theatre performances, entertaining his fellow prisoners. On his repatriation he followed his acting passion. He became best known for playing the title role in the BBC's 1960s television adaptation of the Maigret novels written by Georges Simenon, and was also in Quatermass and Emergency Ward 10.

The squadron was now losing some of those who had replaced the original losses. Titch Harding recalled: 'It was at this juncture that with pleasure we promoted Roy to 'X' Flight commander.' Roy was delighted to at last get recognition for his skills. He now worked much more closely with PO Manning, senior NCO 'X' Flight. Bruce Hawkes continued to be his observer and 'F for Freddy' his aircraft.

That night North Coates was again attacked by the *Luftwaffe*. Clayton recalled another air raid about then:

When working in the hangar, suddenly a tight band seemed to grip my chest and a blast of hot air hit the hangar with an impact which shook the doors and set the sheeting rattling. An avalanche of spare wheels and aircraft parts cascaded from a shelf that had been rigged between the girders. Then Holmes came running into the hangar shouting that the bomb dump had 'gone up'. Shakily, we followed him outside and found everyone gaping at a tall column of orange-coloured smoke rising in billowing clouds into a clear blue sky.

It turned out that the whole underground magazine had blown up, making a crater about a hundred feet across. Corporal McPherson and three armourers had been there, along with an NCO and two of 22 Squadron's armourers. They had been placing detonators on a batch of mines for that night's 'gardening'.

Clayton added:

It took all day to clear the airfield of the debris; twisted girders, split bomb cases, broken chunks of explosive filling, the bent rifle of the sentry who had been on duty and a scorched money belt, with the buckle still done up bearing the name: N. Eardley. His body was never recovered.

On 24 August, the *Luftwaffe* continued its attack on Fighter Command's airfields. The first raid appeared at 8.30 am when forty Dornier Do17s and Junkers Ju88s, escorted by sixty-six Messerschmitt Bf109s, approached the coast. Twelve RAF squadrons went up to intercept but the German raid was a feint. The real attack was timed to catch the British fighters on the ground as they refuelled.

Hornchurch and North Weald took heavy losses; by nightfall heavy bombing meant RAF Manston had ceased to exist as a front-line fighter base. At North Coates, with the dramatic losses of aircrew being sustained by 812 Squadron at this time, replacements were being urgently requested by Cracksie Crawford. A replacement pilot who arrived that month was Anthony 'Puppy' Kennard:

> The squadron was engaged principally in magnetic and acoustic minelaying from the Frisian Islands to Rotterdam at night. Throughout August we used to carry out minelaying ops in formations of two sub flights of three aircraft. This practice had to be abandoned fairly soon after as we were too vulnerable and cumbersome and the 'gardening' was then done individually. During the day we carried out escort duties for east coast convoys around East Anglia.
>
> We flew long hours and there was a steady trickle of casualties. It all came to an end early in 1941 when, much to my fury, I was transferred to 816 Squadron.
>
> I have very pleasant memories of those days because of the pleasant and happy lot in 812 Squadron. Though scared stiff, on and off, we had great fun in between, most of us were bachelors. I can remember heavy beer sessions in many pubs and light-hearted games of darts.
>
> Roy was without doubt one of the nicest men I met in the Navy and his wife Naomi equally pleasant. They had a little house nearby and I can remember many pleasant interludes with them.

Roy and Naomi had quite a reputation for inviting colleagues over to their home for drinks and friendly company to alleviate the stresses of the nightly operations and air raids. As Naomi recalled: 'In our little cottage when Roy got the fire going, we had lovely parties there. Our friends naturally included Titch, who stayed a lot with us.'

Frank Low was particularly fond of the dog and recollected: 'Roy had a beautiful Alsatian named Rex, whom he taught to accompany him down to the flights and to make what he called his DI (Daily Inspection) of Roy's aircraft.'

On 27 August, Roy and the rest of 812 Squadron flew again to RAF Station Detling. Detling was usually full of RAF fighter types such as Group Captain Douglas Bader. Leslie recalled: 'Roy thought "old tin legs", as Bader was nicknamed by Roy's squadron, was rather a big head and show-off, a character that annoyed the RN types, especially his "prima-donna theatrical attitude".'

Bader had three 'dark blue boys' from the Fleet Air Arm in his squadron, 242, including his wingman, Dickie Cork. Another Navy pilot under Bader's command supported Roy's view: 'He wasn't the most diplomatic of people. He had very strong opinions and stuck to those no matter who he was talking to.'

At the time of 812 Squadron's arrival at Detling the air station was in disarray following the air raid of two weeks previously. The Air Ministry had dispersed much of the camp around the surrounding area as far as Sittingbourne.

Air gunner P.O. Pinkerton recalled:

> On 27 August we were sent to Detling in Kent for a minelaying op. It had, however, been heavily bombed in the Battle of Britain and we were unable to go that night, spending our time on settees in the roofless sergeants' mess! The following morning we went into town and, being mistaken for Dutch naval survivors, we were feted and given a cinema show.

We took off that night and arrived at the entrance to Zeebrugge, where at a given signal, we dropped our mines at the exact same time the Germans switched on their searchlights – and a very pretty picture it made as twelve mines dropped from twelve Swordfish – the exact locations of them being recorded by the enemy.

The Swordfish flew to North Coates on their return. Four days later, Roy and six squadron aircraft took part in RAF CCOI Operation No. 50 with the aim of bombing and destroying German fuel supplies at Vlaardingen. They took off and headed out over the sea in bad weather conditions. They sighted a storehouse which was illuminated by searchlight, and bombs were dropped. A large fire was started which was still visible twenty miles away. 'B for Beer' was unable to locate the oil tanks due to poor weather conditions, and found an alternative target, Haamstede Aerodrome, whose boundary lights were switched on. Two bombs were released and dropped on the landing field. The boundary lights were immediately extinguished, and three parachute flares then dropped from 1500 feet in the hope of firing the hangars.

Intense light and heavy anti-aircraft fire was encountered over Rotterdam, with searchlights operating around Vlaardingen and Dordrecht. The flak was so intense that Swordfish 'P' flown by Lt George Villiers-Tothill and Lt Maurice Driver was badly hit by anti-aircraft gunfire over the city.

Villiers-Tothill, who had been a friend of Roy's since his Leuchars days, was killed instantly. His body was recovered by the Germans and buried at Rozenburg General Cemetery.

Driver, who was on his twenty-fifth operation, bailed out of the damaged aircraft but was captured and taken prisoner:

I survived until August 31st 1940, when a small group of Swordfish each armed with six 250-lb bombs took off by night to attack military targets near Rotterdam. My pilot was Lt George Villiers RN. Shortly after crossing the Dutch coast at about 5,000 ft altitude we were attacked by intense and accurate anti-aircraft fire ('flak') and hit several times before a shell burst just forward of an auxiliary petrol tank. My cockpit rapidly filled with flames and I decided to back out. I landed in a small field with stoked grain and freed myself from the parachute harness, which I found very difficult as my hands were badly burnt. After what was probably no more than about ten minutes a small group of German soldiers with flash-lights appeared and took me prisoner.

He was taken to hospital first in Rotterdam, which was being used as a treatment centre for wounded German airmen returning from the Battle of Britain. Driver was subsequently taken to Stalag Luft I on the Baltic, and onwards to Stalag Luft III. He survived the murders of British airmen by the *Gestapo* after the 'Great Escape'.

A second Swordfish failed to return to North Coates, causing great concern for Cracksie Crawford and Titch Harding. The missing pilot was Shorty Shaw who had been flying 'B for Beer'.

At the same time as the Swordfish were over the Dutch coast, the *Luftwaffe* inflicted a second attack on Detling. Messerschmitt 109s and 110s swept low over the boundary at Detling, firing cannon and machine guns. The petrol and oil dumps were set on fire creating a black smoke cloud that hung above the airfield for hours. The main electricity supply cable was cut and the airfield totally out of use for fifteen hours with no communication at all. The main approach roads to the airfield were blocked by rubble from the blasts. Because of the dispersal after the first raid, casualties were low but damage immeasurable.

The *Luftwaffe* succeeded – 812 Squadron was not to return to Detling for a while. That same day, *Luftwaffe* raids were also carried out on RAF stations at Eastchurch, Biggin Hill, Croydon, Hornchurch and Kenley.

Bombing was by then being extended to include London, with the *Luftwaffe* coming by night, dropping high-explosive and incendiary bombs on the outskirts.

Meanwhile, the invasion fleet continued to be built up ready to sail for England, as a contemporary newspaper article stated:

> Berlin, 31 August: Brushing aside the misgivings of his generals and admirals, Hitler has given order for Operation *Sealion*, the invasion of England, to go ahead. Goering has promised to destroy the fighter defences in the south of England in four days and the rest of the RAF in two or three weeks. So the Fuhrer says that he will decide on the invasion date in the next fortnight.

During the afternoon of 2 September, there were cheers in the officers' mess as Shorty Shaw and his observer returned to North Coates. They had ditched in the sea on their return from their operation two days before due to a fuel shortage and been rescued by the destroyer HMS *Jupiter*. They did not take part in the next night's operation of five aircraft, *CCOI No. 68*, with the object being to attack barges in waterways around Terneuzen.

Roy and the other aircrews had been issued with updated recognition charts, illustrating silhouettes of 'types of vessels which might be used in landing operations'. The charts featured a vast array of silhouettes from cargo vessels, car and train ferries, to German river vessels and Rhine cargo vessels, Dutch schoots and typical Dutch motor coasters. Armed with all this new information, 812 Squadron was back in action.

As Roy's Swordfish and the other aircraft approached Terneuzen they encountered intensive AA fire in the vicinity of the target which was lit up by flares and searchlights. Titch was in the first aircraft, which dropped two 250-lb bombs and eight flares. Two hits were registered on barges in the canal basin; ten irregular explosions followed and large fires were visible from a distance of ten miles. The other aircraft dropped bombs, starting fires and destroyed the jetty before returning to base after a total flight time of two hours twenty minutes.

They returned the next day to Terneuzen with six aircraft, again led by Titch. As they arrived there was 'only slight searchlight opposition and inaccurate light gun-fire'. The first aircraft to attack was 'K for King' piloted by Puppy Kennard, who dropped six 250-lb bombs, one of which fell in the target area. The second Swordfish bombed the lock gates at the southern end of the harbour; the fourth and fifth aircraft released their six 250-lb bombs on the dock area which caused explosions and green flashes. One of the Swordfish dropped four parachute flares which lit up the target area, and all aircraft reported that no barges could be seen. All aircraft returned safely to base. The operation took four hours and thirty-five minutes.

On 6 September, a total of six aircraft, yet again led by Titch, went to bomb barges and small vessels off Ostend harbour but were unable to see the target because of poor weather conditions. Titch wrote in his log book 'bombing NBG'! This time Roy sustained damage to his aircraft and it was unserviceable for the next few days.

That day, Cracksie Crawford, after completion of his tour of active duty, was relieved by Lt Cdr W.E. Waters, DFC, RN, as CO of 812 Squadron. Crawford left for the observer school. He was later lost on passage in SS *Almeda Star* when it was sunk by a U-boat on 17 January 1941 en route to RNAS Piarco (HMS *Goshawk* in Trinidad).

The new Commander, Lt Cdr Waters, had the nickname 'Minnie' after 'Hiawatha's Minnie Ha Ha' because of his serious demeanour. Naomi remembered him well and thought him 'a dear old chap'. She was also sorry for him because, as she put it: 'His brother Lt David Waters was, poor chap, taken POW in August 1940.'

That evening there was an air raid over North Coates, rocking Roy and Naomi's cottage as the bombing got closer and closer. Roy later recollected this in a letter to Naomi when comparing it with another bombing raid. 'Our little fun and games in the September blitz seems pretty pathetic altho' my heart was pumping.'

The next morning Roy went to the airfield by motorbike as usual and was told by PO Manning that his aircraft had been further damaged in the night raid. Wilson and Hawkins, Roy's faithful fitter and rigger, were already working hard on getting 'F for Freddy' back to flying condition. Roy carefully considered the matter, characteristically biting his bottom lip, which was a sure sign that he was deep in thought. Clayton recalled he then said: 'Get it fixed as fast as you can.'

On 7 September, British forces were put on invasion alert as 350 German bombers, protected by as many fighters, appeared over London's docks. They were followed by another 247 that night.

A daily newspaper reported:

A few hours later, with 2,000 Londoners dead or injured and the whole area engulfed by flames, all railway links south were blocked, and the decision was taken at GHQ Home Forces to send out the codeword 'Cromwell', and that invasion was imminent. Home Guard and regular troops were called out, church bells rung and some bridges blown.

Fighter Command had reached crisis point as it faced increasingly ferocious attacks on its airfields and mounting losses in the air. Newly trained pilots with only twenty hours' flying time in Spitfires were being thrown into battle and too often shot down on their first sortie.

At this crucial stage, Goering ordered his *Luftwaffe* to stop bombing RAF and Fleet Air Arm airfields and concentrate on London and the big cities. This led to the systematic destruction by night of cities including Plymouth, Southampton, Bristol, Liverpool, Hull, Coventry, Derby, Leicester, Sheffield, Birmingham, Manchester, Glasgow and Belfast.

Goering's new strategy – terrible as it was for city dwellers – meant the pressure was off the airfields and, notably for Roy and his companions, RAF Fighter Command and Coastal Command gained valuable breathing space in which to continue their offensive against the build-up of invasion craft in the Channel ports.

It did not seem like a rest to the exhausted 812 Squadron at that time as overnight on 7/8 September Titch Harding again led five squadron aircraft along with three Beaufort aircraft of 22 Squadron. This was RAF Operation *CCOI No. 71* with the formal objective being to destroy concentrations of small craft and barges in Boulogne Harbour. Roy was detailed for the operation but was unable to take off due to trouble with his aircraft exhaust system following damage inflicted in the raid the previous evening. However, he did not have time to relax as enemy radio signals had been intercepted referring to an imminent attack on North Coates.

Minutes later, all 812 Squadron's serviceable aircraft were evacuated and Roy rushed to the defensive post where he was in command. With him were PO Manning and the 'X' Flight ground crew, including Clayton. Roy's order was for their post to shoot German paratroopers as they landed.

Clayton described what happened:

A white smoke ring appeared in the sky which was thought to be the marker for the dive-bombers and troop-carrying aircraft. The sirens sounded and we were called to man the defences. After the Stukas would come the paratroops and it would be our job to 'pick them off' until the military arrived.

Timber barriers, festooned with barbed wire, were dragged into position to block the road between the hangars and the airfield while we took up our positions with rifles loaded and gas masks at the ready. Tin-hatted armourers came running up with boxes of ammunition and hand grenades and we settled down to wait.

Lt Baker-Falkner was in command at our post, as his aircraft was U/S (unserviceable) and could not fly. He seemed in a reflective mood and remarked that he thought the war was 'becoming dangerous' – an understatement if ever there was one! He went on to say that he had never imagined a career in naval aviation could involve such a long spell on shore-based operations. Though this conversation was really between him and PO Manning, we all listened attentively as each of us contemplated what the next half hour might entail.

We stood-to until dusk. Nothing happened but the experience gave us an inkling of what to expect when the invasion began; indeed it was said that the most likely time would be the next day, September 8th. There certainly was a lot of enemy air activity that night but no bombs fell near the aerodrome. As a precaution, the Swordfish were kept at an inland airfield for as long as possible between operations.

Sqdn Ldr Hearn Philips, RAF, recalled:

I was a sergeant pilot in 22 Squadron at North Coates. At the time of the possible invasion of this country, the airfield at night was covered with all the MT vehicles. The flare path was not lit until our aircraft had made contact with the dummy airfield down the coast, so as duty pilot one had to rush out and get the vehicles off the flare path. The Swordfish had a very slow landing speed and the naval pilots just came in and landed between the vehicles without waiting for the area to be cleared.

I remember 812 Squadron at North Coates well but being a sergeant pilot at the time I had little contact with the officers, particularly as we both lived out, but the naval officer with a huge dog [Roy with Rex] does strike a note!

812 was based at North Coates and operated independently of 22 Squadron though we were both doing minelaying and enemy coastal work at the same time.

Later at night the operational aircraft returned after succeeding in finding and bombing barges in Boulogne harbour even with intense and accurate flak.

On 9 September, 812 Squadron carried out its first daylight attack since the attack on the German panzer tanks at Dunkirk back in May. This was code-named Operation *Flush*, with the formal objective being to bomb concentrations of invasion barges, tugs and small merchant vessels lying outside Flushing near Walcheren island. The desperate decision to fly during daylight for this operation was urgently weighed up against the less hazardous night-time flying, but the benefits from increased accuracy against enemy targets was regarded as worth the risk.

Titch Harding, with the new CO, Lt Cdr Waters, Roy and a total of six aircraft made the intrepid daylight raid against ten groups of barges being towed by tugs, three merchant vessels, and eight escort vessels of about 600 tons in a three-hour operation.

The squadron went in for the attack, encountering medium, accurate flak from two of the auxiliaries. The aircraft proceeded to attack the vessels and 'M for Mother' flown by Lt Bentley dropped a stick of six bombs, hitting an auxiliary ship. There were various results from the other five Swordfish.

Meanwhile, Lt Sier, with air gunner Pinkerton, carried out a hazardous daylight bombing attack on a barge escort off Zeebrugge. Roy's Stringbag and all the other aircraft returned safely to base.

Two nights later four Swordfish attempted an attack on the Carnot Calais basin in Operation *CCOI No. 72*, but were foiled by ten-tenths cloud at 1,000 feet which completely obscured the targets. However, they were still fired upon by accurate light and heavy flak. 'M for Mother' dropped six bombs from 1,000 feet on four flak guns eight miles west of Gravelines. The bombs appeared to burst among the guns and firing was 'immediately discontinued'.

On Wednesday morning, 11 September – at the height of the Battle of Britain – a signal arrived at 812 Squadron office, ordering the squadron to move in its entirety to RAF Thorney Island. The aim was for the aircraft to be nearer targets at Dunkirk, Rotterdam and Boulogne, as well as enemy shipping operating in the Channel. That same day, their companion RAF squadron, 22, flew its first torpedo sortie off Calais.

Frank Low recalled: 'In order to cover the long enemy-occupied coastline we had to migrate, first to Detling then on to Thorney Island and (once) to St Eval in Cornwall. 826 did much the same I gather.'

By then 826 Squadron had replaced 815 Squadron at nearby Bircham Newton. Clayton recalled:

Two large transport aircraft arrived from Doncaster and the ground crew began loading the stores, together with the CO's motorbike, into the larger of the two, a Handley-Page 42.

Some gear was loaded into the Swordfish and most aircraft had a step ladder slung from their torpedo racks when they took off for the flight south that afternoon.

Those of us who were left piled into the other transport, a Ford Tri-motor, X 5000 [transporter aircraft], which had once belonged to the Guinness family. Its cabin was tastefully furbished in pale green upholstery. Mahogany panelling lined the interior, while portraits of racehorses decorated the frieze above the windows; the effect created the illusion of a better-class pub. However, the bar was closed and the rugs had been rolled up, but we thought it was a nice way to go to war.

It was a clear sunny day and the sun-baked countryside showed up in a hazy patchwork of light straw and dark green glimpsed through wisps of cloud. The high-wing configuration of the aircraft offered a wide field of vision; we could also see ahead through the open door of the flight deck. We had crossed the Surrey heathlands and were approaching Petersfield when a large formation of twin-engined aircraft was sighted. I felt my stomach turn over when someone shouted: 'They're Heinkel One-elevens!' But before our pilot had time to take evasive action, they split into two groups and passed to either side and well above us without firing a single shot.

Roy followed Titch's Swordfish across East Anglia, over Surrey and down to the Portsmouth area and Thorney Island. One by one the Swordfish circled the bomb-damaged airfield.

Clayton continued:

> We arrived over Thorney to discover that the *Luftwaffe* had left its ugly mark on the place. Though the runways had been repaired, the airfield was pock-marked with bomb craters and the hangars and workshops gutted. As we circled the field, I noticed that the ground defences were manned and as the pilot brought the Tri-motor round onto the runway, a Bofors gun swivelled in its sand-bagged enclosure as the gunner followed our progress suspiciously.
>
> After landing, both transports taxied across to a tarmac apron in front of the ruined hangars. A Red Warning was in force and a tin-hatted NCO ushered us to a shelter by a heap of rubble that had once been a store. Clearly they took their air raids seriously here!
>
> When eventually the All Clear sounded, we were allowed to retrieve our hand luggage from the aircraft and were shown to our sleeping quarters – a lecture room on the first floor of the Navigation Block, where camp beds had been provided. Bowsers were located and their drivers asked to call. (It was rather like finding a milkman to deliver the daily pint after moving to a new house!) When the aircraft had been refuelled the tent which was to become the Flight Office was pitched, PO Manning brought the case containing the paperwork, the flight desk was erected – we were in business!

Roy's squadron, together with Blenheims of 59 Squadron, with whom 812 Squadron shared the airfield, was ordered to fly their Swordfish on continuous sorties against the barge concentrations at Calais, Boulogne, Dieppe and Le Havre.

That same night the squadron took off to carry out a minelaying operation across the Channel, returning safely two hours and twenty minutes later to RAF Thorney Island, luckily without encountering in the same area the *Luftwaffe* air ace Wolf-Dietrich Wilcke who found and shot down an Albacore from 812 Squadron's sister unit, 826 Squadron, over Dover-Calais. It was his sixth victory.

Sunday, 15 September 1940 was the day Hitler stated that Germany was going to wipe British airmen out of the sky. A stream of bombers headed for London from Northern France and, in response, fighters from nearby Tangmere fighter aerodrome flew sortie after sortie against them. The anti-aircraft fire went on intermittently, day and night.

Instead of the *Luftwaffe* winning in the skies, it was RAF Fighter Command who claimed victory, forcing Hitler to postpone his invasion of Britain which had been due to commence two days later as Operation *Sealion*.

That day – 15 September – it was operations as usual for 812 Squadron. The air and ground crew stood to from dawn, but all was quiet in their sector – no gunfire, no dive-bombers and no sign of any troops landing.

Clayton reflected:

> After all the warnings we had had it seemed too good to be true. Indeed, it was something of an anti-climax. I can recall no excitement and my diary records only that there were five Red Warnings. Of the Red Warnings only one lasted over an hour and that was for the nightly procession of bombers making for London between 20.50 on the 15th to 04.00 on the 16th.

That morning the weather broke, for a diary entry reads: 'Turned out 07.25. Went to breakfast with Greaves (the engine fitter on G). Rainy morning – sky dull, overcast. Red Warning 10.40–11.05. Stopped raining at midday. Brightened up in afternoon. Took charge of petrol and oil issues. By evening, it was blowing a gale from the south west. Red Warning 19.55–03.00.

The immediate threat of invasion may have passed but 812 Squadron still worked round the clock maintaining its 'Cross-Channel Service'. Clayton recalled:

This ran to a tight schedule and was probably the most profitable of the Company's enterprises for, throughout those hectic weeks, not a single life was lost and only three aircraft suffered damage.

The weather for most of those three weeks was perfect, and the ground crew was glad of this, because all maintenance work had to be carried out in the open. When inspections became due, this was done in the bombed-out hangars. Though completely gutted with their heavy steel doors blown out, they provided the necessary level surface to enable rigging checks to be carried out.

They were eerie places where men had died and when aircraft had to go on for a thirty-hour inspection we worked as quickly as we could to get back to the pleasant surroundings of the bramble thickets.

By now it was obvious that Hitler had missed his chance, at least during 1940, and the feeling of relief that we wouldn't have to defend ourselves against paratroops was tremendous.

Roy and the squadron continued to carry out minelaying operations off the harbours, attacks on the docks and aerial spotting for a night bombardment by the warship HMS *Erebus*.

On 16 September, the Swordfish took off for a night gardening operation but they were recalled after ten minutes when Titch had to ditch his aircraft with a malfunctioning engine.

Two days later, Titch Harding and Minnie Waters were again in the air on a roving mission with torpedoes looking for enemy shipping. Suddenly, they sighted a potential target. Waters looked through his ship recognition silhouette book, and the torpedo was released. Titch wrote in his log book: 'We hit Guernsey, but it didn't sink!'

Titch recalled:

Minnie Waters as an observer would often take his 'bird book' with him – easy to make a mistake. It was a very dark night with low cloud and quite a sea running. My log book recorded 'got Guernsey 2 hrs 35'. It was only a slight error! Minnie said that he could find a silhouette of that damned rock in his 'bird book'.

Further 'gardening' work was carried out on 24 and 27 September.

The new replacement pilot, Frank Low, who joined the squadron in September, recalled that bombing was more dangerous than laying mines:

More dicey were the occasional bombing raids in which 812's Stringbags boosted the limited attack strength of Coastal's two Blenheim and two Beaufort squadrons (a Stringbag carried six 250-lb bombs against the Blenheim four, and was, of course, more economical). These ops included Rotterdam, several convoys rich in flak-ships, and airfields.

Roy flew his share of all these kinds of ops and set us all an example of determination and efficient airmanship, though there was little formation work owing to the essential individual nature of the work.

Flights lasted from four to seven hours (and you got a bit cramped sitting in one position for this length of time).

On Friday 27 September, the order came for the squadron to return to North Coates. It was cold, windy and wet. The Swordfish were delayed by the bad weather, but they arrived at North Coates that afternoon, throwing up a thin spray as they landed on the waterlogged airfield.

In Rose Cottage, Naomi heard the recognisable throb of the Stringbags' Pegasus engines and with trepidation counted the aircraft as they came in to land one by one.

A cheer went up from the squadron ground crew as Swordfish 'A' taxied in with the new CO's motorbike slung from the torpedo rack. It turned out that there had been no room for it in the stores lorries so, as a last resort, it had been lashed to the aircraft.

The weather continued to deteriorate and this encouraged the *Luftwaffe* to make lightning attacks out of cloud and retreat home before a warning could be sounded. This made the gunners on coastal defences trigger-happy and was to lead to 812 Squadron losing two aircraft to friendly fire the next month.

On 29 September, six Swordfish flew to Bircham Newton to prepare for Operation *CCOI No. 77* later that night. The object of the mission was to attack shipping and barges in Rotterdam dry dock and harbour. However, a message was intercepted from 53 Blenheim Squadron saying that weather conditions in the target area were unsuitable; the aircraft therefore returned to North Coates.

Four aircraft flew back the next day to Bircham Newton to repeat the operation. They arrived over the target and met heavy 'searchlight menace' and ground flares from up to forty searchlights situated at Rotterdam and the dock area. Intensive flak was also encountered in the vicinity of the target, including from three heavy flak batteries.

On 1/2 October the operation was finally carried out by six Swordfish operating from Bircham Newton, the object again being to attack shipping and barges in Rotterdam dry dock and harbour. Once over the target there was heavy cloud cover and the Swordfish dived down to release their six bombs whilst encountering light inaccurate flak and searchlights. The bombs extinguished or put out of action a number of searchlights. Results could not be observed because of the cloud cover.

The official 812 Squadron report stated:

Landfall was made off the island of Schwoesen, where we throttled back to 65 knots. Searchlights on islands swept for us, but did not pick us up. The time from crossing the coast to reaching the target was forty minutes. Aircraft broke formation just before reaching the target and carried out individual dive-bombing attacks dropping six 250-lb bombs in a stick.

The crew of the first Swordfish to attack, dropped its bombs, and this was followed by two bombs dropped on the petroleum haven at Rotterdam by the second aircraft. The crew of the next aircraft released their bomb load on Rotterdam's dry dock – the bombs were seen to explode and a red glow observed.

Most aircraft were picked up by searchlights at the end of the dive but managed to get clear. Several aircraft returning to the coast came under fire from heavy and light flak. Roy's 'F for Freddy' and all other aircraft returned safely to North Coates, even though enemy aircraft were seen in the air.

In early October, a batch of the squadron ground crew, who were on loan from the RAF, were returned to RAF squadrons. Amongst them was Roy's faithful aircraft fitter, Wilson, as well as Titch's fitter, 'Farmer' Webb. Roy had kind words to say to Wilson, including hoping that they would work together again in the future.

Clayton recalled: 'It was about this time that I first applied for flying training, though my request got no further than the Flight Commander, Lt Baker-Falkner.' Roy carefully considered the matter, biting his bottom lip – the squadron members recognised that this was a sure sign he was deep in thought.

Clayton recalled:

Though sympathetic, he pointed out that I was more use to the Navy as a skilled tradesman. 'Any fool can be trained to fly an aeroplane,' he said, 'you should concentrate on becoming an air artificer and then you could eventually become commissioned as an engineer officer.'

I replied that I hoped to qualify in both engineering and flying. He gave me a long hard look and said, 'It's a pity that you are Continuous Service; if you were Hostilities Only, you could be put up for pilot training as an RNVR under the "Y" Scheme. As it is, I'm afraid it's "no go".' I thanked him and left the office, shrugging off my disappointment.

However, the next day, October 6th, he invited me to accompany him on a dive-bombing exercise. I could see no point in this, except that he was concerned about the performance of the ASI (Air Speed Indicator), though I suspect he hoped I might be air sick and so be put off wanting to become a pilot. Whatever his reasons he certainly threw 'G' about, diving on the meadows around Marshchapel in a way which stampeded the cattle that were grazing there and then zooming up into a stall turn to make another downward swoop. To finish off, he came in for a landing at about fifteen hundred feet and 'slipped off' the excess height with violent tail-flicking manoeuvres. Although I wasn't actually sick it left me looking green about the gills.

The next day Lt Baker-Falkner asked me to go with him again, this time in 'B', to help synchronise the ASI in the bomb-aiming position with that in the pilot's cockpit. This time we headed out to sea and climbed to 3,000 feet. We then dived at the beach (there had probably been complaints about us disturbing the cattle on the previous day). This time I was lying in the bomb-aiming position with one eye on the ASI and one on the slit of a windscreen through which I could see the beach rushing up to meet us. The needle of the ASI reached 270 then, as the Swordfish came out of the dive, my hands seemed to turn to lead so that I couldn't note the speed on the pad until we were climbing again. We repeated this twice before returning to land, this time via a more orthodox approach!

On 15 October, six aircraft of the squadron carried out *Cucumber* operations from Detling. Considerable opposition was encountered from a concentration of searchlights in the vicinity of North Beveland, and from accurate flak, intense enemy aircraft activity was observed round the Dutch islands. All aircraft returned safely from the operation, five machines landing at North Coates and the remaining aircraft at Detling.

From 16 to 28 October, there was a lull with little flying at all. Also, as the evenings drew in, operations were completed earlier, allowing both the ground and aircrew more time to catch up on some much-needed sleep. For Roy it meant it was possible to spend some quality time with Naomi.

However, one exception was on 20 October, when six of 812 Squadron's aircraft, including Roy's 'F for Freddy', were ordered to carry out a diversionary bombing attack while Blenheims of 53 Squadron from RAF Station Detling raided their targets. Fog descended on their return.

A second friendly-fire casualty occurred en route back to North Coates when Swordfish 'H for Harry' was shot down by the Humberstone battery. Sub Lt Sier managed to put his aircraft down safely on the beach at Humberstone, his second forced landing in six weeks. He and his observer, Midshipman Koelges, crawled to safety through a minefield. The Swordfish was left to succumb to the ravages of the sea.

About this time, Roy told Naomi how he had crash-landed on the south coast. Roy was on a sortie testing a new type of Air to Surface Vessel (ASV) radar. It was used to help hunt down German U-boats cruising on the surface.

He flew out on the trip with no mishaps but on his return over the coast his radar and altimeter were faulty, reading 60 feet greater than his true height. Roy crashed, thinking he was still in the air. He hit his harness release button and threw it off then, literally, stepped out onto the beach.

On 28 October, Titch Harding led a bombing raid with the CO as observer, and Roy in his usual aircraft, in a round trip of four hours in Operation *Boul*. Instructions had been received to destroy with 'TIM' bombs, a concentration of barges lying in the wet dock and basin at Laubet at Boulogne. Five Swordfish took off at 5 pm and proceeded to the target area.

Roy and the others arrived over the target which was hidden by dense '10/10' cloud but still encountered intense anti-aircraft fire bursting through the murk. Aircraft 'K' dropped bombs in the centre of the concentration of numerous searchlights. Shortly after releasing the bombs, heavy predictor flak burst within 100 feet of the aircraft which, nevertheless, all returned safely to base.

By the end of October, Roy was exhausted by his work in the Dunkirk evacuations and Battle of Britain. Later he was to receive the Battle of Britain clasp to his medals – awarded solely to '*the Few*' aircrews of fighting aircraft who between 10 July and 31 October 1940 had taken part in the Battle of Britain.

CHAPTER 14

Attacking U-boat Lairs

November 1940 was to see Roy and 812 Squadron continue to remain attached to 16 Group RAF Coastal Command and take part in operations against U-boat lairs in North West France.

In the autumn of that year Admiral Dönitz, C-in-C of the *Kriegsmarine* U-boat submarine force, had begun to focus his activities on the mid-Atlantic. September saw the first wolf-pack operation when ten U-boats intercepted two convoys off the west coast of Ireland and sank sixteen ships.

October had seen the single most successful U-boat operation of the war, when a pack of twelve U-boats, in a four-night operation, sank thirty-two merchant ships totalling 154,660 tons.

In November, the Admiralty decreed that, as 812 Squadron was without a ship, it should continue with 'gardening', provide anti-submarine patrols for the protection of convoys and be ready to mount torpedo attacks against any enemy naval vessels that came within range, including *Scharnhorst* and *Gneisenau*.

As a consequence, at the beginning of the month six aircraft and aircrew, led by the CO Minnie Waters, and including Roy, were detached to RAF St Eval, near Wadebridge in Cornwall. This station was used by the RAF Coastal Command for shipping reconnaissance and U-boat searches over the Cherbourg Peninsula and south-west approaches. The squadron was to be within range of enemy U-boat targets off Brittany, as well as areas of enemy concentrations of shipping and barges.

After a flight of four hour and thirty minutes, they landed at RAF St Eval and were billeted in the officers' mess. Roy wrote to Naomi, who by now was expecting their first child and staying at Norman Cottage near North Coates:

> We had a long trip yesterday, but got here OK and have done nothing since. Sorry that I couldn't ring up but I had hopes of it being cancelled and then we were snatched away so quickly I didn't have time to phone. I did not know beforehand, darling. That's obvious actually 'cos I didn't take my shaving stuff.
>
> Now my darling, I didn't send you a telegram as I thought it might scare you and K.R. [initials for the as yet unborn baby Carole]. Do you think that you'd better go to Annie's [Blackburn] to wait for me? We are here only very temporarily and should be back immediately. Sorry this is such a short note, my darling, but it's all I know at the moment.'

Naomi was unhappy being left alone and continued to worry about Roy being away in operations over enemy territory. Her best friend Mita had left North Coates after Jakes' death but still kept in contact by letter. Fortunately, Naomi had Marjorie Kindell, whose husband, Cliff, remained at North Coates whilst Roy was away.

Roy's detachment's primary objective was to bomb the U-boat pens at Lorient. The port had been heavily fortified with underground bunkers, artillery and machine-gun emplacements, an anti-tank ditch and ever greater concentration of anti-aircraft installations. Most importantly, it was the headquarters for Admiral Dönitz and any successful operation by Roy and the squadron would cause a major blow to the morale of the German Navy.

Delays in the order to fly and atrocious weather meant that Roy, Titch, Minnie Waters and the others were hanging around for almost a week from 1 to 6 November. All they could do was fret and worry about the daunting task ahead. They knew it was highly likely that they would not return alive from attacking the heavily defended U-boat lair. Meanwhile, the ground crew prepared the aircraft, and each Swordfish was painted 'night' black on the underside for the attack.

Roy's next letter read:

I have no idea of the date or day now. It just seems ages since we left and still no news of our return. We are all beginning to get a bit high with no baths and very little water. We just can't get out at all to do any shopping or anything. Just hanging around waiting.

This place is lousy. Our own is a jewel compared to it. P.S. Pinched envelopes – literally.

On 7 November, with an improvement in the weather, all six Swordfish took off at 6 pm to fly to the target at Lorient fully aware of the dangerous situation into which they were going. On nearing the target area at maximum altitude of 10,000 feet, they dropped height and level bombed the dry docks and power station.

The harbour was heavily defended with anti-aircraft guns. Below them was a small spit extending into the harbour with two huge, arched bunkers which functioned as dry docks and were capable of handling two U-boats each. Barrage balloons drifted threateningly in the air above to discourage low-level aircraft attacks. The Swordfish were met by a box barrage of very heavy anti-aircraft fire, but managed to drop their bombs and peal away without being hit. The weary aircrew eventually returned to St Eval at 11.30 pm.

Titch Harding recollected:

On 7 November we carried TIMS [bomb] – a big one. The TIMS drop – it was a very cold night and we were above the 20-mm guns. They used the big but slower firing guns. Our drop was high, straight and level. We were successful – the trip took 5 hours 10 minutes.

One aircraft had to return before reaching the target on account of a broken rev counter. It may have been Roy's Swordfish, as suggested by his letter to Naomi:

I've got absolutely no news this end and I personally haven't done anything yet. The others have and are all OK and longing to get back home.

We are always coming home tomorrow and it's absolute hell the uncertainty of everything. I'm fed up with this place, no bath, no clean clothes, it's horrid. Even if you had come down here it wouldn't have been any use as we can't get ashore and this is miles from anywhere.

Two nights later the weather was fair so Roy's Swordfish and the other five aircraft were ordered to bomb Lorient. This time the aircraft left at 5.30 pm. After about an hour Titch's aircraft had to pull back with its airspeed indicator frozen up and unusable and returned to St Eval. The remaining five Swordfish carried on to the target area and dropped their six 250-lb GP bombs over the Lorient dry docks and power station. They were again met by a terrifying box barrage of heavy ack-ack, but they managed to escape without being hit and returned to St Eval at 11 pm.

Titch recalled his concerns about his aircrew on this most difficult of operations: 'Waters and I stayed in the Ops Room when aircraft were out – to count them back and to be in at the de-briefing.'

On 10 November, Roy's Swordfish and the other aircraft flew back to North Coates in almost three hours. Roy rushed off as soon as he could to Marshchapel to meet Naomi at Norman Cottage. For the next ten days he had no flying duties.

The date 11 November 1940 was momentous for the Fleet Air Arm – it was when Swordfish from HMS *Illustrious* attacked and seriously damaged the Italian Fleet at Taranto in a raid similar to that planned by 812 Squadron, whilst on *Glorious*. Roy's former squadron, 819, including friends Ginger Hale, Tiffy Torrens-Spence, Bobby Going and Cliff Clifford, had played a major role in the operation.

As revealed in the press later, there were two strikes from *Illustrious*, flying the flag of Rear Admiral Lumley Lyster – Roy's former captain on *Glorious*. The first strike, consisting of six Swordfish, was led by 'Hooch' Williamson, CO of 815 Squadron, with 'Blood' Scarlett as his observer. After only twenty-three minutes, the attack was over. The last Swordfish pulled up and away, leaving Williamson and Scarlett, who had been shot down. They were picked up by an Italian destroyer and made prisoners of war.

The second strike of nine Swordfish was led by Ginger Hale, commanding 819 Squadron. Alfie Sutton, Tiffy Torrens-Spence's observer, later wrote:

Because of a shortage of Swordfish, we had no bombers accompanying the torpedo striking force, so there were no diversionary attacks by bombers to draw attention away from us. I gazed down upon a twinkling mass of orange-red lights which I knew was a solid curtain of bursting shells through which we had to fly. It looked absolutely terrifying.

Tiffy Torrens-Spence's target opened fire on his aircraft as he went in for the attack:

The flash of her close-range weapons stabbed at us, first one and then another along her length opened up. We were coming in on her beam, and we were the centre of an incredible mass of cross-fire from the cruisers and battleships and shore batteries. No worries about clear range or gun zones for the Italians. They just fired everything they had except the 15-inch, and I could see the shots from the battleships bursting among the cruisers and merchant ships. The place stank of cordite and incendiaries and was wreathed in smoke.

One by one the Swordfish survivors returned to *Illustrious*, Lt Gerry Bayly and his observer Tod Slaughter, unfortunately, not among them.

Photo-reconnaissance showed the battleship *Littorio* sustained three torpedo hits. Another battleship had to be beached, a third was sunk. A heavy cruiser and destroyers were damaged as well as seaplane base and oil storage tanks.

Later, Williamson and Hale were both awarded the DSO while their respective observers, Scarlett and Carline, got the DSC. Admiral Lyster was awarded the Most Honourable Order of the Bath (CB). DSOs were awarded to Clifford and Going, and DSCs to thirteen others. Eighteen more, including Maund, Bayley and Slaughter, were mentioned in dispatches.

Sadly, Roy and Naomi were never to see their friend Cliff Clifford again. 'He was a wonderful chap,' Naomi reflected 'but sadly after Taranto he later died on the *Illustrious* when it was attacked by the enemy during a Malta convoy.'

The Taranto raid was the biggest Fleet Air Arm success of the war and changed the strategic balance of capital ships in the Mediterranean literally overnight. Roy and his 812 Squadron friends were delighted and celebrated their former colleagues' success.

Roy and the others laughed to see their own photographs taken earlier that summer appear in the *Daily Sketch* under the banner headline 'Another good job well done'. A large centre spread photograph featured Titch Harding, Shorty Shaw, Snowball Edwards and the others in their flying kit walking across the tarmac with their Swordfish parked on the aerodrome behind them.

In the next few days the raid was news around the world, Naomi recollected that Roy proudly cut out an article about the Taranto heroes.

Clayton recalled:

> This was tremendous news, the only regret being that two crews failed to return, and that our late captain in *Glorious* [D'Oyly-Hughes] had not lived to see the day. There was some disappointment among the older hands, who had rehearsed this kind of attack from *Glorious* in Captain Lumley Lyster's time. They felt that they should have been present, together with those others who had been sacrificed for a lost cause in Norway.

If there was good news from the Mediterranean, defences at home had to be maintained and on Friday, 13 November, five aircraft left North Coates for another 'gardening' operation. On returning to base, one Swordfish was hit by the Humber defences but managed to land safely.

There was more grim news on the home front. On 14 November, Coventry was blitzed. In addition to the devastation inflicted upon the city, the Fleet Air Arm was deprived of its only stores depot, according to Clayton:

> Until a new one was built at Almondbank, Perth, spare parts were in short supply and 'cannibalisation' became the order of the day, that is, using parts from one aircraft to keep another serviceable.
>
> Wherever possible replacement parts were made or repaired in station workshops but it was inevitable that one machine had to be sacrificed to keep the others flying. Sadly, this turned out to be Roy's old aircraft 'F for Freddy' which by now was worse for wear after its recent hard work. It was a sad ending for an aircraft that had once roamed the Mediterranean skies and harried the panzer divisions at Dunkirk.

Clayton reflected on his old charge:

> By the end of the month her bare carcass lay on blocks in a corner of the hangar by the doors, through the gaps of which the first snowfall of the winter drifted to cover the fuselage with a white mantle on which some wag had scrawled the legend: 'Fairey Snowfish'.

170

Roy was allocated a replacement Stringbag which was again coded 'F for Freddy.'

On 15 November, three aircraft left for a night bombing raid on *Luftwaffe* air bases in occupied France in cooperation with Beauforts of 22 Squadron. They encountered heavy flak over the targets and Swordfish 'L for Love', flown by Lt Bentley, was hit in the tail by flak.

Frank Low recalled the mission:

I was one of the three pilots detailed to attack one of an elusive collection of airfields in northern France that were being used by the Germans during the Battle of Britain; these were called 'Barley'. Evan David found it by the lucky chance of following in a German aircraft with its navigation lights on but Bentley and I were less fortunate and had to make do with our alternative target which was Boulogne harbour.

He continued:

Bentley was shot down and taken prisoner and my own Stringbag was a bit like a colander. The Swordfish suffered severe flak damage to the tailplane, rudder and port elevator, but was able to make it back to land at Detling – after almost seven hours airborne.

Bentley was listed as having failed to return. The squadron was subsequently informed he had survived and been taken POW.

On 23 November, five aircraft, each armed with six 250-lb GP bombs, carried out a night bombing attack on Quai Chaunzy at Boulogne. All aircraft returned safely.

At the end of the month there were two new observers at North Coates – Kevin Gibney, who remained only briefly with the squadron, and Lt David Buchanan-Dunlop, who was appointed as 812 Squadron's new highly experienced senior observer.

Buchanan-Dunlop, who had previously served on *Glorious* from summer 1937 until spring 1939, recalled:

I was Senior O of 812 from 29 November 1940 for four months. Minnie Waters, another observer, was the CO when I joined the squadron. I did not actually fly with Roy before 29 December '40, but he quickly became my routine pilot. I had served with him previously as Senior O on *Glorious* for seven weeks in 1939. Roy became very quickly a dear friend of mine during the all-too-short time we served together in 812.

In addition to Roy, Titch Harding, and Anthony Kennard, there were as pilots Shaw and Bowman-Smith DFC. They formed a formidable band of experts with whom it was a privilege to fly. Dick Curry was a lieutenant RN who flew normally with Lt Bowman Smith, RN, but who also may have flown with Roy as well.

We were a somewhat isolated little band of dark blue attached to 16 Group Coastal Command RAF. Senior RN officers only visited us very occasionally but I do remember Guy Willoughby (ex-*Glorious*), then commander, later a rear admiral, coming down from the Admiralty. He brought with him his assistant Ralph Richardson, the actor, whom we were all delighted to meet.

At that time, in my opinion, which is not altogether unshared, the FAA's enemies in order of precedence were first the weather, followed by the RAF, the rest of the RN, the Germans, the Vichy French, with such merely misguided clots as the Italians, Bulgarians etc bringing up the tail.

In 16 Group, the station commanders with the exception of those at St Eval, struck me as being ignorant and unfriendly dug-outs: they could somehow never stomach the fact that a Stringbag carried a greater bomb-load than many of their Coastal Command aircraft. At junior level, the feeling and rapport was a lot better though. As a lieutenant RN thirty years of age in 1941, I found the baby wing commanders many years younger than myself trying at times and requiring firm, if polite, handling.

We seldom mixed much with the RAF ashore i.e. off their CC stations. Their drinking habits, and indeed capacity, were quite different to ours and on nights when weather precluded flying, we sought our own fun in our own favourite haunts. We often dined in Grimsby, where a plate of fish was always very well worth while.

Being married, Roy was not of course always with us but I remember his taking part in many a festive evening with his Alsatian in tow.

I remember Roy as an excellent darts and shove-halfpenny player and as a considerable beer-drinker despite complaints on his part that his was a weakish bladder. Naomi was altogether charming and she was present at a number of our many mixed parties.

On 7 December, there was excitement at North Coates when captured enemy airmen were brought under armed guard to the air station. At midday, a blue painted Junkers Ju88 on a reconnaissance mission over the North Sea from Eindhoven was shot down by Spitfires of 611 Squadron at Jackson's farm in North Somercotes, only seven miles from North Coates. The pilot attempted a belly landing and crashed heavily in a field. Armed guards looked after the aircraft and the wounded prisoners who were held in the farmhouse where they were given cups of tea until a contingent from RAF North Coates arrived at 1630 hours to escort them away as POWs.

The next day, Roy and the rest of the squadron flew back to Thorney Island. The pregnant Naomi went to stay with her aunt, Annie Blackburn, near Bradford until Roy's return which was not due for a while.

The evening after, Roy's squadron went on a 'gardening' operation, lasting just over two hours, to renew their bombing and minelaying operations off Boulogne. There were air raids in the area that night which kept him awake even though he was exhausted.

He resumed his letter writing and briefly mentioned the operation: 'We did another job of work last night, I have got one more to do. At least so we all hope. It's the job you don't mind, thank heavens.'

At midday on 10 December, the squadron returned to St Eval in bad weather, for further hazardous ops in the Brest/Lorient area and Roy wrote with relief about how well the Thorney Island operations had gone. He gave no clue to the expected dangers ahead.

Two of our jobs have gone very satisfactory. No signs of activity at all. Most amazing! And we really have been doing the job you don't mind. Also the remaining one is the same thank heavens. We had a certain amount of bombage and gunfire last night. It woke even me up. Today we moved down here in stinking weather.

In the evening of 11 December, Roy and four other squadron aircraft went on a special operation – a minelaying mission to the German-held naval docks at Brest.

The harbour was heavily defended, eventually with more than 1,000 anti-aircraft guns (a quarter of these being heavy calibre), along with several *Luftwaffe* fighter units at nearby airfields. The base was able to hold large German warships such as *Tirpitz*, *Scharnhorst* or *Gneisenau* – and it was hoped that 812 Squadron's mines would hopefully sink these warships if they ever ventured there.

David Buchanan-Dunlop recalled:

Searchlights didn't worry us. They were slow in coming into action. There were exceptions. Our operation to Brest was one of them. Although my visits were during the pre-*Scharnhorst* days, nearly every denomination of flak greeted us and on one occasion I discovered they had a balloon barrage.

That particular Brest trip was an interesting one. It necessitated a long glide approach with the engine shut off, while a simultaneous diversion was provided by a squadron of Beauforts. It was important from our point of view that the Germans should be looking somewhere else while we flew round their harbour.

The operation began with a climb to about 8,000 ft – a long and laborious business in a Swordfish loaded with a mine. I was the first man in [with Puppy Kennard as pilot] – an enviable position, for it was unlikely that the Germans would wake up in time to realise what we were doing. When we arrived over the coast, the diversion was in full swing. An incredible amount of flak was streaking upwards towards the Beauforts which were some 5,000 ft higher up. We throttled back, and began our glide through the curtain of 'lead' towards the inner harbour. None of the stuff was being aimed at us, and in spite of it being so thick, the chances of intercepting something were small. Much of it was obviously old French stick, who but the Gauls would use orange, green, violet and gentian tracer?

Three out of four of us sailed through the curtain untouched, and with a sigh of relief we laid the mine just outside the dry dock which was later to house *Hipper*, *Gneisenau* and *Scharnhorst*. Once the mine had gone, we regained all our natural manoeuvrability and as we were still at 200 ft inside Brest harbour we needed it.

Under such conditions as these there are two possible ways of regaining safety. One is to be as quiet as a mouse, and to stagger with the minimal throttle through the piers in the hope that you will be mistaken for a motor boat – or not to be noticed at all. The other – and the one we fell for – was to cry 'Home, James, and don't spare the horses'. I think our engine revved that night as it had never revved before. We did the length of the promenade at terrific speed for a Swordfish while every light gun in the harbour tried to train round fast enough to get a shot at us.

An error of judgement took us too close to the aerodrome on the southern shore, and we came in for another contribution of lead from its defences. But apart from our stiff collars getting limp through sheer apprehension, nothing else happened, and we set course for home.

On these trips my pilot and I made a rule never to pass the flask until our mine had been dropped in the right place. The precious fluid went down well that night.

'Puppy' Kennard added:

The minelaying op in Brest harbour included him [Roy] and I plus four other Swordfish. There was a lot of light tracer flak. The orange-coloured balls all appeared to be coming directly at one but we were not hit.

I can remember on that Brest trip that on the way back I passed by close to the lighthouse on Ushant and damned if the keeper didn't have a pot shot at us with a rifle! The 6¾ hour trip I can remember as being hard on one's bottom. Also one of the aircraft had to jettison its torpedo due to lack of fuel – we were in formation for the whole trip which made it very tiring. The torpedo was dropped (safe) on the seashore and appeared to be undamaged and was later retrieved.

One aircraft, Swordfish 'M for Mother', failed to return and Sub Lt Edward Hamilton and nineteen-year-old Midshipman Peter Lofts were missing, presumed killed. They were later buried in Brest cemetery.

On the safe return of the other Swordfish, one of the aircrew recorded the dangerous operation in his log books as 'Cucumber. Jellyfish. Successful. A hot spot'.

Titch, Roy and Puppy Kennard flew on a further 'gardening' operation on 14 December and the following day flew back to North Coates. Titch had to make a landing at Abingdon en route but was back in North Coates the next day. Naomi was to follow soon after, returning from Bradford.

A new member of the squadron, Anthony Clayton, recalled:

I was appointed to 812 Squadron in the latter part of 1940. I was proud, and a little nervous, on joining the squadron at RAF North Coates Lincolnshire as 812 Squadron (ex-*Glorious*) was considered to be a crack squadron. B-F, together with the senior observer, Lt Buchanan-Dunlop, made me feel at home. They were both quite senior lieutenants at that time, whereas I was a recently promoted sub lieutenant joining my first operational squadron.

On 18 December, the squadron carried out *Cucumber* operations to Oysters. From the start the weather was bad. However, they all managed to successfully lay their mines in low visibility and return.

Buchanan-Dunlop recalled the event once they had taken off from North Coates:

Looking back afterwards, I think we should have turned back half an hour after leaving base, but the pilot, Bowman Smith, although my junior, was an old hand at the game, and felt sure that he could lay the mine in spite of the weather.

Conditions deteriorated as we progressed, and we crossed the Dutch coast without seeing it. We were actually several miles inland, and flying very low, when I thought I discerned a dividing line between two areas of darkness astern of us. After turning back, we found ourselves quite close to our objective. A few minutes groping round gave us exact bearings, and the mine was duly parked in the appointed place. This turned out to be the easiest part of the night's work.

We then turned for home and a landfall on the Norfolk coast. This we made, in spite of my forebodings, and the mild success made me careless. I gave a course for Skegness, and dispensed with d/f bearings. Like King John's jewels, we came to grief in the Wash, crossing its northern coast without seeing it.

By the time I realised that we had overshot our mark and had got the wireless bearings which I needed, we had the high ground of the Lincolnshire wolds between us and home. This would have been a small matter if the clouds had not been down to 400 ft. As it was, cross-country flying in pitch darkness at any less height was suicidal, so I put in some hard work with the ground stations, trying to find an aerodrome at which we could land. I learned, subsequently, that at least one over which we passed at less than 500 ft was lit up for our special benefit, but the visibility was such that we never saw it.

174

I was contemplating a climb to 7 or 8,000 ft with a view to baling out at this stage but my pilot was made of sterner stuff. Dropping two small flares, against every pyrotechnic regulation, he illuminated a ploughed field long enough to land in it. Another 20 yards farther on was a drop of 150 ft into a ravine, but this menace was mild compared to the Home Guard who approached, shouting, with a pitchfork.

The rest of my memories of this night are confused, but they include the eating of an enormous supper in the village inn, with the village constable standing the last round of drinks at 3 am.

Puppy Kennard recollected:

Bowman Smith was David B-D's pilot when they landed in the ploughed field that night. He [Bowman Smith] was subsequently killed in the Western Desert. He was a great character and when he left us he was employed dropping all sorts of secret gadgets at night in a Swordfish over occupied France.

There was to be leave over Christmas but first Roy and the whole of 812 Squadron had a celebration leaving party for Bruce Hawkes who was due to depart for a new posting at Lee-on-Solent. Roy was undoubtedly sad to see his own observer leave after sharing so much adventure and excitement with just the two of them in 'F for Freddy'. A special bond had been built up between the pair and Hawkes was determined to return to fly with Roy if at all possible.

Over that Christmas leave, Roy and Naomi headed for Devon to spend the break with the Falkner family in Shaldon. Naomi recalled: 'We did return to Shaldon for Christmas 1940 – and were in a very bad air raid in London on our way down.'

Leslie recalled that while driving, Roy accidentally ran over a cat. 'When he and Naomi arrived at our house, he was miserable as sin over the cat. It was amazing that one day he was dropping bombs, the next feeling guilty hurting an animal!'

This was to be the family's first full Christmas together since before Roy and Naomi went to the Mediterranean a few years previously. The family made an occasion of it, bringing back the spirit of Christmases past in Canada, and went on a trip into the countryside in their old Riley using their preciously saved petrol.

Roy and Naomi returned to North Coates and Norman Cottage on Boxing Day, and on 27 December it was back to Thorney Island for the Swordfish 'gardening' operations at Scallops, Jellyfish, Oysters and Mussels.

Roy, as officer commanding 'X' Flight, was to have a new navigator in the back seat, the squadron senior observer, David Buchanan-Dunlop. Titch continued: 'His encouragement and advice from the rear compartment, made him and Roy a good team.'

Two nights later Roy and David were involved in an operation along the Dutch coast. David recalled their operation in aircraft 'A for Apples': 'Roy and I successfully laid two cucumbers, i.e. mines, in "Scallops" on 29 December '40.'

He added:

I never saw any night fighters on our trips and by flying low our approach to the enemy coast was devoid of much risk. This sounds as if we lacked the aggressive spirit but as our business was strictly confined to laying mines, combats with the enemy would have been out of order. In any event, a Swordfish versus a fighter is in the position of a boy with a catapult facing a thug with a Tommy gun.

Searchlights worried us even less. They were slow in coming into action. I always imagined some frozen-fingered old *Landsturmer* fiddling about with his switches in the darkness down below.

In the New Year's Honour List, Titch Harding was awarded the DSC. He modestly wrote:

When the senior pilot was awarded the DSC, it was Naomi who was staying nearby who kindly sewed the ribbon on for me. The citation read 'for leading repeated air attacks on enemy targets' which made it a squadron award, leading following some movement and to get this into the air the ground crew have to do their stuff, which they did under difficult conditions.

The new year got off to a bad start as far as Roy and Naomi were concerned as they were yet again separated. Roy was still at Thorney Island preparing for yet another minelaying operation off the Low Countries of Holland and Belgium, which he reassuringly called a 'job' to Naomi in his letters.

The couple were by now making plans to move into White Cottage, in the village of North Coates, once Roy came back from his operations. He replied to Naomi's news: 'I've got no news at all, darling, except that we seem to be stuck here for a bit longer. Got another job to do. The same kind tho' it's beastly chillsome. How did my old darling usher in the new year. Asleep I expect child.'

The squadron was trying to carry out its duties despite appalling weather conditions. Roy and the squadron were to remain at Thorney Island for another two weeks waiting for good weather.

On 2 January, Roy wrote to Naomi: 'Still being held up by the weather and had a bit of snow today. It's bitter out. Dick [Curry] has got the DSC isn't it grand, he's been posted tho. Also Daddy Hale commander.' Buchanan-Dunlop recalled Dick Curry describing him as : 'A great shooter outer of German searchlights – a practice to be appreciated (in my opinion) unless two, or at least, had you firmly "held".'

The next day, the squadron continued with Operation *Cucumber*, minelaying again. However, they had to turn back in a heavy snowstorm off Beachy Head after forty or so minutes.

Buchanan-Dunlop recalled that evening's bad weather. He and Roy only got as far as the cliffs near Brighton, but had reasons to be pleased about the difficult flying conditions that night: 'The only enemy fighter which ever came our way was off Beachy Head. But we were both in the toils of a snowstorm: we were too busy to shoot at each other.'

Roy wrote to Naomi:

Bloody weather. Had a smack at the job yesterday but forced back by snow down to the sea. Oh, we were fed up.

We are still being held up by the bloody beastly weather darling. It's hell isn't it? We've got nothing to do except tinker with our aircraft and all the paperwork piling up at NC and worst of all, no Billy girl, it's lousy. Even if you were here darling, we don't get released till very late. Shorty has got the DSC, isn't it grand.'

Shorty Shaw flew more missions with 812 than anyone else in the squadron.

At midday on 5 January the Swordfish were out again searching for a missing Blenheim to no avail.

The inability to carry out any operations over enemy territory was preying on Roy's nerves – he just wanted to get the job done and go home. On 6 January he wrote: 'Monday. We are, oh hell, what is the good of going on. It's snowing here now...might be able to do something in the next few days. I'm getting back to bachelor drunken days and it's a lousy life.'

The bad weather continued and still there was no flying at all:

We are all going crazy absolutely and utterly nuts. We know definitely that we've got one more job to do and we can't do it. At least we could go over the other side but we wouldn't do the job. Isn't it hell, we are all longing to get back to NC but can't. Bruce Hawkes came over to see us this evening. He is trying like mad to get back to me for which I am duly grateful. People at Lee just don't believe his stories, amazing isn't it? B-D [Buchanan-Dunlop] and I have been together the whole time. He's an awfully nice bloke.

On 8 January, Roy wrote: 'We've definitely got to do one more job now darling, but God knows when we'll be able to fix it. Soon oh so soon I hope.'

Roy continued to be frustrated with yet another day of no flying: 'It's extremely dismal here, we haven't done anything and haven't been able to get out of camp at all. I've even come down to playing cards sometimes. I hear that our Hammy is married.'

The stress and bad weather was also taking a toll on the health of the aircrew: 'Poor old Puppy has lumbago and feeling very sorry for himself'.

At last, on 10 January, with a slight improvement in the weather, the squadron were given the go-ahead to attack their target, in a night-time operation. They were able to minelay the target code-named *Vineleaves* even though there was poor visibility. Unfortunately, Swordfish 'Q for Queenie,' flew into a hillside near Halton, killing Sub Lt William Hughes, Midshipman Norman Koelges and Air Mechanic Robinson. The remaining aircraft returned to Thorney Island in safety.

That night Portsmouth, only five miles away, lay burning following a *Luftwaffe* bombing raid on the town and naval docks. The next day a bomb fell in front of the Bank of England, causing the ground to collapse into the Underground Station below, killing fifty-seven people. By now, a quarter of the City of London had been destroyed.

On 12 January, Roy's squadron was given the order to return to North Coates – much to the relief of Naomi.

Later that month, there was a heavy snowfall and yet more operations were cancelled. The station commander, who expected the Germans to make another attempt to invade in the spring, took the opportunity to order a practice evacuation of the station.

Clayton recollected:

We tramped two miles up the main road and dispersed into fields where we stood miserably around in a biting wind, waiting for orders. One of 22 Squadron's pilots was likening it to Napoleon's retreat from Moscow when the station warrant officer came up the road blowing his whistle and calling for the officers and NCOs to march the men back to camp!

By that time we were blue with cold, so when we got back to the airfield a snowfight broke out between 'X' and 'Y' Flights which rapidly developed into a free-for-all. I pitched a well-moulded snowball at Dolfuss who ducked, and it caught Lt Baker-Falkner in the chest. He picked me up and threw me into a snowdrift and suddenly everybody began pelting everyone else, though in a good-natured way. The sport lasted until dusk, by which time we glowed with warmth that made up for the miserable retreat up the road!

As soon as the snow had gone we were back on operations. Working on the Swordfish in that weather was bad enough, it must have been hellish sitting in those cramped open cockpits for six hours with an icy gale doing its best to snatch your chartboard out of your lap as you tried to plot a course. And yet they returned, night after night, to lay their mines in the precise position specified by operations in the face of mounting opposition as the Germans deployed more flak ships and alerted their night fighters. Considering the risks involved, it was a wonder there weren't more casualties.

That month new aircrews arrived, including Humphrey Maughan and Paul Wilkinson. Maughan recollected:

> I was trained as an engineering officer and transferred to the flying side because of the requirements for RN engineers to replace the RAF engineers being withdrawn from the Admiralty. I was one of the earliest transferees, flying plumbers, and completed my training in time to join 812 Squadron.
>
> The squadron was then based at RAF North Coates. Sub Lt Paul Wilkinson, a close friend who had been with me throughout the flying training, joined the squadron at the same time but as we were short of night-flying experience, we were sent off to RNAS Crail for some intensive night flying from a small satellite at Dunino.
>
> Baker-Falkner's was a friendship which I have always treasured. His was indeed a fine personality and with great personal qualities of example and leadership.

Clayton continued:

> On the return to North Coates from Thorney Island, Lt Cdr Minnie Waters made changes to the squadron, including the 'trading-in' of the older Swordfish for the new Blackburn-built version fitted with the more powerful Pegasus 30 engine. Other changes included ASV (Air-to-Surface Vessel) radar and the new 'Wurlitzer' radio (so named because of its gaudy array of coloured knobs and switches). This electronic equipment was susceptible to dampness so flameproof paraffin heaters were kept alight in the observer's cockpit whenever aircraft were yanked out at dispersal.
>
> There were frequent gales and the ground crews were often called out to turn the aircraft whenever the wind changed. It was necessary that they faced into wind, otherwise they were liable to be blown over, which, of course, would be doubly disastrous with lighted heaters on board.
>
> At times the wind was strong enough to turn the propellers – an eerie sight at night with the moon casting a fitful half-light through pale-torn clouds. The hardest part of this job was re-positioning the screw-pickets to which the aircraft were secured; it took the combined effort of two men, using a length of steel pipe for leverage, to drive these 3-foot long 'corkscrews' into the gravely Lincolnshire soil.

Roy's squadron was still mainly employed on minelaying in every accessible enemy-occupied port and estuary on the French and Dutch coasts, Cherbourg, Le Havre, Ostend,

Antwerp, the Hook of Holland, Terneuzen, Ijmuiden and the estuaries between the Waddensee islands of Texel, Vlieland, Terschelling, Ameland, and Schiermonnikoog.

Frank Low recalled the squadron's developing technique:

> Minelaying was done at night with as much secrecy as could be achieved by gliding in (weather permitting) from our ceiling of 10,000 ft to the 50–100 foot dropping height. More often than not duff weather meant a lower approach and not always an easy discovery of the precise dropping position, but the chop rate from AA fire was low.'

Buchanan-Dunlop wrote:

> When I joined 812 Squadron, the excitements of the summer were over – the daylight raids on Rotterdam, the planting of infernal machines up against the invasion barges in the French ports, the strangely assorted patrols over the Channel.
>
> We had gone back to a steady job, like clerks after their summer holidays. Our principal business henceforth was to be minelaying, and the more unostentatious we were about it, the better. It consisted of embarking some hundreds of pounds of high explosive in a special cradle slung beneath a Swordfish, and sallying forth by night from some darkened aerodrome to place it with great care in one of the enemy's harbours. The exact point where it was laid mattered a great deal, for the shipping followed a dredged channel, and if it was laid anywhere else it was a waste of the taxpayer's money.
>
> It wasn't a spectacular job; the mine never went off until hours and probably days afterwards. Quite possibly it was swept up and never went off at all.
>
> On the whole, the weather was a greater menace than the enemy on these expeditions. It never seemed to be fine on both sides of the water at the same time, so that we found ourselves setting out on an evening on which we would have hesitated to put the cat out, entering the fine weather zone over the enemy's coast, and returning again through the 'overcast'. There were, of course, several places on the other side which were sufficiently well defended to add nothing to the night's enjoyment.
>
> In between our sorties, we moved from one RAF aerodrome to another – from Cornwall, which was the terminus for St Nazaire and the south, to Norfolk for the Hook of Holland and the east. Our hosts at these aerodromes were prone to be facetious about the Swordfish, but we nevertheless impressed them by demonstrating that they would lift a greater weight than their own Beauforts.
>
> In addition to the extra tank, we usually carried a quota of dried mud, inevitably picked up from the battle-scared aerodromes of the RAF, mud hallowed in the Battle of Britain, but annoying on a chart board or in the observer's eyes. When the mud froze, it frequently knocked the tail wheel off as we were taking off, with the added anxiety of an unorthodox landing when we got home again.
>
> In the air, the freezing level was seldom above 2,000 ft and the pilot was usually forced to fly blind, low down over the sea. The limiting factor was the visibility over the enemy's coast, and if this was really bad the operation had to be 'scrubbed', it was useless laying the mine anywhere except in the right place.
>
> The average round trip took about 5 hrs, although I did one which lasted 6¾ hrs, only to find our landing baulked by a crashed plane, necessitating a further weary ½ hour looking for an alternative landing field.

Roy's squadron was making preparations to move again. Naomi, who was by now seven months pregnant, was preparing to stay more permanently at her aunt's home in Bradford while Roy was on daily operations. Rex, the squadron dog mascot, still went out with Roy for daily inspections of his aircraft, and the squadron looked after Rex when Roy was on operations.

In February, Titch Harding had a major leaving party after receiving news that he had been appointed to the Flying Training School at Arbroath. So soon after losing Bruce Hawkes, Roy was inevitably saddened at losing his friends, but pleased for them that they were going to non-operational postings at last.

Harding's position as senior pilot was taken up by Lt L.E.D. 'Ed' Walthall and the squadron began to prepare for its return to carrier-borne operations. Aerodrome dummy deck landings were practised between operations and, at the same time, the number of aircraft was reduced to nine. The RAF tradition of splitting the squadron into the two flights, 'X' and 'Y', was discontinued to bring it into line with current naval practice.

Three aircraft, together with their crews, were made redundant by this change. They were taken over by Lt Smith, a new arrival. Under his command a new unit was formed which was eventually allocated as 821 Squadron.

On 25 February, Roy in aircraft 'P for Peter', with Buchanan-Dunlop as observer, went on a minelaying mission to Mussels. Even though there was very poor visibility, they were successful in dropping the mines and returned four hours and twenty minutes later.

The following night, whilst returning from a successful sortie off the Dutch Coast, Swordfish 'B for Beer' was seen to lose height and ditch in the sea. Sub Lts Evan David and Kenneth Cole abandoned the aircraft and took to the dinghy. Their position was carefully plotted and at first light all available aircraft returned to conduct a thorough search. Sadly, no trace of the crew or their dinghy was ever found.

Naomi was getting closer to the birth date of her first baby. Since Roy was still going out on ops and expected to return to a ship very soon, she finally moved to Yorkshire to stay with Annie Blackburn. Roy left her in Bradford and travelled alone back to North Coates. Life without Naomi was somewhat empty for Roy. He focused his attention on his other love of his life, Rex the Alsatian.

Roy wrote to Naomi:

Monday. Oh child what hell it was yesterday having to leave you and come back to this place. I got to Retford about 7 being just about frozen. My carriage was bitter and feeling miserable didn't help much I suppose. I went along to the nearest pub about a quarter of a mile away and just drank solidly till 8.30 as the train was due out at 8.50. Eventually the damn thing left at 9.30. Then stopped everywhere. We got to Great Coates and all change. We had to get into buses for the rest of the way. Arriving at Grimsby at 11.30. Not a taxi or anything so I stayed at the Yarboro'. Had a monster breakfast this morning and so to work. Met our hound at lunch time. He'd escaped and been home, I think. He was scared stiff and looking rather sorry for himself. He hasn't really forgiven me for bringing him back to this place yet. He's better now tho!

Now that Naomi was away, Roy took the opportunity to socialise with his squadron colleagues, the first time in ages:

Thank you oh so much, my darling, for your grand old letter and the dog lead and muzzle. It only just fits the old fat head. He's awfully good about it but doesn't understand at all and is awfully sheepish. He is certainly my dog instead of Hunt's. Won't look at H. if I am around.

I got a wee bit pickled this evening. After supper we all went down to our place and played darts and finished off the alcohol. We were a good old squash in Puppy's [Kennard] car. Six of us, also master Rex and a dartboard. Rex is becoming quite good now with strangers.

It's after 11 o'clock and Rex and I have been for a run. Sorry my hand shakes so much but I'm tired.

It was all change in North Coates and housing for the aircrews of 812 Squadron was in short supply. The buzz around the aerodrome was that the squadron was on the move. In a continuation of his letter he told Naomi: 'Naish the squadron leader attacked me this morning on the subject of the house. I didn't know what to say and said that I couldn't let him know yet. However, I have given him permission to live there for two weeks.'

On 13 March, Roy was formally informed that the squadron was soon to stand down from active operations. The Admiralty had at last realised that at least one of its squadrons was absolutely exhausted from non-stop operations against the Nazis for almost a year.

Despite this, there was still more work to be done and the next night Roy's squadron carried out rover flights, with each aircraft flying independently to find targets of opportunity, from the Dutch island of Texel then along the coast to Flushing. The op was relatively uneventful and the aircrew only sighted fishing boats and wrecks.

The squadron was going north to Scotland and preparations for the move started in earnest with Roy heavily involved in ensuring all went smoothly.

Roy wrote to Naomi:

17 March. Written on Saturday. I am so sorry that I haven't written before but we've been going every day and yesterday I was away. We had done our last job of work and landed at another aerodrome. In all we were thirty-nine hours without sleep. We definitely can't do any more now as all our gear and aircraft things have gone north. Rex has gone with Hunt and seemed fairly happy.

At last 812's attachment to 16 Group RAF Coastal Command and their operational tour of duty was at an end. The overload tanks were removed and handed to their reliefs, 816 Squadron.

Frank Low recalled: 'As an indication of the hours our pilots put in on this work, I do remember that from 15 September 1940 to end February 1941, I flew forty-four night minelaying ops – other crews had a similar record.'

Roy's squadron was lucky as two weeks later the two German capital ships *Gneisenau* and *Scharnhorst* arrived in 812 Squadron's former hunting ground, Brest. French Resistance radioed the news to London and 812 Squadron's companion RAF squadron at North Coates, 22 Squadron, was given the task of making a torpedo run against *Gneisenau* with their Bristol Beauforts. If Roy's squadron had remained it may well have had to take part too.

On 6 April, 22 Squadron's three Bristol Beauforts were piloted respectively by Flying Officer Kenneth Campbell, Flying Officer John Hyde, and Sergeant H. Camp. Flying independently, they were to rendezvous near Brest but poor weather prevented this and Campbell made the strike alone.

Gneisenau was secured alongside the wall on the north shore of the harbour, protected by a stone mole bending around it from the west. In this outer harbour near the mole were moored three heavily armed anti-aircraft ships, guarding the battle cruiser.

Flying Officer Campbell came in at almost sea level, passing anti-aircraft ships at less than mast-height. Skimming over the mole, and under heavy fire, he launched a torpedo at point-blank range. The battlecruiser was severely damaged below the water-line and was obliged to return to the dock she had come only the day before.

There was little prospect that Campbell and his crew would survive the attack on *Gneisenau*. The damaged Beaufort crashed into the harbour, from where the Germans recovered it. They buried the RAF men in Brest cemetery. Campbell was posthumously awarded the VC.

CHAPTER 15

Scotland and Malta Convoy Duties

Roy's next posting was to Scotland, as it was time for him to step down from front-line duties and bid farewell to North Coates. On 18 March 1941, he and his 812 Squadron colleagues were posted to a small civil airfield near the village of Machrihanish. It was little more than a grass field in the flat land of The Laggan near Campbeltown on the Scottish west coast. The airfield was too small to have its own RN administration and so it was borne on the books of HMS *Merlin* far to the east at RNAS Donibristle.

Humphrey Maughan remembered: 'We re-joined the squadron just in time to move to Machrihanish in March 1941, which at that time was a small grass airfield used by Scottish Airways. The airfield was known locally as "Mr McGichie's field".'

That early spring, in 1941, a local young teenager, Alastair Black, who lived in Machrihanish, was a cadet in the local ATC and fascinated with watching the first arrival of the Fleet Air Arm aircraft. He readily recalls the ancient Handley Page H.P.42 great biplane monsters with four engines at the Mitchell's Field at Strath (next to the old 1918 Machrihanish airfield), which lay by the Machrihanish to Campbeltown road:

> They had been impressed into Royal Air Force service as transporters at the outbreak of the Second World War. As part of our ATC training at weekends, we went down to the naval airfield, and a group of us were even given a flight in the back of a Swordfish, leaning dangerously out over the edge of the cockpit to look at the views.

Black recollected that one month before Roy arrived:

> Another ATC cadet was not so lucky as we were, and was killed in a Walrus in Machrihanish harbour when it was bombed by an He111, dropping its bombs at low level, maybe 100 ft or less. I can still visualise the whoosh of the spray and water into the air as the bombs exploded. The harbour was full of navy boats. Nearby was HMS *Nimrod*, an anti-submarine detection place – the possible target for the German bomber.

HMS *Nimrod*'s main role was as a training establishment for naval routine and anti-submarine warfare.

At the time of 812 Squadron's arrival a modern and soon to be fully operational air station, the biggest in Western Scotland, was being constructed at Machrihanish and was destined to replace the older airfield. RNAS Machrihanish was finally commissioned on 23 June 1941, officially becoming HMS *Landrail* and unofficially Machrijesus – inevitably it was still considered to be 'in the middle of nowhere'.

Naomi was staying with her aunt, Annie Blackburn, in Bradford and Roy wrote to her the day the squadron was due to depart: 'No hope of us going today darling. Fog has shut down. We were due to go at 10 this morning. We'll go tomorrow tho'. I gather that Campbeltown is quite a nice place and should be very nice in summer. We are off in a couple of days, no more work as we know it to do which is excellent.'

Now that Roy was no longer on nightly ops, the relief of continuous stress was immediate and he took solace in being sentimental about his dog, Rex. However, he had to leave him temporarily with his steward, Sgt Hunt, during the transfer to their new posting.

Roy and 812 Squadron eventually flew northwards but had to break their journey because of 'thick weather' near Catterick.

He wrote at their break en route:

I don't know whether it is Wednesday or Tuesday but we have started on our journey and we've got to a place called Topcliffe. Where it is I don't know. But we have been very nicely sown up by the RAF and generally given a very good time. We were forced down here by bad weather. I don't think that there's much chance of us seeing NC again.

The squadron ground crew, together with Rex, had a more straightforward journey by troop train to Scotland, where they had time to set up temporary camp at the airfield and started to organise the squadron affairs prior to the arrival of the Swordfish.

When at last the aircrew arrived they were billeted at the old gabled Ugadale Arms Hotel overlooking Machrihanish beach. Roy settled down in his shared room to write:

We arrived this afternoon. The hotel where we live is quite nice but nothing out of the way. We are right on the sea. A lovely great sandy beach and rollers and then behind us quite high hills. There is also a golf course just outside the hotel gates, very nice.

Clayton recalled:

A bus took us up to the airfield each morning. This was little more than a grass field that had been used as a landing ground by Scottish Airways until the outbreak of war. There were no facilities and no buildings, only a tattered windsock and a dilapidated Morris Commercial fire tender from whose engine the cylinder head had been removed and never replaced. The previous tenants, 828 Squadron, who had recently left to join HMS *Victorious*, had erected some makeshift shacks built out of four-gallon petrol tins filled with earth. These we improved and extended to provide a relatively comfortable Flight Office and crew room.

At the airfield, Roy was to meet up with old ex-*Glorious* faces, including the officer in command, Cdr Bryant, whom Roy mentioned to Naomi: 'Monkey Bryant who, I think I told you, is the commander here, sends his love to you.'

Squadron life settled down into a routine of training and relaxation: '26 March. We do the odd spot of flying twice a day and nothing strenuous. Suits me beautifully. I haven't been away from here yet and don't want to.'

He continued about Rex: 'My charge has been very good today and he solemnly climbed up a ladder and sat on top when I was inspecting my aircraft then he walked all over the wing.'

To escape the relative isolation and remoteness of Machrihanish and 'Mr McGichie's field', Campbeltown was a highlight for the aircrews, with its hotel bars and shops, overlooking the ancient landlocked harbour at the end of a long sea loch, Campbeltown Loch. Further attractions included walking on Beinn Ghuilean and fishing. On the frequent visits by the aircrew for drinks at the Argyll Arms Hotel and White Hart Hotel, Roy could see the loch crowded with Navy vessels, ranging from corvettes to heavy cruisers and even submarines.

Strict blackout procedures were enforced in the town, with the fire wardens going round checking on suspect lights. The previous month Campbeltown had been attacked by enemy bombers following heavy raids on Clydebank. The bomb damage was quite severe – the *Campbeltown Courier* recorded that the town's procurator-fiscal and an electrical engineer had been killed and fifteen people injured. A large number of houses in the vicinity suffered varying degrees of damage. One old man, seeing Roy, Buchanan-Dunlop and other Fleet Air Arm colleagues in their uniforms in the town, came up to them and defiantly announced: 'If yon wee Hiitlerrh is on his way agin we will give him a right lunerinn' when he attacks Campbeltown!'

The weather was cold and blustery that March and flying an open-cockpit Swordfish in the snow was difficult to say the least. The runways from which Roy flew often could not be seen for snow which also accumulated on goggles. For the ground crew it was a particularly gruelling time, maintaining aircraft in the open, exposed to the Atlantic gales, and refuelling from four-gallon tins.

Clayton recalled:

This necessitated straining the contents through a chamois leather to extract the moisture that always condensed inside these containers. Fortunately the services of the fire tender were not required, nor had its cylinder head turned up. I think we may have been the last squadron to endure these spartan conditions, for a new air station at Machrihanish opened a few miles to the north shortly after we left.

Rationing seemed hardly to have affected this remote part of Scotland and food was plentiful and cheap. I remember that Beery and I used to augment the naval fare provided in the institute with a meal at a local cafe where a plate of bacon, egg, sausage and chips cost only ninepence.

Early war pay for a single Fleet Air Arm or RAF aircrew was about 21 shillings a week, and an extra 1/6 a day flying pay.

Roy was at last settling down after the trials and tribulations of the previous months:

Thursday 20 March. Rex and I are absolutely tired out today. Two miles before breakfast this morning running and walking. Three miles to the aerodrome running and walking at lunch and twelve holes of golf this evening. It's magnificent. We both are awfully well. This place is only eight hours away from Glasgow. Pretty terrific isn't it. We also flew this afternoon.

The weather on 24–25 March was stormy enough for all flights to be cancelled. However, the rest of the month, Roy flew with Buchanan-Dunlop and L/A Joliffe in sub-flight formation dives and ALTs on the Isle of Gigha and flights out over Islay and the peaks of the Isle of Arran.

Roy wrote to Naomi:

> Saturday. We've been working very hard the last week and I have been for quite a
> long walk and I've got to play soccer tomorrow for the squadron 1st team. Rex is
> loving it here but is still pretty scared in crowds. He doesn't order people off now
> tho'. The squadron is settling down well and is really a very happy bunch. At least it
> appears to me. I think the CO is satisfied too.

There were further indications of life returning to normal.

> Friday. I got a letter from Leslie today wishing me all the best. She sounds very
> happy. I am glad Harry has done so well in the Plymouth blitzes. Be marvellous if he
> got a gong or something wouldn't it? Still, he always has been pretty good and a
> plucky little devil. No training today, weather. But I did fire a rifle, first time for ages.
> I wasn't too bad either.

The devastating German air raids of the nights of 20 and 21 March and 21, 22, 23, 28 and 29
April 1941 became known as the 'Plymouth Blitz'. The Falkner family recalled the sky was
lit up for miles around during the raids on Plymouth and they could see the glow of fires in
the sky over thirty miles away in Shaldon. Little were they to know that Roy's brother Harry
was in the thick of it.

Plymouth's air defence consisted of four elderly Gloster Gladiator biplanes on the first
night. At just after 8.30 pm on 20 March the alert was sounded and at 8.39 pm the attack
started. First came a group of Heinkel 111 bombers which dropped bombs, including thirty-
four delayed-action high-explosives. A shower of flares was followed by 12,500
incendiaries and other high-explosive bombs, and then a second wave dropped their bomb
loads, which included seventeen blockbusters, each weighing a ton. Plymouth Fire Brigade
was soon overwhelmed and the army was urgently requested to help.

Harry had been serving with the Royal Army Service Corps near the Royal Navy Dock
at Devonport, Plymouth, when the city was targeted by the *Luftwaffe*. Harry recalled:

> It was Devonport they were aiming at. It was reckoned 2,000 incendiary bombs were
> going off all at the same time. Anything burnable was set alight.
> I was orderly officer that night and the barracks adjacent to ours, the ATS
> quarters, was bombed. I was in charge of transport and organised a lorry and driver
> to get them out. We got forty-nine people in a three-ton lorry. A corporal drove them
> to Seaforth Barracks, everywhere was on fire.

The raid lasted until 12.20 am in the early hours of 21 March. The centre of Plymouth was
aflame. Harry continues: 'I turned up at Crownhill Fort later when the colonel came to see
how troops had fared – I was black from the fires.'

Roy's sister Leslie recalled that on Harry's return to Shaldon he told how: 'He had also
been involved in trying to put out the fires and the fire-fighters quickly ran out of water, so
they had to resort to seawater. The sand kept clogging up their pumps and hampering their
efforts to put out the fires.'

At 8.50 pm the following night, Friday 21 March, the blitz started all over again. There
was no warning and the sudden appearance of the raiders coming in from the north-east
caught the city by surprise. The bombers targeted the area adjoining the previous night's
bombing zone and circled the city for some twenty minutes, positioning themselves before
dropping their flares on the target area. They encountered no resistance from the RAF.

Many of the 292 civilians killed during the raids were buried in mass graves at Efford Cemetery, each wooden coffin draped with a Union flag.

There were raids on 8 and 15 April but they were small in comparison with the previous two raids, although Devonport was the main target. On the night of 21 April, there was a 120 German aircraft raid, killing ninety-six sailors by a direct hit on the naval barracks. The following night an air raid shelter at Portland Square sustained a direct hit and seventy-two people were killed outright.

The final major raid was on 28 April. The enemy aircraft were flying over the city when the air-raid sirens were sounded and on that night the targeted areas were the naval dockyard, St Budeaux, Camel's Head, and HMS *Raleigh*, where forty-three sailors were killed.

Told years later that Roy had written about him, wondering if he would get a medal, Harry merely shrugged: 'I was orderly officer and unfortunately got bombed by the *Luftwaffe*.' The corporal was mentioned in despatches.

For Roy in Scotland there was still plenty of flying: 'Thursday. We really are working quite hard and just the sort of thing I like. I'm loving every moment here except for the one terrific gap in my life – my wife – otherwise it's grand. We don't know any news of how long we're going to be here or anything yet.'

Flying continued throughout the week and into the weekends. Clayton recalled:

The God-fearing townspeople disapproved of our working on Sundays, and when Sub Lt Kindell made a forced landing on a Saturday afternoon, the repair party were warned by one of the elders from the Kirk: 'Nay guid will com o' it if ye attempt to flee yon macheen oot o' ther-re on the Sabbath!' But it did fly out the next morning while the good people were at worship in the Kirk.

Clayton continued:

But they were right, no good came of it, for the Minister prevailed upon Lt Cdr Waters to take the unprecedented step of ordering a compulsory church parade and attendance at the Kirk on the following Sabbath!

It was quite an ordeal as we were paraded in our best clothes and marched into church under the critical gaze of the congregation, but they seemed to accept us better afterwards when they had decided that we weren't completely irredeemable. Thus shrived of our transgression, at least in the sight of the populace, if not in that of the Almighty, we proceeded with the business of working up for sea.

Humphrey Maughan described the daily routine:

There we were engaged in intensive training for carrier operations, including deck landing, torpedo attacks, navigation and anti-submarine ops etc culminating in actual deck landing practice on HMS *Argus*.

B-F batted me down to my first hectic 'arrivals' on the deck of HMS *Argus!* Baker-Falkner was known for his confidence-inspiring calmness when leading a sub-flight in very close formation under bumpy conditions in thick cloud, when our only method of communication was by 'zobbing' – Morse code with the extended forefinger.

The birth of Naomi and Roy's first child was imminent, and Roy sought to give her reassurance: 'Written on Sunday. How grand it was hearing your lovely old voice on the phone tonight. I drank whiskey. I know there is nothing to worry about and you'll find it as easy as shelling peas.'

On Naomi's due date, the prospective dad wrote:

> Today is the great day and how is my precious darling. I have been Officer of the Day today. It's been a bit of a bind I can tell you but I gather that normally it's OK. I tried to ring you up this evening but there was an eight-hour delay so I gave up. I was horribly disappointed cos I should have liked to say hello. Still, there is a war on.

The baby, a daughter, was born on 29 March 1941 at Morningham Nursing Home, Bradford. She was named Carole after Roy's favourite romantic comedy film actress, Carole Lombard.

Roy did not get the news of Carole's arrival until two days later when he was with the squadron carrying out deck-landing practice on HMS *Argus*. Roy wrote:

> Sunday: I am awfully glad it's over and mother and child are doing well. I got the wire in the cockpit of my aircraft at 11 this morning just as we were taking off. In fact I had to throttle back to get it. I told B-D the wonderful news.

The proud father wrote a second time that day: 'Later in fact this evening. I'm trying like mad to get some leave but not yet, maybe with any luck at Easter. How I pray so.'

At the very end of the month Roy's observer and close friend, David Buchanan-Dunlop, left the squadron. Roy was sorry to lose him. However, Buchanan-Dunlop did not leave before Roy and the entire squadron gave him a 'jolly good send-off' in the hotel bars of Campbeltown.

Roy's new observer was Sub Lt 'Pip' Phillips who remained with him for the remainder of the time that Roy stayed with 812 Squadron. Pilot Dane Sinclair recalled:

> I remember Sub Lt Pip Phillips and indeed flew with him occasionally. He was still with 812 Squadron when it was doing anti-submarine patrols from Gibraltar and he was awarded the DSC for an op in which the squadron was credited with being the first ever to sink a U-boat at night with the help of radar. The observer was especially important in such ops of course, because he operated the radar – known in those days as ASV, or anti-surface vessels.
>
> Phillips had flown with Roy, it was customary at that time for crews to keep to the same personnel and to stick to the same aircraft, but there was nothing rigid about it and changes were often made when, for example, a particular crew member was not available or when an aircraft was being serviced.

Wartime duties meant Roy was not allowed to leave the air station to see his new-born daughter but all the squadron joined in congratulating him and sending presents to baby Carole.

Roy wrote to Naomi:

> Wednesday. I've got CN's first present today and I enclose it. I think that the thought is very sweet. It's from Phillips. He also says that if Carole can't understand it she must be a very backward child. I have a wee bit of news. All being well I should get a week's leave in a fortnight or so's time to see Mummy and Carole. The whole squadron sends their love to you both.

Roy's hopes of leave were scuppered when he was hand-picked to go with a contingent of 812 Squadron on an important operation – to take part in a convoy escorting aircraft carriers laden with equipment and urgently needed Hurricanes bound for Malta.

He had to break the news gently to Naomi.

4 April. Sunday. 17 [letters] from you darling. I'm afraid that leave has again receded into the I don't know where. I suppose that we have been very lucky so far but I do get a bit fed up at times when I find people who have done FA the whole time and haven't even been abroad even at the start of the war and just go on doing FA in comfort.

Darling, forgive my toot please altho' I still think it bloody of all the High Ups.'

His clue to Naomi that he was due to leave for foreign parts on board ship was coded as 'PS could you please look for a wee brown book called "Sailors' Pay Book" and send it on to me if you can find it.'

Clayton recollected there was much speculation as to which ship they would join:

This was supposed to be a closely guarded secret not to be divulged until the moment of our arrival on board but in Campbeltown there was a laundry and in that laundry were girls who insisted that they knew which ship we were to join – 'Everyone in Campbeltown knows it,' they would say. 'You are 812 aren't you?' 'Yes,' we would reply. 'Well, you are for the *Argus*!' And, sure enough, when the day of our departure arrived it was confirmed that we were to proceed to Greenock to join HMS *Argus*!

Though we were sorry to leave the friendly folk of Campbeltown, we were not at all sorry to say goodbye to the airfield.

Roy wrote to Naomi:

It's hell not being able to see you and our Carole before I go but it can't be done. The CO is very sorry too and sends his regards. He has tried to let me. Well, Billy girl, we have the satisfaction of knowing that it's a nice easy job. In future, will you always address my letters to C/O Admiralty. We leave here Thursday for destination unknown to the younger gentlemen but it's all right.

I've given Hunt your address so that he can send Rex to you whenever you are capable of having him and some money. It's hell being without you but we have been so lucky so far and I'm so grateful for the love of my lovely old wife and wee Carole. Wives came in for a drink this evening, it made me a wee bit depressed. Marjorie K. is a nice little thing as you say. She certainly does make one laugh.

He wrote the day before departure and made light of the whole matter:

We are off tomorrow for our new abode. Certainly sounds all right apart from the fact of not being able to see you my dearest wife and our lovely wee Carole. Have you seen in the papers that Minnie [Waters] has got the DFC, pretty good isn't it? We are all very pleased as that means that a member of our squadron is the first in the FAA to get an RAF award. It's grand.

On 10 April, Roy and a detachment of 812 Squadron under command of Minnie Waters and with Ed Walthall as senior pilot, embarked on HMS *Argus*. The carrier, nicknamed the 'Ditty Box' due to her similarity to the box in a sailor's kit, was the world's first aircraft carrier, having been laid down in 1914 with a flush deck enabling wheeled aircraft to take off and land. She was relatively small at 14,000 tons with a ship's complement of 270 officers and crew.

Roy's detachment and their Swordfish were destined to provide anti-submarine patrols for a convoy transporting fighter planes to Gibraltar prior to the fighter aircraft being transferred to Malta, in a mission code-named Operation *Dunlop*.

Malta was of strategic importance for the success of the Allies in the Second World War. On the outbreak of war, the island was ill-prepared, having four old Gladiator fighter aircraft, left behind by HMS *Glorious* on her final voyage to Malta, and a few destroyers and submarines.

In April 1941 the situation in Malta was desperate and it looked as though Egypt was going to fall to Rommel's *Afrika Korps* unless reinforcements could be brought in. Supplies to Malta and North Africa had to be through the Mediterranean but the *Fliegerkorps X*, the cream of the German dive-bombers, were in nearby Sicily and Sardinia. Allied convoys were subjected to heavy bombardment from the sea and air. Spitfire and Hurricane fighter planes were badly needed and *Argus*'s role in bringing the aircraft even part of the way via Gibraltar was critical.

Had the island been allowed to fall, the Italian and German armies in North Africa would have had a base from which they could be reinforced easily in the narrows between Italy and Tunisia, British troops in Egypt would have fallen, and the whole of the Middle East with its vital supplies of oil would almost certainly have been brought under Axis control.

For Roy's detachment, the journey to Gibraltar began with preparations on board *Argus* in the Clyde. Easter Sunday was spent inspecting the aircraft inflatable dinghies to make sure they would operate automatically if the aircraft had to ditch.

At the same time, Hurricane fighters were ferried out to the carrier. They were brand new Mark II machines, their wings removed to enable as many as possible to be crammed into the hangar and still leave room for 812 Squadron's six Swordfish. The wings were to be fitted by a RAF working party on arrival at Gibraltar where the fighters would be transferred to HMS *Ark Royal*. The work continued over Easter Monday.

Argus sailed at midnight on Wednesday, 16 April. The ship was described by some as 'a small and snail-like vessel of great age and vulnerability'. One of her engineering officers wrote in the *Naval Review* in February 1945:

> The sight of the *Argus*, firing a pathetic hail of lead from her ancient pieces of ordnance into an assortment of hostile aircraft, weaving wildly to avoid their bombs or torpedoes, flat out and emitting sparks and showers of soot from her funnel ducts and then paddling sedately on her way when it was all over, was enough to provoke paroxysms of mirth in the breasts of the onlookers.
>
> On these occasions she was like nothing so much as an old lady shocked into indelicate exposure while crossing a busy street and letting down her skirts with a sigh of relief on safely gaining the pavement. Shaken: but for the time being, secure.
>
> *Argus* came through the war unscathed.

Roy wrote to Naomi in a hand-delivered letter which escaped the censor's pen.

> Written on Sunday. How I love and adore you Mummy dear and how I hate going off in the *Argus*. We left C.town [Campbeltown] on Thursday and flew to Glasgow where we waited two days before embarking. The CO, Ed and I got pretty pickled one way and another touring the bars in Glasgow.
>
> It was quite fun to see a large city again but it was lousy being on the main line to you and not to be able to nip down to see you. It was hell. Then on the Sunday we embarked our six aircraft. I came down the Clyde in the lighter with them.
>
> We got all our aircraft on board without serious damage to any of them. Then

away to sea with 30 Hurricanes on board to ferry to Gibraltar. The first day trundling past Ireland was nice and fine and sunny and Ed and I provided the convoy escort, submarine spotting.

Roy continued:

Next day. Things began to happen, a beautiful little south-westerly gale sprang up and the old ship began to pitch and heave in the very cold grey Atlantic seas. We and our escort were taking it green over the bows. It was too rough and windy for our young gentlemen to do their deck landing training so again Ed and I did our stuff with only our bomb-load holding us on the deck before taking off, it was grand. All the stomachs of the squadron started to turn up and all the RAF personnel felt very unhappy. How I did want my Billy girl alongside me. I didn't mean I wanted you to be sick, darling but the last time I was at sea was with my lovely old lady and how I loved it and how I do adore and idolize you darling and our wee Carole.

Roy went on:

Next day the storm was even too bad for Ed and I to fly. The poor old ship was rolling 20 degrees or more and everything groaning and grumbling with age. I very nearly had to keep watch but managed to wriggle out of it, which was a good thing. I loved the sea and spent hours watching it and rather cruelly laughing at all the other poor devils.

Clayton noted the maintenance crews' viewpoint from the moment of departure from the Clyde:

We were glad to get away for the previous night there had been an air raid and we had been closed up at action stations until 04.15. Our function on board was to provide anti-submarine patrols to ensure that U-boats were kept at bay. As a precaution against surface attack, we had the heavy cruiser *London*, to be joined later by Admiral Somerville in the battle cruiser *Renown*, flagship of the famous Malta convoy Force H.

The next morning, as the Kintyre coastline receded from view, the first patrols were flown off by Ed Walthall and Roy. These continued throughout the voyage, except when the weather turned rough, for then the risk of attack from U-boats was minimal. By Saturday it was blowing a full gale and double lashings had to be put on the Swordfish. At nights the ground crew slept on camp beds in the hangar, as did most of the other aircraft crews.

As a precaution against surprise attack, the ship went to action stations each evening at dusk and again at dawn. On Sunday afternoon the wind moderated, allowing two aircraft to be ranged on the flight deck and Roy and Ed were detailed to fly, although the windspeed over the deck was 65 mph – slightly over the stalling speed of a Swordfish.

The journey southwards was particularly dangerous; only two weeks previously a Spitfire on a routine reconnaissance mission over Brest revealed that *Scharnhorst* and *Gneisenau* were in the French port of Brest – rather too close for comfort for the convoy as it headed towards Gibraltar.

Roy wrote to Naomi:

Next day. Ed and I again flew with a windspeed of 50 knots over the deck which

191

meant that one was only approaching the ship at 10 mph. Quite easy landing except for the gusts. We were recalled several times because of squalls hiding the ship. I felt a bit lonely when that happened.

Clayton recalled:

> *Renown* rode the Atlantic swell with great elegance and her presence made us feel very important. *London* still held her station in the van. The wind got up and the ship began to pitch and roll about. I didn't mind that so much as the noisy way the hangar and flight deck structure creaked with every movement. The wind increased to gale force.
>
> Certainly the old ship was moving; sheets of spray were flying over the flight deck and the whole structure groaned and creaked with the strain, while the crockery in the messes never ceased to rattle with the vibration.
>
> Around us, the Swordfish strained at their lashings and, as the ship rode the long Atlantic swell, they rose and fell on their sprung undercarriage legs like so many beat-weary constables flexing their aching knee joints. Meanwhile, the ship kept up a melancholy groaning at the way it was being driven as the huge top-hamper heaved and tilted with the swell of the sea. Each time the stern lifted, a harsh vibration shook the whole ship and started crockery and mess traps vibrating in sympathy.

By the fifth day out from the Clyde, it got noticeably warmer; dawn broke later, which made morning action stations less of a shock to the system.

Roy continued: 'Driving ever south, it got warmer and warmer and first pullovers were discarded then vests, and night watches were kept in ordinary uniform.'

The convoy finally saw the familiar outline of the Rock of Gibraltar hove into view on 24 April after seven days and six hours at sea. Roy noted: 'I kept the middle watch that brought us into Gibraltar. Tangier to starboard a blaze of light and Gibraltar as well looked quite light.'

Argus's berth was next to that of *Ark Royal* and a timber ramp was lowered into position to enable the Hurricanes to be wheeled onto her flight deck.

Clayton explained the procedure:

> The next day the Hurricanes were ranged on deck and we helped the working party assemble their wings. We spent the rest of the time between patrols sunbathing in the nets. I think it was then that Admiral Somerville signalled: 'It is a source of great delight to watch your stinging bees alight upon the *Argus* flower!' This was posted on the squadron notice board, and Beery added a cartoon showing a sunflower with bumble bees, labelled respectively 'A', 'B', 'C', etc., buzzing around it with their arrester hooks extended menacingly like stings.

Clayton exclaimed surprise at seeing the modern *Ark Royal*:

> I was impressed by the carrier's spacious hangars; a pleasant contrast to *Argus*'s makeshift arrangements.
>
> The sight of the sleek Fulmars lined up in *Ark*'s light, airy hangars did much to dispel the bad impression formed by my time in *Glorious*. I left *Ark* with a feeling of confidence in the future, for I knew there were more carriers like her coming into service.

After the Hurricanes were hoisted aboard *Ark Royal* and stowed in the hangar, the carrier sailed for Malta, leaving the 812 Squadron detachment in Gibraltar.

Roy continued: 'We disembarked all our Hurricanes to the *Ark Royal* and then sat down to wait for her return.' He and his comrades spent two weeks there. It was good to see bright lights again and find the shops full of luxury goods.

He wrote to Naomi:

The first two nights we were taken ashore by one of the CO's friends and really beautifully sown up. It was lovely drinking beer after six days at sea without any. Today being a day of rest, Ed, the CO and I climbed up the Rock and were dripping sticky messes at the top. It really is a lovely scene.

Much of Roy's and 812 Squadron's air and ground crews' time at Gibraltar was spent sailing in one of the ship's boats.

Clayton looked back with fond memories of 812 Squadron's camaraderie:

These were happy occasions that emphasised the family spirit that had become a feature of 812. The sight of the Spanish town of Algeciras on the other side of the bay fascinated us; we gazed longingly at the tempting shoreline where peace had returned after three years of war and wished that our war could be over too.

Midway across the bay, we dived overboard for a swim, being careful to avoid the colourful jellyfish known as Portuguese men-o'-war, which trailed long tendrils beneath the surface which, if touched, raised painful burns that invariably turned septic.

Roy wrote to Naomi:

I am sailing a lot now trying to teach our young gentlemen how to be naval officers. Their ignorance is amazing, can't keep watch, run boats or anything to do with the sea. Still it's good fun trying to teach them. I kept the morning [watch] and then a cinema tonight on board and it's very hot and I'm very tired so good-night.

While in Gibraltar, Roy bumped into his old Dartmouth friend, Peter Pagett, and also Geordie Carline from 819 Squadron days who was being invalided home. Peter recalled: 'I met Roy again in the Mediterranean at Gibraltar, and together visited the Rock Hotel. By then I had also learnt to fly, April 1940 at Elmdon, Birmingham.' They had a relaxed drinks session and food overlooking the Bay.

In a letter, dated 2 May, Roy wrote:

This morning I took the young uns in a motor boat to try to teach them how to steer and drive one. Some of them made my hair stand on end slightly as it was a high speed boat. This afternoon I've got my usual sailing class. We'll probably be burnt absolutely black and there's no wind but still the sun is very, very good.

The crew were in touch with the rest of 812 Squadron back in the UK. One package of documents that arrived from the squadron office included a series of squadron photographs of Roy's dog, Rex.

Did I tell you I wonder that Mrs S-M [Stewart-Moore] was expecting in a week's time? Ed and I climbed a bit of the Rock today and sunbathed. It's too cold water for bathing. Lots of people did, but not us. No thank you. As usual, we all got a little bit pickled tonight. There's nothing else to do anyway. Billy darling, we've just sailed off.....I am so pleased and excited. It's absolutely heavenly to think that in another seven days or so we should be in England.

On 8 May, *Argus*, with Roy and the 812 Squadron detachment on board, left Gibraltar and, setting course for the Clyde, resumed anti-submarine patrols. With the Hurricanes gone, the carrier was no longer part of Admiral Somerville's Force H and rated only a single destroyer as escort.

The journey did not go without mishap as Clayton recollected:

There was a new rule that prohibited aircraft from landing-on with bombs on board, therefore they were set to 'safe' and dropped astern of the ship before landing.

For some reason 'G', on returning from a patrol, jettisoned hers set 'fused' (four one-hundred pounders!) from a low height, and only about 500 metres astern of the ship. Not only did it shake up the old carrier, it blasted the Swordfish, which returned with a tattered tailplane.

On 14 May, at 2130 hours the action alarm sounded for enemy aircraft. No attack developed and 812 Squadron were stood down at 2345 hours only to be called out again at 0420 for another aircraft, but again the enemy did not find the carrier and 812 Squadron secured at 0435.

The next day the ship arrived in the Clyde, the Swordfish flying off to Campbeltown and 'Mr McGichie's field' via Arbroath.

Roy wrote on arrival:

We disembarked today after quite an uneventful trip back except for one night of alarms and excursion from Jerry aircraft. Nothing happened though. Then we went to C.town [Campbeltown] to see if our luggage etc had been sent on. It had or at least some of it. But unfortunately no letters.

Flew in the afternoon. We came here to Arbroath and met a lot of types, Bob Furlong and Nancy and Mrs Titch [Harding]. I took her out to supper as Titch was away...and then back early to the telephone.

Titch had been posted to the Deck Landing School at Arbroath from 812 Squadron.

On landing, they learned that five days earlier, Hitler's right hand man, Deputy Fuhrer Rudolph Hess, had parachuted from a Messerschmitt fighter near Glasgow and been captured.

The night after Hess's capture, Goering sent 500 bombers to attack London, a raid that lasted five hours, with fires raging all over the capital. At least 5,000 houses were destroyed and provisional figures for casualties were a record 1,400 dead and 1,800 badly injured. The Palace of Westminster was hit and the House of Commons chamber lay open to the sky. Two days later the members met in Church House, Westminster, where Prime Minister Winston Churchill declared defiantly: 'Parliamentary business will not be interrupted by enemy action.'

The war was about to enter an ever more crucial stage for Roy and his Fleet Air Arm colleagues.

CHAPTER 16

Orkney and Twatt

Roy returned to Campbeltown and was ordered to 'report to duty' in the Orkney Islands – but not before he had received a severe reprimand. Unknown to Roy, whilst he was on Malta convoy duties, the rest of 812 Squadron had regrouped at the large air station at Hatston and had been there since 21 April.

Roy's sister Leslie recalled: 'He did not see the posting on the aircrew board, and was seriously reprimanded for missing this – an official blunder and no message was sent to his accommodation.'

On 16 May, Roy and the rest of the squadron aircrew involved in the Malta convoy flew their Swordfish aircraft via Arbroath then northwards, crossing the coast near John o'Groats and across the Pentland Firth to the myriad of islands forming the Orkney Islands.

Phillips warned Roy to avoid the hidden mountainous Hoy and they came in low, avoiding the barrage balloons over the massed Home Fleet at anchor in the protected waters of Scapa Flow. They circled the six large hangars marking RN Air Station Hatston, banked and came in to land on the tarmac runways – an unusual landing surface for Roy and his colleagues who were more used to grass fields. Due to Orkney's damp climate and sodden soil conditions, all runways had to be tarmacadam surfaces or aircraft wouldn't have been able to operate from there.

Roy's steward, Sgt Hunt, was waiting with Rex as Roy landed and came over to welcome him. Roy wrote that Friday:

> We are at Hatston, darling, came up this morning through a bit of snow but otherwise dull trip. Rex didn't seem terribly thrilled to see me at first in my flying clothing but as soon as I took them off he was much more excited over it.
>
> I saw Titch when we arrived. He's very well but has gone back now. Wives aren't allowed here. Mrs K [Kindell] has arrived and it's not popular again. I'm afraid leave is not quite so close as I thought, darling, but it should come I hope. We are training here which is something to the good.

Orkney had been turned into a so-called 'protected area'; it was normally impossible for any civilian to enter or leave the islands without a special pass.

The Royal Naval Air Station at Hatston, HMS *Sparrowhawk*, was close to Kirkwall, the capital of the Orkney Islands. The airfield overlooked the Bay of Kirkwall and was backed by the high ground of Wideford Hill. Kirkwall itself was little more than a small settlement but dominated by the spire of the ancient Viking St Magnus cathedral and by its small stone fishing harbour. The station commander was Captain Henry Lockhart St John 'Fanny' Fancourt, veteran of the Battle of Jutland, who was just recovering from serious injuries received when German dive-bombers destroyed the control tower at Lee-on-Solent. His second in command was Cdr Geoffrey 'Hank' Rotherham.

Hatston was well laid out with four Bellman-type hangars, along with workshops, storage space, compass swinging bases, a magazine and tanks for 50,000 gallons of aviation fuel. It had a complement at that time of 430, including seventy officers.

Clayton recalled:

> In welcoming us to the station, Captain Fancourt confessed that he was at a loss to know what to do with us. (It sounded like Prestwick and Ford all over again!) He regarded us as though we were a lot of vagrants and, indeed, remarked that since we had lost our carrier, we were being passed around like a spare dinner! That sounded ominous, for spare dinners are either consumed or end up in the pig swill, but neither the captain, nor any of us were, as yet, aware of what was happening on the other side of the Norwegian Sea.
>
> However, there was still nothing to do and little to see except the bare, treeless landscape. Yet the place had charm; the air was like chilled wine and every detail stood out in the thin sunlight, the crofters' cottages dotted about the hillside, the dry stone walls.

They were allocated a squadron office and stores behind the main hangars and Roy was accommodated in one of the regulation wooden huts at the entrance to the air station. Sgt Hunt had already readied Roy's hut and had settled Rex there as well.

Life was to be fairly informal and Rotherham recalled that the officers' dress also tended to be pretty informal but the one thing he did insist on was that all officers wore bow ties at dinner. As he put it:

> It was not for reasons of formality, but simply because it was impossible to wear a dirty shirt with a bow tie, as it showed too much! Or maybe this had something to do with the Wrens on the Station, which 812 soon discovered were splendid girls and that their presence was a steadying factor.'

When Roy entered the officers' mess, he learned that a fortnight before there had been the unusual sight of a Walrus aircraft being towed by a submarine.

A Hatston-based Albacore had crashed into the sea fifty miles east of Orkney and a Dutch submarine had picked up the only survivor, the pilot. The Walrus was catapulted from HMS *Shropshire* in Scapa Flow to fly the pilot to hospital in Kirkwall. It rendezvoused with the submarine but with worsening weather could not take off again and had to be towed by the submarine back to Orkney's sheltered waters.

The resident squadron at Hatston was the Fleet Requirements Unit which provided aircraft for fleet exercises. There were two Martin Maryland aircraft which had been taken over from the French air force after the Nazi invasion of France.

Close to Hatston was Scapa Flow, a vast natural lagoon anchorage in the south of Orkney encircled by the mainland of Orkney to the north and a profusion of islands to the south, east and west. That May, the new Vickers-Armstrong aircraft carrier, HMS *Victorious,* had entered Scapa. She was not yet fully worked up, carrying only a few fighters and torpedo-bombers for her own protection.

Lt Cdr Eugene Esmonde, of 825 Squadron, arrived briefly at Hatston, and on 18/19 May, the first prototype Fairey Barracuda dive-bomber made the first deck landing on *Victorious*, with 778 Squadron.

Roy had mixed feelings when he reached the Orkney Islands as this was where his ship,

HMS *Glorious*, and her crew had sailed from to her doom off Norway just nine months previously – the memory of her loss was with all the remaining 812 Squadron members who had served with her.

When Roy arrived, airborne invasion from Norway was considered imminent. Large German troop concentrations in Scandinavia threatened the Orkney peace. Experience had taught the Allies that the blitzkriegs which characterised German progress in Europe, inevitably meant the destruction of airfields was the first step.

By May 1941 there were four operational air stations in Orkney and it seemed likely they would be the first to be targeted; probably followed by an invasion of the east coast of Orkney, possibly supported by airborne troops. The stations were therefore well defended and to test the defences there were several large-scale mock invasions. One of the largest was held three weeks after Roy finally left the Orkney Islands when an invasion force of 18,000 troops supported by tanks landed on the south-east of the Orkney mainland, the main objective being the seizure of Twatt and Skeabrae airfields.

Roy and 812 Squadron had barely arrived when the German battleship *Bismarck*, the most powerful battleship in the world, became the 'buzz of the month'. News came that she was refuelling in a fiord just south of Bergen, less than 300 miles from Orkney. Captain Fancourt ordered all squadrons to prepare. *Bismarck*'s move had put her within reach of a squadron of Albacores which had been specially training at Hatston to strike against the battleship.

On 17 May, Roy's squadron was readied for action stations and the order given for the Swordfish torpedoes to be armed.

The Albacores moved to Sumburgh in Shetland ready for the torpedo strike. A final reconnaissance had to be made before the Albacores carried out the attack, but with bad weather RAF aircraft were unable to fly for three days.

Volunteers from the station's own 771 Fleet Requirement Unit offered to attempt the reconnaissance flight with one of the Maryland aircraft – this was certainly not in line with their normal duties. The CO, Noel Goddard, a most experienced pilot, volunteered along with his TAG, J.W. Armstrong, and air gunner Milne. There was no experienced navigator so Rotherham offered to fill this spot.

They carried out the reconnaissance in the Maryland bomber without incidence, although due to bad weather they were often flying below 50 feet. They ran up inside the fiords to the anchorage, but it was empty of shipping and so was Bergen harbour. Rotherham transmitted the urgent message 'battleship and cruiser have left'.

Immediately the Home Fleet responded to the news and Fleet flagship, HMS *King George V*, HMS *Victorious* and the entire fleet slipped their moorings in Scapa and headed for the Atlantic. The chase was on.

For the 812 Squadron ground crew at Hatston it meant a sudden work overdrive readying the Swordfish. Clayton recalled:

> Nine sets of overload tanks and their associated hardware were produced, and we worked round the clock installing these in the aircraft. Torpedoes were armed and loaded, the crews briefed, but then *Bismarck* and *Prinz Eugen* passed far to the north and beyond the range of 812's Swordfish.

Clayton continued:

> The CO asked for us to be embarked in *Victorious*, whose torpedo squadrons were not fully worked-up, but he was overruled.

In fact, our sister squadron from *Glorious*, 825, now commanded by Lt Cdr Esmonde, were already on their way. Had we been put in *Victorious* our hardcore of experienced aircrews might have meant the difference between damaging *Bismarck* and stopping her in her tracks!

Station commander Fancourt wrote:

When they had established that the *Bismarck* had sailed, there was nothing more I could do from Hatston. I am glad to say that I did not send in the Torpedo Bomber Squadron [812]. It would have been a very difficult operation in the circumstances.

Roy and 812 Squadron stepped down and instead went to an ENSA theatrical show at Hatston followed by catching up with the first-hand news from Rotherham and Noel Goddard over a drink in the station mess.

The next day *Bismarck* and *Prinz Eugen* were sighted far to the west of the Orkney isles in the Atlantic and shadowed by the cruisers *Norfolk* and *Suffolk*, which delivered their quarry within gun range of HMS *Hood* and HMS *Prince of Wales*.

Bismarck shocked the Navy and the whole world by sinking *Hood* in a short engagement in the early hours of 24 May. Three survivors were picked up of a total company of 1,409. *Bismarck* also hit *Prince of Wales* and forced her to break off the action. *Bismarck* then made a run south towards France which would have brought her under the protection of *Luftwaffe* aircraft from the mainland. But by now she was also within range of 825 Squadron Swordfish aircraft from *Victorious*. With the squadron was Roy's friend, 'Feather' Godfrey-Faussett.

The nine Swordfish flew off, followed by three shadowing Fulmars. Swordfish pilot Lt Percy Gick reported later:

Bismarck did what I regarded as one of the most unsporting things of all which was to lob 16-inch shells at us, and in fact caused great inconvenience because one of them landed ahead of us and I flew through the splash.

The whole aircraft gained about thirty feet in altitude, and the only comment that came out of Sayer [PO L.D. Sayer] during the whole four hours' flight was made then, when he said: 'Goddamn, some rotten sod's knocked the bottom out of my house'. In fact, the splash had literally ripped the fabric off the bottom of his part of the cockpit and there he was, sitting gazing into fresh air for the rest of the trip home.

A torpedo hit *Bismarck* but did not slow her appreciably and *Suffolk* lost contact with her. *Bismarck* was not found again until 26 May when she was sighted by a Coastal Command Catalina flying boat. She was so far south that she would soon be under the cover of the *Luftwaffe*. Now, however, *Bismarck* was within range of *Ark Royal*'s aircraft.

On 27 May, fifteen Swordfish, led by Lt Cdr Coode, and including Roy's friend Splash Carver, attacked *Bismarck*. A torpedo hit the German battleship aft and by an extraordinary chance jammed *Bismarck*'s rudder, causing the ship to go round in circles. The end was nigh for *Bismarck* which was eventually sunk by *Dorsetshire*.

Far away at Hatston, Roy's squadron could relax, if only for a short time.

When the news hit the newspaper headlines, Naomi immediately worried that Roy might be actively involved in the pursuit of *Bismarck*. He wrote to reassure her:

24 May. Papa Westray, Orkneys. One week since we came ashore. Thank you, Billy girl, for your lovely old letter. Cross my heart and spit to die we are only training.

I had great fun today, taking things to a forced-landed aircraft on a tiny island. Very small fields and huge bumps. We fixed it alright though. We met one old man of 83 who had never been off the island and had never seen an aircraft at rest and close to until today. The islanders were kindness itself though. By the way, before you think anything, no one was hurt or shaken in the forced landing.

The pilot concerned, Frank Low, gave his version of the story:

I'd forced-landed Swordfish P4095 on a tiny islet called Papa Westray in the Orkneys when we were working-up at Hatston. The landing was OK but the Senior P (at that time Ed Walthall) felt more skill than mine was needed to effect the take-off after repairs had been made to my Blackfish (a Blackburn-built Swordfish). He was no doubt right as Roy only just made it with everything possible jettisoned.

All squadrons saw Orkney, its weather and sea in all their moods. At times they were battered by wind speeds reaching 70 mph or engulfed by sea mists which swirled over the hills. On other occasions they experienced horizontal rain, adding to the anxiety of getting back to base. There were other times when the air was crystal clear with unbelievable visibility.

Air Commodore Brown, former 253 Squadron pilot in the summer of 1941, recalled:

The most abiding impression of Orkney was a sense of freedom, both in the air and on the ground. Apart from the gun defended area of the Flow the islands presented an extensive, uncluttered and unrestricted aerial playground. For the sole benefit of young fighter pilots, this exclusive flying arena provided, from time to time, huge white cumulus clouds with sharply defined edges and deep caverns through and around which to tail chase, twist, turn, dive vertically down the blossoming faces and climb steeply to loop over their burgeoning tops.

At the other end of the aerial scale, at low level, there was the sea rolling in from the Atlantic and offering its broad curving waves with their foaming crests to be skimmed and breakers to be chased along the deserted curving beaches. There were uninhabited islands over which to practise low level acrobatics with no one to complain and, hopefully, a squadron commander blissfully unaware of just how low they were. And if an appreciative audience was required, the lighthouse keepers always seemed to enjoy the show and the unexpected company.

After the *Bismarck* episode, Roy's squadron got down to further intensive training, and focused on the serious business of ALTs on the armed yacht HMS *Atmah* until the end of the month. Only three weeks previously this ship had come to the rescue of 812 Squadron aircrew, when L/A Lock and crew had ditched and been rescued off Papa Westray.

Roy wrote:

29 May. Orkney. Poor old CO is in bed at the moment with a swollen bruised ankle received while playing hockey. Most uncomfortable. Yes darling, Ed Walthall is very nice indeed. The three of us get on very well together. We are the old 'uns. All the others are the young 'uns even though some are older than I am. I must go to sleep after my Middle [Watch] last night and some three hours' sleep.

After eighteen months of war, there was a dwindling number of regular Navy aircrew who had started off on 3 September 1939. As with even Roy's own Leuchars FTS course, whole training courses had by now been wiped out almost to the last airman by accidents on training flights, enemy action and ill-fated operations.

John Winton wrote in *Find, Fix and Strike*, which was published in the middle of the war:

> Those who survived were further depleted by the Navy's own insensitive treatment of aircrews. An air group normally joined an aircraft carrier for the whole commission, just like any other branch of her complement. But the air group was subjected to stresses and strains not experienced by the rest of the ship's company.

The point was well put by Rear Admiral Jamieson, then Ark Royal's engineering officer during the Norwegian campaign in his 1957 book *Ark Royal*:

> The contrast between the risks run by aircrews and by the remainder of the ship's company is always a problem in a carrier. It is strange, and very humbling, for a ship's officer to sit at a table with a pilot or observer who, between breakfast and dinner, has flown to the distant shore and been in action over enemy-occupied territory.

Winton continued: 'In its ignorance, the Admiralty kept aircrews flying until they literally dropped or, in their own words became "bushed or twitchy".' The youngsters who replaced them really were young – they were in their late teens or early twenties. 'Twenty-five,' according to Winton, 'was ancient, while thirty was as old as Methuselah.'

Roy was just short of his twenty-fifth birthday and on that reckoning was now 'ancient'. He was certainly a very experienced pilot and his next letter to Naomi hinted that another operation was on its way:

> Written Wed. It was grand hearing your lovely old voice tonight. I was so glad to be taken away from my company at the time too. Awful moans about how much work they do. As I said on the telephone we are definitely on the up and up [secretly hinting at the next job in the Arctic] but oh aren't I longing for some leave.

Flying continued for Roy, and he and the squadrons regularly practised bombing on an abandoned freighter in Kirkwall bay using flour bombs to mark their hits. Then, on 31 May a huge pall of black smoke could be seen from Hatston towards Birsay village in the north – a crashed Hurricane from 353 RAF Squadron flying from RAF Skeabrae.

Suddenly, on Friday, 6 June, the squadron was sent home on ten days' leave. Roy was at long last going to be able to see his baby daughter, Carole, for the first time. He couldn't believe it that at long last the Admiralty had granted his wish. With mounting excitement he started on the lengthy journey across the water from Orkney and down through Scotland, knowing that every hour he was getting closer to see his little one. At long last he reached the house where Naomi was staying in Bradford, and beamed with pride when Naomi opened the door with Carole on her arm. She was now two months old and he quickly realised she was a very contented baby. The proud father went out and bought a baby diary to record his daughter's progress. Immediately setting to work, he noted her weight at birth – '7 lbs 0 oz' – and the colour of her hair. 'Sadly lacking but fair.'

On 10 June, Carole Naomi was christened at St Margaret's Church, Bradford. The godparents were Roy's sister Leslie, Annie Blackburn, and his best friend from Dartmouth, Lt Robert Boddington.

All too soon leave was over and it was time to catch the Jellicoe Express and endure a dreadfully long train and ferry journey from Yorkshire, through Scotland and ultimately back across the Pentland Firth to Orkney. A travel-weary Roy wrote:

15 June. Sorry that I didn't write last night, but I was sent to the last place in a hurry to do our job and was rather late to get note paper. We had a pretty bloody journey up here and being in town without you was just plain hell.

I got my hair cut and went to a cinema. It was lousy being alone.

I haven't seen our Rex yet but he's Hunt's dog alright at the moment. Apparently he's in tremendous form. Chased a hare and caught it in a straight run last night. I'm not sure whether to be pleased with the once-my-dog, or to be sorry for the hare. I can't help feeling a wee bit proud of Rex – but oh so sorry that I have lost him as mine even tho' it may only be temporary. Goodnight, I must sleep.

The day Roy had written, 812 Squadron, including a new influx of pilots, had moved the twenty or so miles from Hatston to a satellite airfield called Twatt, officially called HMS *Tern*. Preparations were underway to board a carrier for Arctic operations in the near future. Twatt was regarded by the squadrons as being in the middle of nowhere, very primitive, even though it was no more than thirty minutes from Kirkwall. The squadron officers and men hated it.

Clayton recalled:

On return from leave, the squadron moved to the newly-opened airfield at Twatt on the west side of the mainland by the southern shore of Loch Boardhouse. When we arrived bulldozers were still at work, levelling the ground between the runways.

The first party of Royal Navy personnel had arrived at Twatt only two months previously. A small croft served as a galley and dining hall whilst the administrative block housed the wardroom, officers' sleeping quarters, general offices, naval stores and sickbay. The first station command at Twatt was assumed by Lt Cdr Rotherham the same month as Roy's arrival, and his job was to make the place as efficient and happy as possible. No. 812 Squadron aircrew slept two to a room with the exception of Waters as the commanding officer and Ed as the flight commander.

There was little to do in this farmland area after working hours so the officers and men made a football and hockey field. Cinema played a large part in the lives of the men and women in the Orkney air stations. Twatt had its own Nissen hut and brick-fronted cinema, the Orcadia, in which the tickets cost 3d, 4d or 6d. Commander (Flying) kept geese and a squadron commander happily cared for his plot of radishes at Twatt.

Pilot Dane Sinclair recalled:

RNAS Twatt, a satellite of Hatston in Orkney, was still under construction. My crew included Hovington as observer and L/A Lock as TAG. At Twatt we did anti-sub patrols around the islands and the Pentland Firth, as well as doing some working up exercises.

When I joined 812 as a pilot on 6 June '41 soon after finishing my training, B-F, as he was universally known, was then a senior and experienced lieutenant RN, but only, I think, a flight commander. By that time I was the most junior officer in the squadron where Baker-Falkner was very much one of the seniors. He had by then a very distinguished career and is still remembered as one of the outstanding naval officers of his time.

B-F was very much everyone's idea of the professional naval officer – a description which in my book is intended to be entirely complimentary – and that he was by general agreement a superior example of the type. He was respected by everyone both as an individual and for his professional skills.

Roy and the other 812 Squadron pilots recognised they had to be careful and have their wits about them whilst in circuit around Twatt as they were extremely close to the fighter airfield at adjacent RAF Skeabrae and could collide with other aircraft – it was barely two miles down the road and easily visible on the ground even from the officers' mess.

Desmond Scott, a New Zealander of No. 3 RAF Squadron, had arrived at nearby RAF Skeabrae just two months previously and recalled how 'Skeabrae was one hell of a place'. He described how the two asphalt runways were 'a luxury for our Hurricanes' and that everything else was half finished or surrounded by a sea of mud and melting snow. Gale force winds would sweep down from the North Sea almost every day, driving the snow into deep drifts and filling the ditches that had been excavated in preparation for the laying of pipes for the station's drainage system.

Once Roy had been re-united at Twatt with Rex, he was delighted to receive a present for Naomi from his steward and by reciprocation kindly offered Sgt Hunt a short flight in his Swordfish. He forwarded the present on to Naomi explaining:

I am sending you a table cloth from Hunt. It was a very earnest request: 'I've got a table cloth sir. May I send it to Madame.' Rather sweet of him I thought. He's absolutely tickled pink today cos I'm taking him for a flip this evening. He's incredibly thrilled at the idea.

Roy's life involved exercises and aerial explorations around the Orkney archipelago, and walks in the pastures, hills and cliff tops with Rex. At this time he had a motorbike, which he nicknamed Titus, and which he took for forays down the tiny tracks and lanes in the country. There were also excursions with the CO, Ed Walthall, and Phillips to the Royal Hotel bar in Kirkwall but the days still dragged by, particularly when it was raining, which was often.

To while away the time, Roy went on a special trip with Waters, Ed and other pilots to look at an almost intact captured Nazi high-performance medium bomber, a Junkers 88, which had been shot down, barely damaged, at nearby Sandwick on Christmas Day by Roy's fellow Leuchars pupil, Rodney Carver. It was stored in a hangar just down the road at RAF Skeabrae and was the first enemy aircraft of the war to be shot down by a British pilot flying an American aircraft, the Grumman Martlet.

The station diary entry said:

25 December. First blood was drawn, an enemy aircraft, a Junkers 88 was sighted two miles west of base by 804 patrol, Lt Commander Carver, just after the men had finished their Christmas dinner. The enemy aircraft was seen to be flying on only one engine and Carver noticed the enemy aircraft losing height after each burst [of his gunfire] and after the last burst, the aircraft landed with the undercarriage retracted. The crew of four, one of whom was injured, was taken to Kirkwall for interrogation.

Roy wrote to Naomi:

> Wed. It's a month today since we arrived back, what bloody awful ages it does seem. Still, Mugs, when we've fixed this war, won't we have a grand time. It won't be too long now.
>
> We aren't working hard at the moment and as consequence I have a grand time just going over and over our memories.

By June the weather became relatively warm with some magnificent crystal-clear sunny days and big red sunsets over the sea. The cattle grazed contentedly in the meadows around Twatt and the farmers began to cut the hay meadows and form hay stacks. Orchids were everywhere in the grass. Eggs were plentiful in the farms even though they were extremely scarce in the rest of the country due to rationing.

Roy wrote:

> 17 June. We are still working moderately hard and the beer is rather weak so we can't even get a wee bit pickled altho' we admittedly try pretty hard. Still this place isn't too bad.

Some of the station officers were trying hard to resolve the lack of alcohol at Twatt. Tom Johnston, who was then a six-year-old and wide-eyed farmer's son fascinated by the influx of airmen near his rural dairy farm, Bryameadow, recalled the officers 'growing rhubarb in one of the requisitioned croft farms with the express aim of making a potent rhubarb wine'.

Roy wrote on 19 June:

> I've done one job so far Billy girl. The sort you approve of and that's all. This life suits me beautifully except for the beastliness of being away from you my darling. We had a grand game of deck hockey this evening and very nearly sweated ourselves silly. It was terrific fun. As usual we played dice in the evening and so to bed and best part of the day, my letter to my wife.

That day he had flown off with Phillips, navigating out across the flat open cattle pastures of the Isbister plain towards the distant heights of Hoy ahead of them, and the mass of barrage balloons over the Home Fleet in Scapa. They undertook a relatively straightforward three-hour anti-submarine patrol as convoy escort around Orkney and the Pentland Firth and carried out dummy torpedo attacks on HMS *Cumberland*.

In his letter of 21 June, Roy wrote: 'We have been working fairly hard all the time but it's alright though. I don't mind the flying part but proper [paper] work, ugh.'

On 22 June, Germany, Italy, and Rumania declared war on the Soviet Union. Some three million soldiers of Germany and her allies began an attack on the Soviet Union, code-named Operation *Barbarossa*.

Roy wrote defiantly:

> 23 June. We have been working quite hard but nothing excessive. Stalin and Hitler are having fun aren't they? So what, I worship and adore you, darling, and that's all that matters.

Clayton recalled:

> We woke up to hear on the early morning news that Hitler had invaded Russia. This

was terrific news, for it meant that we no longer stood alone. At first it seemed incredible that a man like Hitler had been so foolish as to turn against mighty Russia before he had conquered tiny Britain for, after all, we were still reeling from defeat in France, Greece and Crete.

On the same day the Soviet Union was invaded, Prime Minister Winston Churchill promised to give all possible help to the Soviets. The Admiralty began assembling a task group capable of striking the enemy and deployed the two carriers, *Furious* and *Victorious*. Albacore, Swordfish and Fulmar squadrons were to provide the main thrust of the attack with four Sea Hurricanes to protect the Fleet itself.

A few days later it was midsummer's day and the prospect of flying in pitch black at night was a distant memory. Roy thoroughly approved of the Orcadian tradition of playing golf at the strike of the clock of midnight on Midsummer's Day, when there was still a bright red glow in the western sky.

In the first week of July the *Luftwaffe* resumed operations on a large scale with large numbers of enemy aircraft making attacks on Yorkshire, the Midlands, the south-west and the east coast. Naomi had a near miss with a bomb landing nearby.

Roy wrote on the Thursday immediately after hearing about the attacks:

> I must say that I'm a bit shattered by your bomb news, you be careful, darling. You take the greatest care of my two women Billy with these bombs and take shelter. Quite funny really. If it had been Billy alone I'll bet that you wouldn't have heard them but with T.W. [Carole] up like a flash. Well done Mugs.

A week later, Roy and the squadron received orders to pack up their gear and leave the relative peace of the Orkney Isles to return to shipborne duties. Their new home was to be HMS *Furious*, waiting for them in the Clyde. They were no longer a ship-orphaned squadron.

With mixed feelings Roy took Rex on his final walk around the marshy loch next to Twatt, scattering curlew and oystercatchers as Rex lolloped in the fields full of purple orchids. He knew that Rex would not be with him much longer as the dog would not be allowed onboard ship with his posting to sea. But first there was a farewell party hosted by Captain Rotherham – for some it would be a final farewell as the next operation was to be a tragic fiasco.

Roy wrote to Naomi the next day:

> We had a very, very boozy evening last night. The squadron ratings threw a party for the officers. It really was terrific. Quite naturally, everyone got very beastly drunk.
>
> Some of the impromptu turns put up were very good indeed, others were just plain low, although in the mood that we were carrying, it all went down with a tremendous swing. I did not perform other than raising my right elbow to the horizontal position.
>
> Today being a half-holiday just about saved all our lives. Snores everywhere. I went to sleep in the grass in the sun. And then a very lazy game of deck hockey this evening to sweat some of the beer out.

Roy's squadron was ordered to head south to join *Furious* at Greenock where she was under the command of Captain Arthur Talbot. The carrier was bound for the Arctic.

204

The aircrew were lucky flying; for the ground crew the route was more torturous. Clayton recalled:

We left Twatt and travelled by boat and train to Greenock, where we joined HMS *Furious* to become part of a mixed striking force which, we later learned, was designed to neutralise enemy bases in Northern Finland to clear the way for a convoy route to Murmansk and Archangel.

In *Furious*, there were four Sea Hurricanes of 880 Squadron; nine Fulmars of 800 Squadron; nine Albacores of 817 Squadron and our nine Swordfish. The Sea Hurricanes were the first high performance fighters to operate from a carrier and their presence on board in addition to the Fulmars indicated the importance of the operation.

For two weeks we rehearsed mock torpedo and bombing attacks on quiet coves in the Western Isles, returning to Greenock each evening for shore leave. We joked that it was like peacetime again, working an eight-hour day, but none of us had any illusions over what lay ahead, especially as the captain emphasised the importance of reducing our landing times, adding significantly, that 'we shall soon be steaming close to enemy-held coast'. 812 succeeded in cutting its landing time to twelve minutes for nine aircraft and, as the carrier's outdated lifts could not be made to work any faster, this was reluctantly accepted.

On 18 July Roy received orders to board '*Furious* for full flying duties in 812 Squadron' – they were off to war again.

CHAPTER 17

Attack on Kirkenes and Petsamo

Roy went back to sea in July 1941, and was soon to take part in one of the most ill-fated missions in the history of the Fleet Air Arm, the attacks on Kirkenes and Petsamo.

A month before, Hitler's troops had invaded Russia in Operation *Barbarossa*. In addition, war had broken out between Finland and the Soviet Union with the Finns supporting Nazi Germany, and providing them with Kirkenes as a staging area for its attacks towards Murmansk.

There was pressure on Great Britain to give support to the Soviet Union. A land invasion was out of the question but the Royal Navy could disrupt the flow of reinforcements coming in through the Finnish ports. The operation was to be code-named 'EF'.

Ed Walthall briefed his squadron and later elaborated on the reason for the op:

When Hitler attacked Russia there was immediate political pressure put upon the RN to help Britain's new ally. The Russians pressed for support on their northern flank through attacks on German shipping which was using the two ports of Petsamo and Kirkenes.

Urged by Churchill, the Admiralty persuaded a reluctant C-in-C Home Fleet, Admiral Sir John Tovey, to carry out such an attack which was to be 'a gesture in support of our Russian allies to create a diversion on the enemy's northern flank.'

The aim of the operation was for Albacores and Swordfish to bomb or torpedo the shipping alleged to be 'massed' in the harbours while the Fulmars dealt with German fighter opposition.

He continued:

The strikes were planned for 30 July – on Kirkenes by aircraft from *Victorious*, on Petsamo by those from *Furious*.

Victorious was one of the Royal Navy's newest aircraft carriers, having been launched on 14 September 1939 and commissioned on 15 May 1941 – just two months earlier. Her skipper, Henry Bovell, had been in command during the ship's involvement in the recent *Bismarck* chase. Prior to that he had been the commanding officer of HMS *Argus*.

On 18 July, Roy was ordered to join HMS *Furious* in the Clyde from the squadron's old haunt at Campeltown. The air station was not the old and inadequate 'Mr McGichie's field' but the nearby and very new RN Air Station Machrihanish, commissioned just two weeks previously as HMS *Landrail*.

Roy recalled in a letter received by Naomi the following month:

Our next stop was rather different to when we were there last and it was very crowded and very cold. Still, we saw quite a lot of old faces. Monkey Bryant sent his regards.... The next two or three days were the usual working up ones. I saw Corky Reid and Stewart-Moore for a few hours. They were very well and sent their regards.

James Stewart-Moore would be commanding 827 Albacore Squadron in the forthcoming operation. Since they had last seen each other in 819 Squadron, Stewart-Moore had been with *Illustrious*.

Roy elaborated: 'I had a long talk with him, I suppose about what we had been doing so far in the war.' James Stewart-Moore updated Roy about his own times since they had last seen each other:

From Ford, the squadron flew on board the new carrier *Illustrious*, and she took us to the West Indies. Then Scapa Flow for a week or so, and the day before the *Illustrious* sailed for the Med, I was winkled out. I spent a few weeks ashore, and then was sent to the great *Ark Royal*, the real and famous one.

Roy flew onto *Furious* and was on hand to help the youngsters who were new to deck landings. The skipper was Captain Arthur Talbot who later went on to command both *Illustrious* and *Formidable*.

Dane Sinclair recalled:

Walthall, senior pilot of 812, and Baker-Falkner, supervised my first deck landing, on *Furious*, an old carrier with only four arrester wires and no barrier. I was the most junior and inexperienced pilot in the squadron and the only one with no experience of deck landing so I was last to land on.

It fell to Baker-Falkner, with Ed Walthall, to give me the final briefing and customary pep talk before we took off. The pep talk explained that all I had to do was what I had been taught on the dummy deck and that nothing would go wrong 'just keep your head and do exactly what you were taught in training and you'll find it all quite easy. There's really nothing to it,' explained Falkner.

In the event, I had to circle for an hour and a half while the wreckage of the previous aircraft was cleared from the deck. Such events tend to have a lasting impression!

The incident was played down by Roy in his next letter to Naomi:

Next day we embarked in our present home [HMS *Furious*]. The young gentlemen being definitely a wee bit windy of landing on but all fixed it alright apart from a tyre burst.

Furious had the nine Swordfish of 812 Squadron, together with nine Albacores of 817, nine Fulmars of 800 and four Sea Hurricanes of 880A Flight. *Victorious* had a total of twenty-one Albacores of 827 Squadron and 828 Squadron, together with twelve Fulmars of 809.

On 23 July, the two aircraft carriers, escorted by the cruisers *Devonshire* and *Suffolk* in addition to six destroyers, set sail for the Arctic Circle.

With the fleet was Commander Anthony Kimmins who wrote in a contemporary report:

To make our attack on Kirkenes and Petsamo we had to go so far north that we were sometimes within 15 degrees of the North Pole, and so far east that we were east of Suez. This seems very confusing, but then it is all very confusing up there on top of the world. During the summer there's no darkness; the sun shines at midnight just the same as at midday.

To steam all those thousands of miles just to launch some aircraft for one attack on enemy shipping may seem, on first thought, rather a waste of time, but it was far from that because these were very important ships.

You see, it was known that the Hun was launching heavy attacks against the Russians at Murmansk, at the extreme northern end of the front, with troops based at Kirkenes and Petsamo, and that owing to the very indifferent land communications – there is in fact only one tortuous road – he must obviously supply these troops with food and other war materials by sea. There was also the possibility that he might be going to embark these troops in transports and attempt a flank landing further down the coast. Obviously, then, the sinking of those supply ships and transports was of the utmost importance.

The destination was as yet unknown to the aircrew. As the fleet sailed ever northwards, Ed Walthall and Roy were sent out on a reconnaissance flight to locate Seidisfjord in Iceland.

Weather conditions in the Arctic could range from savage gales and blizzards to freezing fog. Roy was later to tell Leslie about the bitter cold of flying in his open cockpit Swordfish.

In such conditions, getting back to the aircraft carrier was treacherous. Roy would have to watch his fuel gauge closely while at the same time searching for *Furious*, which could be lost in a snowstorm. In an Arctic gale, the old aircraft carrier would pitch and toss in the high seas, her bows cutting deep into the waves and throwing up spray which froze over the flight deck, making it treacherous for the landing parties awaiting the return of the Swordfish.

The crews had been carefully briefed by Commander Flying that if they went into the sea they would have to be rescued in a matter of minutes or die of exposure. Many Arctic veterans recalled that, after hours of sitting in open Swordfish cockpits during their patrols, it was common for aircrews to be so helplessly numb with cold on their return that they had to be lifted bodily out of their seats.

Fortunately, on this occasion the weather was fair and Roy made no particular mention of it when he hinted to Naomi about the sortie following an operational briefing on board *Victorious*:

We eventually arrived in, I think it is Ivan Bastow's place for a couple of hours after Ed and I had been sent out to find it for the ships. We both eventually got breakfast at three o'clock still with our pyjamas on. Not bad, yes – still we were quite happy doing it so that's alright.

We went to a small fjord eventually to refuel. It is rather like Killin [in the heart of the Scottish Highlands] in a way, darling, the same quietness and peace, huge tree-less mountains coming right down to the water's edge but of course there was no darkness as it is never night up here and worst of all, no Billy girl.

Seidisfjord was a desolate place with nothing but a few Nissen huts occupied by the military. Clayton recalled:

As it was high summer, with no period of darkness to mark the passage of the days,

I lost track of time. The weather was fine and clear when we sailed and these conditions prevailed all the way to the Finnish coast. Only then did the captain announce the purpose of the operation: 'To execute strikes against the Nazi-held ports of Kirkenes and Petsamo, which threaten Allied communications with Northern Russia.'

'What communications?' we wondered. That question was to be answered a few days later when we heard that PQ1, the first convoy to Murmansk, had brought much-needed relief to the hard-pressed Russians.

Roy continued his description of the operation:

After thirty-six hours or so, we again steamed north and yet again ever north and usually into thick fog, cold, damp and very dismal fog. One almost expected to see icebergs coming at one out of the murk. They didn't. Then having got within 700 miles of the North Pole, we turned east for our target area.

On Wednesday, 30 July, the ship reached its flying-off position forty miles from Petsamo. At 1230 hours, Action Stations was piped and 812 Squadron's Swordfish were ranged on deck, each aircraft loaded with six 250-lb GP bombs and eight 20-lb incendiaries.

Up until then all had been quiet, but all of a sudden an enemy aircraft appeared on the scene. Though the aircraft fled from one of the carrier's Sea Hurricanes, it was able to transmit a sighting report, thus alerting the enemy to the ships' presence in the area.

Cdr Kimmins described the event:

Then, just as zero hour was approaching, a sudden shout: 'Hostile aircraft, Green 80.' All eyes swung to the direction and saw the escorting destroyers loosing off into the sky. But the Hun aircraft wasn't taking any chances; he had seen what he had wanted to and was off for the beach at full throttle. Now it was a race for time. The gaff had obviously been blown, but in all probability this was their first intimation of our approach. Could our aircraft get there before they got their fighters into the air?

Rear Admiral Wake-Walker, commanding the First Cruiser Squadron, recorded in his diary:

At 1346 just as *Furious* was flying off two Hurricanes, which had to be launched before her TSRs (Torpedo, Spotter, Reconnaissance aircraft) could fly off, an He111 was sighted. An enemy report was made by this aircraft and from that moment the German forces operating off Tana Fiord ceased to transmit. I considered it was too late to call off the attack, and it was launched as planned.

The order came to start up and the peace was shattered on *Furious* by the sound of Pegasus engines bursting into life. The aircrews climbed into their aircraft.

Kimmins elaborated further:

A shout of 'Good luck' from the captain, the order 'Start up', a roar of engines and you couldn't hear yourself speak. The carriers were already heeling over as they turned into the wind and, as the steam jet levelled down the centre line, the first machine was racing down the deck and lifting into the air over the bows. As each one passed the bridge there was a cheery wave from the crew, and in a matter of a few minutes the flying deck was empty, the striking force were in formation and heading towards the shore. And we were left with a rather empty unnatural silence.

Roy was flying his new Swordfish 'F for Freddy' with observer 'Pip' Phillips RNVR as observer and P.O. Gill as TAG. He and the other seven Swordfish pilots of 812 Squadron formed up around the leading aircraft, flown as usual by Ed Walthall with Minnie Waters as observer, and headed towards the Finnish border and Petsamo. They were followed by the Albacores of 827 Squadron, and with the Fulmars of 800 Squadron above and astern of them.

The aircraft flew low above the water to avoid both visual and radio direction-finding detection as long as possible, before climbing to enter the Gulf of Petsamo. Roy and the other torpedo-carrying Swordfish proceeded to Hutoniemi before heading south, using the hills on the east side of the gulf as cover.

Roy's squadron had been ordered to proceed to Trifoni anchorage, but this was empty and instead 812 Squadron went on to attack the jetties at Liinahamari, coming under fire from the harbour defences. The leader, Ed Walthall, fired an enemy recognition cartridge which confused the Germans sufficiently to make them stop firing for a short time. The attack proceeded as planned, but there were again no really worthwhile targets.

A torpedo was fired at No. 1 pier and an explosion was noted. Kindell released his bombs at 100 ft onto oil tanks, making a direct hit; Jones and Maughan saw and felt the force of the resulting explosion. Jones machine-gunned a lighthouse which had opened fire on him.

Dane Sinclair, in a sub-flight of three Swordfish armed with bombs, noted:

We believed, because of a big cloud of black smoke that we left behind, that we had hit some fuel storage tanks. There was some anti-aircraft fire from batteries on the eastern side of the narrow inlet – the torpedo aircraft followed that shore while we, with the bombs, followed the western side – but it was not heavy.

The shipyards were also damaged, but the other results were insignificant and easily repairable. The striking force found no suitable ship targets for torpedoes but there was fighter opposition and two Fulmars and one Albacore were lost.

Roy also wrote about the attack:

On the day it was beautiful, strong sun and no clouds. Of course, there never are clouds when you want them. However, we carried out the attack successfully and I suppose you had heart failure over the casualties. Actually all our squadron got back safely, thank heaven. When I heard the news on the wireless, I spent a hell of a long time, Billy girl, trying to tell you that your stupid, old husband was perfectly alright, even not particularly frightened.

Ed Walthall concluded:

Petsamo was not a success, bad intelligence and bad planning.

There was little darkness in those latitudes at that time of the year, but it might have been expected that the attack would be mounted at night, when German defences were less alert. Instead the aircraft flew off in mid-afternoon after the carriers had been sighted by a German Heinkel reconnaissance aircraft just as the strike was about to be flown off, and so the enemy were well alerted.

Peter Cross added:

> I was No. 3 in the first sub-flight led by Walthall and Lt Cdr Waters and as there were not enough observers to go round at that time my crew consisted of a TAG. To signify that I had no 'O' on board a large red triangle was painted on the side of my Swordfish. 812 attacked the port installations at Petsamo where there was a lot of flak. We were attacking with torpedoes and we went in line astern.
>
> As No. 3 in the first sub-flight, I was immediately ahead of Roy leading the second sub-flight. He would have dropped his torpedo at the correct height and speed, but I as the most junior pilot might not have been so clever. At any rate when we got back to the ship, Roy told me that in his opinion if I had dropped my torpedo any higher it would have bounced up and brought him down! – and he said it in the nicest possible way.
>
> The sub-flights split up after the attack because of the flak and having no observer or intention of being lost in these waters I had followed in Roy's slipstream back to the ship.

Humphrey Maughan recalled:

> Our role was to attack any enemy shipping found in the harbour at Petsamo. Roy B-F was at that time a very senior pilot of 812 Squadron, and he led one of the two sub-flights, armed with torpedoes to attack shipping in the harbour, whilst I led the third sub-flight with six 250-lb bombs each to attack dockside installations and to provide a diversion to enable the torpedo aircraft to press home their attack.

Meanwhile, back on board *Furious*, Clayton and the other 812 Squadron maintenance crew could only wait and watch:

> Enemy destroyers were reported fourteen miles distant, but either this was a false alarm or the sight of our cruiser escort, *Devonshire* and *Suffolk*, scared them off. At 1420 a patrol of Fulmars was flown off for local defence and presently the Swordfish and Albacores returned, followed by the Fulmars. On counting them in, it became clear that two Fulmars and an Albacore were missing. Four aircraft were damaged, one of these being Swordfish 'B', which returned with a spluttering engine and a large hole in both port mainplanes. The engine fitter later found the remains of a half-cooked seabird wedged between the lower cylinders and the carburettor intake.

Clayton continued:

> The news from *Victorious* was grim. Though her Fulmars had shot down a Messerschmitt 109 and a 110, they had lost eleven Albacores and two Fulmars.

Furious's aircrew were indeed lucky in comparison with *Victorious*'s squadrons. Ten minutes after the *Furious* contingent had taken off, *Victorious* flew off twenty Albacores, followed by twelve Fulmars eighteen minutes later. Their destination was Kirkenes where they met heavy resistance and a formation of Messerschmitt Me109s and Me110s of the *Luftwaffe* 'Ace of Hearts' fighter squadron 1/JG 77. The Germans also had Junkers Ju87 Stuka dive-bombers.

Victorious's Albacores fired torpedoes at a gunnery training ship and four smaller ships but the losses outweighed any advantages.

James Stewart-Moore, CO of 827 Squadron, later recollected:

Victorious' aircraft went 10 miles or more inland to Kirkenes. I led the strike. When we reached the harbour, which was well inland, we found no shipping, but plenty of German aircraft. The Germans were expecting us, and we were attacked even by Ju 87s, acting as fighters. The German fighters had a field day among the slow biplanes, so we lost the forty or so torpedoes and achieved nothing in return. Five of the six aircraft in my flight were shot down and my aircraft was severely damaged and a write-off. We were the only aircraft back from the six who flew in with us – I think we lost more than half of the Albacores which took part. Then we were told to do it all once more.

I am afraid that none of the officers who designed the operation had any experience of wartime flying, nor of the impotence of biplanes flying at 90 knots in daylight against the then modern fighters.

When I joined HMS *Victorious* in August '41 as the senior squadron commander following the attack on *Bismarck*, I had found that my aircrews were quite inexperienced and we had no opportunity to train them until we were sent to attack a concentration of German shipping in Kirkenes harbour.

Operation 'EF' was a disaster for the Fleet Air Arm. Altogether thirty-seven officers and men missing – of whom twenty-seven were captured and taken as prisoners of war. One Albacore crew, Sub Lt Burke and L/A J. Beardsley, force-landed and managed to escape to Russian lines. Overall, the Fleet Air Arm lost twelve Albacores and four Fulmars. Eight Albacores were severely damaged.

By comparison, the *Luftwaffe* reportedly lost four aircraft: one Ju87 which was downed by an Albacore flown by Lt J.N. Ball of 827 Squadron, a Me109, and two Bf110s, one of which made a forced landing at sea and both its crew were rescued.

L/A A.E. 'Dickie' Sweet, who had previously flown with Roy in 819 Squadron, recalled his part in bringing down an enemy aircraft: 'I was involved in shooting down a Ju87 on 30 July. I was flying in an aircraft flown by Lt J.N. Ball and observer Lt B.J. Prendergast.' Ed Walthall continued:

Only one of the surviving Albacores returned to the ship undamaged. Lt J.N. Ball and his crew survived a sustained attack by a Ju 87, and then shot it down with the Albacore's front gun.

As it happened, there was hardly any shipping in either harbour. One 2,000-ton freighter was sunk and another set on fire, and four enemy aircraft shot down, and Leading Airman Ford in the back seat of one of the Fulmars had beaten off an Me110 with a Thompson hand-held sub-machine gun.

Newspaper reports of the action emphasised that a German warship, *Bremse*, had been hit twice as well as four supply ships.

Cdr Kimmins, who had been up-beat in his censured report at the time, was later more critical in his post-war 1947 book *Half-Time*:

There can have been no strategical reason for this attack, and one can only suppose that it was a purely political move to impress our latest ally, the Russians. Whether it succeeded in effecting this I have no idea, but to watch those Fleet Air Arm crews staggering off the deck in their antiquated Swordfish and Albacores, in the certain knowledge that they were to meet modern German fighters, provided by far the most unsavoury memory of any operation with which I was connected during the war.

The night before the attack was depressing enough, but the night after was a hundred times more so. At the best of times, naval flying is a far greater strain on the nerves than operating from a shore base. The latter may entail many more operational sorties, but in between whiles the aircrews can get away from the aerodrome and try to forget. But in the aircraft-carrier there is no escape from the hangars, the wardroom or the dormitory, where the empty space, the empty chair or the empty bunk are a constant reminder of the day's toll.

However, the terrible day had not finished for some of the aircrew, notably Lt Lee, Sub Lt Gordon Gorrie and their TAG from 817 Squadron, who had flown out from HMS *Furious* and taken part in the Petsamo attack. On the way back, their Albacore was attacked by an Me109. The pilot was seriously injured in the attack and the aircraft shot up, but he successfully ditched the biplane. The crew spent the next two days and nights in a dinghy. During that time they ate their Horlicks biscuits and urinated on themselves to keep themselves warm. They were eventually washed up on a beach. At that time, they didn't know whether they were in Finland or Russia. The Finns were taking no prisoners, instead, murdering them. They went looking for help, leaving Lt Lee the pilot in the dinghy, on the beach, wrapped in a parachute to keep warm as he was too poorly to be moved. Fortunately, they were found by the Russians, stripped of their uniforms, dressed as Russian kommisars, and interrogated for a week until they believed they were English. They then boarded a Catalina, and were sent to Murmansk. When back on board ship, a message was sent to the captain to say that Gorrie was back, and in good spirits. To which came the reply 'Good show! Has he any caviar in his boots!'

Admiral Sir John Tovey, C-in-C, wrote in a despatch:

The material results of this operation were small and the losses heavy. This had been expected. The heaviest losses occurred in the squadrons from *Victorious* and there is no doubt that some survivors felt that an attack on such poor targets against heavy opposition was not justified and their morale was rather shaken until they appreciated the political necessity of the operation.

The gallantry of the aircraft crews, who knew before leaving that their chances of survival had gone and they were certain to face heavy odds, is beyond praise.

He added pointedly: 'I trust that the encouragement to the morale of our Allies was proportionally great.'

For the aircrew, there was to be no let up. Clayton recalled: 'At 2250 the crews dispersed from action stations and work started on the damaged aircraft to prepare for a second strike.'

The next morning, 812 Squadron transferred to *Victorious* to replace the Albacores lost in the raid on Kirkenes. The plan was to make a strike on Tromsø on the way back to Scapa.

Humphrey Maughan commented:

We were fortunate, and all aircraft returned safely, but the *Victorious* squadrons encountered fighter opposition, and suffered a number of casualties, as a result of which about a half of 812 Squadron, including myself, were temporarily transferred to *Victorious* to provide anti-submarine patrols for the return journey.

Clayton recalled his flight with Roy to *Victorious*:

> Next morning a maritime version of Crawford's Tours was put in motion. 812 Squadron was to transfer six Swordfish to *Victorious* to balance the striking power of the two carriers. PO Manning and I were detailed to fly in a Swordfish piloted by Lt Baker-Falkner.
>
> As we climbed away from the ship, the view was breath-taking. To the south, the cold blue waters merged with a smoky sea mist but, to the north, the polar ice drained all colour from the sky, leaving a chill, pallid glare. Then *Victorious'* squat grey shape loomed through the mist, parting the sullen waters into a wake of dazzling whiteness. At first her deck looked ridiculously small, but B-F put the aircraft down to a good landing, and taxied forward to the lift.
>
> Our arrival was welcomed by everyone except the Master-at Arms, who had never 'in all his service' ever had to 'victual-in' a draft arriving by air! Eventually he was persuaded to pretend that we had arrived on board over the gangway, whereupon he reluctantly agreed to enter our names in the Gangway Victualling Book so that we might be allowed to eat whilst on board! Through such exigencies are long-standing traditions revised.

Clayton continued:

> After *Furious'* cockroach-infested mess decks our new surroundings seemed luxurious. The hangars were bright and spacious – ominously so, for there were many vacant spaces, and those that were occupied had bullet-riddled aircraft parked in them. Next to my Swordfish, a sick berth attendant was busy sponging the rear cockpit of an Albacore with disinfectant which, though strong, barely concealed the stench of death. This was one of those aircraft that had returned with a dead TAG in the back; two jagged holes in the Perspex hood revealed where a cannon shell had passed through the cockpit.
>
> As the previous day's operation had hardly been a success, another strike was planned, this time at Tromsø. By the time we had reached the flying-off position, the weather had deteriorated and, in the event, only Fulmars armed with light bombs took part. They took off in a snowstorm and, although they returned safely, I felt that the results of both operations were a disappointment to the Admiralty, who had expected shipping to be sunk and harbours blocked.

Roy wrote to Naomi from *Victorious*:

> Next day we transferred by air to this great ship leaving all our luggage and maintenance personnel behind. I shouldn't think a squadron has often changed its home in mid ocean. It seems rather queer doesn't it?
>
> However, I have a very nice cabin, running water, radiator lots of shelves, four electric lights. Oh, it's very Cumberlandish, and here, my darling, we stay for God knows how long, with all our goods in one small suitcase. We shall be getting pretty niffy soon I should think.

He continued, giving no hint of the gloom that surrounded the aircrew:

> Friday, 1 August. You will be very pleased to hear, I expect that all of us are perfectly alright. In fact we have had quite a good time altogether although we did

get extremely close to the North Pole. At least, I thought it was fairly close.

Corky Reid and S-M [Stewart-Moore] send you their love. They are in fine spirits and cheerful. We haven't done much work on the way back, just enough to keep from getting too bored. I hope that you weren't worried when the casualties came through. I willed my damnedest to tell you that I was kicking hard.

James Stewart-Moore sadly reflected:

'We had plenty of vacant accommodation by this time. That evening we were quite surprised when a squadron from HMS *Furious* landed on the *Vic* and told us that they were to help us repeat the op in a couple of days. The *Furious* had not enough fuel to do another op, so her squadrons were flown on board the *Victorious* to make up numbers. When I went to the wardroom after the visitors had landed, I was very pleased to find B-F there.'

Stewart-Moore continued:

The op was not repeated. Roy spent a few more days in the ship until we got back to Scapa Flow. Fighter bombers were sent to attack a target, but the Germans got one of these, and then we gave up and went home and I did not see Roy again.

Roy had a little more time to relax:

We are now on our way home, I wonder what our next journey will be. Whether we shall disembark or what and where.

Today we went for a very jolly little trip round the sky pretending to shadow the ship. It was quite good fun but extremely chilly. Still it gave us all a very good blow through. I went a wee bit crazy on the way back and thoroughly enjoyed myself, all at a very safe height about 1½ miles up.

We arrive back in [Hatston – censored] tonight and then on to [censored] we hope and then ashore – maybe. Oh, Billy girl, it is a wonderful thought to think that we are getting nearer and nearer to you. Even if it is only to receive and to write letters.

Not long after he wrote: 'Just sounded off to anchoring stations, good. Another three or four days, then letters. Whooppee.''

The next day he wrote:

I have been doing nothing, just waiting for the great moment for reliefs and getting a wee bit tiddly each evening. This morning, for instance, I have what you might call neuralgia but really I think it is just the old fashioned hangover. Otherwise I have absolutely no news.

When my relief arrives and I get to the next job I shall send for you as soon as it's humanly possible; in the meanwhile we've just got to wait I'm afraid.

Four days later he wrote:

Wednesday. I didn't write to you last night as I had to go to sleep early for a quarter to three trip this morning. Too early for me. Did I tell you that Bowman-Smith has got the DFC. Good show isn't it. He's still at the same old place.

Peter Cross recalled:

> We arrived back at Hatston on 7 August and within a short time were all introduced to HM King George VI whilst still in our working clothes. He came out to see us at our dispersal point – he happened to be at Scapa to visit the fleet at that time.
>
> We all went on leave and when 812 rejoined *Furious* from Hatston on 21 August en route to the *Ark Royal*, Roy was not with us.

Clayton remembered: 'We reached Scapa in a sombre mood, but I was glad to return to *Furious*, despite all the mod. cons. and the plastic-tiled space of the newer ship.'

Clayton recollected the King's visit:

> He looked older than when I had last seen him at North Coates twelve months earlier. He wore a worried expression too, for things were going badly in the Mediterranean at that time. As HM inspected Divisions, I noticed that his face appeared to be made-up, as though to conceal an underlying pallor.

Dane Sinclair added: 'The only other thing that sticks in my memory is that during the next few days the squadron was presented to HM King George VI twice, once at Hatston and once on board *Furious*.'

Furious sailed on 19 August, down the west coast of Scotland, and arrived in the Clyde the next day.

Clayton continued:

> Soon after the mail came on board, I was called to the squadron office where the CO informed me that I had been recommended for advancement to Air Artificer and consequently there was a draft note for me to report at Lee-on-Solent to await the next training course.
>
> Lt Baker-Falkner left on the same day to join 767 Squadron. The realisation that my time with the squadron had come to an end came as a shock. Then we had been like one happy family, all pulling together for the good of the whole. I thought of those who were no longer with us; though I was not yet twenty, I had outlived too many of my contemporaries and it was this thought which accounted for the lump in my throat as I made my way down the gangway to the boat that was waiting to take me ashore.

The memory of Roy's flying skills and prowess were to live on in 812 Squadron well after he had left. Dennis Leach recalled:

> I served as a TAG in 812 Squadron on HMS *Furious* soon after the Petsamo/Kirkenes op in July 1941.
>
> Baker-Falkner was a very well-known, popular, and much respected pilot and squadron CO in the FAA. I heard glowing reports and accounts of his outstanding ability and personality from those who served with him in 812.

Eric Cooper remembered:

> I was the replacement pilot for B-F when he left in the summer of 1941; I only met B-F once but had heard a lot about him from members of 812 Squadron who had been with 812 prior to my joining it. Lt Kindell followed B-F as senior pilot. I did not meet him until the summer of 1942 when 812 had returned from the Med and

when I was sent on a batsman course (Deck Landing Control Officer's Course) to Arbroath where B-F was working his squadron (and wing). We had a number of talks about 812.

812 Squadron went on to rejoin HMS *Ark Royal*, in which ship they operated with Force 'H', where, I understand, they found Admiral Somerville's Club Runs more stimulating than Crawford's Tours. Sadly, *Ark Royal* was torpedoed on November 13 by U-81. The ship's company was transferred to the destroyer *Legion*, but A.B.E. Mitchell, who was on watch below, was trapped by the rising water and drowned.

As all the aircraft were lost, 812's personnel were embarked in HMS *Audacity*, to take passage to the UK, where they were to have reformed. Tragically, *Audacity* was torn apart by three torpedoes and sank immediately with heavy loss of life. So many squadron personnel were lost in this disaster that 812 never again took its place among the Navy's front-line squadrons.

Peter Cross was lucky and did not report to *Audacity* and so avoided her tragic loss: 'I was one of the last to fly off *Ark Royal* on November 4 when she was torpedoed. Then I was loaned to the RAF as a night fighter pilot flying Mosquitoes.

By then though Roy had his new transfer documents – he was ordered to report to Arbroath for a new position and a well deserved rest from front-line duties … or so he thought.

CHAPTER 18

Arbroath Film Star and Instructional Pilot

On 18 August 1941, Roy was posted as an instructional pilot to the Advanced Deck Landing Training School at HMS *Condor*. It was an Royal Navy air station in Arbroath, on the east coast of Scotland. For once, the Admiralty had given Roy what he wanted and he was particularly thrilled to be joining 767 Squadron since Naomi and baby Carole would be able to come up and live with him.

Arriving at Arbroath railway station, Roy found navy transport waiting to take him through the town, along the long straight main road heading out towards Muirheads and Colliston, beyond which ultimately lay the Cairngorm Mountains.

He arrived at a Royal Navy air station quite different to his previous operational aerodromes. At the entrance to HMS *Condor* was the usual military style guard house, beyond which was a large and well-laid out establishment with brick-built administration block, stores and cinema. Roy saw row upon row of well-built wooden huts which lay beyond the parade ground. There was a landing area which had tarmac runways and five modern hangars and the control tower. The buildings even had electricity and facilities with hot and cold running water.

Roy was to look for accommodation off station once Naomi arrived. Meanwhile, he was temporarily billeted in a spacious wooden cabin, furnished with two beds. Another innovation for both Roy and other incoming Arbroath officers was that they had Wren stewards who looked after the young officers and were very efficient.

The morning after reaching Arbroath, Roy reported to his new CO, Lt Cdr James Drummond, a man of considerable experience who learnt to fly back in 1930. However, his experience paled next to that of the station commander, Captain Michael Abel-Smith, who was a very well-known and respected veteran Fleet Air Arm officer. He had qualified on the first naval pilots' course back in 1924 and later became Naval Equerry to the King.

The squadron was equipped with Swordfish and some Fulmar monoplanes. Roy was informed that he would teach deck landings, with each course deck landing on HMS *Argus* in the Clyde in order to qualify. However, he soon learnt that he had to teach a great deal more, including night-flying practice.

James Drummond explained that 767 Squadron was the deck-landing training squadron for torpedo-reconnaissance and bomber pilots. Instructors spent most of their time lecturing or acting as 'batsman' to the pupils landing on the runway. Roy was also told that each officer had some specialised function on the ground, and that he was to be the staff officer responsible for all administration in 767 Squadron.

In the wardroom, Roy was introduced to the instructors and re-united with several former 812 Squadron members, among them Titch Harding and Dick Curry.

John Lang, a friend from Roy's Dartmouth days, was an observer instructor:

> The task of the squadron was primarily to teach trainee pilots the techniques of landing on a deck – a dummy drawn out on the runway – and responding correctly to the signals transmitted by 'bats', the Deck Landing Control Officer.
>
> Roy would be one of these. In addition to approaches and dummy deck landings, our pilots led trainees in formation flying and exercises in deploying for action.

John Lang continued:

> Night flying also took place and as well as trainee deck landings, experienced pilots were taught the techniques of controlled launchings. The main effort therefore of a trainee was circuits and bumps – the pupils becoming known as 'clockwork mice'.
>
> On completing the course trainees went, if they were lucky, to a carrier for practical deck-landing practice, if one was available, but more often or not they went straight to an operational squadron with practical deck landing fitted in as circumstances permitted.
>
> *Argus* was generally the training carrier. Her CO was Captain G.T. Philip, DSC, RN, who would later go on to command HMS *Furious*.

Lang added: 'Roy was one of the very nicest people I've known, a most competent pilot and naval officer.'

Delighted to have met up with his old pals, Roy wrote to Naomi at the end of the first day:

> I'm so excited and thrilled that I am again with Titch and doing the same sort of job. It's heavenly, darling. Now look dearest, can you come straight away for, say a week. Leave T.W. [Tiddly Winks i.e. baby Carole] behind and help me look for rooms for us all. Titch asked me out to supper tonight (I only arrived this afternoon).

The next day, he wrote:

> Willie Ashton and Dick Curry stooged into the mess at lunchtime and we had quite a general party, then your lovely old voice on the telephone and practically immediately afterwards Titch and Barbara breezed in to take me out. Very sweet of them as I did so want to celebrate. Oh roll on Thursday, oh I adore you, Billy.

Inevitably, he had been eager to celebrate because of the relief from his stressful and exhausting tour of duties flying over enemy-occupied territory.

HMS *Condor* was a happy station, close to the town with its romantic ruined medieval abbey of eroded red sandstone, conspicuous on the skyline. The surrounding rolling countryside, with cattle peacefully grazing in green fields, was excellent for both horse riding and playing golf. Not far away down the coast was the pretty little town of Crail with its tiny fishing harbour and HMS *Jackdaw* where pilot pupils learnt basic lessons of flying.

James Drummond, who had resumed command of 767 Squadron in July 1940 after returning from France via North Africa, later recalled Roy: 'I remember B-F very well – he had a most engaging personality and was an excellent pilot and instructor.'

Drummond quickly recognised Roy's natural instructional and leadership qualities and 'above average' flying skills. He and his wife invited Roy over for a meal to help him settle in at Arbroath. Roy was rather daunted by such attention from a CO and wrote somewhat ungraciously: 'Tuesday: Got to go and have dinner with the CO tomorrow. Ouch. And then to cinema.'

Roy plunged into his duties and after his second day he wrote:

Tuesday. It's quarter past eleven now and I've only just finished work. Three trips in the air today instructing and twice control officer doing landings. Still it's pleasant, hard work and that's all that matters isn't it. I haven't been able to get out of camp at all to see about houses or cars today. Maybe I shall have better luck tomorrow.'

His duties were to involve long hours:

Wednesday. Today has been, as usual, pretty busy. In fact, I've just finished work at 11 o'clock. I must say that so far I like the job very much. It's interesting too.

Friday. Titch has been very fatherly all day and looked after me very well. I am playing golf with him tomorrow then supper with him and Barbara afterwards…barring accidents, I should be here for at least six months.

Many of the pupils came from HMS *Jackdaw* to complete their final course at Arbroath on deck landing. The course lasted approximately two months. This was repeated with new intakes every few months.

Roy arrived in the middle of a deck-landing course which had started at the beginning of the month. Titch explained:

By now the vast majority of the incoming trainee pupil pilots to the Fleet Air Arm as a whole, and also at Arbroath itself, were Voluntary Reserve (RNVR) rather than RN types.

Most of our time was spent teaching the young gentlemen how to control an aircraft on instruments. More aircraft were lost through bad weather than in any other way. The boffins were always working on improving instruments and dreaming up new ones.

One of the first pupils that Roy met was Sub Lt George Birch, RNVR, who had begun his course a fortnight before:

The Deck Landing Training Course mainly consisted of us – the pupils – going round the circuit at about 400 ft, while the instructors 'batted' us on to the runway.

Immediately after touchdown, we opened the throttle and went off for another circuit. Each pilot made about half a dozen landings then taxied round to the holding point where another pupil took over, a quick debriefing and that was it until the next time.

Other exercises were navigation exercises over sea and land, practice dive-bombing etc, none of which were carried out with an instructor in the aeroplane.

I ended my naval flying carrier in 1958, having accomplished about 450 deck landings without an accident. I also did a further 11,000 hrs in civil aviation, ending as a training captain on Boeing 707s.

Amongst the pupils that August was John Sayer:

I came to Arbroath for Deck Landing Training which took about two months in July and August 1941, with a few days added to practice on board HMS *Argus* in the Clyde. My recollections are of intensive training by day and night, six days a week with very little time off – this interfered with my courting of a girl from St Andrews! However, we married a year later.

Many of my friends on the course did not survive the war. I went straight to a front line squadron (811), which was employed against German convoys operating along the Dutch coast. I torpedoed a German ship one dark-stormy night and ran out of petrol just as I got to England!

Another RNVR pupil later that year, who remembered and respected Roy, was John Godley, later to become Lord Kilbracken and author of *Bring Back My Stringbag*:

At that time we were confined to doing ADDLS, which stood for Aerodrome Dummy Deck Landings, which were carried out on a dummy deck painted on one of the runways. It didn't have arrester wires, but it was fairly close to the real thing.

Lt Robert Everett was one of the most senior pilots at Arbroath:

I remember Roy, his distinction, charm, and skill! I recall there were two deck landing training squadrons (767 and 769) at Arbroath at that time. I had previously served on HMS *Ark Royal*.

On one of the next courses was Harry Kenworthy:

I served for only one month with 767 Squadron during deck-landing training from 1–27 September. I flew on trips with Titch Harding. All I can remember is having the odd beer together with Baker-Falkner in those days.

Later I remember him visiting Machrihanish to demonstrate the capabilities of the 'dreaded' Barracuda, which he flew magnificently. He was a first-class chap – a splendid aviator.

Sub Lt Dunstan Hadley, RNVR, described his own experience of deck-landing training that year:

Like any other 'ship', we had a captain and commander and a complete crew, but the man who ruled with a rod of iron was Commander Flying or 'wings' a dedicated, fanatical specialist in the wizardry of deck landing.

A month after Roy arrived at Arbroath, HMS *Argus* was available for practical deck-landing training. Tom Esencourt recalled:

Every flight I made at Arbroath whilst I was there during the whole of September 1941 was made in Swordfish and Albacores flying solo, no passengers or instructors. The course included three deck landings on HMS *Argus*, the Lt Cdr Flying of which was James Fenton. Lt Baker-Falkner was one of the instructors. I went on to join 822 Squadron and took part in the North African landings, Operation *Torch* in November 1942.

In mid-September, Naomi made a brief visit up to see Roy and arrange some accommodation. It was wonderful for them to be together again after so many months apart. They stayed at the Seaforth Hotel, on the seafront in Arbroath. For breakfast, the hotel provided them with Arbroath smokies – whole haddock traditionally smoked over oak chips in tiny smokehouses around the harbour. The town, with its busy fishing port, reminded them of Shaldon and Teignmouth.

The couple searched through the *Arbroath Herald* and found a cottage which would soon become available. All too quickly Naomi's trip was at an end and she returned to baby Carole, staying a couple of weeks with her aunt in Bradford whilst Roy made the final arrangements for the accommodation.

Roy kept her up-to-date: '19 September. Billy girl what was your journey like? Night flying, must go.'

Roy was making the most of his leisure time after all the operational strain of the past months:

Friday. I rode today and had quite good fun. I rode Searchlight, the ex-steeplechaser. He seems quite a nice animal and jumps very wide and has got an amazing reach. He is 16.2 hands. Some of the other horses are very nice too – all jumpers. I was out two hours today; only cost me 6/6 too.

The fortnight flew by with Roy riding whenever he could, and the rest of the time filled with squadron office-bound duties and night flying with the young 'gentlemen' as he called the young trainee pilots.

Sometimes work was too demanding for leisure time activities: 'Monday. I didn't go riding today. I was so absolutely tired after flying that I couldn't take it.' Naomi had sent a message to Roy saying that she and baby Carole were on their way North. He continued: 'I was so pleased to get your telegram to know that I was going to see you a day earlier than expected. Hurrah, I am so pleased.'

The work of the squadron progressed well, and every two to three months, Roy and the other instructors were able to sign off another course of young pilots to operational squadrons.

The instructors had to be competent on both biplanes and monoplanes. Roy took every opportunity to fly new aircraft in order to 'gain experience of type' in his flying log book.

During this period, Roy's brother, Harry, was in Perth, Scotland, for army training prior to eighteen months in the Orkney islands. Harry contacted Roy to see if he could meet him in Perth. Roy responded 'No, I can't come to Perth but if you go to Donibristle, I'll pick you up by aircraft and fly you to our place, the flying time is only twenty miles.'

A few days later Harry headed to Donibristle just over the water from Edinburgh and Roy flew down to rendezvous with him. They were happy to meet each other after so long, and soon were strolling out to a lone aircraft by the runway. The aircraft was open cockpit, possibly one of the air station Hornet Moths – Harry did not know exactly. Roy lent him a Sidcot flying suit and leather flying helmet and they climbed in and took off heading out over the Firth of Forth. Roy enjoyed testing his younger brother's nerve and let Harry take the controls, holding the joystick for a brief time.

Harry recalled: 'Roy did the loop the loop. Then he shouted "Do you see that train down there, we will shoot it up." We had to shout at the top of our lungs to hear each other. "Give it a kick in the pants." The journey was nowhere near just twenty miles!'

Once they had landed at Arbroath, they went into the officers' bar. Harry recalled their conversation drifted back to aircraft. 'Roy said he was interested in the new American aircraft coming into the UK at that time.' Later that day Roy left Harry at Donibristle. Harry headed off to Scapa Flow and ultimately North Africa.

Naomi and baby Carole arrived and initially stayed with Roy in the Seaforth Hotel. Later, they moved into their rented rooms at Ballygunge Cottage at the top of the town. The couple appreciated the opportunity to enjoy family life. Naomi recalled: 'Life was relatively normal and we always used to have meals at home every day. Roy had his nose in a book, nothing intellectual, smoking his pipe. He was good at crossword puzzles.'

John Lang commented: 'Roy and Naomi, his very attractive wife, had digs in Arbroath town at that time, as my wife, Jenny and I did, and we got on very well together.'

Naomi continued: 'We had a little social life at Arbroath, most of the entertaining was done at the house or at other friends' houses, nearly all of whom were friends from the Med days. Titch was there as was Splash and David 'Feather' Godfrey-Faussett.'

Feather was a special friend and experienced pilot. Three months previously he had been involved in the same attack on *Bismarck* as Splash Carver. He had been awarded the DSC and twice Mentioned in Dispatches.

Other friends included Lt Andrew 'Aggie' Leatham and Lt Michael 'Pinkie' Haworth who had served on *Glorious* with Roy. Leatham was previously in 813 Squadron operating from HMS *Eagle* in coastal ops off the Western Desert. Of an evening in the Mess, he 'shot his line' about attacking enemy shipping near Bomba and having to force land after friendly fire over Mersa Matruh.

Most weekends Roy and Naomi would go horse riding, Roy kept building jumps too high for Naomi's liking. She exclaimed: 'It made my hair stand on end.'

Roy was not restricted to Arbroath and often led his young 'gentlemen' to nearby RNAS Crail, where he had the opportunity to meet other instructors too.

William Garthwaite was serving at Crail:

I well remember Roy Baker-Falkner – we both served in instructing squadrons in Scotland. Dozens of pupil pilots went through my squadron 785 prior to deck-landing training at Arbroath. I went solo in 1927 on First World War aircraft, the Avro mono.

Prior to that, I had been in the first *Bismarck* chase and from *Victorious* I put the first torpedo into the *Bismarck*, and assisted General Montgomery in the Western Desert, including dive-bombing German tanks.

Roy's sister, Leslie, came to visit during her summer vacation from college. The journey took her thirty hours from Devon; there were lots of delays at Crewe, due to alerts and air raid warnings. The train to Edinburgh was packed full of Canadian troops with their equipment, keeping her company and telling her how the Highlands looked like the foothills of the Rocky mountains. She was amazed when she saw one Canadian officer who she thought looked the splitting image of Roy. Eventually, exhausted, her favourite blue coat and hat smoky from soot of the steam train, she arrived at Arbroath railway station and then on to Ballygunge Cottage.

That first evening Naomi cooked them a wonderful meal and later asked her sixty years later 'Leslie do you remember the cottage pie I made in Arbroath, the best ever.' Leslie added: 'Next morning, Naomi cooked the local delicacy – Arbroath smokies – for breakfast.' Leslie had not seen her young niece Carole since Shaldon and found her a jovial little bundle of giggles and smiles.

Roy told Leslie little about his recent operational duties, more interested in hearing about the family, her college and plans for the future. Naomi told Leslie that the landlady did not approve of a baby in the house. 'So we didn't want to stay too long,' recalled Naomi.

As with all weekends Roy and Naomi went horse riding on Sunday and took Leslie once whilst she was there. Leslie's stay was a pleasant break for her. Roy introduced her to a few of his friends including Andrew Leatham and 'Feather' Godfrey-Fausset. Aggie was invited to visit a number of times, and one evening brought with him a grouse. It was one of the most memorable meals Leslie had ever tasted in wartime or afterwards.

Leslie returned to her final year at Cheltenham, having talked to Roy and Naomi about her future career either as a nurse or, if she passed scholarship exams, entering the Royal College of Music in London.

Roy had time to record Carole's progress in a special baby diary:

29 September: Carole celebrated her sixth month of life having already travelled over 1,000 miles by car and train, including one day of 350 miles and fourteen hours in the car at the age of ten weeks. A remarkably happy little soul with a very well developed bump of curiosity, and an insatiable desire to tear paper and a sadistical habit of pulling hair then shrieking with joy at victims' moans. During Carole's seventh month she rode a thoroughbred 16.2 hand steeplechaser in the stable yard and thoroughly enjoyed it. She also saw eight day-old golden retriever pups and crowed with delight.

The next day was Naomi's birthday and soon after the weather started to get wetter and colder. In October, there were major changes in 767 Squadron. James Drummond was given a new posting in the Admiralty, and Titch heard about his own new posting, which would be as CO of 823 Squadron at nearby Crail, and reliefs were assigned in their place.

There was a leaving event for the departing squadron officers. Drummond recalled, perhaps with a hint of sadness, that: 'B-F was still there when I left to go to the Admiralty in October 1941. I never saw him again.'

Robert Everett took over as officer in charge of 767 Squadron before handing over command to Lt Cdr D.N. Russell later the next month. Titch's replacement, Lt John Welham, arrived on 11 October.

John Welham, who had taken part in the Taranto raid and recently returned from 823 Squadron of HMS *Eagle*, recalled:

Roy Baker-Falkner, I certainly knew him. We were at Arbroath together in 1941/42. I was an instructor in 767 Squadron from October 1941 to September 1942 when I was sent back to Egypt to take command of 815 Squadron.

I transferred from the RAF with seniority from that service, resulting in my becoming a full lieutenant at the age of twenty, and causing much tooth-sucking by the ex-Dartmouth boys. To make it worse, I left Arbroath to command 815 Squadron which gave me an acting half-stripe before my 23rd birthday – more tooth-sucking!

I lived in great comfort when I was there. They were short of space so instructors were encouraged to live out. I found a complete suite in a large manor house which had greenhouses, and its own poultry. The owners were horribly wealthy – in the garage, in mothballs for the war, were two Rolls-Royces!

Instructing there could be quite interesting and was regarded as much more dangerous than operational flying! This was partly due to the fact that the pupils had been trained in Canada or the US. I could find no fault with the standard of instruction they had received, but they had been trained in a peacetime environment, in a blaze of light, so that, when flying at night in the blackout in Britain, they became utterly confused.

I had some hair-raising experiences with them trying to get into formation at night. They kept getting lost; one landed at Montrose, south of Aberdeen, and, on hearing the local accents, thought he had landed in Germany!

The purpose of the Fulmars was for an instructor to sneak around and suddenly jump on the pupils to see if they were keeping alive to the possibility of meeting enemy aircraft. This duty was a popular one, and light relief for the instructors; flying a pleasant and reasonably fast aircraft between towering cumulus clouds, then diving down to make a fighter attack on an unsuspecting Swordfish, was fine entertainment and valuable to the pupils.

If life was easier for Roy, danger was never far away. Tragedy hit the squadron on 17 October when a 767 Squadron Swordfish crashed at Hatton Hill, Frickheim. The pupil pilot, Sub Lt S.J. Carpenter, died three days later.

For the most part, the courses went smoothly and the pupils came and went. Roy enjoyed the bonhomie and opportunity to help the young 'gentlemen' in their own aviation careers, according to Leslie.

She recalled an incident when Roy had been instructing one of his trainees:

The pupil on this particular occasion did not follow the rules and the aircraft crash-landed. Because the pupil was not firmly strapped in, and had not done up his 'jock strap' harness, he smashed his knees, breaking his legs. 'That will teach him to do up his jock strap in future!' was Roy's response as he did not suffer fools gladly if they ignored his sound advice.

Later in the year, Roy was given a major role in the Royal Navy information film 'Find, Fix and Strike', a War Ministry training and propaganda film. Robert Everett arrived with a movie camera crew from Ealing Studios who filmed in and around Arbroath, on board HMS *Argus* and also on *Ark Royal*.

The film profiled the training of Fleet Air Arm pilots from when they first enrolled at HMS *Vincent* shore station. Pilots were shown initially learning to fly in de Havilland Moths and Miles Magisters before progressing to flying in Swordfish, Gladiators and Fulmars, with a later move to HMS *Condor* and Scotland. Filming took several months.

Robert Everett was closely involved in the whole film from inception to just prior to its screening in the cinemas:

When awaiting appointment to command 810 Squadron, I was sent to Arbroath with a crew from Ealing studios to make a film (an antidote) to *Ships with Wings* – that horror comic! I was a keen photographer. I used a camera called the Kine-Exacta which cost about £40, a hell of a lot of money in those days.

The film was made with no professional actors and nearly all on location at RNAS *Arbroath*. Any studio inserts would have been done at Ealing studios. The Ealing film team chose Roy because of his disgusting good looks! The RNVR Sub Lt talking to B-F in the film was a pilot called 'Smoothy' Welham.

Roy was filmed instructing young pupil pilots in the lecture room; bringing them in to land as the officer with the bats; and as CO, sitting in an armchair, in the wardroom of the *Ark*

Royal talking to the main character, Sub Lt Barnes. Leslie recalled that Roy was very relaxed about learning his lines, which included a reprimand for Barnes: 'Tell that fool to wake up!'

Roy, who was depicted as having a wry sense of humour as well as an air of command, was also filmed instructing the trainee pilots on how to land on an aircraft carrier:

> Circuits for landing should be close to the ship at a height of about 300–400 ft so that you can see all that is happening on the deck and so time your approach. An experienced pilot controls your approach and landing with bats: 'Go higher', 'Go lower', 'Port or starboard' or 'Go round again'.
>
> Driving a Swordfish, 1,200–1,400 revs and 60 knots brings you in beautifully. Obey orders and before you know where you are, you have closed your throttle, kissed the deck and been brought smoothly to rest by the arrester gear. Carry out instructions by the bats, don't be ham-fisted and you will find it as easy as falling off a bike.

John Lang recalled 'Find, Fix and Strike':

> This was a bit of fiction with a documentary and propaganda theme. It concerned the adventures of a young FAA pilot who trained with 767 and then went to *Ark Royal* where I was when the action sequences were shot. Roy was involved with the sequences at Arbroath showing circuits and bumps.

Roy also went down to London over three days. He was introduced to Michael Balcon who was in charge of filming, though it is unclear whether he met Lord Elton the narrator. Leslie recollected 'When it came to going to Ealing, Roy was nervous during the studio scenes, putting on his authoritarian rather than natural voice.' In the end the director dubbed over it with a much more clipped accent.

Robert Everett missed seeing the screening of the film: 'Although I was back at sea and missed seeing "Find, Fix and Strike" as an entity, I had, of course, seen all the rushes at Ealing studios and knew the make-up of the film. As a "B" picture it did very well, I believe.'

The film was well received and shown at cinemas throughout the country and overseas – and later regarded as a true classic Royal Navy documentary. Leslie joked: 'After the screening, Roy had to be brought down to earth because he was so full of himself. We teased him awfully.'

The film crew had barely finished filming on board *Ark Royal* before she was sunk. The aircraft carrier had just taken part in yet another ferrying operation to Malta and was returning to Gibraltar on 14 November with her complement of squadrons, including 812, on board, when she was hit amidships by a torpedo. She took an immediate list and despite efforts of a tug and accompanying destroyers to save her, she turned over and sank twenty-five miles from Gibraltar. All the ship's company, save one, were rescued. Splash Carver had been serving with a Skua squadron on *Ark Royal* at the time and was lucky to escape.

Peter Cross recalled: 'When 812 rejoined *Furious* from Hatston on 21 August en route to the *Ark Royal*, Roy was not with us. I was one of the last to fly off *Ark Royal* on November 4 when she was torpedoed.'

Most of the surviving 812 Squadron aircrew lost their aircraft and belongings with the sinking. Ernest Kerridge recalled: 'My log books I'm afraid are at the bottom of the Mediterranean sea, east of Gibraltar.'

On 29 November, Andrew 'Aggie' Leatham was given command of 767 Squadron. Barely a week had passed when disaster struck when one of his trainee pilots, Sub Lt D.J. Elias, was killed in a Swordfish air accident.

Newspaper headlines on 7 December 1941 shocked the world with a far larger disaster when the Imperial Japanese Fleet Air Arm made a surprise attack on the American Fleet at Pearl Harbor in Hawaii.

The Japanese naval air arm attacked with almost 2,000 dive-bomber aircraft from six aircraft carriers and left the American Fleet in chaos: 2,403 dead, 188 aircraft destroyed and at least eight destroyed or crippled battleships. On the same day, Emperor Hirohito of Japan, declared war on the United States and Great Britain.

John Welham recalled the Arbroath instructors' reaction to the attack on Pearl Harbor: 'At the time, we were surprised at their [the Americans] not being more prepared. However, very little detail was published, and it was not until we discussed it at Staff College, and later, that we saw that the Japanese had learnt lessons from the Taranto raid.'

Leslie recalled that the family in Devon were shocked. She added that: 'It changed the whole aspect of the war; however, it did help by bringing the Americans into the Allied war effort.'

Two days later, Roy was confirmed in rank with the seniority of lieutenant, a significant advancement on his old 'acting lieutenant' rank held since January 1939.

On 11 December, Germany and Italy declared war on the United States. All-out global war had started. A fortnight later on Christmas day Hong Kong fell to Japanese forces. The following month the British garrison at Malaya surrendered to Japan. Roy naturally harked back to the days when he was based in Hong Kong and the China Station only five years previously.

In Scotland, the weather continued to get colder with biting wind coming in from the sea. There was some excitement that month when a new Tiger Moth biplane joined the squadron. Welham wrote in his log book '16 December 1941. 35 Minutes. Trying out the new toy.' He went on to add that a few days later he, Roy and the others flew for the film crew.

That Christmas, Roy, Naomi and young Carole spent together as a family for the first time. It was about this period that Splash Carver and his wife Tiny moved to Arbroath – to the delight of both Roy and Naomi.

Splash recalled:

All four of us met up again at the end of 1941 at Arbroath. Roy and Naomi were already there in a rented house and Roy was in a second line squadron flying for the training school. I had been with a Skua squadron in *Ark Royal*. After *Ark Royal* was sunk in November 1941, I was appointed to the Service Trials Squadron – also at Arbroath – which did trials of all new equipment destined for, or of potential use, to the FAA.

Roy and Naomi, very kindly, had Tiny and myself to stay for a few days with them and their little girl, Carole, while we looked for somewhere to live – eventually lodging in a nice farmhouse a mile or so from the airfield.

The next course started at the very end of the month. Phil Blakey recalled: 'As a young Midshipman RNVR I flew at Arbroath on a three-week course between December 31, 1941 and January 17, 1942.' Even with such a short course, the memory of Roy stuck in his mind sixty years later.

Baker-Falkner, or B-F as he was known, was one of the instructors who held the batting wands and stood out on the edge of the runway and signalled us the directions to effect an appropriate landing. I did thirty by day, and thirty-two by night during my period at Arbroath.

I was only a minnow in the big shoals of naval aviators, Baker-Falkner was a fine officer and gentleman.

I gained an 'above average' assessment from the CO of 767 Squadron, Andrew Leatham. At the end of the course we all went on leave and were dispersed to various other appointments. I went to 836 Squadron that was just being formed and three of the other pilots from the Arbroath lot went with me.

In the New Year's Honours List, 1 January 1942, Roy was awarded the DSC for his heroic efforts in 812 Squadron. The award was announced in the *London Gazette* dated 2 January. The citation read: 'For outstanding zeal, patience and cheerfulness, and for setting an example of wholehearted devotion to duty, without which the high tradition of the Royal Navy could not have been upheld.'

Roy's parents Sydney and Grace, were delighted. Brimming over with parental pride, they told all their Shaldon friends and Sid's Home Guard pals.

Early in 1942, Captain Abel-Smith relinquished his command of HMS *Condor* and left to command the escort carrier HMS *Biter*. His relief was Captain Raymond Taylor, who had been executive officer on board HMS *Ark Royal* prior to her sinking.

The incoming chief flying instructor was Simon Borrett. He was a veteran of No. 6 Naval Pilots' Courses of 1927 along with Roy's pal 'Monkey' Bryant. He was a survivor of the sinking of HMS *Courageous*.

One of the pupils on the course over the New Year was George Crowe. On 5 January he wrote off Swordfish P4202 at Arbroath. Later, when posted to the Mediterranean and involved in night strikes from Malta with 821 Albacore Squadron, he sank a 3,000-ton enemy ship, and later became a test pilot in Australia.

Roy and Naomi were saddened to learn in mid-January that Carole Lombard, the movie actress after whom their daughter was named, had been killed in an aeroplane crash at the age of thirty-four. She had died with her mother and twenty others near Las Vegas, during a tour to promote War Bonds. Naomi felt even more strongly that she was lucky that Roy was no longer on ops and was desperate that his next posting should be in a non-operational squadron.

That winter there were heavy snowfalls which slowed down the flying programme. Naomi recalled the weather was very severe: 'Splash Carver and his wife came to stay when their nearby rented farm got snowed up.'

On 11 February, Eugene Esmonde, whom Roy had last seen at Hatston prior to the Bismarck episode, went to Buckingham Palace to receive from King George VI the DSO he won for his part in the sinking of the German battleship.

The next day came the tragic fiasco which saw Esmonde lead six Swordfish of 825 Squadron against the might of the German battleships *Scharnhorst*, *Gneisenau* and *Prinz Eugen* as they made their way through the English Channel. Esmonde was supposed to have been escorted from Manston by five fighter squadrons but the majority of Spitfire squadrons were not ready.

Squadron Leader Brian Kingcombe, of 72 Spitfire Squadron, saw Esmonde lead the first flight of three Swordfish:

I went down to 100 feet, clipping the bottom of the clouds, and we managed to keep most of the German fighters off them. The Germans were firing heavy guns, which threw up great mountains of spray like waterspouts. The Swordfish flew straight into them. Mostly they were caught by *Prinz Eugen*'s flak and I saw the leader and two others go into the drink. They caught fire and went diving in flames towards the water.

The second flight of three Swordfish were all shot down and there were no survivors. None of 825 Squadron's torpedoes scored a hit.

Just five men of Esmonde's flight were picked up. Esmonde was awarded a posthumous Victoria Cross. The four surviving sub-lieutenants were awarded DSOs and the only surviving rating, L/A Donald Bunce, received the Conspicuous Gallantry Medal.

The 767 Squadron officers and ratings were to hear first hand about the strike when the following month Don Bunce was drafted to 767 and 769 Observer Training Squadron.

On 17 February, Roy and Splash, accompanied by Naomi, Tiny and Roy's mother Grace, went to their investiture at Buckingham Palace. Splash recalled 'We had a very happy outing to London early in 1942 when Roy and I went to collect our DSCs from King George VI. Naomi and Tiny were in the audience.'

They took a taxi to the Mall, and entered through the massive iron Palace gates and its attendant guards. They then walked through the central arch into a courtyard beyond, the Palace Yard, which was normally hidden from public view and where the Royal Carriage would draw up after Royal Processions in the Mall. For Roy and Naomi it was very much a feeling that was a memory to be treasured, and that 'Yes they really were at Buckingham Palace and not dreaming.'

Before the investiture ceremony commenced, Roy had to wait with the other medal recipients in an ante chamber awaiting the King.

Naomi recollected: 'After inspection of our admission tickets and ID cards, we were escorted across the Palace Yard by two Guards and met at the door of the Palace by Beef-eaters.'

There was a detail of guards lining the carpet covered steps. They were then taken to their seats in the State Ballroom, a luxurious room decorated in red, white and gold, with many beautiful and large paintings on the walls. It was laid out with rows of chairs in red and gold for the invited guests, with music played in the background by a Royal Marines band.

At this point Splash recalled how he and Roy felt:

Although everyone was briefed on the ceremony and told exactly what to do, what to say and what not to say, there was a delightful air of informality. We were certainly both excited and impressed at the investiture.

Waiting quietly in their seats, Naomi and Grace were thrilled to bits. The women had been concerned about their outfits because of clothing coupons, but fortunately they were able to obtain suitable outfits for the occasion. Around them, proud mothers, fathers, wives and fiancées looked on in excitement. Promptly and on time the King entered from a side door, and stood at a dais, besides which stood the Lord Chamberlain and palace protocol officers.

Immediately after the King's arrival the few hundred people who were being decorated at that investiture came through another door in single file to the platform where the King was standing. Each medal was presented to the King on what appeared to be a velvet cushion. It was a while before Roy received his DSC. The King shook his hand and smiled, saying, 'Well done'. Roy was handed a small black presentation medal box simply embossed with 'DSC' in gold lettering.

When the investiture was finished, all rose for the playing of 'God Save the King' and the King left through a side exit, followed by his guards and palace officials. As Roy, Naomi and Grace left the palace he carefully opened the medal box, with the small silver-coloured cross nestling in blue velvet, the ribbon with three equal stripes of dark blue. Roy explained to his mother that the DSC was the naval version of the Military Cross. Afterwards there were photographs by the press outside the palace. They then returned to the real world as they stepped onto the Mall and had to hail a cab back to Berners Hotel.

Harry, Roy's brother, recalled an incident shortly after:

Just after he had been presented with his DSC by the King, Roy was on leave walking in the street in civilian clothes. He was amazed when a complete stranger presented him with three feathers – the sign of cowardice. Little did they know!

Four days later came shattering news of the British surrender of Singapore to Japan. The loss of Singapore was one of the worst defeats in British history, with hundreds of thousands of troops being taken prisoner of war.

In Roy's previous couple of visits to Singapore, he had made observations about the defences being prepared in the event of a Japanese attack, and now reflected on the words in his midshipman's journal written six years previously: 'The question of the value of Singapore as a large base in the East is being argued over the world.'

Back at Arbroath life had to carry on; many of the trainee pilots were destined to transfer to operational squadrons in the Far East to fight Japan. That month, to Roy's pleasure, Rodney Carver, a fellow pupil from Leuchars days, arrived at Arbroath in command of 885 Squadron, and Roy was able to congratulate him about having shot down the Junkers 88 that he had seen in Orkney when he was stationed at Twatt.

However, bad news continued to prevail. On 9 March, there was yet another 767 Squadron fatality. An aircraft hit high trees when flying low near Forfar. Sub Lt Lawson was unhurt but Sub Lt L.T. Hardy died of injuries the next day.

Two days later, there was an even greater shock for Roy and Naomi when their close friend 'Feather' Godfrey-Faussett was killed near Arbroath. They were quite horrified and could not believe how it could happen. Questions had to be answered. Apparently, the accident occurred while aircraft of 767 Squadron were conducting a low-flying night formation, 'Feather' was killed instantly when his aircraft accidentally flew into the sea one mile off East Haven. His body was never found. He was only twenty-eight years old.

Then a few days after that, on 16 March, a Swordfish of 769 Squadron, flown by Sub Lt J.H.L. Evans, crashed in poor weather. Accidents were becoming too common and the CO, Andrew Leatham, launched an air accident investigation.

For instructors, pilots and aircrew there was little time for grieving and morale had to be maintained, especially in the light of the world situation following Japan entering the war. That year, for reasons of efficiency, centralised maintenance was introduced to the Fleet Air Arm with aircraft no longer assigned to one aircrew.

At the end of March, Carole celebrated her first birthday. Spring turned into summer and father and mother would take their toddler on outings, to see the horses, go paddling in the sea or play on the beach, whenever Roy was free from his long hours of instructing, both day and night flying.

It was not all hard work for Roy. With Splash Carver in the Service Trials Unit, Roy got permission from the CO, Lt Cdr H. Peter Bramwell, to fly some of their unusual aircraft, which at that time included the Seafire and Spitfire Vb, Sea Hurricane, Martlet, and even the Seafire IIc.

Welham also remembered flying aircraft from the Trials Unit:

I flew, of course, dozens of Swordfish, including a Swordfish (T), I believe the only dual one ever built. The Fairey elementary trainer 00-POM, was a prototype for evaluation (hence the unusual number) which Baker-Falkner is likely to have flown.

Regarding my scrounging new types of aircraft to fly, there was no conversion course: one simply read the pilots' notes and was given some advice on handling. At Arbroath, I flew Fulmars, Hurricanes, Seafires and the ghastly Skua.

In the next Deck Landing Training Course that ran from March to April, Paul Housden recalled:

I was under Lt Cdr Roy Baker-Falkner's command at Arbroath in the Deck Landing School from March 1942 for six weeks. During this time I recorded 25 hours' day piloting all solo and 8.35 hours' night.

He was tall and slim, as I remember, and certainly a quite outstanding personality. He was immensely approachable, especially if as a pupil one showed keenness; his manner was quietly effective – without fuss or noise. I acquired a great respect for him at this short acquaintance, entirely because of his helpful manner with all us pupils. At that time I knew nothing at all of his service record nor of his previous operational experience. There was knowledge that he had seen and achieved a very great deal but one did not know the particular. So my admiration was based solely on his leadership in 767 Squadron.

In 767 Squadron we did not fly with instructors in the same aeroplane. B-F and his supporting pilots told us what to do and demonstrated it themselves – we were all standing on the grass verge of the runway at the time. We then emulated their example.

He continued:

My flying assessment was 'average' which was odd because ultimately I emerged as second in the class. I think my second position was awarded by Baker-Falkner. At any rate the result was that Ray Jeffs – the top boy – and I were posted immediately to Cape Town, South Africa. There we were to get ready for a Japanese Invasion which, however, never occurred. I later went on to serve on board HMS *Trumpeter* during Operation *Mascot* against the *Tirpitz*.

On 17 April, there was a further accident when Sub Lt M.H. Stapleton, of 767 Squadron, crashed after hitting high-tension cables.

Back in Devon, Roy's parents in Shaldon were aware the war was getting closer when nearby Exeter was bombed on 24 April, in one of the Baedeker raids, so called because of the German travel guide of that name. The Baedeker Blitz was conducted by the *Luftwaffe* through April until June. Exeter was again bombed overnight on 3/4 May; the medieval centre of the city was badly damaged, with the blaze seen up to fifty miles away.

Overseas, news was grim with the Battle of the Atlantic and the fighting in North Africa between Rommel and Montgomery. The local situation for the squadron was no better for Andrew Leatham and his officer instructors when on 13 May one of 767 Squadron's Swordfish collided with another from 753 Squadron at 2,000 feet. It crashed at Standford Farm, Finavon, near Forfar. Sub Lts F.D.S. Clarke, L/A F.W. Tear and L/A W.W. Calwell, of 767, and the three crew of the other aircraft, were killed.

Roy was cheered up a little three days later, however, when he learned that Malta had been awarded the George Cross for bravery. A national newspaper announced:

> In a dramatic and unprecedented gesture King George yesterday awarded the George Cross, the civilian equivalent of the Victoria Cross, to the Mediterranean island of Malta. A message to the island's governor, Lieutenant-General Sir William Dobbie read: 'To honour her brave people I award the George Cross to the Island Fortress of Malta, to bear witness to heroism and a devotion that will long be famous in history'.

The same day as the Malta announcement Harry was at home in Shaldon on leave from Scotland, and Leslie back from college, when a German hit-and-run Messerschmitt flew at fifty feet over the harbour, machine gunning any people in view. Harry quickly put his infantry tin helmet on Leslie's head and they rushed out of the house to watch as the fighter aircraft roared past by Shaldon towards Coombe Cellars and on up the estuary.

Throughout this period, Roy and Naomi could continue their domestic life with little disturbance. Naomi recalled: 'We had the chance to go to London often. Others from Arbroath would travel down with us. "Pinky" Haworth used to occupy himself on the journey by knitting on the train all the way to London.'

As usual, Roy and Naomi stayed in London at the Berners Hotel. One memory of note was when they visited the London Hilton. 'All big restaurants couldn't charge more than about 7/6d for any meal,' Naomi recalled. 'There were dances, Roy and I picked up an American servicemen, and he was ever so pleased. We had rissoles, the most marvellous ones I've ever had, perhaps it was the garlic.'

As summer arrived, Roy had become one of the most senior instructors at Arbroath. His time was spent increasingly with administration, although he continued to keep a professional eye on the interesting new aircraft at the Service Trials Unit.

Among the June pupils was a young Canadian pilot, Phil Foulds RCNVR, who recalled:

> We practised 'deck landings' on land many times before we tried them on HMS *Argus*. I did 48 practice landings in three weeks, of which 21 were at night (NADDLS) and 27 in daylight (ADDLS). Other sub lieutenants in my course at Arbroath included Ted Edwards RCNVR, George Cronin RNZNVR and Jim Britton RNVR. Britton was later to serve in one of Roy's front line squadrons.
>
> I recall Lieutenant Baker-Falkner's friendliness towards new pilots. It was June 1942 at the Deck Landing Training School at Arbroath where Baker-Falkner was an instructor. After a day flying Swordfish and Albacores, three very young VR sub lieutenants were making our way from the airfield to the wardroom. Baker-Falkner was walking ahead of us but stopped, waited for us to catch up, then walked along with us and in a friendly way asked us how things were going. The pace at Arbroath had been fast with little time for a chat. His gesture encouraged us that, inexperienced though we might be, we were welcome aboard.
>
> After 767, I flew Grumman Avengers in 856 Squadron in HMS *Premier* and 846

Squadron with HMS *Trumpeter* where I received the DSC for an 'air attack on an enemy convoy'.

At the beginning of June, Roy and Naomi celebrated his twenty-sixth birthday. They had much to celebrate as he was informed by the station commander, Captain Turner, that he was going to be offered the command of 767 Squadron once Leatham had been appointed elsewhere.

Three days later, on 6 June, another crash occurred in the squadron when Sub Lt Gilbert struck water whilst low flying. However, a few days later on 10 June the top-secret Fairey Barracuda Mk I was flown to Arbroath for the first time. This aircraft was being tested by Roy's old *Glorious* colleague, Tiffy Torrens-Spence, who was carrying out test trials on this new type of monoplane dive-bomber in the top-secret aircraft establishment at Boscombe Down.

The Barracuda was intended as a replacement to the Swordfish and Albacore. The torpedo bomber had been more than five years in the making, and was later criticised for its lack of streamlined design. A British admiral commented: 'No aircraft which looked like that could possibly be a good aircraft.'

As Welham recalled:

I only flew a Barracuda on one occasion, from Lee-on-Solent, I am glad to say. It was the worst aircraft that I have ever flown. The only one I know where it sank when you pulled up the wheels, because the undercart was so huge. It was not in fact the fault of the designers but the result of the Admiralty specification which required a cross between a fighter, a dive-bomber, and torpedo bomber.

On 17 June, Andrew Leatham left to take up a post as CO of 831 Squadron on *Indomitable*. Lt Williamson was officer in command for just two weeks before leaving for special service with RAF Fighter Command at Middle Wallop. On 1 July, Roy was appointed in command of 767 Squadron, and congratulated, with genuine pleasure, by the CFI and by Captain Turner, both of whom would be working ever closer with Roy in the coming months.

James Drummond, who by now was serving in the Admiralty in London, recalled Roy's new duties: 'As CO of the squadron the duties were largely administrative and supervisory, a little lecturing to the pupils and not much flying. With twenty-four aircraft and a mixture of RAF and RN ratings to maintain them one was kept fairly busy at all times.' Roy was heavily involved with administrative duties and few pupil pilots were to meet him when he was in command of 767 Squadron, although he officially signed their flying log books.

Nigel Hopkins, a young Canadian in the RCNVR on a course that July, recalled:

I was on a three-week course starting on 28 July, 1942, during that period I flew about 20 hours in Swordfish and 10 hours in Albacore. Most of the flights included five or six ADDLs. It was a very hectic time in my young life.

I remember it mostly as a period of intense flying – quite often at night, firstly training and later flying navigation exercises for trainee observers. At that time Lt B-Falkner was CO of 767 Squadron and signed my log book, and Lt Cdr Hall, was Chief Flying Instructor. I did not meet B-Falkner socially, I was a very junior midshipman RNVR in 1942 and he was then a lieutenant commander RN which made him a very senior officer to me.

I had only been in the UK from 1 June 1942 so I was still quite a stranger during the period in 767 Squadron. There were very few Canadians in the FAA, strangely there were many New Zealanders.

At the beginning of August, one month after Roy was appointed as CO, pilot Nigel Hopkins crashed at Fallaws Farm, Arbirlot, three miles from Arbroath. He survived to tell the tale:

> The highlight of the period for me was a night flying accident on 9 Aug. I ran into a hill avoiding another aircraft approaching the airport at night.
>
> I was flying a Swordfish and had just finished a one-hour night training flight. Fortunately I was alone that night. I remember looking up and seeing a red light that looked like a navigation light of another aircraft. I was quite low at the time but I put the stick forward thinking I would go under the other aircraft. I was watching the light and the next thing I knew, I must have hit a tree with a wing tip.
>
> There was a long interval and then a lengthy period when everything was crashing around me. I was quite conscious and waiting to see what would happen. When the noise stopped, I was hanging upside-down by the straps and listening to the gyros running down and fluid dripping somewhere. I knew if a fire started all would be over, but nothing happened, and after a while I started digging away the earth so that I could get out of the cockpit.
>
> This took some time, but I eventually got out and walked to a farmhouse nearby. I can still remember how good the glass of whisky tasted which the farmer poured for me. Obviously I wasn't hurt, because I flew two formation flights of fifty minutes each the next day.

Hopkins continued:

> As a matter of course, even though this was a fairly routine accident, there was an accident investigation. B-Falkner was involved being commanding officer of the squadron. I don't recall who was there since it was a rapid enquiry that lasted only a few minutes. Nobody was blamed since accidents were quite common and no one was hurt.

However, there had already been six crashes in the previous five months in 767 Squadron. Roy felt it was his duty to tighten up procedures as the new CO and no other casualties occurred whilst he was in command.

In August, Bobby 'Grubby' Going, one of Roy's old friends from *Glorious* days, was posted to Arbroath. Since they had last seen each other, Bobby had been badly wounded and lost a leg in the Malta convoys following his involvement in the Taranto raids. Like the famous RAF ace, Douglas Bader, Bobby fought hard to get back in the air. Roy was delighted to help out his old friend, so on 28 August and 1 September 1942, he took Bobby for a spin in the unique Arbroath station dual Swordfish.

Grubby Going recalled:

> I did not meet up with Roy until August 1942 at Arbroath. This was the second occasion of my return to flying after losing a leg when *Illustrious* was bombed in January 1941 and being crashed in an Anson on my first return in March 1942. So after competing with these two incidents and getting to HMS *Audacity* on air staff, I did a course in ASV work at Arbroath and there met up with Roy.
>
> It was a great joy to meet an old friend and to get back to flying with one whom I saw to be a first rate pilot and did brilliantly.

I have one vivid memory from 28-8-42 which was that when Roy and I were flying dual in a Swordfish, we met up with a couple of Hurricanes from a nearby RAF station who proceeded to try and beat us up. This Roy dealt with consummate skill by making a series of such tight turns that the Hurricanes were quite unable to get on our tail and soon gave up.

On 30 September it was Naomi's birthday again, and Roy's second-line squadron stint was fast drawing to an end. Within days he was appointed to a new position at Boscombe Down, in the south of England. His relief in 767 Squadron was taken by Lt C.H.C. 'Pip' O'Rorke. As Splash recalled:

Roy left Arbroath in the autumn of 1942 and I never saw him again. He went to RAF Boscombe Down – the Services' Test Flying Establishment in Wiltshire – to do test flying on the Fairey Barracuda. It was a high-wing monoplane, heavy and ugly and seriously under-powered by one Rolls-Royce Merlin engine and was certainly nobody's favourite aeroplane – I commanded a squadron of them at the end of the war so can speak with feeling.

Nevertheless, greatly to his credit, Roy got the most out of this rather black sheep and it entered service during 1943.

CHAPTER 19

Boscombe Test Pilot

The autumn of 1942 was to see a new phase in Roy's life as he joined the country's foremost top-secret base to become a test pilot flying Britain's hush-hush aircraft. On 8 October he was formally seconded from the Fleet Air Arm and ordered to report to RAF Station Boscombe Down, the Aeroplane and Armament Experimental Establishment (A&AEE) near Amesbury in Wiltshire, under the command of Air Commodore R.B. Mansell.

On arrival, Roy reported to Squadron Leader Gordon Slade RAF and was told he was to test-fly new British-built aircraft and also act as an 'acceptance pilot' for aircraft which the Royal Navy was contemplating purchasing from the United States. Chief amongst his tasks would be to trial Britain's new and top secret naval dive-bomber, the Fairey Barracuda. The job was a dangerous one but Naomi was relieved that Roy was now non-operational. There was also the added bonus that they could live together as a family with toddler Carole. Roy was ordered to sign the Official Secrets Act. No one at all, not even his wife, was to be told about what he was doing!

To Roy's delight, Slade's No. 2 and Boscombe's senior Royal Naval officer-in-charge was Lt Cdr F.M.A. 'Tiffy' Torrens-Spence, Roy's old friend from the Malta days. Torrens-Spence had joined Boscombe Down in January 1942, having succeeded Lt Cdr Stacey Colls.

Torrens-Spence recalled:

I remember Roy and his wife Naomi very well. I was very fond of them both. Roy's position at Boscombe Down was as a temporary appointment to 'C' Flight to learn all about the first production Barracuda and help with putting it through tests.

There were three flights in the test squadron, 'A' for the fighters, 'B' for the heavy bombers, and 'C' for everything in between, including all naval aircraft, except the Seafire. So each flight had several different types at one time, and there was no reason why a pilot if needed for a particular purpose should not then help out with the work on other types, according to his experience. Roy was destined for the first Barracuda squadron.

The object of the test squadron was to clear the production aircraft for service as regards stability, control, and handling qualities, and to measure its performance and fuel consumption with various combinations of load. This had to be done for all types of aircraft, British or American, before issue to service and, in the case of British aircraft, it had to be done first on the prototypes.

The function of the squadron was to evaluate the performance and handling qualities of the aircraft, and establish that the latter was fit for service pilots, and if not why not, and what should be done about it. This work was done first on the prototype and then again on a sample of first production models. The government could not accept aircraft for service purely on the word of its constructor's test pilots.

There were no conversion courses at Boscombe Down. I went there never having flown a monoplane, or a twin-engined aircraft, or one with retractable undercarriage. One was just given a cockpit briefing and sent off.

The A&AEE had been moved at the outbreak of the Second World War to Salisbury Plain from its more vulnerable site near the east coast. It still had a pre-war character about it with a rough and bumpy grass airfield of chalk grassland where take-offs and landings could be made in any direction.

The brick-built buildings of the RAF Station, the airfield and the hangars were all located on the hill plateau above the small market town of Amesbury, which had a number of shops, a hotel and pubs. There was a line of five hangars, around which were several technical buildings, three messes – officers', sergeants' and airmen – some barrack blocks and married quarters, and a myriad of wooden and prefab temporary huts.

There were well over 2,000 people at Boscombe Down, military, civilian and technical. However, even two years after Roy's arrival, there were still only thirty-eight test pilots. Roy was joining a tight knit and select group of aviators. The wide knowledge of new aircraft types gained by pilots at Boscombe Down was unique, especially as there were 100 to 150 aircraft of all types, bombers, fighters and reconnaissance, sitting out on the grass field and in the hangars ready to be tested.

Accommodation was in short supply so Roy and other staff were expected to make their own arrangements and the hotels and publicans of Amesbury and nearby towns and villages enjoyed good business. Roy and Naomi settled in at a conveniently located apartment in the nearby cathedral town of Salisbury.

It was going to be a comparatively relaxing posting for Roy and Naomi, with access to numerous pubs, the Odeon cinema, and the countryside for walks and horse riding. However, for Roy signs of war down south in comparison with Scotland were everywhere. There was an ack-ack gun and searchlights on the cricket field. Salisbury was to be luckier than other historic English towns as it never experienced the full brunt of German bombing raids but there were frequent air-raid warnings when the siren wailed and the townsfolk dashed into the air-raid shelters.

The popular belief was that the Germans used the conspicuous spire of Salisbury Cathedral to fix their position, before heading to the real targets in Bristol or the Midlands. However, whilst Roy was there only a few bombs were dropped on the outskirts of the city, probably jettisoned on the way back to Germany. Yet the town bustled with the military. Being on the edge of Salisbury Plain, it was surrounded by military camps. The town was always full of servicemen and women: Canadians, Australians, New Zealanders, Poles and later large numbers of Americans.

Salisbury was a pleasant place for country lovers like Roy and Naomi. One of their favourite spots was the 'The Meadows', where the River Avon flowed past tall poplar trees.

For Roy, life largely consisted of flying, flying and more flying at Boscombe Down. One of his fellow test pilots at that time, Wing Commander Sandy Powell, described the Air Station in his 1956 biography *Test Flight*:

The whole place was steeped in tradition – Aeroplane and Armament Experimental Establishment tradition and, from the Mess Bar to the hangars, there was but one interest, one topic of conversation – aeroplanes. No one talked about 'flying' that was an incidental matter taken for granted in the discussion upon aeroplanes! Every week new aeroplanes arrived, some were well proven service types with extensive design changes or new operational loads; a few were entirely new prototypes that the Service had only heard of in a hushed whisper.

Each evening, aeroplanes would roar low over the control tower doing 'flame damping' trials to measure the effectiveness of various exhaust systems and each day newcomers would fly equally low, doing position error correction runs along the tarmac.

Roy was ordered to join the Intensive Flying Development Flight which had been established the previous year. The IFDF maintained an existence separate from the other flights and was situated on the extreme southern side of the airfield. His role was to fly 150 hours on each of two early production aircraft, using operational air and ground crews from the appropriate service.

Wing Commander 'Sammy' Wroath, test pilot in command of 'A' Flight recalled:

I remember Lt Falkner coming to Boscombe Down to engage with another naval pilot in a programme of intensive flying on the Barracuda. The two were to test the aircraft, as quickly as was reasonably possible, to see what failed or wore out so that the appropriate modifications and spare parts could be undertaken before the aircraft became operational.

Lt Falkner at the time was a rather nice quiet type of chap. I did hear later that he was involved in the *Tirpitz* attack, in the Norwegian fjords, with the Barracuda and thought at the time, what a brave sort of chap he must have been, remembering my own short experience of the Barracuda.

Roy's unit was like all others at Boscombe in that aircraft were maintained by RAF and RN ground crews – hand-picked men who had to be highly adaptable and proficient to deal with many different types of aircraft and to keep these prototypes and new aircraft serviceable.

The week after Roy's arrival, his team was established when two TAGs, PO 'Ginger' Russell and L/A 'Fred' Townsend, joined him from previous Royal Naval postings. PO Russell had served with Roy in 812 Squadron on board HMS *Glorious*. Roy was also joined by Lt Mike 'Red Mullet' Lithgow, a young naval officer who had just returned on board HMS *Formidable* after providing cover for the landings at Madagascar. He had also played a part in the attack on the German battleship *Bismarck*.

Mike Lithgow recalled in his 1954 autobiography *Mach One*:

On arrival home I was appointed to the Armament Experimental Establishment at Boscombe Down. It appeared that I was required to familiarise myself with the Barracuda, which was soon to go into production as the TBR replacement type. In all probability I would then get a squadron of them and return to Carrier Operations.

As things turned out I was to be bitten deeply by the bug, which is a pretty powerful one, of development test flying and, apart from trial periods, was never to see carrier life again.

Townsend recalled both Roy and Mike:

I was at Boscombe Down from 19 October 1942 until 19 November 1943. Lt Baker-Falkner was at the Intensive Flying Development Flight – together with Lt Mike Lithgow, PO TAG Russell and myself L/A TAF Fred Townsend, under the supervision of RAF Squadron Leader Armstrong. Just the four of us, two pilots and two Telegraphist Air Gunners with the necessary naval ground crew and a RAF corporal radio technician.

Our work consisted of the continual testing of Barracudas I and II, also Firefly and periodic visits of Walrus, Sea Otter for pilot flying experience – plus testing of new equipment in several RAF machines.

Lt Baker-Falkner and Lt Mike Lithgow were much alike, and were sporty types. Baker-Falkner was a gentleman and so was Lithgow. Both pilots were very much respected by all concerned. Being such a small unit, the Fleet Air Arm boys were allowed to work on their own initiative and trust.

Both B-F and Mike Lithgow were truly considerate naval officers and made our work at Boscombe Down a pleasure to conform to the duties. I was an acting petty officer but Baker-Falkner didn't treat me as such, being more familiar with us and regarded me as one of the team. It must be understood that here was no social connection between officers and ratings during the time at Boscombe Down but nevertheless the feelings of aircrews working together on important and sometimes secret operations would lend to a much easier and closer working relationship all round.

Townsend recollected an event during the Malta convoys where he met one of his future Boscombe colleagues:

By amazing coincidence one night one of our aircraft [on *Formidable*] was missing and very much overdue. Suddenly, I heard voices and cries of help in the water. I called out and a passing petty officer enquired what was going on and rang the bridge. After what seemed like ages, the carrier turned round and called for the duty boat crews to assemble. All was complete darkness when suddenly a searchlight lit up the area and the crew was rescued. After the war I obtained a copy of the book by Lithgow that he had written of his experiences and I realised that he was the pilot of the aircraft that was picked up by the *Formidable* – I had flown with him many times at Boscombe Down and never knew that it was he! Amazing coincidence?

Townsend continued:

I was living in Winchester, 13 miles away, I always used to get a lift to Andover, and then another to Boscombe Down. Baker-Falkner had an MG sports car, a green one in which he gave me a lift from Salisbury to Boscombe Down. In his MG, I had a habit of wearing an RAF coloured scarf on cold days. Baker-Falkner would joke about it 'Townsend, I wish you wouldn't wear that RAF stuff.' Blow me, I wore it only a few more times. I used to hide it!

At 'C' Flight, there were many other types of aircraft when Roy arrived. Apart from the top secret Barracuda, there were new types of Swordfish and Fairey Firefly and the Blackburn Firebrand, as well as new American Navy aeroplanes, including the Bermuda, the Grumman Tarpon (later called the Avenger), Grumman Martlet (later renamed the Wildcat), Curtiss Helldiver and Vought Corsair. The prototype aircraft were distinctly marked with a large 'P' painted on their fuselage to show that they were prototypes under test.

Roy's first task at Boscombe Down was to familiarise himself with the latest types of available Naval Torpedo Bomber Reconnaissance type aircraft being developed or in use by the various Allied naval air arms around the world. A large proportion of his test flights involved reporting on the handling qualities of aircraft, obtaining technical data such as speeds, rate of climb, temperatures, and the build up of dangerous concentrations of poisonous engine exhaust gases in the cockpit.

Townsend recalled:

Special instrument testing on Barra I and Barra II was constantly flown with an assortment of armaments attached i.e one torpedo plus one bomb, one bomb only, two bombs (one on each wing) etc. These visits sometimes caused much interest to the manufacturer's workforce when we had to take the plane to the farthest point of the works to get enough distance to take off with enough distance-airspeed etc to clear the perimeter fence. These flights were enough to test the planes for capability landing and take-off exercises.

PO Russell and myself would often communicate with each other from the crew room to one of our aircraft in the centre of the airfield when either a parachute was needed or any test equipment for the flight. This was performed by arm semaphore – much to the amusement and amazement of squadron leader Armstrong and RAF personnel.

Three days after arriving at Boscombe Down, Roy tested a new Mk II production Swordfish, which had been sent from the manufacturers Blackburn because of structural problems which developed on pulling out of dives. Later that week, he returned to this aircraft for control column force measurements, which he carried out with the help of one of Boscombe Down's resident scientists in the back seat. The boffins found that the results of Roy's test flight showed no difference between this newly constructed aircraft and the original Fairey-built Swordfish which Roy had been flying for years. He commented that joystick forces were very low. Following Roy's trials, this aircraft was sent to the Royal Navy Fleet Trials Unit at Arbroath and after six weeks crashed over Millom Bay near Barrow-in-Furness in bad visibility.

Later in the month, Roy's designated aircraft for intensive flight trials, Fairey Barracuda P9647, arrived direct from the manufacturer and was prepared over the following weeks for his forthcoming test flights.

F.J. Costigan worked at the Fairey Design Office during the war. In *Adventures of an Aircraft Designer*, published in 1980, he recalled:

Our basic design project was the Barracuda, the name of a voracious Indian fish, but in our terms a Fleet Air Arm high-wing monoplane torpedo/bomber/reconnaissance aircraft. Its high wing and tail afforded the pilot and the observer a clear all-round view of the sea and terrain below in its reconnaissance role, but this also entailed a very long-legged undercarriage which had a fundamental fault.

With my old Meccano set, I managed to design an emergency hand-cranking mechanism which allowed the undercarriage gear to fall as far as it would under gravity, and then enabled the pilot to wind it down completely and lock it down in the correct 'safe' position. This brought me another patent.

A Barracuda pilot of the day and colleague of Roy recalled its beginnings:

On 7 December 1940 a newly designed aircraft stood waiting to take off. Balanced on its immense undercarriage like a great crab, its Merlin engine purring steadily, it appeared competent and capable. As the pilot opened the throttle it lumbered forward and slowly this prototype of the Royal Navy's newest torpedo bomber, the Fairey Barracuda Mark I, staggered into the air on its maiden flight.

The later Barracuda Mark II had distinctive wings, and bristled with radar aerials, flaps, grab handles, and bomb racks. The wings carried large Fairey-Youngman flaps below the trailing edge, which could be set to 20 degrees to increase lift during take-off or to 30 degrees to act as dive brakes, making the Barracuda a competent dive-bomber.

To any onlooker the undercarriage looked robust as indeed it needed to be for the heavy deck landings it would experience. It had a Rolls-Royce Merlin engine, boosted to about twice its intended power by a big supercharger. It was often quoted that owing to some misguided influence on the part of the 'Lords who rule the waves' it had been designed not so much as a torpedo bomber but as an observer's aeroplane. Indeed, it was designed as a monoplane with the wings set high on the fuselage for an unobstructed view for the observer. It also had two big bulbous clear Perspex-panelled bay windows, one on each side of the observer, and a seat which was almost on the floor. The characteristically long Barracuda legs and its high-set tailplane adversely affected its performance and gave it some of the odd characteristics which made it fatal to those unfamiliar with its handling.

While Roy was to test-fly the Barracuda at Boscombe Down, some other prototype models were also delivered to Arbroath for trials. Gerald Favelle, one of the first Barracuda engine fitters recalled:

After six months training as a special Barracuda maintenance party at the Fairey Aviation Company at Leverhulme Stockport, our first assignment was to HMS *Condor* – Arbroath in about 20 Oct '42 for dummy deck landings ADDLs with the first prototype Fairey Barracuda.

The trials pilot was at that time Lt H.M. Henry 'Brandy balls' or 'Straight laced' Ellis DFC and DSC. We would have absolutely no liaison with any squadron or part of that station life. We also had a Fairey rep, a Mr P. Paterson, who flew with us on assignments. The group was then sent back to Lee-on-Solent to form up the first Barracuda squadron.

At this time, Roy learned the tragic news that his old friend from Dartmouth, Robert Boddington, had gone missing while commanding the submarine *Unique* off Spain. The submarine had been ordered to patrol in the Bay of Biscay while on passage from Britain to Gibraltar. She left her escorts in October 1942 and was not heard from again, the cause of her loss unknown. Roy and Naomi were devastated.

On 4 December, Barracuda P9647 was made available for Roy to fly for the first time. The first Barracuda flight had been two years earlier but with an inadequate engine. Roy's designated aircraft had a more powerful Merlin 32 engine. The additional power was used to increase the weight and thus the stores that could be carried. The Navy wanted a new high-performance monoplane aircraft that could replace the ageing Swordfish biplane for dive-bombing, torpedo work and reconnaissance duties and Roy's task was to ensure that the Barracuda could function in its intended role.

Roy was to fly this aircraft intensively for six months or until it fell apart – as some earlier versions literally had done. P9647 eventually crashed following an engine failure a few days after Roy had completed his tests.

Roy's first impression of the Barracuda was like that of other test pilots, namely that the aircraft was underpowered. It was designed to have the Napier Sabre engine but the priority was for it to be used for Typhoons destined to join the RAF. The RAF got the engines and the Barracuda had to make do with the less powerful Merlin engine. Roy found the early Barracuda was heavy and cumbersome. It needed full power to get it moving. He took the whole length of the runway and then he had to yank the aircraft into the air.

Derek Moore, a 827 Squadron pilot being introduced to the Barracuda about this time, commented:

'B's were noisy brutes. Noise and vibration seemed most severe at morning inspections, concentrated by tarmac, hangar walls etc. nearest I can think of, would be sitting on top of a pneumatic drill!

Roy's initial Barracuda flight was to the test flight facilities at the Royal Aircraft Establishment (RAE) in Farnborough for catapult trials by 'A' Flight. At Boscombe Down there were no facilities for testing short take-off and arresting aircraft on decks. Farnborough was renowned for its experimental aircraft testing and scientific research and had led the world as a pioneer of flying since 1911.

Roy spent the next few days carrying out test flights and handling flights prior to fellow naval test pilot Lt Don Robertson carrying out the catapulting trials. When the pair were off duty, there was plenty of entertainment opportunities for the test pilots. There were two cinemas, the Scala and the Rex, the Navy, Army and Air Force Institute canteen and TOCH for snacks and lounges with comfy armchairs where they could sit down and rest in the evenings. Don and Roy exchanged memories about Canada. Pre-war, Don had flown in Northern Canada, pioneering flights to remote trading posts on the Mackenzie River. He told Roy all sorts of tales about his exploits in the Arctic. Little did Roy know that he, too, would be flying over the Arctic in less than a year's time.

Roy returned Barracuda P9647 to Boscombe Down on 9 December where she was tested for maximum weights for baulked landings, weights and loading, then take-off trials with various flap settings, and engine cooling trials.

Roy encountered stalls to the starboard which he described as 'vicious', not surprisingly so as the aircraft would flip upside-down. He identified that with flaps in the air brake position, stalls were even worse. In dive recoveries, application of rudder past a certain point caused airflow breakdown; the rudder overbalanced, the elevator was pulled down momentarily and the nose pitched down violently. Roy had to be extremely level-headed and calm not to crash.

The Navy wanted the Barracuda aircraft in operational service as soon as possible, and contracts worth thousands of pounds were involved. However, during the spring of 1943, accidents in the first squadrons equipped with the Barracuda led to two investigations at Boscombe Down by Roy and his colleagues.

After these test flights and Roy's observations, amendments were carried out, including the fitting of a dorsal fin, a metal-covered rudder and a spring balance tab to the rudder. Those modifications were incorporated immediately; other modifications suggested were to await confirmation by further trials by the RAE Farnborough.

Flight commander Charles McClure, a Farnborough test pilot, recalled:

I find from my log book that I did 15 hrs on Barracudas, one of the ones I flew was P9642. It was a terrible aeroplane. It was underpowered with a single Merlin engine. Most of my flying was trying to sort out troubles with its airscrew-engine combination when used as a dive-bomber; I don't think we ever got it working properly.

Sandy Powell, based at Boscombe Down, recalled:

At this time the naval aeroplanes were much to the fore and we did a great deal of flying on the Martlet fighters and the Barracuda, a replacement for the Swordfish torpedo bomber reconnaissance aircraft. The Barracuda was undergoing an intensive handling programme, much of which involved very steep dives and pull-outs.

Lt Cdr F.M.A. Torrens-Spence was away one morning, diving the Barracuda, and had become somewhat overdue. Presently the phone went – 'Oh, hallo Sandy,' he said 'had to force-land the Barracuda at "X", can you possibly come out and pick me up?' I asked what had caused the trouble. 'Well' he said, 'halfway through a dive there was a loud bang and an oil leak which covered the windscreen with oil. I'll tell you the rest when I see you.'

This must be one of the finest understatements on record – in fact, the entire propeller and reduction gear had come off in the dive; this certainly had covered the front of the aeroplane and pilot with oil! It presented him with a sudden change of centre of gravity which made it only just possible to fly the aeroplane in level flight, let alone land it. And, of course, this all occurred in a near vertical dive not very far from the ground.

Roy's tests on the Barracuda were on the whole less dramatic. He was instrumental in making improvement changes to the performance of the aircraft, not least by his suggestions to replace exhaust manifolds with those based on the ones used by the Lancaster.

Test pilot Dennis Cambell was more generous than most in his assessment of the Barracuda:

I think the Barra had the usual teething troubles but I don't recall it had any bad characteristics, considering what it had been designed for – dive-bombing and torpedo carrying – and as Roy B-F himself proved, it did the former role very well. Roy and his team put it to good use when the opportunity arose.

Roy's talents in flying were needed for more than just the Barracuda. Following the signing of the Lend-Lease Agreement with America, a flood of new US Navy aircraft began to arrive at Boscombe for assessment, including the Wildcat, Avenger, Hellcat and Corsair.

Roy embarked on a series of tests with American aircraft – the first involved the seaplane Vought-Sikorsky OS2U-3 Kingfisher, which had already proven its value in the US Navy and was comparable in its versatility to the Fairey Swordfish for training, reconnaissance and search-rescue duties. Next, Roy flew in his first big multi-engined aircraft, a brand-new Mitchell B25 bomber. He acted as co-pilot in the Mitchell flown by Torrens-Spence, for wireless telegraphy tests.

Recollections of performance testing the Mitchell were made by a young TAG, Ken Mitchell:

Lt Cdr RBF was a very good pilot indeed and a grand chap to work with. In the flight in the Mitchell with W/Cdr Slee as pilot, I was supplied with about four football bladders and a hand pump to enable me to take samples of the air in the cabin when the bomb doors were opened. Naturally I was wearing an oxygen mask during the test, apparently there was a problem when the planes were used in action, because of the exhaust fumes which entered the plane when the bomb doors were opened for action.

A few days after that, Roy flew a Supermarine Sea Otter. It was a biplane designed for the role of reconnaissance, communications or air-sea rescue. The Sea Otter was the last biplane to enter RAF and Fleet Air Arm service in 1944. Roy carried out handling trials and radar tests. He found the aircraft was 'sedate, pleasant and very stable'.

As Roy's flight tests continued, the first front-line Albacore squadrons were ordered in December to re-equip with the new Barracuda TBR aircraft. The first was 827 Squadron followed by 810 Squadron.

There was a personal crisis for Roy at the end of December 1942, when Naomi became desperately ill with fever, headache and sickness. A doctor was called and diagnosed influenza. Roy had to leave for the airfield but was so worried he returned soon after to find Naomi feverishly calling 'turkey, turkey'. She was trying to ask for medicine but her brain was confused. The doctor was called again and she was rushed to Salisbury Hospital suffering from the killer disease, meningitis. For days her life hung in the balance.

Roy was at a crucial stage of his secret work and was not allowed to give up his duties. He therefore sent a telegram to his sister Leslie who was still studying at the Royal College of Music in London asking her to come urgently to look after Carole because Naomi was seriously ill.

Leslie rushed down on the train from London and was met by Roy at Salisbury railway station. She recalled: 'When I first arrived Naomi was worse and for one week was in intensive care on the danger list. She was put on a course of antibiotics, M&B, one of the first ever antibiotics.

Leslie continued: 'In total, I must have stayed there for about one month over the Music College's Christmas holidays whilst Naomi gradually recovered in hospital.

Roy used to go out to work each day by car, travelling over the Downs from the centre of Salisbury to Boscombe, leaving Leslie at home with little Carole. For Leslie, life became fully occupied with looking after the toddler, and in the evenings attempting to cheer up the extremely worried Roy. He spent all his spare time at the hospital – Naomi was at death's door and it was not clear whether she would survive.

As Christmas drew closer, there did not seem to be anything for the young family to celebrate. Alone with Carole in the Salisbury home on Christmas Eve, Leslie received a message from Roy saying he would be out all night. That evening she felt very lonely, having to make her own entertainment. On Christmas Day itself, Leslie had a thoroughly miserable day. 'All I can remember is washing the floor and cleaning the flat. Roy later apologised for coming in late as he had crashed his aircraft.'

On this occasion, Roy had been warned not to fly at a speed greater than 400 mph. However, the dial on the instrument panel tipped beyond the 400 mark during a dive and his engine cut out, and he was forced to take emergency action. This high-speed stall caused the wing to drop sharply and he fought to recover the aircraft immediately, by relaxing the pressure on the control column. Once the aircraft was under control, he managed a forced landing. Luckily he stepped out unhurt.

Naomi later recounted her Christmas in a letter to her brother Bill who was by that time a captain serving with the British Army Medical Corps in North Africa:

Lieutenant R S Baker-Falkner acting in the Royal Navy information film 'Find, Fix and Strike' onboard HMS *Ark Royal*. (*Author's collection*)

Test Pilot Lieutenant R S Baker-Falkner at RAF Boscombe Down, 1942. (*Photograph reproduced with the kind permission of the Fleet Air Arm Museum*)

st pilot B-F with his trusty motorbike JB6584 at his residence near Amesbury.
(*ker-Falkner family collection*)

test piloting an American Lend-Lease Grumman Avenger (Tarpon) FN767 at RAF Boscombe
wn, 1943. (*Author's collection*)

Barracuda Mk I P9659 of 827 Squadron on dive bombing exercise at Stretton, 1943. (*Author's collection*

...rracuda Mk IIs of 827 Squadron in flight. (*Kevin Gibney collection*)

...et carrier HMS *Furious* at anchor. (*Author's collection*)

B-F and HMS *Furious* chaplain, Rev Cyril Warner. (*Cyril Warner collection*)

Barracuda Mk II 'K' of 827 Squadron taking off from the flight deck. (*John Stark collection*)

0 Squadron aircrew including CO Lt Cdr 'Dickie' Kingdon, HMS *Furious* in 1944.
avid Brown collection)

8 TBR Wing Leader, B-F, with Guy Micklem, Wing Observer, Kevin Gibney, 827 Squadron CO,
d 'Dickie' Kingdon, 830 Squadron CO at Scapa Flow, 1944. (*'Puck' Finch Noyes collection*)

B-F with personal Barracuda Mk II '4K' LS577 on the flight deck of HMS *Victorious* following raid ⟨ German battleship *Tirpitz*, April 1944. (*Author's collection*)

(*Left*) Lieutenant Howard Emerson RNZVR B-F's wingman and senior pilot of 827 Squadron. (*Roy Emerson collection*)
(*Right*) No 8 TBR Telegraphist Air Gunner, Allan Thomson of 830 Squadron, in flying gear, 1944. (*Allan Thomson collection*)

evin Gibney in his cabin drafting material along with B-F for the Naval Air Fighting Instruction, '43. (*Kevin Gibney collection*)

aily Mirror headlines about B-F leading the strike on the battleship *Tirpitz* in Operation Tungsten, '44. (*Author's collection*)

AILY MIRROR, Saturday, April 8, 1944

Daily Mirror

APL 8   No. 12,576   ONE PENNY   Registered at the G.P.O. as a Newspaper.   ✦ ✦

The boys tell how they smashed Tirpitz

BOMBS HIT HER 16 TIMES

THE men who bombed the Tirpitz are back —with vivid stories of how they smashed Hitler's 42,000-ton battleship.

The Tirpitz got at least sixteen direct hits—one is believed to have crashed into her magazine. She is thought to be aground on her stern.

Each covey of Barracuda dive-bombers dropped twenty tons of high explosives in less than a minute.

The Tirpitz guns were silenced, flames leaped to her topmast, and no German plane went up in her defence.

Our losses were three dive-bombers and one fighter.

Here is the story of the attack, as correspondents aboard the aircraft-carrier from which it was launched told it yesterday:

"THE OFF." It is 3.30 a.m. The Arctic sun glints on lines of grey-green Barracuda dive-bombers.

The flight deck officer waves his green flag. One by one the bombers climb away; wing-tip to wing-tip they streak off for Alten Fjord.

Canopies of Fighters

Hellcats, Wildcats and Corsairs—canopies of fighters from escort-carriers—fill five miles of sky.

Lieutenant Commander A. B. Baker-Falkner, Torquay, who led the attack on the Tirpitz, was educated at Dartmouth College. His wife told the "Daily Mirror" yesterday, "The only thing he was really good at was boxing."

Those (absent) fish

FISHMONGERS answered the Ministry of Food's appeal to stay open to handle "exceptionally heavy landings" of cod and other white fish yesterday.

Housewives queued outside London fishmongers' shops—and gazed at almost empty slabs.

● There wasn't any fish for most of them.

Only 316 tons were landed at Billingsgate—a normal day's supply for wartime—compared with as much as 800 tons on a peacetime Good Friday.

Some of the queues for the fish that never arrived were fifty yards long.

● Where was the fish? It had been landed at Hull and Fleetwood, said the Ministry of Food, but it would take a few days for it to be distributed.

"The fish will be coming to London and other large towns, and we are hoping that it will be available for tomorrow and Monday."

About 320 tons, mostly Icelandic cod and haddock, were discharged at Fleetwood. Hull's wholesale fish merchants handled almost as much.

Supplies had not come up to expectations, said Mr. J. Bailey, Hull Fish Merchants' Association president. "But we are busy, and expect busy times ahead." he said.

WE STOP EIRE COAL

The ban on the export of coal to neutral countries announced by Major Lloyd George, Minister of Fuel and Power, in the House of Commons on Thursday, applies to Eire.

ADVERTISER'S ANNOUNCEMENT

Where's OUR

NFS men ready to invade Europe with 2nd Front troops

THE NFS, which fought and helped to beat the blitz in Britain, is ready to invade the Continent with our Second Front armies.

Cutaway by Wladislaw Tirpitz in Kaafjord, North Norway, under disc bombing attack by No. 8 TBR Wing led by R. E. Casti, leader, 3 April 1944. (Author's collection)

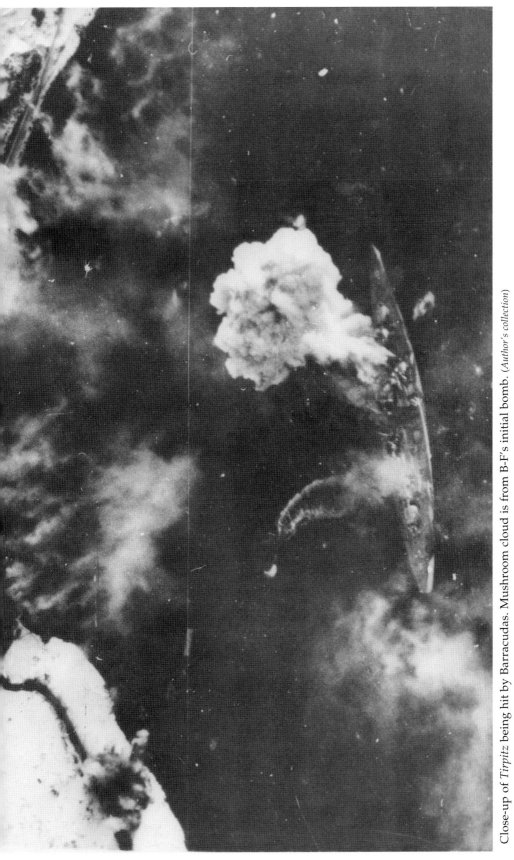

Close-up of *Tirpitz* being hit by Barracudas. Mushroom cloud is from B-F's initial bomb. (*Author's collection*)

John Jellie and fellow 804 Squadron fighter aircrew on board HMS *Emperor*. Fighter aircrew played an invaluable role in Operation Tungsten to subdue enemy positions during the strike. (*John Jellie collection*)

B-F and his personal aircrew, Guy Micklem and air gunner Arthur Kimberley, at attention meeting King George VI following the successful *Tirpitz* raid. (*Author's collection*)

...ntgomery being introduced to *Tirpitz* aircrews on board HMS *Victorious* by Captain Denny weeks ...ior to the D-Day Normandy invasion. (*Author's collection*)

...et carrier HMS *Formidable* at sea. (*Patrick Duffy collection*)

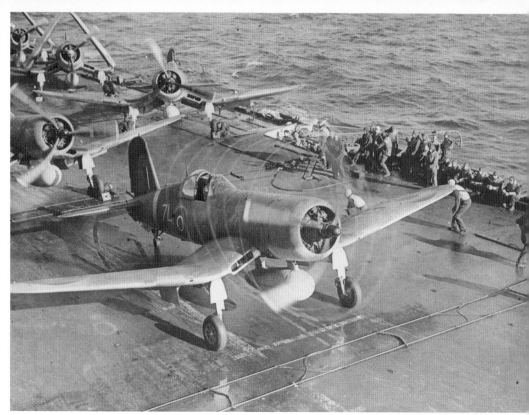

Vought Corsair '7L' of 1841 Squadron preparing to take off from *Formidable* for Operation Mascot, July 1944. (*Author's collection*)

Aerial view from B-F's Barracuda over Kaafiord showing smoke screens protecting *Tirpitz* from FAA attack in Operation Mascot. (*Gilbert Clark collection*)

Sub Lieutenant Harold 'Matt' Mattholie RNVR, senior pilot of 1841 Corsair Squadron whose aircraft was lost over Norway with B-F, July 1944.
(*Matt Mattholie collection*)

Area in region of the Lofoten Islands in Arctic Norway where B-F's aircraft was presumed lost, 18 July 1944.
(*Author's collection*)

Dr Gilbert Clark, last person to fly with B-F prior to the lost patrol.
(*Author's collection*)

Limited edition commemorative envelope and card for the 50th anniversary of B-F's strike against battleship *Tirpitz*. (*Author's collection*)

Fleet Air Arm operations against the TIRPITZ in Norwa

50th Anniversary
1944-1994

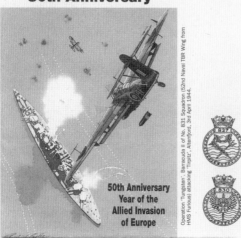

FLEET AIR ARM ATTACK
ON THE TIRPITZ
50th Anniversary

50th Anniversary
Year of the
Allied Invasion
of Europe

Operation 'Tungsten'. Barracuda II of No. 831 Squadron (52nd Naval TBR Wing from HMS Furious) attacking 'Tirpitz', Altenfjord, 3rd April 1944.

Members of No 8 TBR and families, accompanied by B-F's sister Leslie (eighth from the left), at the Wing's 50th anniversary reunion at RNAS Yeovilton and the Royal Navy Historic Flight, 1994. (*Author's collection*)

Well dear, I sincerely hope you had a better Christmas than I did! I spent a most cheerful Christmas dying – I certainly don't recommend it! – I expect you have had all the details from Eira by now – I have never had such a headache and been so sick in all my life – by the fourth day I was quite crazy with pain and was even unconscious for a wee while.

Roy returned to Boscombe Down on 1 January 1943 after a short leave and carried out further flights tests, commencing with the US single seater-carrier fighter, the Martlet/Wildcat IV. The Martlet was the name the Royal Navy had given to the American Grumman Wildcat, but with subsequent confusion its name was officially reverted to Wildcat by 1944. Roy found it had uneventful handling but was pleasant to fly, with straightforward stalls. He described the narrow undercarriage which took thirty seconds to retract manually as 'twitchy'. He reported that contamination by carbon monoxide was bad, but much improved when boffins had sealed the cowling and cockpit.

As well as his flying duties, Roy also had to arrange a move of house for his sister and small daughter over the New Year period. The lease of Roy's Salisbury flat came to an end and he found a stop-gap solution by arranging to stay at the George Inn in Amesbury High Street, whilst he searched for more suitable long-term accommodation elsewhere.

The George Inn was a typical old rambling coaching inn, with wonderful nooks and crannies for mischievous little Carole to explore and play hide and seek with Leslie. It also provided a centre for Leslie to explore the area whilst Roy was away at Boscombe Down, including taking Carole up in her pram to see the ancient stone circle at nearby Stonehenge. Roy also introduced her to Mike Lithgow who she thought was very dashing, but she was too shy to visit him and other test pilots at the officers' mess or to go to the Boscombe Down Christmas and New Year parties.

Meanwhile, Naomi responded to the antibiotics and in early January she was allowed to leave Salisbury hospital and return home to Roy and Leslie in Amesbury. Soon after, Roy found accommodation for his family at Nag's Head Cottage four miles north of Amesbury out towards the pretty village of Durrington. It was an isolated building nestling at the foot of Bulford Hill, reached by walking across fields or across an old ornate bridge over the river.

Leslie thought Nag's Head Cottage was a beautiful place; it was tiny with the deep flowing waters of the River Avon at the bottom of the garden beyond the bulrushes. With Naomi now recovering, Leslie went back to London and her college studies. Roy and Naomi settled down to family life again. Roy loved gardening and pottering around, reading or doing the odd crossword puzzle whenever he had time off from his heavy schedule of flying duties.

On 1 February, Roy had to leave Naomi and Carole at Nag's Head Cottage for a few weeks whilst he went northwards to Scotland. He took Barracuda P9647 on deck-landing trials to Arbroath and elsewhere in Scotland for a three-week period. He was to log eighteen flights totalling 17.15 hours. The Arbroath mission was to involve carrying out a series of aerodrome dummy deck landings, followed by trial deck landings on HMS *Illustrious*. Roy flew up with L/A Townsend, although he did not use a TAG for the actual deck landings.

A young budding naval test pilot Eric 'Winkle' Brown recalled the Arbroath event:

Roy was an accredited test pilot who was attached to 'C' Squadron at Boscombe Down specifically to get acquainted with the Barracuda II before taking over the first squadron to be equipped with the new type. This was a fairly common practice to arrange such attachments for designated COs of squadrons introducing a new aircraft type.

In 1942, I knew Roy by sight at Arbroath as one of the 767 Squadron pilots, but I did not actually meet him until the end of January 1943 when he brought a prototype Barracuda to Arbroath prior to deck-landing trials on HMS *Illustrious* in the Western Approaches and when I was in No. 778 (Service Trials Unit) at RN Air Station, Arbroath (HMS *Condor*) in 1943. I remember Roy as a tall, good-looking lieutenant, with a somewhat serious but pleasant personality.

He arrived at Arbroath, one of a team of four prototype aircraft and test pilots who were to make initial deck-landing trials. The others were: Cdr D. Cambell – Firebrand I from Blackburn aircraft; Lt Cdr F.M.A. Torrens-Spence – Firefly I from Boscombe Down; and Lt Robertson – RATOG Seafire from RAE Farnborough.

At Arbroath they did endless landings there, and I acted as 'batsman' for these four during their aerodrome dummy deck landings practice from 1–4 February, and then accompanied them to *Illustrious* where I was to carry out trials with a Wildcat IV and a Seafire IIC fitted with a Merlin 32 engine on February 8–9.

Then I was told to go out with them to *Illustrious* and bat them on. I was no professional batsman, and I was not looking forward to coping with these very fast aircraft. However, the *Illustrious*' own deck-landing control officer felt so keenly slighted by my appointment that he persuaded his captain to stop me from batting. The trials went off without mishap. The Firefly looked like a useful machine, but the cumbersome Firebrand was one of those machines which make test pilots shake their heads in disgust.

The trials' pilots stayed in the wardrooms of RNAS Arbroath and then RNAS Machrihanish, but whereas the four from down south were free after their daily stints of ADDLs, I was fully engaged in flying in the Service Trials Unit so I did not have much time to socialise with them. However, we did debrief together after each ADDLs session, and Roy was certainly the most relaxed, possibly because he was flying the easiest of the aircraft to deck-land. I was responsible for reporting to the CO of 768 Squadron when I considered each pilot ready to go to the deck.

The trials went well, so Roy was obviously a very capable pilot and had a distinguished naval career.

On Roy's return to Boscombe Down, he carried out level speed tests, aileron handling, carbon monoxide measurements, followed by an exchange with Swordfish V4570 for take-off measurements. Carbon monoxide gas, present in the engine exhausts and gun firing fumes, posed a significant threat to aircrew at the time.

The technique used on this trip was for PO Russell to use balloons inflated by small bellows at various times in flight, and the sample was analysed later on the ground. The work of the A&AEE was then to identify and cure the source of the carbon monoxide poisoning, often by simply lengthening exhaust pipes, or sealing the tailwheel opening.

On 25 February, Air Commodore D. D'Arcy Greig, took over from Air Commodore R.B. Mansell, as the overall officer commanding at Boscombe Down. He was yet another pilot with a distinguished aviation career who had been a Schneider trophy pilot, served with distinction in the Great War, won an airspeed record in the RAF High Speed Flight and had been Chief Flying Instructor at the Central Flying School.

That day, Roy test-flew the first production Barracuda Mk II, P9667, which had been delivered to 'C' Flight after Christmas. He carried out flights with aileron handling trials, and three days later he made handling and dive tests. Subsequently, he flew the thirty-second production Barra Mk II. Roy carried out an air test, then followed through with further handling trials. The aircraft was later tested for flame damping and carbon monoxide contamination tests at dusk at low altitude over the airfield.

He also flew a Barracuda Mk I for carbon monoxide measurements, the first of a number of flights on this aircraft over the next few months. It had been fitted with a shroud fitted over the air-cooled fishtail exhausts. Roy's conclusion was that it failed to meet requirements. The aircraft was returned to Hucknall, near Derby.

By March, the number of different types of aircraft Roy was to fly increased. That month Roy flew the Barracuda, the Sea Otter, Swordfish, the Martlet, and the Vengeance. He daily switched from one type of aircraft to another, memorising the layouts of the various cockpits, engine settings, take-off speeds, and the different instruments and gauges of the US aircraft.

On 6 March, Mike Lithgow pranged Barracuda P9677, coded '77' – it had only achieved 119 hours when it hit a ridge on take-off at Boscombe Down. He recalled:

I hadn't been there very long when I succeeded in blotting my copy book by damaging a Barracuda. Boscombe Down was a very rough, bumpy grass field and in a certain direction the ridges were such that it was possible on take-off to start a sort of divergent bounce rather akin to 'porpoising' when taking off the water.

On this particular day I encountered it as usual, and since the indicated speed appeared to be sufficient to 'unstick' the aeroplane, I pulled the stick back and hitched the wheels up, thinking we would climb nicely away. To my horror, the next thing I knew was small pieces of wooden propeller flying past the windscreen, so thick that they were almost like spray. The Barracuda had a rather 'draggy' undercarriage which was best retracted as soon as possible if one wished to climb away, but that didn't alter the fact that next day I was on my way to the Ministry of Aircraft Production to explain the matter away as best I could.

Fortunately, the commander to whose presence I was summoned had done something very similar in a Fulmar a few weeks before, so all was soon forgotten and forgiven.

Townsend recalled the event: 'I had returned to Boscombe Down from overnight leave and PO Russell said to me "there's your plane Fred" and pointed to 77 in the middle of the drome "pranged" – he said "no flying today for you".' He was disappointed but went on with Lithgow to fly another aircraft.

At the same time, Roy's flying activities were not without incidence whilst visiting RNAS Stretton where 827 Squadron was working up on the new Barracuda. L/A Sawyer recalled:

Baker-Falkner appeared on the scene, not as a squadron member, but continuing in the flight-testing with which he had been involved at Boscombe Down. He was introduced to us, according to my log records, as an Admiralty test pilot! I first flew twice with him in Barra P9681 on March 26, 1943, and by July had flown with him ten times.

One event, perhaps worthy of mention, that involved Baker-Falkner, I distinctly recall. We TAGs, previously working with Albacores which required chest-type clip-on parachute packs to be used by the back-seat crews, had been issued with seat-type parachutes for the new Barracudas. It had quickly become our custom to leave our 'chutes in the rear cockpit, in between flights, rather than 'hump' them back to the parachute section each time the aircraft landed.

On the particular occasion, Baker-Falkner wanted to try a certain manoeuvre in the aircraft in which we'd both been airborne and he wanted to fly solo. It didn't occur to me that he was going to fly inverted. After all, the Barra was not really intended for rolling, but roll it he did, the 'chute fell out of the back seat, pushed open the rear cockpit cover, burst open and solemnly descended, carrying only my seat-pack and dinghy, right over Stretton airfield!

On landing Roy went up to L/A Sawyer and reprimanded him but soon let him off as no harm had been done. They were in the air again together soon after. Sawyer added:

> There were early troubles with the Barracuda – beginning at Stretton. A problem with the Barra was its apparent inability – until the cause was discovered – to build up power to recover height after pulling out of a dive, and with those unique dive-brakes, the Barra could, and did, dive almost vertically!

Whilst Roy and 827 Squadron were at Stretton they were visited by a Hurricane squadron. Sawyer recalled:

> I well remember the arrival of the Hurricanes – a lot of showing off over the airfield and then snappy sequence landings. Except for one bright-spark who ran off the runway (possibly a bit of side-wind caught him unawares) into soft ground and turned right over on his back. A group of us spectators ran out to release the pilot (he was unhurt!) and I noted that painted on his aircraft engine cowling was '*simper in excreta*'.

Roy's first flight in the Lend-Lease supplied American Vultee Vengeance was on 14 March. The Vengeance was designed in America for the RAF, who at the time recognised the need for dive-bombers following the early achievements of the German Stuka. Roy made carbon monoxide tests on this dive-bomber which was to find little favour with the Royal Navy or the RAF.

During this time Townsend recollected a strange and secret visit to their Air Station:

> Two visits were made to Boscombe Down by the Lancasters of RAF 617 Guy Gibson's squadron preparing for a hush-hush op – by coincidence one of his rear gunners was a neighbour of my wife so I brought him home to stay overnight in order to spend some time with his parents. We returned next morning. 617 Squadron later went on to become famous as the 'Dambusters'.

Sawyer continued to describe his squadron's Barracuda activities:

> During March the whole of 827 Squadron moved south to Lee-on-Solent, to show off the new TBR monoplane to various 'bigwigs'. Roy flew one of his Barracuda aircraft to meet up with the squadron. This was to carry out chase-me-Charlie aerobatic test flights with Lt Bailey in command of 827 Squadron to show the flying capabilities of the aircraft.'

Roy continued these Barracuda chasing flights with this squadron until 23 March with Sawyer as his TAG. He returned to Boscombe three days later.

One of the young 827 Squadron pilots, Lt Howard Emerson RNZNVR, wrote in his secret diary about his visit to the A&AEE at the same time. He excitedly noted having seen twenty-nine different types of new aircraft:

Flew down to Boscombe today in a kite going to Lee for ASV – to relieve Eaton. This is a big RAF experimental place. All types here, Lancs, Stirlings, Halifaxes, Manchesters … including the old Barracuda undergoing Intensive Flying Trials. This is a very rough drome, but handy to Salisbury.

Whilst there Emerson noted:

My kite has been u/s for twelve days... Had two flips in a Mitchell, and one in a Mosquito. These are superb, climbs 2,000 ft a min at sea level. Most cruising 300 mph. Top speed 410. Stalls at 115 very gently.

Beaufighters are carrying fish up there, & Mosquitos are to try deck landings. Lots of other secret gen from there.

At the end of the month, Roy again flew a Barracuda Mk I for handling trials with 250-lb smoke curtain installations (SCI) – gas-spraying tanks. Two days later he was in a de Havilland Mosquito as a passenger with Torrens-Spence as pilot in a handling flight.

In April, the first trip of the month was again as a passenger with Torrens-Spence. They flew to Lee-on-Solent to meet incoming production Barracudas which were being handed over to operational squadrons converting to this new aircraft type.

By now, the first re-equipped squadron – 827 – was settling in to flying its new aircraft at Dunino, a satellite of Crail where it moved to that month. Jeff Gledhill, a young New Zealander of 827 Squadron, recalled:

We started a torpedo and armament work-up. In fact, this was the first real trial of the Barracuda in the weapons role. A large number of Attack Light Torpedo (ALTs) were carried out, in my case about thirty without any rogue characteristics appearing. Why no aircraft losses had occurred in the time since we took delivery of the Barracuda, despite so many dives, remains a mystery.

Meanwhile, Roy carried on with his other duties test flying new American aircraft, including the Tarpon. Called the Avenger in America, it was first delivered to the UK at the end of January and first flown by Roy in April. It was a three-seater monoplane carrier-borne torpedo aircraft and light bomber.

Roy was to fly this aeroplane for the next two months, to trial if the Avenger was suitable to form the backbone of the Fleet Air Arm instead of the Barracuda. He carried out air-to-air recognition, dives, air tests, level speed climb performance, take-off measurements, fuel consumption measurements and radio trials. Roy was destined to spend almost as much flying time with the Avenger as the Barracuda, and his name was getting known for his successful trials of this aircraft.

At the end of Roy's Avenger trials, partly based on success of these test flights, the Royal Navy started to allocate these aircraft for operational squadrons in the Pacific Theatre, disposing of the less efficient Barracuda. In this role it operated as a bomber, and as a search and anti-submarine aircraft, rather than as a torpedo plane.

A few days later, Roy was to fly the Brewster Bermuda, a land-based, three-seat dive-bomber, to test handling and contamination. His testing led to the original short exhaust pipe being identified as the cause of high levels of cockpit fumes.

Soon after, Roy was one of the first British test pilots to fly the American Curtiss Sea Mew, which had been delivered to the UK two months previously. This aircraft was intended for ship use in an observation role. He was to fly it only once again, in June for contamination tests – the aircraft was considered underpowered and had a mediocre climb. Tests on one other aircraft were subsequently cancelled and the Sea Mew quietly retired.

He also flew a multi-engined aircraft, the de Havilland Mosquito, on a short air test of only thirty minutes. A few days later Roy was back with 827 Squadron further re-equipping with the Barracuda.

On 13 May, Roy led a demonstration flight of the Barracuda at Lee-on-Solent in front of Mr Cox, MP, and the Fifth Sea Lord, Lord Bruntisfield, the Parliamentary Secretary to the Admiralty and other high officials. 'High Ups' as Roy called them.

Whether Roy was apprehensive or not it was impressed upon him by his superiors that the success of this demonstration was crucial to the future of the Barracuda. It was agreed that with 827 Squadron's CO, Lt Cdr Bailey, that their senior pilot, Sub Lt Robert 'Jock' Smith, RNVR, should also assist in the demonstration in a second Barracuda. Once Roy and Smith were ready in their cockpits, at the allotted time, contact, and they were away. Banking steeply over the Solent, they flew out towards the Isle of Wight and then back towards the display area and the waiting VIPs.

The two pilots then carried out a series of flights to show the manoeuvrability of the aircraft. The programme consisted chiefly of individual ALTs on a stationary target at Gosport, carrying loads of four 500-lb bombs. Mr Cox had spoken in the House advocating the abandonment of Barracuda production, so this demonstration was to try and impress him.

An entry in the 827 Squadron line book stated:

About this time a Mr Cox, MP, made such unpleasant remarks about Barracudas that Fairey's employees went on strike. To put a great wrong right the squadron was entrusted with the task of showing the Hon Member the errors of his opinions.

In fact we supplied him with *all the answers* but our own Senior 'P' Jock Smith and expert Lt Baker-Falkner RN had the job of throwing round the sky the aircraft so questioned before Mr Cox, the Fifth Sea Lord and his numerous braided staff.

Mr Cox, who had to be hoisted into Roy's aircraft by crane because of a lame leg, was then taken for a flight after their display, which 'included some very spectacular flying' according to the 827 Squadron line book.

The next squadron being equipped with the Barracuda at Lee-on-Solent was 830 Squadron. Leading Airman Allan Thomson TAG recalled the high-level visits at Lee-on-Solent and remarked on Roy's flying skills:

The 830 Squadron office, inside a camouflaged, bomb-damaged hangar from 1940, was a huge wooden packing case for a Grumman Martlet which had been shipped across the Atlantic.

Questions had been asked in 'THE HOUSE' about the safety of the a/c.

At Lee, we first witnessed a demonstration dive of a Barra. We had been told the official dive angle was 87°. This a/c, flown by Baker-Falkner, was vertical. It appeared to be lying on its back on the way down. So we knew what we were in for. I never heard if the two Members of Parliament in the back were afterwards more or less doubtful about Barracuda airworthiness.

After all this VIP demonstration work, Roy's next flight was relatively mundane. On 17 May, he flew up to the east coast of Scotland in a Fulmar to see a problem Barracuda at 827 Squadron's new home at RNAS Dunino, a satellite of RNAS Crail.

Things were not going too well for the squadron, although training was continuing at a good rate, as written about by Lt Emerson at the time:

> Flying is going on at a pace. We are dropping fish and doing formation attacks. Our serviceability is poor, and has now dropped to 2 a/c out of 19. .....I went into a pressure chamber today. Spent an hour in it and went to 40,000 ft. Took the mask off and only lasted about 4 minutes. Was very intoxicating and good practice for taking oxygen, & showing the need of it at height.

After consulting with 827 Squadron, Roy went on to carry out dummy deck-landing trials, thence to Finningmere and then back to Boscombe and on to Lee-on-Solent.

Reg Elliot recalled Roy coming to Crail:

> I had the pleasure of meeting Lt Baker-Falkner when I was an instructor at the Torpedo School at Crail in 1943. We had begun to change over from Swordfish and Albacores to Barracuda aircraft and being a new type, there were the inevitable teething problems.
>
> A squadron was also working up with Barracudas and was based at Crail, and they too had problems with the aircraft. I recall that Lt Baker-Falkner was sent to Crail to see exactly what those problems were. The old methods of torpedo attacks were altered to suit the new aircraft, following Baker-Falkner's visit.

'Winkle' Brown recalled: 'The TSR Training School was located at Crail on the Firth of Forth and they had a series of fatal accidents with the new Barracuda, and Roy and Doc Steele-Perkins had gone there to investigate.'

Jan Steele-Perkins was an aviation medicine specialist and surgeon commander RN. He was closely involved with naval flying at Boscombe and Farnborough and his duties focused on medical and psychological problems of Fleet Air Arm aircrews. His job on this occasion was to assess any medical problems arising from the new Barracuda squadrons.

Tom Darling, a young Canadian pilot who later served in 827 Squadron, recalled:

> My first sighting of B-F was in the wardroom at Crail in the spring of 1943 – I was taking the Torpedo Dive Bomber course exam then. B-F's name became a kind of fable/legend as the test pilot from Boscombe Down for the Fairey Aviation 'new' Barracuda aircraft.
>
> He could perform any manoeuvre with it in safety whilst others with less skill and experience when (near) vertical diving on several occasions plunged into the Firth of Forth on their backs. He found that the cure/antidote was found to overcome 'skid' by turning the rudder tail all the way to the right to compensate – this adjustment being made just before plunging into the steep-dive. It worked!
>
> Unknown to us B-F was at work researching climbing high and performing the same antics but pulling out with sufficient height to correct afterwards. He found that if one did not trim into the dive – and one usually didn't bother – at some point there developed a violent yaw which because of the combined turn etc went unnoticed – this yaw put the aircraft in or close to a high speed stall.

Aircrew were losing confidence in the Barracuda aircraft and one was passed to the research branch at Farnborough for evaluation. 'Winkle' Brown was ordered to test fly a Barracuda and thought the rudder was overbalanced. Accordingly, he took it up to 14,000 feet, did a simulated torpedo attack, pulled up and banked sharply to port. The aircraft promptly flipped over on its back. After losing a considerable amount of height, Brown recovered and repeated the exercise. The same thing happened again. It was certainly the overbalance of the rudder. Alterations were made to the pilot's notes – to prevent any more accidents.

Brown later remarked:

> I shudder at the thought of what the inevitable consequences would have been had I actually performed the test at sea level. I cannot leave the accident investigation without paying tribute to one of the flight-test observers involved in those tests – Mrs Gwen Alston. Mrs Alston was a truly remarkable 'lady boffin' who, despite having lost her scientist husband in a fatal crash while on a similar duty, never flinched at any risky flight and in all circumstances displayed the essence of courage.
>
> As part of her work as a RAE scientist, she was called upon to fly as an observer on many hazardous test flights. Perhaps her best known work in this field was a series of trials flown in 1944 to try and discover the cause of the fatal accidents involving the Fairey Barracuda, five of which had crashed into the sea after releasing torpedoes.

On 16 May, Roy carried out fuel consumption measurements on Barracuda P9647, the first Barracuda he had ever test flown. This was to be Roy's last intensive trial flight on this aircraft. Four days later while it was being flown by Flight Lieutenant E.S.T. Cole, RAF, and Sgt Thornily, there was an engine failure at 11,000 feet. They managed to return the aircraft to Boscombe and force-land with wheels and flaps down. However, the undercarriage entangled on the airfield's perimeter wire fence and collapsed. Both men survived.

In June, Roy again flew a variety of aircraft, including the twin-engined US Lend-Lease Lockheed Ventura, an aeroplane similar to the Hudson.

In the middle of the month, Barracuda P9646 was being tested with 778 Squadron at Dunino conducting radio altimeter tests. It lost power and went through telephone wires and a tree, bounced off a hillock, and hit invasion poles and two brick walls. 'Winkle' Brown and crew, amazingly, survived.

Nine days later, on 21 June, Roy flew one of the new Grumman Martlet Mark Vs delivered from the States the previous day. The same day, Roy flew the advanced US carrier single-seat fighter, the Grumman Hellcat Mk I, for airspeed calibration. The month after Roy's first assessment, the Hellcat started to be distributed to operational squadrons. This aircraft became widely used in the Fleet Air Arm, and was very successful in combat operations later to be led by Roy.

During June a new Royal Naval Officer arrived at Boscombe, Lt L.P. Peter Twiss. He went on to become a Fairey Aviation record-breaking test pilot. 'I was considerably junior to Baker-Falkner being a midshipman in 1941. He was a well-known and respected FAA pilot, and I met him once or twice.'

Meanwhile, Roy had other aircraft problems to solve. On 19 June, 827 Squadron lost its senior pilot, 'Jock' Smith, in a Barracuda crash at Crail. Roy was rushed there to assess the problem. Jeff Gledhill recalled the accident:

> Without warning in June 1943, the senior pilot, who was a competent aviator, dived

into the sea during ALT. In the space of the next few weeks a total of four aircraft and eleven aircrew had been lost. No one came back to tell what went wrong but from eyewitness reports, aircraft were flicking into the sea near the bottom of steep dives. Test pilots and Admiralty representatives hastened to Dunino but no remedial measures were taken.

Sawyer also recalled the event:

> I had a lucky escape when Lt Smith took off from Crail on 19/6/43 in Barracuda BX682 with just an observer, leaving me free to return to Dunino with Lt Emerson in another a/c.
>
> BV682 it seems failed to pull out of its dive, went straight into the sea and of course the two crew were lost. Needless to say it was thought at first that all three of us had been in the aeroplane and I was about to be posted missing when I turned up later in the day at Dunino (near St Andrews) guardroom.

Roy's assessment was used in a subsequent major inquiry into the unexplained crashes. Sawyer recalled:

> I believe the findings involved a defect in the constant-speed unit on the propeller. As far as I understand it, the prop blades went into fully coarse pitch in the dive, overriding the pilot's selection of 'fully fine' to give him the power to gain height after levelling out at the bottom of a dive, thus instead of climbing away, the aeroplane continued to sink and in a number of instances failed to clear the surface, usually the sea, although some were over land, and a write-off was inevitable!

Roy was back at Boscombe a week later and straight away launched into carbon monoxide measurements and airspeed calibration tests on Martlets and Hellcats. However, another Barracuda accident occurred, this time with 830 Squadron.

L/A Allan Thomson recalled:

> I was detailed to fly, but arrangements were changed and it was decided to embark some ground crews to service the kites en route to Orkney. While coming in to land at Arbroath RNAS – this a/c plunged into the deck with loss of pilot and two ground crew (we guessed he may have selected the dive position of the massive flaps instead of lowering them for increased lift as the a/c slowed for landing). No official explanation was given to us.

Roy remained at Boscombe to carry out anti-icing trials on Swordfish HS553. This was a novelty as it was one of the very few Swordfish which had an enclosed cockpit and was destined for Canada and cold weather climate flight training at the end of the year.

At last Roy's secondment to Boscombe Down was coming to a close, and he and Naomi prepared to pack up their belongings in Nag's Head Cottage. Roy's final flight whilst at Boscombe was in a Martlet V for dive trials, bringing to a close a most stimulating chapter in his career, and the opportunity to spend so much quality time with his young wife and daughter. Overall, during the previous nine months he had flown at least fourteen different types of new or secret aircraft.

American aircraft had been coming to the UK and now the Admiralty decided to send some British fighters and dive-bombers to America for assessment by the US authorities. Roy was given this overseas assignment. It was planned that he would travel to America with the aircraft, supposedly for three or four weeks of demonstration flying. Firstly he would go to the flight-testing section of the British Air Commission, then on to Patuxent River, Maryland – the naval base built by the US Navy as a test centre for all their new aircraft.

He had long conversations with Naomi about the task ahead, and whether she and toddler Carole would be able to join him in America. However, their careful plans were scuppered with the escalating number of crashes suddenly occurring in 827 Squadron. Roy was desperately needed to sort out the Barracuda problems and raise squadron morale. He was appointed squadron commander and ordered to Scotland, so his young single colleague, Mike Lithgow, was sent to America in his stead.

Lithgow wrote:

> The Admiralty hit on the happy idea of sending over to America a Barracuda, Seafire and Firefly, just to let them see what we were doing.
> By a stroke of good fortune I was accorded the tough assignment. I crossed in the *Queen Mary* and waited for nearly three weeks in New York before any news of the aeroplanes, which came, via the northern route, by slower means.

He continued:

> It is difficult to describe the awe with which the arrival of the Barracuda was regarded. We managed to induce a burly American commander into it for a short flight. When he landed I asked him what he thought of it, and I'm sure my many friends at Fairey's will forgive me for quoting his reply which was 'Well, there's only one thing will supersede this, and that's the aeroplane!'

Back at Nag's Head Cottage, Roy and Naomi finished packing up their belongings and with a heavy heart they closed the door for the last time. Roy finally departed for front-line duties up in Scotland, and Naomi and little Carole went to stay with family in Shaldon. It was an agonising separation after eighteen months together.

Of the many letters Roy was to write home to Naomi over the succeeding months, one letter stood out, hinting at his possible disappointment at not going to the States. It was written aboard HMS *Furious* six weeks after they left their cosy little cottage: 'I think Mike [Lithgow] has gone off on the job that I was originally going on, good show I feel 'cos he does at least know his stuff which is a lot more than most do nowadays.'

As fate would have it Lithgow went on to have a very successful test pilot career, never going back to sea. After the war he became chief test pilot for Vickers Supermarine and held the world airspeed record for a short time, flying the Supermarine Attacker. He joined the British Aircraft Corporation in 1961, but was tragically killed while testing the BAC-111 airliner prototype in 1963.

On conclusion of Roy's intense period as a test pilot at Boscombe Down, his fellow Royal Navy aircrew member L/A Townsend recalled: 'RBF's log book entries – with the number of one, two or three flights per day in so many types of planes – puts emphasis on the importance of secrecy, and his loyalty and dependability to the IFDF – intensive flying development flight!'

CHAPTER 20

In Command of 827 Barracuda Squadron

In the early summer of 1943 Roy faced a new and difficult challenge – to command 827 Squadron which had recently experienced a series of fatal accidents in the Fairey Barracuda.

On 26 June, at the age of just twenty-seven, he was granted the rank of acting lieutenant commander and Naomi carefully sewed on the extra half ring to his uniform sleeve – he was now proudly a 'two-and-a-half ringer'.

Three days later he made the painful parting from Naomi and two-year-old Carole. This time the parting was especially poignant as Naomi was four months pregnant with her second child. Roy set out by car on the long journey to rendezvous with his new squadron at Dunino in southern Scotland.

Lt Howard Emerson, a young New Zealand pilot and Volunteer Reserve Officer in 827 Squadron, had notable views about the place at the time: 'This is a hell of a hole, much dispersed and a cold northerly wind blows all the time. We are in huts a long way from the mess and very browned off.'

Dunino, which had been taken over by the Royal Navy six months prior to Roy's posting, was not far from his old haunt at Leuchars and was a satellite to the adjacent training aerodrome at Crail where 827 Squadron did much of their flying.

Splash Carver recollected:

> Roy was the CO of one of the first Barracuda squadrons. The fact that he was filling such a post, as an acting lieutenant commander when he can't have been out of his twenties, is a great tribute to his determination, skill and leadership.

Roy was to join a squadron which already had a number of respected aviators, not least Lt Kevin Gibney, a young Irishman who was senior observer. Kevin had originally been in 812 Squadron at North Coates and had served in the Western Desert campaigns of Egypt and Libya in 1941. There was also CPO 'Ginger' Topliss who was senior TAG and NCO. Topliss was a real squadron character who got to know Roy very well. 'I flew with him many times in the Barra as his telegraphist air gunner. I was known as "Red" or "Ginger" Topless because of my hair colour.'

At the time of Roy's arrival, morale in the squadron was very low. In the previous two months the squadron had suffered three fatal flying accidents, losing six aircrew. The most recent accident, which occurred ten days before Roy's appointment, saw the loss of the squadron's experienced senior pilot, Lt Robert 'Jock' Smith.

Support from the senior officers was insufficient as Leading Airman Sawyer recollected: 'During the period of losses, the captain of Crail who was learning the elements of flying in a Tiger Moth, came to address aircrew at Dunino and informed us that we didn't know how to fly the aircraft!'

The flying accidents and prangs had occurred in the Barracuda aircraft during weapons trials and particularly during diving manoeuvres.

To assist Roy in raising morale another experienced pilot, Lt E.S. Linstead, was appointed on 1 July. Straight away he found fault with both the airfield and the aircraft:

Dunino was a grass airfield with a central rise so that no matter from which direction the approach was made, the aircraft initially landed uphill and then ended in a downhill braking. The pilots and observers were mainly directly from training, or had been Swordfish and or Albacore crews with other squadrons, the important point being that no pilot other than myself and Baker-Falkner had ever flown, to my knowledge, a single-wing aircraft outside of training.

My involvement was meant to be of assistance to the CO in helping these biplane pilots to come to grips with a very demanding and unusual aircraft, in that it was grossly underpowered, and under-controlled especially as regards the rudder – however this situation was not communicated to the powers that be.

Roy had an extremely difficult job in trying not only to introduce an aircraft which was totally different to any in service but to also cope with an airfield which was a 'disgrace' for such an enterprise.

Linstead continued:

Due to the factors involved, the squadron had suffered much more than the average training losses of crews and aircraft.

Morale was also being investigated by Surgeon Cdr Steele-Perkins who was described as the Twitch-Doctor by aircrew.

The Barracuda had become the object of much derision as indicated by a poem penned by Roy into a Wren's scrapbook:

That Thing

Why should the unoffending sky,
Be tainted and corrupted by
This product of a twisted brain,
That's aeronautically insane
This vile and hideous abortion,
Devoid of beauty and proportion,
That people call the 'Barracuda'
Whose form is infinitely cruder,
Than any other scheme or plan
As yet conceived by mind of man.
To see it stagger into space
Would bring a blush upon the face,
Of the most hardened Pharisee,
Within the aircraft industry.

256

But I suggest we don't decry
This winged horror of the sky,
But keep it till the war is won
And then we'll all join in the fun,
Festoon its wings with fairy lights
And wheel it out on gala nights,
And so help to dispel the rumour.

Roy's first task was to try and restore faith in the flying attributes of the Barracuda and he began by giving a demonstration flight. Linstead explained:

In order to give the pilots confidence, Lt Cdr Baker-Falkner demonstrated the aircraft to the maximum of its ability, including slow rolls over the airfield carrying a torpedo, slow flying and dive-bombing runs, and in doing so showed the excellence of his piloting abilities, enthusiasm and leadership in the most discouraging circumstances.

New Zealander Sub Lt Derek Moore remembered:

Baker-Falkner joined us at Dunino as did a flying psychologist. To begin with B-F just explained the problem and we went up skywards playing Chase-Me-Charlie in and around the clouds. He explained that the crashes occurred in the final stage of the dive when we returned 'in' to attack the target. Up to that time, the drill had been to dive with brakes at over 300 knots – pull out and turn and raise brakes in quick succession.

On 11 July, the squadron took part in a training exercise known as the 'Shattock Shambles' which involved all the Barracudas. This was a tactic devised by a fellow named Shattock in which all the aircraft attacked at the same time, all from different directions. The aim was that in combat, this avoided a concentration of defensive fire and meant that whichever way the target turned there would be torpedoes coming at it from the side. A nasty snag was that, after dropping, each aircraft was flying towards half a dozen others, some still flying straight and level before dropping. The aim then was to turn away so that they were flying on the opposite course to the target, thus opening the range as fast as possible.

Lt Emerson, who had been newly appointed senior pilot, was anticipating radical changes in the squadron with the appointment of Roy as their CO. He wrote at the time:

Still at Dunino. Lots of changes though. Smith crashed in June. I was made senior pilot. Put in for ten days leave and got it. Connie managed time off at the same time & we went to Thirsk together. Bailey has been replaced by Lt Cdr Baker-Falkner as CO. He is a very fine chap & makes a great CO, much respected by the men. Everything was going fine.

New blood was also coming into the squadron; two of the first included Sub Lt Ian Robertson and, from Canada, Lt Tom Darling RCN. Robertson recalled: 'I first met RBF [Roy] at the little airfield at Dunino. I was joining 827 on the same day as RBF and recall sitting with him on the ground at Dunino.'

Roy explained to him that: '827 Squadron had suffered a lot of casualties at the hands of the Barracuda – a high winged monoplane – because the pilots, ex Swordfish and

Albacore, were not experienced in the different techniques of piloting required.'

Robertson had done a Master [monoplane] conversion course and had flown Lysanders at Arbroath but had not yet flown a Barracuda II. He was assessed within the week 'Under RBF's briefing I see that on July 5th 1943 I made my first solo in a Barracuda II. I see RBF signed my cockpit drill certificate.'

An increasing number of pilots and aircrew were now volunteers – 'Wavy Navy' – Royal Naval Volunteer Reserve (RNVR) officers. Many had been trained in Canada or the United States and came from far away dominions or colonies, mostly from Australia and New Zealand.

Tom Darling was from Toronto in Ontario. He recollected that as Roy also came from Canada he got on particularly well with the Canucks and other overseas crews: 'I had great admiration and liking for Roy B-F. He always joked about being a "colonial". I know he spent his boyhood in Victoria and went to school there.'

Jeff Gledhill added:

Roy B-F was a very good leader and a very human and understanding person. He took command of 827 Squadron when the previous CO and most of the aircrew had either done a very long time in the squadron or had lost faith in the Barracuda as a result of all the crashes, which had no explanation. B-F had the task of trying to identify the cause of the aircraft crashes and to mould a virtually new squadron.

From the lower rank perspective, Sawyer recalled:

My impression of B-F, I see him as a tall man, a man with definite style. A sort of Lord Louis Mountbatten kind of naval officer, who wore his cap at just a slight angle and from whom you could expect a ready smile rather than a scowl.

After two weeks of assessing the flying skills of the pilots and the reliability of the aircraft, Roy led one of the first squadron formation flights. Senior Observer Kevin Gibney and Leading Airman Sawyer flew with him in 'M for Mother'.

They flew to Crail for ALTs with the station instructors. Roy was deep in concentration at the time and Sawyer recollected the flight with him: 'About the only words he would have addressed to me would have been "Are you secure in the back? Right, let's go then". But I took to the man! I liked him.'

Roy organised intensive flight exercises for the whole squadron almost every day, focusing on formations, intensive torpedo attack and dive-bombing.

Then disaster struck again on 14 July when another aircraft was lost, killing Sub Lt Neville Eaton RNZNVR. He was buried in Crail cemetery. It was difficult for Roy to write to the next of kin. With a heavy heart, and whilst characteristically biting his bottom lip in deep concentration, he wrote the letter of condolence to Eaton's parents in Wellington, New Zealand. That evening, fellow New Zealander, Emerson, described the mood of the squadron:

Eaton crashed during live bombing. Twitch is about again. Mike & Andrew & Hutch have had it, & several others are likely to go. I expect radical changes soon, and lots of new blood. Will be here another six weeks or so. Hope to get leave to marry soon.

Roy ordered immediate changes in the way the Barracuda was flown.

Jeff Gledhill recollected:

> Baker-Falkner decided that dive brakes would no longer be used and particular care should be taken to watch turn and bank indicators to ensure that during a dive no skid developed whatsoever. Aileron turns would be used at the bottom of the dive instead of the usual turn on to target bearing.
>
> It was clear that the aircraft had characteristics which in certain conditions could cause catastrophic loss. However, Baker-Falkner's decisions on handling techniques eliminated further casualties in 827 during diving manoeuvres.

PO Norman Austin who was to become armourer for Roy's aircraft recalled another alteration:

> Baker-Falkner soon discovered that the engines of the Mark 1s were not powerful enough to carry out evasive action with the dummy torpedo still attached. Eventually we received a batch of Mark 2s with Merlin 32 engines, things then improved and we finished the programme with no further loss.

Once Roy had addressed the technical problems, he then launched into improving the mood in the squadron, and assessing the flying skills of each of his pilots. By doing so, he could start the process of replacing the squadron with new and refreshed aircrew.

The squadron line book – an informal, often satirical, record of events recorded by the aircrew – commented:

> ...the 'High Ups' considered the squadron should be almost completely reformed.
>
> When the axe eventually fell the only heads left unsevered were the CO, Lts Gibney, Emerson, Kirby, Yorke, Sub Lts Collett, Jamieson, George, Moore, Gledhill, and Parker.
>
> It was decided to form a 'Twitch-Proof' Club of people who were in the squadron when it first flew in Barracudas until after the re-formation.

Roy was made an honorary member.

CPO Topliss remained part of the squadron and played an important roll in maintaining confidence in the non-commissioned squadron members. His wife, Anne, who was then a young Portsmouth Naval Wren recalled:

> Ginger adored Baker-Falkner and always kept the morale high of the squadron. He was on the entertainment side of things, on one occasion he played a fairy in front of the King of Norway. He was always full of nonsense.

Roy's replacement pilots in the reformed squadron were selected on the basis of having been trained on the latest monoplanes as opposed to the more antiquated biplanes.

Towards the end of the month, aircraft manufacturer representatives from Fairey Aviation visited Dunino and test flew with Roy.

At the beginning of August, further incoming crew replacements included Sub Lt George Green. 'Duff Gen' was a bright and enthusiastic, likeable young man, so called because he was rather quick off the mark with optimistic and wild rumours about what was going on in the war.

Roy was delighted when he learnt that Naomi and Carole were coming up to Dunino. Naomi worshipped Roy and every reunion meant so much to her that she could hardly bear to contemplate leaving him: 'In many ways the best moments were just before I met Roy because I then knew I had not yet spent any of the precious minutes with him...'.

A transfer back to sea was inevitable. The squadron morale and skills had improved such that it was working up to operational standard and would soon be ready for combat operations. Emerson wrote in his diary:

> August 10. Big changes made. 14 of the Boys have had their draft chits. All the doubtful ones are gone. Only Collett, Yorke, Jamieson, George, Pethick, Colin, Moore, Gledhill, CO and self left. All the rest are new, and everything is going fine. There is a great spirit among the troops and nothing can stop us. Serviceability is much improved, and we have stopped going to Crail for torpedo work. I did a ground loop today.

On 12 August, Roy and 827 Squadron left the relative quiet of Dunino and flew their aircraft the two-hour journey westwards to the new RN air station at Machrihanish, HMS *Landrail*, in preparation for aircraft carrier training. The air station had grown enormously since Roy had last been stationed in this part of Scotland. The squadron members were to be lodged in Nissen huts away from the main buildings, in what was nicknamed 'Nissen City'.

Once installed, training began in earnest. Some of the New Zealanders had not experienced landing on a carrier so scheduled ADDL exercises and then actual deck landings were to be carried out on HMS *Furious* in the Clyde.

Naomi had to remain alone at Dunino and was almost distraught. She wrote to her brother Bill:

> 20 August. I'm up in Scotland at the moment, had just got up here when Roy got moved to the other side and now I'm stuck here till Roy can find me a room of some description – it's just infuriating to think I can't be with him because I'm stuck for accommodation – it's quite hopeless to get anywhere during August and September on the coast of Scotland. Roy embarks very soon so I feel almost desperate to have the last week or two with him.

Roy was back in familiar territory on returning to Machrihanish – known as 'Mac' to aircrew – with memories of its open and wild countryside. He felt it was aeons ago when he was last stationed there back in 1941 with 812 Squadron. Back then he had enjoyed walks on the sandy beach in the company of the squadron mascot – his Alsatian dog, Rex. Times were now so different with squadron responsibilities weighing heavily on his shoulders.

In a previous letter to Naomi he had described the local scenery: 'A lovely great sandy beach and rollers. And then behind us quite high hills.' One of Roy's first priorities was to find accommodation for Naomi and little Carole. After much searching, he eventually succeeded in acquiring rooms in Machrihanish village for no more than a couple of weeks.

Naomi met some of Roy's friends, including Kevin Gibney, who she thought was kind and softly spoken with his mild Irish lilt. In her turn, she made quite an impression on the young flyers. Tom Darling described her as 'very quiet and attractive with blonde/golden hair and complexion'. Jeff Gledhill called her 'a very beautiful lady'.

All too soon Roy and Naomi's time together was at an end as it looked as if he would soon be off to sea. There was no prospect of their being together in the foreseeable future for more than a few days at a time. With nowhere to stay near Roy, Naomi was forced to head back to her aunt's house at Bradford. Roy would not have had much time for relaxed family life anyway, as the squadron entered an intensive work-up programme, including night flying. Roy's usual aircrew were Gibney and CPO Topliss and the majority of the flights went without any mishaps; however on one occasion there was a dramatic incident in his aircraft when the ASV radar unit caught fire. He, however, managed to land the Barracuda and the crew all escaped without any further worries.

Exercises continued unabated, including night flights dropping aerial flares, and exercises over the sea. This experience was to form an invaluable contribution to a revised guard book of Naval Air Fighting Instructions in the foreseeable future.

Squadron pilot Clifford Lock recalled:

> The Barra had some unusual flying characteristics over the sea – a normal procedure for us much of the time – and we were used to a very stable aircraft. It was to loop and roll occasionally if no one was looking, and could dive vertically if necessary – and was a good deck-landing aircraft.

Four squadrons were based at Machrihanish. Among Roy's colleagues now were Lt Cdr F.H. 'Baldy' Fox, CO of 830 Squadron, which was ultimately to come under Roy's command. He had family near to Roy's parents in Devon so they had got to know each other well.

Emerson wrote in his diary:

> August 30th. We moved to Machrihanish on the 12th, for Wing Training. 4 Barra squads here. Got a week's leave, and Connie and I were married quietly on the 16th. Jeff and Topsy were Best Man and Maid. Then back to work. Bags of night flying here, no rest at all. We all average over 2 hours per day. We are definitely the top squad here. The CO has all the drill on tactics, consumptions etc. He is also keen on sport, and we are getting in lots of deck-hockey, squash, badminton, tennis and footy.

Allan Thomson, 830 Squadron TAG, recalled the heavy workload of the time:

> Much and continual work seemed to be the most noticeable thing at Mac. We were kept at it. Sometimes near 50 per cent of aircrew were in sick bay – colds etc and with 12 aircraft to man those who remained fit had plenty to do. My own pilot was grounded with raging T/B. Perhaps an indication of the strain of dive-bombing practice.
>
> Because of the dive-bombing element in the flying, involving a rapid pressure change of anything up to 10,000 feet (average say 6,000) then even a heavy cold was enough to take flying personnel off flying duties.
>
> One incident at Mac. There was a Barracuda lost from some other unit stationed at Mac. We were airborne on search till 2 am. In the air again by 6 am credited with a night's sleep between what? 3 am and 5 am? Don't mind when there's a purpose. But it gives an indication of how the pressure was kept up.

Roy resumed his letter writing to Naomi. The months of intensive training of the young aircrews, and hard work was beginning to take its toll on him: 'I'm just waiting to go night flying again now. Too strenuous this, but interesting.'

Internationally, the tide of the war was turning as the British 8th Army landed in southern mainland Italy on 3 September. Among the invading forces was Roy's younger brother, Captain Harry Baker-Falkner, although Roy did not know he was involved at the time.

In Roy's next letter he wrote:

Friday. What price the news today? Moving again which is something in the right direction. But when is the b... thing going to end so we can be together again just the three of us. I'm still tired after last night and today's efforts. What a life, just on and on and on it seems to me, no breaks and no comforts and no my three.

Two weeks after moving to Machrihanish, Roy got into trouble with his superiors following a letter of complaint from squadron members about the quality of food being served at the air station.

Derek Moore admitted it was his fault:

Whilst back at Dunino we had run the mess ourselves. One member did the work and what with our allowances and rations and imagination – we ate very well. At Machrihanish the food was ghastly and very expensive. It was run by the commander who lived out.

He continued:

Some of us and I must own up to being a ring leader – suggested a mess meeting – since a naval mess is supposed to be democratic – eventually a round robin was resorted to with signatures from almost all the four squadrons. It was presented, I believe to the captain by Baker-Falkner who, I'm sorry to say, got severely reprimanded with almost Bligh'ish calls of mutiny etc. I think B-F was hesitant about presenting it but we urged him to. I was very sorry the way it turned out. But he did it and took the can for us.

To the squadron, Roy outwardly appeared unfazed by the reprimand. However, he may have taken the criticism to heart as indicated by an unusually gloomy letter to Naomi.

Friday: Yet another letter to you today but I feel so low and so old. I called at a house today for rooms and a young well-educated man in plain clothes answered the door and immediately started calling me 'Sir'. I felt, oh so ancient, and then just before that I asked a youngster the way and he said 'To the right, sir'.

Darling Billy I am so much older and it's awful. My lovely old wife is such a babe compared to me and all the weight on me at the moment, wet nursing isn't in it. I can neglect my own pity and have to deal with everyone else. It's almost too much as everyone is so ignorant and incompetent. Don't I sound smug, darling but I'm afraid that I've tremendously got that impression. Thank God for my three darlings.

I'm awfully sorry but I have only got you and I'm too old for everyone else including people miles senior and older than I am. They just haven't a clue. So please bear with me when I'm not quite as cheerful as I might be.

Another reason for his depression was exhaustion from night flying. A further letter in the same envelope said: 'Written after night flying. I guess I'm rather tired and have been plugging away rather a long time without leave.'

Roy had come a long way since he first joined the Fleet Air Arm but the intervening years had seen the loss of so many friends. There were few people he could turn to share his experiences and he was feeling the weight of responsibility for the young men who now made up his squadron.

However depressed Roy might be, he was transforming his squadron into a first class fighting unit and his men knew it. Derek Moore commented:

I greatly admired him. In fact for some of us he was the tops – someone we dangerously hero worshipped.

Under Baker F we became a proud bunch. *Esprit de corps* shot up. Our confidence was restored in the aircraft (I always liked it) and we were knit together into a grand team. I can safely say I felt stimulated by the presence of B-F.

He brought out the best in all of us. He was a great leader – dignified but comradely – indeed good company. He took flying seriously – we all did – but could make his machine really perform. As I recall he would listen to your stories with interest and give encouragement when needed. He was not afraid to take on his superiors in our interest.

Ian Robertson, who was later to become an admiral, said:

RBF was a very respected senior pilot with much experience of flying. I admired him enormously and count him one of the four men who have made an impact on my life. At the time I 'worshipped' him for being an RN officer and a 'natural' pilot. I had to work awfully hard at my flying all my career!

Clifford Lock commented:

Lt Cdr Roy Baker-Falkner, we called him Sir to his face, B-F or Daddy between ourselves, was immensely popular. He was a friendly, calm, authoritative father figure to us young and inexperienced RNVR people.

Into September, intensive training, night navexs, or naval exercises, and bombing exercises continued. There was even a 'strike' on the escort carrier HMS *Tracker* and bombing on towed targets at sea.

Roy was delighted to meet and start liaising with Lumley Lyster, his former skipper on *Glorious,* who was by this time a full blown vice admiral, and Flag Officer Carrier Training and Administration. He wrote on 5 September about this meeting to Naomi who had last seen Lyster in Alexandria before the war: 'I saw Lyster today. He hasn't changed at all except for more and more gongs and gold braid. He was looking very well.'

Lyster had previously informed Roy that he was to put in a lot of time to re-write the handbook or bible of the Fleet Air Arm – the Guard book for Naval Air Fighting Instructions (AFIs). This was effectively the King's Regulations and Admiralty Instructions for operating the Fleet Air Arm throughout the world. He had indicated that Roy would be expected to test and apply the instructions practically, both in training exercises and in multi-aircraft carrier operations against enemy targets. Roy had already been implementing and testing many of these navexs with the squadron and in cooperation with the other squadrons on the air station.

Lyster had gone on to explain that the existing Admiralty policy was hopelessly out of date given the advancements and increased complexity in the Fleet Air Arm since the instructions were last drafted earlier in the war. Larger aircraft carriers with greater aircraft capacity were becoming available, with the ability to fly off more, newer and faster aircraft, all of which provided opportunities to restructure and develop new strategies, and reconstruct Squadron and Wing tactics.

He informed Roy that there were few officers in the Fleet Air Arm who had the range and breadth of expertise to achieve the job and he had every confidence in him to carry it out. He reminded Roy that the final product as Confidential Admiralty Fleet Orders (CAFO) would be circulated and lodged not only at the Admiralty, but in *all* Fleet Air Arm establishments and aircraft carriers.

Tellingly, he also indicated that revising and updating Naval Air Fighting Instructions was an absolute requirement with the imminent invasion in Europe and bringing the fight to the Japanese in the Pacific.

Roy stood carefully considering the matter, biting his bottom lip, a sure sign that he was concentrating hard on what Lyster was saying. Roy's immediate reaction was to be daunted, but it was a task for which he knew he was entirely competent, and that he could build on his experience as an operational pilot, instructor and test pilot. Some of his doubts and frustrations came through in his letters back home but he never uttered a word about the real reason.

Roy's first task was return to his squadron and to settle down and carefully review all the existing documentation and then to formulate new instructions. Detailed chapters were to include the following:

Guard Book for Naval Air Fighting instructions

Part I.	Instructions to Reconnaissance Aircraft;
Part II.	Air Attack Instructions;
Part III.	Instructions for the Employment and Direction of Fighter Aircraft;
Part IV.	Higher Tactics by day;
Part V.	Higher Tactics by night;
Part VI.	Defensive Fighting Tactics;
Part VII.	Instructions to Spotting Aircraft;
Part VIII.	Instructions for Operating Aircraft Formations from Aircraft Carriers in Company.

It contained everything from procedures for pre-flight briefings, to aerial evasion and attack tactics for fighter and bomber aircraft.

Roy spent many a long hour revising the plans, whilst the squadron were resting, on exercises or out training. Kevin Gibney soon became an important assistant in the task, not only providing the additional 'observer' perspective but also by bringing in his many years of experience. Together they worked out squadron and wing tactics and put them to practical test in many exercises with 827 and later 830 Squadrons. The results became the instructions 'Air Attack Instructions; Higher Tactics by day and night; Defensive Fighting Tactics and Instructions for operating aircraft formations from Aircraft Carriers Company.' They had to completely re-write sub-section in Part VIII including on 'Aircraft instructions for formation flying from aircraft carriers at night and day' and the important sub-section on 'Instructions for the conduct of striking forces from aircraft carriers'.

Next on their list was the important section on 'Instructions for the conduct of striking forces from aircraft carriers'. The depth of instructions were required to a fundamental level such as the following:

> The Striking Force Leader should be ranged as the leading aircraft on deck. Although not essential, it will facilitate the forming up of the force if the aircraft are ranged in the order they will subsequently fly.
>
> Each sub-flight is given a forming up height, intervals of 500 ft being allowed between sub-flights if the cloud base permits. The striking Force Leader's sub-flight should be the lowest and the rear sub-flight the highest.

Roy and Kevin then went on to write:

> When the Strike Force Leader is satisfied that the force is ready he should take departure over the flame float marker....The importance of accurate navigation should be stressed. It is of great help to the rest of the formation if the leader passes back from time to time the course he is actually steering.

Roy and Kevin carefully sketched out the carrier waiting and circling positions – line abreast, line ahead, and at night with circles depicting aircraft around flame floats.

Roy totally rewrote Part VI Defensive Fighting Tactics. Sections were varied and included:

> Principles of evasive tactics, general instructions, characteristics of Naval TB and TB aircraft in air combat, Tactics of the gun, Evasive procedures for naval aircraft other than fighters, organisation in the air, escort by fighters, evading attack by night fighters, and avoiding gunfire and searchlights.

It started with:

> The following instructions have been framed upon the fact that it is the function of TBR aircraft to deliver a concerted and co-ordinated attack rather than shoot down fighters. The principles of evasive tactics are – a thorough appreciation of the fighter's problems and limitations, together with a knowledge of the characteristics of our own aircraft and limitations of their armament is essential. The object is to make things as difficult as possible for the fighter.

Roy and Kevin further practically tested their draft instructions on the Fleet Air Arm squadrons on the air station. These included a combined fighter evasion exercise in company with 801 Seafire Squadron, from *Furious* against the sloop *Londonderry* in the Clyde.

Recognising the larger number of squadrons and aircraft available to the Fleet Air Arm at this stage of the war, in comparison with the miniscule number in the dark days of 1940, Roy wrote:

> If the striking force is six to eight squadrons or larger, considerations should be given as to dividing the force so as to divide the enemy's defences. If this is done, each group should contain all the elements of attack ie dive-bomber, torpedo aircraft etc.

Again, much time was spent writing in minute detail the various evasion techniques, based on their own experiences and that of others. The chapter ended with a whole series of drawings showing the various flight formations and evasion techniques which had largely been practically tested with No. 8 Wing.

Next for Roy and Kevin to tackle were the Air Attack Instructions, with sections on standard methods of torpedo attack by day, to types of bombing attack, including probability of hitting, perforation of armour, dive and glide bombing, and low-level bombing, attack on submarines, minelaying and attack on harbours.

Roy and Kevin went into detail about the role of the new structure of naval air wings, led by the strike leader, with the instructions to the air striking force stating:

The Admiral or Senior Officer aircraft carriers, will indicate the policy for the guidance of the Striking Force Leader, before the air striking force is briefed. Instructions for flying-off and forming up are given in Admiralty letters. The Striking Force Leader should order the attack and squadrons will then be led in independently.

INSTRUCTIONS FOR THE CONDUCT OF THE ATTACK

The Striking Force Leader should indicate at the briefing the general direction in which he intends to retire and reform. On return, the Striking Force Leader must report that the attack has taken place and the estimated number of hits.

The last major chapter to be reviewed and re-written was on 'Instructions for Operating Aircraft Formations from Aircraft Carriers in Company', with sections on launching and landing-on of day escort strikes, forming up procedure, launching and landing-on of night strikes, return to the carrier and aircraft carrier flying signals. This final chapter was to be practically implemented by Roy and his men during operational flights in the Arctic over the coming months.

After many weeks of writing, consultation with fellow officers, and practical exercises, at last Roy and Kevin were confident to submit the completed document to Lyster and the Naval Air Warfare and Flying Training Division. After a round of meetings and conferences with 'High ups' as Roy called them, it was approved by the Admiralty and signed off by H.V. Markham, hurriedly copied and circulated throughout the Fleet Air Arm. It was implemented immediately and was to stand as a legacy for Roy and his expertise in the Fleet Air Arm, played an important role in the forthcoming invasion of Europe and in the Pacific, and was used until at least into the 1950s. In some cases a few instructions drafted by Roy were still active Fleet Air Arm policy well beyond that period.

It was a valuable document to be copied to 'all Flag officers, captains, commanders, and commanding officers of HM Ships and vessels concerned.' Printed on each and every copy were the words: 'This Order is to be kept locked up when not in use. When necessary to dispose of it abroad it should be destroyed by fire.'

Roy was about to meet up with another name from the past, Cdr 'Monkey' Bryant, who had been station commander at Machrihanish when Roy was posted there in 1941. He wrote to Naomi: '7 September. Darling I expect to see Monkey Bryant in the near future. It'll be nice seeing him again. He's a Commander Flying.' Soon afterwards Roy flew his Barracuda from Machrihanish and landed on board HMS *Furious*, batted down by Bryant – so commenced a series of deck landings to test the Barracuda's qualities and train *Furious*'s deck-landing crew. He then flew that evening back to Machrihanish.

'Written Wednesday. I did three landings today for Monkey's edification and expect to see him again very shortly.' Roy had obviously recovered his usual buoyant self and wrote the next day about his squadron's co-ordination with 830 Squadron: 'Sat 10 September. We are still progressing most magnificently as regards the squadron and also mixing beautifully with Fox.'

The squadron was still involved in intense flight training and practice including bombing towed targets – it was all part of the practical testing of the revised Naval Air Fighting Instructions, but secret plans were obviously brewing somewhere in the Admiralty and kept the squadron aircrew guessing.

Roy wrote:

9 September. Night flying again tonight. I shall be tired as usual I suppose. I must admit that we are not wasting much time. I said that we would work. We certainly are. I am so sorry I wrote those so depressed letters to you. Poor darling, as if you hadn't got enough without me.

Roy was intensely proud of the young men under his command and subsequently wrote: 'Everything has gone very successfully in the last couple of days. All my boys have passed their landings OK.'

More and more rumours floated around as to what would be expected of the squadron when it joined the Fleet and it was imperative that pilots and observers were as ready as possible for battle. Training was still not without mishap but no longer fatal.

Derek Moore recalled:

Off Machrihanish our aircraft was involved in a mid-air bump while formation flying over the sea. The other Barracuda's wing tip smashed down on top of our rudder. What is a wing tip? Something of not much consequence. The damage to our tailplane was almost critical, the cantilevered top part of the rudder was bashed down on to the fixed part of the fin. The rudder could only be moved from one side to the other with great difficulty.

Emerson wrote on 20 September:

Go aboard the *Furious* next month with 830 Squad. Expect embarkation leave. *Furibox* has been doing a re-fit, & will have a Spit Squad aboard also. Looks like cold waters for us. We are reduced to 9 a/c. ..... Serviceability much improved. Stores position still poor. Bags and bags of night flying. I now have over 200 Barra hours. 180 day & 20 night.

Roy felt team spirit in the squadron was important and played rugger whenever he could. He also wrote on 20 September, though he made no mention of the Barracuda aircraft training to Naomi:

Like a sucker I played rugger for the squadron again tonight and as a result I am so sore and stiff that I can hardly move. Sheer agony. We are as a matter of fact top squadron at rugger. We have beaten everyone else so far fairly convincingly. I play as and when circumstances permit.

On 22 September came the amazing news that the German battleship *Tirpitz* had been badly damaged by British midget submarines in a daring raid. A newspaper reported:

At 8.12 this morning Germany's biggest battleship, the 46,000-ton *Tirpitz*, was blown up by British midget submarines. The blast lifted the ship, moored in Altenfiord, in northern Norway, several feet out of the water, disabled her three main engines and left her with a 15-degree list. Repairs could take over six months.

The attack was an amazingly heroic feat and was to have an immediate effect on Roy's squadron. The line book recorded: 'September 24 – October 4. The whole squadron went on leave on 24 hours' notice.'

There was major work ahead for 827 Squadron but now a brief respite meant Roy could at long last meet Naomi in London after weeks and weeks of uncertainty. The journey down from Scotland to London was long and tiring. With the pressure of work, Roy was exhausted but delighted to see his dear wife and cuddle little Carole. 'How much she has grown!' he exclaimed when he first saw her again.

He and Naomi, together with Carole, stayed as usual at the Berners Hotel, near Oxford Street. By now there were fewer air raids in London and the metropolis was bustling with servicemen of all nationalities. London was in ruins after the recent blitz bombings but life still carried on – the theatres and concert halls were beginning to open up again to entertain the troops and Londoners alike.

During his leave, Roy went with Naomi and Carole to the Queen's Club, where in earlier days they had played lawn tennis and dined in its elegant restaurant. They also visited Roy's sister Leslie who was in digs in South Kensington whilst continuing her studies at the Royal College of Music.

In the break, he was ordered to visit Admiralty House and was briefed about his forthcoming new position to implement the Naval Air Fighting Instructions through the setting up of a naval air wing, a new concept for the Fleet Air Arm. His rewritten Defensive Fighting Tactics with his subsequent additions was printed on 7 October 1943, the week of his return to Scotland.

Leave was over all too soon and Roy and the squadron were back in Machrihanish.

While 827 Squadron was on leave, 832 Squadron and its CO, Frank Low, arrived in Machrihanish. Low was another old colleague of Roy's from the 812 Squadron days – so it was a pleasant surprise for Roy on his return.

Two days after leave ended, on 6 October, Roy embarked on HMS *Furious*, or the *Furibox* as she was still affectionately called. Her commanding officer was now Capt. George T. Philip who Roy knew from when he was in command of HMS *Argus*.

For Roy it was the first time he had been at sea since the Petsamo raid from HMS *Furious* two years previously. The old 'Box' had changed since Roy's day.

Allan Thomson of 830 squadron recalled:

The story of *Furious*, how she grew like 'Topsy' and finally became one, is a tale of improvisation. Her final shape was unique though her sister ships *Glorious* and *Courageous* were fairly similar. The deck was most unusual. A flat platform aft giving adequate space to range nine Barracudas; sloped down, by about 2 feet, to a long flat waist with the two a/c lifts one forward and one aft. The flight deck sloped up again and under this at its foremost part there was the ship's bridge. Catapults and a screen which could be erected as a wind break – there was no crash barrier – were fitted on this forward part of the flight deck. The deck was almost a 'flush' deck but on the starboard side near the forward lift there was a small deckhouse which housed the a/c tractor and sheltered the asbestos clad stoker who stood by on crash duty.

Thomson continued:

> The ship was riveted not welded and when she made a tight turn into wind at high
> speed the deck plates aft in the upper hangar vibrated by a good 6 inches.
>   There were pom poms at each end of the shelter. There were only four arrester
> wires aft on the waist section and on either side aft by the round down, were the
> gratings to allow fumes etc to escape from engine room. Twenty-seven Seafires
> were stowed in the wider upper hangar. The lower hangar was narrower because she
> still carried her original side armour on what had been the main deck when she was
> a battle cruiser. The hangar narrowed in amidships and that part accommodated four
> Martlets (Wildcats) with nine Barracudas in front of them and nine more behind.

Initially, Roy had to share a cabin. He wrote to Naomi: 'I hope to get a cabin to myself very
shortly and then I can put up all my pictures in all their glory. At the moment I've only got
your two and four snaps.'
    The squadron line book recorded on 7 October: 'Certain sadistic "Os" were heard to
remark something about Grim Menace Ahead. Won't they ever have faith in their own
navigation?'
    Almost a week later, a further entry in the line book stated:

> Nine pilots and various gash hands gathered up the pieces and shook Machrijohnson
> mud off their wheels for good an' all. Landing on was uneventful except for the
> excessive zeal of one hardy Scot, who thought he could see the wardroom bar better
> by putting one wheel over the side.

The entry continued: 'Off the beach: 827 gets its third carrier' and featured a cartoon headed
'Flying on the *Furious*'.
    A new ditty, to the tune of 'Lambeth Walk', quickly became 827 Squadron's theme
song:

Land On Crawl
Any night on FURIOUS
If you're rather curious
You'll see them all
Doing the land-on stall.
'Bats' is stood there – all lit up,
Hoping the engines don't go 'phut',
'Hang on the prop'
Don't let the darned thing drop'.
Down go the bats – go lower,
Over the Round-down – slower,
On to the wires – no more
Flying – sighing.
Over the hill and down the lift
Into the hangar – it's a gift.
You've seen them all
Doing the land-on stall.
When the lift has made the grade

You are sure to feel afraid,
You'll see us all,
Doing the flight deck crawl.
If we jay walk on the deck
We will break our ruddy neck,
Slip stream and sound
And all the props go round.
Watch where you move – go slower
Look out! – you must bend lower,
One little slip – no more
Blighty – Crikey!
And when the last machine's flown off
Thankful we stand there out of puff,
You've seen us all
Doing the flight deck crawl.

Emerson was not as enamoured as Roy to be on board *Furious*:

> Monday Oct. 11th. We have night flown on some horrible nights, and the other squadrons have had six put down in different drones about Scotland. All lost. All four Barra squadrons have had their share of prangs.
>
> We did 6 deck landings each on *Furious* in the 8th and flown aboard on the 10th. Thee deck prangs so far – none serious.
>
> We go out & exercise each day, & anchor off Gourock each night.
>
> The *Furious* is a very old and dirty ship, also very small, much too small for Barras. Landing on is OK but hangar & stores spaces etc are very cramped. The Squad ratings have to sleep in the hangar etc – a very poor arrangement – still we will manage.

Roy's operational training of the Barracuda squadrons on board the Fleet carrier began in earnest as he wrote on 13 October: 'My poor feet – I've walked so many miles on steel decks my Billy girl that my feet are growing armour plated soles and am undergoing terrible hardships.'

He allowed himself a rare pat on the back about his and fellow test pilots skills but was just as pleased with his squadron: 'Tiffy [Torrens-Spence] and Stacey [Stacey Colls, formerly of Boscombe Down] are still the best plus me. We are coping very well indeed and my young are indeed first class. Thank you again for a magnificent leave, Billy.'

The next day he wrote again:

> Thursday. I have been very pleased with my young during the last few days. They have coped and settled down most magnificently for which I certainly am thankful. Everyone on board seemed to be in the old ship's style, very nice indeed and very helpful. I walk miles on board Billy girl; you really wouldn't recognise your husband, he moves so fast up and down and round about.

The squadron line book at this time included a cartoon of a bomb-laden Barracuda about to land on *Furious*. A naval officer on the bridge is exclaiming 'Oh Daddy!' The words underneath read: 'The CO does bomb-load trials. *Furious* had never heard of such a thing before – we hope, never again!'

270

Roy confided on 22 October:

Work is going very very satisfactorily here and Baldy Fox, you know the one Carole fell for, and I do get on so magnificently together. It's really magnificent and the skipper [Capt. Philip] is awfully pleased. The ship is extremely happy and we have got a magnificent skipper and commander so everyone is hunky dory. Tomorrow just about makes my second week without going ashore.

His senior pilot, Emerson, was also pleased with the situation and wrote in his secret diary about the same time:

Tuesday. Everything going well. We are flying all day & every day doing carrier training. Landings all going off OK. All pilots have had a dozen now. We are working in the Clyde area, down to Stranraer. We anchor off Greenock or in Lamlash every night. There are lots of carriers here. Looks like an invasion soon. Have seen *Vic, Formidable, Unicorn, Argus, Illustrious* (?), 6 Woolworth carriers & 4 Macs in the Clyde area. We are to do night deck landing this week.

By the time that working up to operational standard was completed, morale was sky high and such a contrast with the early days when Roy first joined 827 Squadron four months previously, as Tom Darling elaborated:

Suffice to say that our leader Lt Cdr Roy Baker-Falkner DSC to me exemplified the very epitome of a fine naval officer RN, in qualities, character, flying skills, and as a first class leader of his squadrons, wing and the men who served in them. He was the bravest and best.

Bill Pethick concluded:

The spirit in the squadron was always good. Our *esprit de corps* was very good. We had come through the bad patch early on, we all worked well together. We reckoned that because of the skills and experience all parts of the squadron had gained from being the first squadron ship-born, we were part of *Furious*, but loaned to the other ships to help them to learn how to handle and fly Barracudas! *Furious* was 'our' ship, excellent in every way. 827 the best squadron.

Roy had excelled at his work.

CHAPTER 21

Clyde's Own Naval Wing Leader

> The Old Order Changeth: The boss got a good report this term and becomes Head Prefect. He has been appointed Wing Commander of the TBR squadrons and is now 'Daddy of Them All'. Good luck! But we hope not goodbye!

The entry, recorded in the 827 Squadron line book on 25 October 1943, marked the appointment of Roy as one of the first-ever naval wing leaders. Scotsman Jimmy Watson, 827 Squadron pilot and the line book diarist, also pasted in a photograph of Roy's daughter Carole.

The wing was to consist of Roy's own 827 Squadron together with Baldy Fox's 830 Barracuda Squadron and be called the 8th Torpedo Bomber Reconnaissance Wing. Roy's place as Commanding Officer of 827 Squadron was taken by Kevin 'Fangless' Gibney who became the first observer CO of any Barracuda squadron. Lt (A) T.M. Townsend RNVR was to be No. 8 Wing Air Engineering Officer (AEO), to manage his magnificent 'troop' of mechanics, fitters and deck handlers, who kept the Barracudas in such splendid running order. As Allan Thomson of 830 Squadron recalled: '830 moved to Machrihanish. Shortly afterwards 827 arrived and No. 8 Wing was formed, operating as one unit. The squadrons kept their individuality, separate quarters and structures.'

Roy heard the news while on board HMS *Furious* and wrote briefly to Naomi about the appointment: 'Gibney has taken my place with an acting ersatz Lieut Commander's rank. I'm boss of both now.'

Gibney commented:

> I assumed command of 827 Squadron in October 1943 when Roy was appointed wing leader. We had been together a close unit, Roy and I – that's either life or death. By then we had become not only close colleagues but close friends.

Roy had now been on board *Furious* continuously for a fortnight and appreciated returning to the sea. Capt. George Philip was delighted for Roy on news of his appointment, and called him into his cabin to congratulate him personally. The skipper was central to making the old 'Box' a very happy ship.

The new wing's aircrews consisted of a range of characters and expertise. The men came from all walks of life and from all over the world, the majority were from the dominions and the colonies – Australia, Canada, New Zealand, South Africa, Kenya as well as the Republic of Ireland. All were young, in their late teens or early twenties. Few had flown hostile operations against the Germans; some had not even served on board ship.

There was a short spell at Machrihanish where the two squadrons were combined essentially into one fighting unit. Allan Thomson recalled:

The training was intensive and continuous with no weekend breaks. Memories are of having to contend with a lot of mud. The NAAFI van with its tea and buns the only break.

Thomson went on to illustrate just how close 827 and 830 aircraft flew to each other, with the wing of one aircraft between the wing and tail of the other:

Flying over water, west of the station, in close formation, one day with an 827 a/c. Its wing tip smashed down on the top of our fin. A wing tip hardly matters, but it was only with great difficulty our rudder could be moved from side to side. Both planes landed safely.

Roy led the entire wing for the first time in open vic formation to HMS *Furious* in the Clyde and landed on in text book fashion. Other landings were not so perfect. Norman Austin recalled:

I flew on with Lt Darling who missed the arrester wires the first attempt and managed to crash on the second, finishing up hanging over the side of the flight deck. No one ever got out the wrong side of a Barracuda quicker than me.

Allan Thomson remembered another near miss involving 830 Squadron:

I was flying with Sub Lt Clarabut known for his dash and impulsiveness. It was reckoned that if a Barracuda missed all the arrester wires (only four on *Furious*) then there would be no time to open up and go round again.

We made a good landing and should have picked up a wire. We passed the point on deck where the jolt should have come – nothing! Our deck hook jammed back up when we landed on deck. His instant reaction was to immediately bang on full throttle and with a struggle we were airborne, the aircraft just managed to gather enough speed to get airborne again over the bows. Because Machrihanish was nearby we made a safe landing there.

There had been some argument beforehand about what would happen if a Barracuda missed all four arrester wires in a landing on deck. It was reckoned that there would not be enough time and distance along the deck to get above stalling speed again. He proved it could be done – but not to be recommended – especially for anyone whose reactions were any slower than his were.

Dave Clarabut himself explained:

One snag in HMS *Furious* was that, without barriers, if you missed the arrester wires you had it, there was insufficient power in the engines despite them being the most powerful existing at that time to take off again. The first time 827/830 Squadrons landed on the carrier the batsman got the angle of approach wrong and we had a lot of accidents but none at that time fatal.

Furious, now equipped with the first Barracuda wing to go afloat, carried out a working up programme in the Clyde Estuary. The Firth of Clyde had one of the deepest sea entrance channels in northern Europe. It was very beautiful, even though it was so close to Glasgow, with wide lochs and distant views of hills and snowy mountains. The routine was to pass through the anti-sub boom at Gourock, exercise in the lower reaches and return before the boom closed in the evening.

Allan Thomson noted that after the oily and dirty waters of port it was such a difference to see clear water with phosphorescence. Ploughing through the Firth, *Furious* was often followed by harbour porpoises and even whales and basking sharks.

Roy's task was to work up the combined wing to shipborne combat operational standard as soon as possible. Reflecting about one exercise involving Barracudas in formation evading a Seafire fighter aircraft, Allan Thomson recalled:

> Shortly after take-off the attacking Seafire watched in consternation as the two Barracudas – one from each squadron – attempted a formation corkscrew evasion. Instead of corkscrewing as one unit they took opposite paths and crashed into each other.

Accidents were not confined to the inexperienced aircrew. A few days later Roy wrote to Naomi:

> Saturday: I've got no news particularly, just work and more work, of course the odd drink or two. I must say the old girl is certainly a very happy ship. One of my boys went swimming the other day. He found it very cold but otherwise OK.

Roy deliberately failed to mention to Naomi that it was actually Baldy Fox who had crashed into the sea.

Allan Thomson was at lunch at the time in the TAGs' mess:

> There was an extra loud thump on deck followed by a splash. I managed to get my head out of the porthole in time to see our CO Lt Cdr Fox, the Senior O, and CPO George Carr scrambling out of their Barracuda before it sank alongside near the stern.

Roy had already dedicated much time and effort to 827 Squadron and now focused attention on 830 Squadron and support for Baldy Fox. Dave Clarabut commented:

> Once B-F became wing leader he flew more with 830 Squadron and I later flew alongside him as his No. 2, that is in squadron formation the first aircraft on his starboard side. A great privilege to me as I was the youngest pilot of the two squadrons and the most junior.

The routine of the wing evolved as the two squadrons worked hard together to form an effective strike force involving protective fighters, and testing the newly drafted Naval Air Fighting Instructions. As Clifford Lock, an 827 Squadron pilot, pointed out:

> A mixed strike of dive-bombers and torpedo bombers could proceed in formation together, in our case in double line-ahead, to a point nearly over the target. Then as the fighters went in to cool the flak down, the dive-bombers would aim at the targets while the torpedo bombers dived to their dropping points, trying to get deployed about 1,200 yards on the target's bow – depending on its evasion action.

The line book recorded a wing exercise to carry out harbour reconnaissance photographs of Campbeltown 'flying at wave-top' – or in the case of Johnny 'down at zero'. During the autopsy, Commander (SA) was rather pointed about the height 'we took our photographs. We didn't like his tone when he said we'd probably have spent longer than we expected if it had been the real thing!'

On 18 October, Vice Admiral Lumley Lyster, now head of the Fleet Air Arm and Flag Officer Carrier Training and Administration, visited *Furious* for secret discussions on the success of the practical implementation of the Naval Air Fighting Instructions by the new naval air wing structures being established across the Fleet Air Arm. That evening 827 Squadron pilot George 'Duff' Green was detailed by Roy to fly Lyster and Lt Cdr Johnston to RAF Ayr. Green failed to report on landing and take-off, resulting in 'considerable confusion and the Admiral not met', according to the 827 Squadron line book.

Roy's next letter to Naomi showed his eagerness to get on with his new task while recognising that the protocol for dealing with admirals and other 'High Ups' was not as straightforward as was his existing experience with fellow aircrews. The letter also obliquely referred to his work on the Naval Air Fighting Instructions which he realised had to convince all concerned:

27 October. HMS *Furious*. My recent promotion appears to mean absolutely sweet FA but it will do in time when I've convinced various personnel that I do know something about the job. It's jolly nearly three weeks since I went ashore if you count that other dump [Machrihanish] as home and curiously enough I have no longing whatsoever.

At the end of October, Roy was ordered to attend a meeting at HMS *Monck*, the Royal Navy's shore base at Largs. This was the headquarters for Combined Training and its Flag Officer, Lumley Lyster.

Also at HMS *Monck* at the time was Lt Cdr Duncan Lewin, whom Roy had known back at Dartmouth and in their Leuchars days. He had gone on to command 808 and 885 Squadrons. They were now destined to work together on operation tactics in a few weeks' time.

Roy wrote:

31 October: I had to see Lyster yesterday and was then taken to his place for lunch. Mrs [Lyster] sent her regards to you and said all the nice things. She called you that very pretty girl with the lovely eyes. How right she is.

As usual Roy gave nothing away about the reason for this secret meeting.

Lyster was in command of one of forty-five separate Combined Operations establishments. The Combined Operations Command drew on the best practices and expertise from the Royal Navy, the Army and the Air Force. With Roy being summoned, there was something afoot that went well beyond normal carrier training. Roy reported to Lyster on the status and readiness of his new wing and discussed the possibilities for an operation against the enemy with dive-bombers over enemy-occupied Europe.

Roy made a further oblique reference to the Naval Air Fighting Instructions when he wrote to Naomi on 1 February 1944: 'Oh yes, a while ago I wrote some paperwork on our job and got commended for it by old Lyster.'

Meanwhile in Devon, Naomi was also busy. She had bought the couple's very first home – St George's Flats in Torquay. When Roy heard the news he wrote excitedly:

Just got your letter telling me that you've bought a flat or something. Obviously your other letters describing it have gone astray at the moment as I don't know where or what it is, but it sounds a very excellent idea and you were a very clever old thing to find it and also not to waffle but to buy straight away.

Naomi proudly wrote to her brother Bill:

I have bought quite a large house, practically opposite the golf links – it has been turned into two flats – both with separate gardens and entrances – I think it's delightful – and I consider that I've got it incredibly cheap – they asked £2,500 – and I got it for £2,000.

Back in Scotland, working up the squadrons carried on apace. Allan Thomson recalled:

On 4 November every aircraft on board the *Furious* took part in an exercise – a dummy attack on Londonderry to exercise their defences, air raid precautions etc. The weather was rough and during this one land-on, three Seafires and two Barras damaged their undercarts. Strangely enough for a long time there was no more bending of undercarts after that.

Roy still maintained close contact with Boscombe Down and Tiffy Torrens- Spence. He wrote to Naomi: '6 November: Did I tell you Tiffy got another eighteen months' seniority. I am so pleased but it ought to have been more.'

Over the next few weeks, his new work as a wing leader increasingly involved administration and staff assessment duties:

13 November: I'm absolutely worn out just doing nothing but stand round and advise and tick off and criticise for just on twelve solid hours today on deck and gosh was it cold.

Howsoever, everything is going very well and seems to be appreciated to a certain extent. I am so delighted that you are so happy in the house. Incidentally I am one of four [wing leaders] in the Navy, not bad. Our wee Winkie's sayings keep me shrieking with laughter all day. Thank you for writing them down, Billy. I love and adore you so much, my darling, and oh boy Xmas leave if we get it.

Evenings in the wardroom were a time to relax as Dave Clarabut noted:

On the social side Roy very much joined in wardroom life, always setting a very good example. He was not one of the rowdy boys but would always join in on a party and also the lower type of sing song that squadrons used to embark on from time to time.

Eddie Gale, one of the Squadron aircrew, added: 'Roy was not "gung-ho" but a quietly effective CO with a wry sense of humour.'

Roy was tiring of the war situation as shown in his next letter to Naomi: 'Monday. I do, oh, so long to finish this war and then come back to mine own. I am so delighted that I have at least got a home to come back to now anyway.'

At the end of the week after an exhausting session to revise the guard book for Naval Air Fighting Instructions he wrote:

Things are going very well up here as regards the work but I'm getting a little in need of a rest and leave. Gosh, I am looking forward to it. I'm very glad that you haven't come up here I should have seen nothing or practically nothing of you.'

Fox, whose family still lived not far from Naomi in Devon, whilst on leave hand-delivered some letters and presents to Naomi, including chocolates from Kevin Gibney for Carole. Chocolates were normally impossible to get hold of during wartime rationing in civvies life, and so were greatly appreciated. Roy noted in a letter to Naomi: 'I always find a very sweet note from Gibney: "To Miss Carole with Lt Cdr Gibney's compliments" alongside his chocolate. Rather nice I feel.'

He later wrote:

> We have been definitely working pretty hard of late but all the better say I and then the sooner I can get back to my darlings and grow our pigs on Dartmoor. The captain seems to be satisfied with our two squadrons and yesterday called Fox and I 'Baldy and Daddy'. Rather a nice touch, I feel.

Roy was not the only one under pressure. Allan Thomson recalled: 'After a while the pace began to tell on aircrew.' He then went on to describe the reaction of one of the new aircrew in the wing, TAG G. McInally, who admitted being terrified when he thought his aircraft was not coming out of the bottom of a dive: 'He pleaded ear trouble (which could not be proved or disproved) and so was grounded. His hair went piebald black and white patches in a very short space of time.'

Thomson continued:

> ...near the end of our time at 'Mac', three of us were sitting round a table in the crew hut, each playing 'patience'. At that time almost 50% of our aircrew were in sick bay. With twelve serviceable aircraft and only six to seven crews to man them those of us still 'fit' had no respite. One night there was a Barracuda missing at sea, not one of No. 8's. I was the one out searching till 0200 and airborne again by 0430. That credited as one night's sleep! Back on duty again in the morning as usual.
>
> So having observed that the three card players no longer had the wit to play together, I spoke to our CPO, Geo Carr, and suggested that if the pace continued the number of fit aircrew would decline further. He said 'Allan glad you've spoken. I'll see the Senior O temporarily in charge of 830. Lt Cdr Fox being in Sick Bay.' Result we had a normal weekend break from Sat morning till Monday.

The heavy workload and increased sense of responsibility was gradually exhausting Roy with its relentless schedule:

> 14 November. I am absolutely deadbeat at the moment, as I have been thirteen hours on the go, absolutely non-stop. The job is getting better and things are going quite well. I am so longing to be with my two women and see our new home.

The next day, there was further tragedy when Sub Lt 'Jamie' Jamieson, Lt Charles Kirby and Leading Airman Stanley Bridges flying in an 827 Squadron aircraft were killed in a flying accident in the Clyde.

Emerson wrote:

> Still in the Clyde area. Flying day and night and sweating like hell. The ship is flying all aircraft all day. There is no rest for the wicked. We have ALTs, ARTs, A/S & dive-bombing, searches, strikes, shadows, fighter evasion, navexs, w/t exs, sub exs, sub patrols etc. All have done night landings. FOCT has been aboard. Mathew (830) collided with Jamieson yesterday at 7,000 ft & both went in. Chas. Kirby and

Bridges were in the back. No survivors. They fell abreast Ailsa Craig.

For Allan Thomson it was an extremely lucky escape, as he was meant to be in the 830 Squadron aircraft that crashed:

> The exercise was to practise 'fighter evasion in formation' – and our 827 and 830 were to be the first to try it.
>
> For some reason known to himself, Wilf 'Dinger' Bell who was normal crew for the 830 aircraft was missing. The senior O sent Andy Anderson, a farming type from Aberdeenshire, to replace him. CPO TAG Geo Carr sent me. By the time I had collected my kit and got to the aircraft Andy was already there. He said 'I'm in here, I might as well stay here now.' Little did he know what he was saying. The two aircraft were supposed to perform a circular motion in close formation. Instead they circled in opposite directions and crashed heavily when they met halfway, much to the consternation of the 'attacking' Seafire.

The ship searched around Ailsa Craig for a couple of hours. No trace was found.

Roy was naturally concerned and felt somewhat responsible by the sudden deaths especially since the aircrew were trying out the new aerial tactic 'the Fighter Evasion in Formation' which he had devised. There was a speedy air accident investigation and more condolence letters to be written.

Roy did not want to worry Naomi and made no mention of this crash in his next letter:

> 15 November. We have been working extremely hard recently and damned cold too. Billy girl, it seems such ages since we were all together on leave. I am longing for some more; maybe we'll be lucky at Christmas and be able to move in together. The whole ship is calling me 'Daddy' now from the captain down.

The following day, he joined in a game of rugby for relaxation and exercise, sandwiched between his hectic Barracuda wing preparations. He injured himself and was ordered to rest:

> 17 November. Such are the plans of mice and men. I was going to ring my darling up tonight ashore but unfortunately I played rugby first and twisted my damned knee and consequently can only just hobble. I had to get a car ride back and of course I can't go ashore. It's infuriating and just my luck.

The day after he elaborated:

> My knee is pretty unpleasant today and I have had to hobble on a couple of sticks. I have quite naturally done nothing today again, I could have rung you up. It's damned silly too, just a lousy knee the size of a tennis ball.

The Medical Officer made his decision – he was grounded. Roy was confined initially on board HMS *Furious*, and banned from flying for almost one month from 17 November. Fortunately, the wing finished its working up period in the Clyde two days later and was declared 'operational'. However, night flying was to continue until the projected visit of Vice Admiral Lyster on 22 November. Roy was incapacitated but knew he would have to meet Lyster for secret discussions.

By now, Naomi was nine months' pregnant and her due date was imminent. Roy wrote anxiously to her: 'Look after your darling selves, Billy girl, and be oh so so careful and make sure the doctor does everything for you. How I hope I get some Christmas leave. One never knows tho'.

Roy's two squadron commanders continued the set flying programme. Flying continued and on 21 November there was another night flying accident killing one airman; two others were lucky to escape with minor injuries. Emerson elaborated in his diary:

> We lost Jan McKay on the night of Nov. 21. Jim Watson burst a hydraulic pipe in the front cockpit at 900 ft. He was blinded & crashed in the sea. Jim got out, Adam was thrown out, but Mac's hood was jammed & Jim couldn't get to him. The a/c sank in 15 secs & Mac went down with it. The boys spent 30 minutes in the water, and were picked up OK by a ML.

The next day Lumley Lyster was flown by Swordfish to *Furious*. The 827 Squadron line book recorded: 'FOCT flew aboard in a Stringbag, and was received with medieval pomp and ceremony on the flight deck.' Underneath a cartoon of stepping out of a Stringbag onto the flight deck, the entry continued with glee: 'What do we care, though. He has SUSPENDED NIGHT FLYING.'

Roy could only hobble to dockside transport with the help of his batman to drive to the air station to come and watch the show for the admiral's benefit.

Allan Thomson recalled:

> The culmination of our training at Mac was a visit by the 5th Sea Lord who was then the direct highest ranking officer in charge of the Air Arm. The wing did a formation take off in pairs down the runway; followed by a demonstration fly past and display over the airfield. The verdict – we were fit to go on board *Furious* [as an operational wing].

About the same time, the RAF's Battle of Berlin operation started and by 24 November, Berlin was reported as a 'sea of flames'. Roy wrote to Naomi:

> Wed. It is wonderful to receive your letters. They are always so interesting Billy girl, totally unlike mine I'm afraid. Cor hasn't Berlin had a pasting. Our little fun and games in the September blitz seems pretty pathetic altho' my heart was pumping. My dearest, my leg is almost recouped now and I manage to hobble a couple of hundred yards at a time in about quarter of an hour. Pretty good going but then I never did like walking. I'm not allowed to do my job yet of course or go ashore, even if I wanted to.

That same week Roy's worries for Naomi were eased. On 29 November, Naomi gave birth to another baby girl in a Torquay nursing home. Roy received the news from Naomi's sister-in-law, and excitedly wrote to Naomi:

> I've just got Eira's telegram. I can't say how delighted I am that this awful waiting is over and our wee Kay Leslie has at last decided to say 'How do you do' to the world.'

When Roy had received the news of Carole's birth two years previously, he had been sitting in his Swordfish about to take off – now, laying on a sickbed in his cabin on *Furious*, it was just not the same!

The wing joined in the congratulations the next day. Jimmy Watson noted in the squadron line book: '"The new and improved model" – the Falkner MK II. Congratulations to the Wing Leader for the mod – a daughter.'

Naomi wrote to her brother Bill, now with the Allied liberation forces in Italy: 'Mount Stuart Nursing Home – I've just produced another baby and am disappointed above all possible words that it's a girl – not a boy.'

Roy wrote as the proud father:

> Darling I'm so pleased about Kay Leslie, can it be those names please? Young Gibney is demanding to be Kay Leslie's godfather. What do you think, darling, and curiously enough the commander is saying that we ought to have a ship christening. A very nice thought but I don't think that that is quite us.

Furious was operationally ready and on 3 December sailed northwards to join the Home Fleet at Scapa. The 827 Squadron line book recorded: '*Furious* dug the hook out and we waved our last farewells to Two Ton Tess before turning our faces towards Mecca – Sorry Scapa (Same idea anyway!). We appear to be the sole aerial comfort for the Home Fleet!'

On arrival at Scapa, *Furious* was acknowledged by Admiral Bruce Fraser, Command-in-Chief Home Fleet, on board his flagship, the battleship *Duke of York*.

By now, the large open water expanse of Scapa Flow was filled with warships with masses of barrage balloons flying above to ward off low-level enemy air attacks as elaborated by Emerson:

> Saturday Dec 4th – just arrived at the glorious holiday resort (?) of Scapa Flow. Typical weather, fog and rain. We left the Clyde PM the 3rd, and anchored here at 9 am this morning. There is not much in here. 2 KGVs, the *Richelieu*, an American cruiser, 2 *Dido*s, 2 *Southampton*s, & a few odds & sods. Also *Kent*, *Edinburgh*, *Belfast* and *Nelson*.
>
> Capt Philip has gone sick, and the old commander is now acting capt in his place. Philip handled his chief nearly as well as Troubridge & that says a hell of a lot.
>
> Guess we will go ashore to Hatston. I think there is something in the wind. Lots of buzzes.

They had barely arrived in the Orkney Isles before training for 827 and 830 Squadrons continued apace, and Roy, who was still grounded, was to work closely alongside the operations officer in Ops Hatston. The Hatston sector ops room was a great concrete blockhouse in the hill above Kirkwell, nicknamed the 'Black building' by the locals. It had a central role at Hatston, and functioned as the main communications centre for the Orkney Islands. It was built in 1940 to control the aerial defence of Scapa Flow. With the Nazis in control of Norway and the *Luftwaffe* just an hour's flight away, it was crucial to the defence of the UK.

Roy's work was to assist in the implementing of the Naval Air Fighting Instructions and advise the operations officer and his team in their readiness for the forthcoming strikes against the Germans in the Arctic.

Third Officer Wren Catherine 'Puck' Finch-Noyes worked directly for the operations officer:

> I knew Roy very well. He was not able to fly for a fortnight or so owing to a rugger injury and came to work in the Hatston Operation Office. So that's how I got to know him well. My husband, Lt 'Ned' Finch-Noyes, had been shot down and killed over Norway in 1940.

'Daddy' we called him as he was a senior officer of two squadrons and used to say 'I'm the Daddy of them all'.

It was no desk job – aircraft were in and out being briefed, issued with maps, charts etc – one of the things I did at the time was to find out which ships were leaving the Flow and wanted dummy attacks by our squadrons in training – so I was always in touch with the C-in-C Home Fleet Gunnery Officer's Assistant. Ships and aircraft took photographs and so results of attacks could be analysed. I stayed in that job until the end of the war.

In preparation for hostile operations, exercises were conducted at sea by HMS *Furious* together with other carriers. Fighters and bomber squadrons took off from different ships simultaneously to practise forming up into a single strike force, with fighter squadrons providing cover for the bombers at various heights. No. 8 TBR Wing then carried out mock dive-bombing attacks on pre-arranged targets.

There were occasional lighter moments at Scapa, as Allan Thomson recalled:

Captain Philip would extend an invite to all aircrew including ratings to dinner in the wardroom. This was preceded by a film show in the after lift-well. There was always much laughter at the ribald remarks thrown out by all the wits in the frequent breaks in each film as the operator stopped the show to change each reel. Drinks and an excellent meal followed. These gatherings, an unusual event in the service in those days, were almost the only occasion when all aircrew mixed socially.

New Zealander David Brown, an 830 Squadron observer of about the same age as Roy, recalled:

My recollections of 'B-F' are of a quiet-spoken, most friendly person, irrespective of rank or pecking-order. He certainly took part in most of the off-duty activities of the wing, both afloat and ashore, but did not overly socialise or mark out any favourites.

Most of the time Roy and the aircrews were detached to RNAS Hatston. George Green explained: 'HMS *Furious* had joined the Home Fleet in Scapa in December 1943 and when not engaged in operations, the squadron flew ashore for exercises in RN Air Station Hatston.'

The Hatston posting was to be a pleasant alternative to *Furious* for Roy and his wing. It seemed a long time ago that he had last been there during the *Bismarck* flap. He was again billeted in one of the wooden huts on the air station. His steward was a reliable chap and survivor from the sinking of *Repulse* by the Japanese.

'Honest' John Grieveson, 827 Squadron observer, noted:

Hatston as a base was quite comfortable in spite of the bleak wintry countryside. The nearby small town of Kirkwall was there to lure us with its bright lights from time to time. The cinema was always well attended and when dances were organised, it was a great scramble to get tickets (something to do with seeking female company!). Any excuse to hold a party in the wardroom (flying duties permitting!) was not hard to find.

Thelma Lancaster, one of the aircraft maintenance Wrens stationed at Hatston, recalled:

In comparison with Machrihanish, Hatston was civilisation! Only a mile from Kirkwall as it was. And Kirkwall was the Mecca for all 'off duties' on a Saturday afternoon. At teatime, the officers went to the Royal Hotel, those with cash went to the Albert café, those – of the girls at any rate – went to the Church of Scotland canteen often for a magnificent meal of poached egg on toast. Brothers or boyfriends were admitted but otherwise it was 'our' territory.

Hatston itself was very windy most of the time. In summer it could be very beautiful (not the camp, the surroundings). The main runway was the original road to Finstown. To use it they had to build another round the airfield! The other runway was almost at right angles and out towards Scapa Flow.

There were eight hangers, six in two parallel lines, and hangars 7 and 8 at right angles to them down on the flank. Visiting squadrons used No. 1 & 2. The squadron offices were on the bank above 1 & 3. The airfield stretched down to the shore beyond 2, 4, 6, 7 and 8. As I remember it, the path to the security gate was between 3 & 5, and the Officers' Mess was along it. Outside the security gate, and across the road, was the farm among the trees where you could get milk and eggs.

At the time in question, there were four Wren 'aircraft checkers' at Hatston. We had an office/storeroom in a Nissen hut alongside No. 7 hangar, also one of those pot stoves. They were in use all over the camp and they never seemed to be a shortage of coal. One of us stayed in the Nissen to answer the phone and make sure that the fire was burning and to heat the kettle and make the toast ready for 'stand easy'. 830 Squadron visited frequently.

Everything else apart we were pretty well fed up there. Beside it was a track that led up to the Wrennery. There were a lot of 'goodnight sweethearts' on that hundred yards.

The men had their quarters on the camp, between the main gate and security gate. The cinema where everything took place was right at the bottom.

Most of the squadrons had their dances in the cinema, but No. 8 TBR went one better and had theirs in the drill hall in Kirkwall when there was a spring floor. That was the only time I saw Baker-Falkner close to.

Hatston commanding officer, Geoffrey Gowland, who had served with Roy in *Glorious* in 1938, commented:

After a year in Arctic convoys, I found myself in command of the four naval air stations in the Orkneys. I had a nice little Queen Anne farmhouse as my official quarter and part of my job was to keep open house for any illustrious great men or women who might find themselves weather-bound – they'd skip back to my little farm – we'd put our feet up before the peat fire, and begin opening bottles.

He continued:

Roy B-F was several years younger than I was – but soon he was making a name for himself – commanding air squadrons with great success, with skill, technical know-how, and fine leadership. He was one of those who had natural impeccable manners – one felt 'here is a really fine model of a young officer who should go far.' I certainly wrote him a very appreciative personal report as part of my 'goodbye' duties when posted to my next duty.

The new Barracuda aircraft in the Orkney Isles came in for some comment from other squadrons, as recorded by Jimmy Watson:

At Hatston, from 848, our beautiful aircraft came in for a lot of unhealthy criticism – 'The Barracuda was called a "Flying Prostitute" since it had no visible means of support' and 'The Barracuda is a wonderful invention, but it will never take the place of the airplane.'

A song deriding the Barracuda and entitled 'They Will Not Fly' was sung to the tune of 'As Time Goes By' from the film, 'Casablanca'. The first verse ran:

> *You must remember this,*
> *A Barra's poor as piss,*
> *On that you can rely.*
> *No matter what the future brings,*
> *They will not fly.*

'Puck' Finch-Noyes at Hatston Ops recalled an event soon after Roy was able to fly again, where he showed the doubting Hatston aircrew really how well a Barra could fly if you really believed in it:

Roy's squadrons had new aircraft called Barracudas and some of them did not like them very much. One fine day Roy took an aircraft up and flew it over the airfield doing turns and turns, loops etc. Commander Flying stormed in to Ops and screamed 'Who is that idiot up there? Send him to me – as soon as he lands!'

However, Roy and his wing were not beyond mocking their own 'beloved' Barracuda, and would raucously sing in the gin and tonic laden atmosphere of their wardroom around the old piano.

Old Iron
> *Any old iron, any old iron, any any any old iron*
> *Easy meat! Protection for the Fleet!*
> *Stooge for any old Messerschmitt you meet.*
> *Oh what fun! No front gun,*
> *And engine you can't rely on.*
> *You know what you can do with your Barracuda II.*
> *Old iron, old iron!!*

The Hatston wardroom was manned by thirty or so Wrens, not least three indomitable Wrens – the three musketeers, Panda, Mac and Betty. They got to know Roy and his aircrew well in their daily visits after flying exercises. The Hatston girls had very exotic nicknames; there was Margueritte 'Kittenpuss' Carter, Amy 'Cleopatra' Barron, Violet 'Jackie Bookworm' Jackson and Hannah 'Matelot Mag' Tait. June 'Panda' (Common) Blakey, wife of one of Roy's old 767 Squadron pupils, recalled:

B-F is the man who christened me 'Panda'. I was a Wren serving in the wardroom mess office at RNAS Hatston, where officers settled their mess bills. One of my friends, the late Sub Lieutenant Alan Walling, was asked by B-F who his companion was, and on learning he said 'Oh, that little girl that looks like a Panda?' She had dark rings under her eyes.

From that time forward I have kept this nickname and am still known as Panda Blakey by the vast majority sixty years later.

Others of their friends included Elizabeth or Betty 'Mac' MacIver who recalled that 827 and 830 Squadron aircrew were the most frequent visitors, and got to know them all personally. She greatly admired Roy. When new squadrons came to Hatston and their officers visited the wardroom she was quick to get out her scrapbook for them to inscribe a line or two. Roy's penned an amusing handwritten poem for her in her book:

> *It was only an old beer bottle*
> *A' floating on the foam*
> *So many miles from home*
> *Inside was a piece of paper*
> *With these words written on.*
> *'Whoever finds this bottle*
> *Will find the beer all gone.'*

She and her fellow Wrens naturally took part in the many crazy evenings in the wardroom, and outside. On one occasion they were dragged into a great snowball fight between the 'Illustrious' Wrens pyjama clad, in boots and macs, with the 'cheeky chaps' from *Furious*'s No. 8 Wing aircrew.

827 Squadron aircrew were so taken by Betty, Sophia and Mac in the wardroom that they drew up and signed a certificate dedicated to them:

Dear Betty, Sophia and Mac,

We the undersigned wish to convey our humble thanks for the most efficient services rendered during our frequent visits.

Although occasionally the ale bears a close resemblance to 'A bit of old boot' we realise that you exert every effort to satisfy your thirsty customers.

Signed by members of 827
Squadron and the Wing Leader.

The squadrons continued their intensive flying practice from Hatston. The day for the real thing, an operational strike, was getting ever closer.

Whilst the wing were jesting about 'Danger unexploded bombs' and 'Lumme is it a live un, sir?' Roy ordered his armourers to bomb up his aircraft for a day's trials back on board *Furious*. Thumbs up to the deck crew and then he lifted off to test the bombs in flight and to demonstrate the approach to his pilots. The 827 Squadron line book wags wrote: 'Capt Philip, the Wing and Furibox had never heard such a thing – Oh Daddy!'

Pressure and drama increased day by day as live bombing practice brought its own hazards. Allan Thomson recalled:

In the first live bombing exercise, the aircraft were newly fitted out with oxygen. Flying from Hatston, the wing set off on a live bombing practice on one of the skerries off Shetland. Each aircraft carried one old, live 500 pounder.

The intention was to fly in pairs spaced out about 200 yards between each in the column. As we taxied along the runway for take-off, smoke and sparks appeared from our tail so take-off was aborted. We had blown a tailwheel as we attempted take off. When the aircraft stopped at the end of the runway the tailwheel was ground away, at least as high as the axle.

So the rest of the wing, now only eight pairs with a single somewhere in the middle, proceeded towards Shetland. Suddenly one aircraft which had no partner blew up in mid air. Oxygen or bomb to blame? Who knows? The one which blew up should have had, self and crew locked in very close formation with it.

Immediately on return to Hatston an inquiry was launched. Thomson recalled that Roy ordered the oxygen systems be stripped out and dispensed with from all Barracuda aircraft. Yet again Roy sat down in his office summing up the will to write to the next of kin of the young airmen.

About this time, the 827 Squadron line book wryly recorded a breach of security:

This book has suffered for the past year from the fact that the thing we fly has been one of the Admiralty's pet secrets – so no fame or headlines for us. But that's all over now because look what we found...

Pasted into the line book was a newspaper cutting which announced:

Secret Aircraft on Show – Shock at a model exhibition

The Air Ministry is to investigate circumstances which led to the discovery on Saturday that models of two of Britain's secret aircraft had been hanging for nine days among nearly 100 models at an exhibition organised by the Soldiers', Sailors' and Airmen's Families Association in Edinburgh. One of the models was of the Barracuda, a new torpedo bomber. Photographs of it are still banned.

The Barracuda by now had its defenders. David Brown reflected:

My belief is that those of us who were the first operators of the machine, pilots and observers/TAGs alike, were greatly impressed with its versatility, in spite of all the duties that it was called upon to perform – torpedo dropping, dive-bombing, 'long-range' reconnaissance, etc. – it also had to be strengthened sufficiently to withstand a force in excess of 7G when used in dive-bombing.

Brown continued:

We in No. 8 Wing were even more enamored of the machine, knowing that B-F had been a test pilot on and had thoroughly approved of the Barracuda.

I think that, only following the addition of No. 52 Wing ...in late 1943, did we begin to hear rumours of dissatisfaction with the Barracuda 'underpowered' (which it probably was after all the ancillary gear (radar etc) had been draped over it, and 'wing falling off' (we had never had any authentication of such mishaps, nor did we ever experience any such trouble during the innumerable dive-bombing exercises and the attacks on German shipping along the Norwegian coast).

At the time when these rumours were circulating, we put it down to 'twitch' on the part of other FAA units, who had not had the benefit of sufficient training, flying experience, and proper aircraft maintenance, such as we had under the direction of B-F.

Roy's enforced rest due to his injured knee was merely a brief respite, and by now he launched straight back into a heavy workload which included briefings with Admiral Lyster and attending conferences in preparation for all-important new operations.

Roy wrote to Naomi after a rare phone call together between important meetings with admirals:

> 8 December: Sorry I couldn't stay longer listening to you but I'd only just arrived back and Lyster had seen me arrive and had sent for me when your call came through so I decided that he could wait for a couple of minutes.
>
> Things are happening very quickly now and I don't seem to get a moment to myself. It's awful.

Earlier that day the wing had carried out live dive-bombing practice on the Shetland Islands. The wing repeated the live bombing for the next couple of days by which time Roy was given a clean bill of health to fly again.

On 11 December, the wing carried out a full dress rehearsal dive-bombing attack on the Shetlands and ALTs on the warships *Valiant* and *Queen Elizabeth* in preparation for their first operation against the enemy.

Emerson wrote in his diary:

> Monday, Dec 13th – Have got all the gen. now. We are to do an attack on the Norwegian coast, with bombs & fish looking for shipping. It is nice to be going at the enemy again, but I don't like it all. We only have a cover of 8 Seafires for 14 Barras. If they have much dog-fighting to do, the fighters won't get back to the ship. The range is too great & there are not enough spots to cover us. We hope to go in at 50 ft, so we shouldn't be picked up until about 30 miles off. Then we climb all out & search up the coast in the leads for ships. We have a Norwegian naval officer aboard & he says the ships hide in the numerous fjords all night, & creep up the coast by day.
>
> We have been ashore at Hatston for 4 days doing sweeps out westwards & coming back to Shetlands & bombing Roona Stacks. Carrying 6 x 250 lbs for 3 hrs at 50 ft leading a formation of 14 Barras & 8 Spits is no fun. However, the consumption figures have been good. Clipped wing Spits from Sumburgh have attacked us and shown that 8 fighters are too few to cover us. We have got some intelligence from the RAF & that is not too bright. We are to make a landfall off Kenda Island, and this is now a fighter drome with 5 x 109s or 5 x 190s as well as a few 210s & 88s. The RAF have given us pictures of it and all the gen. All the COs concerned are against it. This strike is just a political move to boost the Barra. We reckon the losses will be too high.

These inexperienced aircrew might have been worried but Roy also had other personal concerns – his new baby daughter was dangerously ill during her first few weeks of life. By 19 December, Kay Sandra as she was now known, was getting better. Roy wrote:

> How lovely it was to hear your voice again tonight and to know that our weeist babe Kay Sandra is better or at least an improvement. I must admit Billy that I prayed a bit last night and didn't sleep very well. Sorry, but true.
>
> I was so delighted to hear our eldest Wren's voice tonight, Billy. To hear you two certainly does take one away from this stupid war and bring one's mind fresh thoughts and beauties.

In late December, Roy selected Lt Guy Micklem RN, a young and up-and-coming naval officer with operational experience from 841 Squadron, to be his wing observer. He appointed nineteen-year-old Petty Officer Airman, TAG 3rd Class Arthur Howard Kimberley to be his air gunner. His friends called him Kim.

Guy Micklem wrote later to his brother Hugh in India Command:

> I am afraid it is some time since I last wrote to you but as you can guess I have been kept busy getting used to my new job. I have been made a wing observer which is quite a lift in the world for me. Obviously it doesn't mean a thing to you but, I assure you it is big stuff. I am still rather in the air about my duties but I am gradually feeling firmer in the saddle.

Guy was well liked as Clifford Lock recalled:

> Guy Micklem, B-F's observer, was a super chap, a delightful man. In fact the RN element in the wing were very helpful to us – they seemed to be competent professionals of high morale who were a steadying influence.

Christmas was fast approaching and Roy was fated to be away from Naomi until after the New Year. He wrote on Christmas Day: 'Merry Christmas my darling and I hope that it's a much better one than I've had. Just booze. Absolutely the only thing to do.' However, he had not elaborated the full story and explained how he was looking after his wing. An entry in the 827 Squadron line book recorded: 'Thanks to Wing Leader, CO and a few others for supplying the squadrons thousands of jugs of ale to the angry multitude.'

Roy wrote on Boxing Day: 'No news of anything in particular, only the devil of a hangover from Christmas and that's all.'

All was to change at Scapa shortly after he wrote this note. A force of the Home Fleet, Force 1, including the battleship HMS *Duke of York*, had that morning been in engagement with the German warship, *Scharnhorst*, as the latter threatened to attack an east-bound Arctic convoy carrying vital munitions to the Soviet Union.

At 10:25am Force 1 lost radar contact with *Scharnhorst* and there was ensuing panic as the rest of the Home Fleet back at Scapa Flow prepared to assist in a chase to trap the German warship.

Roy's wing embarked fully armed on *Furious* but *Scharnhorst* was already heading back to Norway. Later in the afternoon, *Scharnhorst* was relocated by *Duke of York* which thundered her main guns broadside. One of the last *Duke of York* shells hit a vital spot on the German battleship, penetrating the boiler room and severing the turbines. At 19.45 hours, a tremendous explosion caused *Scharnhorst* to sink rapidly.

Allan Thomson reflected:

> Early Xmas morning, ashore at Hatston, the news came through '*Scharnhorst* is out.' We scrambled to get back on board ship. By the time boarding was complete, word came through. She had been sunk by the guns of the fleet!

A few days later the victorious Home Fleet ships returned to Scapa watched on by Emerson and the rest of the wing:

> The *Duke of York*, *Jamaica* and 7 destroyers have just entered the Flow. *Nelson*, *Rodney*, *QE*, *Kent*, *Belfast*, *Richelieu*, *Anson*, *KGV* & ourselves all cleared lower deck & cheered the ships entering harbour. The destroyers flew affirmatives &

numerals on their torpedo tubes. 1st – 1 hit, 2nd – zero, 3rd – 2 hits, 4th 2 hits, 5th and 6th zero. 7th – skull and cross bones (Norwegian DR). That shows that the *Scharnhorst* received 5 hits. We are disembarking again on Monday.

The alert was described by Jimmy Watson in the 827 Squadron line book in his usual flippant style:

Boxing Day – Flap!!! Stand by to embark (and we did). *Dramatis Personae* – The whole ruddy squadron. *Why*??! – God knows! The thing was 1100 miles away. *What*?? The *Scharnhorst*.

CHAPTER 22

Preparing for Secret Missions in Norway

The sinking of *Scharnhorst* meant that the battleship *Tirpitz* was now the greatest maritime threat and Roy was to play a major part in annihilating it.

Prime Minister Winston Churchill declared that 'destruction, or even the crippling, of the *Tirpitz* is the greatest event at sea at the present time. No other target is comparable to it. The entire naval situation throughout the world would be altered.'

Tirpitz, sister ship to *Bismarck*, was a 54,000-ton battleship armed with 15-inch guns and a complement of 1,500 crew. She was the world's largest warship, a veritable floating fortress. The Germans thought *Tirpitz* was virtually unsinkable – her lower deck armour was 150 mm thick.

To respond to Churchill's declaration, the First Sea Lord explored the possibility of RAF or USAAF bomber attack support or diversion with a combined carrier-borne strike. Finally, it was agreed that the best option was that the Fleet Air Arm should attack *Tirpitz* in her lair in the Norwegian Arctic Circle in a carrier-borne daylight raid. On 29 January 1944, the Admiralty ordered the Commander-in-Chief of the Home Fleet, Admiral Sir Bruce Fraser, to prepare the plan. Fraser had significant experience of carriers, having been captain of *Glorious* prior to Lumley Lyster. Vice Admiral Sir Henry Moore, Second-in-Command, Home Fleet, was to oversee and mastermind the air strike, code-named Operation *Tungsten*.

Previous *Victorious* commanding officer, Captain Lachlan Mackintosh of Mackintosh, the Vice Admiral's Chief of Staff, was to be invaluable in planning and carrying out the operation. In charge of fighter aircraft was Rear Admiral Escort Carriers, Rear Admiral A.W. Bisset, and his Senior Naval Officer, Duncan Lewin.

The aim was to send two waves of dive-bombers, flanked by fighters, in a daring operation deep into enemy-held territory to strike *Tirpitz* at anchor in Kaafiord in the far north of Norway near North Cape. Kaafiord was approximately four miles long, one mile wide, with a spit of land protruding from its southern end where *Tirpitz* lay at anchor. *Tirpitz* herself was protected within strengthened defences, anti-submarine and torpedo fencing.

The main attack was dependent on the dive-bombing capabilities of the Barracuda, and Roy was the obvious choice in the Royal Navy to lead this mission. Under the utmost secrecy, Roy was called to meet Vice Admiral Moore and informed that he would play a strategic role in leading, preparing and coordinating the operation. He would be in overall command of the entire strike.

Roy made an oblique reference to the plans when he wrote to Naomi on 1 February referring to his role in re-writing the Naval Air Fighting Instructions which he had completed the previous year.

Roy would lead the entire strike with the first wave of dive-bombers, his No. 8 TBR Barracuda Wing. Lt Cdr Vic Rance was detailed to follow closely with his No. 52 TBR Barracuda Wing in a second wave of bombers. The bombers would be protected by a screen of fighter aircraft. Lt Cdr Dick Turnbull of *Victorious*, was to command the Corsair fighters, whilst Lt Cdr Jimmie Sleigh and Lt Cdr Mike Fell from escort carriers *Pursuer* and *Searcher* were to command the American-built Wildcat and Hellcat fighters in the first and second strikes respectively. It would be a complex task and Roy would have to liaise with scientists, carrier captains and other wing leaders.

Dick Turnbull recalled:

> In the planning and preparation for the attack the various wing leaders were more closely involved than was normally the case with such operations. We had several meetings with the Flag Officer who was to command the force and the carrier captains, and it was at these meetings that I got to know Roy.

Roy requested each of the wing leaders to make a detailed plan of action and to report back to him so that all of the various elements could be pulled together for the very detailed operation. A whole round of briefings and meeting were held over the next few weeks.

By now, there was increasing urgency to the operation. *Tirpitz* had been damaged by Royal Navy midget X-Craft submarines during September 1943, but Norwegian Resistance reports to Admiralty's Operational Intelligence Centre indicated that temporary repairs would be completed by March 1944. The battleship was probably not completely fit for sea operations, but it constituted a potential threat to Atlantic shipping, North Russian convoys and preparations for the imminent D-Day invasion of Normandy. It was therefore imperative to put her out of action as soon as possible.

Roy acknowledged that he could not let Naomi know anything about the forthcoming operation and his letters to her were non-committal: 'I've got no particular news at all just chugging along in the same old way, just longing to come home again and be with my women and their puppy, Bruce.' This new addition to the household had been named in honour of Roy's C-in-C. He continued: 'Gosh it will be heaven when this beastly war is all finished and over and we can live our own lives again and know what is going to happen from day to day.'

Roy was to mastermind many of the techniques and tactics to be employed in the *Tirpitz* air strike, based partly on his experiences built up early on in the war. With these top secret plans, subtle changes were made to prepare for the strike against *Tirpitz*, now scheduled for only ten weeks' time. Lt Cdr 'Dickie' Kingdon took over from 'Baldy' Fox and became the new CO of 830 Squadron.

Guy Micklem, who already knew Kingdon through family connections, wrote to his brother Hugh:

> 15 January. I have just heard that Richard Kingdon (Leslie's husband) is coming up here to take over command of one of the squadrons in my wing. I look forward to his arrival with mixed feelings as I am darned if I am going to stand any bullshit from him! But on the whole I think it will be rather an amusing situation.

The preparations were exhausting but Rotherham had arranged a series of ENSA entertainments to keep the personnel happy when not working. Roy took the opportunity to wind down during a rare break from his hectic preparations: 'January 10. Went to a pantomime with Gibney tonight. It was very good. As usual we laughed at jokes other people hadn't seen thereby causing a bit of a black.' He wrote a few days later:

I've just seen a Tommy Handley show. It was very funny indeed but in some parts definitely a wee bit raw. I'm just stooging along in the same old fashion. Gibney paid us a huge compliment today. He asked if you and I would hold his hand when he eventually goes to the Palace to see the King to get his DSC. A very nice gesture indeed, I thought.

As preparations for Operation *Tungsten* continued, Roy's duties changed somewhat with increased assessment of the flying skills of the aircrew to take part in the strike and lecturing on the various components that made up the strike. For Roy it was important to build up the comradeship of individual Barracuda crews so that they would eat, sleep, think and drink together – and fight together as cohesive units when the time came. It was so successful that many crews were together for over one and a half years and kept in touch for almost seventy years afterwards.

He wrote to Naomi: 'Monday: I haven't got any particular news. I'm writing this on my knee in the office hence the phoney writing. I've been having a lousy time the last few days examining people. Hateful business altogether.' The following Monday he added: 'I've been on my feet all day examining people and am so tired of asking the same old question time and time again. Finished after 6, absolutely beat.'

At midnight on 22 January, the tide was changing favourably for the west as Allied Forces at last landed on the occupied European mainland – on the Anzio beaches close to Rome. To Roy it looked as if the war was going to end at long last.

He wrote to Naomi the next day about her new young nanny, Violet Matthews:

Two lovely letters from you today saying that Violet seems to be a nice girl. I'm so pleased. I'm so delighted that our wee babe Sandra is progressing satisfactorily. [Roy had still not seen his now two-month old, baby daughter.] A dull day nothing very much to do and also an unattractive day. Be alright if I were with my women though in front of a lovely log-fire, oh boy. I am so longing to see the latest edition of the Falkner breed. Still things are looking slightly more hopeful anyway all round, war and everything.

We, of course, are just soldiering on in the same old way, and all longing for leave somewhat naturally. Gibney and I, of course, pretty well twins now and certainly manage to sink back the old noggin of beer. How I do long to be with my three wonderful women and to see our flat. It must look wonderful with all our own knick-knacks up. Things that we haven't seen for years. Still maybe it won't be long now, anyway the war situation certainly looks better and better.

On 27 January there was more headline news as Russian troops relieved Leningrad from the occupying German forces.

Roy later wrote: 'Saturday. I told you that Fox has left us and got his own party like me.'

Every day the aircrews were carrying out intensive flying exercises to get the wing to operational standard for the strike, yet none of them knew what they would attack – it was still top secret and unknown to all except the highest-ranking officers.

John Grieveson recalled:

In early '44 our days were occupied with a great deal of working-up practices in dive-bombing, torpedo attacks, air fitting, navigation, fighter evasion, wing formations etc – plus numerous lectures on the ground.

I had joined 827 in January '44 and recall seeing a Barracuda for the first time. I had been with a Fulmar squadron in the Indian Ocean previously. The Fulmar – slow, two-seat fighter – had always looked like an aircraft – but the Barra had little grace about it – an 'incredible creation'. However, little did I know that I would spend the next twenty-two months in that kite – but it did see me through – with Cliff Lock's expert driving, of course! We spent eighteen months together as a crew.

At Hatston, Roy was delighted to meet an old friend from the past, David Buchanan-Dunlop. Roy wrote to Naomi on 2 February: 'I saw Commander B-D for a few minutes to-day. He is very well, sends his love and asked after the family. He hasn't changed the least tiny bit.'

Roy had not seen Buchanan-Dunlop since they were flying together at North Coates in 1941. Their reunion was on board B-D's new aircraft carrier, HMS *Indefatigable*. Over a gin or two at the bar, he told Roy that he had been awarded the DSC, taken part in anti-submarine patrols and bombing strikes in Madagascar, and had survived the bombing of HMS *Indomitable* during Operation *Pedestal* to Malta. Post war, as Captain Buchanan-Dunlop, he was to serve on the British Delegation at the Nuremberg Trials.

As a relaxation for aircrew, on 4 February a No. 8 TBR Wing dance was held in Kirkwall Drill Hall. The 827 Squadron line book noted: 'We took this opportunity of expressing at the same time our thanks and condolences to the Wing Leader for the way he carried out the "task" that was foisted on him.'

About the same time, the wing was grounded for a week while all wing pins were checked to see if they were mild steel or high tensile. A Barracuda had failed to pull out of a dive somewhere.

Roy, along with Capt Philip, Monkey Bryant, Gibney and Kingdon, agreed on an interim plan to test the Fairey Barracuda in action against the enemy, prior to Operation *Tungsten*. On 8 February, the wing embarked to *Furious* for Operation *Posthorn* which was scheduled for three days later. The plan was for an air strike from the carrier against enemy convoys in the waters near Stadlandet on the German-occupied Norwegian coast. A heavy support force was to consist of the battleships *Anson* and FS *Richelieu*, the cruisers *Belfast* and *Nigeria*, together with three Canadian warships, *Athabascan*, *Haida* and *Iroquois*.

For many of the wing this was the first-ever taste of operational flying against the enemy. Emerson elaborated on the plans for the operation and his own thoughts as the day drew closer:

Feb 8th – Had 10 days leave. We are now back. Flew on yesterday & and are off on a do soon. It is the same place, Norwegian Leads. We have only 12 Barras aboard, & some of 880 (Moose Martyn) fighters extra, in addition to 801. We have picked a better landfall. Stadlandet Point, halfway between Osen & Bergen. We patrol 30 miles north. There is a drome 60 miles north & 60 miles south of us. Our greatest danger is from flak ships escorting the convoys, and the heavy coastal batteries.

The ship flies us off at dawn. We attack at 11, and hope to return to the ship at noon & return to Scapa with the tit pulled. I have left instructions for this [diary] to be smuggled to Connie if I don't come back.

It is still a political stunt to justify the Barra Wee Wee. It will be its first operation. Will probably take place on my birthday. It is more sensible than the last one drawn up by the Admiralty.

Beaufighters do the same operation regularly from Wick & for 8 torpedoes they have an escort of 8 RP & 8 cannon fighters. The fighters carry 3,000 rounds each & the RP carry 6 x 60-lb heads each to strafe the flak ships whilst the fish are aimed and dropped. We shall have 12 fighters 6 for top cover & 6 to shoot up the flak ships as we dive, but they have only 60 rounds of cannon ammo, a ten second burst and then they have lost their sting. Our search is to Stadlandet, past Vaeger. We are all carrying some empty beer bottles to throw out. Also 10 illuminating cartridges against fighters.

We put to sea tomorrow morning with *Anson, Richelieu, Belfast, Nigeria* and *Bermuda*. TO [take-off] is 0900 on Thurs 11th. Attack about 1030, land at noon (we hope) & return to Base.

Cheerio folks.

Clifford Lock recalled the pre-operation pep-talk when Roy sought to reassure the young aircrew using low key 'no dramatics' sayings typical of his quiet, thoughtful approach to life and flying. 'He ended with his trademark "Just follow Daddy!"'

Tom Darling commented: 'To us B-F was irreplaceable, but of course, if you had put that to him at any time he would have laughed! John Grieveson observed: 'His leadership qualities were highly respected by us all, and gave us confidence in carrying out the job we had to do.'

The Fleet left Scapa and steamed at top speed northwards to the flying off position near to the Norwegian coast. At 09.05 hours Roy lifted off from HMS *Furious* in Barracuda 'A', an 830 Squadron machine, with Gibney in the observer's seat and CPO Topliss as TAG. They were followed in formation by five other Barracudas. The object was to strike enemy shipping at Ervik Bay, an inlet on the Norwegian coast directly east of the Shetland Islands and to the north of Bergen.

Emersen described the operation in his diary:

We took off at 0900, & circled the fleet at 50 ft. Spits took off at 0930 & we set course 0940 for Norway. Fleet was 100 miles off the coast, the weather was lousy. Cloud base 2,000 ft, very overcast & frequent rain squalls. We flew in at 50 ft through heavy rain. It is a great sensation to go so near the sea at 160 knots & see the bombers on each side of you in formation & spits covering the vic.

Emerson continued:

We made landfall and turned north. Cloud base was from 500 ft to 2,000 ft varying. This handicapped our flak evasion but no bursts were seen. Five Me 109s attacked and were chased by our spits. A couple knocked down & one Spit missing.

We flew up the coast to Ervick and to Stadlandet Point. Only small fishing smacks sighted. There was a small convoy in Stadt Bay, but the cloud base was down to 100 ft, so we did a 300° turn to seaward and came back to Ervick.

Once Roy and the strike force reached the distinctive bay and peninsula, the anticipated shipping was sighted. He then gave the command for the strike force to follow him in for the attack. Flying over a series of islands and mainland they came to an inlet bay and over the village of Ervik itself.

Emerson noted:

Our target was a beached ship of 6,000 tons in Ervick Bay. It was pranged by Torp-Beaus on Jan 20th and is being salvaged. Cloud was at 2,000 ft, hills are 1,500ft. We slipped over the coast and stall-turned into the Bay from 2,000 ft, aimed, dropped, out at 900 ft and away all out. I dived 6th & both halves were burning & smoking as I dropped. Experienced some light flak from the Point on the way out. Throw the old kite around a bit.

A beached merchant vessel was attacked, the *Emsland* was hit, and one enemy aircraft, an Fw 180, confirmed as destroyed. One Seafire of the escort was shot down by the Germans. Overall, it was an auspicious start to the Barracuda's operational career.

The 827 Squadron's line book recorded the event:

The First Op…well, what d'ye know – we're on our way to the rodeo! Target was convoy, if found! Unfortunately there was no convoy, so an alternative was chosen, in the form of a beached merchantman, which was in process of being de-beached. The tonnage was around 6,000 tons – and approximately nine hits were scored with 500 pounders. All our aircraft returned safely.

Roy then led the strike safely back to the aircraft carrier and landed on with no difficulties. He jumped out of his aircraft as soon as was safe, rushing to de-brief Captain Philip about the result of the mission, and proudly watching the flight deck like a mother hen as his aircraft came in to land one by one – then with relief went off to a well earned rest.

Guy Micklem, who was sitting in the observer's seat of Roy's aircraft throughout the strike, recalled the operation in a letter to his brother in India on 13 February: 'For me things are very much the typical wartime existence – long periods of boredom punctuated by moments of intense excitement.' Gibney added: 'I always went out without eating, and boy did I eat when I returned.'

Furious returned to Scapa and the aircrews disembarked for RNAS Hatston where Roy learned he was to get leave to see Naomi and the children at last:

I've just had the extreme pleasure of sending you a wire saying that I shall be home on Saturday unless something very unforeseen happens. It's a wonderful thought. I can't really believe that it's true that I shall see my darlings after such a hell of a long time. Lovely, lovely.

He mentioned nothing of the attack and was delighted to focus solely on family matters.

Roy took the first available train down to London and onwards to Torquay railway station. His new house was on the northern outskirts of the town in St Marychurch. At last he was home; there was Naomi, little Carole and their baby Sandra. Naomi had been busy and many of the souvenirs they had collected over the years were on full display, from the small treasures acquired in China to the two horse head reliefs that Naomi had bought him as a birthday present in Cairo before the war.

On 24 February, Sandra's christening took place at Stoke-in-Teignhead Church, where six long and eventful years previously Roy and Naomi had been married. The godparents were Splash Carver and Nan Hauser.

At long last, Roy could snatch a brief taste of family life with his wife and children. The weather was atrocious but he did have time to explore a little, strolling with Naomi down the lane to the cliffs of Petit Tor Point and to Oddicombe beach.

St Marychurch had only a few months previously been at the forefront of the attacks by Germans. One eyewitness recalled to Naomi how she had been:

> ...gazing down at the harbour, when the peace was broken by the loud drone of planes. We could not believe what we were seeing – six planes, so low, they seemed to skim the water, were making for Torquay. The next minute the dreadful 'thud-thud' of bombs which were all too familiar to me. Thank God, within minutes the all clear sounded, but the Germans had done their work, a bomb had fallen on St Marychurch and killed twenty-one children at Sunday School.

With the bad weather Roy appreciated nothing more than to quietly sit with his family in front of a roaring fire. He knew that with Operation *Tungsten* set to take place he may never see Naomi or the children again.

Little did Roy know what was happening back up in Scotland in his absence. On the same day as Sandra's christening, Emerson wrote:

> Thursday Feb 24th – We flew on board yesterday, in a flap. We are at sea again & off on another raid on the Norwegian coast: this time 100 miles farther north. We have picked an open stretch of water halfway between Trondheim and Bodo, both dromes. It is still in the embryo stage, but the fighters won't act as anti-flak, so we are asking 4 dive-bombers and 6 torpedo a/c. I am not at all keen & consider it is very fraught. The Wing Leader, CO Flight Sgt and Chief TAG are all on leave.

Roy's leave seemed to flash by and on his return after a long journey by sleeper trains up from Devon via London he wrote to Naomi:

> Thank you my darling for the most happy and wonderful leave. It was infuriating not having decent weather but, Billy girl, it was such heaven to be able to hibernate with my darling wife and the two Wrens, the eldest of whom's charms seem to wrap themselves round one's heart more and more each day. And the newest edition just seems to grow on one as everyone else seems to find. It's lousy being back.

He also wrote:

> I was very touched today the squadron sent for me and gave me a Christening mug for Kay Sandra engraved 'Kay Sandra Baker-Falkner from 827 Squadron'. I thought it was a very grand gesture don't you. Will you also write and thank them.

Once back at Hatston, work started again in earnest, and at least some of his aircrew were appreciative of his and Gibney's return. Emerson again: 'Feb 29th – Will be glad to see the CO back and hand over to him. I have been acting CO this past 10 days. Bags of worry & flap.'

Roy was busy at all levels and frequently had to inform the flag officers, captains and his other superiors of the progress in preparing for the operation and its tactics.

Central to Roy's strategy was to provide as much tactical and practical information as possible to his aircrews and to try and simulate the actual operation by a series of programmes, firstly formation and wing flying, then live dive-bombing practice, including on terrain similar to the target area in North Norway.

Based on the scientific information supplied, Roy ordered a series of dive-bombing trials on targets to find the best height and angle to attack *Tirpitz* as she lay in her anchorage.

There were major discussions between the aircrews and about the tactics drummed into them, recounted Clifford Lock:

For dive-bombing strikes, the aim was to get all the aircraft in position to start their aiming dives at the same time and thus avoid taking turns at being the focus of unwelcome attention which could impair accuracy and lower morale. A wing on a bombing strike therefore divided into two squadrons of nine planes each and these formed in line ahead to get in position on either side of the target at about 6,000 ft.

Ideally all aircraft would dive together just after the fighter escort went in for their strafing runs to keep the flak down.

Meanwhile, scientists advised Roy about the capability of the new American armour-piercing bombs that the Barracuda aircraft were to use. As Roy's No. 2 pilot, Dave Clarabut, later explained: 'The boffins worked out the general plan of campaign with the operational commander, prior to us putting it into practice.'

Lock continued:

On these practice attacks we were releasing the bombs from a much greater height than had been normal, so as to give the armour-piercing properties a chance. When a dive-bomber releases a bomb it goes into free fall and arrives on the deck somewhat short of the aircraft's aiming point.

This distance between the aiming point and the bomb strike increases as the height of release increases which could result in errors of range since we were dropping from this unaccustomed height.

Roy's increasing involvement with admirals, flag officers and staff officers soon came to the attention of even the naval wing air gunners. Allan Thomson recalled:

As a leader Daddy was highly regarded by the TAGs. The impression was of a man whose authority far exceeded his rank. He sometimes had occasion to parade in full uniform and wore distinguished 'lines' of gold braid in a rope form round one shoulder. I believe this marked him as a staff officer with direct and frequent contact with Admiralty. Hence his apparent enhanced authority over others of Lt Com rank.

At heart Roy was still a modest man as indicated in his letter of 3 March: 'I went out to dinner again last night with the High Ups and again the most sumptuous spread. It really was terrific, but I still prefer my dried eggs and beans with my Billy girl.'

Roy later reported: 'I think that today is Thursday but I don't honestly know. Everything is going very well my end but I'm beginning to think that it is almost time that I went ashore, I haven't yet apart from one conference.'

This meeting had been with Vice Admiral Moore, Lyster and other senior officers and concerned the final briefing preparations for the attack on *Tirpitz*. Those attending the confidential briefings were shown the very latest high-level RAF reconnaissance pictures of the target, given a description of the target area and the enemy aircraft strengths which might be brought to its defence.

Roy was on an ever increasingly demanding schedule and apologised as soon as possible to Naomi that he was not able to write his daily letters as normal: 'I'm so sorry that I didn't write to you yesterday but it was a fairly busy day and I guess I was pretty tired by the time I turned in.'

For many weeks fighters and Barracudas had been practising for this operation, until they 'finally had everything buttoned-up' as Roy put it. There was then frustration waiting for the action to begin. 'It's been a wonderful today I don't think, standing by to do things and then just not. Plain aggravating and even worse no letters.'

In order to minimise the risk from U-boats and also to give the assembled task force of battleships, aircraft carriers and support vessels a good chance of making their advance undetected, it was decided to synchronise the operation with the passage of an outward-bound convoy to Russia, JW.58 – the largest ever such convoy to date, which might have attracted *Tirpitz* out of its lair.

On 17 March the wing embarked on *Furious* in preparation for live dive-bombing practice and the carrier prepared to steam southwards from Orkney, though the aircrew had no idea what was happening, as seen in Emerson's diary:

> Friday March 17th – We are on board again. All sqdns, & personnel and stores. What for we don't know. Fighters landed on at 1400, 827 at 1500. Ship was rolling and pitching like hell. Brown was last on and collapsed oleo leg. 830 landed on after 1600 & Massicks and Browse both wrote off both legs in heavy landings. No clue. Don't know what we are in for yet. Bags of buzzes going.

Emerson continued:

> Monday, March 20th – we are still in the Flow. The weather has been lousy these last 4 days. And full scale exercises have been cancelled each day. Four Woolworths carriers have arrived, *Fencer*, *Emperor*, *Searcher*, *Pursuer*. We have no gen at present, but there are several possibilities.
>
> 1.   I think the escort carriers are for more Russian convoys. There are bound to be more and bigger ones as time goes by.'
>
> 2.   The *Tirpitz* is due to go south for repairs. She will have to be docked for her underwater repairs which can only have been done temporarily by divers in the fiord. She is bound to move soon, and may attack a Russian convoy en route, though I doubt this. She is still tying up the Home Fleet. & she is our main target?
>
> 3.   The second front will be on inside 2 months I reckon. Things seem to be coming to a head now with pretty continuous bombing. We may assist in it, or cover it, or even make a point of a foray with the other carriers.
>
> At any rate this is something in the wind & are doing intensive bombing practice. It is bloody cold water round these parts to ditch in.

The weather finally improved and *Furious* eventually reached the coast off Loch Eriboll, where on 22 March Roy's wing commenced live bombing practice on a mock-up German battleship. The objective of the operation was still top secret.

Clifford Lock recalled:

> Our training was, I think, first class in accordance with good naval tradition. Before the strike on *Tirpitz*, an island in Loch Eriboll near Cape Wrath in Scotland was selected as a target similar to the German battleship in Kaafiord.

The dummy *Tirpitz* was on the island in the loch. The ten Barracudas travelled around, in three sub-flights of three aircraft with one spare coming along behind. The sub-flight formed a tactical unit which was designed to carry out a dive torpedo attack with the aircraft deployed to drop simultaneously spread out along the vulnerable sectors of the target, which were the outside bow or the inside beam if the target were turning to take evasive action.

Four days later the two Barracuda wings had their final bombing exercise using live bombs. Confidence among the aircrews was high. Dave Clarabut recalled: 'There is no doubt that 827 and 830 Squadrons formed a very efficient and professional fighting arm of the Navy and Roy can take a very great deal of credit for having lead us to the standards we attained.' Allan Thomson:

As far as No. 8 Wing and its early crew members were concerned the Barracuda was a good aircraft to fly in. No use for torpedo work – almost suicidal – but possibly the most accurate dive-bomber and at near 90-degree dive gave minimum likelihood of being shot down by ack-ack.

The dress rehearsal was not without event as Clifford Lock recalled:

We rehearsed by mounting a full-scale strike against the island and returned to the Fleet at sea off the Orkney's. It was returning from one of these dummy strikes, at low level over the sea, that I picked up a seagull through the windscreen of my Barracuda with nearly disastrous results. Luckily the body of the bird, a herring gull I think, hit me mostly on the lower part of the face and my eyes although scratched were not badly damaged. It just took out the starboard panel of the windscreen.

We were very glad to land safely back again – the [nose art] painting on the Barracuda panel on my plane 'Stormy petrel' was in memory of this incident. I had my eyes cleaned out in *Iron Duke* moored by Scapa and soon after we sailed north on Tungsten.

His observer John Grieveson also recalled the event: 'Our Barra hit a seagull on the way back and good old Cliffy Lock flew with this wretched bird in his windscreen flapping in his face – and put us down safely on the deck again!'

The next day, Operation *Tungsten* commenced when the convoy of fifty mainly American ships set sail from Loch Ewe for Murmansk in the Soviet Union.

Early in the morning of Tuesday, 28 March, Roy flew to *Victorious* from RNAS Hatston, and reported to her commanding officer Captain Michael Denny, a short stocky man with bushy eyebrows, known as a strict disciplinarian. The following day Roy met with the admirals, captains and staff officers overseeing the operation and hosted a wing leaders' meeting, and, still bound by the utmost secrecy, could not resist writing to Naomi about the subsequent evening activities:

Wednesday – Just back from a dinner party with the High Ups, Captain, Commanders etc. It was terrific exactly the same as pre war almost. Soup, lobster, chicken, savoury sweet. It certainly was big eats with a vengeance.

With the end of the operation now so nearly in sight he concluded his letter with: 'Maybe my leave won't be too terribly long now with a bit of luck. I sure hope so.'

Hatston was all abuzz about the possibility of a major strike about to take place though no one on the station had any inkling of the actual operation. One of the Wren aircraft maintenance crew or 'checkers', Thelma Lancaster, recalled:

> I remember very well the days immediately before the *Tirpitz* raid. The weather was bad, high winds and rain when they took off, and not all of them landed safely on the carriers. So of course back they came for replacement aircraft. We were working flat out that afternoon. At the end of it I was soaked to the skin. Literally you can't climb the side of a Barracuda in an oilskin. We of course had no idea of what was going on, save that this was an emergency.
>
> I was walking up the hill to the Wrennery when the last of them went over my head, and it seemed as if they were no further up than would be needed to clear the spit of land between Kirkwall bay and Scapa Flow. A friend told me that the vibration had shaken everything off the dressing table they were so low.

Victorious took on board the Barracudas of 827 Squadron, as well as her own 829 Squadron aircraft and a full complement of Corsairs. *Furious* had her normal complement of 830 Squadron as well as Barracudas belonging to 831 Squadron of No. 52 TBR Wing of *Victorious*.

Emerson wrote:

> March 28th Tues. We flew off to Hatston on the 22nd, having done nothing the week aboard. Weather had been lousy & stopped our programs each day. *Vic* arrived here three days ago, & today we flew aboard her. We are off on an op & 831 have gone to the Box so that No. 8 Wing & No. 52 can each range at once at one hour interval & go off for a 2 wave strike. We did a big rehearsal this afternoon on post ZH with live bombs. The 4 escort carriers supplied fighters, 40 to each Wing (Corsairs, Martlets and Hellcats).
>
> *Vic* is a beautiful ship, similar to *Indom*. 12 Wires and 2 Barriers. The ship's organisation is lousy & and she is not a happy ship at all. More flap and panic than I have ever seen before. The offices, stores and cabins etc are excellent, but the food is poor. We get stooged for lots of ship's duties.

On Thursday, 30 March, *Victorious* left Scapa Flow with the main battle fleet, Force 1, in company with the battleships *Duke of York*, flying the flag of Admiral Sir Bruce Fraser, and *Anson*, flying the flag of Vice Admiral Sir Henry Moore, the cruiser *Belfast*, five destroyers and the Canadian warships, *Algonquin* and *Sioux*.

In the evening *Furious*, with 830 Barracuda Squadron on board, departed along with the second battle fleet, Force 2, including four escort carriers and headed northwards to rendezvous off the coast of Norway.

Operation *Tungsten* and the latest bid to destroy *Tirpitz* had begun.

CHAPTER 23

Attack the *Tirpitz*

'Our target is *Tirpitz*' Roy announced to fighter and bomber aircrews on board the carrier *Victorious* once the ship was at sea. There was momentary silence and then murmurs of approval from amongst the aircrew hanging onto every one of his words. Up until now under great pressure, Roy had kept this most secret of confidential information even from close friends in the wing. So it was with relief he filled in the outline details of the operation in the rest of his presentation; every now and again there were the usual gags breaking the ice notably from the seasoned 827 Squadron aircrew.

Roy was under tremendous strain – with the D-Day invasion of Normandy now secretly scheduled for only eight weeks away, Operation *Tungsten* was of immense strategic importance. It was imperative to put *Tirpitz* out of action immediately.

At the same time as Roy made his announcement on *Victorious*, Captain George Philip on board *Furious* also gave aircrews the news, announcing over the ship's tannoy: 'Now hear this, this is the captain.' He then gave a very short rousing speech of support ending with 'The Fleet Air Arm will go in and smoke the old badger out of her hole.'

With the Fleet now steaming northwards towards their target, detailed briefings were held on board both aircraft carriers to bring aircrews up to date with the latest top-secret information.

Dave Clarabut recalled the briefings by Roy:

> The planning of any action was activated from sources above squadron or wing levels. The actual manner in which the action was to take place was up to Roy and the two squadron commanders of 827 and 830. It was advised to us at a pre-action briefing by the ship Commander Flying on information the captain of the ship received from the Admiralty who in turn, particularly in the case of Operation *Tungsten*, were guided by what they had received from resistance sources in Norway.

David Brown and other aircrew in 830 Squadron praised the talks called by Roy when he flew over briefly to *Furious* and returned later that day:

> Full briefings were really well done and the gunroom in *Furious* was fitted out with a large-scale relief model of the Alten Fiord area of which Kaafiord is a small inlet, showing light and heavy flak positions, air landing strips etc. Photos and maps were plentiful, and close study models of routes, so that all concerned had a clear picture of the operational set-up.
>
> A daily reconnaissance by a PRU Mosquito was being maintained over the area and we had up-to-date knowledge of *Tirpitz*'s whereabouts.

Aircrew from 827 Squadron recalled: 'being assembled in the wardroom for a lecture on

Norway – what to do, where to go and why – if we got stranded there.'

Emphasis was also placed on informing the aircrew about the efforts to get them home after the operation. Dave Clarabut recalled in the briefings:

> The route back to the carriers was up to each pilot and crew because after the attack the various aircraft were all split up and you made the best way home you could.
>
> In Operation *Tungsten* this was to be helped by the C-in-C Fleet positioning destroyers at intervals on the homeward track with their forward guns pointing in the direction of the Fleet. So that if you were lost and came across a destroyer you flew down the gun barrel which direction took you to your carrier!

Roy's presence generally boosted confidence. Arthur Towlson, a pilot in 829 Squadron, noted: 'He was a striking figure, standing out in company, tall, confident, energetic and much respected and admired by all in his squadrons. That much was obvious to us in the *Victorious*'s squadrons 829 and 831.'

Cdr Anthony Kimmins later broadcast on the BBC the build-up to Operation *Tungsten*:

> During the first part of the passage up north and into the Arctic Circle, the weather grew more bitter every day, and in no type of warship is there any place so exposed to the elements as the flying deck of an aircraft carrier. The whole ship has been specially designed to produce the maximum uninterrupted wind flow over that long open deck, but when that wind flow is a forty-mile-an-hour snow blizzard, and the spray breaking over the fo'c'sle is freezing before it touches down, those flight deck parties have one of the toughest jobs imaginable.

Then came a major alert, as recalled by Norman Austin, armourer for Roy's aircraft:

> A few days after joining the convoy, a 'Jerry' plane was spotted shadowing us, the *Victorious* was supposed to be supplying the fighter escort. On failing to start, the first Corsair it was pushed out of the way to try to start the second, which caught on fire.
>
> In the meantime the *Furious* ranged a Seafire from below, took off, shot the intruder down, came back over the convoy doing a victory roll, receiving a tremendous cheer from 827, much to the chagrin of the Commander Flying *Victorious* who ordered us below for demoralising his crew. Baker-Falkner was really 'chuffed' by our action in taking the micky out of the *Victorious*.

Austin continued:

> The difference between the *Victorious* and *Furious* was like chalk and cheese; whilst the *Furious* was warm and most seaworthy the *Victorious* was wet and cold. The water was up to 3 ft deep, rushing from one end of the hangar to the other as she pitched and tossed.

Emerson wrote on Saturday 1 April:

> In the Arctic Circle. This is our 4th day at sea. We have sailed north all the time, and it is bloody cold now. We steam through frequent snow and hail showers, blizzards etc with a biting wind.
>
> We have 25 Corsairs and 21 Barras aboard. We are doing A/s patrols & the fighter boys are a readiness all the time.
>
> There is a Russian convoy 150 miles ahead of us (the largest yet) and *Furious* and

the 4 ECS are covering us 100 miles astern of us. We follow the convoy round the North Cape & then return, going in to bonk the *Tirpitz* on the way. Boy what a show. She is lying in Alten Fiord & is suspected to have been repaired since the midget subs hit her at Xmas.

It is a big show for us. A bit fraught, but we expect about 30% casualties. We will have 40 fighters to each wave of bombers, & given good weather conditions (at least 8,000 ft) we can weave like hell to avoid the flak, & yet damage her to a fair degree. If only we can get enough 1,600 lb AP bombs. They want to give us 25% APs, 500 lb MC, 500 lb SAP & 500 lb SP. The ratios are all wrong.

We have Andy Tye and Anthony Kimmins aboard, so big things are expected of us.

Last time 827 did an op from *Vic* was July 31st 41 when we sustained 4 deaths and 14 POWs at Kirkenes. Let's hope we have better luck this time.

Plans had to be suddenly advanced when the Admiralty learnt from decrypts that *Tirpitz* was likely to set sail almost immediately. Roy and the other wing leaders were called in to discuss options with Vice Admiral Moore. With a growing sense of urgency Roy and Vic Rance flew over to *Furious* to update the captain and Monkey Bryant in his role as commander flying. Then he broke the bitter news to the Barracuda aircrew of the change of plans.

'B-F informed us that the C-in-C had decided, following Nelson's maxim never to trifle with a fair wind, to advance the operation by 24 hours' recalled David Brown.

Furious, the oldest operational carrier in the world, seemed in danger of shaking herself to pieces when she steamed at top speed to meet the new deadline. Whilst still on board her, Roy wrote to Naomi: 'Sorry my writing is so bad but the old girl is shaking powerful cruel and it's impossible to write properly.' Roy later returned to *Victorious*.

In the afternoon, 2 April, Force 1 led by *Victorious* and the flagship *Duke of York*, met up off the Norwegian coast with the second battle fleet, Force 2, under Rear Admiral Bisset, consisting of the flagship cruiser *Royalist*, *Furious*, the escort carriers *Emperor*, *Fencer*, *Pursuer*, and *Searcher*, the cruisers *Jamaica* and *Sheffield*, with two Fleet oilers screened by seven destroyers.

Between them, the two forces embodied in excess of 15,000 naval personnel, and the overall command was handed over to Vice Admiral Moore while the C-in-C in *Duke of York* set sail to support the convoy bound for Murmansk and hopefully confuse the enemy of the impending strike. Emerson and the other 827 Squadron aircrew aboard *Victorious* were beginning to get excited:

Sunday April 2nd – Bed early tonight. We take off at 0400. We joined forces with *Furious*, *Royalist*, *Pursuer*, *Emperor*, *Fencer* and *Searcher* today. We have heard that the activity with the Russian convoy has shot down 5 shadowers. Convoy have bagged 2 subs also (1 to HMS *Stirling* – Capt Walker).

Roy, having returned to *Victorious*, by now had a vast array of over a 100 aircraft and a dozen squadrons to coordinate in this operation. During the trip north preparations for action were made – emergency rations, escape aids and side arms (if desired) were issued. Aircraft were checked thoroughly along with all their equipment then loaded with either one 1,600-lb bomb slung underneath on the torpedo belt, or three 500-lb bombs in the wing racks. At a predetermined position the strike force peeled off from the decoy convoy towards the Norwegian coast where *Tirpitz* was hiding in her lair.

Norman Austin recalled: 'On leaving the convoy to continue its journey to Russia, we prepared to carry out the first strike on the *Tirpitz*. The day before the raid the weather was atrocious with a blizzard blowing all day.'

Tension was building in the whole Fleet as the minutes ticked away towards zero hour. On Sunday 2 April, the evening before the operation, Roy and Vic Rance again flew over from *Victorious* to their wing squadron crews on *Furious* for a further briefing. Roy gave up-to-date information and answered last-minute apprehensive questions, helping a little to calm their fears.

Dave Clarabut, 830 Squadron pilot, asked what would happen if Baker-Falkner was shot down before the dive-bombing attack and who was then to lead the attack in. Roy replied 'You'.

Once the briefing was over, Roy and the rest of the aircrew tried to relax before he returned to *Victorious* for the night. David Brown recalled:

During the evening in the wardroom of *Furious* prior to the attack, I was with a group of officers, talking about the next day's operation. Half jokingly, I said: 'Anyone break my arm for ten bob?' A voice from outside the circle said: 'Make that two (people), Dave' at which I muttered '*Who* said that?' turned round and to my great chagrin found B-F (Roy) and the skipper grinning fit to burst themselves.

On Roy's return to *Victorious*, Kevin Gibney had already completed their briefing to 827 Squadron. Sub Lt Clifford Lock recalled: 'As usual Roy was in the wardroom that evening chatting and talking things through with the aircrew, a listener and advisor rather than a "holder forth".'

The ship piped down at 8 pm and then closed up to Action Stations. *Victorious*'s Aircraft Direction Room log recorded: 'From 20.00 silence was the policy from sunset until first strike take departure.'

Cdr Anthony Kimmins continued in his recorded broadcast for the BBC:

There was little sleep the night before the attack, for we were now in the danger zone as we steamed close in to enemy waters. Look-outs and gun crews – only their eyes visible through scarves and balaclava helmets – searched the sea and sky. Supply and damage control parties never left their posts.

Down in the huge hangars there was feverish activity. On one side were the long lines of Fairey Barracudas – the new Fleet Air Arm torpedo-bombers which were being tried out in action for the first time. They looked rather like enormous beetles with their wings folded back over their bodies. On the other side were the American Corsairs with their wings folded vertically and almost touching overhead at the tips, like enormous butterflies just after they have dropped on to a leaf.

While mechanics swarmed over their aircraft making final adjustments, great yellow bombs were being wheeled down the narrow gangways, loaded up and fused. Each, of course, bore the inevitable chalked message.

The 'bomb-head' armourers chalked graffiti including: '*Tirpitz* it's yours!'

That night alone in his cabin onboard *Victorious*, Roy was inevitably wondering whether he would survive the forthcoming operation, as were *all* other aircrew. Putting aside his own fears, he eventually sat down at his desk to write his letter of farewell to Naomi in case he didn't get back alive from the operation.

Sunday: Yesterday was yet another anniversary of our becoming engaged when I had the sense to ask you to marry me and thank God you said 'yes' seven whole years ago. They have gone so terribly quickly Billy mine and have been so wonderfully happy. Thank you, darling, for all your love always.

Now Billy girl we have got two young women to care for and look after. What a responsibility and wonderful care.

Billy girl, looking back on all these years brings back the most wonderful memories doesn't it? – Killin, Lanark, Malta, Alex, Cyprus, Arbroath and always just us.

Take the greatest care of your very darling self Billy. I love and adore you so much. You and the widgers are my all. All my love to my women, Dil [Darling I love you].

From now on Roy had no time to write to Naomi who became increasingly desperate and anxious. 'Roy writes to me every day and when for several days he didn't, I knew he was in some operation. I was afraid he was in danger.'

Roy was woken at an extremely early hour on the morning of the strike by his steward and went on deck to talk to his personal mechanics and bomb crew and check that all was well with his own aircraft.

Norman Austin was already waiting and recalled: 'On the morning of the strike the weather for us was perfect. Jerry was not so lucky, as all his aircraft were snowed in and unable to intercept our bombers.'

Cdr Kimmins broadcast continued:

Just before dawn, pilots and crews, having had a good night's rest and a hot breakfast, started to drift into the hangar in their flying kit and yellow 'Mae Wests'. For a few moments there were little groups round each aircraft, as they chatted with their mechanics before going up to the bridge for their final briefing. This was the first chance they had of sniffing the air and having a look at the weather. And now – as they found perfect conditions, calm sea, clear sky with patches of cloud, and an assurance from 'Schoolie', the Met officer, that conditions would be even better inshore – there was a sigh of relief. Their one worry had been bad weather, delays or even a postponement.

Roy and Kevin Gibney mustered the aircrew for their final briefing in the bowels of the ship. Captain Denny, fatherly watched over proceedings and wished them Godspeed. They crowded around and inevitably were anxious before the strike. The majority were in their late teens or early twenties in comparison to Roy's ripe old age of twenty-seven. He calmed their fears and ended with his usual 'Just follow Daddy'.

On *Furious*, Dickie Kingdon, called his aircrew for their final briefing in the ship's canteen, a large covered space on the foredeck, forward of the upper hangar. Allan Thomson said:

This large area combined with its position was conducive to seasickness. Some people not normally afflicted were inclined by the motion to succumb towards sickness, Johnny Whyte piped up 'Let's get airborne! Before I am seasick!'

PO Jan Lock, also of 830 Squadron, reflected:

> After five years of war, I still got butterflies, and I'm sure we were all the same. Most of the lads had never had a go before. However, all members of the wing had the highest regard for B-F, as one of them put it very succinctly 'I think we'd all willingly have flown into hell with him' and in fact the first attack on *Tirpitz* must have looked as near as hell as one could imagine.

From now onwards timing was absolutely critical. Lives were at stake. Every second in the operation counted; if not adhered to the attack would unravel, the strikes could fail in their mission and *Tirpitz* would remain the biggest threat to the preparations for the D-Day landings.

At 2 am on 3 April before dawn, Captain Denny ordered *Victorious* to close up at Action Stations, the flight deck and hangar were the scenes of frenzied activity. Aircraft were moved into pre take-off positions, bombs pushed along on their trolleys to be fitted underneath the Barracudas, fighters were fully armed. The flight deck handling party stood ready for action. There was an air of expectancy waiting to get the go ahead.

Vice Admiral Moore recorded: 'By 3 am it appeared that everything was in our favour. So far as we knew we had not been sighted, and flying conditions were perfect for putting the operation into effect.'

On *Furious* David Brown recalled: 'The rest of the aircrews were also finally briefed and the captain gave us his blessing. The skipper spoke to us over the tannoy, wished us well, and added that he didn't expect all of us to return from the operation.'

Cdr Kimmins continued: 'In the early morning twilight at that high latitude, the ghostly shapes of the other warships could be seen with the destroyers fussing about to take up their new positions in the screens as the Fleet manoeuvred towards the flying off position. The sky was clear.' Battle ensigns were flying.

By 4.05 am all aircrews on *Victorious* had already made their way up to the flight deck where there was a buzz of activity as the aircraft were ranged and bombs checked, until finally 'Wings' voice came over the flight deck tannoy: 'Pilots man your aircraft.' Ducking under wings and dodging propellers, each clambered into their polished aircraft.

Roy climbed into the cockpit of his personal Barracuda coded '4K for 'King', clipped on his parachute, fastened his straps, tested rudder aileron and elevator controls, glanced quickly over the cockpit instruments and then checked the intercom with Guy Micklem, his resident observer, and young Arthur Kimberley sitting apprehensively in his telegraphist air gunner position. Their aircraft's grey-green painted wings glinted in the Arctic dawn. The side of his cockpit was decorated with a small painting of bombs with swastikas to denote the first mission earlier that year. Roy's lucky mascot Pop-eye was as ever in his cockpit.

Behind Roy's aircraft, Lt Cdr Kevin Gibney, commanding officer of 827 Squadron and his closest friend, sat waiting in his Barracuda, recently freshly painted with the words 'Heaven can wait'. In front of Gibney, his pilot, Howard Emerson, was making last-minute checks.

When Roy was ready in his cockpit, characteristically he called back to Micklem and Kimberley on the intercom: 'Are you secure in the back… right, let's go then.' He gave thumbs up to the flight deck crew.

One by one all the other pilots confirmed to Norman Austin that they were also ready to take off: 'I received the thumbs up from all our pilots, prior to take-off, some, I am afraid for the last time.'

Cdr Kimmins continued: 'At first light – at exactly the pre-arranged minute – Commander Flying shouted the welcome order: "Start up".'

Roy rammed down on the starter button. There was the tell-tale puff of black smoke from the Merlin engine as the Coffman starter cartridge was fired. Then, as Cdr Kimmins noted: 'The words were hardly out of Commander Flying's mouth before there was a roar of engines....'

The propeller turned hesitantly and then fired. The growl of the engine reassured Roy that all was in order. He then ran through his cockpit checks, whilst Micklem had a last glance at his charts and Kimberley tested his radio and gun mountings.

Cdr Kimmins continued:

By now the carriers and the escorting ships were all heeling over, swinging into the wind. As the steam jet up in the bows – to show when the ship is dead into wind – was opened up, lumps of ice shot into the air, went slithering down the flying deck, got whirled up in the propeller slip-streams, and were sent cracking against the flight deck crews clinging to the wing tips and lying on the deck tending the chocks.

A final nod from the captain, a signal from Commander Flying, the flight deck officer raised his green flag, the engines started to rev up, the flag dropped and the first aircraft were roaring away over the bows.

At zero hour – 4.16 am – the first Corsair from 1834 Squadron roared off *Victorious*'s flight deck at the flying off position, 120 miles west of Alten Fiord. It was followed by the rest of Lt Cdr Turnbull's Fighter Wing.

Roy sat ready in his cockpit, carefully reviewing in his mind that nothing had been forgotten and that all was going to plan. Precisely nine minutes later, the waiting was at last over, and Roy took off with heart beating fast and a sigh of relief. He was already lined up along the centre line painted on the flight deck. He quickly checked that his throttle lever was tight and that he had twenty degrees' flap on. The flag whirled round and round in the air. Roy, hard on his brakes, pushed the throttle wide open. The Merlin growled, the Barracuda juddered, the flag dropped, brakes off and he rolled forward, the propeller cutting through the air. They were past the bridge and the forward pom pom, and then suddenly at the end of the deck and airborne, with the aircraft carrier receding behind him.

Once he has taken off from *Victorious* he was followed by the other twelve Barracudas of 827 Squadron, and at exactly the same time the rest of his wing, the nine Barracudas of 830 Squadron, were airborne from *Furious*.

Lt Cdr Jimmie Sleigh led his wing consisting of thirty fighters, including Wildcats of 881 and 882 Squadrons, which took off from *Searcher* and *Pursuer*, and Hellcats of 800 Squadron from *Emperor*. Then, once aloft, Roy gradually throttled back, the controls sluggish at this speed, and dropped two smoke floats at short intervals to indicate to the fighter escort the course to follow, 126 magnetic. The fighters took up station on the quarters of the bomber strike.

Once the Barracudas were airborne they formed up on Roy's aircraft. His wing man, No. 2, positioned close by as the aircraft on his starboard flank. The wing flying in close formation followed him to the south-east heading for Kaafiord. It was a dramatic sight, the aircraft filling a full five miles of sky with bombers and fighters. The first strike took departure from the Fleet at 4.38 am.

Allan Thomson described the scene: 'The aircraft flew in pairs very close together. The wing tip of one aircraft was locked between wing and tailplane of the other where the TAG sat with a wing tip waving up and down a few feet from his face.'

It was a perfect morning with a slight haze, the distant white coastline of Arctic Norway already visible. The attacking aircraft, fighters and bombers, skimmed over the waves below 50 feet to avoid detection by enemy radar for as long as possible.

Roy reported later: 'At 04.57 the striking force began to climb when we were 25 miles from the coast.'

As they approached land, Roy broke the strict radio silence, broadcasting as briefly as possible his personal call sign 'Headache Leader', and brusquely ordered over the VHF radio: 'Get some height.' In unison the bombers and fighters responded by climbing to 10,000 feet on full throttle in open V-formation in preparation to climb above the snow-capped mountains directly ahead of them.

Roy continued:

Two minutes later Loppen Island was identified on the port bow, and our landfall close to the westward of that island was established. We crossed the coast at 05.08.

The route they followed passed close to the westward of the head of Lang Fiord and thence to the eastward down the valley to the target anchored in Kaafiord.

As the striking force advanced towards Oksfiord glacier, Arthur Kimberley in the rear seat of the leader's aircraft recounted: 'We picked up our landmark and then stooged inland. The sun was shining. We streaked inland crossing over some gun positions, but they seemed to be fast asleep.'

They were undetected and unopposed even though they saw two destroyers and a big tanker lying in Lang Fiord. Kimberley continued: 'They seemed asleep also. We altered course towards our target.' They swept into the head of the valley of Kaafiord and emerged from above the protective cover of the steep snow-covered mountains in perfect weather, and there was *Tirpitz* lying exposed below them.

As the strike was approaching her, *Tirpitz* was weighing anchor to commence post-repair trials. The second anchor was coming in when the smoke screen ashore began and thirty-two Allied aircraft were reported heading south. The ship's alarm was sounded and guns manned.

Roy reported later:

At approximately 05.25 the striking force was deployed and began its initial dive from 8,000 feet. At the same time it began to come under heavy, but inaccurate, fire from HA batteries at the head of Kaafiord and elsewhere ashore. The smoke screen started to operate as we arrived in sight but was too late to be effective. Smoke all round the fiord.

Thanks to our briefing we had no difficulty in finding the *Tirpitz*. She was just where we expected to find her. She looked very large against the grey fiord.

Roy continued: 'About ten miles from the target I disposed 830 Squadron aircraft astern of 827 Squadron's twelve aircraft.' He ordered the Corsairs to patrol over the whole area as top cover at about 10,000 feet, as a defence against possible attack by enemy fighters. He said: 'We had fighters ahead of us, astern and on either side, above and below.'

Dickie Kingdon reported: 'At about 5,000 ft and three miles range the target was sighted inside her boom defence close to the near shore under the hills.'

Then Roy gave the order to 'double line-ahead' – to deploy a formation of two parallel columns, with all the Barracudas of 827 Squadron in the lead, followed closely by the Barracudas of 830 Squadron to a point nearly over the target.

Two columns of Barracuda parted and swept round to form a circle about a mile radius above *Tirpitz* in order to carry out the synchronised attack. The port wing took advantage of hill cover at 3,000 feet, whilst the starboard column, with no cover at all, experienced only very light flak.

Roy continued: 'Sighted target in position expected, then dived to keep hill cover sending all Wildcats and Hellcats down to strafe guns and target.' The fighters dived down after the pre-agreed call sign 'lights out! Groups of aircraft accelerated downwards, and, with all guns blazing, swept the decks of the *Tirpitz*.'

Lt George Cockburn-Yorke described the action:

Our Wildcat fighters were playing merry hell with enemy guns positions, shooting them up all over the place.

The Hellcats and Wildcats of the escort flew low over the battleship, machine-gunning her gun positions and superstructure. Others banked around, strafing any suitable targets and set *Tirpitz*'s supply tanker alight with cannon-fire, riddling anti-aircraft battery posts and roaring to and fro across the battle area waiting for the German fighters which never came up.

Emerson watched as:

Martlets strafed AA positions as they dived. They made a very awe-inspiring sight as they went in streaming red tracer. The flak started coming up in waves, and I was sitting in position to dive waiting for the wing leader to go in. I decided not to wait for him as the smoke generators round the fiord were building up, I was going to weave down through the flak. Then the wing leader dived over the hills due west went past and beat me in.

The battleship responded by firing her short-range ack-ack guns on either beam, reportedly at 8,500 rounds per minute.

At 5.29 am precisely, the dive-bombing attack commenced. Barracudas peeling off over *Tirpitz* from three directions, Roy turned into the centre, gave his 'Go! Go! Go!' order and put his aircraft into a steep dive. Green and red streamers came shooting up at his aircraft as he dived directly towards the stern of *Tirpitz*, eyes glued on her funnel.

Roy continued:

My aircraft dived towards the mountain NW of the target, pulled up over the top and dived steeply towards the target itself from a height of approximately 4,000 feet. I then lost sight of all aircraft and carried out a dive from stern of target, releasing bombs at 1,200 feet.

His three 500-lb bombs whistled down and *Tirpitz* was hit on the bridge superstructure, causing heavy explosions and flames, and silencing the ship's own flak. He reported: 'We dived and got two direct hits. They got off some light red tracer stuff at us, but it was nothing like the reception we expected.'

A moment of heart-stopping terror was experienced in the air gunner seat of the rear of Roy's aircraft. Kimberley was stunned as he heard a loud noise and feared that the aircraft had been hit and was disintegrating. He recalled:

We screamed down and let go our bombs as everything opened up on us. Just as we were pulling out of our dive there was a loud 'whoomph' astern of us. I thought our tail had been blown off by flak. But we were alright.

Once Kimberley had caught his breath in the midst of the strike, with sixty-one aircraft milling around, he was able to later describe the ordered chaos and marvel at its strength: 'Everybody was there, bags of fighters, top, bottom, and both sides I could see dozens of American Wildcats, Hellcats and Corsairs.'

Roy pulled sharply out of the dive, harnesses tightened around him and his crew as they were pushed back into their seats with the high G-force. Roy pushed the control column, forcing the aircraft sharply starboard and climbed rapidly away. He reported:

The Barracuda then levelled up to avoid the mountains all around. We left at full speed, hedge-hopping over the countryside thick with snow. The rest of the Barracudas followed closely behind peeling off over the *Tirpitz* from three directions.

Roy's attack was followed at rapid intervals by the rest of the wing. Dickie Kingdon, piloting the second aircraft, started counting as he turned in and dived when he got to ten. So it went on, one after the other, peeling off in turn from each side and diving almost vertically. They released their various bomb payloads of high explosives from heights from 3,500 to 1,200 feet.

The third Barracuda to attack was piloted by Howard Emerson, and in the seat behind him Kevin Gibney was deep in concentration watching the scene unfold:

We saw a great black swastika painted on the fore-castle of the *Tirpitz*. We had one of the big 'cookies' aboard – an armour-piercing, high-explosive bomb – and our wings lifted as it went down. I watched it hurtling down towards the *Tirpitz*. I couldn't see it hit, but the tail gunner of the following plane said it exploded in a cloud of smoke and flame.

Arthur Wells, 830 Squadron air gunner later reflected:

I recall the confidence which came across the R/T from the CO as he led the wing into the dive. The flak came up from the *Tirpitz* and from all sides of the fiord. I have a tremendous admiration for all our pilots who just put the aircraft nose down and screamed 'here we go chaps' weaving all the way down and out to avoid the flak.

Clifford Lock watched wide-eyed as his leader's aircraft entered the dive:

The first strike on *Tirpitz* was very spectacular. B-F scored the first hit with a bomb on the superstructure – a great pink flash as it went off – but things rapidly became rather confusing. The heavy anti-aircraft fire did not seem to be very close – but the light flak was daunting – you could see it coming up for what seemed ages before it shot past.

After dropping its bombs, each aircraft dived sharply away from the *Tirpitz* and the sheer cliffs behind her and then headed inland up the fiord individually. Most aircraft flew overland to Silden Island, which lay at the entrance to Alten Fiord, then set a course low on the water for the Fleet.

Sub Lt Roy Eveleigh, an observer of 830 Squadron, looked back and could see 'a huge pall of smoke rising 1,200 feet over the *Tirpitz*. From there on we flew over valleys and glaciers, twisting and turning all the time to avoid flak which came up at us from odd batteries here and there.'

In the last aircraft to dive was Allan Thomson:

> Getting out was not so easy! There was still a lot of flak! And it was a case of circle and climb for enough height to get into the shelter behind a ridge high between hills. Someone had a gun ranged on that gap. Perhaps it was one of the shore batteries. It was a case of wait for a shell to explode then plunge for the gap, hopefully before the next one arrived. Then we were through and formed up with another Barracuda, hugging the ground as we made our getaway. Something moved behind us and I watched intently till it broke the skyline. Hurrah! A Wildcat!

As his aircraft left the snowy scene of devastation, David Brown observed:

> ...the aircrews' last view of Kaafiord was of a myriad of red flash bursts, dozens of milling aircraft, and most conspicuous, the flash of guns from a heavy battery at the south end of the fiord. It was an awe-inspiring show and *Tirpitz* must have been fairly stunned, little knowing that another strike was already on its way.

At 5.30 am, exactly sixty seconds after the first bomb had been dropped, the attack by twenty-one Barracuda aircraft was over.

En route back to the Fleet, Roy, Micklem and Kimberley flew over small Norwegian houses, but saw nobody. 'It was too early' recounted Kimberley. Roy could take stock of the situation and recognised 'visibility throughout was exceptional and weather in general could not have been better. It is clear that a considerable element of surprise was achieved.' He was relieved to report that 'no enemy fighters were sighted and the flak, in general, was sporadic, erratic and inaccurate.'

On his return flight, Emerson's aircraft was attracting enemy fire: 'A mobile heavy gun gave us a hot reception & plenty of close blasts. Very accurate. Boy was I sweating, it seemed a hell of a long way out, doing 200 mph.'

At last Roy's aircraft hove into sight of *Victorious* and prepared to land-on. The Barracudas circled the carrier while the fighters landed on. In the back seat TAG Kimberley expressed the feelings of Roy, Guy Micklem and himself: 'Then we sighted our carrier. Were we delighted?' Roy throttled back his engine and landed on to the cheers of the deck-handling party. By 6.21 am, all the Barracudas of the first strike had landed on. The other part of the wing having returned safely to *Furious*.

David Brown exclaimed with relief:

> I shall always remember the splendid feeling of homecoming when *Furious* hove in sight out of the north Atlantic mists, and the skipper, that fatherly figure Captain George Philip, would be waiting to greet each aircrew individually as we landed on.

Kingdon sadly had to report to Roy that one of his aircraft had failed to return. The twenty-one-year-old pilot Sub Lt Bell, his observer Sub Lt Drennan and L/A Burns were missing. They had last been seen in their damaged aircraft making a controlled glide after the attack, and may have made a good forced landing according to Kingdon.

Allan Thomson's reaction was also one of relief on returning to the ship:

> Back in the hangar it was a case, for me, of 'head down' stretched out on the pad of the gymnastic box, for a while till the ship was stood down from Action Stations.

310

Then aircrew breakfast (special egg – traditional) and de-briefing. Praise B-F's and everyone else's organisation, my log book shows a surprising 2.00 hours trip for this operation. Slick! Wasn't it!

The score for the first strike was out of twenty-one aircraft – forty-six bombs dropped with ten hits claimed by the aircrew. Subsequent Admiralty analysis confirmed six certain hits and three probables for the first strike alone.

The return of Roy and his strike force was watched and filmed by cine and press correspondents. He was later inundated by their questions at the press meeting. Asked about his role, he replied:

What did I do? Just piloted my Barracuda. There were a few flak ships about, but nobody bothered. Guns ashore too, but nobody bothered. We came down low. Nobody on the *Tirpitz*'s deck. I'll tell you why. Because of our fighters. They haven't had the praise due to them. They went in first, fired at by the flak ships, shore guns, and all the *Tirpitz*'s guns. They shot up the *Tirpitz*, and the flak ships and the shore guns – shot 'em so they shut up.

Then we went in – and nobody on the *Tirpitz* decks. We dropped smaller bombs first, to keep Jerry below and to scalp those in the turrets, and then our big bombs.

Just after 6.36 am the second wave of nineteen Barracudas of 52 Naval TBR Wing with their escort of forty fighters, led by Vic Rance, struck *Tirpitz*. As the bombers banked and turned high over the fiord, the battleship gradually became shrouded in smoke, had ceased firing and was burning fiercely amidships. Her magazine was believed to be hit, and she was aground on her stern.

L/A Victor Smyth, of 831 Squadron, later recollected:

As we manoeuvred into position for the dive, the sky was full of bursting shells which rocked the aircraft violently when they were near. A few seconds later we were speeding down into a mass of exploding shells so thick that the target can hardly be seen through the thick cloud of black puffs. It took my breath away.

The explosions which rent the *Tirpitz* were so terrific that her stern whipped round in the water, and flames leapt as high as her topmast.

The second strike scored one 1,600-lb and one 500-lb hit for certain and two probable 500-lb hits, while the fighters again strafed *Tirpitz*'s upper deck. For a bit of light relief, nineteen-year-old L/A Robert Bacon recollected how he 'had great joy in hurtling four empty bottles over the side at *Tirpitz*; they made a lovely whistle going down.'

The overall outcome of the two strikes was that *Tirpitz* took sixteen bomb hits and was left blazing fiercely in two places amidships, and smaller fires were plainly seen burning at other points. Above her was a colossal column of smoke now rising even higher, to more than 3,000 feet.

Ninety-four bombs totalling 26 tons had been dropped on *Tirpitz*. The Germans admitted 'fifteen direct hits on the *Tirpitz* and two near misses', along with 'heavy damage to the upper deck leaving it on fire'.

Despite anticipated heavy aircrew losses, casualties from the two strikes had been remarkably light, two Barracudas, one from each strike, having been shot down and a third crashed in the sea after a successful take-off. One damaged Hellcat had been ditched. *Tirpitz*'s casualties were 122 killed and 316 wounded, including her commanding officer, Captain

Meyer.

Tirpitz was severely disabled, and proved to be no further threat to the North Russian convoys and provided the green light for Eisenhower and Montgomery to go ahead with the ultra secret D-Day preparations scheduled for now only eight weeks later. The operation had even caused the German High Command to believe that an invasion was imminent on the Norwegian coast, safeguarding the secret of the real invasion zone in France.

That evening at 5.30 pm, Vice Admiral Moore signalled to the Fleet 'Prepare to Repeat *Tungsten* tomorrow', so re-enforcing the impression of a forthcoming invasion of Norway. Emerson wrote: 'C-in-C ordered a repeat to-morrow. Everyone has twitch. It was later cancelled. Whew! Am off to join the PU.'

Allan Thomson said:

We were due to repeat the performance next morning. Turned in early, there was some hammock talk from 831 on a sort of 'Fancy having to go back there again' theme. Admittedly they had had a better reception than the first wave. However an 830 voice of sanity pointed out it would be better in the morning than in six weeks or three months' time when the defences would be repaired. And 'if we don't get some sleep we won't be fit to go anywhere' brought silence and swinging hammocks soon put all into a good night's rest.

However, the aircrew had mixed feelings when at 9 pm Captain Denny announced over the tannoy in *Victorious* that the repetition of *Tungsten* was cancelled. Vice Admiral Moore had revised his original intention to follow up the attack in view of the damage to *Tirpitz* and the fatigue of the aircrews.

Allan Thomson reacted: 'An anti-climax in the morning, no attack! Enough damage done! In the ensuing months we were to remember the prophetic words about "their Lordships" not being content till *Tirpitz* was on bottom'.

Jan Lock added:

As soon as we got back onboard we re-armed and re-fuelled ready for another strike. The Vice Admiral decided it would not be worth it, much to Baker-Falkner's disgust. We were finally credited with sixteen hits, and according to reports she burned for days.

Arthur Wells recalled: 'The Admiral was so pleased with the result and that we returned safely that he entertained us all to a meal and drink in the wardroom – I think for ratings to be entertained in this way was unheard of at that time..

Roy was awarded the ship's battle pennant to commemorate his invaluable achievement. That evening Clifford Lock recalled the antics of Monkey Bryant:

Commander Flying in *Furious* entertained the wardroom with one of his favourite exercises which was to make a barrier of furniture across one corner of the wardroom, and 'come on, let's go over the top – whereupon everyone in the room was expected to dive headlong over the pile and end up in a sprawling heap on top of each other. By the time everyone was sorted out it was time for another gin...

Allan Thomson concluded: 'There was an Admiralty Fleet Order (AFO) published which suggested that the rest of the FAA take an example from No. 8 Wing (attack on the *Tirpitz*). Surely it was a tribute to B-F who put it all together.'

312

CHAPTER 24

Hero's Return from Orkney

Roy and the *Tungsten* force returned to Scapa Flow in triumph on 6 April 1944 to splice the mainbrace. Reuters' correspondent Desmond Tighe recorded the moment:

> The carriers were welcomed home with full honours. As we passed each ship the officers and ratings lined the quarterdecks, took off their caps and cheered, the sound reverberating across the blue waters.

Another correspondent, Leo Disher, later reported in the *Daily Telegraph*:

> The force which knocked out the *Tirpitz* came back to their base today to one of the most rousing welcomes of the war. As they rode through to the anchorage they were cheered along from ship to ship of the Home Fleet.
>
> The demonstration was led by Admiral Sir Bruce Fraser, the C-in-C. He stood on the quarterdeck, with the entire company of his flagship, waving his cap as the aircraft-carriers and other ships of the attacking force sailed by.

Allan Thomson recalled:

> As the ships turned into Scapa we formed up in a long line on deck for the 'cheer ship' routine as the carriers did a lap of honour, round the ships at anchor. We were then steaming into wind and while it may have been a heart warming reception it was a bone chilling experience and we were very glad when it ended and we would finally break ranks and move around in an effort to restore circulation.

As *Furious* took her leave, Captain George Philip signalled to the escort carriers: 'Au revoir and thank you. Once again the loving care and attention to my fishes when covered by your chickens was much appreciated. An unnatural but very effective combination.'

Roy was just relieved to be safely back, and on his return wrote to Naomi in classic understatement about the *Tirpitz* attack: 'Thursday. Just had a very good trip and expecting lots of mail.'

The post was not long in coming. The day after the *Tirpitz* raid the following Naval Message was received and handed to Roy personally: 'H.M. The King wishes the following message to be passed to those who took part in yesterday's attack: "Hearty congratulations on your gallant and successful operation. George R."'

A further Naval Message from the Commander-in-Chief read: 'I have received the following from the Prime Minister: "Pray congratulate the pilots and air crews concerned on this most brilliant feat of arms so satisfactory to the RN and to whole world cause."'

A third from the First Sea Lord given to Roy read: 'Please congratulate all those concerned in the gallant and well-executed attack on *Tirpitz*. Only the most careful and thorough planning and preparation could have produced such a successful result.'

Vice Admiral Sir Henry Moore made a general signal to the Fleet: 'Hearty congratulations: That's prime.'

All of the congratulatory pink signal messages were distributed by Roy to the aircrews aboard ship on their return. As David Brown put it: 'The Powers that Be in Great Britain in April 1944 proved Themselves more than satisfied with the success of the operation.'

The public did not hear of the attack till three or four days after the event when it broke on BBC broadcasts and in the headlines of national papers across the country. Naomi first heard on Good Friday about Roy's involvement. A reporter arrived, knocking on the door and asked: 'Did you know your husband had done this?'

The paper reported Naomi's response:

'Just his line of duty: I wondered if he had been in it,' dark-haired Mrs Baker-Falkner commented when the *Daily Mirror* told her that that her 28 year-old husband had led the *Tirpitz* attack.

'I don't mind admitting I've been anxious for the past few days, as I've heard nothing from my husband lately.'

The report continued:

A few minutes later a telegraph boy arrived.

'Oh good,' she exclaimed; 'He's getting leave. I'd have opened this in fear and trembling if you hadn't told me what he's been doing.'

The telegram from Roy told Naomi he would soon have ten days' leave. It went on – 'meet me Paddington, Roy.'

The rest of the Falkner family heard the news on the wireless on 7 April and over the next few days Leslie collected national and local newspapers about Roy's exploits.

The front page of the *Daily Mail* of 8 April was dominated by a photograph of *Tirpitz* ablaze and the headline read: 'The *Tirpitz* Bombed Out of the War'. Correspondent Leo Disher wrote:

The *Tirpitz* has been knocked out of the war. Dive-bombing Barracudas of the Fleet Air Arm scored at least 24 direct hits on her decks with more than eight tons of armour-piercing bombs in their daring dawn attack last Monday and rendered Germany's sole surviving naval giant useless as a battleship.

Another newspaper recorded in massive bold headlines:

Major Blow to the Enemy
SMASHING OF TIRPITZ

AT LEAST 24 HITS ON BATTLESHIP COMPARABLE WITH SINKING OF *SCHARNHORST*

Torn by terrific inner and outer explosions as a result of the brilliant and gallant attack by Fleet Air Arm pilots at dawn on Monday, the *Tirpitz* is useless as a warship.

Assailed by the largest formation of carrier-based aircraft ever concentrated against a single ship, the *Tirpitz* was hit at least 24 times.

Crews of the Barracudas (acting as dive-bombers) and pilots of escorting Seafires, Hellcats, Wildcats and Corsairs returned from the attack jubilant, reporting violent flashes on the target and the steady dull glow of fires as heavy armour-piercing and medium bombs struck home.

The *Daily Mirror* ran a photograph of the blazing *Tirpitz* on its front page and also a photograph of Roy with the caption:

Lieutenant Commander Baker-Falkner, Torquay, who led the attack on the *Tirpitz*, was educated at Dartmouth College. His wife told the *Daily Mirror* yesterday: 'The only thing he was really good at was boxing.'

The *Daily Sketch* reported:

Barracudas Dived At Dawn
Tirpitz 'Asleep'
As Bombs Fell

The Barracuda dive-bombers which attacked the 42,000 ton *Tirpitz* at dawn in two waves last Monday in Alten Fjord took the Germans completely by surprise, it was revealed yesterday. Bombs rained down at more than 20 tons a minute. At least 16 direct hits were scored – four by 'cookies', heavy armour-piercing bombs. 'I believe the *Tirpitz* is now useless as a warship,' said the captain of one of the carriers.

Not one German fighter came up to protect the battleship. The attack, made by 42 planes, was led by 27 year-old Lieut. Commander Roy Baker-Falkner, DSC, whose home is Torquay.

Naomi's sister-in-law Eira wrote to her husband Bill, now with the advancing Allied troops in Italy:

Well, my darling, we have a hero in the family. Nao has just phoned me to say that Roy led the raid on the *Tirpitz*. She has been worried stiff since reading about it yesterday as she hasn't heard from Roy for ten days and as you probably know by this time, three Barracudas were lost and the radio announced that the next of kin were going to be informed.

Well, she received a wire from Roy this morning, saying he was safe and that he was having leave and could she meet him at the Berner's tomorrow. Since then she has had lots of reporters from different daily papers all wanting information about Roy – they wanted to take a photograph of Nao and the children but she wouldn't let them – isn't she a silly?

However, in Roy's next letter to Naomi he had to defend his role in the *Tirpitz* attack.

Friday: I don't honestly know what to write about. I know that my darling wife is worrying again but that I'm afraid, Billy, it can't be helped. I'm sorry Billy girl and it's all over now – we've done our stuff and quite well too.

Naomi left Carole and Sandra in Devon and rushed up by train to London to meet Roy at Paddington Station as arranged. She had not seen him for weeks and was shocked to see how gaunt he looked. The couple went to church to give thanks for Roy's safe home-coming.

There were several reporters around and Naomi later said 'I was a bit overwhelmed. We were just coming out of church and the Fleet Street press came to photograph us, I tried to get out of it but it was all over the papers after that.' Roy just wanted to go home to Devon for Easter, and to some gardening. But first there was an official duty to undertake – Roy and Guy Micklem had been invited to meet the King of Norway who was in exile in London.

Guy Micklem wrote to his brother in India:

Did Mum and Dad tell you about the lunch party with the King of Norway? He wanted to hear my story and so Admiral Evans arranged this particular festivity. His son Prince Olav was there too. The lunch was excellent, and with a second glass of port the atmosphere was nothing if not matey and I thoroughly enjoyed it all.

Prince Olav also remembered this meeting, even when contacted fifty years later. Soon after the meeting with Roy, the prince was appointed Chief of the Defence by his government in exile.

Roy and Naomi at last caught the train down to Devon, getting out at Torquay's Torre Station. The press, however, were still after Roy and met him off the train. The resulting report by the *Daily Express* featured a full-length photograph of Roy and Naomi and announced:

Barracuda Flier Baker-Falkner Comes Home

TIRPITZ ATTACK LEADER TURNS TO LAWN-MOWING 'DON'T LET ME STEAL ALL THE THUNDER'

Back from crippling the *Tirpitz* Lieutenant-Commander Roy Baker-Falkner, DSC – 27 year-old leader of the Barracuda attack which left Hitler's last battleship blazing in Alten Fiord – stepped from the 11.16 train at Torquay tonight with his dark-haired wife, Naomi.

Tomorrow, neighbours in the St Mary Church district of Torquay will probably see the six-foot Lieutenant-Commander contentedly mowing the lawn in front of his new house, Petitor.

'I thought of doing it myself but then decided to save it up for Roy,' said Mrs Baker-Falkner.

'You see, it's the first time we've had a lawn to mow, the first time we've had a home of our own in the six years we've been married.'

Her husband had two things on his mind.

One (because of that lawn) was: 'Mm – I hope the weather is fine for a few days'.

The other was 'Look – don't make me steal all the thunder on this show. I wish somebody would give those fighter boys the big hand they deserve for going in smack against the *Tirpitz* in their single-seaters with only four guns apiece. They made it easy for us.

'Then there's Rance – Lieutenant-Commander Victor Rance. He led the second strike.

316

'And Gibney – Lieut-Commander Kevin Gibney, only we call him "Fangless". He's bitten Jerry hard enough on ops in Norway, Coastal Command, Malta, Egypt and now in Norway again, but he had two teeth knocked out playing rugby, so he's "Fangless" to us.

'There are plenty more I'd like people to know about. Good types, all of them. That's why the action was such a piece of cake. It went like clockwork, exactly as planned, because they all did exactly as they were told.'

The Falkner family did not celebrate in a major way. Leslie recalled: 'At that time we could not celebrate parties as we do now. We probably celebrated by opening a tin of peaches. However, the village was awash with the news. People were coming up to my parents and congratulating them.'

'Shaldon Family's Pride' was the headline on the front page of the *Teignmouth Post and Gazette* on 14 April:

People were thrilled over the weekend by the exploits which led to the crippling of Hitler's biggest battleship, the 45,000 ton *Tirpitz* in Alten Fjord, Norway, it was a surprise attack by planes and 42 Barracuda dive-bombers scored at least 24 hits on the ship.

The attack was led by 28 years-old Lieut.-Commander Roy Baker-Falkner, RN, DSC, son of Mr and Mrs Baker-Falkner, of Shaldon.

At long last in St George's Flats he could wind down and relax with his family, and to appreciate his little children – after all he had only seen tiny Sandra two times since she had been born.

Yet he couldn't be left alone to relax, and the next accolade was from the Mayor of Torquay as reported in a local newspaper:

The Mayor of Torquay (Mr E. H. Sermon) has sent a telegram of welcome to Lieut.-Com. R. Baker-Falkner congratulating him on his attacks on the German battleship *Tirpitz* and welcoming him home to Torquay. Lieut.-Com Baker-Falkner has also been invited to the Mayor's Parlour to sign the distinguished visitors' book.

Soon after the Right Worshipful the Lord Mayor of Exeter honoured him with the freedom of the City.

Bill Lord wrote to Eira from Italy:

I was very thrilled to hear about Roy's magnificent achievement – but above all delighted that he survived. I wonder what he will get – maybe a VC. Poor little Naomi – what a terrible time she must have had waiting for the telegram – am not sure but that she ought to have a DSO or something too.

During this period after the *Tirpitz* raid, Roy applied for a desk job, news of which he was awaiting over the forthcoming weeks. Eventually, he was signalled that he would be going back to Boscombe Down and become non-operational again as a test pilot, although there had been offers involving him taking up a posting with the British Delegation in Washington to test display aircraft.

Violet Matthews, the Baker-Falkners' young nanny, who was aged seventeen at that time, remembered meeting Roy:

He was a very nice man, very pleasant, very kindly. He was delightful.

He came on his final leave; it was to be his last leave doing operational flying. He was going to be made a commander. He was going to be grounded for a while – he had done his hours, and his quota of flying.

He said to me: 'Now Vi, I am hoping you are going to come with us. We want you to. We are going to get a pony for each of the children. I could get one for you. One thing I can assure you, we will have lots of fun.'

Roy's leave ended and in mid-April he reluctantly returned to the Orkney Isles and Hatston.

On the return journey north by train he bumped into his old Dartmouth friend, Donald McEwen, whom he had not seen for the previous seven years. McEwen recalled:

On completion of the sub lieutenants' course, in the summer of 1937, we went our separate ways; I was appointed as Sub. of the new cruiser *Glasgow* and B-F had gone off to do a flying course. After that I saw him only once, briefly, boarding a train at Edinburgh, just after he had returned from the successful attack on the *Tirpitz*.

They had a lot of catching up on old news and then finally parted ways.

CHAPTER 25

Ultra Secret Operations –
Prelude to D-Day

Roy had led a successful raid on *Tirpitz*. The battleship had been severely damaged and was out of the war for the foreseeable future. 'What next?' he thought.

The Royal Navy now had a golden opportunity to release capital ships for the war effort in other theatres around the world. Most importantly, the removal of the *Tirpitz* threat against Arctic convoys and the invasion fleet building up in the English Channel, meant the Supreme Allied Command could give the final signal for the forthcoming Invasion of Europe to go ahead.

However, there was to be no let-up for Roy or his wing who were now unwittingly part of a major deception plan in the prelude to D-Day – Operation *Bodyguard*. *Bodyguard* was the deception plan that supported the Normandy invasion – Operation *Overlord*. Its objective, as stated in the initial plan dated 20 January 1944, was to push Germany into making 'faulty strategic dispositions'. The deception planners wanted to convince the Germans to mis-allocate their Forces away from Normandy and instead reinforce the Nazi effort in Norway, the Mediterranean and the Balkans.

Bodyguard consisted of three primary operations – *Fortitude North*, *Fortitude South* and *Zeppelin*, and numerous secondary operations. *Fortitude North* affected Roy and his wing in that it involved a deceptive strike on Norway. Accordingly, in the spring of 1944 false information was spread that the Western Allies were about to attack Norway.

As part of this story, the Allies created a fictional Fourth Army in Scotland that contained three corps with 250,000 troops – eight divisions overall. The fictitious British VII Corps was to capture Narvik while the other two corps were to capture Stavanger. To further convince the Germans, the Allies used numerous double agents, false radio broadcasts, and decoy camps. The Soviets colluded by dummy offensive preparations aimed at Finland and northern Norway.

This played into Hitler's express wish which was not to withdraw from any occupied country. The German leader was in particular concerned with Norway. He had been reported to have described Norway as 'the zone of destiny of this war'.

The Allies' fictitious 'Invasion of Norway' was scheduled to be launched from Scotland in May 1944, and to be followed by an 'invasion' of Germany by way of Denmark. The Allies falsified the Swedish stock market so that it appeared that Norway would soon be liberated.

To further this deception, the British Home Fleet continued their own unwitting contribution to *Fortitude North* throughout mid-April with a series of further air strikes on *Tirpitz* and German shipping along the Norwegian coast. Within this context, unknown to all but the highest levels of the Admiralty, Roy and his wing returned from their twelve days' leave during which time *Furious* was in Rosyth 'getting her bottom scraped'. The well-deserved break, as written into the 827 Squadron line book had 'brought the boys back to the "Box" feeling fighting fit – just as well as we flew on board the *Vic* the following day for another Do-bodo-do-do....'

This was an operation code-named *Planet*, planned for 24 April, in which Roy would lead another Barracuda strike against *Tirpitz*. It intended to involve *Victorious* and *Furious* together with *Searcher*, *Emperor*, *Striker* and *Pursuer* on the appointed day. In preparation the Fleet steamed northwards to its old hunting ground off the Arctic Norwegian coast.

However, prior to departure No. 8 was stormbound for four days by the crosswinds of a gale at Donibristle. As Allan Thomson recalled:

> During a lull on the morning of 20-4-44, No. 8 managed to take off and fly to Hatston at about 1700, with the 80-knot gale and the carriers steaming at 4 knots. There was just enough to keep them head to wind.

Thomson then went on to elaborate what happened when the wing approached Hatston and Scapa Flow:

> A signal had been sent to the RAF asking if all the barrage balloons in the area were down – they confirmed *yes*.
>
> We were on circuit waiting our turn to land on when there was a bang up front and the engine went very rough with a loss of power and tremendous vibration. The certainty of a ditching followed.
>
> About six weeks later, at the Board of Enquiry, aboard 'KG5' it was confirmed that we had cut a balloon cable with our prop. The answer to our question, had omitted to mention that there were four balloons tied to buoys in the middle of the Flow. They couldn't take them down because of the storm. With the poor visibility and the balloon hidden in the cloud there was little chance of seeing the cable. The RAF gave us an official apology.

Two days later, Emerson wrote:

> Saturday – Back on board the *Vic* and off to do a repeat on *Tirpitz*. Admiralty reckon she is not damaged enough.
>
> ... the weather is lousy and may hold off the op. With usual dimness their Lordships are only giving us 18 x 1,600 lb AP bombs out of 40. Should be 30. The world's largest battlewagon, specially built to withstand air attack & and we have mostly MC, SAP, and a/s. Bloody silly. If we had had enough the first time we wouldn't be going back now. We have orders to release them higher (4,000 ft) too. That will mean more misses.

At 9.03 am, zero hour, Roy roared off the *Victorious* in a strike of forty Barracuda bombers and forty escort fighters heading again towards Kaafiord, in Operation *Planet*. En route the weather conditions deteriorated too much for them to be successful. Roy had no alternative other than to cancel the strike using the pre-assigned signal – firing two red Verey lights from his Barracuda. The entire force returned to the Fleet two hours later. Roy was not to realise that the strike had succeeded in deceiving the German High Command into thinking that the Allies were unusually interested in Norway.

The next day, on 25 April, Emerson wrote: 'Operation just cancelled. Weather is lousy. Stood here at 500 ft for 6 days on end. Lots of snow too.'

The Barracuda squadrons continued their unwitting deception campaign elsewhere in Norway to add to the impression that the Allies were not solely after *Tirpitz*.

A further plan was hatched by the Admiralty, to be executed again by Roy as strike leader. This operation – code named *Ridge Able* – would involve strikes against a series of targets of opportunity along the Norwegian coast, the objective being to intercept German ships carrying valuable cargoes such as Swedish iron ore destined for the German furnaces.

So two days after the abortive Operation *Planet*, Roy was again in action over Norwegian skies. The plan was to be a daring attack on a German convoy off the occupied Norwegian port of Bodø, south-east of the Lofoten islands. It would be led by No. 8 and No. 52 Wings again from *Victorious* and *Furious*. The dive-bombing force was to be divided into two strikes using Roy's textbook tactics he devised for the Naval Air Fighting Instructions, synchronised formation tactics as last applied at Kaafiord – one strike to go straight to Bodø harbour as its objective, the other strike sweeping the area south and north of Bodø for any shipping underway.

Emerson elaborated:

> We are going south and will do an attack on Bodø, a convoy anchorage. We are the same force as last time. We will attack about 0500. We hope to find something or another in the bay. If not there are docks, & fish oil factory for auxiliary targets. There are 4 AA batteries & 10 light round the drome. The second strike will be 829 Sqdn only, and they will fly off with us & search the leads from the south, & arrive at Bodø what 20 minutes after us & finish off where we stopped.

At 4.30 am on 26 April, the first aircraft was flagged off the deck of *Victorious*. Thirty minutes later Roy took off leading his escort of ten Barracudas. At 5.06 am the force departed for the target. The fighter escort of sixteen Hellcats and twelve Wildcats and Corsairs formed up on the Barracudas and they headed in formation towards the Norwegian coast with Roy in the lead. They had to alter course several times to avoid snow storms. As usual, Micklem and Kimberley were Roy's back-seat companions.

Emerson recalled later that day:

> We took off at 0445. Weather lousy. Cloud base 1,500 ft. Set course 0500 but couldn't maintain time owing to heavy snow storms. We met 5 of these, all of which we had to skirt.
>
> We had hoped to fly straight in to Bodø but made a landfall well south, turned north and followed the coast up about five miles out. Visibility very poor.

Then through the snow clouds a convoy was sighted. In the Leads of Bodø below them, between Arn and Sandhorn islands, they could see a convoy of four merchant ships of between 2,000 and 5,000 tons in line ahead together with five escort vessels and flak ships.

Roy immediately reported in code that targets 'Rally of trucks south of foundry' (rally = convoy, trucks = merchant shipping, foundry = Bodø) had been sighted. He ordered the wing to climb for height, and then deployed the aircraft into squadron line astern. They then opened up so as to position themselves for action against the enemy at 6.00 am.

There was a snowstorm when they commenced the attack against a barrage of flak. Roy fired two green Verey lights and broadcast over the R/T 'Out Lights' – signalling the

Wildcats to strafe the shore batteries at Arn Island and the convoy precisely sixty seconds before the first Barracuda would commence its dive.

One minute later Roy announced to the other Barracuda crews 'Leader over', the special signal warning them he was about to commence his dive. As he dropped down towards the targets he noted 'the flak was pretty hot but we dived in and scored several hits on several ships. Shooting from the flak ships was very fierce too, and I saw one Hellcat go down in flames.'

The rest of the wing followed through with their synchronised strike including Emerson:

> We turned in to attack & deployed our ARN. There were 3 heavy AA batteries opening up. We went in in 4 columns weaving like hell. We each had a sector, & I hit my column over to approx 4–5,000 tons just in our sector. We had to go right over a flak ship – a 15,000 ton job. All the ships mounted Oerlikons fore and aft – there was a gorgeous display of tracer. Red, green and pink coming up in lines all around the clock. We were in snow cloud at 2,000 ft, so there wasn't much future in it. It was all my splat. A hell of a course round the lines of flak.
>
> We turned 180° and dived on the target. Dropped and away out weaving and undulating. And out to sea for peace and to get our breath back. Johnny was on my tail and got all the stuff that missed me. It was lousy shooting.

Johnny, was Sub Lt Herrold, the young New Zealander of 827 Squadron. He dived down onto his target and dropped his bombs, scoring direct hits on one of the ships, but was hit by flak and crashed into the sea. No survivors were seen.

Roy continued: 'Visibility was rather bad – it was snowing hard – and it was difficult to see what was happening, but I saw four motor vessels hit by bombs and three of them were well alight when we left.'

The second strike of No. 52 Barracuda Wing, under Vic Rance, penetrated to Bodø harbour where one large supply ship at anchor was hit with bombs and set on fire amidships. Their orders received on board ship had included 'that a damaged ship is more trouble to the Hun than a sunken ship, as his facilities are already over strained. Alternative targets: aerodrome, fish factory and docks.' The getaway was made to the westward over Arn Island and 'follow-my-leader' through the snow storms back to the Fleet, where they had all landed on by 6.45 am.

The attack led to the beaching, sinking or left burning of five merchant ships.

The strike was deemed an excellent success and an important propaganda triumph to confuse the German High Command about an imminent invasion. Under the headline 'Barracudas' Fierce Attack in Dawn Snowstorm', Reuter's correspondent Arthur Oakeshott described the event from on board an aircraft carrier:

> High above the spray-swept flight deck, in the early hours of a bitter Arctic dawn, I watched Barracudas of the Fleet Air Arm roar in to strike a smashing blow at a German Convoy in the leads of Bodo. The raid was divided into two 'strikes'.
>
> Stamping our feet and buffeting our arms to keep warm in the icy wind, we heard the announcement that the strike had been 'most successful' and that one of the aircraft had been forced to 'ditch'.
>
> Then a quiet voice on the loud-speakers said: 'Group of aircraft green 110, friendly.' Dashing to the starboard side, we saw through binoculars tiny black dots getting larger and larger.

In a few minutes they roared over the carriers, doing the victory roll, indicating that the 'party' had been a success.

It was a successful operation but for the loss of five aircraft, including the Barracuda flown by Johnny Herrold.

Later that day Emerson wrote in his diary: 'This afternoon 6 Corsairs did a fighter swoop over Narvik, across Sweden and back, just to make the Jerries think.'

On their return there were celebrations as Emerson wrote:

At Hatston now. We flew ashore yesterday and held a great party last night. Somewhere about 1 am B-F confided that he had recommended me for a gong? I feel I did more to earn one last June to Sept, when we had all the Barracuda trouble & twitch etc. than I have done on these recent ops. B-F is a great leader anywhere, & all of us would follow him as one man. He certainly knows his TBR tactics. His own I mean. He was torn off a strip by Admiralty because on the *Tirpitz* attack he dived at 70°. Admiralty Barracuda tactics No. 11 logs down that the best angle of dive is 50° & we have been ordered to comply with that. What a lot of hooey.

The ultra secret deception plan continued with more Norwegian ops. Roy's next strike was to be Operation *Croquet* scheduled for 6 May, again as part of the D-Day deception plans of Montgomery and Eisenhower.

Immediately prior to this operation, Roy was rushed off his feet at Hatston making sure last-minute preparations were in place. He wrote to Naomi: 'May 1. Monday. Oh what a heavy day, dashing here and there and everywhere and as a result am so ready for bed. In fact I feel rather over tired – you know that rather horrid feeling that one won't sleep'

Naomi was also not getting sleep as she confided to her brother Bill:

I was nearly crazy with worry over Roy in the *Tirpitz* raid – and so relieved and happy when I knew he was safe and then after his leave he was sent straight off again for another 'Do' – all my worry started all over again – it seems so endless.

Operation *Croquet* was planned as a combined dive-bombing and torpedo attack on two convoys off Kristiansund on the extreme southern tip of Norway. The force was to fly off from HMS *Furious* which was escorted by *Searcher*, the heavy cruiser *Berwick* and six destroyers. The attack was in the area where the Allies wanted the Germans to believe the supposed 'invasion' would take place.

Allan Thomson recalled:

The strike was in the waters off Kristiansund north, located between Averoy and Smola islands off the southern approaches to Trondheim fiord. *Furious* had on board her normal complement of twenty-seven Seafires, eighteen Barracudas and four Martlets as we called them, the Wildcat.

Our arrangement was that, if the targets were close enough, the strike force would operate as one unit; if not, then four Barracudas and four Wildcats were to attack the two lone ships. In all we had fourteen dive-bombing Barracudas and four carrying torpedoes.

Emerson wrote in his diary:

Thursday May 4th. Back on board the Box, and glad to be here. The whole squadron hates the *Vic*, and we have named her '*Altmark*'. We are doing another op tomorrow morning. We have *Searcher* with us, also *Berwick* & 6 destroyers. We take off in two ranges, form 1 strike with 25 Wildcat escorts and hope to make a landfall just north of Gossen. We search north of the coast past Kristiansund. We are carrying 8 torpedoes 10 x 3 MC, 500 lb bombs. This is a strike laid down on our own orders and should be OK. TO is 0630. Our landfall is easily recognisable as we weave to the north of 5 islands that rise from 0 ft to 2,000 ft in layers. The same landfall is 12 hrs steaming north of Stadlandet point which is always passed at night (bit late to find that out). I am bombing, for which I am thankful. I don't think there is much future in fishing these convoys.

Emerson continued:

Saturday May 6th. Op was cancelled yesterday owing to the weather, but it was perfect this morning and we took off at 0645, circled whilst 830 were ranged & took off, set course 0730. Hit coast at 0800, we sighted it 25 miles away, the sun on the snow – it looked beautiful.

We climbed to 2,000 ft and turned north. Weather perfect no cloud.

Allan Thomson added:

The predicted position of the convoy was exactly as expected. On making our landfall just south of Kristiansund, two enemy merchant vessels, escorted by two flak ships, were sighted. 4 Barras were carrying 18" torpedoes, we reckoned they were unsuitable for torp attacks.

Emerson noted: 'Sighted 2 MVs and Wing Ldr detached Black section to attack.' This was a flight of four Barras including one with Allan Thomson on board. Meanwhile, Emerson was with Roy's main strike force:

We continued north, climbing & off Kristiansund sighted a convoy of 2 large MVs about 7,000 tons escorted by a *Narvik* destroyer & 6 flak ships.

Heavy AA batteries on the coast put up a barrage so we started weaving and deployed. I got about 2,000 ft above the Wing Leader. There was lots of medium flak, pom-pom and Bofors & Oerlikons etc. We dodged in and out at full tap, detached the torpedo bombers & went in. I saw 1 bomb burst short as I dived then dropped (Robbie saw mine hit) and down to the deck.

There were 2 enemy a/c circling the convoy, an He115 and a B&V 138, both of which the Martlets shot down. We got in between the dog and the rabbit twice in the getaway. There was a hell of a lot of stuff falling all around us. We got out safely & landed on about 9.15. Brown and Reynolds are missing from our squadron. We don't know how many hits were made yet. There are 3 or 4 torpedo claims.

Allan Thomson was flying with part of the Black section detachment of aircraft left behind by Roy when he led the main convoy strike:

I was in a minor group of 4 Barras and 2 Martlets attacking two ships. I was in the third dive-bombing Barracuda of the small force.

Since dive-bombing at 87 degrees was extremely accurate, both ships were hit and one was left on fire and smoking heavily. They were so close together when last seen that a collision seemed almost certain.

Our bombs were dropped from 1,500 feet and, as we pulled up out of the dive and made our getaway, I glimpsed an aircraft down in the water about a mile ahead of the targets. It looked like one of the Wildcats with square wings, but on checking the remaining aircraft we had only three Barracuda and the 2 Wildcats were still with us so it was obviously it was the torpedo Barracuda I had spotted. I only had a fleeting instant to observe it on the water as changing light patterns obscured it, or, more likely, it had sunk.

Flotation time was about 40 seconds with full tanks, perhaps two minutes if empty. The crew was Jimmy Grant as pilot, ACP Walling as observer and D. Bussy, TAG.

One of the three torpedo aircraft was lost in Roy's part of the action also, but no dive-bombers were lost that day. Barracudas were reckoned by we crews to be almost suicidal in dropping torpedoes. They could drop and bank away almost over the target or plough overhead at best 180 knots; either way presenting a point-blank target to the enemy.

I believe lots were drawn before this attack to see who should be unfortunate enough to carry torpedoes. With two out of four lost and no dive-bombers lost on this occasion, I think their Lordships at the Admiralty finally got the message and did not use Barras for torpedo attacks.

Overall, the operation was a success both in terms of tonnage of shipping sunk and also in terms again of confusing the Germans about imminent Norwegian invasions. In total, one ship, the ore-carrying steamer *Almora*, of 2,500 tons, was sunk and destroyed – she was on her way to Germany, and the the 7,900-ton tanker *Saarburg* was also sunk. An escort vessel was hit by bombs and a merchant ship probably damaged by near misses. In the second convoy – one ship, probably the *Sabine Howaldt* of 6,000 tons, appeared to break in two after being hit by two bombs and one torpedo. A second ship, the Norwegian *Sommarstad* of 5,900 tons, was hit by bombs and two torpedoes, and a large escort vessel trawler was also hit by a bomb.

Naval Message To *Berwick/Searcher* from *Furious*

1. First convoy going southwards. Two ships of 2500 and 1800 tons. Larger ship hit by one bomb and appeared to be hit by torpedo as well and destroyed. Smaller ship not hit but probably damaged.

2. Second convoy two ships going southwards. First ship seems to have been *Sabine Howaldt* 5956 tons hit by two bombs and one torpedo and there are indications that she broke in two. Second ship is tanker of about 5500 tons in ballast and may be the Norwegian *Sommarstad* of 5923 tons. Hit by one bomb and two torpedoes. A large escort vessel trawler type or armed whale catcher of about 150 ft in length also hit by a bomb.

Roy was satisfied with the success of the attacks and contented his aircrew coped so well, but no longer wanted to worry Naomi and so made no mention of the operation in his next letter to her. The day after the attack he wrote: 'Sunday. Just had all the crew's photographs taken. I think we all look more like a bunch of apes than anything else but I'm very proud of them however.'

On 8 May, there was an unexpected visit; General Montgomery came up to Orkney for a top secret conference, and to visit the Fleet and Hatston. Roy met him in the officers' wardroom. Geoffrey Gowland, commanding officer of all the Fleet Air Arm Air Stations on Orkney, recalled this high-level secret visit and recognised in hindsight that it was probably to discuss further plans for the Operation *Fortitude North* attacks in Norway and Home Fleet preparations for Normandy with Admiral Sir Bruce Fraser and his staff.

Gowland elaborated:

Time went on, and people began to speculate about D-Day and Normandy. One day, Monty appeared, rather tight-lipped. He was picked up by my car and brought home to the farm-house. He wouldn't smoke or drink. He thought he'd be off next morning. When morning dawned there was a fog again, a really first class one, really shattering fog. We got a helicopter ready to take him to the flagship – but it began snowing hard and the C-in-C said 'NO'. So I had got my commander to warn the ship's company that we should *all* be attending a talk by Monty in B hangar – I was sure we could persuade the men to attend, clap, and cheer – by which time, with any luck, the snow should have stopped.

Monty and I padded round one or two hangars: occupied by male and female aircraft riggers and fitters, radio men and girls, and engineers – and some ordnance boys and girls. By dint of a quiet wink here and there, I managed to get a little party of buglers to sound off 'cooks to the galley' – steered Monty into B hangar before he had a clue about what was going on. He talked for 50 minutes, the hands lapped it up: and at a suitable moment the buglers sounded off and the chief quartermaster had a posse of his mates piping 'awa-a-y captain's motor boat', alongside Scapa jetty.

He was whisked off to the flagship, and I never saw him again. It was a fortnight before D-Day. So he had plenty to think about. There was clearly no doubt that Bernard Montgomery was the greatest personality in his little world: that others must expect to be climbed over, on his way to the very top. After four or five days in the wardroom, and many gales of laughter at BM's idea of how to tell a funny story, he left us, quite quietly and bade us a perfectly friendly and attractive goodbye. In another few days time they were put ashore in Normandy after some noisy hours of bombardment.

Montgomery went on to visit the C-in-C, and discussed the success of the recent crippling of *Tirpitz* and whether the ship could now attack Allied shipping destined to take part in the D-Day landings in France. They then discussed the detailed plans for the Home Fleet in leading the forthcoming Normandy invasion. The meeting was a resounding success, after which Montgomery's private pilot flew him back south to his headquarters where he would remain for the final preparations of D-Day.

Roy never mentioned this visit in his letters to family and friends. However, the next day's letter to Naomi was more upbeat: 'It looks as if I shall get my leave about the right date my darling or a few days later. Unless something very unforeseen pops up. Gosh, I hope it doesn't.'

Naomi was suffering an increasing agony of fear for Roy. She wrote to Bill:

May 14: I do hope you are still at the same place. I feel a bit worried in case they may have moved you. As for Roy, I'm nearly out of my mind over worry over him.

He has been mentioned twice since the big event and each time I've been tormented with worry till I've heard from him again. This wretched beastly war, will it ever end? I'd almost give my soul for Roy to get a safe job.

Something else was afoot – as recorded in the 827 Squadron line book:

During this time, the old Box (*Furious*) was in the process of being 'got tiddley' – painted, polished and all dead seagulls scraped from off the deck. The reason was soon obvious – HM The King arrived in Scapa to visit the Home Fleet – at least those who were home.

King George VI paid a visit to the Home Fleet immediately before the invasion of Europe, to take leave of his captains and bid them and their ships' companies Godspeed before the battle. In four crowded days he boarded fourteen different ships and inspected representative detachments from nearly every ship in the Fleet.

Emerson wrote about the visit in his secret diary:

Friday May 12th – The Flow is full of ships at present. ...Reason HM the King is inspecting the Home Fleet. He arrived here Wednesday the 10th, and that evening there was ceremonial sunset aboard D of Y. I was invited to attend in charge of 6 Dominion ratings from the ship. It was very impressive. They had massed RM Bands aboard, 20 Buglers on Y turret and they beat the retreat. The Bands played a switch of musical numbers including Rule Britannia, Abide with me, Land of our fathers, etc and the 20 Buglers sounded off colours and the Last post. The 5 Dominion flags were flying from the yard arm and were struck with the white ensign.

The quarterdeck port side was filled with Dominion troops who were inspected by the King (he spoke to me) and the starboard side was filled with C-in-C, VA2, 4 Commodores, 40 Captains, 60 commanders, and many 2½s and Lts.

Today the King has been on board *Furious* and inspected the ship's log in the lower hanger and the aircrews on the flight deck.

Before he boarded the cruiser to return at the end of the visit, the King attended Admiral Fraser's staff conference in the flagship and took part in highly secret discussions of impending operations against the enemy. Roy was to present the latest diversionary plan – which was scheduled to get underway later that day – Operation *Brawn*. Roy was inevitably complimented on his recent *Tirpitz* raid.

As a royal compliment to the Fleet Air Arm, the King put to sea in *Victorious* and saw a thrilling display of flying by Roy's strike force in a repeat performance of their strike on *Tirpitz*.

A newspaper correspondent reported the event:

Standing on the Admiral's bridge with the Commander-in-Chief Admiral Sir Bruce Fraser, the King watched a swarm of deadly Barracuda dive-bombers, with a strong escort of Corsair fighters, suddenly swoop out of the clouds ahead of the great ship.

Twelve fighters flashed across the bows in a low-level attack, firing live ammunition only a few yards ahead of the ship to punish the AA gunners, while the Barracudas, splitting into two sections, attacked simultaneously from port and starboard, diving to fling their dummy concrete torpedoes into the water so close alongside, and with such accuracy that, turn and twist as we might, it was utterly impossible for their ship to dodge them all.

Captain Denny delegated his Number 2, Cdr Ross, to escort the King to lunch in the wardroom. Roy, as leading squadron commander from the morning's flying, was invited to the King's small table for lunch along with Engineer Commander Cronk, and Lt Cdr Pollock, torpedo officer. Their meal was not at all like typical rationed fayre and consisted of grapefruit, fried chicken and vegetables, tinned pears and rice, cheese and biscuits and coffee.

The King, along with Admiral Sir Bruce Fraser, then inspected and shook hands with the lined up aircrews on each carrier's flight deck to thank them personally. Roy was honoured with being requested to inspect, alone with the King, the line upon line of his men, rigid at attention.

Guy Micklem was duly impressed and wrote to Hugh in India:

The other day we had a visit from the King. He asked me how long I had been in and I told him two years. I think this shook him a bit as he must have wondered how I could have collected two stripes so quickly! But I thought he meant my time in the Fleet Air Arm. Anyhow have got some photographs which I will look forward to showing you when you return.

Roy's comment to Naomi on the Royal visit was restrained: 'We were inspected by a big personage yesterday not that I was unduly excited by it.' Perhaps this was not surprising as he had more worrying concerns on his mind – the start of the afternoon's operation.

Thelma Lancaster recalled:

The King came up and reviewed No. 8 Wing and then came to Hatston. He looked at every kind of aircraft we had on the station at the time. I understand he climbed into them all, perhaps the highlight of his afternoon!

We paraded for him too. RN and WRNS from Kirkwall. All of us from Hatston, detachments from the Army and the Royal Marines.

And the marines marched past...! I saw nothing to equal it till the Queen Mother's funeral fifty-six years later.

The 827 Squadron line book recorded:

The same afternoon, 'The Old Lady' set course for Norway, round Alten Fjord somewhere! The objective was very obvious but unfortunately or otherwise, the weather was duff over the coast, so we turned about smartly and landed on board again.... For two days the weather closed down, so there was nothing else to do but return to dear old Scapa – and Hatston this time.

Emerson elaborated in his diary:

Monday May 15th – have been at sea 3 days now with *Vic*, *Kent*, *Norfolk* and 6 DRs. VA2 is in *Vic* & CS10 in *Kent*. We arrived in the Arctic Circle yesterday and have been hanging around as the weather has been lousy. Today is beautifully sunny with little cloud and zero hour is 5 pm. *Vic* has 13 Barras & 28 Corsairs to range and we range 14 Barras & 4 Wildcats. The Spits remain behind as Fleet Cover. The W/Ldr leads in same as before with 52 Wing just astern. 20 Corsairs go in as anti-flak and 8 stay up as top cover. 4 Wildcats stay with No. 8 Wing in case any position gets annoying and then they will be sent in. Should go well providing the cloud base over the target is high enough.

I am not going on this do as there is another op planned for early tomorrow morning. We are to attack 6 heavy coastal defence batteries outside Narvik, & I shall be leading our lot. I consider this is just a feint to make Jerry think, and there may be a dummy run up here at invasion time.

The following day Emerson wrote:

We are on our way back to the Flow now. The strike returned last night at 1830. At the coast they struck a cloud back from 1,500 to 7,000 ft that was a solid layer and they couldn't find the target – no holes in the cloud anywhere.

During the final lead up to the invasion of Europe and Operation *Overlord*, further diversionary sweeps were made by the Barracuda squadrons of *Furious* and *Victorious* against occupied Southern Norway to simulate pre-invasion reconnaissance.

The strains of continual operations and command of the wing were increasingly taking a toll on Roy's health: 'Sunday. I haven't been able to sleep for quite a time except when pickled. I have no news of course, just the usual routine.'

There was yet another diversionary strike against *Tirpitz* just one week before the launch of the Allied invasion. Operation *Tiger Claw* on 28 May was planned but was again cancelled due to bad weather. The 827 Squadron line book recorded that 'the squadron flew on board *Furious* for another uneventful trip to the Arctic regions – and back again to dear old Hatston – at least to Scapa which is as far as we got...' Emerson elaborated: '*Tirpitz* do cancelled again. We steamed through fog all one day & ran out into perfect weather, but reports told us that it was right down at the coast.'

There was some news, however, set out in an official letter to Roy from the Admiralty:

I have the pleasure, as chairman of the Honours and Awards Committee, to inform you that, on the advice of the First Lord, the King has been graciously pleased to give orders for your appointment as a companion of the Distinguished Service Order for undaunted courage, skill and determination shown as Strike Leader of the 1st strike of dive-bombers in the daring attack carried out on the German battleship *Tirpitz* on 3rd April 1944.

Notification of the award was published in the *London Gazette* on 30 May. Roy's comment to Naomi was brief: 'I've got the DSO and Kevin bar to the DSC.'

That evening they celebrated with everyone else in the wing by hosting a major all-night party at Hatston. The next day he wrote:

Sunday – As a result of the gong receiving there were, as you can imagine, a few shambles last night and one feels somewhat sleepy. Still a good party but nothing to get excited about anyway altho' I was very pleased that my young got gongs. Gosh I'm longing to see you all again. Let's hope it's soon, even the London jaunt would be fun.

Guy Micklem was less pleased and wrote to his brother Hugh about the awards:

Some members of the wing have been decorated. My pilot (the wing leader) got the

DSO, Richard Kingdon and four others got DSCs but little Guy missed out. However, I am assured that there is one of these letters on the way for me. So I will write and tell you the glad tidings as soon as it comes through!

A few days later Roy wrote eagerly to Naomi about recent correspondence he had received from Washington DC: 'I got a letter from Stacey saying he was trying to get me back! Don't bank on it Billy girl.' Presumably the news was about the secondment duties in the United States which he had originally been offered whilst still serving at RAF Boscombe Down two years before.

Lt Cdr Stacey Colls AFC was a veteran of No. 14 Pilots' Course in 1929 and then went on to be CO of 702 Flight in 1936. He was with 812 Squadron in *Glorious* pre-war and later 809 Squadron up to just before Petsamo, leaving in July 1941 with the rank of commander. He went on to be CO at Boscombe Down before joining the British Air Commission in the United States. In the June 1944 edition of the *Navy List* he was listed under HMS *President* for duty at the Ministry of Aircraft Production.

Roy's next task was to lead Operation *Lombard* on 1 June – five days before D-Day. It was to be a strike on enemy convoys off Stadlandet in southern Norway – again to make the Germans believe an invasion of Norway was imminent and tie down enemy troops away from Normandy.

Roy's strike was part of the overall Operation *Skye*, a major sub-plan of Operation *Fortitude North* – with its fictional 'British Fourth Army' now building up for its invasion of Norway. The British media cooperated with this effort by broadcasting fake football scores and even wedding announcements for the non-existent troops. Seventeen German divisions were tied down as a result of this deception.

The 827 Squadron line book recorded:

> The Box put to sea again, but not too far north – just as far as Stadlandet, where the Wing found and attacked an enemy convoy which was heading northwards. The results were good enough – two ships (merchantmen) sunk, three ships (merchantmen) left on fire, 50% of flak ships burning or sunk. No aircraft were lost from the wing.

Aircraft from *Furious*, *Victorious* and *Fencer* were involved, including thirty Barracudas, twelve Seafires and twenty-two Corsairs in the attack. En route north to the target area, on 30 May, an acoustic torpedo attack on HMS *Victorious* by U-957 failed.

This operation was the first time that teenage air gunner L/A Roy Matthias, of 827 Squadron, had seen action. He recalled:

> The observer and I saw hits on the ship we had attacked, and then I noticed red and white streamers coming up at us as we pulled away, and asked what the hell were they, only to be told 'You bloody fool, that's anti-aircraft fire'. Even then I was too keyed up to be afraid.

Intercepted German reports by the Admiralty showed the success of the operation:

> At 21.45 hours the convoy passed Haugsholmen lighthouse and at the same time they were attacked by aircraft and the cargo bay in the hold of *Hans Leonhardt* caught fire, and Captain Held wounded. At 22.10 the crew rushed to their lifeboats. *Hans Leonhardt* drifted north and exploded at 22.30 hours and sank. D/S *Florida* and *Sperrbrecher 182* were beached with much damage.

Roy was still news and Arthur Oakeshott, Reuters' special correspondent filed a report of the strike:

'Tirpitz DSO' at Nazi Ships
Convoy Wiped Out Off Norway

Aboard HMS —— off Norway. From the bridge of an aircraft carrier I watched the striking force of the Fleet Air Arm take off to hammer yet another German convoy in Norwegian waters.

The operation took place at night. But at this time of year in these latitudes there is no darkness. It is broad daylight all the time.

Barracudas, Corsairs, and Seafires roared into the Arctic skies, led by Lieut.-Comdr R. Baker-Falkner, DSO, DSC, RN (Torquay), who won the DSO for his attack on the Tirpitz.

These were the results achieved:

Two 6,000 tons ships hit

One 3,000 ton vessel hit – stern blown off

Four flak ships silenced and left burning.

Gibney commented that this mission was 'very fraught', writing in his flying log book on his return of a 'glorious first' – both the Allied and German sides could claim to have been successful in this attack. The Glorious First of June was the first and largest fleet action of the naval conflict between the Kingdom of Great Britain and the First French Republic during the French Revolutionary Wars and both sides claimed victory in this battle.

Micklem wrote to Hugh after a further report:

We have been kept very much on the hop during the past two months and have had further successes. The ship herself being mentioned on the wireless a couple of days ago. All of which is very gratifying.

Meanwhile, the international situation was giving Roy more hope, particularly since it was looking inevitable that he would be sent back to Boscombe Down or even out to the US as a test pilot. The fall of Rome to the Allies on 4 June brought further hope of the end of the war. Roy wrote to Naomi: 'Monday: I suppose you heard the news – good show about Rome isn't it?'

Back home in Shaldon and Torquay, as the weeks went by everyone was wondering when the invasion of Europe would happen. Aircraft were very busy in the lead-up and the Teign estuary was crammed with landing barges and boats in readiness. Waiting was hard for everyone, particularly Naomi. She wrote to Bill:

June 4. I sometimes feel I'll go crazy as Roy has been in the news (not actually his name) about six times since he was so much in the news – I think a wife's part of waiting is far far harder than the actual doing.

At last on 6 June, the wireless announced that the Allies had commenced the invasion of Normandy, as paratroops landed and invasion troops poured onto the beaches from Allied landing barges. The deceptions were to continue. Overnight on 5/6 June, while the invasion fleet headed for Normandy, German radar was fully occupied in the Dover Straits. Small flotillas of motorboats, fitted with radar reflectors to make them seem much larger, headed towards the French coast between Boulogne and Le Havre, while RAF bombers flew complex patterns overhead, dropping a dense screen of radar-reflective aluminium strips.

Once the actual invasion force had come ashore, deception efforts were redoubled. Even after the troops had landed in Normandy, the Germans believed for several weeks that these were in fact a diversion and that the real invasion, on an even bigger scale, was still planned for Calais in mid-July. As a result, the Germans held back most of their reserves, rather than rushing them straight to the fighting in Normandy during the critical first few days of the invasion.

Whilst troops started to land on the Normandy beaches early on 6 June, Roy was very aware of what was going on and was obviously becoming ever more hopeful about the end of the war and being able to have a normal family life at long last. He wrote that same day: 'What price the news of the second front. Glad I'm not over Dunkirk again.' He sounded more relaxed and went on to add: 'I've had such wonderful fun the last couple of days. We've got a wonderful artist in the squadron and he's been copying your "Alex" photograph.'

Later in the week he wrote:

According to my calendar it's Thursday but I haven't really got the faintest idea. Hours, days, weeks seem to go so quickly and yet at the same time so slowly when all the time I want to be with my darling Billy girl. Sorry to have to ask this Billy but I got very little pay last month with odds and ends taking my money. Not wine bills either. I had a very pleasant afternoon today. Nothing to do so I lay on my bunk.

In the next correspondence he was still pre-occupied with Naomi's letters: 'Thurs: I am so longing to receive a letter from my adorable old wife. I suppose the invasion is generally to blame for it all but still that's a good thing so it can't be helped.'

He continued: 'Did I ever tell you "Moose" Martyn, the tall Canadian in Monkey's squadron in Malta, is with me as CO of the fighters. It's wonderful being with him again. He's doing his stuff for me personally!' The letter referred to Lt Cdr Martyn, the Calgary-born CO of 880 Squadron, as the personal fighter aircraft escort of Roy's Barracuda.

Roy went on in optimistic vein: 'This Second Front news has enabled me to write so much better. At last it really looks as if you and I are going to be ourselves after five long years. Darling, do take care of yourself with these bombs and things. I'm petrified and I do adore you.'

Roy had just heard from Naomi that Torquay had been subject to a German bombing raid. When the air raid sirens had started, Naomi calmly took Carole and Sandra to shelter from the bombs.

In the build-up to D-Day, German raids on coastal areas were expected and Torquay was attacked on the night of 28–29 May. Some twenty aircraft were believed to have been in Torbay laying mines and dropping bombs. The worst affected property was Bay Court Hotel where twenty-four were killed and rescuers dug for days for survivors. Carole thought back to her recollections of that event and even though only two years old at the time clearly remembered the bombing at Torquay when she hid and cowered under the table with her mother and baby sister.

Roy didn't have to wait long after his last letter, and on 7 June he and the wing were granted ten days' leave. Immediately, he sent a telegram to Naomi with the wonderful news and arranged to meet at their normal London haunt, the Berners Hotel. On their return to London, Naomi's first impression was that Roy 'was very tired and exhausted looking'. She had left Carole and Sandra in Devon with family.

Leslie came to visit and they went to Roy and Naomi's favourite pubs and restaurants. She told Roy about having her own share of bombs. Leslie recalled: 'The air raid sirens used to make your heart beat faster. I would never be caught going down in the shelters, claustrophobic'.

The very first V-1 doodle bug flying bomb flew into London during Roy's leave period on 13 June 1944. By 16 June, 199 had reached England. Leslie recalled:

> You could recognise the airplanes by the engines and tell whether they had dropped their bombs or not. During the period Roy was on leave I remember walking down my road from music college and the church had disappeared – bombed! We could cope with the bombs but doodle bugs and their chug-chug like an untuned car – oh no when their sound cut out, and as for the V-2 rocket that was just a horrible whoosh and bang of the exploding building.

Leslie also recollected that whilst they were together in London: 'Roy also mentioned to me having seen a sailor in the train with a beard which was supposedly bad luck.'

Roy and Naomi didn't have time to go down to their Torquay home and to the children. He had some work duties in the Admiralty. Days later Roy took the long journey back to Hatston in a refreshed mood. The next day he wrote home to Naomi:

> Sat: My wonderful holiday is over and now just memories but what heavenly memories they are my darling. Not a bad trip up really altho' I felt very miserable as always leaving my darling. Still one thing is better, we have got more hope this time.

He was pleased to hear that Kevin Gibney was to be CGI (Chief Ground Instructor) at Crail and ever more confident that his own time as operational wing leader was coming to an end. He wrote to Naomi: 'June 17. I'm feeling very pleased at the moment 'cos Kevin has got his draft chit too. So he won't be left all by himself when I go. He's joining John. Quite a good job I think. He doesn't go for a wee bit yet.'

Bill wrote to Eira about the same time:

> I have just received your letter dated 7 June, 1944 – the day after the invasion. I guess you must all have been thrilled – and like you – I was quite satisfied that I was in Italy at that time if never before – I'm not made in the heroic mould, I fear. I suppose Roy is off performing more noble deeds, and poor old Nao on tenterhooks as usual but if one will marry a hero one can expect nothing else.

At Hatston, Roy was getting ever more optimistic about his new job after receiving his draft chit and there was a hint of life getting back to normal. He wrote to Naomi:

> Monday. I had a grand game of golf today with Kevin. It took us 2½ hours to play eight holes due to a lost ball. We just mooched round and round in almost summer weather and thoroughly enjoyed ourselves. My spies have hinted that my job might be for the middle of July. I hope.

Kevin Gibney was due to leave at the end of June so before he went Roy granted him one of his wishes, a flying lesson in one of the station's aircraft as a goodbye present. Gibney was proud of this kind gesture from Roy who was busily preparing for this next operation. Gibney treasured this memory for many years.

Roy's final task for Kevin was to write an official note in his friend's flying log book. 'Gibney has been an above average observer who has done very well as Squadron Commander. He has taken part in many operations and has shown himself to be a cool and determined leader.'

There was yet another abortive attempt in the Arctic. Emerson recorded his frustration:

June 24th – Flew back to Hatston yesterday. The strike took off early on the 23rd. No one sighted anything & they landed on again at 5.30. Fleet returned to the Flow, and we are to carry on 'B' bombing trials again. Plenty of time ashore when weather permitting.

On 24 June, Captain Gowland and the RNAS Hatston held a dinner in honour of the wing. Roy might be a hero but he was still a very private person:

Written Friday. I have very little news, we had a dinner given to us last night. It was very good fun but I had to reply to a speech. Awful business. I coughed and spluttered and stammered but they did at least laugh once or twice.

CHAPTER 26

Back to the *Tirpitz* Again – Operation *Mascot*

In June, a high-level meeting was held at the Admiralty with the C-in-C Home Fleet who had come down especially from Scapa to London for the event. It looked as if there was still more dangerous work being planned for Roy to do. The admiral wrote:

TOP SECRET: HUSH
From: C-in-C Home Fleet
Address: Admiralty

Intend to carry out attack on *Admiral von Tirpitz* with carrier borne aircraft about mid July including *INDEFATIGABLE* and *FORMIDABLE*, which will be placed under my command in addition to *FURIOUS* for this operation. Request that carriers arrive Scapa no later than 8 July and the complement of aircraft may have adjusted as arranged at meeting which I attended at the Admiralty on 20 June.

On the C-in-C's return to Orkney, Roy was summoned to his flagship, and informed of the outcome of the meeting. His orders were to leave Hatston for the Clyde forthwith and assess the aircraft preparations in *Indefatigable* and *Formidable*.

Over the next ten days Roy, accompanied by his observer Lt Micklem, travelled by aircraft across the country to visit both aircraft carriers and attend a series of conferences. The first was a staff officers' conference with Admiral Lyster at his HQ at HMS *Monck* at Largs.

On 25 June Roy wrote to Naomi prior to his return to Hatston: 'I am down at another conference at the moment with our ex-Malta captain – remember?'

After the meeting conference Roy went on board the two Fleet carriers which were scheduled to play a leading part in the forthcoming operation. The intention being to brief the wing leaders, squadron COs, the captains of the two ships, Captain Ruck-Keene of *Formidable* and Captain Graham of *Indefatigable*, and their respective Air Staffs about Operation *Mascot* and practical application of the latest aerial tactics in the Naval Air Fighting Instructions.

Roy was delighted to renew acquaintance with his old observers from 812 Squadron, both Cdr Buchanan-Dunlop RN, now the Air Staff officer in *Indefatigable*, and Bruce Hawkes, Lt Cdr Flying in *Formidable*. He was interested to see the newly commissioned *Indefatigable*, an *Implacable*-class aircraft carrier of 32,000 tons and over 1,800 crew. She had joined the Royal Navy only a few months previously, from John Brown's Shipbuilding yard on Clydebank. She had an enormous flight deck of 760 feet and her hangars and deck park could accommodate up to eighty-one aircraft.

Briefings were very time consuming and tiring. The operation was planned on much the same lines as was Operation *Tungsten* on 3 April 1944. However, Roy's wing was now to fly from HMS *Formidable* and HMS *Furious*, along with No. 9 Wing under Lt Cdr Temple-West with his 820 and 826 Barracuda Squadrons. Lt Cdr Ronnie 'Biggy' Bigg-Wither's Corsairs from *Formidable*'s 1841 Squadron would provide fighter support along with *Furious*'s new 1840 Squadron Hellcats.

HMS *Indefatigable* was at that time undergoing sea trials and exercising the Fairey Fireflies of 1770 Squadron. The squadron CO, Major Cheesman RM, found Roy's test pilot expertise invaluable for preparing his Firefly squadron for their forthcoming first operational strike.

On 25 June, 1840 Hellcat Squadron was transferred to HMS *Indefatigable*, and the day after her 820 Barracuda Squadron, under Lt Cdr Nowell, was detached as part of No. 9 Wing to *Formidable*.

Sub Lt Richard 'Dickie' Douglas-Boyd, a pilot in 820 Squadron, recalled:

On June 26th I flew from *Indefatigable*, via Machrihanish to *Formidable* with my Observer Andy Anderson and TAG Mitch Mitchelson, and flew from her for a week. It was obviously a very happy ship with probably a tighter regime than that of *Indefat*. I was later, in the Pacific, aware of the personal attention given to aircrew by Captain Ruck-Keene, the only carrier captain in pilot's wings. I was therefore under 8 Wing, Roy Baker-Falkner's control and I met him before the five glide-bombing exercises we carried out before returning to *Indefat*. I can only remember the general warmth of his welcome and firm leadership.

The aircraft carrier already had three Barracudas on board. Sub Lt (A) Gilbert Clark RNVR recalled:

When HMS *Formidable* left Harland and Woolff's Belfast yard after a refit earlier in 1944, three Barracuda aircraft were sent to her from an operational training unit at Fearn to take part in 'working her up' to the pitch of efficiency necessary to join the Fleet. I was the observer in one of them. My pilot was Sub Lt Donald McLachlan, and Telegraphist Air Gunner PO Patrick Coogan. The observer in one of the other Barracudas was Sub Lt (A) John L.E. Smith RNVR who post-war was destined to be knighted and became MP for the City of London and Westminster. The three aircraft were known as the *Formidable* Flight, and when the working up period was over *Formidable* sailed to Scapa Flow. The 'Buzz', the ship's gossip at the time we headed for Scapa Flow, was that we were to load with aircraft and transport them to the East Indies Fleet based at Trincomalee in Ceylon. Indeed, loading had begun when intelligence from Norway told of *Tirpitz* moving in the northern fiords and testing her armament. Instantly the aircraft already loaded were unloaded and *Formidable* switched to preparations for Operation *Mascot*.

The *Formidable* Flight included the Barracuda with picturesque names – Meteoric Dustbin, *Per ardua ad aqua*, and Rita.

Gilbert Clark added:

The officers in *Per ardua ad aqua* were old friends from Eton and chose something they thought was classical. 'Meteoric dustbin' was the crew's interpretation of a view widely held at the time of the characteristics of the Barracuda. And last, my aircraft 'Rita'. My pilot Sub Lt Donald Maclachlan's girlfriend was called Rita, but in painting the figurehead the technician went wild and produced a blowsy blue floozy with more bosom outside the dress than in it. The crew loved this and she was soon translated by word of mouth into 'Blue Titty Rita'. I was not amused.

During this busy period Bruce Hawkes, now second-in-command of the Air Department, was responsible for all activities on the flight deck. As a gesture of superstitious good luck, Hawkes would pat the roundel on the port side of the fuselage each time Bigg-Wither prepared for take-off.

Roy wrote home to Naomi: '27 June. Oh so tired after a pretty hard day's work and rather late stuff too – still I suppose it's a good thing, keeps us interested at any rate.'

Two days later he wrote:

Tues: Billy girl I went down to see old Lyster and then on to see B-D [Buchanan-Dunlop] and of course got stuck and couldn't write. Anyway I saw him and transferred to Peter Bramwell and again got stuck. Bruce Hawkes is with Bramwell. It was very nice indeed to see all the old faces again after so long. They send their love. Oh yes and O'Rorke too. His second is a son, I think he said.

Roy's youngest daughter had been poorly and he tried to make light of his own extreme worries: 'I do so hope poor babe Sandra hasn't got German measles or some horrid complaint. Not very patriotic of her if she has.'

Micklem had been accompanying Roy on conferences and other appointments, and the strains of such duties were beginning to show on him. He wrote to his brother:

I am afraid I have been an awful time in writing but I had seven days' leave from the 19th June and since my return we have been touring the kingdom in an aeroplane indulging in a series of the most appalling conferences. This is literally the first moment I have had to myself for a fortnight.

You ask me what I have been doing recently but I am afraid that any details are definitely not allowed. However, I can say that we have sunk many thousands of tons of Hun shipping and we certainly haven't finished with them yet.

Roy and Micklem flew back to reunite with No. 8 Wing at Hatston on the evening of 5 July. Immediately after their return, Roy launched 827 and 830 Squadrons into wing exercises with No. 9 Wing, including joint dive-bombing attacks on the Loch Eriboll dummy *Tirpitz* target. This was a frame of the same dimensions as *Tirpitz* and there was a Crown Colony-class cruiser HMS *Jamaica* on hand to make smoke if necessary. The new boys to join Roy were flying Fairey Fireflies of 1770 Squadron. Their role was to provide protection to the Barracudas for the forthcoming strike. One member wrote into their squadron diary at the time:

6th July – by day bomber escort of 8 and 9 of Barras from Hatston. Flew at 50 ft from Brough HD to Cape Wrath in a terrific gaggle turned East and climbed to 9,000 ft, 8 Wing leading. Lt Cmdr Baker-Falkner RN reckons on climbing to this height in 9 or ten mins (very credible indeed) this being about ⅓ of the time taken usually by 9 Wing. Target was in a loch 30 miles East of Cape Wrath.

Timing was perfect. Baker-Falkner giving the 'stand by' 10 miles away & the 'go' just at the right time. There were 8 of us escorting 36 Barras.

It is most noticeable in these exercises that the Barras bombing is pretty good stuff & their leader is the right man.

As the time drew closer to the next operation Roy increasingly became apprehensive: 'Thurs. I suppose Billy girl I shall see my daughters grow up but it does seem such an awful waste of time just soldiering on...'

On Sunday 9 July, the squadrons landed on *Formidable* in Scapa Flow, in readiness for the impending operation. Emerson was frustrated:

My leave has been stopped and I am at present in HMS *Formidable* for another stab at the *Tirpitz*. *Formi* & *Indefat* arrived up in the Flow on the 3rd & Nr. 9 Wing from *Indefat*. Flown ashore. We have been doing live bombing on Loch Eriboll with No. 9 Wing and 50 fighters. 3 per day for days on end. Everyone is fed up with them. Both squadrons are aboard, and all 9 Wing is aboard *Indefat*. *Furious* is full of fighters (detachment of Hellcats) except for 6 Stringbags for A/S Patrols. Guess we will do several exercises from the deck before we go out on the job again.

Roy was anticipating a transfer to his new job in a fortnight. He wrote to Naomi that evening:

Sunday: At the moment my darling lying on my tummy in the sun just waiting. It's absolutely heavenly but oh so acutely uncomfortable trying to write. Do you remember Alex days, darling? I've got absolutely no news, darling. My spies seem to say about two weeks from now.

Meanwhile, on 13 July, Emerson recorded details of the forthcoming operation. *Tirpitz* had by now been temporarily patched up from the damage she had sustained on 3 April and intelligence from Norway spoke of her moving and testing her guns in the Northern Fiords:

The strike is timed for Sunday 11 pm. Both wings at the same time with 50 fighters. Then if losses are not too high we refuel & rearm and strike again. Then we do another club run off Stadlandet. A nice quiet time we are in for.

The flight deck party are clueless and prang a/c all the time. There is more panic than that at present and everyone is very discouraged. Especially the troops here who have to work all night replacing ailerons, flaps, elevators, folding edges & mainplanes. Only to have them broken again next day.

Gilbert Clark added:

The flight deck handling party was composed of those who could not be fitted in elsewhere. They belonged to that section of society which England finds to do her dirty work. Strong, smiling they push the aircraft about at the command of the flight deck officer. There was indeed a problem during the rehearsal of arranging aircraft. It fell so much below par that Captain Ruck-Keene removed the officer in charge pronto and brought in a substitute. All went well thereafter.

Roy's letter, also dated 13 July, showed his own frustration with the situation and held a rare trace of bitterness:

Wednesday. Mail is so lowsy these days that it almost seems impossible. Troops in the invasion areas get theirs. Stand fast poor old Fleet Air Arm, they've only been doing their stuff the whole war.'

However, recognition of Roy's work was forthcoming the next day, when a naval message was handed to him from Admiral Sir Henry Moore who had taken over from Admiral Bruce Fraser as C-in-C Home Fleet the previous month. It read:

> 14th July Following received from C-in-C HF begins. *Furious* from C-in-C HF, the King has approved the following awards for operations PLANET, VERITAS and RIDGEABLE. Mentioned in dispatches Lt Cdr Baker-Falkner, Lt (A) Emerson, Sub Lt (A) Eveleigh, Flight Sergeant Taylor.

The next letter from Roy was brighter and made first mention of the newly appointed CO of 827 Squadron, Graham Woolston:

> Thursday. I'm having quite a good time with Bruce Hawkes and see a fair amount of B-D. Kevin's relief is a very good hand and an excellent addition to the wing. Married, three children, two are step children. No more news my darling.

Roy was expecting further news of his shore job at Boscombe Down but first there was to be another major attempt by the Fleet Air Arm to damage *Tirpitz*. Operation *Mascot* was scheduled for 17 July, 1944. This time the Fleet included the carriers *Formidable*, *Indefatigable* and *Furious*, with up to ninety-five aircraft, the largest Fleet Air Arm air operation against a German battleship and the largest in the war to date. The cruisers HMS *Bellona* and HMS *Jamaica*, and the flagship battleship HMS *Duke of York*, along with numerous destroyers, formed the covering force for the carriers.

Once again it was to be commanded by Roy. It comprised forty-four Barracudas from No. 8 TBR Wing from *Formidable* and No. 9 TBR Wing (820 and 826 Squadrons from *Indefatigable*, under Lt Cdr Temple-West). They were to be escorted by 801 and 880 Seafire Squadrons, eighteen of *Formidable*'s Corsairs (1841 Squadron), eighteen Hellcats from *Furious* (1840 Squadron) and twelve Fireflies of 1770 Squadron from *Indefatigable*.

At 7.58 am on 14 July, the Fleet sailed from Scapa. A young pilot in 826 Squadron, John 'Johnnie' Baggs, recalled:

> It was probably the following day after we had left Scapa and were headed northwards, all aircrew were called to the wardroom ante-room and were addressed by Commander Operations, Cdr Buchanan-Dunlop, who opened his remarks with the words 'Gentlemen, the ship has sailed on Operation *Mascot*'. We were advised that we had set out to attack the *Tirpitz*.
>
> Until B-D stood up and spoke, the aircrews had no definite idea where they were going or what they required to do. By the time B-D sat down, we knew everything there was need for us to know, so complete and masterly was the scope of his briefing. His remarks were supported by further briefing from the strike leader, wing leaders, squadron commanders, the ship's intelligence officer, and 'schoolie', who was also the ship's meteorological officer.
>
> We spent the next few days studying models of Alten Fiord and Kaafiord, discussing the method of attack, checking known German gun positions etc.
>
> It was during this stage that Baker-Falkner flew over to *Indefatigable*. We knew he was to be the strike leader and he came to tell us how he wanted the attack carried out.
>
> He had some surprises in store for us. To avoid German radar, no aircraft was to fly above a height of 150 feet, which explained why we had spent so much time

flying at 30 feet above the fields of Orkney and frightening all the sheep.

He certainly impressed me as I can remember him talking to us, explaining the terrain – the problems and how it was proposed to overcome them.

One of the things which was worrying us most was the long distance we would have to fly inland to get to the target. Roy told us we were to fly [our engines] on full throttle from the moment we reached the coast until arriving at the target. This would enable us to proceed faster, at 165 knots.

Baggs continued:

At the time this was almost revolutionary to us. Most of us had been taught to treat our engine gently – it was the only one we had and we needed it to get us back to the carrier. Full throttle was therefore only used on take-off or, in very short bursts, in an emergency.

We expressed our fears that a long period of full throttle would overheat the engine and perhaps cause it to fail. Roy replied 'Nonsense you have a Rolls Royce engine which will thrive on full power and in any event your main objective is to get to the *Tirpitz* and hit it. If you do that you will have succeeded.'

Sub Lt Richard Douglas-Boyd also recalled the briefing:

He stressed the need for tight air discipline – the highest Barracudas in our formation should not be above 150 ft until we neared the coast of Norway. We must expect anti-aircraft fire from the ground, and particularly from the sides of Kaa fjord. He gave us a clear picture of the position of the target, the plan of attack and re-forming afterwards.

Another pilot, Roy Hawkes, a junior pilot of 820 Squadron, recalled Baker-Falkner:

...proceeding to give us a pre-battle briefing and pep talk which fired us with determination and allayed some of our apprehension. After all, he was a convincing example of someone who had done it all before and come back to tell the tale. There was no reason why, by taking his advice, we could not do likewise. He was a skilled and convincing leader.

The aircrews retired early to be as sharp as possible for the next day's activities. Roy wrote yet another of his 'goodbye letters' just prior to the Operation *Mascot* in case he wasn't going to get back from the operation. She didn't know it at the time, but this was to be the last letter that Naomi was ever to receive from Roy:

Tuesday. No mail today consequently it's not so hot. How I do love to see your darling handwriting always and your news about the babes. They must be an adorable pair. Wee Sandra must be a cuddly little slogger. I've been unlucky not seeing her grow up and our darling Carole at her best age. DIL [Darling I Love you]

Allan Thomson recalled:

HMS *Formidable* lived up to her name. In the short time the wing was on board, the ship's crew managed to damage more than a few aircraft. I cannot recollect an occasion on board *Furious* when a single aircraft 'got bent' as a result of mishandling by the deck handling party. Trouble arose on *Formidable* because all the Barracuda aircraft of the strike force were embarked on the one ship. The attempts to range them on deck and fly them off as a mass unit (American style) led to a lot of minor damage to wings and tails etc.

In the early hours of 17 July, Operation *Mascot* began with the Barracudas ranged up for flying off forty minutes after midnight The *Formidable* flight had been attached unceremoniously to the main body.

David Clarabut, Roy's wingman, recalled:

> The wing was closely packed on the after end of *Formidable* ready for take-off. Roy would take off first and me second.
>
> Roy opened his throttle and as he did so, the ship did a lurch, Roy's plane swerved to the right into mine which was stationary tucked in behind him and my propeller (they were wood) cut into his wing tearing a great hole in it. He quickly got out, evicted the crew from the aircraft on his left side and he duly took off.

As Allan Thomson recalled:

> The crowning example occurred just before take-off for the attack on *Tirpitz*. A/C 'B-F' was due to lead attack in, but had a wing root chewed by someone's propeller whilst still on the flight deck. He immediately commandeered another 'kite' which I believe had no radio telephone and a strange crew.

Sub Lt (A) Gilbert Clark RNVR, the observer in one of *Formidable's* Barracuda flight aircraft nicknamed 'Rita', further described the incident as they unfolded for him:

> The day came, fine, clear, and with a light wind from the south east. All was hectic on *Formidable*'s flight deck as aircraft manoeuvred for the take-off. One Barracuda went an inch or two too far forward and his propeller clipped the end of B-F's tail. He leapt from his cockpit, ejected my pilot (we were the next convenient aircraft) and climbed in. Not a word had been said to me about the change, and when I saw my pilot standing on deck giving a farewell wave I undid my belt and got up to see what was happening. As I did so B-F took off and I was flung back into my seat. Our air-gunner of course was completely oblivious to the situation, as he was facing aft! It took me a few seconds to realise what had happened. I had been promoted by fate from being a 'tail end Charlie' doing 'following navigation' only, to strike navigator in the twinkling of an eye! Effectively, if this had been the Lord Mayor's Show I'd have been pitch-forked from the corporation dustcart at the tail end of the procession into the Lord Mayor's carriage in the lead. All inside five minutes! A junior observer who had never 'smelt cordite' or been officially appointed to a front-line squadron. My duty now was to make an accurate landfall.
>
> B-F's first words to me were 'Observer'. He had not the slightest idea who he was speaking to – 'I require the first course in five minutes, the smoke float is away to starboard'. The smoke float, indicating the position of latitude and longitude for departure, had been dropped by a destroyer. I gave him the course, but such was the necessity for speed that he did not go over the mark but left it well to starboard. I had no choice but to depart from a position obtained by a bearing and estimate of distance from the smoke float. Not an ideal start, but 'needs must when the devil drives'.We had roughly speaking 100 miles to go. Sixty over the sea and forty from the coast to Kaa Fiord.

We were flying at something in the region of 60 feet above the water, the propellers of the lower aircraft leaving wind lanes in the calm sea. All this by the light of the midnight sun at 01.31 British double summer time.

Clarabut took up the story:

Meanwhile, on the assumption that my propeller would have been badly damaged I was pulled clear and stopped my engine whilst all the other aircraft took off and when they had gone my propeller was inspected very quickly, and given the OK. So in some trepidation I took off last of all. However, all was well. I caught up the others, tucked myself into my No. 2 position next to Roy, and to this day I can see the surprise on Roy's face as we formated closely at seeing me there thinking most naturally that my aircraft was U/S.

Gilbert Clark continued:

We proceeded at this low altitude hoping to avoid detection by enemy radar until B-F ordered: 'Tell me when we are 20 miles from the coast. Then we'll climb'. I did so and he started the climb. It was a remarkable sight to see that strike of about 90 aircraft rising as one.

The fighters took station, and on we went. Now for the landfall. This was of prime importance. I was inexperienced, and I had never been over Norway before. Add to that the fact that my pilot was the doyen of British TBR pilots and around me were some of the Navy's best I must confess to a slight sweat!

With some anxiety I tried to compare by the light of the midnight sun, from 10,000 ft, and moving at 145 knots, our position over the rocky coast, with that I'd marked on the chart. Nothing looked the same, then suddenly it all clicked into place. The wide mouth of Alten Fiord, the island of Silden, and most important of all the island of Loppen (Loppa.) My plotted track ran straight over Loppen and our ETA there was 02 hrs 02 mins BDST. A glance at my watch showed 02 hrs 02.5 mins. Dead on, what a relief. No time for sitting back however, map reading showed that we were moving south of our intended track. This could only mean that the wind strength and direction at 10,000 ft was different from that lower down. That was quite natural and an appropriate correction was made.

B-F levelled out and the armada went on. We should have passed the tip of Lang fiord, which is a projection on the SW side of Altenfiord, but I noticed we were altering course very slowly. The reason soon became plain. There were three enemy destroyers moored on a trot (that is one behind the other) near the end of the fiord, and by working to the south, B-F had placed a mile or two between us and their guns. As it happened, they spoke not a word.

The manoeuvre had however put us off course a little and his next command was 'next course'. I gave him 120°. It was 0215 – the scenery superb.

Flying in formation with 826 Squadron, Johnnie Baggs noted:

By now we were above 10,000 ft and still climbing on full throttle. Ahead and slightly to the port side of the formation we could see the long stretch of Alten Fiord and Kaafiord at the end of it. I could see the *Tirpitz* at the base of the huge mountain and sheer cliff-face on the southern side of Kaafiord, but much worse, the long streams of smoke pouring out of the canisters across the fiord and gradually covering it with a layer of white cloud.

Gilbert Clark continued:

At 0217 *Tirpitz* opened the bowling with fire from her 15″ guns – we were 14 miles away from her.

Her 5.6-inch (150-mm) guns soon joined in as we pressed on. B-F had by now started to 'weave'. The aircraft rose and fell relative to each other like the model horses on a fairground carousel, and of course spread out. It was a ploy to baffle the enemy radar. My (Irish) air gunner was to say later 'Foine it was, like bein' rocked in a cradle' Some cradle!

As one of the strike's rear gunners, Gordon 'Blondie' Lambert, of 820 Squadron, recalled:

One flight of fighter bombers had, in addition to their bombs, parcels of aluminium foil strips – window – which they were to drop in the hope of confusing the German radar system, but despite their efforts the enemy were ready for us.

Baggs continued: 'The signal came from the strike leader "commencing attack", and we all eased the control column forward, closing up into a tighter bombing formation.' The two Barracuda wing formations went down steeply in a dive together.

Clark continued:

Sad to relate, it seems that a German submarine had seen us and given warning, so that when we reached the target, the smoke screen was in full swing. The smoke filled the fiord and we had to dive blind, aiming at the red glow of her gunfire. The fighters raced down like the traditional bats out of hell, tearing into any gun emplacements they could find. But – we were baulked.

Some of the Barracudas were carrying four 500-lb bombs and others including ours one large 1,600-pounder with an armour-piercing snout. It had chalked on it by a member of the maintenance crew, 'here's one for Coventry'. Our intention was to dive from 10,000 feet and drop from 4,000 feet so that these bombs could get up sufficient momentum to pierce the armoured deck, 12 inches thick.

In a determined attempt to try and find her, B-F went down to 2,000 feet. The place was a cauldron of ack ack fire. The *Tirpitz* of course, apart from her own guns had helpers ashore and afloat.

Roy himself recalled in his official debriefing that if he 'had not been there before he might not have recognised the locality as a fiord at all.'

Baggs was concentrating hard:

The smoke was rapidly filling the fiord, but I had my aiming point firmly fixed, even though the *Tirpitz* had practically disappeared. It was darker underneath the cloud and as I circled round looking for the target, all hell was breaking loose around me.

Intense light and heavy flak issued from this pall of smoke in the form of a barrage directly over what was assumed to be the target, as well as accurately aimed fire from gun positions recently established on the hillsides above the smoke level. Under these circumstances the majority of pilots dropped their bombs blind through the murk in the position from which most of the flak seemed to be coming. No hits were claimed on *Tirpitz*, although a column of smoke with a mushroom top was seen to rise above the general smoke level to a height of about 1,500 feet. An explosion with a large jet of flames was observed.

Lambert continued:

> I felt the aircraft lift slightly as the pilot released the bomb, and then started to pull out of the dive, but not before we had entered the smoke. It was a relief to fly out of this, so that we could at least see where we were, but then of course so could the AA gun crews.

In Dickie Kingdon's Barracuda, Joe Armitage the observer was standing up when they dived on *Tirpitz*. The jolt when they pulled out of the dive wrenched a knee-joint severely and his shout of pain was heard clearly over the intercom.

Emerson noted that 'Most of us bombed blind at where she might have been, but we didn't see the *Tirpitz* at all. Vertical vision poor & all the fjords in deep shadow. Flak was intense.'

By now Baggs was in the thick of it:

> The *Tirpitz* and the shore batteries were putting up a box barrage around 4,000–5,000 ft. Aircraft were weaving about all over the place looking for an aiming point and trying to avoid each other while flying around in circles. One thing that showed clearly through the smoke was the flash of the *Tirpitz* guns, which outlined her position clearly and I was able to dive from 5,000 ft, line up on the gun flashes and release my 1,600-lb semi-armoured piercing bomb. I had certainly seen a number of deep red angry eruptions of exploding bombs, but there was no way of telling exactly where they landed.

A near miss was felt in *Tirpitz* at 2.21 am but by 2.25 am the battleship was totally obscured and no other bombs fell near.

On Roy's return flight, Clark recalled:

> Now for home. Initially we turned and going low over the Norwegian mountains, made best speed, like grouse over the butts. It was now every man for himself – and out to sea. We powered low over the mountainous terrain and then climbed up over Alten fiord.

Thomson recalled the escape and intense flak: 'One fighter mis-timed the run and disintegrated in a ball of fire.'

Gilbert Clark added:

> The destroyers in Lang fiord were now wide awake and to avoid their fire B-F dived to sea level. He had seen them peppering the sky round those who had got ahead higher than us on the return journey, and by this tactic avoided that danger. Off the island of Silden, smoke floats had been dropped to give the direction of the Fleet and the destroyer *Verulam* stationed 15 miles nearer than the main body, to help those who may have needed it on the way home.

Before they finally left the Norwegian coast Clark recalled 'Flying low over Norwegian houses, some brave souls were hanging out of the upstairs windows waving Union flags.' He continued:

At 0300 we made a perfect landing on *Formidable* and Lt Cdr Baker-Falkner leapt out [of Barracuda 'Rita's' cockpit] and sped to report to his superiors. That was the last I saw of him and had never spoken to him face to face!' All was disappointment – and in record speed the aircraft were refuelled and bombed up – to go again. However the weather had deteriorated and the attack cancelled. I had breakfast, and a few hours' sleep.

Meanwhile, Roy's ejected aircrew, Micklem and Kimberley, had not been quietly waiting for the other aircrews to return from the strike. Clark recalled:

My pilot S/Lt (A) Donald McLachlan RNVR had been ejected from his seat by B-F and left standing on deck together with their [B-F's] observer Lt Guy Micklem DSC and their TAG Arthur Kimberley. McLachlan was a fire-eater and after a quick examination of B-F's damaged aircraft, jumped in, hauling Lt Micklem in with him! Whether they got Kimberley in with them I can't be sure. Admiral Sir Henry Moore, Captain Phillip Ruck-Keene RN and others on the bridge, including Captain Miller an invited observer from the United States Navy and a specialist Norwegian meteorologist, gazed with incredulity as they saw the damaged aircraft roar into life and race away up the deck without official permission from anybody! Maclachlan trailed the main body by about five minutes and passed through them on their return journey.

When they reached the position of the *Tirpitz* they found her totally covered in smoke. Mac decided that it would be a waste of bombs to go for the gun flashes and decided to go instead for three fleet destroyers moored on a trot in Lang Fiord, on the way home. One destroyer was more than a match for one Barracuda let alone three; that lay in the realms of lunacy! Unfortunately they only succeeded in achieving near misses. However, their grit was rewarded with a DSC for Sub Lt Maclachlan and a Bar to his DSC for Lt Micklem.

Tirpitz had fifteen minutes' warning and although there was still no German fighter opposition when the Barracudas attacked, the flak was very heavy and *Tirpitz* herself was almost entirely obscured by smoke. There were rumours prior to the attack that the Germans had a squadron of fighters at Bardufoss some distance to the south. True or false, none were encountered. The smoke from *Tirpitz* and from shore generators reached to about 600–700 feet above the target.

One Corsair and one Barracuda were lost and due to the effectiveness of the smoke-generators, the Barracuda force was unable to judge the success of the attack. One near miss was felt in *Tirpitz*, but nothing else.

Just before the operation, Naomi sent the only surviving letter from her to Roy. It was postmarked 14 July 1944 and was returned to her on 18 October 1944, unread. She wrote:

Oh, when will this rotten war be over. Winkie gave me a good heart ache today – she suddenly shouted 'Daddy, Daddy, Daddy – Daddy's coming soon.' Glad you're seeing Bruce H. but am a bit worried over that news. I'm getting so, so war-weary – I love you so terribly much it really hurts me.

CHAPTER 27

Lost Patrol, 18 July 1944

Roy and his wing were back on board HMS *Formidable* to calm down after the strain of once more attacking *Tirpitz*. A planned second strike scheduled for later that morning was cancelled owing to the sudden appearance of fog.

On board HMS *Indefatigable*, Johnnie Baggs recalled the events as they unfolded:

As we were debriefed the aircraft were refuelled and re-armed for an immediate repeat attack. Approximately an hour and a half after landing on, all aircrew were again sitting in their ranged aircraft, once more awaiting 'Wings' staccato 'Start-up'. This time the fuel gauge for my starboard tank registered only one quarter full. Flt Sgt O'Keefe climbed up on the wing and gave me his assurance that the tank had been filled fully. He said the fuel gauge in the cockpit must have become faulty. I was far from happy. 'Start-up' crackled across the flight deck. I quickly ran the engine up as the ship swung into wind ready for take-off.

This time, *Formidable* was directly ahead of us, as engines were revving up, suddenly *Formidable* disappeared. The fleet had run into a bank of fog and cloud and within minutes we were also swallowed up by it. It intensified, damping down over the whole fleet and the second attack had to be cancelled.

On board *Formidable*, after debriefing and breakfast, sleep was the order of the day for the exhausted aircrew throughout most of the morning and afternoon. Emerson, however, realised they still were not safe and stayed up to write in his secret diary just after returning from Operation *Mascot*:

We landed on at 4 am, re-armed and refuelled and stood by for the second strike. We all knew it would be a waste of time and useless, but CS-1 ordered it and we started up at 8 am. However, fog was soon up. Thank God, and it was cancelled.

We are now going south for another stab at Stadlandet. There is a belt of subs lying in wait for us and relays of Cats and Libs are patrolling the area.

Many of the squadrons had taken heavy losses in the strike, which weighed heavily on the fighter boys who had encountered stiff resistance from the Germans. 'Ron Dubber my senior P was shot down and taken POW and I also lost pilot Woodward, and several others returned badly shot up by small arms and cannons, doing low level attacks on flak positions,' recalled 'Biggy' Bigg-Wither, CO of 1841 Corsair Squadron.

Lt Cdr Anthony 'Tony' Freire-Marreco RNVR, the ship's Fighter Directions Officer (FDO), was also concerned for the fighter boys, and noted: 'On their return from the *Tirpitz* attack the pilots were very tired and so as we steamed back to Scapa the Commander who was a stickler for tradition, did the almost unheard of and opened the bar.'

At long last Roy could relax knowing that he had completed his last operational mission. He was ready to go on leave with Naomi and the children as soon as the ship anchored back at Scapa. It was now only days before his being posted non-operationally back to Boscombe Down as a test pilot.

Biggy noted that whilst they were relaxing in the bar:

...that night – the weather was ghastly and the forecast grim. We were all most relieved as other squadrons had had similar losses and consequently we had quite a party in the wardroom. We were *alive* and that was something to celebrate!

Roy, too, was relaxing in the wardroom looking distinguished in his No. 2 Mess uniform, waistcoat and black bow tie, a sharp contrast to his flying kit he had been wearing only a few hours before. For him this was the final evening to unwind on board ship before his shore posting, and he had no idea what the future would hold or even if he was ever going to sea again. However, not all of Roy's wing were celebrating; neither David Brown nor Roy's wingman David Clarabut were at the party. 'I am "teatotal"' reminded David Brown. Clarabut had gone to bed exhausted. He had no doubt that Roy was there to socialise and give support to his men after the trials of that morning over Norway.

Meanwhile, unbeknown to the vast majority of the Fleet, the return journey was starting to look increasingly perilous. That morning ULTRA intelligence from British cryptologists at the top-secret establishment at Bletchley Park had intercepted and decoded enciphered messages from the German Enigma machines. A few hours after the attack on *Tirpitz*, *Kriegsmarine* Captain U-boats Norway had signalled coded orders for some of U-boat Group *Trutz* to move at high speed south-eastwards to intercept the British force on their return journey to Scapa. It was known to intelligence that the Arctic flotilla numbered at least thirty U-boats. Moreover, all submarines carried the most up-to-date flak armament to defend against Fleet Air Arm and RAF aircraft attacks. Yet none of this highly classified information was made available to *Formidable*.

Developments progressed, when, in the afternoon the Admiralty and the RAF also received communication from Norwegian resistance agents that U-boats were out to sink the Fleet. Completely without the knowledge of the vast majority of officers on *Formidable*, No. 18 Group RAF Coastal Command were allocated an anti-submarine patrol area of its hunter-killer flying boats out to the west of the Lofoten Islands. As such the RAF aircraft were to patrol over and protect the Fleet until the ships had passed the danger area. The intelligence gleaned from decrypts of the German Enigma codes, code-named ULTRA, informed them of the submarine search area for the Fleet.

No. 18 Group RAF therefore inaugurated special sweeps by long-range aircraft to cover the track intended to be taken by the retiring naval forces. The first two aircraft left their RAF base in the Shetland Islands early in the afternoon of 17 July and both later sighted U-boats in the area. The early reports received from RAF aircraft confirmed the ULTRA decrypts were correct and that there was indeed a concentration of U-boats ahead of the Fleet and it was estimated they would be met in the early hours of 18 July.

By the evening, whilst Roy and the other ship's officers were relaxing in the wardroom, an RAF Liberator and a Catalina patrolled across the centre of the Fleet's projected path and attacked U-boats at 9.48 pm, and 9.56 pm respectively, which they went on to sink.

Catalina Y/210 was piloted by Flying Officer John Cruickshank of 210 RAF Squadron flying out of Sullom Voe. He had sighted a U-boat in the vicinity of the projected route that HMS *Formidable* would sail later that evening.

Cruickshank recalled that their orders were 'to conduct a reconnaissance sweep to cover the withdrawal of the Royal Navy aircraft carriers which had attacked the German battleship *Tirpitz*.' He later recalled: 'I never sighted the naval force and I had no knowledge of its position, course or speed. We had no radar contact with it.'

It was almost 10 pm but the Arctic sun was still bright enough to see by as the Catalina approached the Lofoten Islands. Suddenly, a blip appeared on their radar screen, and, through a break in the sea fog, a U-boat was sighted on the surface.

Cruickshank put his Catalina into a dive and prepared to release six depth charges. The submarine was ready as the Catalina searched for gaps in the fog. A hail of flak shells from the U-boat ripped into the flying boat fuselage, killing the navigator and hitting Cruickshank seventy-two times with shrapnel in his legs, body and lungs. But he stayed on target, dropping the charges. He himself had suffered serious wounds in the action and during the five and a half hours of the flight home he lost consciousness several times, but insisted on helping to land the Catalina. He was awarded the Victoria Cross for his bravery. Enigma intercepts later confirmed the sinking of the U-boat, *U347*.

Cruickshank and his fellow RAF pilots' actions had changed the whole situation for the Fleet and by their enforced withdrawal put it in greater jeopardy. Cruickshank continued:

Both aircraft Y/210 and U/86 carried out attacks on separate U-boats between 2130 and 2200 hrs after which neither were able to resume their patrols. The result of these attacks was the naval force had no other protection against U-boats while it was traversing what was clearly hostile waters – at least the aircraft due to relieve us were to arrive probably between 0200 and 0300 hrs on 18 July 1944.

I would expect Naval HQ would have advised the Naval Force Commander of this situation. The selection and decision about patrol areas is not a matter decided at squadron level – it would have been done at 18 Group Headquarters, and the HQ was located in the proximity of Naval Headquarters at Rosyth.

Could it be that the Naval Task Force Commander then decided to provide an anti-U-boat patrol from his carrier aircraft?

The next scheduled patrol by RAF aircraft over the Fleet's path was not due until 0006 hours with the arrival of the next Catalina 0/210, piloted by Flight Lt French. Therefore it left the admiral commanding, Home Fleet Second in Command, Rear Admiral Rhoderick 'Wee' McGrigor, on board *Formidable* no alternative but to close the gap by sending up Fleet Air Arm aircraft from the Fleet's aircraft carriers.

On board HMS *Formidable*, the ship's navigating officer Jack Frewen, was on the main bridge. 'The plot showed submarines ahead which probably came from an Admiralty signal in the main Admiralty Ops room in the citadel in London,' recalled Freire-Marreco, or Marreco as as he was commonly called.

Rear Admiral Commanding, 1st Carrier Squadron, McGrigor subsequently wrote in his operational report:

I therefore arranged with the approval of the Commander in Chief, Home Fleet for a patrol of one Barracuda and one Corsair from *Formidable* to search on either bow during the critical period. While a normal anti-submarine patrol ahead of the Fleet was to be carried out by a Swordfish from *Furious*.

He further elaborated that:

> A strike force was kept ready in *Indefatigable* who were also to extend the patrol with a Barracuda and Firefly to a depth of 60 miles on either beam if weather conditions were favourable.

He ended with a telling point explaining his interest in flying the patrol even in bad weather: 'I had hopes of hitting several U-boats.'

By this stage of the war, German U-boats recognised that all Fleet Air Arm TBR aircraft were comparatively slow and did not carry any forward-firing guns. They decided to stay on the surface and fight it out instead of diving. To make sure this ploy did not succeed the Admiralty started to send out fighters with their TBR aircraft when on anti-submarine patrols.

With the decision by McGrigor to go ahead with an anti-submarine patrol, Ruck-Keene ordered Roy and other COs to the ops room to elaborate on the plan and to confirm that the Stadlandet strike was cancelled. In the ops room, under the bridge in the island of the carrier, were the admiral, captain, ops room staff, the senior Fleet Air Arm officers, including Roy, and the FDO. Marreco presented the situation:

> From bridge plots there were reports of U-boats so the Captain decided that since the pilots had been drinking, to let the squadron commanding officers undertake the first anti-submarine patrol. This had been after Baker-Falkner, Bigg-Wither and others had got into a little huddle with Commander Flying, Cdr Bramwell, and the ship's navigating officer, Jack Frewen.

Frewen plotted the patrol route on the gyro table, a table with a light shinning up onto the Admiralty charts. Outside, the weather was 'not good and visibility very poor indeed, banks of fog/heavy mist met constantly' recalled Frank Grainger of 826 Squadron.

Present at the meeting was Patrick Duffy:

> I was Assistant Air Staff Officer under Cdr Griffiths in the commanding operations room, so formally central to, and partly responsible for, operational control.
>
> My role was to carry out the commands of the Air Staff Officer in the ops room. It was known that RAF aircraft were operating in the area.

Biggy added:

> I had just turned in about 11 pm when a messenger came to my cabin and said I was wanted in the ops room. B-F was there and told me that they had news of a pack of U-boats which had been detected by aircraft some 100 miles ahead of us, and that they were on the surface.

Duffy continued:

> The weather gradually worsened and became foggy. Due to the bad weather aircrew were not mobilised straight away. B-F, Kingdon and Bigg-Wither discussed with Ruck-Keene the patrol. He let the flyers have their way.
>
> Implications in hindsight included perhaps B-F's judgement to fly off in the bad weather. Who did agree to the patrol? Not Griffiths and not me!

Duffy then went on to state: 'It was because B-F wanted to go!' The atmosphere was fraught, and appeared to stem from concerns over differences of opinion, or even antagonism between, the RN and RNVR officers.

However, it emerged that in the small group discussing the patrol with Captain Ruck-Keene, Roy had explained to him that the weather was quite unsuitable for flying. But the captain continued to be firm and concluded that the patrols had to go ahead, perhaps with secret knowledge of orders direct from the Admiralty, which he could not disclose to those around him. In the end Roy insisted that if anyone had to go up, it would be him.

As Roy's No. 2, his wingman David Clarabut, put it 'with the weather foul, it was typical of him to go on the mission in those conditions when he could easily have ordered others to do it.'

Des Rowe, the Kiwi 830 Squadron pilot, elaborated:

> B-F was against us carrying out a/s patrols as the crews had had a very tiring day but he couldn't persuade the captain. He therefore elected to carry out the first patrol although he would not normally carry out a/s patrols at all. This was immediately after dinner and both he and Guy Micklem were wearing bow ties, we had a bit of a joke about that.

Roy's old friend Cdr David Buchanan-Dunlop, now in command of *Indefatigable*'s ADR room, even went on to say:

> ...after their all out, if unsuccessful, efforts against *Tirpitz* some aircrews of 827, so I was told, were somewhat browned off being required to fly such patrols and B-F, to set a good example as always, decided to fly the first of them himself – typical of him.

Biggy went on to describe the details of the patrol:

> Baker-Falkner said that he proposed that the senior people should carry out two patrols of square searches ahead of the Fleet.
>
> He selected Dickie Kingdon, CO of a Barra squadron, myself, and my new senior P [pilot] Mattholie [Sub Lt Harold 'Matt' Mattholie RNVR]. Matt took the place of my Senior P who had been shot down on the previous day. It may seem odd that we should go off on what was after all a routine a/s patrol. Indeed in B-F's mind there was a good reason for it. Firstly it was reported that a wolf pack of U-boats had been deployed to intercept the Fleet on its return to Scapa – secondly – several day/night operations having been concluded there had been quite a celebration in the wardroom amongst aircrew that night. The bar closed at 10.30 pm and orders for these patrols came through shortly afterwards. So B-F selected himself and those he considered to be the most experienced, reliable and least likely to have been affected by the celebrations. I was 26, Matt 23 and the remainder of my squadron 19 or 20 at the time – more or less fresh out of Pensacola so the choice was fairly obvious. Bob Woolston, Kevin Gibney's replacement as the new CO of 827 Squadron, had turned in when all this was going on!

However, as Lt Cdr Woolston himself recollected: 'We were all tired yet Roy decided to do the first anti-submarine patrol and I would do the second.'

David Brown also thought this typical of Roy and that he would have been up to the job. 'B-F would not haven taken strong drink before the flight.'

Biggy continued:

I was to form up on B-F and Matt with Dickie – the idea being to strafe U-boats on the surface so that the Barras had a clear run to drop depth charges.

Trouble was that the Barra's speed was around 120 knots at which the Corsair was sluggish and floppy so we would be zigzagging around the Barras keeping always within sight as we relied on them to navigate.

By the end of the meeting, Duffy appeared to have felt aggrieved:

I viewed some of the decision-taking and tactical direction with the utmost misgiving at the time. Ruck-Keene, a strong-willed character, was a good captain and a good leader, however at the same time his leadership was questionable. Ruck-Keene adored his flyers. Rear Admiral McGrigor was not a strong character and was pulled along by Ruck-Keene – he really could not stand up to Ruck-Keene at all.

By comparison, Cdr Griffiths in charge of the ops room didn't have the confidence of the captain. The operation itself really consisted of Ruck-Keene and his relationship with Kingdon, Bigg-Wither and Baker-Falkner rather than those in the ops room.

Ruck-Keene did not favour fools gladly, if you got on the wrong side of him: 'If you were difficult.' Lt Cdr Flying, O'Rorke had until recently been in charge of the flight deck; Ruck-Keene had him off the ship the second time he didn't agree. He should have considered his ship's officers more.

Meanwhile, whilst those in the ops room were apparently unhappy with the situation, according to Marreco 'Baker-Falkner would have organised the patrol with the navigating officer in the bridge.'

The other aircrew for the patrol were given messages to prepare for their flights scheduled for 1 am. Biggy's second in command, Matt, recalled:

The *Tirpitz* op had been a long, and exhausting day, and, that evening after a bit of a party, everyone went to bed. Later that night I was woken up to be told that I was to be catapulted off within the hour. I had to be ready for an a/s patrol in response to a definite sighting or threat of a U-boat in the area. I was told that Lt Cdr Baker-Falkner was to be protected by Biggy's covering Corsair. He was marked as a man who would make admiral grade and was a first class pilot and leader. I was to give cover to the other Barracuda.

As the aircraft made ready for the patrol, preparations were almost complete in the Aircraft Direction Room (ADR) – all *Formidable*'s aircraft, when airborne were subject to control from the ADR. The ADR was manned by radar plot ratings and Fighter Direction Officers, under the control of the senior FDO. In command of the ADR that night was Marreco. 'He ran a good FDO. He was a biggish, darkish, charming and able man and later became a politician. He had a very important role,' recalled Duffy. 'We were in adjacent cabins under the bridge.'

Marreco himself noted:

During the working up period of *Formidable* early in 1944, I designed the FDO position and trained up the ratings. It was during this period that the ship's crew refused to obey orders – the only known mutiny on a capital ship during the war.

Eventually the situation did calm down but the troublemakers remained. Many of the radar operators under me had been central to the mutiny. The *Tirpitz* op cheered the crew up a bit.

That night when fully operating, although much was happening, the dimly lit room was very quiet with only the hum of machinery and low voices. Dominating the room was the vertical plot, a large Perspex compass rose, the centre of which represented the ship, with intersecting lines representing distances from the ship. Behind the plot sat the ratings, each of whom was connected by internal phones to the various radar sets around the ship. These ratings, who had been trained to write backwards in special symbols and words, marked down the information on the plot. Each one was responsible for different echoes being received.

The senior FDO's task that night was to interpret the various tracks, to decide whether they represented friend or foe and monitor the patrol aircraft movements. Although radio silence was to be adhered to during this patrol so close to enemy-occupied Norway, he could communicate with Roy and the other aircraft crew by radio telephone (R/T) to establish their positions.

One of the ADR ratings, AB Ron Tovey, recalled:

Seated around the room were further members of the crew manning the low and high frequency R/T sets, their task being to listen out for messages and to log all incoming and outgoing calls in a special R/T shorthand. These log books could be called for in the event of any questions arising over incidents that may occur..

Another rating, George Andrews, explained his role:

In the ADR, I would wear earphones connected to the radar. I would stand in front of a large vertical circular map that was transparent and which was covered with grid references of 360 degrees. The report from the radar would say 'Bogies bearing 0 3 0'. And then they'd estimate the distance: for example 16 miles. I would then plot that on the circular map with coloured pencils, red, blue.

Finally all in the ADR was ready to track the movements of the patrol.

Down below the island on the flight deck, the maintenance crews were already busy at work making last-minute checks to the aircraft.

The flight deck was ready under the command of Lt Cdr Bruce Hawkes, Roy's old observer from 812 Squadron, in his capacity as second-in-command of the Air Department. The *Tirpitz* strike aircraft had already been serviced, refuelled and bombed up in readiness for the anticipated second strike which was later cancelled. The maintenance crew had finished their daily inspections and signed both the office and travelling copies of the Form 700 – the certificate of maintenance. The aircraft to be used on the patrol were released for use.

Meanwhile, the flight crews were making their final preparations. 'We were all about to go on the op when the captain called us up onto the bridge and wished each of us in turn "Good luck old chap" but when he got to Matt "good bye old chap",' recalled Biggy.

Two gull-winged Corsairs and three Barracuda aircraft were readied on the flight deck. Roy's personal wing aircraft was still being repaired after the accident of the day before, so he climbed into LS556, an 830 Squadron Barracuda coded '5F'. Roy was still wearing his bow tie under his flying gear. He appeared to have made a good choice as Des Rowe recalled: 'It was our aircraft that B-F was flying, mine and David Brown's. It was a lovely aircraft and well maintained.'

Near Roy's aircraft, not all were at ease in a small huddle of aircrew. 'A few of us were chatting with Kim [Roy's TAG Kimberley], who was not too happy at flying anti-submarine patrols,' recalled Frank 'Bing' Bingham, another aircrew member on board the carrier.

I was on *Formidable* with 826 Squadron at the time.

Normally a wing leader did not go on anti-submarine patrols, this was left to we lesser mortals. It's a very boring job looking for submarines. Most of the time you circle the Fleet at about 10 miles radius looking for something you rarely see. We chided Kim that he had the best crew to fly with, so 'What's the worry?' Going round and round the Fleet was no big deal.

Why the wing leader went on anti-sub patrol with a Corsair escort doesn't ring true. But who were we to argue, we were flying ourselves within hours. The other thing that makes me wonder about the mission was that the Barracuda had a fighter escort, a luxury we never had.

Also readying on the flight deck in the second Barracuda 5A was Dickie Kingdon with David Brown as his navigator. David explained:

I volunteered to go on the first anti-submarine patrol on the orders of Vice Admiral Moore. We were by then west of the Lofoten Islands. The patrols were ordered out ahead of the Fleet to port and starboard. Without calling for volunteers, the wing leader assigned himself and crew, Guy Micklem and Arthur Kimberley, to the starboard stint and the CO of 830 Squadron Lt Cdr Kingdon, myself and an air gunner, CPO Carr, off on the port stint. So we were in fact going down the line of the Fleet, B-F to starboard away from Norway and we to port towards Norway.

'Three crews on the flight deck were ready to take off for anti-submarine patrols,' recalled Ron Hibbs, an 827 Squadron TAG who had joined the squadron relatively recently. 'My pilot on the *Tirpitz* raids was Sub Lt McCandless. I was in the third Barracuda ready on the flight deck.'

The Corsairs of Biggy and Matt were scheduled to fly off first and then circle above the carrier whilst the Barracudas were readied on the flight deck. Matt recalled:

I went to get ready my aircraft but the one available had radio aerial difficulties and so I asked for my personal one of the day before, this a/c had also had radio trouble earlier in the day, aircraft serial JT404, it had no cartoon emblem. An earlier aircraft of mine had been called *Bucephalus* – my air fitter wasn't very learned and was totally perplexed with a word much like syphilis.

At last all was ready and Roy made his final pre-flight checks, after Ron Humphreys, one of his personal flight deck handling party crew, had strapped him into the pilot's cockpit.

The ship's log recorded: '01.58 the a/s patrol, delayed from 0100, by the uncertain weather conditions, took off.' In the ops room, Duffy noted: 'The weather was, by the time the aircraft took off, dreadful. It was almost 2 am on board, and 150 miles west of the Lofotens. There was a slight south westerly breeze.'

On deck Matt had also completed his final instrument checks: 'I lifted off from the carrier as escort of one Barra whilst Biggy took off as escort to Baker-Falkner's Barracuda.'

Then it was Roy's turn to take off as part of the first anti-submarine patrol with his normal crew.

Hibbs was watching the proceedings whilst still parked and waiting in the third Barracuda: 'Baker-Falkner in my mind's eye shot off first. The weather wasn't very good at all. Another aircraft shot over to the left.'

Biggy noted:

I was flying the other Corsair and started to circle the ship. The Barras took off after us as they needed a full run of the deck to set off with their load (depth charges) so that made it difficult to form up and of course at that stage one preserved radio silence. I should have been with B-F but in the terrible weather – the cloud base was about 100 feet to 200 feet – we did not connect. It was still light of course in those latitudes.

Matt added:

I was the last Corsair to be catapulted off and my misery began. When we lifted off I was escorting the second flight, but the cloud cover was so dense and so low it was difficult to see, so each aircraft flown off was flying 'on instruments' at less than 100 ft. In the climb up through the clag, I was worrying that any moment I might collide with the plane somewhere ahead of me. As the aircraft couldn't see one another we became separated.

Suddenly I found myself only a few feet away from a Barracuda, and as it was imperative that I stayed that close – I lined up with it. Once the pilot in the heavily loaded bomber knew he had his fighter escort he headed off on a set course for anti-submarine patrol. I had to stay in tight formation with the Barracuda.

Both aircraft, climbing steeply, we were not far from the point of stalling, and at any moment our engines might cut out, which would have meant 'curtains' since we both had insufficient height to give time to get out of any spin.

The next forty minutes were hellish, until, at 10,000 ft, we broke out of the cloud, into a bright blue sky. The relief was fantastic. Then came the first surprise. The bomber I was 'covering' was that of the Fleet Commander which meant that Biggy (my CO) must be 'covering' the other Barracuda.

Biggy added:

Radio silence had to be strictly observed so there was no way of knowing that I was not with B-F. Then, we now know, but I didn't at the time, I formed up on Dickie K [Kingdon], CO of the other Barracuda squadron.

Corsairs had one drop tank which gave us at least 4.30 hours flying time. My log book tells me I did 3.30 hours that day and I reckon I had about 30 minutes left so perhaps 4 hours would be more accurate.

Matt added: 'The Corsairs were armed (as normal) with 0.5 machine guns (plus drop tanks of fuel), Barras (I believe) had only depth charges.'

The ADR now presumed that the two patrols were on their pre-determined course pointed out Marreco: 'The two Corsairs and Barracudas flew off for their 3-hour search patrols ahead of the carrier. They then were due to commence step aside searches ahead of the Fleet. We were alone at the time except for a screen of destroyers.'

However, Roy and Matt's aircraft were already not able to achieve their objectives. The weather was worse than feared for flying; cloud cover was now no more than 100 feet and was unbroken until 10,000 feet. Matt exclaimed:

The whole project was now looking stupid. We were airborne, to search, seek, and destroy, enemy submarines. Flying at 10,000 ft, and with thick cloud blotting out any visual contact with the sea, left us with no chance of doing that job.

B-F frequently let down to see whether we could get under it – and we couldn't so up again.

I had difficulty in keeping slow enough to keep up with the much slower Barra and so for much of the time circled around fast keeping a visual on the Barra whilst he did his work. I was only really needed to strafe submarines or enemy aircraft.

This went on for a long time – can't remember how long. We were in open formation and if he wanted me closer for a hand signal he would waggle wings, and I would close up. I had some 'conversation' with the skipper – but only in hand signals and then we moved comfortably away from each other.'

Once at the top of the climb I tried to switch to my auxiliary fuel tank – the drop tank, which had been fitted for a possible *Tirpitz* strike. The extra tank was bulky and hindered flight so I attempted to use that fuel up first. But as it happened when I switched there were a few jolts and then nothing – the fuel wasn't feeding through and so with heart in mouth I attempted, and succeeded, to switch back to main tank.

David Brown, in the Barracuda flown by Kingdon, explained what was happening in their patrol:

We kept company along with B-F on a pre-determined mean advance of 200° for about 15 minutes to the SW. Then we would have disengaged on our respective tracks. B-F to starboard, Dickie Kingdon to port.

The plan was a single triangular pattern to be repeated again after returning to *Formidable*.

The Fleet's mean line of advance was 240° and we were told to go at right angles after a prescribed time.

We patrolled at 1,000 feet, for us the sky was clear and our port tack was 1½ hrs, the total a/s patrol would have been 3 hrs.

At about 3 am on board Roy's Barracuda, they had been attempting to follow the prescribed route of down the line of the Fleet, then starboard at 90° right angles away from Norway – the ETA of the first leg would bring them straight to the Fleet steaming ahead of them in an hour or so. Roy's and Matt's first leg was drawing to a close without seeing any targets through the dense cloud cover. Micklem calculated that by then they would be anticipating crossing the path of the advancing Fleet.

Coming up to one hour thirty minutes' flying time, David Brown reported to Kingdon: 'Now at 330° the Fleet came up dead ahead of us and we could see them miles away.'

However, at the ETA Roy's flight appeared to be in difficulty and the Fleet was not where they expected to see it. Matt continued: 'Failing to rendezvous, we carried out a short square search'. After requesting Micklem to re-check plots and charts, and when the Barracuda's ASV gave no indication of the path of the Fleet, they made signs to Matt in his Corsair to come alongside.

Over in the Corsair, Matt noticed activity in the Barracuda:

After what seemed a couple of hours the Barra waggled its wings to indicate come alongside. Baker-Falkner somehow then indicated to me by sign language that they wanted me to tune in on the homing beacon as they weren't getting beacon themselves. The 'crystal' of B-F had stopped working and couldn't contact the carrier. God knows how they conveyed it to me but they did. So I tried to pick up the beacon myself. I don't think I was getting anything and so said that to B-F. But then I started to get a bearing … a faint bleep some of the time.

Presumably Micklem had calculated that the flying time for Barracuda II, taking into account reduction of weight for fuel use, was about 4.00 hours in total. So they had just less than 2.30 hours to find and return to the ship.

For the patrol we would have been over the Fleet and likely no further than 50–60 miles away from it. No concerns – routine.

What I don't understand is once we had completed our square searches we didn't just let down through the cloud and 'there she is, there's mother a mile ahead.'

We only needed to be 10° off course in the a/s patrol to be far enough away to be in trouble. Something going wrong with the compass is the most likely theory.

There must have come a point whether it was 5 mins or 25 mins, I don't know, when B-F called me up and asked if I was receiving any messages from base – and I wasn't – but I was alerted to there being a problem otherwise R/T silence would have been maintained.

They asked me to break R/T silence and dial up the carrier. Since B-F was the most senior man flying at that moment, and if anyone was going to break R/T silence it would have been him in his aircraft first.

In which case, in my opinion, he would have got on the radio and said 'I'm lost', but he didn't which tells that his radio contact with the vessel wasn't there.

For the talk way I would have said we had VHF. At the time very few of the Barracudas had VHF. The Germans could not pick this up.

Matt sent the message using the R/T call signs allocated to TBRs and fighters for the previous day, 'Hassan' and 'Tinker' respectively. He then tried W/T but received no reply. So the situation for Roy's patrol was beginning to look even more serious. 'It now looked like the communication problems lay mainly in the Barra – on top of which they may have had compass problems.'

Meanwhile, back in the ADR on *Formidable*, ratings were marking on the glass plotting board the positions of Roy's aircraft and of the other three aircraft involved in the patrol. By now it was clear to them that Roy was in trouble and Ruck-Keene and senior officers were informed of the worsening situation.

Marreco recalled:

I was asleep in the ops room [ADR] whilst the patrol was on and left the control of the room to my assistant Philip 'Pip' O'Rorke. He awoke me when the patrol started to get into difficulty to say that they had lost the patrol off the screen. I don't recall the exact time.

I then took full command. It was my job to get Baker-Falkner back.

The ops room included a ½ dozen or so radar screens feeding into the main plot.

Two ratings were plotting on this from the peripheral screen. There were about 12 radar operators, Philip O'Rorke and myself.

The main radar was a Type 283 or 270 [Identification Friend or Foe, IFF].

By 3.15 am, Roy should have been nearing the Fleet. But there was no indication of him on the radar screens even up to its maximum range of 80–100 nautical miles. This was a newly fitted radar, type 281 or 79B. This modernised aircraft warning equipment had been installed three months previously to provide efficient cover at all altitudes – so in theory it was up to the job.

George Green recalled that when members of Roy's wing heard that he appeared to be getting into difficulty:

827 Squadron members asked to be allowed to go and fetch him back but the senior officers sent, I believe, a couple of Corsairs but to no avail. Our CO was flying east away from the ship and was obviously not in radio contact.

The FDO decided to send up a Barracuda and Corsair to search for the missing pair. The Corsair was up by 3.20 am and the Barracuda, flown by Roy's No. 2, David Clarabut, at 3.27 am. Clarabut recounted:

Observer Bob Knight was my navigator for the flight which we took off on a search to look for Baker-Falkner..

That night I was still asleep in my cabin in bed, and woken up being told that Baker-Falkner was missing and the need to bring him back. I don't know why our senior pilot didn't go up. I said I will go up, a voluntary job.

My job was to find him, and that's what we did – and failed. My volunteering to search for him and his crew proved abortive but we tried. I can't recall a patrol more than 3 hours and normally 2½ hours. We went off for a search not an a/s patrol. We started on a square search, first leg 15 mins, 2nd leg 15 mins then gradually increase 30 mins, 45 mins and so on.

They were effectively flying on a box spiral flight path outwards from the carrier. 'We didn't see any aircraft at all and were up about 2 hours.'

Immediately after Clarabut's Barracuda had lifted off, David Brown's aircraft flown by Kingdon landed on. David Brown recalled:

On our return to the Fleet on the first leg at 03.30, three minutes after David Clarabut had taken off, instead of continuing on the second ordered stint which we were ordered to do, we requested to land on with a suspected oil leak. We were ordered not to resume our second planned patrol. The Fleet continued on its way at 20 knots.

Hibbs, still waiting in the third Barracuda, had watched as the second Barracuda circled the carrier preparing to land, noting the aircrew had:

...started to flash their Aldis lamp for an emergency landing. We didn't take off, we were put to one side.

It came down, the aircraft landed on and said that their compasses were all spinning.

The movement of the two aircraft was duly written into the ship's log: 'An hour into the two anti-submarine patrols one Barracuda returned with compass trouble and a relief patrol of one Barra and one Corsair were flown off at 03.25.'

David Brown continued:

> After we landed on we went to the ops room for a de-briefing and were informed the wing leader had not returned and had disappeared off the radar screen.

David Brown was surprised Roy had not seen the carrier yet:

> The Fleet consisting of a battleship, two Fleet carriers, three cruisers and a sizable destroyer screen – so that fleet on a perfectly calm day must have been making a very big wake – so that makes it difficult to believe that B-F wouldn't have spotted that wake if he was anywhere near on the return tack.
>
> There may have been a front out to the west which they ran into.

Matt and Baker-Falkner were asking for a homing by now, according to the 1841 Squadron diary.

Biggy added: 'When Dickie landed on I stayed in the air in case I was needed to help. The whole Fleet had to alter course 180° to receive us and did not wish to do so twice.'

David Brown recalled that earlier on 17 July:

> Sub Lt Bob 'Digby' Knight, 830 Squadron navigator for Barracuda 5B and Compass Officer for the wing, had made the rounds of the aircraft in the hangar and found that the aircraft 5G (LS556) that Lt Cdr Baker-Falkner had taken had a defective gyro-compass, and listed it as 'Not to be flown.' When he came down on the 18th for his own flight later that morning he found the aircraft had gone. Roy had taken it – it was our Barracuda – he took LS556.
>
> This would have had a gyro-compass and an ordinary standby compass which is not terribly reliable in that high altitude because of the magnetic dip – but at least I thought that the navigator would have noted that the gyro track was not in accordance with the sun – so seriously out that he was not able to re-cross the track of the Fleet when he came back from the starboard stint.
>
> I can only assume that the aircraft was not picked up by the carrier radars scanning ahead and the destroyers scanning at the rear – so he may have passed astern of them.

Duffy explained that back in the Ops room: 'We should have been running things. However, plotting on the reversible glass in the ADR the radar operators were tracking the wrong aircraft.'

In the Aircraft Directions Room, Marreco was carefully following developments after Roy's aircraft blip had disappeared off the radar screen. 'There was a bloody admiral on board, "Wee willy" McGrigor, who kept looking over my shoulder annoyingly.'

Bob Woolston recollected the mounting tension: 'I was in the ops room dozing, when I gradually heard Roy was in difficulties and couldn't make it back to the carrier.'

Marreco recalled: 'A new blip on the radar screen confirmed an unidentified aircraft. For a while I was sure it was Baker-Falkner, since it was where he was supposed to be, and even told this to Ruck-Keene.' 'The radar was recording a bleep West North West,' added David Brown. Marreco continued: 'By now Ruck-Keene was very worried about the situation.' By this time the Fleet was far enough out from the enemy coast to consider breaking radio silence 'At the time we certainly couldn't see the Norwegian coast on the screen – though if we had been close enough we would certainly have been able to do so,' mentioned Marreco.

Biggy recalled that: 'The radar screen apparently showed the others going off in a northish direction and Ruck-Keene decided to break R/T silence to send them a vector.' On the captain's order Marreco started to transmit *Formidable*'s newly designated call sign 'Uncurtain'. 'We then started to transmit bearings to try and get the Barracuda back to the carrier.' There was no reply from Roy and Micklem to the carrier, though they heard the transmission.

Biggy commented that in the Corsair above the Fleet: 'I could hear them [Roy and Matt] asking for a repeat.'

'The radar screen showed him to be following a course more or less due *north* away from the ship,' recalled Woolston who was now closely watching the radar. 'The track finally disappeared and we lost contact.'

Biggy then explained what happened next: 'After 15 minutes or so they lost contact but I could still hear both so relayed *Formidable*'s messages to B-F.'

According to the 1841 Squadron diary: 'By 0400 Matt and Baker-Falkner were off the screen completely. 0428: Ruck-Keene ordered a further pair of aircraft sent off to cover the water left open.'

In the lost patrol, Matt continued describing his and Roy's increasingly concerned actions:

Once we knew we were in difficulty, finally we got up above the cloud. I heard snatches of transmission.

My memory is hazy as to when I picked up a faint plain language call, which I recognised as Biggy asking whether I knew my position, and did I know the course to steer, to get me back to the carrier. I had to reply 'no' to both questions. He then 'rattled' off three numbers which would have been the course to steer but the voice became muffled and crackling, I got no answer to my request to repeat those number. I relayed to B-F which he acknowledged and which (presumably) we then followed. B-F's compass was not wrong but they were not steering the compass directions that had been relayed to me. Often the broadcast to us was unclear but here was a very clear relay 'head in direction', I forget what it was let's say, 210 or 217°.

On picking up the transmission I relayed it to them. And only 5 minutes later I took a glimpse at the compass which I was not doing regularly, mainly monitoring visual with the Barracuda, we weren't steering 217° but gradually drifting 10° off course – something was definitely wrong with their compass.

I had such implicit faith in the torpedo boys since this was their life blood, whereas we chaps stooged around like nobody's business. So even if I had seen their steering come to ass, I don't think I would have had the temerity even to ring them up to say 'by the way you're steering the wrong course.'

Biggy continued in his rescue attempts:

The radar screen continued to show them going north at about 10,000 feet so I was vectored accordingly. Visibility there was perfect but no sign of them. I must have been some 50 miles north of the ship.

Eventually, when I lost touch I decided to fly north to try to pick them up. I broke cloud about 10,000 feet – it was still 300 ft cloud base at sea level – and again made contact giving vectors for homing.

Hibbs continued: 'By that time, Baker-Falkner was all over the sky according to the radar – the compasses were just haywire. He had to steer by the compasses and they weren't giving true bearings.'

Increasing numbers of aircraft were now in the air above the Fleet, potentially confusing the radar operators tracking Roy. One such aircraft was RAF Catalina O/210 flown by Flt Lt French, which had been over the area from 3.05 am until 6.59 am. French was patrolling over the Fleet at 800 feet looking for U-boats in a search sector allocated by RAF Coastal Command. His crew sighted the Fleet as well as a Barracuda and Corsair, potentially that of Roy and Matt, during their square searches which was duly logged in the 210 Squadron Operations Record Book. The Fleet made no effort to contact this aircraft.

Wireless operator mechanic/air gunner F.W. Hammett who was on board the Catalina recalled:

Radio frequencies of RAF and naval R/T transmitters would have been different and they would not have been able to hear each other. Catalina O/210 was not requested to radio or assist the missing Barracuda nor Corsair which it apparently had sighted and was not aware they were in difficulty when they were sighted. But this appears to be the very last visual sighting of the lost pair. But at no time when I was on the receiver did I hear anything but routine messages, nor did any one of the crew mention anything about a call from an aircraft.

The 1841 Squadron diary recorded:

Radio communication was very poor. To make things more difficult for the FDO, Sub Lts Morten and Woodward with two more Barras as well, were patrolling in the area of the ship. At one moment it was decided that Sub Lt Brown of 1841 Sqdn should be sent off and vectored on to Sub Lt Mattholie, but this idea was given up almost immediately.

In fact they were ordered not to go as the success of a rescue mission was looking less and less hopeful, as Hibbs recalled. 'I remember the fighter boys wanted to go off and see if they could get him back and they said it was too risky and couldn't do it.'

Matt continued: 'My feeling is that we were so far away from the carrier that we were out of reach of their signals and even Biggy transmitting from 10,000 feet was barely audible.'

Another aircraft was soon afterwards heard flying overhead by *Formidable* but it was thought to be Roy's Barracuda returning to the carrier. In fact, it was another of the 210 Squadron RAF Catalina flying boats, Q/210, flown by W/O Stothers who reported seeing the Fleet at 5.15 am.

By now, the Fleet knew about the various RAF aircraft, although there was initial confusion. Marreco recalled: 'We heard flying over the Fleet. A star shell was fired to try and attract the aircraft as it was thought to be the Barracuda. I believe there was an RAF flying boat in the area, it could have been the one whose engines we heard.'

At 5.30 am, Roy's Barracuda was in theory towards the limit of its range, and the seriousness of the situation was so extreme that the C-in-C ordered action from his flagship.

This last ditch effort from the flagship battleship HMS *Duke of York* included her making smoke and firing High altitude (HA) shells, star shells from her 5.25-inch calibre guns, to light up the sky and assist the lost patrol aircraft.

From the ops room Duffy realised they were failing: 'We sent up a star shell above the clouds but B-F saw nothing.'

Even Biggy, circling in his Corsair, was too was too far away from the Fleet by now:

The ship fired the star shells at 12,000 feet in the hope of visual contact. I passed this on to B-F who acknowledged.

Meanwhile, I continued to give vectors to either Matt or Micklem who acknowledged them, but contact became weaker so I flew further north to try to regain contact. I never saw this firework display myself but shortly afterwards I lost contact altogether with B-F and neither could the ship hear me.

Matt saw nothing of the HA pyrotechnics.

I saw no star shell nor did I register any call from Biggy alerting us to it.

After some time came an even fainter Biggy call, again giving a course but which I couldn't plainly hear. With R/T silence already dumped, I now replied to Biggy but got no response. It was after that (I think) that I dropped to sea level, following discussions with B-F, and agreed to later rendezvous.

Meanwhile, the ADR in *Indefatigable* was also monitoring signals. Ian Easton explained:

I was Assistant Directions Officer in *Indefatigable*. Our radar detected an aircraft flying ahead of our Force and towards the west. We established from *Formidable* that Baker-Falkner's aircraft was overdue, obtained the call sign and called him up. Received no reply. *Formidable* also was calling him with no little luck.

At about the same time that we began calling, we began to hear Baker-Falkner's aircraft calling, asking for a course to fly. We obtained D/F bearings on successive transmissions from Baker-Falkner's aircraft that established with reasonable doubt that the radar echo that we were plotting was Baker-Falkner's aircraft, and that by then was well out to the westward of the force – I think about 60 miles, and it continued on its course to the westward.

However, this could not have been the lost patrol which was, it later transpired, heading to the east towards Norway.

Easton continued:

I recall hearing the news with a sense of impotence as we watched the aircraft echo move slowly away aware that its fuel must be very low and hearing Baker-Falkner's voice, never other than calm, while he was unable to hear us.

Biggy himself was now nearing the end of his fuel supply:

Then, *Formid.* who I could hear, failed to receive *me* – panic on board as they thought they might lose me too!

So I was instructed to fly back to the carrier and they kept repeating 'Return immediately to base.'

I had little idea where I was by that time and flew due south and eventually regained contact. I was getting worried as my fuel was dangerously low and reckoned I had only ½ hr flying left. I dropped down through the cloud to 100 feet and miraculously found the destroyer screen and *Formid.*, and greatly relieved I was to see them!

Formidable turned into the wind and Biggy landed on at 5.38 am. Biggy speculated whether Matt and Roy had any hope at all.

If I had ½ hr fuel left, Matt would have had roughly the same which would have taken him about 120 miles at cruising speed.

Matt's compass was reasonably accurate whereas I think B-F's was faulty. His observer Guy Micklem had mentioned that it went haywire in the previous day's op.

Ordinary compasses went haywire in those northern latitudes but I had set my gyro as usual on take-off so navigated on that. Matt, I am sure did the same so when he parted from Baker he could fly due east to Norway and make it practically out of gas.

Meantime, on board Corsair JT404 Matt was still battling to return to the carrier:

As a guess estimate as being 40 minutes after we first got into problems, maybe much later, we were still flying at 5,000–10,000 feet and I saw a gap in the cloud, approaching a huge pillar of cumulus, I radioed B-F for permission on the R/T: 'There is a gap what do you say I go down and have a quick look and see what the visibility was like down there.'

B-F had been averse to going down through the cloud and climbing up again since it would have wasted limited fuel. And also his range of picking up the beacon would have been diminished significantly by going down to too low an altitude – giving himself maximum opportunity at a distance to pick up the homing beacon.

'Ok' said he to my suggestion of going down 'but we have got to meet up again' and we came up with this idea of rendezvousing around a particular stack or column of cumulus cloud which towered above the other clouds and Baker-Falkner was to fly around it until I returned.

I cannot forget as I was about to peel down under the cloud, I looked over to the Barra and saw B-F with mask on looking down at his instruments, Micklem the navigator concentrating presumably on his maps, but the air gunner, with wireless off, was just looking and he gave me a wave, but not a cheery wave of a chap saying 'Let's go and get them boys.' Looking back I am of a strong opinion he was a worried lad at that moment. It must have been a farewell wave.

I peeled down to check the cloud base and the visibility was poor. It was still almost zero. When I had finished looking around, I climbed again and broke cloud cover and vectored to what I believed was the pillar. I then called B-F to report and asked him the position he was in. The R/T transmission between us was still clear. He was no longer there. In going down 5,000 feet and stooging around you can easily move off 7–8 miles.

After failing to sight one another he fired a Verey light which I did not see. I contacted them by radio and was told to fire my Verey pistol. The flare from the pistol would be seen about 5 miles but he said he couldn't see anything. Possibly I was completely the other side of the cumulus cloud (about 20 miles) which was in the middle between the two aircraft, and so the light couldn't have't been visible from that distance – we would always be opposite and couldn't see each other.

Alternatively, since these cumulus clouds were moving and so when I came up and found a cumulus column cloud it was a completely different cloud column and so I was circling one cloud and they another.

Matt was by now getting anxious:

It was only when I came up out of the clouds again that I became worried and had no idea where I was.

We were possibly widely separated by now and I was pretty low on fuel in my main tank – and the drop tank (still attached) was u/s because it would not feed.

B-F, recognised both our fuel situations. He calculated that he had only just enough petrol for the distance which he calculated as about 200 miles.

I replied that I had sufficient petrol to stay for another half hour and wished him 'good luck'.

He gave me a course to steer for the nearest landfall in Norway, said that he too was heading for the coast on that bearing and hoped that he would make it. The boss wished me good luck, and long life. After that, no more R/T.

By now Roy's fuel situation must have been becoming critical, and he was trying to fly as economically as possible to save dangerously low amounts of petrol – the depth charges had probably long been jettisoned to save weight.

Meanwhile, Matt's situation was also bleak:

I had no idea even slightly where I was and knew if I followed his general last bearing I would most likely also be heading for land. I estimated that I had sufficient petrol for 250 miles, but steered slightly south of the course given me by the Barracuda. I was then steering a general SE direction, 145 maybe 135°.

Matt continued:

Presumably Micklem had checked the map and found the best course for the minimum distance to the coast and the border with neutral Sweden.

My guess is that we were 600 miles WSW maybe more W than SW of the SS position.

SS was the aircraft rendezvous point on the run in to *Tirpitz* the day before. Matt continued:

The way B-F said 'I am running low on fuel. I have no alternative, I am heading for Norway' certainly in my memory tells me or gives me the impression that he knew he wasn't going to make it.

The Barracuda hung on too long in hindsight, but the last thing you want is to throw away your aircraft by flying to enemy territory.

I had no means of telling how good was the course given to me by B-F, however, the Scandinavian coastline is pretty lengthy! I had no maps aboard of the coast other than the escape map sewn into my flying suit. Not being issued against any specific operation such maps were very small scale.

Meanwhile, far away in the ADR of *Indefatigable*, David Buchanan-Dunlop recalled:

When with his escorting fighter, Roy became lost, I remember the mounting tension in *Indefatigable*'s AD room as we listened in to ineffectual efforts by *Formidable*'s AD officer to home him, which went on and on. I remember hearing Roy's last calm order to his escorting fighter to break away and head for the Norwegian coast – after that silence. God rest his soul.

On *Formidable*, as the four-hour endurance limit of the Barracuda ticked away, the senior officers waited with mounting tension in case there was a final glimmer of optimism. 'The four hours stretched and stretched, then you give up hope.' recalled 'Bing' Bingham. Des Rowe, the pilot that normally flew the aircraft that Roy was now piloting, was still hopeful:

I am sure that B-F would have ditched the depth charges, and provided they were heading in the right direction would have had sufficient fuel to reach Norway. It would have been feasible for his aircraft to reach inland. They could have been trying to reach Sweden.

Another Barracuda aircrew member, Allan Thomson, recollected a separate flight where he had been up in the air 4.20 hours. So there was great hope that Roy could reach the Norwegian coast. However, he added 'This is probably the limit for a Barracuda as our own fuel tanks were below the 10-gallon mark when we landed.'

Matt continued:

Meanwhile, I was on economic cruising because the Barra had earlier been holding me back during the patrol, it was giving me optimal operational conditions whilst I was up in the clouds. That would leave me 4 hrs plus the drop tank of another ⅓ extra.

At about 6 am, or four hours into the Barracuda and Corsair's flying time Matt noted:

By now I was also getting extremely low in fuel (must be the 4-hour range of the fuel tank) and since I didn't have much to lose I decided to try and again switch to the auxiliary drop tank. After a few seconds whatever had blocked the connection earlier came free, then the engine spluttered and finally fed smoothly. I was using this extra fuel. I realised that I had maybe 40–80 gallons left and could comfortably make land. I was fortunate I had made the mistake of retaining, rather than ditching, my external fuel tank.

I can recall at that time, without having heard from the carrier for quite some while that I radioed 'Am heading for the coast' end of message…shut up.

On board *Formidable*, by now Ruck-Keene, Tony Marreco and the ops room staff having heard the final transmissions from the Barracuda and Corsair about heading for the coast, gave up hope of recovering them and so called off any further search patrols. So at 6.07 am the final Barracuda and Corsair landed on. As an exhausted and dejected Marreco put it: 'After a long time we felt it was hopeless and so decided to stand down, sometime in the morning.'

The RAF flying boats had resumed their patrols, and had now fully taken up positions above the Fleet which they occasionally sighted. No further anti-submarine patrols were carried out by *Formidable* that day.

However, about the same time far away a rather anxious Matt had less than thirty minutes' flying time of fuel left:

Alone I was flying east or SE, still holding about 4,000 feet, being maximum altitude possible not because there was anything magic in that, but if you are thinking ahead of running out of petrol then you want as much altitude as possible to give yourself the maximum time for gliding down a clear flight path. In the end, I was following the last bearing they gave me and I made landfall but hardly surprising given the length of the coastline.

By 6.20 am, at the absolute maximum of his Barracuda's range, there was no Mayday or any other message from Roy's aircraft and all was presumed lost. Roy had either ditched, crashed or been shot down over the Norwegian coast by the *Luftwaffe* or coastal defence. Matt presumed they would have: 'Ditched when the fuel ran out; they probably managed to get out and into an inflatable dinghy, but, several hundred miles from anywhere, and with no 'shipping lanes' they were doomed.'

At 6.37 am *Formidable*'s log recorded firing off six rounds of 4.5.

Matt's aircraft still had fuel and at about 7 am, with the weather at altitude 'superb', he suddenly saw land to his great relief:

With peaks poking up through the cloud I believed it to be the Lofotens. Flying at about 5,000 feet I spotted two peaks sticking out of the clouds and got the impression they were at my level. Now came the options, bail out, or do a 'wheels up belly landing. I chose the latter. With unbroken cloud beneath me, I decided to let down, still out over the sea, and at sea level fly in towards the land looking for a possible crash site.

I circled and since the gauge was almost zero I decided to let down through the cloud and see what was around, even though it was against all rule books to fly down near mountains when you couldn't see what was there.

I broke out of the murk at around 500 feet and then down to some 60 feet. I was horrified to realise that I was ploughing through the tops of pine trees and above the occasional house instead of water.

Visibility below the cloud was good and I instantly flew over a small island connected to the mainland by a spit.

I had no intention of ditching. A year earlier I had great difficulty in extracting myself from my cockpit as my aircraft sank and left my parachute (and attached to it my dinghy) in the cockpit at a depth of about 50 feet. I had no wish to repeat the act.

When I reached the coast I had been heading on a 145° or a 131° bearing, generally SE direction. I could have been flying for 5.00–5.20 hrs duration.

Matt continued:

The flat land adjacent to the water looked good enough – but it was barren rock. I circled the base of one of the mountains looking for somewhere to land. I selected a reasonably level spot and crash-landed on the flattest part of land.

A large rock stopped the plane with a great jolt, I bashed my head on the compass and, took a few seconds to realise my plight.

Matt had actually flown right over the cloud-covered Lofoten Islands and landed on Hamaroy, part of the mainland between Bodø and Narvik in German-occupied Norway. It was about thirty miles from neutral Sweden as the crow flies.

In the hamlet where Matt crash-landed, two local farmers, Ludvik Nilsen and Mathias Sørensen, were awoken by the noise of the aircraft overhead. They quickly rushed outdoors to investigate when they realised the sound was getting nearer and that an aircraft was likely to land. They were the first to the scene. Ludvik's heavily pregnant wife was at home in labour; their son Hugo Rønring was born later that memorable day.

Mathias recalled: 'The aircraft flew from the NW and came around the mountain I circled and then came in to land.'

They helped the dazed pilot out of the aircraft.

The aircraft had circled twice and then landed by the cross roads between the track and the road in the potato field. We spoke to the pilot who talked of another aircraft. At that time, the weather was good, with mist only out to sea. We helped him and gave some old clothes.

Locals then hid Matt's parachute, Mae West life jacket and flying helmet from the Germans. One enterprising farmer even siphoned off the few gallons of remaining aviation fuel from the stricken Corsair, which he proudly boasted about years later.

The stunned Matt remembered:

Next, I fired a Very pistol into the plane hoping that it would set on fire. Then I ran across the rocky shore and into the shelter of forest. I looked back expecting to see the Corsair on fire – but saw only a thin plume of smoke.

Matt had no plans but knew it was hopeless looking for Roy, Micklem and Kimberley.

After several hours of difficult climbing, I found a huge pile of rocks with a small 'window' that I crawled through, and sat down to rest.

One button of my uniform was a minute compass. Sewn into my jacket lining was a thin, silk map of Scandinavia – but it didn't show me where I was. There was also a small packet of concentrated food tablets that would keep me going.

He then started to walk, heading generally eastwards towards neutral territory and freedom.

Walking in any direction, in a straight line in Norway is impossible. The fjords all run NE to SW and I spent so much time in going down a mountain side to come to a fast flowing, wide, stream or river, and having to climb back again, in a direction that might not be taking me east.

By now, I had lost one shoe in a bog and had to use my long silk scarf as a wrapper on that foot.

I lost track of time. I made one contact only, with a Norwegian hill farmer who gave me a 'goat milk cheese sandwich' and hurried me off into the forest again.

However, the Germans had either seen his aircraft flying over or plotted it on radar, as the next day they were waiting for him. He was captured and spent the rest of the war as a POW in Germany.

Nothing was officially recorded by the Germans of Roy's Barracuda and there were no sightings of it having landed near the Corsair. In the nearby village at about 7 am local time an eyewitness in a shop thought he heard the sound of two aircraft engines circling overhead. In the manner of a good Norwegian he didn't report it to the police who were working for the occupying forces.

But rumours abounded that there were other Allied airmen who had landed. In another nearby hamlet local people heard the crash of an aircraft in the mountains though weren't sure of the exact date. There were even unsubstantiated reports of an Allied aircraft in a lake on Hinnøy, Norway's largest island, between the Lofoten and Andoya.

Other eyewitnesses much later reported to Trond Inge Mathisen of the Hamaroy Museum saying that two Englishmen's bodies had been found dead floating in the sea washed up on Hamaroy. There were other stories of Allied airmen being shot nearby. But no clear confirmation that it was from Baker-Falkner's Barracuda. His patrol was declared lost by the Admiralty and next of kin were to be informed.

Emerson wrote in his secret diary:

Now back at Hatston. Stadlandet do was cancelled owing to weather, and Fleet returned to Scapa. Had a fight with subs on the way. There is strong feeling against *Formid* for losing Daddy. I am very shocked, as are all the boys.

The following was recorded in the 1841 Squadron diary for 18 July 1944:

At 10.30 all pilots were called to the Admiral's cabin – the intelligence room – for a talk by the captain. This amounted to the explanation of the operation as a whole and most particularly, of why Matt and Baker-Falkner were lost. He assumed that they must have had a very large compass error and that Matt's YE beacon aerial had been snapped off by his belly tank when he'd released it. Apparently the FDO had requested that all the other aircraft be landed on during the most critical period so as to clear the screen. However this had been refused because of the U-boat menace at the time. There is a possibility that the FDO was vectoring the wrong section of Corsairs and Barracudas. In short, no one really knew what went wrong. The fact remains that 1841 had lost an excellent senior subby and the FAA one of their 'finest' TBR commanders.

CHAPTER 28

Missing in Action and the Aftermath

Each person in No. 8 TBR was deeply upset about the catastrophic loss – and were even jointly considering mutiny due to the incompetence of the senior carrier officers. Roy Eveleigh recalled:

> We were shocked to a man when it became apparent Baker-Falkner would not be returning to the carrier. After his loss, the wing and the ship were never quite the same. To us he was irreplaceable, but of course, if you had put that to B-F at any time he would have laughed!

The sad news spread across the Home Fleet, even reaching one of Roy's former pupils at Arbroath, Paul Housden, by then serving on board HMS *Trumpeter* during Operation *Mascot*. He recalled:

> The news of his loss quickly reached the ears of all the aircrews, in all the carriers and brought great sadness.
> We all felt it personally, especially as the manner of his going seemed so unbelievable. It was a long time before we at last gave up hope for his safety; I pinned my faith on him reaching the Faeroes or Shetland. I still grieve sixty years later.

There was little hope of now finding Roy or his crew. The following morning RAF Catalina Q/210, piloted by W/O Stothers, flying over the Fleet's path of the night before, sighted at 9.10 am a yellow box, with no sign of life near, and soon after spotted an oil patch annular of 800 yards diameter which had the appearance of fuel oil. Whether it was from a crashed aircraft or sunken submarine was not recorded or followed up.

There wasn't any news from Norway either. 'We got no intelligence about the whereabouts of B-F from our Norwegian agents who were already giving us results of the strike and reports about the operation,' recalled Duffy. Two days later reconnaissance flights were made over the Lofoten Islands and along the coast where Matt had crash-landed. Navigator Flt Sgt Eric Hill was flying in an RAF 544 Squadron Mosquito at low level over the Norwegian coastline on a reconnaissance mission:

> Our brief for the trips on July 20th and 22nd was, roughly, to look at the 100 fathom line and keep an eye open for any important shipping lurking in any of the fjords. Consequently, we did all this under cloud. We did recces along the coast, having photoed the *Tirpitz* in Kaa Fiord. As far as I remember we were under instruction not to go as far as Alten on these occasions.

As far as I recall, there was never talk of a crashed aircraft on Lofoten.

The Mosquito's pilot, Flt Lt Frank Dodd, added:

> Weather was bad on 22nd – down to 100 feet at times. Obliques of the Lofotens were taken but nothing unusual was seen. The brief for the flight on the 22nd was to follow the 100 fathom line from Andenes, north of the Lofotens, to the west of Trondheim. I am sure I would remember if we had been briefed to keep a lookout for a crashed Barracuda and I cannot recall any talk of one having been lost near or over the Lofotens.

Far below them, Matt had already been captured by the Germans after only one night on the run. He was interrogated, and then flown to Germany and prison camp. He was not surprisingly unhappy with the whole situation:

> I do not believe that B-F made it to dry land: firstly because he himself doubted that he had sufficient fuel and secondly had he made land *and* been captured, it would have been information that would undoubtedly have been used by the Germans when they were interrogating me.

Matt continued:

> Once in the bag I was sent to Stalag Luft 3 prison camp near Breslau (Sagan), the wooden horse camp in Silesia. At some point whilst POW I had a couple of letters from someone in the Admiralty, I don't know the author, asking apparently quite innocently, innocuously, 'What had happened to the B-F.' I wrote back in my next letter saying as guarded as I possibly could that 'B-F wasn't here nor did I think in any other.' I got another letter three months later still from the Admiralty asking much the same sort of questions, clearly there was a lot of interest being evinced in what had happened to Baker-Falkner.

Matt concluded:

> I always felt that somewhere along the line if I had done something different, I don't know quite what, we would have got back.
> I still have a strong memory of the three faces, looking out at me as we parted. What an inexcusable loss of lives, on a pointless sweep, after a failed attack, and B-F such a highly respected wing leader.

A Court of Enquiry into the loss of the Barracuda and Corsair was held almost immediately on board the flagship *Duke of York*. Marreco was there in his capacity as FDO:

> We returned to Scapa where Ruck-Keene and I were sent to court martial at the Court of Enquiry, on the flagship. There was the C-in-C, also involved was Commander Flying Bramwell, and navigating officer Jack Frewen. Ruck-Keene was very worried about going to the court martial, however I was not so concerned.

Lt R.H. Kelsall, RNVR air electrical officer, was one of the officers who gave evidence at the enquiry, mostly concerning gyro-compasses, their sensitivity and the problems faced by them after dives against *Tirpitz* the previous day. Other evidence included the ADR log of all radio telephone messages between the ship and the aircraft. 'I do remember that these were taken for the purpose of the enquiry that was held next day,' recalled Tovey.

Marreco continued:

During the Court of Enquiry, it became apparent that the unidentified 'radar blip' or aircraft was indeed an RAF flying boat searching for submarines.

Overall the findings were that once lost there was nothing that could have been done to save the aircraft.

The verdict was accidental loss. The court exonerated Ruck-Keene but I was court martialled as being 'unduly self confident'.

Biggy added:

...the FDO was blamed quite unjustly for the loss of B-F and my senior pilot H.S. Mattholie – it resulted in Tony Marecco being relieved of his appointment – quite wrongly in my opinion – soon after we arrived in the Pacific later in the year – which I thought was disgraceful as I don't think it was his fault at all but I suppose that someone had to take the rap.

David Buchanan-Dunlop concluded:

I happened to be appointed a member of the Court as one of the commander operations of the carriers involved in the operation. No blame the court attached to anyone could ever bring dear Roy back to life.... I cherish his memory, and it will not be long before we happily meet again in that Valhalla where, surrounded by so many, many FAA mutual friends and comrades, we shall together drink hot spiced mead out of the skulls of our enemies.

The sad news quickly spread to all personnel at Hatston and at Scapa. Roy's petty officer steward, who was a survivor from the *Prince of Wales* and *Repulse* sinkings off Singapore was devastated. On relating Roy's loss to friends back at Hatston he broke down in tears.

Communications Wren at Hatston, CFT Cath Thomson, recalled: 'I well remember when the sad news of his loss was received. The talking point at Wrens quarters was 'have you heard' and how shocked everybody was.

But the effect on Naomi was even more dreadful. She may well have had a sixth sense that something awful had happened. Hours before she received a telegram from the Admiralty, she wrote to Bill in Italy:

July 19, St George's Flats: How are you, dear? I'm feeling just about as fed up and worried as it's possible to feel if that's any consolation to you! This appalling worry gets one down in time. I think I shall have to ring and ask dear old Eira to come and cheer me up – she is always cheerful – bless her.

She ended the letter:

Well dearest – no news – I feel really almost too depressed tonight to write – have hopes of Roy getting a change of job – but when? It seems such ages coming.

The telegram she received next day read:

It was with deepest regret that I learnt that Lt Cmdr Baker-Falkner was in the Barracuda missing this morning. He has led the attacks on *Tirpitz* and enemy shipping with such gallantry and success. We can only trust that both the Barracuda and Corsair succeeded in making a landing in Norway.

Grace and Sydney Baker-Falkner and Violet Matthews were with Naomi when the telegram arrived. Violet recalled: 'She reacted very badly – she fainted. It was the shock, I suppose. Always in the back of her mind, she knew it could happen but when it did, she could not cope at all.'

Eira broke the news to Bill in Italy:

Two Gates July 21. Oh, my darling, what we have dreaded has happened – Roy is missing. The B-Fs were with her when the wire arrived yesterday – thank goodness she had someone. They got in touch with me about 8 pm and I went round there as quickly as I could. Nao of course is half-demented. One feels so useless – of what use is sympathy?

The doctor was leaving as I arrived – she of course could do nothing but gave me some very small tablets – with instructions to give two and no more at night-time. The B-Fs eventually left and I stayed the night with Nao – never have I known such a long one.

Roy's mother, Grace, received a personal letter of sorrow from Admiral Sir Bruce Fraser which stated:

Roy went missing when the Fleet was returning from an operation against the *Tirpitz*. His aircraft went missing when he flew off to look for and rescue a ditched crew. There was a storm which blew up and the instruments on his aircraft stopped working and they got lost out at sea, just ran out of fuel.

Captain Ruck-Keene, of HMS *Formidable*, visited Grace and told her that Roy was lost off the Lofoten islands and that his compass went wrong due to the magnetism of the islands.

On Leslie's summer break from her music college in London, Grace had to tell her the dreadful news that Roy was missing. The family continued to hope – Grace refusing to believe her son would not return, almost up to the time of her death. She never gave up the idea that 'he had survived and was in an institution in Norway'. Her letters to the Red Cross and the Norwegian government are a testimony to endless grief. In the early years of 1942, during a promotional drive to raise money for the Wings for Victory campaign, she had bought National Savings Certificates. She saved them for Roy on his return from his travels and kept them for when he might appear after the war. Many, many years later, after Leslie had married and given birth to a son, Graham Roy, the certificates were given to him. So steadfast was Grace in her belief that Roy would return, that she refused to allow his name to be added to the war memorial in Shaldon. Only in the 1990s, well after her death, was this to be done.

Naomi's first letter to Bill after Roy went missing was a mixture of despair and hope. She wrote from Annie Blackburn's home at Ashfield Avenue, Frizinghall, Bradford:

2 August: I haven't written to you before because I was feeling just too terrible – whatever happens in the world to me now can never be worse than what I've experienced in the last few days, twelve actually.

Death in any form must be child's play compared to what I have suffered. As you know Roy is my earth and to suddenly get a telegram to say he was missing the very week he was due to be grounded was just too terrible. But I do feel a little better today as I received a letter yesterday saying that Roy's last message was that he was heading for Norway to try and force land there.

Oh, Bill darling, this terrible waiting, it's nearly sending me crazy – nothing could be worse. I can't be brave as it's far more than my life and nothing else matters – if Roy doesn't return my life will just be a living death but I do feel so strongly that my precious is alive – when we parted in London I thought we were going to be together for good in three weeks.

Bill dear, it does seem so cruel – Roy was so tired and war-weary. He should have been grounded so long ago – immediately after his big effort – instead he has been in action after action since.

On 25 July – a week after he went missing – Roy was mentioned in a Despatch for Distinguished Service: 'his bravery, leadership, skill and devotion to duty operating from, or serving in HM Ships, during successful strikes at enemy shipping off the coast of Norway'. Later Roy's father, Sydney, was to go to Buckingham Palace to receive Roy's DSO from the King.

Meanwhile, Roy's new posting to RAF Boscombe Down as a test pilot had been confirmed – but now too late. Torrens-Spence recalls: 'Roy and his wife Naomi, I was very fond of them both. Baker-Falkner would have been returning to take over my position in the Naval Performance Testing Squadron.'

On 12 November 1944, *Tirpitz* was at last sunk by the RAF in a strike involving thirty-two Lancaster bombers. However, by then her fighting capacity had long since ended and the victory was hollow.

For Naomi as the weeks went by, hope got less and less. There was no news from the POW camps. At the end of the war, she received a letter from the director general of the British Red Cross saying that there was no further information. After his release from a German POW camp, the surviving Corsair pilot – 'Matt' Mattholie – contacted Naomi. He told her he knew nothing and there was no hope. He also wrote a letter to Admiral Boyd at Lee-on-Solent on his repatriation:

3 September 1945

Dear Sir,

I would like to thank you for your kindness in writing to me in Germany. I regret that I couldn't and cannot now give any definite information of Lt Cmdr Baker-Falkner and his crew.

It seems fairly certain to me, Sir, that Lt Cdr Baker-Falkner must have been forced to ditch some miles off shore, and in poor visibility. While I was held in Norway I heard no news of the Germans rescuing any crew from the area in which he may have ditched.

I have written to Mrs Baker-Falkner, Sir, but I did not feel that I could honestly offer her any hope that her husband had reached land safely.

I am, Sir, Your obedient Servant

H S Mattholie Lt (A) RNVR

Roy's good friend, Splash Carver recalled:

Roy's tragic loss over the North Sea in 1944 was one of the cruellest strokes of fate. It was not due to enemy action but to a defective compass and a concurrent fault in his homing beacon receiver. The last transmission heard from him was that he was 'making for Norway' but he never got there.

Of course, I didn't know of his loss straight away but it was devastating news to Tiny and myself when it came. Roy is remembered by many FAA people still. He was something of a role model – highly skilled and professional in his job, highly decorated and handsome too. His death was a very great loss to the Navy and the FAA in particular. God bless them.

On 8 May, 1945, at 3 pm, Winston Churchill announced in a broadcast from Downing Street that the war with Germany was at an end. There was dancing in the streets of London, people waved flags, blew whistles, climbed the lamp posts and sang.

But there was no singing in the little household in Torquay. Peace had come too late for Roy and too late for many of the brave young men who had sailed and flown with him and lost their lives. They included: Ken Gurr, from the Alexandria days, who was shot down over Dunkirk; Robert Boddington, Roy's Dartmouth friend, who was lost in his submarine off Spain; Eugene Esmonde, who had been lost in the suicide mission against *Scharnhorst* and *Prinz Eugen*; Jakes Barnes, the live-wire from the Egypt days, who was killed in a mid-air collision during a mock battle; 'Feather' Godfrey-Faussett, a pal from the Malta era who died in a night-flying exercise when his aircraft went into the sea; Bobby Dundas and Robin Grey killed at the time of Dunkirk; 'Cliff' Clifford killed during the bombing of *Illustrious* during the Malta convoys; Cracksie Crawford who was lost after a torpedo attack whilst he was on passage to the Caribbean in a transport ship; as well as the ship's complement of HMS *Glorious*, lost in the terrible dark days of 1940.

Naomi was utterly devastated when Roy went missing and continued to be completely distraught as the months went by. A year after his disappearance she wrote to Bill, still with the RAMC in Italy:

July 4, 1945: St George's Flats, St Marychurch, Torquay. Many thanks for your many letters – I do appreciate them but I just haven't answered them because I have no heart – just don't know what to say – I'm so utterly and completely heartbroken. I just really don't know what to do with myself. I realise now that only a miracle could bring my adored darling back – every day my hopes fade a little more – it nearly kills me and my one and only wish is to die myself.

Eira Lord continued to be a tremendous support as was Annie Blackburn and Violet Matthews. Naomi found she grew closer to Grace and Sydney in their shared loss. Naomi's former nanny from her childhood, Edith Allsopp, returned at this time, arriving on the doorstep with a suitcase and saying: 'I've come to look after your children.'

Eventually, when all hope of Roy's return was lost, Naomi set sail for a new life in South Africa. She was accompanied by Mrs Allsopp and Carole, then aged six, and Sandra, aged four. She bought a house in Pinetown, near Johannesburg, and made good friends at Moir River but the move to Africa was not a success. Naomi returned to England in 1948 and initially stayed with Bill and Eira at their home, Culross, in Torquay. In 1951, she moved to Dial Cottage at Frensham to be nearer to Annie Blackburn who by now lived in London. After Annie's death, Naomi moved back to Devon where she was to remain for the rest of her life.

In the early years after Roy died, Naomi and Grace would go to spiritualist churches in a bid to contact him. She and Grace also consulted mediums and regularly were told that a tall, naval officer was present. On one occasion a message was read out to contact 'Norma Svendsen', a name that hinted of links to Norway, but neither Naomi nor Grace knew how to reach that person.

The message Naomi particularly wanted to receive was a Morse code message. In their early days, Roy would tap out in Morse code 'BILY – Beautiful, I love you.' In almost her last decade of life, Naomi went to a medium who, as usual, told her there was a tall, naval man present and he was trying to say something to her. The medium reported that she was having difficulty hearing because of some background noise. The medium said the naval man was getting very frustrated with her but the noise was getting ever louder. 'It's a tap, tap, tapping noise,' complained the medium and then she exclaimed: 'It's Morse code!'

Naomi died on 12 March 2000. She was laid to rest in Gidleigh churchyard; buried with her was a photograph of her and Roy in their Egypt days. The tombstone in the tiny Dartmoor churchyard bears the epitaph: 'Naomi, much loved wife of Lt-Cdr Roy Baker-Falkner, and dearly loved mum and gran.' In Morse code at the bottom are the letters 'BILY'.

Epilogue

Roy's two children, who were so small when he went missing, grew up and were successful in life, but sadly never knew their father. Sandra had only been eight months old when he went out on that fateful anti-submarine patrol.

Carole married Gilbert Molland, and after living for a while in Shropshire, the couple came back to Devon to run a Post Office Stores. They had two sons, Richard and Noel. Sandra went to Trinity College, Dublin, before becoming a journalist. She married a Merchant Navy officer, Peter Coventry, and they had a daughter and son, Lynn and Duncan.

Roy's father, Sydney, remained in the Home Guard until the end of the war. He and Grace retired to Poole, in Dorset in the 1950s. Sydney remained for ever Canadian at heart and received his invalidity pension from the Ottawa government until he died in 1964. Grace died still believing that Roy would return.

Harry was away in North Africa and subsequently in Italy and Greece when Roy was lost. He was demobbed in 1947. He later married Helen Bell and they had two children, Helen Anne and David.

Leslie completed her music course at the Royal College of Music and took part in the VE Day celebrations at Trafalgar Square and outside Buckingham Palace. She got a job in the Carl Rosa Opera Company, and subsequently the Yorkshire Symphony Orchestra where she met her future husband, Gerald Drucker. They married in 1948 and went on to have three children, Victoria, Graham Roy and Stephanie. Vicky went on to teach languages, whilst Stephanie studied geography and subsequently settled in Canada where her family now live.

Bill Lord returned to Devon after the war and ran a private practice as a doctor from his home at Culross. He and Eira had two daughters, Victoria and Penelope. Bill died of a heart attack in 1972. Eira died in 1993.

Leslie's son Graham followed his two passions – animals and learning all about Roy and Fleet Air Arm history. He has worked for over thirty years in nature conservation, including working with the European Commission and United Nations from the 1990s until 2008.

Graham grew up being fascinated by his uncle who went missing a decade before he was born and after whom he was named. He first made enquiries to the Fleet Air Arm Museum and was saddened that they knew little of Roy's naval career. That started his goal to ensure that the world would not forget the sacrifices made by Roy Baker-Falkner.

In 1994, Graham co-organised with Roy Matthias, a former TAG of 827 Squadron, the one and only reunion of Roy's naval air wing, No. 8 TBR, with veterans from *Furious*, *Formidable* and *Victorious* commemorating the fiftieth anniversary of the attacks on *Tirpitz*.

They contacted the ever-diminishing surviving shipmates from around the globe and were successful in getting over sixty of Roy's air and ground crews, to participate in the two-day meeting in RNAS Yeovilton. They came from all over the UK and as far away as Australia. Guests of honour were Kevin Gibney, Naomi and Leslie. Guy Micklem's brother and Arthur Kimberley's sister and nephew also attended. A film was made of the proceedings by former BBC cameraman, Nigel Kinnings.

In 2005, Graham's first son was born, and proudly named Roy in honour of his great uncle. Roy's name also lived on in the daily lives of the families of his former aircrew. Howard Emerson, former senior pilot in 827 Squadron, had returned home to New Zealand after the war. He never forgot his commanding officer, and proudly named his newborn son Roy in 1952.

Roy's aircraft was never found. It was long thought the Barracuda was lost at sea west of the Lofoten Islands. However, Graham has investigated a further possibility that it reached Norway.

Graham travelled into the Arctic Circle towards Tromsø, the final resting place of *Tirpitz*. Then he visited the area where Corsair pilot 'Matt' Mattholie told him he had crash-landed the morning that Roy was lost – a potato field east of the Lofoten Islands and only a few miles from neutral Sweden during wartime.

Of Roy's aircraft there was no more news, except for a possibility that a tiny piece of wreckage found on a mountain glacier was that of a Barracuda. There had been no other aircraft wrecks in that area during the war. Roy's aircraft fitter in No. 8 TBR was at the fiftieth anniversary reunion and thought he recognised a photograph of the remnant as an exhaust manifold pipe of the Fairey Barracuda – he was sure as Roy had developed that manifold at Boscombe Down to improve the Barracuda's performance. It could be that the Barracuda made it as far as the coast of Norway and then crashed, or even ditched in a lake. It is possible that the mountain and its glacier form the beautiful and peaceful last resting place of Roy, Guy and Arthur.

In the words of H. Glynn-Ward, who wrote from British Columbia in 1932:

Men come, live their little lives, and are gone, leaving but a memory behind them. Human beings are full of tears and laughter – mostly tears – but in the brooding mountains and in the still waters there is eternal peace.

Glossary

*	After a medal or decoration for valour, denotes Bar to that medal
£/-/d	Pre-decimal pounds sterling, shillings, pence
(A)	Air Branch
(A)	Acting rank
AA	Anti-Aircraft (ack-ack)
A&AEE	Aeroplane and Armament Experimental Establishment (RAF Boscombe Down)
a/c	Aircraft
AC	Companion of the Order of Australia
ADDL	Aerodrome Dummy Deck Landing
ADM	Admiral
ADR	Aircraft Direction Room
AFC	Air Force Cross
AFI	Naval Air Fighting Instructions guard book
AFO	Admiralty Fleet Order
AI	Airborne Interception – airborne radar
ALT	Attack Light Torpedo or Aerial Light Torpedo (attack)
AM	Air Mechanic
AP	Armour piercing bomb
ART	Airborne radar tests
A/S	Anti-submarine
ASI	Air Speed Indicator
ASP	Anti Submarine Patrol
ASV	Air to Surface Vessel radar
ATA	Air Transport Auxiliary
ATC	Air Training Corps
AVM	Air Vice Marshal
AW	Air Wing
Barra	Fairey Barracuda
BEM	British Empire Medal
B-F	Lt Cdr R.S. Baker-Falkner
Box	Nickname for HMS *Furious*
BPF	British Pacific Fleet
BRNC	Britannia Royal Naval College
Bt	Baronet
CAP	Combat Air Patrol or Constant Air Patrol

Capt	Captain
CB	Companion of The Most Honourable Order of the Bath
CBE	Commander of the Order of the British Empire
CCOI	Critical Contact of Interest
Cdr	Commander
CFI	Chief Flying Instructor
CGM	Conspicuous Gallantry Medal
C-in-C	Commander in Chief
CO	Commanding Officer
CPO	Chief Petty Officer
c/s	Call sign
CS1	First Cruiser Squadron
CVE	Carrier Escort Vehicle
CVO	Commander of the Royal Victorian Order
Daddy	No. 8 TBR nickname for Lt Cdr R.S. Baker-Falkner
D/B	Dive Bombing
D/C	Depth Charge
D/F	Direction Finding
DFC	Distinguished Flying Cross
DFM	Distinguished Flying Medal
DH	De Havilland aircraft
DI	Daily Inspection
DL	Deck Landing
DL	Deputy Lieutenant
DLCO	Deck Landing Control Officer (batsman)
DLT	Deck Landing Training
DSM	Distinguished Service Medal
DSO	Distinguished Service Order Medal
DSC	Distinguished Service Cross Medal
Dt	Detachment
e/a	Enemy aircraft
E-boat	German motor torpedo boat
ETA	Estimated time of arrival
FAA	Fleet Air Arm of the Royal Navy
FDO	Fighter Direction Officer
FDU	Fighter Direction Unit
Ffd	Full Flying Duties
FIU	Fighter Interception Unit
FL	Forced Landing
Flak	*Flugabwehrkanone* /German anti-aircraft gunfire
Flt	Flight
F/Lt	Flight Lieutenant
Flt Sgt	Flight Sergeant
FTS	Flying Training School
F/O	Flying Officer
FOCT	Flag Officer Carrier Training

FONA	Flag Officer Naval Aviation
FONAC	Flag Officer Naval Air Command
FRU	Fleet Requirements Unit
ft	Imperial foot measurement
FTR	Failed to Return
FTU	Fleet Trials Unit
GBE	Knight's Grand Cross of the Order of the British Empire
GCB	Knight Grand Cross of The Most Honourable Order of the Bath
GCM	Good Conduct Medal
GM	George Medal
GP	General Purpose bomb
Gp	Group
HA	High Altitude shell
HMAS	His Majesty's Australian Ship
HMCS	His Majesty's Canadian Ship
HMNZS	His Majesty's New Zealand Ship
HMS	His Majesty's Ship
IF	Intensive Flying
IFDF	Intensive Flying Development Flight
IFF	Identification Friend or Foe
JP	Justice of the Peace
KBE	Knight Commander of the Order of the British Empire
KCVO	Knight Commander of the Royal Victorian Order
KM	*Kriegsmarine*/German Navy
KMS	*Kriegsmarine Schiff*/German Navy Ship
L/A	Leading Airman
L/Air	Leading Airman
LAC	Leading Aircraftman
Lt	Lieutenant
Lt Cdr	Lieutenant Commander
Lt Cmdr	Lieutenant Commander
LDV	Local Defence Volunteer
LS	Leading Seaman
LW	*Luftwaffe*/German Air Force
MAC	Merchant aircraft carrier
Mae West	Life jacket
Martlet	Grumman Wildcat
MBE	Members of the Order of the British Empire
MG	Machine Gun
MID	Mentioned in Dispatches
Mid	Midshipman
MLD	*Marine-Luchtvaartdienst*/Dutch Naval Air Service
MP	Member of Parliament
MP	Military Police
MV	Merchant Vessel
NAFI	Naval Air Fighting Instructions

N/A	Naval Airman
N/air	Naval Airman
NAS	Naval Air Station
Navex	Naval exercise
NAW	Naval Air Wing
NCO	Non Commissioned Officer
NF	Night Fighter
NFW	Naval Fighter Wing
NO	Naval Officer
NTW	Naval TBR Wing
NW	Naval Wing – Squadrons grouped into numbered wings (from June 1943)
OBE	Officers of the Order of the British Empire
Op	Operation
Ops Room	Operations Room or HQ
OTU	Operational Training Unit
OW	Operation Tungsten
Plot	Radar sighting
PO	Petty Officer
P/O	Pilot Officer
PoW	Prisoner of War
PR	Photo Reconnaissance
RADM	Rear Admiral
RAE	Royal Aircraft Establishment Farnborough
RAF	Royal Air Force
RAN	Royal Australian Navy
RCN	Royal Canadian Navy
RCNVR	Royal Canadian Navy Volunteer Reserve
Recco	Reconnaissance
RM	Royal Marine
RN	Royal Navy
RNAS	Royal Naval Air Station
RNAS	Royal Naval Air Service
RNC	Royal Naval College
RNethN	Royal Netherlands Navy
RNR	Royal Naval Reserve
RNVR	Royal Naval Volunteer Reserve
RNZNVR	Royal New Zealand Navy Volunteer Reserve
R/T	Radio Telephone (radio equipment)
Sandra	Beacon guiding system
SANF	South African Naval Force
Senior Pilot	Second in command of FAA squadron
SF	Station or Ship's Flight
Sgt	Sergeant
Skipper	Ship's Captain
S/L	Sub-Lieutenant

S/Ldr	Squadron Leader
Senior O	Senior Observer
Sqdn	Squadron
SS	Steam Ship
Stooge	Fly unobjectively
Stringbag	Fairey Swordfish
STU	Service Trials Unit
Sub Lt	Sub-Lieutenant
TAG	Telegraphist Air Gunner
Tarpon	Grumman Avenger
TBR	Torpedo Bomber Reconnaissance
Toc H	Christian Service Club
TSR	Torpedo Spotter Reconnaissance
TT	Torpedo Training
u/c	Undercarriage
ULTRA	Intelligence resulting from decryption of German radio communications – Enigma
u/s	Unserviceable
USAAF	United States Army Air Force
USAF	United States Air Force
U-boat	German submarine
USN	United States Navy
USS	United States Ship
VAD	Voluntary Air Detachment of nursing
VADM	Vice Admiral
VC	Victoria Cross
VE-day	Victory in Europe day
VHF	Very High Frequency radio
VRD	Volunteer Reserve Officers' Decoration
Wing	Squadrons grouped into numbered wings (from June 1943)
W/C	Wing Commander
Wing Leader	Commanding officer of Naval Wing (from October 1943)
WL	Commanding officer of Naval Wing (from October 1943)
W/O	Wireless Operator
WRNS	Women's Royal Naval Service
WSR	War Service Rank
W/T	Wireless telegraphy – Morse code
YG Beacon	Homing beacon

INDEX